D1602832

Litigation and Inequality

Litigation and Inequality

Federal Diversity Jurisdiction in
Industrial America, 1870–1958

EDWARD A. PURCELL, JR.

New York   Oxford
OXFORD UNIVERSITY PRESS
1992

Oxford University Press

Oxford   New York   Toronto
Delhi   Bombay   Calcutta   Madras   Karachi
Kuala Lumpur   Singapore   Hong Kong   Tokyo
Nairobi   Dar es Salaam   Cape Town
Melbourne   Auckland

and associated companies in
Berlin   Ibadan

Published by Oxford University Press, Inc.,
200 Madison Avenue, New York, New York 10016

Oxford is a registered trademark of Oxford University Press

Library of Congress Cataloging-in-Publication Data
Purcell, Jr., Edward A.
Litigation and inequality : federal diversity jurisdiction in
industrial America, 1870–1958 / Edward A. Purcell, Jr.
p. cm.   Includes index.
ISBN 0-19-507329-0
1. Jurisdiction—Social aspects—United States—History. 2. Civil
procedure—Social aspects—United States—History. 3. Courts—
United States—History. 4. Actions and defenses—United States—
History. I. Title.
KF8858.P87   1992
347.73'12—dc20   91-35869   [347.30712]

9 8 7 6 5 4 3 2 1

Printed in the United States of America
on acid-free paper

For Dan and Jess

Preface

This study began as an effort to write a political and intellectual history of the civil jurisdiction of the federal courts since the Civil War. In the process of reading congressional debates and academic writings, I grew increasingly curious about what was actually going on in the federal courts and how the political and doctrinal debates of the time related to what litigants were actually doing. At some point in my research, prompted in part no doubt by the fact that I was then no longer a practicing historian but a practicing litigator, I found myself trying to answer the latter question rather than the ones with which I had started.

This book is the result. It is neither a political nor an intellectual history, and it touches only minimally on those areas. It is not, at least directly, a study of legal institutions or, in its emphasis on litigation behavior, an examination of legal doctrines as such. Nor is it primarily a study of the United States Supreme Court, though in some part it inevitably became one. Finally, it is not a study of the desirability of maintaining or abolishing federal diversity jurisdiction.

The principal subject, instead, is the sociolegal process of disputing, settling, and litigating claims. In particular, the book focuses on the litigation process involving disputes between individual plaintiffs and national corporations over contract claims for insurance benefits and tort claims for personal injuries, and its analysis concentrates on the three-quarters of a century from the 1870s to the 1940s. The periodization results from the fact that litigation strategies and patterns, like other social phenomena, are historically specific. The period from Reconstruction to the mid-twentieth century witnessed the emergence, spread, and decline of an identifiable combination of such strategies and patterns.

A basic argument of the book is that the strategic uses and social significance of jurisdictional and procedural rules shift over time as a result of changes in the characteristics of the adversarial parties, relevant legal rules and institutions, and prevailing social, economic, and political conditions. Thus, the book argues that however much certain issues may constitute "perennial" or "classic" problems of jurisdiction and procedure, however much they may be constantly present or regularly recurring as formal legal issues, their social meaning and practical import may differ substantially at different times and places. The social significance of "technical" procedural and jurisdictional rules, in other words, is as historically contingent as is any other aspect of law or society.

The book examines some of the ways in which litigants and their attorneys attempted to use the resources available to them in order to prevail in claim disputes, and it explores the ways in which courts, legislatures, and the legal profession helped shape and in turn responded to those efforts. Its focus on litigation and the tactical utility of legal doctrines means, among other things, that legal philosophy, legislative proposals, and arguments of social policy are relatively peripheral. Conversely, existing common and statutory law, the structure of the judicial system, the practical problems of conducting a litigation, the relationship and relative resources of the parties, and the effort to gain tactical advantage over the adversary are central. The book views the law not only as something that establishes norms, adapts to social change, and responds to internal pressures toward rational consistency, but also as a grab bag of tools that parties attempt to use if they can or when they must during private litigations that are often of the greatest importance to one if not both of the participants.

Two preliminary matters should be noted. First, a word about the book's expected audience seems appropriate. My goal was to make the discussion accessible and useful to a variety of readers. In particular, I had in mind at least four different groups: general American historians, especially those interested in the late nineteenth and twentieth centuries or in the social and political role of the Supreme Court; specialists in legal and constitutional history; scholars from a variety of disciplinary and intellectual perspectives who are interested in studying the relationship between law and society or law and economics; and law professors who specialize in either procedural issues or the problems of the federal judicial system. With those diverse groups in mind, I have tried both to provide sufficient background information to make the discussion intelligible without going into elaborate detail and also to highlight the issues that are central to my argument without exploring all of the ramifications that one or another of those groups might find desirable. The book seeks to bring relatively technical legal subjects more fully into the realm of history and society or, stated from the opposite viewpoint, to bring the study of historical change and contingency more deeply into the realm of technical legal analysis. In doing so, I hope to offer to diverse groups of scholars the advantages of integration and synthesis.

Second, it seems appropriate to emphasize that this is a work of history, not of current legal commentary. There are, of course, numerous ways in which the discussion inevitably implicates contemporary debates that revolve around the federal courts. Examples come readily to mind. On a methodological level the book suggests that the social impact of procedural and jurisdictional rules changes over time and that to truly understand them one must persistently ask who uses them, how they use them, and what results they achieve with them in the litigation process and, even more important, in the out-of-court process of claims disputing and settlement. On a doctrinal level the book suggests that any effort to advance a historically based concept of "federalism" as an unchanging or specific normative standard is unsupportable. On a practical level the book illustrates how and why parties have so frequently struggled to gain the forum of their choice, and that fact points, among many other things, to the immense and unfair disadvantages that forum-selection clauses inserted in standard retail sales contracts often impose on individual consumers. Finally, in terms of the connections between legal doctrines and social results, the book shows that use by the courts of jurisdictional and procedural devices to favor or disfavor identifiable classes of litigants is anything but new, just as it shows that use by litigants of available pretrial procedural tactics to gain advantages and impose burdens on their adversaries is also a time-worn if not time-honored practice. The former suggests that the goal of "trimming the federal caseload" does not justify any specific action but provides at most a mere starting point for analysis. The latter underscores the importance of studying jurisdictional and procedural rules not only as rational methods for allocating judicial business or for achieving just and efficient results at trial but also as tactical devices that allow parties to impose different types and degrees of risks, costs, fears, burdens, and uncertainties on their adversaries and thereby to pressure them to accept relatively unfavorable out-of-court settlements. In spite of such obvious points of contemporary resonance, however, this book is no place to explore such issues. It is and was designed to be historical, not contemporary, analysis.

It is both appropriate and deeply gratifying to thank the many individuals who contributed to the completion of this book. I relied heavily on a vast and illuminating secondary literature, and I am particularly in the debt of those scholars who have begun the extremely burdensome and often frustrating task of subjecting the work and caseloads of the courts to quantitative analysis. I have also profited greatly from the comments and criticisms of friends and colleagues who contributed immeasurably to sharpening and strengthening the final manuscript. In particular, I would like to thank Richard Bernstein, Robert G. Bone, Erwin Chemerinsky, William W. Fisher, III, Lawrence M. Friedman, Alon Harel, Sneed Hearn, Jon Heller, Peter Charles Hoffer, David A. Hollinger, Morton J. Horwitz, Randolph N. Jonakait, Robert J. Kaczorowski, Alfred S. Konefsky, William P. LaPiana, David W. Levy, Park McGinty, Martha Minow, Eben Moglen, William E. Nelson, Robert C. Post, John Phillip Reid, Judith Resnik, Edward B. Samuels, John Henry Schlegel, Henry Steiner, G. Edward White, and William M. Wiecek. The members of the New York University Legal History Colloquium, numerous and changing over the years, deserve a special collective thanks for reading and commenting on two separate early drafts. I am grateful to Celis Whyte, Stephen Douglas, Gemma Jacobs, Kathleen Moore, and Andrew Young for their consistent care and cooperation in printing innumerable drafts of the manuscript. Finally, I would like to thank my research assistants, Geri Schaeffer, Mary Jane Oltarzewski, Rachel Rabinowitz, and Kenneth Shuster, whose work has been consistently reliable and helpful in preparing the final version for publication.

In addition to friends and scholars, a number of schools and organizations have also assisted me in completing this book, and I want to express to them my deep appreciation. Early research efforts were supported by grants from the American Philosophical Society, the Social Science Research Council, the Harvard Law School, and the University of Missouri. The law firm where I practiced, Paul, Weiss, Rifkind, Wharton & Garrison, allowed me long periods of time off and provided much needed secretarial assistance. A fellowship from the National Endowment for the Humanities enabled me to complete a first draft, and another from the American Council of Learned Societies allowed me to see that the first draft really contained two separate books and to complete a draft of one of them. Finally, assistance from the New York University Law School, where I was a Golieb Fellow in 1988–89, and from New York Law School, where I began teaching in 1989, allowed me to complete the book.

My biggest thanks, of course, must go to my family. My wife, Rachel Vorspan, offered steady support and encouragement, and she gave the manuscript the invaluable benefit of her professional skills as both lawyer and historian. My in-laws, Max and Sandy Vorspan, repeatedly furnished an exceptionally pleasant place to work on vacations and provided me with every possible comfort. My son, Dan, and my daughter, Jess, consistently showed patience and understanding when work called me away from them, and they continually delighted me with their love and companionship.

New York   E.A.P.
October 1991

Contents

Litigation and Inequality

Introduction

This is a study of what I call a social litigation system, by which I mean a coherent and dynamic set of patterns of claims-disputing behavior that arises from an identifiable combination of social and legal factors.[1] The idea assumes that historical conditions regularly lead certain types of parties to dispute a relatively limited number of issues against one another in certain consistent ways and that most of the legally-related activity in any given period can be broken down into some number of different behavioral patterns that are recognizably "legal" and at the same time markedly different.[2] Social litigation systems are defined by prevailing historical conditions, the social characteristics of the parties, the types of issues that the parties are led regularly to dispute, and the special subsets of legal rules—both substantive and procedural—that are particularly relevant and useful to their litigation strategies.

The concept of a social litigation system offers a way to think about the complex relationships that exist at any given time between the variety of elements we subsume under the misleadingly simple labels of "law" and "society." It represents an attempt to bridge the gap between the broadly social and the technically legal, between quantitative studies of caseloads and the doctrinal analysis of cases, between the tumultuous and changing sources of disputes on the one hand and the rules and institutions available to channel formal litigations on the other. Its purpose is to integrate a consideration of changing social and political conditions with the study of technical legal issues into a synthesis that illuminates their complex and dynamic interactions without minimizing or losing sight of the particular significance of either.

We commonly recognize, at least implicitly, that distinct types of litigation differ as much in the social conditions that shape them as they do in the legal issues that they present. Antitrust litigation in the federal courts is profoundly different from landlord–tenant litigation in the housing courts of large cities. Securities actions have little in common with deportation proceedings, and suits involving personal injuries are quite different from school desegregation cases. Even within such a relatively narrow category as corporate litigation, the distinctively social differences that mark various types of cases may be particularly significant: Contract disputes, for example, contrast sharply with hostile tender offers. Yet in spite of the various social differences, we generally identify such types of litigation, as I have just done, by their legal rather than their social characteristics. The former may not always and for every purpose be the most useful way to categorize, examine, and understand them. Indeed, litigation involving a wide range of diverse substantive or procedural legal issues may in many

3

cases be far more profitably studied together as aspects of social conflict centering on race, class, gender, ethnicity, inequality, sexual preference, or economic competition than as compartmentalized illustrations of anything narrowly "legal."

The concept of a social litigation system is thus not primarily legal but rather historical and synthetic. It examines legal doctrines and categories but attempts to root them in a distinctively social–historical analysis. The focus is not doctrine as such but the social factors and group conflicts—and especially the available legal and practical opportunities for strategic maneuvering—that generate and channel claims disputing in general and formal litigation in particular. The concept of a social litigation system encourages exploration of the legal aspects of those relations and conflicts free from the power of legal categories to delimit the subject matter and foreordain the criteria of relevance.

Although the focus of the book is litigation, it is not on litigation in the abstract or in general. It concentrates, instead, on litigation that occurred in a specific historical period, essentially the age of industrial America. The roughly three-quarters of a century from the 1870s through the 1940s constituted a period of rapid and massive industrialization that helped transform social and economic relations in the United States. The period also witnessed the emergence of large national corporations and their rise to positions of social and economic power. That complex historical development, in turn, produced an essentially new social type of legal dispute, one between aggrieved individuals and national corporations, and it generated literally millions of such disputes.

This book looks at the patterns of claims disputing and litigation between those two unequal groups of litigants that developed around federal diversity jurisdiction, the jurisdiction of the federal courts to hear suits between citizens of different states. It focuses on the problems that relatively ordinary individuals faced when they were forced to dispute claims against national corporations that were capable of invoking the jurisdiction of the federal courts. In terms of substantive law issues, it considers two types of disputes that became particularly common and important to ordinary Americans in the late nineteenth and early twentieth centuries: negligence actions brought against manufacturing and railroad companies, particularly by injured employees; and contract actions brought against insurance companies, generally though not exclusively by claimants under relatively small personal life, health, and disability policies.[3]

Two related facts combined to create the mainspring of this social litigation system as it emerged after 1870. First, the adverse parties were drastically unequal in the social resources they brought to their disputes, and second, their forum preferences tended to be conflicting. Individual plaintiffs generally wanted their suits tried in the courts of their states, whereas national corporations favored the federal courts. Those two basic social conditions provided much of the dynamism that created and shaped the system. Although the legal categories of negligence and contract determined the substantive rules that were relevant to the system, the persistent attempts of the companies to have their cases heard in the federal courts—and the resolute efforts of their adversaries to avoid that result—determined which procedural rules would be critical. Not surprisingly, the procedural rules often proved to be far more important than the substantive ones. For convenience, the book refers to this social litigation system as "the system of corporate diversity litigation" or, more briefly, "the system."

Two qualifications are in order. First, the concept of a social litigation system implies the existence and persistence over time of relatively large scale and regular behavior patterns, and detailed quantitative evidence is not available to measure those patterns with exactitude. In spite of the difficulties, however, there is sufficient evidence to identify the nature of the patterns and to chart the ways in which they changed. Statistical data, though spotty, establish the system's outlines with clarity, and congressional reports and hearings fill in much of the detail. Case reports reveal both the persistent reappearance of critical fact situations and the repeated use of specific litigation tactics and countertactics. Statements by judges, lawyers, litigants, and legal writers further delineate the system's scope and operation. Political evidence—though only touched on here—is confirmatory, showing that national corporations and their attorneys consistently defended the legal rules that allowed them access to the national courts, whereas populists, progressives, New Dealers, and plaintiffs' attorneys criticized those elements repeatedly.

Second, it is important to emphasize that the general patterns the book identifies were subject to considerable variation. Of greatest importance, each of the states and federal judicial districts probably presented a somewhat different pattern, depending on any number of specific local factors. Economic organization, ethnic composition, political culture, the nature of the local bench and bar, the particular state substantive and procedural rules in force, and the nature of the federal judge or judges who sat in the local federal court could combine to create numerous diverse and divergent subpatterns.[4] As a general matter, too, it is clear that the system operated most pervasively in the states of the South, Midwest, and West. It is equally clear that the system changed over time. It operated most broadly in the decades around the turn of the century, and the advantages that corporate defendants enjoyed in the system began to shrink after about 1910. It is also clear that the system developed differently in tort suits than it did in insurance actions. The strategic considerations and tactical opportunities in the two types of cases were different, and their litigation patterns accordingly diverged. Tort litigation in the system reached its most intense phase during the quarter-century from 1885 to 1910. Insurance litigation, in contrast, was relatively staid through World War I but suddenly escalated in intensity during the 1920s and 1930s. In spite of variation and change, however, certain dominant patterns did emerge in the late nineteenth century and for more than half a century characterized the dynamics of litigation practice in both tort and insurance actions between individuals and national corporations.

In analyzing the operation of the system of corporate diversity litigation the book emphasizes the importance of claims disputes and settlements that occurred outside the formal legal process. As important as the formal processes were, they accounted for the resolution of only a small percentage of claims against corporations. Most of those claims, in fact, were never brought to the courts, and a majority of those that did become lawsuits were discontinued before final judgment. Studies of injured workers, for example, show that only a small percentage, probably no more than 5 to 10 percent, converted their potential claims for redress into formal legal actions. Similarly, of the relatively small number of disputes that did give rise to formal actions, well over half were dismissed or discontinued without judgment.

The practices involved in negotiating and settling claims outside the courts I refer to as "the informal legal process." Although the adjective "informal" seems appropriate for fairly obvious and generally accepted reasons, it may seem less clear why the process should also be termed "legal." I use that characterization for three reasons. First, the informal process disposed of claims that were or at least purported to be legal claims recognized and established by the formal law. Although defendants denied their validity, they nevertheless often paid to settle them and required formal written documents to attest to the fact that the claims had been extinguished according to the forms prescribed by law. Second, the process impinged directly on the formal law by drawing actions out of the legal system before the courts had found the relevant facts and applied the controlling law. The process was a substantial and regular supplement to the formal law, and the formal law recognized it obliquely and even relied on its existence and encouraged its use in numerous ways.

I also use the adjective "legal" for a third reason, one meant to reflect a central thesis of the book. The informal process of claims disposition was in practice an integral and essential part of the overall system of corporate diversity litigation. Without gaining some understanding of the relevant informal process, we cannot begin to understand how the formal process actually operated or what its general social significance was. Because the relation of the informal to the formal process was so integral, it seemed appropriate to denominate it as legal.

Many scholars, of course, have analyzed and illuminated aspects of the informal legal process, and several have referred to it with the phrase "bargaining in the shadow of the law."[5] I prefer the term "informal legal process" because I am concerned with the extent to which the claims disposition process is removed from the process of formal adjudication and the extent to which the relevant bargaining factors may be extralegal and purposely hidden from public view. The phrase "bargaining in the shadow of the law" might be taken to imply that rules of law generally shape or "influence" the outcomes of private negotiations, even though the parties might sometimes distort or ignore them. I believe, instead, that in many disputes the formal law is largely or wholly irrelevant, especially in those cases where parties have a prior relationship, where they are substantially unequal, where one of them is not represented by counsel, where social or cultural factors restrict the ability of one of the parties to enforce his or her legal rights, or where a lawsuit would impose on one of the parties disproportionate personal, social, or economic burdens.[6] This is not to deny that the law may have a vague but real influence on negotiations, does cast a "shadow," and does give "regulatory endowments." Nor, of course, is it to deny that in some types of negotiations the relevant legal rules may have a major or even controlling influence. It is merely to say that the nature of the influence, the shape of the shadow, and the size of the endowments depend in each case and in the first instance on extralegal factors such as the character of the disputing parties, their relative bargaining positions, and the social context in which their dispute occurs.

The effort to explore the informal legal process presents particularly difficult evidentiary problems. The ways in which parties settled, discontinued, or simply abandoned their claims took place, for the most part, beyond the purview of the law reports and outside the pages of the public written record. Further, parties able to use social pressures to impose unfavorable settlements on their adversaries had every incentive to obscure their negotiating practices and to keep them out of the public view. Thus, it is difficult to obtain evidence on out-of-court settlements, let alone evidence that is detailed and comprehensive. The massive and obviously critical role played by the informal legal process, however, requires an effort to identify and study its significance to the fullest extent possible. Fortunately, in spite of the difficulties, a range of sources—docket statistics, congressional reports, judicial opinions, and the testimony of individual litigants and their attorneys—bring the private process of negotiation and settlement into view, even if somewhat indistinctly. The evidence seems sufficient to establish the pervasive importance of the informal legal process and, further, to identify fairly specifically its role in the system of corporate diversity litigation.

By examining the litigation and out-of-court settlement patterns that characterized the system of corporate diversity litigation, this study attempts to cast light on a number of issues. Most broadly, it tries to explore the difficult and complex question of the practical significance that law and the legal system had in the lives of ordinary individuals. Focusing on the relationship between the formal and informal legal processes, it identifies some of the powerful extralegal forces that shaped the ways in which parties used the legal options open to them and suggests that the formal law determined the results in only a relatively small percentage of claim disputes.

More particularly, the book argues that the dominant patterns of litigation behavior and claims disposition had an adverse economic impact on individual litigants, and it reconsiders both the so-called subsidy thesis and the more recent efficiency thesis that scholars have used to explain tort law in the late nineteenth and early twentieth centuries.[7] The book argues that the legal system did confer a kind of de facto subsidy on business enterprise, but it also suggests that the economic advantages that corporations enjoyed did not arise for the most part from the formal rules of tort law or from the alleged social biases of the judiciary. Rather, it maintains that the advantages arose primarily from a variety of social, procedural, and institutional factors that allowed corporations to impose steep discounts on the amounts that they had to pay individual claimants to induce them to settle out of court.[8] With respect to the efficiency thesis, the book illustrates some of the ways that those social, procedural, and institutional constraints combined to hold down the amount and frequency of claimants' recoveries. By identifying the extent to which common law tort rules failed to determine the aggregate legal costs of accidents, the book shows that those rules failed to impose the "true" costs of accidents on corporate enterprise and, consequently, failed to bring about an economically efficient level of accident prevention.

The book also examines the impact that changing litigation tactics had on the operation of the legal system itself. By identifying some of the ways that parties used jurisdictional and procedural rules to gain great and sometimes compelling advantages in their disputes, it shows how the patterned use of certain litigation tactics repeatedly helped induce both Congress and the Supreme Court to alter federal law in response. The pressures of a dynamic and escalating litigation practice, in fact, became a major factor in forcing them to restructure various parts of the national judicial system.

Further, the book questions the standard assumption that corporations used federal diversity jurisdiction primarily or exclusively to protect themselves against local prejudice and to secure the benefits of a uniform federal common law. It suggests that the identification of local "prejudice" is a complex and problematic matter, that prejudice against corporations may have had much less influence on the state courts than has often been assumed, and that corporations may have benefited from various prejudicial factors as much as they suffered from them. More important, the book demonstrates that, regardless of the presence or absence of any operative local prejudice, corporations gained powerful legal and extralegal advantages by using the federal courts. It argues in addition that the independent federal common law was probably less significant to corporate defendants than were extralegal factors in leading them to prefer federal forums and that, insofar as the federal common law did attract corporate litigants, it was its favorable substantive nature rather than its national uniformity that accounted for its appeal.

The book also addresses the long-disputed question of whether and to what extent the federal judiciary favored business and corporate interests, and it qualifies and refines ideas about the social role of the national courts in the late nineteenth and early twentieth centuries. It explores striking and previously unrecognized ways in which the federal courts, and especially the Supreme Court, both assisted corporate litigants and disfavored them as well. Moreover, it argues that although the federal courts were generally favorable forums for business interests, the reasons why they were favorable were largely independent of the social attitudes and values of federal judges. The book suggests, too, that the Supreme Court was often relatively less favorable toward corporate enterprise than were many of the lower federal courts and that on critical procedural issues the Court often adopted rules that worked to the advantage of plaintiffs who sued national corporations. Those procedural rulings, it also contends, were often of far greater practical importance than were the Court's substantive common law rulings.

Finally, the book identifies the decades that bracketed the turn of the century as a pivotal period in the evolution of the federal judicial system. It highlights the tumultuous years from approximately 1892 to 1908 when the Supreme Court twice reversed its course in shaping the scope of federal jurisdiction. From the late 1880s to the early 1890s, the Court began methodically and broadly to restrict access to the national courts, including the access of corporate litigants who sought to invoke federal diversity jurisdiction. Beginning in approximately 1892, however, it changed course and made conscious efforts to expand corporate access to the federal courts. Then, after 1900 it again reversed course and suddenly began to limit that access. The book shows how the Court's abrupt and repeated reversals in dealing with ostensibly technical procedural and jurisdictional rules represented complex responses to changing social conditions and to the tactical battles that marked the system of corporate diversity litigation. It argues, too, that the second reversal between 1900 and 1908 effected a major reorientation in federal law that helped shape the national judicial system for the remainder of the twentieth century.

Because this book ranges back and forth from the broadly social to the narrowly doctrinal over a period of some three-quarters of a century, an outline of its structure seems useful. In broadest terms, its story falls into two parts. The first six chapters examine the emergence and growth of the system of corporate diversity litigation from its formative period in the 1870s and 1880s to its most expansive and most socially divisive phase in the two decades around the turn of the century. The next four chapters explore the system's third stage, its evolution and decline after 1910 to its disintegration in the 1940s and disappearance in the 1950s. Finally, Chapter 11 considers the overall significance of the system.

More specifically, Chapter 1 discusses the legal and social background that gave rise to the system of corporate diversity litigation, describes the system's basic characteristics, and explains why it was particularly advantageous for national corporations to litigate in the federal courts. Chapters 2 and 3 look at the two most important general advantages the federal courts offered to corporations: the de facto ability to impose severe practical burdens on plaintiffs and thereby to pressure them to discount or drop their claims; and the availability in the national courts after the 1880s of a "federal common law" that was, on critical issues, distinctly more favorable to corporations than was the common law of many states.

Chapters 4 and 5 focus on "The Battle for Forum Control," the parties' efforts to use available procedural tools to ensure that their disputes would be heard in the court that would, in their view, give them the greatest leverage possible over their adversaries. For the reasons discussed in the first three chapters, plaintiffs understandably sought to bring their suits in the state courts, and equally understandably, corporations sought to "remove" those suits to the local federal courts. These chapters analyze the two principal tactical devices that plaintiffs used to defeat federal jurisdiction and thereby avoid the federal courts. One was discounting claims below the minimum required for federal suits, and the other was "joining" parties whose presence in the action would destroy the requisite "complete" diversity of citizenship between the adversary parties. Chapters 4 and 5 also explore the ways in which corporations tried to counter those efforts and the economic consequences of the general systemwide struggle for forum control. In addition, the two chapters begin consideration of the ways in which the United States Supreme Court responded to the developing tactics in the system, identifying the changes that occurred in the decades around the turn of the century when the Court first restricted, then expanded, and then again restricted the opportunities that corporations had to remove suits to the federal courts.

Chapter 6 concludes the first half of the book by considering the role that local prejudice played in the system. Using two special removal statutes that dealt specifically with that problem, the chapter develops three arguments. First, extending the analysis in Chapter 5, it concludes that the Supreme Court's treatment of the right of corporations to remove was the result not of doctrine or logic but of the Court's efforts to deal with the intense social conflicts that arose in the system of corporate diversity litigation. Second, considering the claim that corporations preferred the federal courts because they feared "local prejudice" in the state courts, the chapter suggests that the danger of local prejudice has been inflated and that it was probably only a relatively minor threat in the state courts. Third, showing that the concern about local prejudice in the federal judicial system was itself biased and highly selective, the chapter concludes that—regardless of the presence or absence of local prejudice—the right to remove gave national corporations a procedural advantage that was both exceptional and unnecessary.

Chapter 7 begins the story of the system's contraction and evolution after 1910. It shows how legislative reforms, the rise of a plaintiffs' personal injury bar, and improvements in transportation and court administration combined to lessen the burdens that federal litigation imposed on plaintiffs and consequently to ameliorate the system's harshness. The Supreme Court contributed to the process by upholding most reform legislation and by moderating parts of the federal common law. In other areas, however, the Court extended its own lawmaking powers and in minor areas even expanded the scope of the system itself.

Chapters 8 and 9 return to the battle for forum control, analyzing the ways in which the new social and legal conditions of the early twentieth century helped spur an escalation in litigation tactics on the part of both individuals and corporations. Sizable numbers of plaintiffs began to bring their suits in distant states that offered relatively favorable laws and the lure of larger jury verdicts, a practice known as "interstate forum shopping." For their part, defendants countered with a variety of tactics designed to ensure that plaintiffs sued near their homes. In addition, changes in federal law created new opportunities for insurance companies to use the federal courts, and during the 1920s and 1930s, insurance litigation became increasingly innovative, volatile, and complex. For the first time, federal equity became a major force in the system, and the Supreme Court struggled throughout the two decades to control the new volatility and limit the sharply escalating tactics. Chapters 8 and 9 also establish the breadth of the pattern of restriction–expansion–restriction that marked the Court's removal decisions in the decades around the turn of the century by identifying two additional doctrinal areas in which the same familiar pattern recurred.

Chapter 10 traces the disintegration and disappearance of the system from the late 1930s through the 1950s. The new Roosevelt Court abolished the federal common law in 1938, and during the following decade the New Deal transformed the political orientation and image of the entire federal judiciary. In combination with continued improvements in transportation and court administration, those changes meant that by mid-century individual plaintiffs no longer had any general incentive to avoid the federal courts. The chapter concludes by showing how in the decades after 1937 Congress and the Supreme Court restricted both interstate forum shopping and the corporate use of federal equity.

Finally, Chapter 11 reflects on the long history of the system of corporate diversity litigation. Providing an overview of the system's evolution, the chapter considers the concept of a social litigation system and some of the ways an understanding of the system helps illuminate a number of issues in American legal history in the late nineteenth and early twentieth centuries. It focuses on the utility of the local prejudice rationale of diversity jurisdiction, the merits of the "efficiency" thesis, and the political orientation of the federal courts in the long period from Reconstruction to the New Deal. It ends by stressing the pivotal importance of the Court's decisions from 1905 to 1908 in shaping the social role of the national judiciary in the twentieth century.

One last comment seems in order. The book gives relatively little attention to individual judges, litigants, and lawyers and to the influence of politics, ideas, and culture. I regret that lack and by no means intend to detract from the importance of any of those factors. I hope, in fact, to explore their significance in another work. The focus of this study, however, is intentionally and necessarily on the structure and operation of the system of corporate diversity litigation itself—its social and legal preconditions, its characteristic patterns of behavior, its social and institutional consequences, and its rise, evolution, and disintegration over a period of some three-quarters of a century.

By itself that story seems sufficiently complex for one book. Indeed, the story involves in one way or another a wide range of legal issues and most of the major events that marked American life from Reconstruction to the Cold War. And in spite of the emphasis on general patterns of behavior and the relative absence of individuals, the reader should nonetheless get some sense of the underlying human conflict, vitality, and creativity that continuously fed the litigation process and ultimately helped shape the twentieth-century American judicial system.

Chapter 1

Origins of a Social Litigation System

When Newton D. Baker's Cleveland law firm became regional counsel for the Baltimore & Ohio Railroad in 1934, it immediately took on the defense of several tort suits. Baker, a progressive Democrat who had served as Woodrow Wilson's Secretary of War, informed the railroad that his staff had "worked up a technic which ought to assure the best possible results."[1] The staff tried the cases in federal court.

Baker's firm enjoyed striking success. During 1934, an official of the B & O boasted privately, the railroad set "an all-time low record" for the amount it paid out to tort claimants.[2] One of the suits involved an eight-year-old boy who, admitted another B & O official, had "lost his leg by reason of having been run over by one of our locomotives at a dangerous crossing." Two other suits involved automobiles struck during the night at crossings. Both drivers, according to the B & O, sustained "serious injuries."[3] The boy won a verdict for $2,750, and the two drivers received a combined total of $1,250. The B & O normally paid its regional counsel in Cleveland approximately $20,000 per year, and in 1934 it paid all of its regional federal tort plaintiffs a total of $4,100, barely one-fifth of that amount.[4] "I just want you to know," the railroad's general counsel congratulated Baker at the end of the year, "how pleased we all are with the magnificent work."[5]

The existence of federal diversity jurisdiction allowed the B & O and other large corporations to take their cases to federal court regularly and often, and a variety of incentives induced them to take advantage of the opportunity. Diversity jurisdiction was the matrix within which a disparate collection of legal rules, practices, and institutions interacted with specific and changing sets of social conditions to create systematic practices for resolving legal claims that tended in the long run and over the mass of cases to favor national corporations. Some of the system's formal legal elements were consciously designed to foster business enterprise while others were developed to achieve traditional legal goals of fairness and equality or such practical institutional ends as operational economy. The social conditions resulted from massive demographic changes, the complex processes of industrialization, and the existence of widespread de facto inequality. The synergism of formal elements in the legal system, changing social conditions, and the dynamics of mass litigation between drastically unequal parties generated new patterns of litigation behavior that determined the scope, structure, and significance of the system of corporate diversity litigation.

The Legal Elements of Diversity Jurisdiction

The existence of parallel state and federal courts in the United States has been basic to the American judicial system, and that dual system established the legal framework out of which the system of corporate diversity litigation evolved. The states had long maintained their own judicial systems, and their courts possessed "subject matter jurisdiction" to hear and decide almost any kind of case that came before them. In contrast, the federal courts exercised only limited and narrower types of jurisdiction. The Constitution restricted the judicial power of the United States to certain specific categories of cases, the broadest and most important of which were cases "between Citizens of different States" and those "arising under" the Constitution and laws of the United States.[6] The former category became known as "diversity jurisdiction" and the latter as "federal question" jurisdiction. With the exception of the United States Supreme Court, however, the Constitution did not create any federal court or confer any jurisdiction. Rather, it granted Congress the authority to "ordain and establish" whatever "inferior Courts" it chose and, by implication, to determine what jurisdiction—within the outer limits allowed by the Constitution—such lower federal courts would exercise.

In the Judiciary Act of 1789[7] the First Congress established a system of federal trial courts, and from that date the nation's dual federal–state judicial system, though altered subsequently in various ways, has remained continuously in operation. In the First Judiciary Act Congress made a number of decisions that would prove critical to the evolution of that dual system. First, it granted the lower federal courts diversity jurisdiction but not federal question jurisdiction, establishing diversity as the "original" and "ancient" jurisdiction of the national courts.[8] Second, it accepted the idea that federal jurisdiction over cases involving citizens from different states should be "concurrent" with that of the state courts. Any case, that is, that could be brought in a federal court on the basis of diverse citizenship would remain cognizable in the state courts. Third, Congress decided to limit diversity jurisdiction to cases in which the "matter in controversy," the subject of the dispute, involved a minimum of $500. That monetary limitation was generally referred to as the "amount in controversy" or the "jurisdictional amount." Finally, Congress enacted a general "removal" provision that allowed a defendant who was sued in the court of a state where he was a nonresident to "remove" the suit from the state court into the local federal court. To be removable, the suit had to meet the requirements of diverse citizenship and the jurisdictional amount, and the plaintiff had to be an alien or a resident of the "forum" state—the state where the suit was brought.

Removal was perhaps the most significant innovation that the First Judiciary Act made. The Constitution did not mention such a jurisdiction, and it was a powerful device to assert the primacy of the national judicial power over that of the states. Removal not only authorized federal courts to preempt state jurisdiction, but it also established a one-way process. Whereas a case in a state court could be removed to the local federal court, a case properly brought in a federal court could not be removed or transferred to any state court.[9] Finally, removal countered the traditional assumption that the plaintiff, the party who initiated the legal action and had allegedly been wronged, had the right to determine the forum that would decide her claim. Removal allowed defendants to trump that choice and force plaintiffs out of their chosen forum. A clear device for asserting national authority, removal was also a potentially powerful strategic tool for defendants.

For almost eighty years the basic structure of the federal judicial system remained unchanged, but the political and social pressures generated by the Civil War and its aftermath forged a number of modifications. In a series of Reconstruction statutes the Republican Congresses expanded the jurisdiction of the federal courts to help enforce their new national policies. They increased the availability of the writ of habeas corpus, broadened the right to remove general diversity suits, and granted both original and removal jurisdiction to the federal courts over causes of action arising under the Civil Rights Act of 1866. The Republican policy of expanding federal judicial power culminated in the Judiciary Act of 1875 which pushed the reach of the federal courts toward their outer constitutional limits. The statute conferred general "federal question" jurisdiction on the national courts for the first time,[10] and it allowed plaintiffs as well as defendants to remove suits from the state courts.[11] Its elaborate procedural sections bristled with provisions aimed at quashing any effort by the state courts to obstruct removal. It authorized the federal courts to order state courts to grant removals, allowed them to hold plaintiffs in default if a state court blocked removal, and provided that a state court clerk who refused to effectuate a removal was guilty of a misdemeanor punishable by a year of imprisonment and a $1,000 fine.[12]

The high tide of Republican Reconstruction quickly receded. Expanded jurisdiction under the 1875 act brought increasingly heavier caseloads to the federal courts, and pressure grew to relieve the growing burden. Far more important, Reconstruction faltered and then failed, and the nation's politics underwent a fundamental change. The years after 1877 brought renewed Democratic strength to Congress and a growing resentment against the national judiciary in the South and West. The triumph of white "Redeemer" governments and an ingrained hostility to the federal courts inspired much of the southern opposition, while growing hostility to eastern financial interests and national corporations—increasingly identified with the federal courts—animated much of the Midwest and West as well as the South. Beginning in 1878, southerners and their allies mounted a persistent campaign to restrict the federal courts, prevent corporate removals, and limit diversity jurisdiction.[13]

Twelve years after the Judiciary Act of 1875, in a political and social world that seemed light years from Republican Reconstruction, Congress reached one of the last compromises that ended the era of the Civil War and one of the first that responded to the new era of social and political conflict over industrialization and the role of the corporation. Although sectional conflict continued and states' rights attitudes remained strong, in the 1880s economic issues became more and more important in spurring the opposition to diversity jurisdiction.[14] Unlike the compromises that northerners made regarding the rights of black Americans, however, the jurisdictional compromise of 1887 gave the South and West only a small part of what they wanted. The Judiciary Act of 1887, reenacted with corrections in 1888, retained the new federal question jurisdiction and narrowed the scope of diversity jurisdiction only slightly. It eliminated the provision that allowed plaintiffs to remove and shortened the time for filing removal petitions. Most important, it raised the jurisdictional amount from $500 to $2,000.[15] An ambiguously drafted statute that gave rise to innumerable problems of construction, the Judiciary Act of 1887–88 established the basic statutory scope of federal jurisdiction that remained in effect until the revision of the federal judicial code in 1948.

Industrialism and the Rise of National Corporations

Although Congress expanded and then restricted the scope of diversity jurisdiction between 1866 and 1887–88, the social and economic developments that transformed life in the late nineteenth century made far greater changes in diversity jurisdiction by profoundly altering its social significance. The latter half of the nineteenth century was a period of rapid and tumultuous change. A predominantly rural, agricultural, and decentralized society unevenly but swiftly gave way to an urbanized, industrialized, and centralized nation. The 9,000 miles of railroad track that existed in 1850 multiplied to almost 200,000 by the end of the century, while between 1870 and 1900 the gross national product grew at the spectacular rate of almost 15 percent per year.

Corporations became the dominant units of business and commerce. Providing limited liability to stockholders and allowing for the aggregation of huge amounts of capital, the corporate form of organization became the norm for large-scale business enterprise. In the early 1850s only a handful of major railroads had been capitalized above $10 million, but by 1893 twenty-seven separate railroad systems were capitalized above $100 million. The Pennsylvania Railroad Company, the nation's largest, stood at almost $850 million and employed more than 110,000 workers. The capitalization of the largest manufacturing companies rose above $10 million by the 1880s and above $100 million by the turn of the century. The size of the corporations allowed them to dominate employment, manufacturing, transportation, and distribution. In 1900 corporations produced approximately 60 percent of the total value of American manufactured goods and employed well over half of the nation's work force.[16]

With industrial expansion and the dominance of the corporate form of business, determined efforts to consolidate market control soon followed. A range of pressures spurred the efforts—the drive for larger profits, the need to protect massive fixed investments, the practical demands for capital created by ever-wider markets, and the drive for stability inspired by the increasingly bureaucratic structure of big business and the recurrence of economic depressions. The railroads went through the process first, followed by basic industries such as oil and steel, and then by a dozen others. The consolidation efforts peaked in the decade after 1895. Almost three thousand separate business units disappeared in a sweeping merger movement, and by 1910 narrow oligopoly structures characterized many basic industries such as rubber, chemicals, electricity, and food processing. "It is no exaggeration," wrote one historian, "to say that the structure of the twentieth century American economy had been reshaped by the end of the century's first decade."[17]

State law nourished the corporate expansion. Until the middle of the nineteenth century corporations not only were small in size and number, but their existence also depended on special legislative charters. Beginning in the 1840s, however, states began passing "general incorporation" laws that allowed individuals to obtain state corporation charters merely by complying with certain standard and relatively minimal requirements. By the 1870s, general incorporation laws were common, and the states began to grant more liberal terms both to those starting new businesses and to those interested in reincorporating established ones. Some competed vigorously for lucrative corporate filing and other fees by offering generous and ever less restrictive corporate charters. The competition allowed companies to select their state of incorporation freely and to do so on the basis of a careful analysis of the relative advantages offered by each. The New Jersey incorporation statute of 1875, for example, encouraged out-of-state businesses to incorporate in the state by granting charters regardless of the residency of the incorporators or of the company's principal place of business.[18] Other advantages included lower local taxes, expansive charter powers, hospitable political climates, and more favorable statutory and common law rules.

Beyond the specific and increasingly sweeping powers that corporate charters conferred they also granted legal authority to engage in interstate commerce throughout the nation. The United States Constitution required states to recognize the rights that other states created in their charters, and it protected corporations with out-of-state charters—termed "foreign" corporations in all nonchartering states—against discriminatory laws designed to restrict the "interstate" activities that they carried on in any state. The states could, within limits, set the terms on which foreign corporations could do "intrastate" business, and they could also—within unclear but generally narrowing limits—impose some regulation on even interstate business. The line between interstate and intrastate commerce was, of course, disputed in every context imaginable.

While the adoption of general incorporation laws spread, the Supreme Court gave additional significance to a company's choice among chartering states by infusing new meaning into the federal jurisdictional statutes. In a long series of not always consistent decisions the Court developed the doctrine that a corporation was, for purposes of federal diversity jurisdiction, to be treated as a citizen of its chartering state. The development proceeded in three stages.

First, beginning in 1844 the Court began to alter earlier doctrine in order to allow corporations to sue and to be sued more easily in the national courts on the ground of diversity of citizenship. By the end of the 1850s it had established its new doctrine. For purposes of federal diversity jurisdiction, the law would irrebuttably presume that all of the individual stockholders of a corporation were citizens of the corporation's chartering state. Hence, the corporation would be treated jurisdictionally as a citizen of that state.[19]

Second, two decisions in the 1870s extended the doctrine to create an essential jurisdictional prerequisite of the system of corporate diversity litigation. Before the Civil War orthodox legal theory had assumed that a corporation, as a mere creature of the law of its chartering state, could not act or be "present" outside that chartering state. Accordingly, foreign corporations were generally thought to be liable to suit only in their home states. The realities of a growing national market and of the burgeoning interstate activities of large corporations, however, compelled a revision of the theory. On various grounds, such as a corporation's consent to be sued or the purposeful acts of its agents within a nonchartering state, the courts of the states began to assume personal jurisdiction over foreign corporations. The Supreme Court generally approved their efforts,[20] and in *Railroad Company v. Harris*[21] in 1870 it expanded federal jurisdiction along similar lines, holding that the federal courts could hear suits involving corporations that were chartered outside the state in which the federal court sat. Eight years later in *Ex parte Schollenberger*[22] it held that the jurisdiction of the federal courts to hear suits involving foreign corporations included suits that foreign corporations removed from state courts. *Schollenberger* was critical to the development of the system, in other words, because it established the right of foreign corporations to remove in every state except the state of their incorporation. Less than a month after the decision came down, southerners and westerners in Congress began pushing to restrict or terminate the corporate use of diversity jurisdiction.[23]

The third step in the development of the doctrine of corporate citizenship came in 1896. On the ground that the presumption of corporate citizenship for diversity purposes "went to the very verge of judicial power," the Court in *St. Louis and San Francisco Railway Co. v. James*[24] refused to allow the further presumption that corporations could, by state law, be made citizens of additional states. "The presumption that a corporation is composed of citizens of the State which created it accompanies such corporation when it does business in another State," the Court ruled, "and it may sue or be sued in the Federal courts in such other State as a citizen of the State of its original creation."[25] *James,* in other words, ensured that corporations could restrict their jurisdictional citizenship to only one state and thereby preserve diversity with citizens of every other state in the union.[26] It blocked statutes in a number of states that attempted to stop foreign corporations from removing by "adopting" them as domestic corporations and hence destroying their diversity of citizenship with the citizens of the adopting states.

James was typical of the attitude that came to mark the Supreme Court in the 1890s. Although *Harris* and *Schollenberger* had opened the federal courts to foreign corporations in the 1870s, both explained that they did so to assist individuals who wanted to sue those corporations in federal court. By allowing individuals to bring federal suits in their home states, the decisions relieved plaintiffs from the potentially heavy burden of having to conduct their federal suits in the corporation's distant home state.[27] If the proplaintiff rationale of *Harris* and *Schollenberger* was plausible in the 1870s before the system of corporate diversity litigation had formed, however, it had no relevance in 1896 when the system was fully operational. By then it was thoroughly and widely understood that plaintiffs did not generally choose to sue in the federal courts and that they seldom had either the desire or the resources to file in a distant federal court. Instead, they sued at home and in the state courts, and defendants frequently and regularly removed to the local federal court. In the context of the fully developed system of corporate diversity litigation, *James* defined the citizenship of corporations in the way that offered the maximum possible scope for the corporate use of diversity jurisdiction. Unlike *Harris* and *Schollenberger,* it offered no social reasons for its decision. It rested, instead, on a general assertion about the limits of judicial power that failed to provide a logical justification for the Court's decision.[28] *James* was, in fact, part of a concerted effort that the Supreme Court made in the 1890s to expand substantially the ability of corporate defendants to remove diversity actions.

By the end of the 1870s, then, corporations could generally be sued in states where they were doing business, and they were treated as "citizens" capable of invoking diversity jurisdiction and removing state suits to the federal courts. They were also able to select among competing and hospitable jurisdictions as chartering states and, if they chose, to restrict their jurisdictional citizenship to a single state. In 1896 *James* guaranteed that last right. The result was that a corporation could invoke federal jurisdiction in an original suit against citizens of every state but the one that had granted its charter or by removal in every state but its chartering state unless sued by a cocitizen of its chartering state.[29] Corporations, in short, could for the most part invoke federal jurisdiction when it suited their purposes and preserve the right to remove in every state but one.[30]

By the late nineteenth century, corporations of all types were exploiting the availability of out-of-state charters. Further liberalization of the corporation laws in New Jersey and Delaware, restrictive actions in a number of other states, and the competitive economic pressures that intensified in the 1890s combined with decisions like *James* to spur a wholesale movement. In 1900 and 1901, for example, 264 and 211 Massachusetts businesses took charters from their home state, while 423 and 524, respectively, sought theirs out of state. In contrast, in only the first seven months of 1899, New Jersey chartered 1,336 corporations, most of which operated primarily in other states.[31]

Large national corporations had the legal sophistication, economic resources, and doctrinal opportunities to utilize diversity jurisdiction, and they increasingly had powerful incentives to do so. The development of a national market and the dominance of corporate enterprise meant that more and more individuals came into contact with foreign corporations. Railroads and streetcars, mass-produced consumer products, machines powered by steam and electricity, and the escalating dangers of industrial labor all combined to cause an enormous increase in the number and severity of accidental injuries to persons and property. In Boston the number of trolley car accidents rose from 200 in 1889 to more than 1,700 by 1900, and the number of resulting tort suits jumped from fewer than 20 in 1880 to more than 1,400 only twenty years later.[32] After 1900 industrial accidents of all kinds caused an estimated 35,000 deaths and 2 million injuries each year.[33] Tort suits brought against those who owned the machines multiplied dramatically.

The railroads were the paramount sources of danger. Although injury to livestock and property located near the tracks became common, it was the human toll that seemed staggering. Per-capita injuries to railroad workers doubled between 1889 and 1906, running in the 1890s at about 2,000 killed and another 25,000 to 35,000 injured each year. The numbers escalated sharply in the two decades after the turn of the century, averaging 3,000 to 4,000 killed and about 100,000 injured each year. Workers were not alone in bearing the impact of steam and iron transportation. Passengers, shippers, bystanders, trespassers, and employees of third parties also were victimized. Although fewer nonemployees were harmed, their injuries were more frequently fatal. In the 1890s, for example, railroad accidents annually injured about 15,000 nonemployees, but almost a third of the total were fatalities. In the two decades after 1900, railroad accidents killed 20 to 30 percent of the 15,000 to 35,000 nonemployees injured each year.[34]

Similarly, noncommercial contract litigation involving private individuals, particularly cases raising insurance claims, expanded enormously. Although commercial insurance had become common by the early nineteenth century, the private life and health insurance business did not boom until the last third of the century.

Then, the pressures and fears generated by an industrializing and urbanizing society helped inspire stunning growth. From 1850 to 1900, life insurance companies increased their total assets by 12,000 percent, and per-capita coverage rose from just over $40 in 1885 to $179 in 1910.[35] So-called industrial life insurance, generally covering some medical expenses and final burial costs, grew in popularity. In 1880 approximately $13 million in industrial insurance was in force, but by 1897 the total had jumped to almost 1 billion dollars.[36] The conditions against which the policies were meant to protect were harsh. In 1898 an industry spokesman explained that companies writing industrial insurance faced "a death-rate among adults over twice as great as that which has prevailed among the companies doing an ordinary life insurance business."[37]

Up to 1870 the American law reports contained a total of approximately one hundred appellate cases involving insurance contracts. The following decades produced thousands. During the 1890s, appellate decisions involving the major national insurance companies grew more rapidly than did the companies' skyrocketing overall business.[38] In one five-year period at the end of the 1920s, forty-two life insurance companies alone litigated almost eighteen thousand separate cases.[39]

The changing economic system thus generated significant new classes of cases that repeatedly pitted injured or aggrieved individuals against national corporations. By the late 1870s and early 1880s those national corporations were beginning to invoke diversity jurisdiction regularly to take their cases to the federal courts. Diversity suits were "the largest and most rapidly-increasing class of Federal cases," a House of Representatives report noted in 1876. They arose from the nation's rapid economic development and "the formation of numerous great corporations whose business connections extend into many States."[40] Twenty years later another House report found the situation unchanged. The cases in the national courts arose "chiefly" from corporations involved in interstate commerce, it explained. "Such litigants naturally seek the Federal court and are invited there by the law."[41]

The System of Corporate Diversity Litigation

A study of Supreme Court decisions between 1855 and 1885 points to the growing corporate preference for the national courts. Not until 1862 did the Court hear a diversity suit that had been initiated as a federal action by a corporation, and at no time after 1872 did it hear a diversity case in which a corporation opposed an adversary's attempt to remove. Of approximately one hundred removed diversity suits, eighty-four were removed by corporations, primarily railroads and insurance companies.[42] Most of the corporate removals presumably came after 1878 when *Schollenberger* first authorized the federal courts to hear such suits. Even after *Harris* in 1870, the Court explained in *Schollenberger,* "the practice in the [lower federal] courts generally has been to decline jurisdiction in this class of suits."

If *Schollenberger* gave foreign corporations the right to remove and *James* guaranteed that they could use the right broadly, the beneficiaries took full advantage of the opportunity. Successive editions of a late nineteenth-century treatise on *The Law of Insurance* listed prominently among the insurers' "remedies" against policyholders their "Right to remove Action."[44] A report by the House of Representatives in 1900 readily assumed that "outside capitalists now investing within the State [of West Virginia] will naturally take their cases to the Federal courts."[45] The "great majority" of all removals were effected by corporations, a 1928 treatise on federal jurisdiction explained, "and to these this right of removal is one that is cherished and valued."[46] An Arizona federal judge agreed. "[N]early all of the [local] personal injury cases," he observed in 1930, "were removed to the federal court on account of diversity of citizenship by the mining, smelting, railroad, and other large corporations doing business" in the state.[47]

Available statistical data confirm the picture. A study of litigation in Alameda County, California, between 1880 and 1900 found that of a total of 340 personal injury suits, plaintiffs initiated only 29 in the local federal court. Of the 110 personal injury actions that the federal court heard, 81 were there by way of removal. Thus, plaintiffs instituted more than 90 percent of their actions in the state court, and for every 1 case that plaintiffs brought in the federal court, defendants removed 3. Corporations, too, removed at a somewhat higher rate than did individual defendants, and common carrier defendants accounted for almost 60 percent of the removals.[48] The same pattern appeared in insurance suits. Of 631 federal actions against forty-two life insurance companies from 1927 to 1931, plaintiffs initiated only 99. The remaining 532 were removals. Thus, companies preferred the federal forum at least five times more frequently than did plaintiffs.[49] In addition to forcing plaintiffs into federal court by removing, however, insurance companies could accomplish the same result in some cases by seizing the initiative and launching preemptive actions in the federal courts. During the same five years, the forty-two companies filed 488 such suits.[50] Thus, of the total 1,119 insurance suits heard in the federal courts involving the forty-two life insurance companies, fewer than 10 percent were brought there by the claimants. The companies were responsible for more than 90 percent, almost half as initial federal actions and slightly more than half as removed ones.[51]

The outline and some of the details of the pattern emerged most clearly in a massive study of 9,852 civil cases that were terminated in thirteen federal judicial districts during the year 1929–30. The study, conducted for President Herbert Hoover's National Commission on Law Observance and Enforcement and subsequently published by the American Law Institute (ALI), found that approximately 70 percent of all diversity cases (1,816) and 86 percent of all diversity actions at law (1,493) were tort or contract disputes. Insurance contract cases made up 13 percent of the law docket, and negligence actions 52 percent. Foreign corporations were defendants in well over half of the cases, and residents of the forum state were plaintiffs in almost 60 percent. Of all actions brought by resident plaintiffs, 86 percent were against foreign corporations, and of all actions brought against foreign corporations, almost 93 percent were brought by resident plaintiffs.[52]

The ALI study highlighted four characteristics of removal jurisdiction. First, it showed that tort and contract actions dominated the removal docket. Together, they constituted 77 percent of all removals and 87 percent of all removals at law. Actions on insurance contracts probably accounted for 12 to 15 percent of the removals at law, and negligence actions about half. Second, the study showed that removal was overwhelmingly a product of diversity litigation. Cases removed on the basis of diversity of citizenship accounted for 92.6 percent of all removals on the federal docket. Federal question cases, in contrast, accounted for only 2.3 percent of all removals. Third, the study showed that removal was a major part of the overall diversity docket, accounting for just over half of all diversity actions. In contrast, barely 1 percent of federal question cases were removed from the state courts.[53] Fourth, the study showed that corporations were the dominant removing party. Of 877 removed diversity suits, foreign corporations removed 759, or approximately 87 percent of the total.[54]

The ALI study also suggested that corporate defendants did quite well by removing. Whereas plaintiffs voluntarily dismissed or discontinued approximately 45 percent of the diversity actions that they filed as original federal suits, they dismissed 64 percent of the diversity actions that defendants removed.[55] The figures suggest that the mere fact of removal convinced substantial numbers of diversity plaintiffs to dismiss their suits. Further, diversity plaintiffs fared relatively poorly when their actions were decided on the merits. Plaintiffs prevailed less frequently in diversity actions at law than in cases brought under other jurisdictional heads. In civil suits in which the United States was a party, plaintiffs won at the rate of 5 to 1 over defendants, and federal question plaintiffs won 3.3 to 1. Diversity plaintiffs, however, won at the rate of only 2.7 to 1, and those who asserted negligence claims won at an even lower rate, a mere 2.3 to 1.[56] Other data, too, suggest that plaintiffs in state courts won two to four times more frequently than did the diversity plaintiffs that the ALI charted.[57]

In addition, other studies have shown that corporate defendants repeatedly fared better in the federal than in the state courts. The study of state and federal trial courts in Alameda County, California, between 1880 and 1900, for example, concluded that "[p]laintiffs did not do as well in federal court as they did in [state] superior court,"[58] and a follow-up study for the period 1901 to 1910 found that plaintiffs in the state court won approximately 70 percent more frequently than did plaintiffs in the federal court.[59] Consistent with those conclusions, a study of litigation in West Virginia from 1870 to 1940 found that corporate defendants there prevailed more frequently in the federal court than they did in the state courts.[60]

Three general conclusions stand out. First, the diversity docket was dominated by negligence actions and by suits on insurance contracts, most of which were between resident plaintiffs and foreign corporations. Second, removal was overwhelmingly the tool of corporate defendants.[61] Third, corporations enjoyed a relatively high degree of success when they removed diversity actions. Whatever the variations by time, district, and legal subject, the basic characteristics of the system of corporate diversity litigation were clear.

In regularly seeking federal jurisdiction, then, corporations seemed to follow the time-tested advice of a late nineteenth-century handbook entitled *The Conduct of Lawsuits*. "The forum of your choice," it advised litigators, was an advantage "to be looked for with wide-open eyes and clutched with unslipping hold when found."[62]

The Corporate Preference for the Federal Courts

Forum choice in the system of corporate diversity litigation was confined by practical factors almost wholly to a choice among courts located relatively close to plaintiffs' residences. Although plaintiffs were often able to choose between state and federal courts or among different types of state courts, they seldom had either the resources or the sophistication to take their claims out of state or far from their homes. As the ALI study showed, as late as 1929–30 almost 93 percent of all suits against foreign corporations were brought in the plaintiffs' home states. Corporate defendants, in turn, frequently had no choice of forum, if, for example, the suit were filed in federal court or if the requirements for diversity jurisdiction did not exist. When they did have a choice, they were limited to that between a state court and its local federal counterpart. Indeed, that was the pivotal choice on which the system of corporate diversity litigation centered. That choice was not random or manifold or unpredictable. Rather, it was specific, binary, and regularly recurring, and in most individual cases the tactical advantages to be gained by removing— whether in any particular case they were nonexistent, significant, or fully dispositive—could be rationally calculated in both legal and social terms.

A number of factors contributed to the corporate preference for a federal forum. Most corporate attorneys, for example, probably believed that the federal courts were simply better and more prestigious than the state courts. The federal courts were the "national" courts; they had much smaller dockets and almost no "petty" cases; and their judges were generally reputed to be more highly qualified than state judges. As a result, large national corporations probably viewed them as more "appropriate" forums for their business, and their attorneys saw them as representing a higher caliber of practice that brought with it an enhanced professional status.[63] Convenience undoubtedly also played a significant role. Although national corporations retained local counsel, in many states they relied primarily on attorneys in the larger cities which, unlike smaller cities and towns, regularly hosted terms of the local federal court. Thus, when faced with a lawsuit filed one or two counties away, local corporate counsel would often prefer removal to the nearby federal court as a matter of personal convenience. Of course, by forcing the burden of distance onto plaintiff's attorney, removal in such cases also served broader tactical purposes.[64]

It is important to recognize, of course, that any attempt to explain massive patterns of forum selection in broad and general terms is subject to serious limitations. In individual cases the role of the attorney in selecting a forum is critical, and the reasons for making one choice over another must in many cases have been highly individualized. Lawyers may select a forum on the basis of idiosyncratic considerations regarding the individual case, the opposing attorney, the trial judge assigned, or other similar and case-specific factors. Lawyers may also select a forum for relatively personal reasons, such as the presence or absence in the forum of other cases that the attorney is handling, personal relations with the administrative personnel of various courts, or some informal arrangement with an opposing counsel for mutually convenient trade-offs.[65]

Whatever the significance of such particular factors, however, the fact remains that as a general matter corporate defendants frequently and regularly preferred to litigate in the national courts and their individual adversaries did not. Over three-quarters of a century and literally millions of lawsuits, the general pattern was clear, broad, and steady. Indeed, few corporate spokespersons denied that corporations valued removal highly or that they often preferred a federal forum.

When publicly explaining their preference for the federal courts, corporate spokespersons usually relied on two justifications. The first was that the federal courts, in contrast to the state courts, applied a nationally uniform common law that was essential to business planning and security. Because the common law still governed most commercial transactions, they maintained, widely varying state rules were disruptive and archaic. The federal courts offered an alternative. In 1842 the Supreme Court decided in *Swift v. Tyson*[66] that the federal courts were not required to follow the decisions of state courts in matters of general commercial law. They were, instead, free to follow their own views as to the nature and application of the principles that controlled a case. Under *Swift* the federal courts developed their own "federal common law" in many subject areas, and they applied it with some uniformity across the nation. In some subject areas they even succeeded in winning agreement from a good number of state supreme courts.[67]

The second reason that corporations gave for removing was their need for protection from local prejudice. With historical and judicial authority to support them, they maintained that the very purpose of diversity jurisdiction was to provide out of staters with a forum free from local prejudice when they litigated there against local residents. In utilizing diversity, national corporations insisted, they were simply claiming the jurisdictional benefit that the Founders had intended for those who engaged in interstate commerce.

Two structural characteristics of the federal courts seemed particularly useful in deflecting local prejudice. The first was the political independence and institutional authority of the judge. Unlike most state judges who were elected to office, federal judges were appointed for life and could not be removed except for serious misconduct. Life tenure was designed to make them less susceptible to popular feelings and to guarantee their political independence.[68] Institutionally, they had the right to exercise firm control over the jury, generally regarded as proplaintiff and unsympathetic to corporations.[69] Federal judges, for example, had the right to "comment" on evidence presented to the jury, a right denied by statute to most state judges. As long as a federal judge did not appear to coerce the jury or foreclose its right to determine the facts, he could explain to the jury his views concerning the quality and weight of the evidence.[70] Moreover, federal judges not only had the duty to instruct the jury as to the law, but they also had authority to set aside jury verdicts and to instruct the jury that a certain verdict was required as a matter of law. Although state judges also instructed juries in the law and in most cases could direct verdicts, the standards under which they acted seemed more restrictive and the leeway they gave the jury often seemed broader.[71]

The second characteristic of the national courts that seemed useful as a counter to local prejudice was the nature of the federal jury. It was drawn generally from wider geographical areas than were state juries, and corporate attorneys argued that the practice lessened the possibility of prejudice in favor of a locally known individual plaintiff. There was also some evidence that a higher percentage of jurors in the federal courts came from middle-class backgrounds, and that perception may have influenced the views of corporate defendants. An insurance company attorney believed simply that "you get a better class of citizens on the juries in Federal courts."[72] Perhaps most important, the federal courts required a unanimous verdict of twelve jurors. In contrast to the jury systems of a number of states, where smaller numbers of jurors were used or nonunanimous verdicts allowed, the federal jury was clearly more favorable to defendants.

Beyond the perceived benefits of uniformity in the federal common law and protection against local prejudice, additional and quite practical advantages made removal a tactical option that corporate attorneys valued highly. One was that removal allowed corporations the luxury of being able to choose between alternative judges, enabling them either to avoid one they considered potentially troublesome or to gain one they regarded as particularly favorable. Although seldom admitted publicly by the legal profession, the ability to choose one's judge was widely recognized among practitioners as a major advantage. Judges came in many types, and their differing individual qualities—from temperament and training, to specific views on issues of doctrine and practice, to basic political and social philosophy—could create differences between their styles of judging and the outcomes of the cases before them. "You must watch the bench, especially in a large city," advised one personal injury attorney in 1906. Those attorneys who did could identify "this judge or that judge who is strong for the defense" and "this judge or that judge who favors the plaintiff."[73]

Divergence among judges, however, did not need to determine results in order to be tactically important. Even seemingly minor differences in the extent to which they required briefs and other formal papers or dealt with matters promptly or tardily could have a telling impact on the conduct of a litigation. Because federal judges enjoyed almost complete freedom in the way they administered their courts and managed their dockets, variation from judge to judge and district to district could be substantial.[74] When the parties were unequal, even ostensibly minor practical or procedural differences could impose disproportionate practical burdens on the weaker party.

Augmenting the standard advantage that parties enjoyed when they could choose among judges, removal in the late nineteenth and early twentieth centuries probably gave to corporate defendants an additional edge, allowing them across the overall run of cases to obtain judges whose basic social values disposed them to view with relative sympathy the doctrines on which corporate defendants regularly relied. As a general matter, federal judges may have shared the values that fostered national corporate enterprise more than state judges did. The latter generally held elective offices, and their need to face reelection likely made at least some of them more sensitive to popular feelings against corporations. Further, state judges tended to be more closely tied to local politics and interests than did federal judges, and that probably made them less concerned with the interests of national corporations and less protective toward interstate commerce when there was a conflict with local interests and policies. "One of the most characteristic features of our state courts," Woodrow Wilson wrote in 1897, "is what I may call their *local attachment*."[75] Federal judges, too, especially at the appellate and Supreme Court levels, were more frequently chosen from the ranks of prominent and successful corporation attorneys. Despite best efforts to be neutral and fair, their social and professional backgrounds may have disposed many of them—at least after 1890—to better understand and more readily sympathize with the legal views and implicit social policy arguments that national corporations advanced.[76]

To whatever extent the social and political attitudes of federal judges made them more sympathetic to corporate interests, from the late nineteenth century through the 1930s Americans certainly regarded them as relatively probusiness.[77] While defenders of the national courts proclaimed them fairer, more neutral, and simply better forums, their critics accused them of social and political bias in favor of corporations. In the 1880s, for example, the national courts began using their power to appoint receivers to provide special protection for corporate reorganizations, a process that seemed to link them closely with both the new national corporations and the emerging elite corporate bar.[78] "The 'friendly receivership' is distinctly a product of the Federal courts," declared a law writer in 1904.[79] Others made the same connection more broadly. A North Carolina attorney insisted in 1896 that "it is known to all men that the Federal bench is the stronghold of the money power,"[80] and in 1903 the *American Law Review* praised a retiring Eighth Circuit judge because he "did not, like so many Federal judges, do his thinking on the side of the rich."[81] In 1909 the progressive publicist Herbert Croly noted "the constant extension of a protecting arm to corporations by the Federal courts,"[82] and three years later a muckraking series of articles in *Everybody's Magazine* labeled the federal courts the "Last Refuge of the 'Interests'."[83]

For half a century, populists, progressives, and New Dealers repeatedly attacked the federal courts as biased forums. William Jennings Bryan, the presidential candidate of the Populists in 1896 and of the Democrats on three occasions, charged in 1907 that corporations "have constantly defied the states and sought shelter in the federal courts."[84] There was going to be "dangerous agitation," Theodore Roosevelt declared privately in 1910, "unless the Federal judiciary is willing to submit to temperate criticism where it goes completely wrong."[85] The following year he began his campaign for the recall of judicial decisions.[86] A decade later Senator Robert M. LaFollette of Wisconsin, the 1924 presidential candidate of a new Progressive party, expressed similar views. "For years I have seen the day coming when the Federal judiciary must be made, to some extent at least, subject to the will of the people," LaFollette maintained. The national courts had become "a Frankenstein which must be destroyed."[87] During his presidential campaign in 1932, Franklin D. Roosevelt continued the attack, charging that the Republican party "was in complete control" of the federal judiciary.[88] Five years later, after a triumphant reelection, he brought a half-century of populist and progressive attacks to their culmination when he launched his campaign to displace the Supreme Court's anti–New Deal majority by "packing" the Court with new appointments.

From the late nineteenth century until the 1930s, then, the social image of the federal courts was firmly set. Although the level and focus of political criticism varied, the attacks recurred broadly, continuously, and sometimes intensely. The image of the federal courts as probusiness forums, in turn, contributed to the rise and endurance of the system of corporate diversity litigation. The belief that federal judges tended to favor business was a widely shared part of American political culture, particularly among the less well-to-do and members of the working class, especially those affiliated with or sympathetic to labor unions. Whether or not the belief was well founded, either generally or in any individual instance, its strength and persistence sharpened the desire of corporations to have their cases heard in the national courts and helped convince plaintiffs that removal to a federal forum most likely harmed their chances of success.

In terms of the choice between judges, then, the right to remove gave corporations several advantages. Perhaps most important, it gave them in all cases the valuable opportunity to choose between two or more different individual judges.

Further, across the general run of cases it gave them the opportunity to take advantage of the likelihood that federal judges would be more sympathetic to their positions than would state judges. Finally, it gave corporations the ability to force plaintiffs to appear before judges whom large numbers of plaintiffs regarded as biased in favor of their corporate adversaries. Removal thereby allowed corporations to increase the de facto pressure they could exert on plaintiffs to lower their claims and settle out of court for relatively small amounts.

Although the significance of the ability to choose between different judges was largely individualized and relatively random, the right to remove also gave corporate defendants two additional advantages that operated in patterned and regular ways. First, removal often gave corporations a dramatically increased ability to exploit their social and economic power when confronting relatively weak individual litigants. An ordinary suit heard in a federal court was or could easily become far more burdensome and expensive than it would have been if heard in a state court, not for the most part because of the relevant legal rules, but because of the nature and structure of the federal judicial system. Those higher costs and burdens weighed with disproportional force on weaker individual parties. Removal was a powerful litigation tool, in other words, because it magnified the power of corporations in the informal legal process. Second, removal sometimes gave corporate defendants the opportunity to choose between conflicting state and federal common law rules. In a number of areas the federal common law was not simply more uniform than state common law but, especially after 1890, more favorable to business interests. Removal was also a powerful litigation tool, then, because it often enabled corporate defendants to change the applicable substantive law from a less favorable to a more favorable rule.

Corporate lawyers exploited their advantages in whatever ways they could. Although the practical significance of both the social burdens of removal and the federal common law varied according to geographical area and time period, their general impact was widespread and substantial. It was around their predictable operation that the practices that marked corporate diversity litigation coalesced into a recognizable set of patterns.

Chapter 2

The Social Structure of
Party Inequality and
the Informal Legal Process

In disputes between individuals and national corporations, inequality between the parties was a paramount fact, and it conditioned the operation of the system of corporate diversity litigation. National corporations were able to take actions and use resources that were beyond the knowledge or means of most individual claimants. A corporation could freely and carefully select the state in which it would hold jurisdictional citizenship, and by virtue of that single incorporation it enjoyed as a matter of course the choice between state and federal courts in every state in the union but one. In most instances, individuals lived where they were born or where they could find work, and when they moved they seldom did so for purposes of litigation planning. Corporations employed permanent legal counsel who could oversee and develop legal strategies, and they retained local counsel who could advise on the best tactics in each district. Individuals rarely went to court more than once in their lives, and rarely did they possess the resources necessary to offset the advantages of their powerful adversaries. Corporations had the long-term incentive to seek out favorable laws or to litigate and lobby to establish new ones. Individuals normally had to settle for whatever rule existed in their particular state when they suddenly found that it was important to them.[1]

Corporations, of course, did not intend to be unfair or harsh in their dealings with individuals. Indeed, evidence suggests that their officials often showed considerable sympathy for the plight of individual claimants. In many instances they exhibited special concern for badly injured workers, particularly for workers known to be reliable and who had been victimized by forces beyond their control. Corporate officials often made special efforts to provide some relief for such people, and they did not purposely try to deprive them of what they regarded as "just" compensation.[2] At the same time, however, corporate officials were caught up in the effort to manage large-scale operations, to impose general rules of policy, and, above all, to minimize their costs of operations. The cultural world view of a relatively successful but new and insecure bureaucratizing business class not only helped justify their efforts but also filtered out the kinds of considerations that could impair their chances of success. To a larger extent, for example, corporate officials held to the belief that industrial injuries were overwhelmingly the result of some kind of "fault"—ignorance, carelessness, recklessness, stupidity, drunkenness, or even defiant wilfulness—on the part of workers. In the late nineteenth and early twentieth centuries there was an apparently widespread belief among employers that the great majority of injuries—95 percent by some of their estimates—were caused by the carelessness of employees. Although some empirical studies suggest that workers' fault was probably responsible for only 20 to 30 percent of industrial accidents, the common assumptions about employees' fault that corporate officials shared, together with rules of law that made such fault a bar to legal recovery, convinced most of them that personal injury claimants, especially workers, seldom had valid legal claims against their companies.[3] Thus, in spite of personal goodwill and a frequent sympathy for the unfortunate condition of many claimants, corporate officials treated claims and litigations as difficulties to be overcome like the other problems they faced. They had to manage them, control their effects, and, in the end, minimize their costs.

In the late nineteenth century the institutional advantages that corporations enjoyed in claim disputes with individuals were immense. Pressed by the demands of competition and the burdens of high fixed costs, railroads led the movement to strengthen and rationalize internal corporate management techniques and to use their increased organizational powers to expand control over the external forces that affected their operations. By the late nineteenth century streamlined, cost-conscious management structures and techniques were in common use among railroad companies and were spreading to larger corporations involved in manufacturing and distribution.[4] As part of the process, the office of general counsel grew in importance and staffing. Corporate planning reached increasingly into litigation practice, anticipating a company's problems, improving its legal posture, and raising its litigation learning curve.[5] Corporations had the time, resources, incentives, and sophistication both to litigate selectively in order to maximize their chances of developing favorable common law rules and to lobby the legislatures persistently in an effort to have statutory law tailored most closely to their interests.[5]

By the 1890s railroads and insurance companies had settled or litigated many garden varieties of cases hundreds or thousands of times. In only one California county, for example, from 1901 to 1910 the Southern Pacific Railroad defended 82 personal injury actions.[6] Nationwide, during the three years from 1908 to 1910, the New York Central lines handled almost 11,000 personal injury cases.[7] The New York Life Insurance Company began using its own full-time attorneys in 1893, and an incomplete count showed that in the next seventeen years it handled some 2,000 litigations and was a party in at least 133 appellate decisions. Its legal costs jumped from about $10,000 a year in the early 1890s to $140,000 in 1904.[8]

The volume of their litigation gave corporations critical economic advantages over individual litigants. First, they were able to lower their average litigation costs by spreading them over a large number of cases. Whether individual litigants were paying costs and attorney's fees or, far more likely, relying on some kind of contingent fee arrangement, their one possible recovery had to cover all their expenses as well as their original loss. Moreover, relative to the cost burden that a litigation placed on the corporation, the costs that individuals faced were extremely heavy. Even small attorney's fees could constitute a high percentage of an individual's wages or savings, and contingent fee arrangements would generally take about a third of her recovery—after deducting other costs and fees. Second, large corporations generally had little incentive and no pressing need to settle. Given their fixed overhead for legal matters—permanent internal staff, local counsel on retainer, and budgeted funds to cover regularly recurring costs—it made little difference whether any single case was settled or vigorously contested. Usually, in fact, because a settlement would require a payout, it was cheaper not to settle on any but the most favorable terms. This was particularly true if the outcome of a suit was relatively uncertain and a final judgment would be delayed for years. Conversely, individuals had no litigation budgets and no legal resources on call. Moreover, because of the nature of their injuries and resulting expenses, they were usually financially pressed and often desperate.[9]

Corporations also enjoyed the advantages that flowed from their ability, founded both on financial resources and legal sophistication, to retain throughout the country the attorneys who would likely provide them with the most effective representation. They commanded the best, or at least the most reputable, legal talent available. Joseph H. Choate, William M. Evarts, William D. Guthrie, Paul D. Cravath, Elihu Root, and Charles Evans Hughes were but a few of the nation's most prominent lawyers who reached the pinnacle of professional success by representing the new national corporations. At the local end of the spectrum corporations were equally on the hunt for talent. When Thomas J. Walsh, the future progressive Senator from Montana, made a particularly impressive argument before the Dakota territorial supreme court in 1889, he was immediately approached by the assistant solicitor of the Milwaukee Road and retained as its local counsel.[10] "[T]he Illinois Central operates in about 70 of the counties of the State of Illinois," one of the railroad's attorneys told Congress. "In each of those counties we have a local attorney, and we do try to get the best man we can get."[11] A spokesman for the Brotherhood of Railroad Trainmen agreed. "It is notorious that the railroads retain the services of the leading doctors in every community," he charged, "just as they do the leading lawyers."[12] Simeon E. Baldwin, a governor and supreme court judge in Connecticut, was a railroad lawyer who wrote a leading treatise on *American Railroad Law,* and John F. Dillon, a federal circuit judge and chief justice of the Iowa Supreme Court, was a railroad lawyer who wrote the leading treatise on *Removal of Causes from State Courts to Federal Courts.* Together, in fact, the two treatises constituted a significant part of the corporate legal learning curve of the late nineteenth century. From the 1870s onward, corporate lawyers emerged as the acknowledged leaders of the bar, and ambitious attorneys across the country anxiously awaited the opportunity to represent one of the great national corporations.[13]

Corporations probably had a further advantage in being better able to secure honest, competent, and conscientious attorneys. Their litigation experience and in-house counsel enabled them to monitor local attorneys and to evaluate their overall performance. The attorneys they retained also had strong incentives to impress their clients with favorable results in order to hold their business. Conversely, most individuals were unable either to evaluate fully an attorney's skills or to monitor his performance. Attorneys representing individuals undoubtedly enjoyed greater leeway in deciding on tactics and greater de facto authority in evaluating and accepting settlement offers, and their own interests—such as reaching certain accommodations with adversaries they regularly faced or disposing of large numbers of cases with minimal effort—likely induced them in a number of cases to settle on terms less favorable than might otherwise have been obtainable.[14]

In addition, the needs of the new corporations for continuous and substantial legal work allowed them to foster the growth of large law firms devoted for the most part to the protection and expansion of corporate rights. The new generation of elite lawyers created larger and larger firms to service the legal needs of national corporations, and by the turn of the century, such elite firms were developing into powerful new institutional and professional supports for corporate interests. The ability of the corporations and elite national and local firms to confer professional status and financial rewards seemed to enable them to attract to corporate work a relatively high percentage of the most talented young attorneys who entered the profession each year.[15]

Suggesting that those advantages made a difference, a study of almost six thousand cases decided in sixteen state supreme courts from 1870 to 1970 found that in suits against individuals large companies—railroads, manufacturers, banks, and insurance companies—won somewhat more frequently than did other types of litigants, that in suits against their employees the corporations held "a significant net advantage," and that they enjoyed their greatest relative advantage over individuals in the years around the turn of the century. The study concluded tentatively that "the net advantage won by business organizations flowed primarily from their litigational capabilities."[16]

As the system of corporate diversity litigation developed from basic human limitations and necessities on the plaintiffs' side, so it developed on the corporations' side from the processes of market competition, economic rationalization, legal specialization, and the need to cut variable costs in the context of mounting fixed costs and declining profit levels. Those broad social and institutional factors structured the parties' legal capabilities, incentives, tactics, and goals. In large part they determined the nature and results of the system of corporate diversity litigation, both its formal adjudications and its informal settlements.

Corporations and the Informal Legal Process

Two principal characteristics marked the informal legal process of out-of-court settlement. First, the process was vast, private, and to some extent unknowable. It disposed of the great majority of potential claims without formal legal action, and it disposed of most legal actions without a formal judgment.[17] Because there was almost no record of the former and often very little of the latter, the existence and merits of the claims and the justness of their dispositions were largely beyond evaluation by outside parties. The claims—and particularly the processes and terms by which they were settled—were for the most part invisible to the formal law. Second, the process disposed of claims to some unknown but often substantial extent on the basis of social context and extralegal pressures, not on the basis of legal rules. Because there was no necessary, and in many cases even indirect, relationship between the terms of settlement and the applicable legal rules, the process could bring results inconsistent with or even contrary to those required— and presumably regarded as just—by the formal law. A House of Representatives report noted the problem in 1886. When parties were "unable to meet the expenses incident to litigation in the federal courts remote from their homes," their adversaries were in a position to "obtain unfair concessions and compromises."[18] Sixty years later a government study of the operation of employer liability acts drew a similar conclusion. "It is plain that the provisions of the liability acts are only indirectly and remotely related to the settlements arrived at as a result of the bargaining process" between employers and employees.[19]

By the late nineteenth century the overwhelming majority of claims, including those liable to be swept into the system of corporate diversity litigation, were settled or otherwise resolved out of court. Among injured workmen most claims were never filed, and only a small percentage of all claims reached judgment. Between 1887 and 1915 only about 5 percent of more than three thousand miners injured in one West Virginia county filed suit,[20] while in Washington State during the first decade of the twentieth century only about one injured worker in eleven did so.[21] Among injured railroad workers from 1908 through 1910, less than 5 percent of the claims based on death or permanent disability went to judgment, and less than 1 percent of all claims did so.[22]

Statistics also show that in the late nineteenth century the number of filed lawsuits grew but that increasing percentages of those actions were terminated before judgment. From 1875 to 1885 approximately one-quarter of all private federal civil suits were voluntarily discontinued, dismissed, or settled. During the 1880s, the percentage began to rise, reaching 50 percent by 1890. After the turn of the century, cases discontinued on one ground or another consistently accounted for more than half the civil cases terminated and, in some years, for more than 60 percent. Studies of state court litigation show similar patterns, with more cases filed, smaller percentages proceeding to final judgment, and larger numbers terminating in private agreements or other informal and unrecorded ways.[23] To the extent that those trends characterized claims disputing in the late nineteenth century, they suggest two trends: first, an increasing bureaucratization and formalization of claims disputing, perhaps with a concomitant decline in consensual community-based patterns of effecting compensation; and, second, the pervasive influence of social and cultural factors that discouraged plaintiffs from pursuing their formal legal actions to a conclusion.

The informal legal process was not, of course, necessarily bad, nor was litigation to judgment necessarily good. In the abstract, at least, the opposite seemed far closer to the truth. Because litigation was expensive, time-consuming, and socially disruptive, it was a burdensome way to resolve a dispute.[24] If freely and fairly negotiated, private settlements would almost always have been preferable.

The problem for plaintiffs suing national corporations in the late nineteenth and early twentieth centuries, however, was that the amounts they received in out-of-court settlements were held down by a variety of extralegal factors unrelated to the merits of their claims. In court, the amounts they could win depended on the perceived merits of their claims discounted by their legal costs and attorneys' fees. Out of court, the amounts they could obtain were limited not only by the perceived and discounted "merits value" of their claims but also by the additional discounts that practical social pressures compelled. Plaintiffs were frequently induced to settle cheaply because of ignorance of their legal rights, the gravity of their injuries, a desperate need to get money quickly, or fear of employer retaliation. Moreover, corporate defendants could pressure more aggressive claimants to settle out of court by adopting or threatening to adopt a legal strategy that would drive up plaintiffs' costs and thereby drive down the amount they would collect if they won a judgment. The threat of intransigent litigation tactics—making every possible preliminary or post-trial motion, obstructing plaintiffs' efforts to secure necessary witnesses or physical evidence (both of which were often under defendants' control), and exhausting all avenues of appeal—often made the much smaller amounts available in out-of-court settlements appear markedly more attractive. Although corporations often enjoyed an advantage over individual plaintiffs in the courts, they usually held additional, and in most cases far greater, advantages in the informal legal process. As a general matter, then, they worked assiduously to keep their disputes out of court and to resolve them privately.

Evidence suggests that corporations used the practical advantages they enjoyed over individuals regularly and methodically to avoid both liability and litigation, to induce or coerce claimants to settle for minimal amounts, and to keep settlement values at the lowest possible levels. Only when unavoidable or particularly advantageous would they litigate to judgment.[25] In 1875, for example, 27 injured workers and the family of 1 worker who had been killed refrained from bringing lawsuits and asked for compensation from the employer, the St. Louis & Southeastern Railroad. Only half received anything from the company, and the 14 successful petitioners received an average award of $66.75, about two months' income. In Illinois the following year, 262 railway workers were killed and another 102 injured, but only 24 managed to obtain any compensation. The average recovery for the fortunate few was $152, and the companies' total outlay equalled about $10 per worker injured or killed.[26] Although in the late nineteenth century the railroads often made some payment to injured workers or their families, the compensation paid was tiny, unpredictable, and often based on factors other than the seriousness of the injury suffered or the number of dependents affected.[27] Other industrial workers fared little better. Studies of industrial accidents in the early twentieth century found that employers in Pittsburgh gave some form of compensation to fewer than half of their employees who were killed or injured and that those in Wisconsin gave no compensation to a quarter and nothing more than part or all of their doctors' bills to another two-thirds.[28] In the early twentieth century in Illinois, Ohio, and New York, only 6 to 12 percent of injured workers received any compensation.[29]

Although corporate spokesmen insisted on the fairness and benevolence of their compensation practices, they acknowledged that their goal was to minimize costs. An attorney for the New York Central System exemplified the contradiction when he testified before Congress in 1911. He insisted that the railroads were fair in dealing with injured workers and were "the most liberal people in making settlements as compared, for instance, with the street-railway companies." However harsh he may have thought the streetcar companies in comparison, the attorney nevertheless acknowledged that "[t]he lawyer for the railroad company is trying to [settle cases] from an economical standpoint." The goal, in other words, was the bottom line. The railroad lawyer "is trying to bring about the end of the year with the smallest amount possible to be paid in the aggregate so far as his company is concerned."[30]

Insurance company records reflected their desire to hold down the costs of settlement. The New York Employers' Liability Commission found that between 1906 and 1908, companies paid more than $23.5 million in premiums to liability insurers but that the latter paid out only $8.5 million in benefits. Sixty-three percent of all premiums, the study concluded, went to profits and operating costs, including "the salaries of attorneys and claim agents whose business it is to defeat the claims of the injured."[31]

Corporations used a variety of tactics to hold down their settlement costs. Most generally, they simply insisted on their lack of liability, attributed injuries whenever possible to the fault of the injured person or of third parties, and offered minimal settlements on an essentially nonnegotiable basis. "I am trying the Chicopee method of settlement," wrote the manager of a New England cotton mill in 1902, "i.e., waiting till they get hungry for money before going to see them."[32] In 1933 an Illinois policyholder described a similar approach from the claimant's point of view. Seeking about $1,300 to cover the costs of an accident, he reported the response of his insurance company's claim agent. "We will not pay your claim," the agent told him.

> We will not say that you could not win at law and that you would not be awarded the full amount of your claim; but in such an event, if the decision went against us we would appeal the case, and if we lost again, we could still keep you out of your money for a year or longer. A judgment, as you may know, is easily avoided or delayed under one pretext or another. We have attorneys employed by the year. Even at that we would still have some expense in connection therewith. It would cost you at least $500.00 in attorneys [*sic*] fees and court expenses. You have your own time to consider and the annoyance to which you would be put. We figure that if you win and are able to collect, which we will not say you cannot, your expenses, your own time and all, would give you a "NET RETURN" of not to exceed $200.00. We will give you that now. It is all you could expect to get in the end. I personally regard this as a most generous and magnanimous offer on the part of our company. Take it or leave it.

The tactic, "which I understand is quite usual," explained the policyholder, "is laughingly termed by their claims agents as the 'Net Return' or Starvation Plan."[33]

At even cruder levels, companies used harassment, pressure, and sometimes deceit to control potential claims and secure prompt, minimal settlements. "The employer, in danger of litigation, is desirous of securing a settlement as promptly as possible," explained the congressional Employers' Liability and Workmen's Compensation Commission in 1912 after an extensive inquiry into railroad injuries and compensation practices. "His representative or claim agent keeps persistently in touch with the injured man, with a view to a possible control of the situation and for the purpose of effecting a settlement as cheaply as possible."[34] A review of industrial tort litigation practices in 1906 identified the same tactic. "[N]aturally enough the first object of the successful adjuster is to get a release before a lawyer can catch the claimant," it explained. "The bedside settlement is generally the cheapest."[35] The *Virginia Law Register* agreed. Company claim agents "fly with the wings of an eagle to the scene of the accident," it reported in 1905, "and before the victim has an opportunity to get advice often induce him to sign iron-clad releases for entirely inadequate compensation." Sometimes, it continued, the agents used "the most dishonest strategy and misrepresentations to that end."[36] One railroad worker who had been injured and eventually became an attorney described his experience:

> When I was injured the agent came to me in the hospital in 1911. I was a youngster
> 19 years old and I did not know the law. The claim agent told me I did not have any

claim because of the fellow-servant law. Some years later I found it was abolished in 1908, but he got a release from me in 1911. I was glad to save my life.

Such tactics, he declared, were "very common."[37] An official of the Aetna Life Insurance Company seemed to acknowledge the companies' general strategy. "In settling claims," he explained in 1913, "considerable money can be saved if done in the early stages before the case falls into the hands of an attorney."[38]

Corporations systematically and aggressively sought releases from those with potential claims against them, usually offering small and often token settlement payments. In numerous cases they obtained releases under dubious conditions, sometimes shortly after injury when the injured person was in pain or under medication. They secured releases from people who were unable either to read or to speak English. Most important, they persistently sought releases immediately after accidents, before the nature of a person's injuries were known and before the injured person had been able to consult counsel. The president of the Brotherhood of Railroad Trainmen described the process:

> The companies do not fight fairly; they do not give the [injured] man an even chance for his defense, but are after his release before he recovers from the anaesthetic in the hospital; they hound him in his delirium; they haunt him with demands for adjustment under pretense of benefiting him or his family. . . . The injured employee is at every disadvantage.[39]

In 1912 the Eighth Circuit described one episode:

> The release was procured by a claim agent of the defendant the day following the injury, when the plaintiff was in bed suffering from the injury and stupefied by drugs administered to him to relieve his pain, and when the full effect of the injury was not, and obviously could not then have been, known to either the plaintiff or the claim agent.[40]

A claim agent for another railroad worked even more quickly. Affirming a verdict for plaintiff in 1894, the Massachusetts Supreme Judicial Court summarized the evidence that in an accident the plaintiff

> had received a shock which had finally resulted in serious damage to him; that he bore marks of the direct injury upon his face; that while he was in this condition, about an hour and a half after the accident, in the office of the defendant's superintendent, the defendant's agent prepared the two papers for him to sign, and passed the release to him, saying, 'this is merely a form,' and said the second paper was merely a receipt for the trousers and hat; that both of these statements were false.[41]

In numerous cases plaintiffs charged corporations with deceiving them about the extent of their injuries, the circumstances surrounding the accident, or the nature of the papers they were asked to sign.

Although it was not uncommon for courts to void releases on the ground of fraud or mistake,[42] corporations found them extremely valuable and used them widely. Often, of course, the releases held up in court.[43] Their primary importance, however, lay in the informal legal process. The intimidation potential of a signed release could be ruthlessly effective, and its very existence undoubtedly dissuaded innumerable claimants from bringing suit. Further, releases loaded heavy increased burdens on those who were determined enough to force a court challenge. In order to void a release on the ground that it was obtained fraudulently or mistakenly, plaintiffs faced difficult evidentiary problems and a particularly demanding standard of proof.[44] Moreover, prior to suit they generally had to return the settlement money they had received.[45] That requirement by itself could pose an insurmountable practical obstacle to those who had settled originally because they desperately needed money to pay their medical bills or to support their families. The attempt to void a release meant further delay, extra litigation efforts and expenses, and additional uncertainty about prospective recovery. Reported cases challenging releases were surely the tip of an iceberg.

The availability of diversity jurisdiction and removal often compounded the problem of plaintiffs who had signed releases. Because law and equity remained separate in the federal courts and because the remedy of cancellation of a written instrument was available only in equity, the federal courts with few exceptions held that plaintiffs could not, in a tort action at law for damages, avoid a release on the ground that it was fraudulently or mistakenly obtained. Instead, federal plaintiffs were required to bring a separate suit in equity to cancel it.[46] Beyond the added delay and expense of a second lawsuit, the necessity of going to a court of equity also meant that plaintiffs in the federal courts were unable to have a jury decide their fraud claims. In contrast, in more than twenty states where procedural reform had merged law and equity, plaintiffs could challenge releases on grounds of fraud or mistake in their tort actions for damages.[47] The merger of law and equity in the states, however, did not alter procedures in the federal system.[48] Accordingly, in release cases removal to the federal court could offer defendants special advantages, delaying plaintiff's action at law, forcing her to prosecute two suits instead of one, and depriving her of a jury on her claim of fraud or mistake in signing the release.

Ephraim Lumley's suit against the Wabash Railroad illustrated some of the problems that plaintiffs faced. Injured while riding as a passenger, Lumley executed a release for $75 in October 1890 when the company's doctor assured him that he would be fully recovered in eight weeks.[49] His physical condition worsened, however, and within a few months he wrote to the doctor claiming that he had been misled.[50] Three and a half years later, in March 1894, he brought an action for damages in state court. He had not acted earlier, Lumley stated, because he had been unable to work or hold a job since the injury and "had no money wherewith to fee lawyers" or retain medical experts.[51] The railroad removed, and the federal court ruled that the release Lumley had signed could not be attacked at law. Lumley then filed a bill in equity seeking cancellation of the release, and the circuit court dismissed it on the ground that he had waited too long to challenge the release. In June 1896 the Sixth Circuit ruled his delay excusable and reversed,[52] and Lumley returned to the trial court where he eventually prevailed in his equity suit. In October 1899, only four days short of nine years after Lumley had executed the release and five and a half years after he had originally filed suit, the Sixth Circuit affirmed a decree voiding the release. The decision did nothing but clear the way for Lumley to pursue his action at law for damages.

While corporations used releases to settle claims quickly and to foreclose legal action, some also used them to exploit the ignorance of accident victims. An established rule of the common law held that a release given to one of two or more "joint tortfeasors"—persons whose actions combined, intentionally or not, to cause injury—released all of them from liability. Presumably every lawyer who handled tort cases knew that rule, but most likely few if any nonlawyers did. Over the years the courts heard and dismissed any number of tort suits brought by accident victims against one joint tortfeasor after they had released the other. *Abb v. Northern Pacific Railway Co.,*[53] decided by the Supreme Court of Washington in 1902, seemed typical. Frank Abb, a passenger on a streetcar who was injured when it collided with a railroad train, signed a release with the streetcar company and sued the railroad. He alleged that his settlement with the former was

> in partial satisfaction only, of his damages suffered in said collision, as was understood by said street railway company and [Abb] at the time, and that it was not the intention on the part of either [Abb] or said street railway company to in any manner release or discharge [Abb's] cause of action or to surrender any claim for damages that he might have against [the railroad].[54]

Although Abb could reasonably have believed that freedom of contract allowed such an agreement, the attorneys for the streetcar company undoubtedly knew otherwise. Anxious to secure his release and possibly hinting at least implicitly that the railroad was a more promising party to sue, they apparently did not share that information. The court followed the settled rule and dismissed Abb's claim against the railroad.[55]

The elaborate practice of companies in attempting systematically and persistently to obtain releases from injured persons points to the crucial role of the informal legal process as well as to the importance of the formal legal rules that determined the validity of releases. Scholars studying the treatment of personal injuries in the late nineteenth and early twentieth centuries have focused mainly on the substantive rules of tort law. They have paid relatively little attention to release cases which, formally, are contract actions. Although the informal legal process dwarfs the immediate social significance of both tort and release cases, the latter may be of equal or even greater importance than the former in understanding how the substantive law related to the de facto compensation patterns that characterized the late nineteenth and early twentieth centuries.

In addition to their tactics for obtaining releases, corporations also used their positions to maintain control over evidence relating to injuries and accidents. Because they usually held authority over both the property or equipment involved in accidents and the employees who might be witnesses, they were in a particularly advantageous position both to investigate the facts and to deny their adversaries access to critical information.[56] Insurance companies repeatedly instructed manufacturers not to allow anyone representing injured parties to examine machinery or equipment involved in accidents.[57] A number of railroads, in fact, went so far as to publish formal rules that required employees to provide all information they had about accidents to designated company officials while prohibiting them from speaking about accidents with any other party. The roads enforced the rules and dismissed employees who violated them. The Baltimore & Ohio Railroad, for example, defended its use of such rules on the ground that they ensured worker loyalty, protected employees involved in accidents, and prevented workers from being harassed by "ambulance chasers."[58]

In 1939, when Congress amended the Federal Employers' Liability Act

(FELA), it examined the railroads' practice of controlling evidence and dismissed the B & O's arguments. "The railroads maintain well-organized and highly efficient claim departments," the Senate report explained. Immediately after an accident or injury the departments attempted to gather "all available information considered necessary to protect the railroad company," including statements from all witnesses and whatever relevant physical evidence existed. "On the other hand, the claimant may be seriously handicapped in his attempt to procure the information necessary."[59] The report viewed rules prohibiting employees from providing information to claimants as a major obstacle for potential plaintiffs, and the 1939 amendments to the FELA made it a crime for anyone to use any device, including threats or disciplinary actions, to prevent persons from furnishing information to injured workers.[60]

While corporations aggressively sought to use out-of-court techniques to limit their liability to all potential claimants, they were able to apply particularly intense pressures to their own employees. Increasingly in the late nineteenth century corporations sought to cut their operating costs and to control their labor force. Their methods ranged from company welfare plans to intimidation and violence, from the calculated mixing of divergent ethnic groups designed to fragment worker unity to the sponsorship of cultural values that encouraged deference and passivity. As corporations struggled for control of raw materials and markets, so they struggled for control of their employees.[61]

One widely adopted tactic was to require employees to sign contracts in which the workers agreed to assume all risks of their job and to hold their employers harmless from liability for injuries. The Santa Fe Railroad, for example, used a contract in which employees agreed to assume literally dozens of broadly specified risks and hazards while accepting the personal responsibility—manifestly impossible to fulfill—to "examine the condition of all machinery, tools, tracks, switches, cars, engines, and all the appliances thereto" before using them.[62] The American Express Company required workers to agree to "assume all risks of accident or injury" however and by whomever caused and, in the event of an injury, to "execute and deliver to said company a good and sufficient release" covering "all claims, demands, and causes of action arising out of such injury or connected therewith."[63] Union representatives protested to Congress that the worker was deprived of his rights "through mere contracts of employment, which, by force of circumstances, he is required to sign in order to be allowed to earn a living."[64]

A second tactic was to bar injured workers from returning to work after an accident until they signed written releases.[65] Some railroads made the practice a formal rule of employment,[66] and company pressure could be particularly intense on workers whose injuries had been relatively serious but who had recovered and were ready to return to work.[67] Often the tactic proved successful. Releases signed by workers to regain their jobs defeated many subsequent tort suits,[68] and in a far greater number of cases they must have dissuaded employees from even attempting suit. On occasion some companies may even have induced injured employees to sign releases by misleading them about the seriousness of their injuries. Proof of fraud in such cases, however, was particularly difficult.[69]

Workers often feared, and were sometimes threatened, that their refusal to settle quickly and "reasonably" would endanger their jobs. A review of industrial tort litigation in 1906 concluded that "putting the claim in the hands of a lawyer means inevitably the sacrifice of the claimant's job."[70] A study of tort suits against railroads in West Virginia between 1890 and 1910 found that railroad workers were, in fact, far less likely to pursue their claims to judgment than were nonemployees. Whereas nonemployees went to trial in 57 percent of their cases between 1890 and 1899 and in 85 percent between 1900 and 1909, employees did so in fewer than 15 percent of their cases during both periods.[71] A 1915 study of New Jersey's workmen's compensation statute found that meritorious claims were not pressed because workers feared for their jobs and that for the same reason employee-witnesses sometimes changed or shaded their testimony to help the company.[72] A study conducted by the United States Railroad Retirement Board for the period from 1938 to 1940 reached similar conclusions. "When interviewed," the report stated, "the employees frequently indicated that they feared, or had been threatened with, loss of job if they filed suit against the employer."[73] More significant, the Retirement Board's study found substantial evidence to support the employees' claims. Considering only those workers who were physically able to return to work and whose records suggested no disciplinary or other reason why they should not have been able to do so, the study found a striking difference among those who settled informally, those who retained attorneys, and those who went so far as to bring suit. In two different categories of injured workers, those who settled informally and without an attorney returned to work in 97.7 and 98.5 percent of the cases. Those who merely retained attorneys returned less frequently, taking their old jobs in 83.8 and 84.7 percent of the cases. Those who actually filed suit returned in barely half of the cases, 55.6 and 51.6 percent respectively.[74]

A third corporate tactic, the establishment of employer-sponsored benefit or insurance plans, appeared benevolent. If such plans provided compensation that injured workers might not otherwise have received, however, they were also designed to keep corporate costs down and employees out of court. In 1880 the Baltimore & Ohio Railroad Company established its Employee Relief Association, an institution that became a model adopted by a number of larger corporations, particularly those in mining, transportation, and metals production.[75] The companies managed the relief departments, paid their administrative costs, made some initial contribution, and often forced their employees, expressly or in effect, to join. The plans generally required employees to contribute monthly payments, scheduled benefits commensurate with individual contributions, and made the funds largely self-supporting. For the nine-year period from 1886 to 1894, employee contributions paid for more than 88 percent of the total costs of the Pennsylvania Railroad's relief department, and between 1903 and 1907 the relief departments of five major roads paid out more than $17 million in benefits but collected from their employees more than $500,000 in excess of that amount.[76] Most important for litigation purposes, the companies required all members of their relief departments to sign agreements waiving their right to sue for injuries and agreeing that if they did sue, they would forfeit the benefits otherwise due from the relief association—the benefits the employees themselves had funded.[77] The tactic was thus particularly powerful and cost effective from the companies' point of view, pressuring employees to settle with the carrot of their own money and the stick of its threatened loss.

In combination with other pressures on workers, the relief department plan seemed particularly successful in discouraging litigation. "It is customary," Simeon Baldwin wrote in his treatise *American Railroad Law* in 1904, "to require servants injured by accidents who receive relief from such a department to waive any right of action which they might otherwise possess against the company." He added that "such a requirement is valid."[78] The president of the Baltimore & Ohio told the United States Industrial Commission that "the effect of the relief department has been to almost entirely wipe out litigation with employees on account of injuries."[79] By the first decade of the twentieth century, only about 1 percent of all injured railway workers and 5 percent of those with permanent injuries carried actions in the courts through to final judgment.[80]

A fourth tactic centered on the use of company work rules. The railroads issued to their employees elaborate rule books, often leather bound and running more than a hundred pages, that identified lines of authority and established standards of behavior. The books were intended to help enforce discipline and ensure greater safety, and they set out detailed instructions for the performance of various tasks for each level of employee. Regularly and often, however, employees ignored the work rules. Sometimes they did so out of carelessness or even defiance, but often they did so because the rules in the book were inconsistent with the practical requirements of their jobs. In many cases workers simply did not have time to perform the tasks as instructed, or they were given more or different work than they were supposed to have, or they confronted unanticipated or emergency situations.[81]

Beyond their necessary and benevolent functions, work rules gave the railroads significant tactical advantages. Legally, it was sometimes held negligence per se for an employee, absent special justification, to violate a work rule that was made for his protection.[82] If a company could show that an injured employee had failed to follow the rule book, it had at least a prima facie defense to his claim for damages. The tension between written rules and practical job requirements thus put employees at a substantial disadvantage. They had to get their jobs done and perhaps in many cases violate the rules to do so, but if they were injured in the process, the law cast on them the burden of proving that their violation was excusable.[83]

The railway unions charged bluntly that "many of the rules were made for the purpose of protecting the railway companies against personal injury suits."[84] They argued that rules were often unrealistic and that the companies knew that employees could meet their timetables only by ignoring them. "All of the elaborate safety rules read well," explained one union official, "but it is not expected the employee will observe them." Instead, the "rules go to the public," while "the unwritten order goes to the employee to keep traffic moving at all hazards, and it is the latter order that he obeys."[85] A study of work injuries in Pittsburgh in 1906–7 confirmed the pressure to "keep traffic moving," if not the motives behind the companies' work rules. Underlying the problem of work-related injuries on the railroads, the study concluded,

is the pressure for speed in handling the fast-increasing tonnage. The public demands it, and the whole railroad, from the president down to the yard brakeman, feels the demand. There can be no doubt that this accounts for much indifferent inspection, and for much of what is called carelessness.[86]

In spite of tensions between work rules and job practices, the existence of the rule books—like the presence of signed releases—was a powerful tool for the companies in the informal legal process. If an injured worker had violated a work rule or if there was some basis for arguing that he had, the employer could bring additional pressure on him to settle or drop his claim. Even if there was a general practice among employees inconsistent with the rule, that practice might not be sufficient to overcome the company's prima facie defense. Moreover, even if such a showing would be sufficient, the injured employee faced a heavy burden of proof. He had to show that the practice existed and that the company knew or should have known of it. Proof would require the testimony of several fellow workers to establish the inconsistent practice, and workers able to provide such testimony would be particularly vulnerable to company pressure. If they gave such testimony, the company could inform them, they would be admitting that they knew of or participated in systematic rules violations. Their failure to report those practices and violations subjected them to fines or dismissal. The Santa Fe Railroad's employment contract, for example, required that workers "always have a copy of the rules at hand when on duty" and "immediately report any infringement of them to the head of your department."[87] An injured employee "knows that he can not depend upon his associates to testify in his behalf if he brings suit," declared the president of the Brotherhood of Railroad Trainmen in 1912, "for it means the job of the man who bears witness against his employer."[88] Whether or not purposely designed in some part to protect the company from employee suits, work rules gave the companies another effective method of pressuring employees in the informal legal process.

Although it is extremely difficult to quantify the advantages that corporations reaped from those and similar tactics,[89] available statistics suggest that they were frequently able to force large discounts and small settlements on individual litigants. A 1920 study of New York's workmen's compensation law, for example, revealed both the use and profitability of harsh settlements. It found that insurance companies and employers were implicated in a variety of dubious and fraudulent practices involving underpayments to injured workers that amounted to millions of dollars. Most relevant to the informal legal process, the study examined the operation of the compensation law's "direct settlement" provision that allowed insurance companies to negotiate directly with individual claimants. Out of a sample of 1,000 direct settlements in which the amount of compensation was governed by state law, the report found that serious underpayments had nevertheless been made in 114. Even more striking was the amount of the underpayments. Although the claimants received a total of $13,712.40 from their direct negotiations, they had been entitled under the statute to a total of $65,992.24. Negotiating directly with the insurance companies, in other words, the claimants had received barely 20 percent of the amount lawfully due them. If the sample were representative of all the 140,000 direct settlements reached since the law went into effect five years earlier, the report noted, the underpayments "would reach a total of $5,700,000."[90] And, it concluded, the insurance companies and employers were not without the traditional motive in settlement negotiations. "All of the underpayments have inured to the financial benefit of insurance companies, self-insurers and others, such as employers."[91]

Similar evidence appears from a comparison of settlement amounts paid to employees with and without legal representation. One of the characteristics of the informal legal process was that large numbers of claimants were not represented, and those without counsel seemed almost invariably to receive less than did those who were represented.[92] The Department of Legal Counsel of the Brotherhood of Railroad Trainmen, for example, reported that between 1946 and 1949, 8,003 of the union's members chose to settle directly with their employers, and another 2,431 retained counsel to handle their claims. The former group averaged $1,880 in settlements, and the latter group averaged $10,990, approximately five and a half times the amount paid to those without counsel.[93] The Railroad Retirement Board study of injuries during 1938–40 confirmed that legal representation made a major difference in settlement amounts. Although companies increased their initial offer by an average of about 60 percent when negotiating directly with employees, when dealing with represented parties their offers on the average "at least doubled, often trebled, and in some cases increased by even higher proportions."[94] Perhaps most revealing, the Railroad Retirement Board study also showed that there were significant differences between represented and unrepresented claimants even when comparing only those who had suffered similar types of injuries. In permanent total disability cases unrepresented claimants received an average settlement of $6,797. With attorney representation the average settlement was $10,360. When the attorney filed suit, the average jumped to $13,930. Similarly, in permanent partial disability cases, the numbers were $2,581 without counsel, $6,301 with counsel but without filing suit, and $8,316 with suit filed.[95]

Retaining counsel, however, was not a simple or obviously wise choice for employees. Although settlement would almost certainly be much lower without representation, the use of an attorney would increase the worker's overall risks. The divergence between the amounts paid to represented and unrepresented claimants was particularly suggestive, for example, in connection with the Railroad Retirement Board's finding that the retention of counsel by an employee who would be physically able to return to work reduced the likelihood that he would actually do so.[96] Retention of counsel, in other words, raised the strong possibility that a larger settlement amount would nevertheless bring to the claimant a lower net recovery. Counsel would increase a claimant's actual recovery, the Railroad Retirement Board pointed out, "only if the attorney is able to raise the settlement amount sufficiently to cover his fee and the additional incidental expenses, and to compensate for both delay in settlement and possible loss of job."[97] In a large number of cases, attorneys were unable to achieve that goal,[98] and employers' claim agents dramatized the risks persistently and skillfully. "[T]he decision to hire an attorney is clearly a gamble," the Railroad Retirement Board noted. "The hazard is naturally exploited by the [company's] claim agent to the best of his ability."[99] Innumerable numbers of workers refrained from obtaining counsel because they were keenly aware of those risks. The companies had them in a bind, and the costs and risks—social as well as legal—of simply retaining an attorney often persuaded them to settle quickly and for relatively small amounts.

The 1912 report of the congressional Employers' Liability and Workmen's Compensation Commission cast light on the general economics of the informal legal process as it affected railroad workers in the first decade of the century. First, and not surprisingly, it showed that settlements averaged much less than judgments and saved immense amounts for the corporations. On death and permanent disability claims settlements were consistently less than one-half to one-third the average amount of legal judgments. Railroad workers who suffered permanent partial disabilities, for example, received average settlement amounts of $1,296 compared with average judgments of $3,515.[100]

Second, the report illustrated the negotiating advantages that corporations had over individuals. Dealing with hundreds and often thousands of claims, corporations could adopt intransigent bargaining tactics and keep settlement offers low because they knew that 95 percent or more of all claimants would eventually settle. Further, they knew that they could spread the extra costs of litigation and of the relatively small number of high judgments over a large base of claims and that their savings from the settlements would more than offset the higher costs of litigation expenses and any adverse judgments. Statistically it made little difference to them which cases settled and which went to trial. Conversely, individual workers had only one claim to assert, and they depended on it for all their lost wages, litigation costs, and other expenses. Generally, they had little or no ability to put pressure on the company, and the retention of an attorney would likely cost them 20 to 40 percent of whatever recovery they might win.[101] The compulsion was to settle and guarantee that they would at least obtain something for their losses.

Third, the report suggested that settlements were even less expensive to most of the railroads than the raw figures seemed to imply. Given the average settlement amounts, it was apparent that a large part of the settlement payments—often the entire amount—could come from the funds of the companies' relief associations. Up to some limit, in other words, the contributions of the workers themselves, not company funds, paid for settlements. On the Baltimore & Ohio Railroad, for example, the maximum benefit that a worker could obtain from the relief association was $1,250. That was only $46 less than the average settlement for permanent partial disability claims and almost $100 more than the average death settlement.[102] It was also more than ten times the average settlement amount in the most numerous and, in terms of total cost, the most expensive class of injuries, temporary disabilities. As the general counsel of the Baltimore & Ohio admitted when he testified before Congress in 1912, the workers themselves paid for the benefits they received, and the company had not incurred significant liabilities under its plan.[103] Relief departments shifted the bulk of the cost of injuries and death from the companies to their workers, and they provided ample funds with which the companies could either dissuade workers from suing or settle the actions that they brought without subjecting the companies to any significant financial risk or uncertainty.[104]

Finally, perhaps the most revealing aspect of the commission's statistics was the difference between the ratios of judgments to settlement amounts in death and all permanent disability claims, both total and partial, on the one side and temporary disability claims on the other. For temporary disabilities—defined as injuries that required an absence from work of more than two weeks—settlements averaged only $70, whereas judgments averaged $932. The ratio between the two was an exceptionally high 13.3 to 1, about four to five times the comparable ratios for death and permanent disability claims. In part, the difference between the $70 and $932 figures was the result of differences in the severity of the injuries. Those who settled averaged forty-one days away from work, while those who took judgments averaged sixty-five days away.[105] By itself, however, that difference was insufficient to explain why awards in the latter category were about 1,200 percent higher than those in the former.

The explanation of the difference between the $70 settlement average and the $932 judgment average reveals essential characteristics of the informal legal process. When dealing with temporary disability claims, corporations had both a greater ability and a sharper incentive to force settlements at minimal levels than they did in dealing with claims for permanent disabilities and deaths. They took advantage of the former and profited handsomely from the latter.

Their greater ability stemmed from the fact that those with temporary disabilities were particularly vulnerable. Legally, they could count on relatively little sympathy from a judge or jury, especially because they would almost certainly have recovered from their injuries and be back on the job by the time their cases came to trial. Further, they could well face more serious problems of proof regarding both physical injury and economic damages than would a permanently disabled worker. Moreover, because their potential recovery would be relatively small, litigation costs and fees would consume a relatively high proportion of any recovery. The difficulties of proof, too, could compound the latter problem by requiring the worker to retain a medical expert. Finally, a worker with a temporary disability was especially vulnerable to threats that he could lose his job by suing. Unlike those permanently injured, he would be physically able to return to his old job. After the layoff and the medical bills, he would most likely also be desperate for a paycheck and happy to return to work.

The numbers confirmed the analysis. Those with temporary disabilities were far less likely to sue than were those with permanent injuries. Less than a third of 1 percent of those with temporary injuries took their cases to judgment. The families of deceased workers were fifteen times more likely to do so, and those with permanent injuries sixteen to eighteen times more likely.[106]

Equally important, corporations had powerful incentives to hold settlements for temporary disabilities to an absolute minimum. The reason was that those injuries accounted for approximately 90 percent of all injuries, and their numbers more than made up for the relatively small amounts of the individual claims. A simple computation illustrates the point. If all claims settled for death and for permanent disabilities were valued at the average judgment amount for their category, the railroads would have had to pay an additional $15 million for the years from 1908 to 1910. If all temporary disability claims were valued at their average judgment, the railroads would have had to pay an additional $68.4 million for the same three years. Even discounting the latter amount to compensate for the less serious nature of the temporary disability claims that were settled, the additional amount due for temporary disabilities would still have been $43 million, almost three times the combined additional amounts due for all claims for death and permanent disabilities.[107]

If the railroads held the line tightly on temporary disability payments, then, they controlled their largest potential cost category for worker injuries. They knew the advantage they held. "No employee," declared the second vice-president and general counsel of the Baltimore & Ohio Railroad in 1908, "could afford to sue the company for a disability of that temporary character."[108] The commission's numbers showed that the roads controlled that cost with great effectiveness.

Corporations used their advantages in the informal legal process to discourage litigation and compel settlements on highly favorable terms, especially when their adversaries were their own employees. It was in the context of that informal legal process that the availability of federal jurisdiction and the right to remove took on their special salience in the system of corporate diversity litigation. Put simply, the right to remove magnified the practical advantages that corporations held against their individual adversaries. In the late nineteenth century geography, demographics and the institutional characteristics of the national courts combined to make federal litigation more expensive and burdensome than state litigation. And when the contending parties were radically unequal, the added costs and burdens of federal litigation bore with much greater force on the weaker. The result was that the threat of removal often gave corporate defendants another powerful weapon in the informal legal process. In the system of corporate diversity litigation removal, or the threat of removal, functioned in the first instance as another disincentive for plaintiffs to bring suit and an additional reason for them to lower their claims and settle out of court.

The Informal Legal Process in the System:
The Impact of Geography and Demographics

The demographic changes that marked the period from the 1870s through the 1930s were rapid, sweeping, and unprecedented. The nation's population grew from 39.8 million in 1870 to 75.9 million in 1900 and then to 122.7 million by 1930, while the "new" immigration of millions of southern and eastern Europeans, largely Catholics and Jews, altered its composition. Frontier and rural conditions continued past the turn of the century to characterize some of the eastern half and most of the western half of the nation, and seventeen western and plains states that had been largely uninhabited in 1870 were for the most part settled, though sometimes sparsely, by 1920. More than half the nation's population lived on farms in 1870, but by 1916 slightly less than a third did so.[109] Urbanization was dramatic. The census in 1870 counted 663 cities and towns with populations greater than 2,500, but in 1910 it found 2,262.[110] The massive growth, spread, and concentration of the population created a social environment that corporate litigators could exploit.

The first conditioning social fact that helped shape the system of corporate diversity litigation was distance and the burdens of travel. To the extent that Americans were a mobile people, they might change jobs, move from town to town, or even "light out for the Territory." They did not, however, regularly travel far from home on personal business. "[N]ot more than three per cent of the people go fifty miles away from their homes during a year," estimated one journalist in 1895.[111]

Those who remained in sparsely settled rural areas or small towns east of the Mississippi or who spread into the vast and largely unsettled areas to the west found themselves located far from the nearest federal court and often with no transportation available except horse and wagon. One particularly punctilious federal territorial judge in the late nineteenth century discovered a juror without his coat and directed him to go home to get it. The juror did as he was told without informing the judge that he lived eighty miles from the courthouse. He returned with his coat in three days.[112]

The problem of distance was most common and acute in the trans-Mississippi West. The annual reports of the attorney general in the last quarter of the nineteenth century repeatedly voiced the requests of federal officials there for extra travel and subsistence allowances. Special allowances were necessary, the 1885 report stated, in "the districts of California, Oregon, Nevada, and all the Territories." Those "territories" contained ten future states, six coming into the Union in 1889–90 and four more entering between 1896 and 1912. "[T]he places of holding court in the districts mentioned are at great distances apart, often 200 or 300 miles," the attorney general explained, adding that "the necessary mode of travel is by stage." Business could be conducted only "at a great pecuniary loss and personal inconvenience."[113] In succeeding years the attorney general's report called attention to the distance problem in additional states such as Colorado and Wisconsin and, on the circuit level, to the entire eighth and ninth circuits which covered almost the entire trans-Mississippi West.[114]

Although the first transcontinental railway was completed in 1867 and the nation's basic rail system was in place by 1890, most of the West and large parts of the South and Midwest continued without convenient local lines into the first decades of the twentieth century. In the West cattle drives continued well into the 1880s, and wagon freighting remained common in the 1890s.[115] Outside the Northeast, it was only in the years from the end of the depression of the 1890s to World War I that systems of closely knit local rail networks filled out across most of the country. Total route mileage reached 163,597 in 1890 and increased by another 55 percent during the next quarter-century. In 1900 it reached 193,346 and then hit its all-time peak of 254,037 in 1916. More to the point, the new construction was concentrated in the Midwest, West, and South. In the decade between 1900 and 1910, for example, when the roads added 47,000 miles of new track, they built almost 90 percent of it in the South and West. Eleven southern states added 13,000 miles during the decade, and the twenty-one states west of the Mississippi added another 28,000.[116]

Even though relatively convenient local rail networks filled out after the turn of the century, travel remained a significant problem. For some people, the nearest depot remained at a distance, and for many the railroad was an expensive form of transportation. Based on the average income of American workers in 1900, the fare for a single two-hundred-mile round-trip cost a week's wages.[117]

Although the burdens of distance and travel were heaviest west of the Mississippi, they also weighed on people in parts of most states. As late as 1938 a federal judge in Virginia informed the House Judiciary Committee that his district extended "in length for a distance of approximately 450 miles" and that parts of it "may be reached only by the use of considerable time and inconvenience."[118] In spite of better transportation and shorter distances, many rural areas east of the Mississippi remained relatively cut off and fifty to a hundred or more miles from the nearest federal court. Even in the late twentieth century, the age of the superhighway and the airplane, attorneys in some districts still regard the requirement of intrastate travel as a useful burden to impose on local adversaries.[119]

The problems of distance and travel had particular resonance in diversity actions because state courts were held in so many more locations than were the federal courts. There were approximately 2,700 counties in the United States in 1890 and about 2,900 in 1910, almost all of which had a county seat that hosted one or more terms of a state court of general jurisdiction.[120] In contrast, federal courts convened in fewer than one county in every ten. In 1885 they sat in 186 locations, in 1895 in 227, and in 1910 in 276. By 1937, after the population had long since risen above 100 million and filled the entire West, federal judges held court in only 376 locations.[121]

Although conditions and distances varied considerably from state to state, the structure provided in the Judicial Code of 1911[122] told much of the story. Federal courts were authorized to sit in fewer than one in every ten counties in at least sixteen southern, central, and western states,[123] and in another half-dozen they were authorized to sit in only about one of every eight or nine counties.[124] In the far western states the ratios were smaller because the states generally had fewer counties, but the actual distances between federal court locations were much greater. In seven far western states the national courts sat in a total of only twenty-six cities and towns, fewer than four locations per state.[125] To compound the distance problem, federal judges did not actually hold court in all of the locations authorized by law, and in some they did so only sporadically or briefly.

The federal courts held their terms in the largest cities and in many smaller ones, but the number of sizable cities and towns that mushroomed across the country meant that millions of people remained distant from the national courts. In the 1880s less than a quarter of the population probably lived in cities that hosted terms of a federal court, and by 1910 only about a third did so. Considering only those who lived in urban settings—assuming that they were more likely to have claims against corporations, at least for personal injuries—the numbers affected by distance were still substantial. Of the nation's urban population, almost half in the 1880s and more than a quarter in 1910 probably lived in cities without a federal court. In 1895, for example, railroad workers, among the most common victims of industrialism, lived in more than seventy different towns in Iowa, thirty-six of which were home to fifty or more railroad workers each. The federal courts, however, sat in only eight of them. Indeed, seven different Iowa towns were home to more than one hundred railroad workers each and had total populations in excess of ten thousand yet did not host a federal court term.[126] For tens of millions of Americans, including millions of urban Americans, the federal courts were distant courts.

Throughout the late nineteenth and early twentieth centuries towns, cities, and counties repeatedly petitioned Congress for improved access to the national courts. Although they often asked for additional judges, they particularly sought methods of reducing the burden of geography. They asked Congress to divide districts, to add new divisions within existing districts, to provide for additional court locations within existing districts and divisions, and to shift counties from one district or division to another as improvements in transportation altered the calculus of travel convenience.[127] Seeking a new court term in Beaumont, Texas, in 1897, a House of Representatives report emphasized the distance problem. "The people in the locality of Beaumont who now have to attend court must go either to Tyler or Galveston," it explained. "The first is 175 miles and the other 135 miles distant."[128]

Although the desire for prestige, patronage, and federal funds helped fuel the efforts of localities to obtain a term of the federal court, the practical burdens of geography and travel were nonetheless real and oppressive. In 1900 California sought a term of court for Fresno, which had "a population of about 15,000" and was "the industrial center of the great San Joaquin Valley." The federal courts sat only in Los Angeles and San Francisco, a House report explained, and "[l]itigants, witnesses, and attorneys are now compelled to go enormous distances and at great expense."[129] Four years later Missouri sought a new court term in Cape Girardeau. "[T]he people of the whole southeast section of Missouri, who have any business with the Federal court," a House report declared in 1904, "are compelled to travel from 100 to 250 miles up to St. Louis and back again, making an average total distance of nearly 400 miles for each individual."[130] Oregon complained of even greater distances. "[T]hose who live in eastern Oregon having business before this [federal] court," a House report stated in 1905, "are required to travel from three to six hundred miles, at great expense to themselves and to the Government."[131]

The problem was not simply distance but also the inconvenience of delayed, indirect, and roundabout railroad connections. In 1904 Iowans sought a new division that would hold terms in Davenport, a city of forty thousand people. "To attend a session of the Federal court it is necessary that attorneys, litigants, and witnesses from Davenport shall travel about 140 miles and change cars twice, being sometimes subjected to long delays between trains and being subjected to large expense and to great annoyance." Litigants from Muscatine, a town of seventeen thousand, suffered the same inconveniences of travel, though they had to go only about 110 miles. "The expense to which poor litigants are subjected because of traveling expenses and in paying counsel for the time expended in traveling to and from court," the House report stated, "results in great injustice."[132] In Mississippi one county was only about 50 miles from the nearest federal court located in Oxford, but there was no direct rail connection between the two places. "In order to reach Oxford, however, on the railroad, which is of course the way all parties go to court now," a 1907 House report explained, "it is necessary to travel from 150 to 200 miles over three different railroads and spend the night or day in Memphis, Tenn., going and returning." Those coming from a second Mississippi county had "to travel over two railroads from 100 to 150 miles to reach Vicksburg, the present site of their [federal] court, and spend a day or night in Greenville, going and returning."[133]

The distance problem could also be acute in the older and smaller states of the Midwest. Although federal judges were authorized to hold terms in five locations in Indiana, for example, they confined themselves largely to Indianapolis. It "has been for a long period of time the practice of the [federal] courts to hold their sessions in the city of Indianapolis, seldom devoting more than a day or two in the year in any other point and holding no session at all at some of these places." Round-trips between Indianapolis and four of the state's larger cities ranged from 226 to 364 miles. "To make this trip from Evansville or Fort Wayne, the cities next in size to Indianapolis, and to attend to the slightest court business," noted a House report in 1906, "requires two days, unless a night be spent in traveling." The result was "inconvenience, expense, and injustice to litigants remote from Indianapolis" and widespread efforts to avoid removals "by lessening the demand or molding the cause to avoid Federal jurisdiction."[134]

Participants in the system repeatedly noted the practical burdens that removal could create. Remanding a case to state court in 1887, a federal judge condemned the practice of parties who would "harass their opponents by capriciously removing a case upon slight grounds, from the state to the national court hundreds of miles distant, and not readily accessible for trial."[135] A standard treatise on removal, published in 1901, noted the desire of many plaintiffs to avoid "the resulting delay, annoyance, and expense of a removal."[136] A plaintiff's attorney in Iowa was more blunt. "The reason for such removal," he charged in 1933, "is to make it as difficult and place the greatest possible burdens upon the [insurance] beneficiary in the prosecution of the action, to discourage that prosecution, and to force a settlement at a minimum figure."[137] Even dedicated defenders of removal acknowledged the social burdens that it created. In a decision that strained to uphold a defendant's right to remove and suggested—as only the most ardent defenders of removal did—that the right was of constitutional stature, a South Carolina federal judge stated the matter plainly in 1904. "[C]ases often arise wherein it is a great hardship upon a plaintiff to have his cause removed from the county where his witnesses reside, to a forum where, by reason of his poverty, he may ill afford to carry a case."[138]

In large numbers of suits, a hearing in federal as opposed to state court meant extra time, money, and inconvenience. Given the relative distances involved, particularly where convenient rail transportation was wholly or partly unavailable, those increases could be substantial. Distance, of course, meant not just travel expenses but also added costs for food and living accommodations. If the case went to trial and the plaintiff had to bring several witnesses in addition to himself and his attorney, the added costs could multiply quickly. For an average income earner, the escalating expenses and the further burden of additional time away from work could dissuade all but the most determined litigant. If he had been injured and was unable to work, they could be prohibitive.

While the burdens of cost and distance constituted one set of conditioning social factors that shaped the system of corporate diversity litigation, the problem of delay created a second. Those who congregated in the larger cities were generally closer to both state and federal courts, but their sharply growing numbers and the multiplication of their interactions increased the demand for legal services. At the same time the problems generated by the new urban industrial society forced governments on all levels to expand their activities in an effort to cope with them. Together a rapidly multiplying number of public and private lawsuits flooded the courts, and by the 1880s judges and lawyers were beginning to express heightened anxieties about the dangers of delay and "congestion" in the courts.

Put simply, the more time that must pass between filing a complaint and obtaining a final judgment in a court system, the more the court system tends to confer advantages on defendants.[139] The longer the period before judgment, the longer defendants can hold their funds and hope to outwait their adversaries. "On the theory that 'delay is always good for the defense'," explained a Chicago attorney in 1906, "counsel discourage either the settlement or speedy trial of personal injury claims."[140] For plaintiffs, who carried the burden of proof, delay compounded their risks that memories would fade, witnesses die, and evidence disappear. It allowed them to recover from injury and return to work, reducing jury sympathy and decreasing the likelihood of success or, if successful, the amount of damages they might win. It heightened their sense of frustration and helplessness, wearing down their determination to persist and making low settlement offers appear ever more attractive. Perhaps of greatest significance, it put intense pressure on poorer plaintiffs who desperately needed money, especially when they were unable to return to work after injury and faced mounting medical bills and the expenses of their families.[141] An injured coal worker in Kentucky testified about the statements made to him by his employer's claims agent. "Of course, you might sue us and get a judgment in this court," the agent told him, "but we would carry it further, and you might be an old man by the time you received anything out of it." The worker settled.[142] "That delays were systematically used by defendants and by the liability insurance companies in particular to defeat or impair rights," concluded a Carnegie Foundation study in 1919, "is common knowledge."[143]

From the 1870s to World War I the business of the federal courts rose steadily. Total case terminations rose from 17,000 in 1876 to 29,000 in 1900 and then to 50,000 in 1916. In the same years terminations of private civil cases rose from 7,000 to 10,000 to 19,000. The docket of pending cases, however, bloated even more noticeably. Total cases pending swelled from 28,000 in 1876 to 50,000 in 1900 and then to almost 90,000 in 1915, and the number of private civil cases pending jumped from 14,000 to 39,000 to 55,000.[144] By the turn of the century the average length of time between commencement and termination of a federal civil action was about three and a half years, and in 1912 it lengthened to slightly more than four years.[145]

Moreover, although the average length of time between commencement and termination was three to four years, the time required to prosecute a suit to final judgment—as opposed to settling—was even longer. In 1905, for example, of the 12,085 private civil cases terminated in the federal courts, only 5,880 were terminated by a final judgment for one of the parties. The majority were settled, dismissed, or voluntarily discontinued.[146] Thus, parties who refused to settle and insisted on carrying their cases through trial were often forced to wait much longer than the average three or four years.

There was, of course, great variation among districts. While the average ratio of pending to terminated private civil cases in all federal judicial districts in 1905 was about 3.7 to 1, many districts showed ratios as high as 5 and even 10 to 1. The ratio was much higher in many heavily urbanized districts, including those that covered Pittsburgh, New York, Detroit, and New Orleans.[147]

If litigants in many populous districts suffered long delays, those in less populated areas often suffered from the same problem. The ratio of pending to terminated cases in 1905 was far above the average in a number of less populated districts, including districts in Mississippi, Kentucky, Montana, Virginia, Oregon, and Wisconsin. Though the dockets in such districts were much smaller than those in heavily urbanized districts, so too was the time available to move cases along. In the overwhelming number of locations the federal courts held terms only once or twice a year. In 1901, for example, they held only one term per year in 45 of their 203 locations, and only two terms in all but a handful of the remainder. The terms in smaller cities and towns were frequently short, and any number of preliminary pleas or motions—to amend, abate, dismiss, remand, compel witnesses, or join or sever parties—could have the effect of delaying action for up to a year or forcing the parties to attend a term at another and more distant location. Another motion, or complications resulting from the decision of the previous motion, could push the case over yet again.[148] In any event, removal—absent settlement or discontinuance—meant that most plaintiffs would have to wait several years for a final judgment.

Beyond delay as an absolute factor in federal litigation, there is no reliable basis to generalize confidently about delay relative to the state courts. As in every other area, there was almost certainly great variety among and within the states and, of course, among individual lawsuits. There is some reason to believe, however, that delay in the federal courts was in at least many districts worse than it was in the state courts.[149] A study of more than twelve hundred appellate decisions in 1895 and 1905, for example, found that the mean duration of tort suits from initiation to judgment on appeal ranged from about two and a half to three and a half years and that the duration of state and federal suits was, on average, comparable. The study also found, however, that there were significant differences by time and region and that delay increased somewhat in the federal courts. By 1905, when the mean duration of civil actions in the federal courts had grown to forty-one months, in the state courts it was thirty-six months in the West, thirty-two months in the border states, and only twenty-eight months in the South. Thus, around the turn of the century the burdens seemed to compound. In twenty-nine border, southern, and western states, where the burdens of distance weighed most oppressively, the federal courts lagged behind the state courts in disposing of cases by a period of five to thirteen months.[150]

Scattered data dealing solely with state courts strengthen the conclusion that, although the caseloads of the state courts also rose throughout the period,[151] at least many of them managed to dispose of most their cases in less than the average of three to four years in the federal courts. A study of Boston in the 1890s discovered that the state courts resolved 60 percent of the tort suits on their dockets in less than a year.[152] Similarly, a study of two counties in California, one rural and one urban, found that in 1890, 1910, and 1930, well over half of the state actions reached final judgment within one year of filing and that between 75 and 95 percent reached final judgment within two years.[153]

Because the federal courts generally took several years to dispose of a case and in at least many areas moved cases along more slowly than the state courts did, diversity jurisdiction and removal often allowed corporate defendants to force their adversaries to bear the resulting burdens of time, expense, and frustration that long delays imposed. Hiram Johnson, the progressive governor of California, charged in 1911 that corporations purposely tried to "delay suits against them for interminable periods."[154] If Johnson's politics made his statement suspect, Judge John F. Dillon's did not. A prominent railroad lawyer and a leader of the conservative bar, Dillon consistently supported the expansion of federal judicial power and the protection of private property. In doing so, however, he acknowledged that "removals, especially by foreign insurance and railway corporations, often have the effect to delay, if not to oppress, those having claims against them."[155]

Many individuals, especially those who had suffered personal injuries and sought to collect from the corporation involved or from an insurance company under a disputed policy, were simply unable to endure a wait of several years before trial, especially when a favorable verdict would quite likely lead only to further delay and expense while the defendant took an appeal. "Litigation in Federal Courts to-day is so expensive," claimed an attorney in Kentucky in 1928, "that it is denied a poor litigant."[156] Congested dockets, like the burdens of travel,

created conditions that allowed corporate defendants to impose harsh and sometimes prohibitive extralegal handicaps on individual plaintiffs that pressured them
relentlessly to settle cheaply and obtain at least something for their claims.

The Informal Legal Process in the System: Structural
and Procedural Burdens in the Federal Courts

While the burdens of distance and delay gave corporate defendants many opportunities to impose informal social costs on plaintiffs, the internal structure and
procedures of the federal courts lent themselves to the same practice. One factor
was the difference in formal legal "costs," such as filing fees or the expenses of
preparing the record, which were generally somewhat higher in the federal courts
than in the state courts. The differences were likely exacerbated by the fact that
until 1919 the clerks in the federal courts were paid on the basis of the fees they
collected and not by salary, a practice that encouraged abuses. "[T]he court officers, the clerk and the marshal, have not failed, especially in the Federal courts,"
William Howard Taft noted in 1908, "to make the litigation as expensive as
possible."[157] As late as 1923 the attorney general called attention to the various
small fees that the federal courts required which, he believed, were both unnecessary and "vexatious to private litigants."[158]

More important, the nature of the removal process itself imposed burdens on
plaintiffs. In theory, the rules were clear and the process almost automatic. The
general removal statute and the decisions construing it sought to protect the right
of defendants by providing that the federal court, not the state court, would
decide contested issues relating to removability.[159] To begin the process, a defendant needed only to file a petition and bond in the state court before the federal
statutory deadline. If the case appeared removable on the face of the petition, it
was in law removed and the state court divested of jurisdiction.[160] Although the
state court could examine the face of the petition to determine whether it presented a legally sufficient ground for removal, it could not decide any disputed
issue of fact. Such issues were for the federal court alone.[161]

When removal proceeded smoothly, it cast an immediate burden on the plaintiff. After a proper removal petition was filed, the plaintiff no longer had an action
in state court. Instead, he found himself in a different court and in many instances
in a different town or city. In some federal districts, in fact, a removed plaintiff
could not even attempt countermeasures until the first day of the court's next
term, often several months away.[162] Regardless of the merits of defendant's removal petition, the plaintiff's case would likely stay removed unless he took
action. Although the federal court could on its own motion return a case to the
state court if federal jurisdiction were lacking, such *sua sponte* remands were
unlikely. If the removal petition were drawn with skill or if removability turned on
disputed issues of fact, the plaintiff would have to contest the matter if he hoped
to escape the federal court.[163] Moreover, if the removal was faulty for other than
jurisdictional reasons—if, for example, the petition or bond contained errors or
had been filed late—the plaintiff would waive his right to object if he did not act
promptly.[164]

A motion to remand the case to state court was the plaintiff's device to challenge removal. It required additional lawyer time, quite possibly travel, often the

preparation of one or more affidavits, in some cases the use of discovery, and occasionally the conduct of a hearing or trial. The disputed issues usually involved the citizenship of the parties, the nature and amount of the claim, the bases for joining or not joining other parties, and the "good faith" of either or both of the litigants in their efforts to secure or avoid removal. At a minimum the motion had to be made on written papers and, in many districts, accompanied by a brief. It required, in short, a significant effort.[165] Although the purpose of the procedure was to protect the right to remove and to ensure that a federal court would determine any disputed issue of fact, its usual effect in all but facially obvious instances of improper removal was to force plaintiffs either to accede to the removal or to take steps that could delay their actions and drive their costs upward.[166]

In those cases in which the removal did not proceed automatically, where the state court ruled that the petition did not present a removable suit, plaintiff's situation could be even worse, at least if the removability issue were a close one. A corporate defendant whose removal petition had been denied in state court had two useful options. One was to proceed immediately to the federal court and have it decide the removability issue without regard to the state court's decision.[167] The state court could not, in other words, prevent a defendant from having a federal court decide its right to remove or from being able to force a plaintiff to carry the burden of litigating a remand motion in federal court. In the event that the federal court disagreed with the state decision and held the action removable, the corporation could put the plaintiff to difficult choices: to abandon her state court action, even though her suit might ultimately be held nonremovable on an appeal through the federal system; to continue in state court and run the risk of suffering a default judgment in the federal court; or to shoulder the burden of conducting two separate litigations.

Alternatively, the defendant could remain in state court and, by taking an exception to the state court's denial of its petition, raise over plaintiff's head the sword of an eventual nonmerits, jurisdiction-based appeal. Although a remand order from the federal court could not be appealed, the denial of a removal petition by a state court could be reviewed on appeal from a final judgment. If the defendant opted for the appeal preservation tactic, the plaintiff would know that her preliminary procedural victory might cost her years of wasted effort. If the state court's ruling were eventually reversed, she would lose whatever judgment she had won and be compelled to try the entire suit a second time and in federal court.[168] The cost in both time and money to an individual with minimal resources could be severe, and the mere threat could serve to press settlement values further downward.

Thus, removal procedure posed significant problems for plaintiffs.[169] When the state court accepted the petition, the procedure immediately placed on plaintiff the burden of appearing in the federal court and fighting to reverse the action. When it induced a state court to retain a suit, it forced plaintiffs to make difficult choices and run the risk of additional uncertainties. The law of removal, concluded one treatise writer, "may be justly characterized as a snare and a delusion."[170] Again, the advantages went to those who were most experienced and knowledgeable. Considering the complexities of removal proceedings, a federal judge in Iowa declared in 1912, "there is no other phase of American Jurisprudence with so many refinements and subtleties."[171]

A second procedural characteristic of the federal courts imposed a somewhat different type of burden on plaintiffs. In equity the federal courts followed their own procedures independent of those in the state courts, and at law they followed a hybrid of federal and state procedural rules that frequently proved confusing. Under the Conformity Act of 1872[172] the federal courts were required in actions at law to follow "as near as may be" the practices and procedures of the state in which they sat. The statute itself excepted the rules of evidence from its coverage. Other federal procedural statutes further circumscribed its reach, and over the years decisions by the federal courts repeatedly carved out additional areas of procedural independence. In 1889 the Supreme Court declared that the statute did not apply to a federal judge's general administration of his court or limit his inherent common law powers to process cases.[173] By the beginning of the twentieth century the federal courts followed their own rules or had discretion to follow their own rules in numerous areas, including parties, appearances, continuances, trial procedures, bills of exceptions, and motions for new trials.[174]

Federal practice was thus quite different from state practice, in equity clearly so and at law unclearly so. The ambiguities that grew up around the Conformity Act made federal practice confusing and frustrating. "When removed," protested a Missouri lawyer in 1927, "the case will be tried in a court in which the law is administered in many respects vitally different from a state court."[175] Removal, a California attorney complained five years later, forced attorneys to confront "the intricate mazes of Federal practice and procedure."[176] In the federal courts, concluded one scholar, procedural "principles and their applications are often hazy and uncertain, and they vary very widely in the different states."[177] Successful navigation through trial required either long familiarity with the local federal practice or some serious preventive research. Reliance on procedural "conformity" proved as often a trap as a guide to attorneys who appeared in the federal courts only rarely.

The great majority of lawyers, including most of those who represented poorer individuals in ordinary tort and contract actions, fell into that last category. The attorneys who represented corporations and who frequently or habitually removed often did not. By the last quarter of the nineteenth century, in fact, the legal profession itself was dividing into elite and nonelite tiers, with the former servicing the corporations and the latter individual middle- , lower-middle, and working-class litigants. "The ordinary lawyer prefers to sue in a State court, when he has the choice, on account of his greater familiarity with the practice there," explained Simeon E. Baldwin in 1905. "Many American lawyers have never brought an action in a federal court."[178] A Missouri lawyer pointed to the practical consequences of that fact in 1931. Removal often forced a plaintiff to incur "almost prohibitive expense by way of employment of additional counsel, as the average small town lawyer is unfamiliar with federal practice."[179] An Iowa lawyer who represented insurance claimants agreed. "Unless a lawyer specializes in federal practice," he declared, "he is at a considerable disadvantage, in the federal court, all of which acts as a handicap to the dependent beneficiary."[180] The social conditions of corporate diversity litigation and the sharpening stratification of the bar turned the ambiguities of practice under the Conformity Act into another source of increased costs and unpredictable risks for individual plaintiffs.

Institutionally, two structural features of the national courts also worked to the advantage of corporate defendants. One was the court to which cases were removed, the "circuit court." Since 1789 Congress had provided for two types of federal trial courts, the district court and the circuit court. Their jurisdiction was different though partially overlapping, and the latter had limited appellate jurisdiction over the former. The district courts held jurisdiction over one federal judicial district, either a single state or a part of one state; the nine circuit courts each exercised jurisdiction over several states. Most immediately relevant, the circuit courts had jurisdiction over all removed actions. The circuit courts were originally held by Supreme Court Justices traveling "on circuit," but in 1869 Congress provided for the appointment of an additional "circuit judge" for each circuit. By the late nineteenth century the dual federal trial court system was confusing and redundant. Supreme Court Justices continued occasionally to sit on circuit; circuit judges were often unable or unwilling to hold court at the many times and locations mandated by Congress; and district judges held the great bulk of circuit court terms.[181]

The nature of the circuit court system contributed in three ways to the advantages that corporations enjoyed in removed actions. First, the ability of district judges to sit as circuit judges offered removing defendants additional opportunities for judge shopping, in this context between different federal judges. Second, until the first decade of the twentieth century the circuit courts apparently met somewhat more irregularly than the district courts did and, perhaps as an accommodation to the traveling circuit judges, held terms in fewer locations than did the district courts.[182] Third, because circuit judges held court in several different states, their procedural practices were more likely to diverge significantly from "conformity" with the practice of any single state than were the practices of district judges who sat permanently in only one. Litigating before a circuit judge probably gave advantages to those attorneys, more likely corporate attorneys, who practiced commonly in the circuit court.

The second and far more important institutional feature, the appellate structure of the federal courts, imposed significant burdens. There were, of course, extra costs, including the special requirements for preparing the record of the proceedings below and printing briefs on appeal. The formal papers required on appeal, the attorney general reported in 1895, imposed "very great and unnecessary expense."[183] In 1904 the Supreme Court held that the federal *in forma pauperis* statute did not apply to appellate proceedings and that, in the absence of a statute, the federal courts had no authority to allow poor persons to prosecute appeals.[184] In 1910 Congress attempted to alleviate some of these problems, though for several years the new statute seemed to bring little improvement, and the problem of excessive costs on appeal remained.[185]

The problems of distance and delay in the federal appellate structure were extreme. In the 1870s and 1880s, appeals from the circuit courts went directly to the Supreme Court, a fact that forced poorer parties to choose between incurring heavy travel costs and foregoing representation on appeal.[186] Further, in many cases the losing party had up to five years to file an appeal,[187] and even after the appeal was filed it often took years to obtain a decision. By 1890 the average time required from filing an appeal to a hearing in the Supreme Court had reached four years.[188]

In 1891 Congress restructured the federal appellate system and moderated some of its most burdensome features.[189] The Evarts Act retained the earlier system of dividing the country into multistate circuits and created in each of nine circuits an exclusively appellate United States Circuit Court of Appeals. In a range of suits, including those brought under diversity jurisdiction, the act severely limited the opportunity to appeal to the Supreme Court but gave litigants an appeal as of right to a circuit court of appeals. Although the act modified the jurisdiction of the federal trial courts and stripped the old circuit courts of their limited appellate jurisdiction, it retained the dual system of district and circuit courts as courts of first instance. The old circuit trial courts retained jurisdiction over removed suits until Congress abolished them in 1911.

Although the Evarts Act represented a significant improvement, the federal appellate system continued to impose serious burdens on most individual plaintiffs. For a large part of the population the new circuit courts of appeals were located out of state and farther by a great distance than were the appellate courts of the states. All of the circuits reached across hundreds of miles. The smallest, the First Circuit in New England, covered four states. The Second and Third in the East and the Seventh in the Midwest included three states each. The heaviest burdens fell on much of the Midwest and all of the South and trans-Mississippi West. The Sixth Circuit covered four states—Ohio, Indiana, Tennessee, and Kentucky—and the Fourth encompassed five—Maryland, Virginia, West Virginia, North Carolina, and South Carolina. The Fifth was larger still, spanning more than a thousand miles from Florida to Texas and including Georgia, Alabama, Mississippi, and Louisiana. The Eighth and Ninth were huge, gathering in between them a total of twenty states. The former included Colorado, Nebraska, Minnesota, Kansas, North Dakota, South Dakota, Wyoming, Iowa, Missouri, Arkansas, and the incoming states of Utah, Oklahoma, and New Mexico; the latter covered California, Oregon, Nevada, Idaho, Montana, Washington, and the new state of Arizona.

The distance problem remained acute because the new appellate courts generally sat in only one or two locations. The most burdensome phase lasted from 1891 to 1902 when the courts of appeals sat in only one city in each circuit.[190] Thereafter, Congress began to ease the distance burden slightly by requiring some appellate courts to sit in additional cities. The alternative locations, however, offered only limited relief. They were few in number and often little used. By 1916, for example, both the Sixth and Eighth Circuits were authorized to sit in additional cities. The Sixth, however, remained for the most part in Cincinnati and only occasionally sat at its alternative site in Detroit. The Eighth Circuit, though authorized to sit in St. Louis, Denver, and Cheyenne, heard an estimated 95 percent of its cases at its base in St. Paul.[191]

In the circuits of the Midwest, West, and South, an appeal could easily require a round-trip of five or six hundred miles, and in the Fifth, Eighth, and Ninth Circuits it could take over a thousand miles. In the years before World War I a one-way train trip of two hundred or three hundred miles—especially one originating in a smaller city or town—could take an entire day and sometimes two. As late as 1916 a House of Representatives report concluded that a round trip to St. Paul from the farthest point in the Eighth Circuit "requires about a week."[192] Between time spent traveling and awaiting oral argument, an appearance in any of the federal appellate courts in the Midwest, West, or South could easily consume several days of an attorney's time.

In addition to increasing the burden of distance, the larger size of the circuits in the West and South also compounded the problem of delay. Although concentrated population and commercial activity imposed a perennially heavy docket on the Second Circuit, centered in New York City, demographic and economic expansion over their larger areas increasingly pressed heavier caseloads on the circuits in the West and South. By 1915 four circuits in the West and South—the Sixth, Seventh, Eighth, and Ninth—accounted for 65 percent of the appeals pending in the federal system. In the Sixth Circuit the time between docketing and final decision rose to between eighteen and twenty-four months,[193] and by the turn of the century the Eighth Circuit consistently had more cases pending—and longer delays—than did any of the other circuits. A House of Representatives report in 1916 estimated that the time from docketing to decision in the Eighth Circuit would shortly reach three years.[194]

Because the losing party had an appeal as of right and corporations often used it, the threat of appellate costs was always present.[195] One sample of more than fifteen hundred appellate cases found that defendants appealed more than twice as frequently as did plaintiffs.[196] Other studies confirmed the pattern.[197] In 1905 a Maryland attorney paraphrased the reasoning he heard from defendants:

> "Oh! it will not be very expensive to take this case up, there is a chance that I may win out, and if I do not, the additional time I shall gain before the day of final reckoning will be worth more to me than the cost of the appeal."[198]

The following year an attorney who specialized in the defense of personal injury actions acknowledged the way that defendants used the appeal process to delay final judgments and to impose added costs on recalcitrant plaintiffs:

> Supplied with ample means for defense, they determine to defend to the bitter end, often from a high sense of what is due to themselves and to society in resisting injustice. The result is that almost every adverse judgment is appealed from. In the course of the trial, with an appeal in view, all manner of questions are raised, having but remote connection with the real merits of the case and ultimate rights of the parties; instructions, having any purpose but to instruct, are drawn and requested; and often the summary brief on motion for new trial presents but little resemblance to the elaborate one submitted in the higher court.[199]

Where plaintiffs lived a great distance from the nearest appellate court or their circuit had a heavy backlog, the burden of appeal was particularly oppressive. The circuit court of appeals was "several hundred miles" away, complained a Wisconsin attorney in 1932, and the fear of that added expense helped discourage his poorer clients.[200] The mere threat made by a New York insurance company to remove and then appeal, a Nebraska attorney wrote the same year, forced him to settle a widow's insurance claim for one-quarter of the amount he thought was properly due.[201] Even if a corporation did not overtly threaten that it would appeal an unfavorable verdict, a plaintiff would still have had to include the likely costs of appeal in evaluating settlement.

Indeed, in the federal system it was even possible for the losing party to take a second appeal, carrying the case to the Supreme Court in Washington. Though only a tiny percentage reached that level, some did. The threat of an ultimate appeal to the Supreme Court made by an aggressive corporate attorney could have helped further discourage some litigants. If such threats did not intimidate plaintiffs, when they were carried out they often proved too expensive for plaintiffs to counter. As two students of the early twentieth-century Supreme Court noted, injured plaintiffs failed to appear "all too often in tort actions against railroads which reached the Court."[202]

Social and economic inequality, the rules of federal jurisdiction and procedure, and the demographic and institutional conditions of late nineteenth- and early twentieth-century life combined to forge distance, delay, and procedural complexity into powerful tools of litigation. If settlement was the most cost-effective method for a plaintiff, the system of corporate diversity litigation helped drive down settlement values by forcing up the costs and burdens of litigation.[203] The result in innumerable cases was a decision to settle a claim on a steeply discounted basis, with or without previously filing suit. In either case the result had no necessary connection with the "law," the merits of the underlying claim, or the extent to which the claimant had been injured.

The patterns and practices in the informal legal process that surrounded the system of corporate diversity litigation bear critically on two major and related questions about the judicial system in the late nineteenth and early twentieth centuries, whether it provided a de facto "subsidy" to business and whether its rules brought economically "efficient" results. A more complete answer to those questions requires a more thorough consideration of the whole system of corporate diversity litigation, but the massive scope and unequal balance in the informal legal process suggest preliminary but nevertheless clear answers. The structural organization and the procedural rules of the federal courts expanded the scope of the informal legal process, augmented the extralegal pressures that corporate defendants could exert against individual plaintiffs, and helped limit the amounts that corporate defendants had to pay to settle claims and obtain releases. To that extent, the federal courts—irrespective of the substantive rules they applied—did provide corporations with a kind of subsidy and, at the same time, helped prevent the substantive rules of the common law from achieving efficient social results.[204]

Chapter 3

The Federal Common Law

Tort and contract actions, whether brought in state or federal court, were governed by state law. Absent a controlling state statute, they were governed by the state's common law, that is, by judge-made rules and principles embodied in earlier decisions of the state's courts. Although legislation increased in the late nineteenth and early twentieth centuries, the common law remained a dominant force in both tort and contract law. And even when legislation altered or abrogated judge-made rules, the common law continued to provide the methodological and conceptual tools that the courts used to construe and apply statutory enactments.

The common law in the United States was complex. The courts of each state developed their own common law which, in spite of broad similarities in method and substance, contained numerous conflicting rules. Even more problematic, the national courts applied their own special version. In theory federal judges applied the common law of the states in which they sat, but in practice they developed their own conflicting and to some extent nationally uniform "federal common law."

Removal thus gave corporate defendants an opportunity to avoid the common law rules that the state courts applied and to have their cases decided under the rules the federal courts applied. This became increasingly important in the late nineteenth century because in the 1880s significant parts of the federal common law began growing more and more favorable to corporate defendants. As removal often allowed defendants to impose heavy practical burdens on their adversaries, it also enabled them to improve their formal legal positions.

Rooted in the Supreme Court's 1842 decision in *Swift v. Tyson,*[1] the concept of a federal common law caused difficulties throughout the late nineteenth and early twentieth centuries. For one, federal judges repeatedly stated that there was no such thing as a "national" common law, though they occasionally said that there was and, in any event, tried to build up just such a body of rules. Most took the position that common law issues were matters of state law but that the federal judiciary had a right and duty, when the issues were "commercial" or "general," to make an "independent judgment" as to the nature of that state law. Regardless of theory, however, when "state" law properly controlled a case, as in tort and contract claims heard in diversity actions, federal judges often ignored the decisions of state courts and applied their own independent federal rules which were in many cases inconsistent with the state rules. As instances of independent judgments piled up, especially when the Supreme Court made them, a particular and somewhat unusual kind of common law resulted. This was the common law that was termed "federal" or "general," or sometimes "federal general."[2] Its exact nature was unclear, confused, and disputed.

In practice, the federal common law was state law for some purposes and federal law for other purposes. For example, it was clearly not federal law in three important senses. First, a claim under the federal common law did not present a "federal question" for purposes of either original or removal jurisdiction in the lower federal courts or appellate jurisdiction in the Supreme Court. Second, any rule of the general common law—absent congressional preemption or constitutional bar—could be altered or abolished by a state legislature. Third, a federal common law rule was not binding on the state courts. They were free, rather, to ignore the federal rule and apply their own contrary or inconsistent rules. The general common law was federal law, however, in two other senses. It could and frequently did allow federal courts to disregard the common law rules enforced in the states, and it tended to create over time a set of rules that were enforced in federal courts throughout the nation and that, once in existence, could not be altered by the decisions of state courts.

Although state statutes could change state common law and make those changes binding on the federal courts, the latter enjoyed some leeway in applying them. First, if a statute could be construed as merely "declarative" of the common law, the federal court could ignore it.[3] Second, if the state's highest court had not yet construed the statute, the federal court was free to place its own construction on it and, more important, to maintain that construction even if the state's highest court subsequently construed the statute differently.[4] Finally, even if the state's highest court had construed a statute before the federal court did so, the latter was bound only if the construction given decided the precise point at issue.[5]

Although the rules relating federal common law to state statutes were relatively clear, the rules that determined when state judicial decisions were properly binding on the federal courts were not. In theory, state decisions were binding on the federal courts if they dealt with "local" matters. Conversely, they were not binding on the national courts if they ruled on issues of "general" law. In part, the distinction itself was unclear. What, after all, could not be properly included in the "general"? In part, too, the federal courts simply kept expanding the scope of the general, defeating any attempt to draw and maintain a clear and coherent line. The 1914 edition of *Bouvier's Law Dictionary* tried valiantly to explain the scope of federal common law, but it could do little more than describe and categorize dozens of cases. "It is difficult," it confessed, "to deduce from the cases any general rule or principle."[6]

Although the lines were not clear, the cases generally recognized two specific situations as particularly local. One was the decision of a state's highest court construing its own state constitution or statutes, assuming that a federal court had not yet placed a different construction on them. The other was a clearly established "course of decisions" that created a specific local rule of "property." In both of those situations, state decisions were supposed to be binding on the federal courts.[7] Outside those two areas it was clear that federal courts could make an "independent judgment" on state law issues or at least possible that they might do so.

Growth and Reorientation

In the years after the Civil War and peaking around the turn of the century, the federal or general common law developed along three lines that were fundamental to the operation of the system of corporate diversity litigation. The scope of the federal common law expanded; its disagreements with the common law rules enforced in the state courts multiplied; and some of its basic rules came increasingly to favor the interests of national corporations.

Swift v. Tyson itself had dealt with a narrow question involving negotiable instruments, but the federal courts gradually altered the focus of its doctrine from the relatively narrow limits of commercial law to the far broader and more amorphous realm of "general jurisprudence." By the 1870s federal common law covered a large part of both tort and contract law, and for the next three decades it stretched its reach ever further. In 1888 the Supreme Court itself admitted that the problem of identifying the scope of general jurisprudence was "an embarrassing one."[8] By the beginning of the twentieth century the federal common law had taken over almost the entirety of contract and tort law and extended its sway to numerous other areas, including wills, deeds, mortgages, and many rules relating to evidence and measures of damages. In 1910 the Supreme Court expanded it once again to include important elements of local property law.[9]

The expansion of the *Swift* doctrine brought a growing divergence between state and federal common law. Because common law rules were formally state law, the Supreme Court could not impose its general common law on the state courts. Its appellate jurisdiction did not even allow it to review state court decisions insofar as they were based on state common law grounds.[10] Hence, there was no judicial authority in either the states or the nation capable of reconciling divergent views or compelling uniformity in the common law decisions of the federal and state courts.

Throughout *Swift*'s reign judges, lawyers, and scholars debated the extent to which the federal common law differed from the rules in the various states. Its proponents minimized the divergence, and its opponents maximized it. Because of the nearly infinite variety of legal rules, the existence of over forty state jurisdictions, the fact that the common law was changing dramatically throughout the period, and the extent to which analysis turned on subtle issues of interpretation, no one attempted to determine precisely the extent of the divergence that *Swift* engendered. The evidence, though spotty, suggests that the divergence was considerable.[11]

Beginning in the 1880s and culminating in the years around the turn of the century, the rules of the federal common law grew more favorable to corporate business. The Supreme Court seemed to shed its suspicion of large-scale corporate enterprise and gradually embraced the corporate form as the instrument of national wealth, power, and progress. Many judges and lawyers, too, believed that the Constitution provided for federal diversity jurisdiction specifically to protect business and encourage interstate transactions, and *Swift* itself was at least in part an effort to facilitate a burgeoning national commercial order by strengthening the principle of negotiability.[12]

The expanding scope and shifting orientation of the federal common law roughly paralleled the rise of substantive due process in the 1890s, and both developments expanded the role and lawmaking power of the federal judiciary. The federal common law and substantive due process were obverse sides of the same coin of federal judicial activism and centralization, and they both seemed to make the federal courts the protectors of corporate interests. Although the former was vulnerable to state legislation, the latter imposed limits on what such legislation could accomplish. Substantive due process emerged, then, as the constitutional trump that stood guard over the domain of the federal common law. If states could not legislate in certain areas, then those areas remained within the realm of the common law where the federal courts could exercise their independent judgment.

Although never the major political issue that substantive due process became, the independent federal common law nevertheless emerged in the late nineteenth century as an issue of significance within the legal profession and one that occasionally flared in national politics. Legal writers frequently attacked both its theory and its constitutionality, and they repeatedly pointed to the anomaly produced by the existence of conflicting common law rules in the same state. Some emphasized the extent to which the federal common law seemed to favor corporations, and others stressed the intrusion it made on the sovereignty of the states. The federal common law, charged the *American Law Review* sweepingly in 1894, revealed the "manifest purpose and tendency" of the federal courts "to make themselves the supreme interpreters in all cases and over all questions."[13] In spite of the variety of their criticisms, opponents of the federal common law—like those who opposed other central elements of the system of corporate diversity litigation—tended to come from the South, Midwest, or West, to be populists or progressives in their politics, and to sympathize with or represent individuals as opposed to national corporations.[14]

The Supreme Court helped cast the image of the federal courts as guardians of business interests in 1864 when it initiated a major line of cases, analogous to *Swift* and frequently brought under diversity jurisdiction, that used the federal common law to protect investors in municipal bonds. In *Gelpcke v. Dubuque*[15] the Court overlooked evidence of widespread fraud and illegality on the part of bondholders in order to prevent state repudiation. *Gelpcke* and the cases that followed it held that the federal courts were not required to follow the decisions of a state's highest court changing the construction of state constitutions or statutes when the result of the change would be to invalidate local government bonds previously marketed. By the end of the century the Court had heard over 350 such cases from more than twenty states, involving between $100 million and $150 million in bonds. In the great majority the bondholders won, and their ability to invoke diversity jurisdiction and thereby avoid the state courts often meant the difference between the validity and invalidity of the bonds. Perhaps more than any other specific line of cases before the 1890s, *Gelpcke* and its progeny came to symbolize the role of the federal courts as the protectors of investment capital.[16]

By the 1890s a wider range of cases seemed to show that the national courts often treated business and property interests favorably. "The policy of the nation," announced the Eighth Circuit in 1904, "is to enlarge, not to restrict, commerce."[17] The Corporation Trust Company of New York City, which specialized in helping businesses exploit the procedural advantages that diversity offered, emphasized in one of its pamphlets the importance of differences in substantive law. A principal benefit of incorporating out of state, it explained, was the ability to bring or remove suits to federal court where "a study of the decisions" indicated that the law tended to be much more favorable to property interests than it was in the state courts.[18]

Although as a general matter the federal common law seemed to grow more favorable to business interests after the 1880s, it is important to emphasize the extreme diversity that marked individual cases as well as the variations that occurred by state. Compared with the federal courts, the state courts were in many instances equally or more favorable to business interests.[19] Further, federal law sometimes favored plaintiffs. The national courts, for example, placed the burden of proving contributory negligence on the defendant, and at least outside the employer–employee context they limited the defense even further by applying the rule of "last clear chance."[20] Similarly, the rule that a federal court could not compel a personal injury plaintiff to submit to a medical examination before trial also favored plaintiffs.[21] Naturally, too, in some instances federal judges themselves seemed especially solicitous toward injured parties who were suing corporations.[22] The resulting legal situation was thus complex, and in any individual case either a federal or a state court might have offered a plaintiff the more favorable substantive law. Conflicts between federal and local law, and differences in the social sympathies that might be shown, varied by state, time period, doctrinal area, specific legal rule, appellate circuit, and individual judge.[23]

Although such variations limited the scope of the system of corporate diversity litigation, they did not alter its nature. The essence of the system, after all, was not that social and legal conditions remained unchanged, that state courts were always preferable forums for plaintiffs, or that the federal courts invariably or purposely favored national business. Its essence, rather, lay in the fact that a large-scale, long-term, and regularly recurring conflict between identifiable groups of adverse and unequal litigants occurred under a set of legal and social conditions that combined to produce—in the specific historical context of the late nineteenth and early twentieth centuries—results that generally and for the most part favored national corporations. Those results also were probably skewed even more favorably toward corporate interests by the fact that national corporations had a greater ability to minimize or neutralize the impact of unfavorable local variations. Compared with individual litigants, they were more likely to know of the variations in advance, to be able to develop strategies of avoidance, and to have the long-range incentives to do so.

Beyond the direct benefits that many of its substantive rules provided to corporate defendants, the existence and nature of the federal common law also gave them added leverage in the informal legal process. One of the fundamental justifications of the federal common law was that it would allow the development of a uniform national law and thereby facilitate rational economic planning. By the late nineteenth century, if not before, it seemed clear that *Swift* was not achieving that goal. Even assuming that the doctrine brought some significant uniformity to the commercial law, it nevertheless failed to bring complete uniformity, failed to bring any uniformity in many other areas of general law, and failed even to draw a clear and workable line to identify its own domain. If *Swift*'s contribution to legal certainty and business planning was mixed, however, its contribution to business litigation tactics seemed clearer. The very existence of the federal common law could contribute an additional element of uncertainty to a case. Would state or federal precedents control? Was the issue in dispute "local" or "general"? Were the state precedents sufficiently clear and numerous to constitute a "settled course of decision?" Could the court be induced to expand the reach of the federal common law to a new fact situation?

By expanding the area of uncertainty, the federal common law loaded additional practical burdens onto plaintiffs. First, because many state court practitioners were no more familiar with federal common law than they were with federal practice under the Conformity Act, a federal action tended to require more attorney's time and hence to be more costly. Second, to the extent that it was unsettled whether state or federal common law would control, removal increased the likelihood that additional and sometimes complicated issues of law would become pivotal and require formal briefing. Third, the added element of uncertainty as to controlling law increased the general unpredictability of outcome and therefore the overall risks of litigation. Given the social resources of the respective parties in the system of corporate diversity litigation and the drastically different economic significance their disputes had for each of the parties, those uncertainty factors created additional incentives for plaintiffs to discount their claims and settle. Similarly, they created additional incentives for defendants to exploit those uncertainties, to see them as opportunities to make new and more favorable law, and to stress their significance in pressing plaintiffs to drop their claims for small settlement amounts. However bad uncertainty may have been for business planning, it was not bad for business litigation, at least not in the system of corporate diversity litigation.[24]

In spite of variations, in many areas the federal common law imposed particularly narrow standards of liability. After the 1880s it increasingly adopted rules that favored corporate defendants, and in at least many states its rules seemed to conflict significantly with the local common law. Those tendencies were evident in the two substantive law areas that were central to the system of corporate diversity litigation, insurance contracts and industrial torts.

The Federal Common Law of Insurance Contracts

The law of contracts was a core area of the federal common law, and in 1842, on the heels of its decision in *Swift,* the Supreme Court held that insurance contracts presented issues of general jurisprudence on which the federal courts would render independent judgments of state law.[25] A quarter-century later the Court ruled that the insurance business did not constitute "commerce" within the meaning of the commerce clause.[26] Hence, Congress had no direct constitutional authority to regulate the insurance business, and legislative control of the industry seemed destined to remain with the states.

By the 1870s, the states were beginning to assert broad control over the activities of insurance companies, and they attempted to protect policyholders in a variety of ways. State insurance statutes mandated that certain substantive provisions be included in policies, regulated rates and coverages, and prohibited excessively harsh provisions that could too readily lead to forfeitures or lost coverage. Further, they imposed on the companies a variety of procedures designed to ensure adequate notice to policyholders concerning premium payments, terminations, and forfeitures. Generally, the federal courts gave state legislatures leeway in regulating insurance, recognizing it as a special area "affected with a public interest" that justified the broad exercise of the states' police powers.[27] Where protective state statutes applied, they frequently allowed policyholders to recover when their claims were otherwise in jeopardy.[28]

In spite of numerous state statutes, however, the law of insurance contracts offered the federal courts a wide area for the application of their general common law. Some areas of contract law escaped legislative supervision completely, and other areas were regulated in only some states. Many statutes, moreover, were brief and general, and in specific cases they raised questions of construction that allowed the federal courts considerable flexibility in deciding whether and how to apply them. Further, in cases where the laws of more than one state were arguably applicable, the federal courts were able to choose among them and to limit on constitutional grounds if necessary the "extraterritorial" reach of state laws.[29]

To a large extent both federal and state courts looked favorably on policyholders. As a class they represented to both state and federal judges the frugal, the self-reliant, and the economically rational. The courts usually gave them a sympathetic hearing and, when policyholders seemed deserving, sometimes noticeably stretched the rules to protect them.[30] There was, a treatise writer concluded in 1910, "special and exceptional favor shown by the courts to policyholders."[31]

Although the federal courts shared in the general judicial solicitude toward policyholders, their common law nevertheless differed from state law and in many cases proved relatively less hospitable to claimants. In 1894, for example, the Supreme Court increased the obstacles to recovery that many insurance claimants would face. *Imperial Fire Insurance Co. v. Coos County* presented a typical dispute.[32] A fire insurance policy provided that the insured, the county of Coos, New Hampshire, should not make certain repairs on its building without the knowledge and written consent of the insurer and that violation of the condition would void the policy. The county made the repairs, and after their completion the building caught fire and burned. The company claimed that it was not liable because the unauthorized repairs had voided the policy. The county claimed that the forfeiture clause could not be interpreted to preclude ordinary repairs, that the repairs had been completed by the time of the fire, and that the repairs had neither caused the fire nor increased the risk of fire. In such circumstances, the county argued, to hold the policy void would contravene the basic principles of insurance law that policies should be construed liberally in favor of the insured and that forfeitures were not favored. The Supreme Court nevertheless reversed a jury verdict for the county and ordered a new trial.

In *Coos County* the Court was unwilling to rest its order for a new trial on the narrow ground that the record failed to support the jury's finding that the repairs had not increased the risk of the fire or caused its occurrence.[33] Instead, it decided to assume those findings, hold them irrelevant, and rest its decision on broad principles of federal common law. First, it emphasized that insurance policies were contracts that, like other contracts, should generally be enforced as written:

> The compliance of the assured with the terms of the contract is a condition precedent to the right of recovery. If the assured has violated, or failed to perform the

conditions of the contract, and such violation or want of performance has not been waived by the insurer, then the assured cannot recover. It is immaterial to consider the reasons for the conditions or provisions on which the contract is made to terminate, or any other provision of the policy which has been accepted and agreed upon. It is enough that the parties have made certain terms, conditions on which their contract shall continue or terminate. The courts may not make a contract for the parties. Their function and duty consist simply in enforcing and carrying out the one actually made.[34]

Second, the Court held that the policy's forfeiture clause—providing that a violation of its conditions would void the policy "wholly independent of any increase of risk"[35]—was "not unreasonable" and that a violation therefore voided the policy "without reference to the question whether such [violations] had increased the risk or not."[36] Uncoupling "reasonableness" from objective risk, *Coos County* allowed insurers wide latitude in imposing conditions and forfeitures on policyholders. "[T]he insurer had a right, in its own judgment, to make [its conditions] a material element of the contract and, being assented to by the assured," the Court explained, "it did not rest in the opinion of other parties, court or jury, to say that it was immaterial."[37] In such a case, "the only inquiry will be whether the [action] in question comes within the category of changes which by agreement shall work a forfeiture."[38]

Coos County seemed to announce a relatively narrow role for the federal courts in supervising insurance contracts and to suggest a concomitant expansion of the areas in which they would simply enforce as written whatever agreements private parties made. Given the immense bargaining advantages that insurers enjoyed against most individual policyholders, the decision promised the companies the regular opportunity to protect their interests and to impose unwanted risks on unsuspecting policyholders. Consistent with the orientation of *Coos County,* the federal courts sometimes interpreted insurance policies narrowly against claimants[39] and often rigorously enforced provisions that denied recovery.[40] Insurance companies consistently sought access to the federal courts, on occasion expressly claiming, as the United States Life Insurance Company did in an appeal before the Supreme Court in 1903, that "the law is more favorable to insurance companies as administered in the Federal than in the state court."[41]

The "more favorable" nature of the federal common law was manifest on the question of the import of a policyholder's failure to pay on a note given in payment of a premium. Notes were commonly used to secure policies, and the courts disagreed widely on the scope to be given the forfeiture clauses that companies usually put in their notes or policies. Some courts held that a company could cancel a policy only after a reasonable time following notice to the policyholder that payment was past due, and others held that forfeiture provisions could be enforced only to the extent necessary to provide the company with security. The federal rule, followed in only a few states, was the harshest. "[I]n the federal courts," summarized a Washington federal judge in 1911, "the rule is well settled that failure to pay such a note, containing a provision of forfeiture, works an absolute forfeiture of the policy."[42]

The leading federal authority on the note forfeiture rule was the Supreme Court's 1902 decision in *Iowa Life Insurance Co. v. Lewis*.[43] The record on appeal showed that the failure to redeem the note had occurred on September 24 and that

Thomas M. Lewis, the insured, was on that date "confined to his bed with typhoid fever." The company's agent came to collect on the note on September 29. When Lewis promised to have it paid "at once," the agent told him that the note could be paid anytime before October 1. On the next day, September 30, two of Lewis's friends tendered payment to the agent. The agent refused the tender because, on the same day, he had received instructions from the company not to accept. A week later Lewis died of typhoid fever. The company maintained that the policy had been forfeited for nonpayment. The Supreme Court announced that it would not follow certain "cases in the state courts" that restricted policy forfeitures but would, instead, "follow our own decisions."[44] It then ruled as a matter of federal common law that the provisions of the policy controlled, that the payment had been due on September 24, that the agent had no authority to modify any of its terms, and that the company had not waived the payment requirement. The Court reversed a judgment in favor of the policy's beneficiary, Lewis's wife.

Similarly, in numerous cases the federal courts applied federal common law to deny recovery on policies against "accidental" injury and death where either the applicable state law allowed recovery or the federal court faced conflicting lines of state precedents and chose the one that denied recovery.[45] Over an anguished dissent by Justice Benjamin N. Cardozo in 1934, the Supreme Court in *Landress v. Phoenix Insurance Co.*[46] embraced this line of federal decisions and confirmed that there was a critical difference "between accidental external means and accidental result."[47] Essentially, the distinction—difficult to articulate and more difficult to understand—meant that recovery was allowed when an unexpected external means caused an injury but that it was denied when an expected external means unexpectedly caused injury. *Landress* illustrated the distinction, denying recovery for death suffered from sunstroke by a man playing golf. Although the sun (the "accidental external means") was to be expected on a golf course, the Court explained, death from the sun (the "accidental result") was not. In reaching its decision the Court ignored state law. Alone in dissent, Cardozo argued that the Court's distinction was so incoherent that its adoption would "plunge this branch of the law into a Serbonian Bog."[48] More important, Cardozo pointed out, acceptance of such a distinction was simply misleading and unfair to policyholders. The "average" person reading an insurance policy would never think of such a distinction, and if she did, she would naturally and reasonably assume that an "accident" policy would cover both types of "accidental" injuries.[49]

Perhaps the most common issue over which policyholders and companies battled throughout the period was the role and authority of the insurance agent. The lines were clear. Trying to control risks and prevent fraud, the companies limited as much as possible the authority of salesmen, brokers, and employees while requiring written approval from specified company officers before considering any policy or amendment to be in effect. Claimants repeatedly attempted to establish the validity of disputed policies or to avoid the effect of provisions that could deny recovery. They usually claimed either that whatever their applications stated, they had made satisfactory and appropriate disclosures to some agent of the company or that in failing to meet some requirement or condition of their policies, they had relied reasonably on statements made to them by some company agent that they need not comply with the provision. In the overwhelming majority of cases, the alleged statements at issue were unrecorded oral statements. Such cases, commented a standard treatise on insurance law in 1910, "confront the insurance lawyer in court perhaps more frequently than any other issue."[50]

To succeed in such cases, policyholders needed to prevail on two preliminary matters, the admissibility into evidence of the oral statements—so-called parol evidence—and the authority of the agent to bind the company. The first issue was controlled by the "parol evidence rule" which provided that evidence of oral statements made at or prior to the signing of a written contract were inadmissible to contradict or modify the terms of the written contract. The second issue was subject to the law of agency, which bound a principal to an agent's actions when the principal either conferred authority on the agent to take the acts in question or acted in a way that reasonably led people to believe that the principal had conferred such authority.

In the 1870s the Supreme Court showed considerable sympathy to claimants raising such issues. In *Insurance Company v. Wilkinson*,[51] decided in 1871, the company refused to honor a life insurance policy on the ground that the application contained false statements about the medical history of the insured's mother. The beneficiary claimed that he and the insured, his wife, had informed the company's agent that they did not know the mother's age at death or the cause of her death. He explained that they had then introduced the agent to a family friend who confirmed their lack of information and also, under questioning by the agent, provided information that the agent used to complete the application. The beneficiary testified that neither he nor his wife assented to the friend's statements, though he admitted that the statements proved to be untrue and that he had signed the completed application.

Affirming a jury verdict for the beneficiary, the Court ruled that the parol evidence was admissible and that the agent's acceptance of the answers bound the company. The striking fact about *Wilkinson* was the extent to which the Court merged the two issues of parol evidence and agent authority by resting its decision on the general need to protect policyholders from both insurance agents and companies. The parol evidence was admissible, the Court ruled in essence, not because of any technical limitation in the rules of evidence, but because the parol evidence showed on the merits that the insured had not intended to mislead the agent.[52]

In *Wilkinson* the Court ruled that the company was bound by the agent's knowledge for a blunt and practical social reason:

[I]t is well known, so well that no court would be justified in shutting its eyes to it, that insurance companies organized under the laws of one State, and having in that State their principal business office, send these agents all over the land, with directions to solicit and procure applications for policies, furnishing them with printed arguments in favor of the value and necessity of life insurance, and of the special advantages of the corporation which the agent represents. They pay these agents large commissions on the premiums thus obtained, and the policies are delivered at their hands to the assured. The agents are stimulated by letters and instructions to activity in procuring contracts, and the party who is in this manner induced to take out a policy, rarely sees or knows anything about the company or its officers by whom it is issued, but looks to and relies upon the agent who has persuaded him to effect insurance as the full and complete representative of the company, in all that is said or done in making the contract. Has he not a right to so regard him?[53]

Insurance companies persistently argued that their salesmen did not have authority to bind them, *Wilkinson* explained, and some courts accepted that doctrine in one form or another. The Supreme Court of the United States, however, would not accept it, at least when it would be inequitable to do so. *Wilkinson* rejected the position of the company with surprising emotion:

> But to apply such a doctrine, in its full force to the system of selling policies through agents, which we have described, would be a snare and a delusion, leading, as it has done in numerous instances, to the grossest frauds, of which the insurance corporations receive the benefits, and the parties supposing themselves insured are the victims.[54]

Its decision did not reject the parol evidence rule, the Court concluded deftly. It merely held that when a writing was not truly the statement of a party, the other party was estopped from relying on it.

Wilkinson made it relatively easy for policyholders to use parol evidence, and well into the 1880s the Court remained particularly solicitous toward policyholders who seemed to have substantively just claims.[55] In *Insurance Company v. Norton*,[56] for example, the Court seemed to acknowledge stretching to find that an agent had authority to waive a policy provision and thereby maintain the policy in force. It relied on cases that "show the readiness with which courts seize hold of any circumstances that indicate an election or intent to waive a forfeiture."[57]

Conflicting strains, however, began to appear. In *Norton,* handed down in 1878, three Justices dissented. The company had not given its agent authority to waive conditions, the dissenters noted, and the policy itself "declared that agents should not have authority to make such waivers."[58] Eight years later the Court denied recovery to an unsympathetic plaintiff and in doing so seemed to state the parol evidence rule in a broadly preclusive form.[59]

The slow and somewhat erratic shift in the Court's views came to completion in 1902, the same year it handed down its decision in *Lewis* on the federal note forfeiture rule. *Northern Assurance Co. v. Grand View Building Association*[60] quickly established itself as the leading federal case on both the parol evidence rule and the scope of the insurance agent's authority. The policyholder had obtained fire insurance from one company and subsequently purchased additional coverage from the Northern Assurance Company. The value of the two policies together was approximately equal to the value of the insured property.[61] The second policy contained a condition making it void if the insured had other fire insurance, and it also contained provisions that required any waiver of conditions to be in writing and limited the authority of the agent to make alterations. After fire destroyed the insured building, the policyholder attempted to avoid the "no second policy" condition by showing that the Northern Assurance agent had been informed about the first policy and had knowingly waived the condition. The claimant's evidence was strong. Both its president and the agent of the other insurer testified that they had informed the Northern Assurance agent of the first policy. The testimony of the Northern Assurance agent was equivocal at best. Although he denied knowledge of the other policy, he admitted that the insured's president "might have mentioned that there was an existing policy."[62]

The insured won a jury verdict, but the Supreme Court reversed. On the ground that the provisions of the policy were "unambiguous," it ruled that parol evidence was not admissible to vary any of the terms of the written agreement. It also ruled that it was reasonable for companies to deny their agents authority to waive or vary any term or condition, that such a limitation of authority contained in a policy was valid and enforceable, and that "where such limitation is expressed in the policy, executed and accepted, the insured is presumed, as matter of law, to be aware of such limitation."[63] Plaintiff's only remedy lay in a suit in equity to reform the contract.

Northern Assurance was a landmark in the federal common law of insurance contracts. It was, declared one treatise writer, "a decision of perhaps greater practical moment than any other rendered in the law of insurance within a half century."[64] The Court devoted more than forty pages to a discussion of judicial precedents from England, Canada, eight different states, and the federal courts, and it announced "the principles sustained by the authorities" that properly controlled.[65] The principles that the Court identified placed insurance companies in a highly advantageous position. They made a rigorous parol evidence rule applicable in the federal courts and increased the likelihood that policy provisions would be enforced there to the letter. They upheld the right of insurers to impose on their policyholders the burden of creating or securing properly drafted and executed documents whenever the policyholder faced a potential problem concerning the policy's scope or meaning. Finally, they allowed companies to limit the authority of their agents and to avoid any policy change or waiver that was not in writing and approved by a specified company officer.

The advantages that *Northern Assurance* gave to the companies were magnified by the practical inequality that existed between them and most of their policyholders. A broad parol evidence rule benefited the more sophisticated and knowledgeable party who could carefully craft an agreement, covering every eventuality and protecting against every risk and ambiguity imaginable. The freedom to impose various favorable provisions strengthened the more powerful party, the one capable of understanding the significance of such provisions and insisting on their inclusion. Insurance companies were geared to take advantage of such rules. Except in rare cases, individual applicants could not fully understand most policies, even if they read them, and they were unable to compare and effectively evaluate alternative policies. Moreover, the equitable remedy left standing by *Northern Assurance,* a suit in equity to reform the contract, posed special complications, could cause additional delay and expense, and forced plaintiffs to try their cases without a jury.[66]

In announcing its principles of federal common law, the Court revealed how radically its views had changed in the three decades since *Wilkinson.* Gone was its earlier concern with the "numerous instances" when insurance companies profited from "the grossest frauds." In its place was a concern for the companies. "[T]he community at large have a deep interest in the welfare and prosperity of such beneficial institutions," *Northern Assurance* explained.[67] Gone also was *Wilkinson*'s assumption that policyholders reasonably relied on statements made to and by company agents and that "supposing themselves insured," they should not be made "victims." In its place was a concern for investors.

> It would be very unfortunate if prudent men should be deterred from investing capital in such companies by having reason to fear that conditions which have been

found reasonable and necessary to put into policies to protect the companies from faithless agents and from dishonest insurers, are liable to be nullified by verdicts based on verbal testimony.[68]

In *Northern Assurance* the Court saw only two risks, "faithless agents" and "dishonest" policyholders. It decided "to protect the companies" from both and—contrary to *Wilkinson*—to place the risk of the "faithless agent" on the policyholder. Gone, too, was *Wilkinson's* social analysis, its focus on the nature of the business of national insurance companies and the vulnerability of individual policyholders. In its place were fleeting references to the fact that a strictly applied parol evidence rule would "protect both parties" from such risks as the loss of a critical witness to an oral statement.[69] Gone, finally, was *Wilkinson's* implicit criticism of state courts for treating insurance companies too favorably. In its place was a warning that the states were treating them too harshly. "Increased importance should be given to the rules involved in this discussion by the fact that, in latter times and in most, if not all, of the States," the Court concluded, "statutory changes have opened the courts [of the states] to the testimony of the very parties who have signed the written instrument in controversy."[70]

In its striking emphasis on the conflict between federal common law and the laws of the states, the peroration in *Northern Assurance* was highly unusual. In other respects, however, the case exemplified the more typical approach of the federal courts in dealing with that conflict—minimizing or ignoring it when possible. *Northern Assurance* attempted to minimize the conflict by reviewing at length parol evidence decisions in eight states and concluding that "the decided weight of authority is to the effect that a policy of insurance in writing cannot be changed or altered by parol evidence."[71] The Court did not explain how this conclusion related to its later assertion that statutes "in most, if not all, of the States" had made parol evidence admissible. Apparently, the Court seemed to think it appropriate to include in its weighing process those judicial decisions that had, by statute, been restricted or negated in their own jurisdictions.

Northern Assurance also adopted an even simpler way to minimize federal–state conflict. It did not state the fact that, as the Eighth Circuit pointed out[72] below, the common law of Nebraska, the state whose law applied, would have admitted the parol evidence, found that a waiver had been made, and allowed the insured to recover. Not surprisingly, the defendant Northern Assurance Company had removed the original suit from state court.

Throughout the reign of the federal common law *Northern Assurance* stood as a leading case that made the national courts highly attractive to insurance companies. Repeatedly the Supreme Court reaffirmed it,[73] and the lower federal courts applied it, frequently either rejecting or otherwise avoiding local law.[74] The states, for their part, generally ignored the federal rule, creating an area of fundamental disagreement between federal common law on one side and the laws of most of the states on the other.[75] By the end of the 1920s, a leading treatise writer concluded, the general rule in the state courts was that they would not enforce policy provisions that attempted to relieve insurers of liability for the knowledge and actions of their agents. Under *Northern Assurance* the federal courts enforced such provisions[76] and sometimes construed state statutes narrowly to deny that they made the agent's knowledge chargeable to the company.[77] Moreover, a leading insurance scholar concluded, evidence of oral statements that *Northern Assurance* refused to allow in the federal courts "may be shown in the courts of every state of the Union except Massachusetts and New Jersey."[78]

Northern Assurance not only made it easier for companies to win their litigations, but it also made it easier for them to win them cheaply. By foreclosing the admission of parol evidence and establishing the validity of certain restrictive policy provisions, *Northern Assurance* increased the likelihood that companies could win judgment as a matter of law and avoid the burden and expense of a trial and the danger of putting their case to a jury. In 1937, for example, the federal courts directed verdicts in 14 percent of all private civil cases tried by jury, and in three separate classes of contract actions tried by jury they directed verdicts in 13, 23, and 24 percent of the cases. By contrast, in insurance contract actions, the federal courts directed verdicts in 37 percent of the cases.[79]

The companies learned from the case, too, adding restrictions and conditions to their policies along the lines that the Court had approved. In *Aetna Life Insurance Co. v. Moore,*[80] for example, the Court rejected conflicting Georgia common law and reversed a judgment against the company. It relied in part on policy provisions that severely restricted the company's liability. "The competency of applicants for insurance to make such agreements, and that they are binding when made," the Court pointed out, "is decided by *Northern Assurance.*"[81]

Moore illustrated a general advantage that the companies had over most individuals. Not only were they better able to select and impose favorable policy terms, but they also were able to plan systematically and continuously in order to put themselves in the most favorable legal position possible. In *Moore* the company adopted the kind of stringent policy provisions that the Court had approved in *Northern Assurance* and, as a result, defeated a subsequent recovery. Within certain not clearly settled limits, insurance companies could select the state law that would control the construction of their contract.[82] By carefully controlling their operations, they could avoid application of the laws of states with unfavorable rules.[83] And by adjusting quickly to adverse decisions, they could obtain future victories.[84]

The Federal Common Law of Industrial Torts

By the 1870s the federal courts were regularly exercising their independent judgment in tort cases, and by the late nineteenth century the federal common law had expanded to include almost the entire law of industrial accidents. In contrast with the law of insurance contracts, tort law until the end of the nineteenth century was less affected by legislation. The major exception was railroad law. Even before the Civil War the states recognized the dangers created by the new steam and iron transportation system and began to protect the public by imposing statutory safety requirements and more rigid standards of liability. Legislation increased after the war, and in the 1880s the federal government began to assert its authority over interstate commerce and, in the 1890s, to impose its own safety requirements. For the most part, as with insurance regulation, the federal courts were hospitable to such legislation, though they sometimes construed statutes narrowly when they were "in derogation of the common law."[85]

In spite of legislation, however, the federal common law of torts thrived in the decades before the turn of the century. Much of the law remained unaffected by legislation, and even when statutes applied their construction was largely determined by the use of common law concepts and techniques. The federal common law came in the late nineteenth century to impose relatively narrow standards of liability. Restricted standards of care, exacting requirements for establishing causality, and a capacious idea of the kinds of risks that people properly "assumed" all combined—particularly in suits by injured employees—to give frequent advantage to defendants.[86] Compared with insurance claimants, tort plaintiffs often confronted courts that were unsympathetic or, if sympathetic, unable or unwilling to stretch the rules of liability.

To many courts narrow standards of liability had the virtue of fostering business enterprise. In 1904, the Seventh Circuit applied the general rule that an injured consumer could not recover against a seller or maker of goods with whom the consumer was not in "privity" of contract, that is, from whom she had not directly purchased the goods. Economic policy, it declared in *Galbraith v. Illinois Steel Co.*,[87] was the foundation of product liability law. If the law held "all the builders and makers and doers in the land" to a duty to everyone who might use their product, "we fancy few persons would be willing to do business, in the face of the insufferable litigation that would ensue." With unusual candor, the court admitted the corollary, that its decision could have been different, as it was based on policy and not on necessary or unchanging rules of law:

> True, the common law—that inexhaustible fount, of which the taps are in the hands of the courts—might have been turned to watering plaintiff's contention; but we think it evidence of the perception of a sound public policy that the courts, with virtual unanimity, have refrained from opening the gates.[88]

If the federal courts imposed narrow rules of liability in suits brought by those who were injured by a company's products, they seemed to impose even narrower rules in suits brought by a company's employees. Generally, the common law imposed on employers the "personal" and "nondelegable" duty to provide employees with a "reasonably safe workplace." The duty was limited, however, and the employer was required only to use "due care" in making the workplace safe. The duty included providing tools and equipment that were reasonably safe and suited to the work, using care in selecting competent employees, and establishing proper work rules, especially if the work involved numerous employees or complicated and dangerous machinery.[89]

The Supreme Court repeatedly emphasized that the employers' obligation was limited to the exercise of due care and that it did not require them to "guarantee" a safe workplace. In 1901 it stressed the significance of that limitation in *Patton v. Texas and Pacific Railway Co.*[90] The Court seemed to impose on plaintiffs particularly demanding standards for proving that defendant's negligence was the cause in fact of injury and, further, to deny to employees the right to rely on the doctrine of *res ipsa loquitur.* The latter doctrine often eased the evidentiary burdens that tort plaintiffs carried. If plaintiff established that an otherwise inexplicable accident had occurred involving equipment or instruments over which the employer had responsibility and control, the *res ipsa loquitur* doctrine shifted to defendant the burden of proving that it had not been at fault.[91] *Patton,* however, allowed no such leeway. "The fact of accident carries with it no presumption of negligence on the part of the employer," the Court insisted. Rather, the employee had to prove as "an affirmative fact" that "the employer has been guilty of negligence." Further, it was not sufficient to show that "the employer may have been guilty of negligence." If the evidence "shows that any of a half dozen things may have brought about the injury, for some of which the employer is responsible and for some of which he is not," the Court continued, "it is not for the jury to guess between these half a dozen cases." In such a case the plaintiff must fail.[92]

Although *Patton's* evidentiary rule may have seemed rational if exacting, in practice it forced particularly heavy and sometimes insurmountable burdens on injured workers. The evidence relevant to causality was often either in the employer's control or under its influence. Other workers and superintending personnel were susceptible to real or imagined pressure from above, and relevant physical evidence was usually owned by the employer and located on its property. Even more damaging, conclusive evidence that equipment had been faulty was often—especially in railroad cases—destroyed by the very collision, derailing, or explosion that caused the injury.[93] In 1902 the final report of the congressionally sponsored United States Industrial Commission—which reviewed economic and social conditions in the United States and other countries in nineteen lengthy volumes—pointed to the bewildering problems of proof that industrialization imposed on injured workers:

> Another hindrance to the workingman in securing compensation, which has been experienced in all countries, is the growing difficulty, under modern conditions, of fixing definite responsibility for accident upon any one individual. In the large industry of the present day the individual worker is no longer able to carry on his own work on his own responsibility, with the conditions attending it under his own control. His actions depend on the actions of others. He has to take his place at some one stage of a long and complicated process, involving the use of complicated machinery, where the fault of one is liable to involve all the others, and yet it can not be plainly shown who has committed the fault.[94]

Patton, with its exacting requirement that workers prove that their employers were negligent and that such negligence was the sole cause of their injury, imposed a heavy burden in theory, but a far heavier and sometimes impossible one in practice.[95]

O'Brien v. Chicago & Northwestern Railway Co. illustrated the practical consequences of the federal rule. J. J. O'Brien, a railroad express messenger, was killed when the train he was working on derailed in August 1899. Encouraged by an Iowa statute that provided favorable substantive law, his wife, Mary O'Brien, brought suit against the railroad. After defeating the defendant's pretrial motions in 1902,[96] she won a jury verdict that was reversed on appeal in 1904. The Eighth Circuit, relying on *Patton,* refused to allow an inference of negligence from the circumstances of the accident and ruled that plaintiff's two witnesses had not provided sufficient testimony to support the verdict.[97] O'Brien tried again, and at the second trial she put on one of her two original witnesses and eight new ones. The new witnesses were two railway mail clerks and her late husband's assistant, all of whom had been riding on the train; a railroad telegrapher who had seen the wreck from a half-mile distance; and four locomotive engineers who gave essentially expert testimony about speed, the use of brakes, and the track grade at the wreck site. She won the second trial, and in March 1907 the Eighth Circuit held that her evidence of negligence was sufficient and affirmed the verdict.[98]

The exacting federal evidentiary rule imposed heavy costs and burdens, and it sharply decreased the likelihood that plaintiffs would be able to persist to a successful judgment. O'Brien's attempt to win with a relatively small scale and economical first effort boomeranged and deprived her of the first verdict. Ultimate success took numerous court appearances, two trials, two trips to the appellate court, seven and a half years of litigation, and the assiduous work required to identify, locate, and prepare ten witnesses, to persuade each of them to testify, and to ensure that they were present when needed. The effort may well have also required the cooperation of a whole community of railroad employees, some of whom may have endangered their own jobs by helping or testifying. In any event, the evidentiary effort required energy and resources that were simply beyond the means of many and probably most individuals.

Consistent with *Patton* and *O'Brien,* the federal courts generally applied rigorous evidentiary standards to workers' claims. They held that the *res ipsa* doctrine was inapplicable in master–servant cases,[99] imposed exacting standards of proof concerning both negligence and causality,[100] and often gave narrow scope to the safe workplace rule.[101] Where state law provided different rules for allocating the burden of proof, they sometimes emphasized that the issue was one of federal common law over which they exercised their own independent judgment.[102] In contrast, at least some states apparently applied *res ipsa loquitur* and similar evidentiary doctrines more commonly to mitigate the harshness of substantive rules.[103]

As important as *Patton* was in the courtroom, it was probably far more important in the informal legal process. It stood at the door of the federal courts, warning injured workers that they had little chance of prevailing unless they were able and willing to mount a major evidentiary effort that could establish their case with little room left for doubt. Such a major effort, in turn, would magnify the practical burdens of litigating a case and multiply the costs involved, especially if the federal court were a comparatively distant court. *Patton* undoubtedly helped channel innumerable plaintiffs away from the courts and into relatively unfavorable settlements.

The obstacles to recovery posed by rigorous evidentiary requirements were compounded by three substantive defenses that the law gave employers. Each severely restricted the scope of the employer's duty to provide a safe workplace. If the employer could show that the injured worker's own negligence had "contributed" to his injury, that he had "assumed the risk" of the injury, or that the injury had been caused by an act of a "fellow servant," the employer could avoid liability entirely.[104] The federal courts enforced all three of the employer's common law defenses, and by the mid-1890s they did so more rigorously than did the courts of many states.[105] Indeed, the contrast between the federal and state courts grew more acute in the decades bracketing the turn of the century. As pressure in the states pushed their legislatures and their courts to moderate or eliminate the fellow servant rule, for example, the United States Supreme Court began to apply it in its broadest and most rigorous form.

The three defenses magnified the importance of *Patton's* evidentiary requirements. Even if the employer could not prove one of the defenses, his evidence might be sufficient to prevent plaintiff from proving that the employer's negligence was the sole cause of the injury. If the injured worker or a fellow worker appeared to have contributed to the accident, even without negligence on their part, that showing might be sufficient under *Patton* to prevent the worker from carrying his burden of proof and hence defeat the claim.[106] Combined with the strict evidentiary requirements imposed by *Patton,* the three employers' defenses made the federal courts highly desirable forums for employers.

Into the first decade of the twentieth century the law of employer and employee—still referred to as master and servant—remained largely within the domain of the common law. As late as 1906 statutes had abolished the fellow servant rule in only seven states and modified it in only eighteen others. In twenty-two states it remained untouched by legislation. The assumption of risk defense, though modified by statute in many states, still retained wide scope in almost every jurisdiction. Contributory negligence stood almost universally as judge-made law, with only three states having altered it by statute.[107] In dealing with employees, then, the federal courts enjoyed much leeway in developing their own common law.

The history of the fellow servant rule illustrated the way in which the federal common law expanded in the late nineteenth century, the ways in which the social views of the Supreme Court changed after the 1870s and early 1880s, and the extent to which the Court around the turn of the century enforced in at least some areas substantive rules of law that favored national corporations. The rule held that a master was not liable to his servants for injuries caused by other servants of the master, and it created in effect a massive exception to the safe workplace rule. A product of the antebellum period, the fellow servant rule became one of the most bitterly disputed legal and social issues of the late nineteenth century. "The difficulty has been in [the rule's] practical application to the special circumstances of particular cases," the Court commented in 1879. On that point, it noted, "much contrariety of opinion exists in the courts of the several States."[108]

In the early 1870s, in fact, the Supreme Court approached the fellow servant doctrine with suspicion. In two cases decided in 1873, it questioned the doctrine and refused to apply it. *Railroad Company v. Fort*[109] involved a "mere youth" who was injured performing a dangerous job that was beyond "what his father engaged he should do."[110] The Court had little difficulty avoiding the fellow servant rule and finding the company liable "either upon the maxim of respondeat superior, or upon the obligations arising out of the contract of service."[111] In the other case, *Packet Co. v. McCue,*[112] a temporary employee was injured by the negligence of other employees while on the company's property. The Court refused to overturn a jury verdict against the company, accepting the proposition that the jury could have found that plaintiff's temporary employment had ended prior to the accident and that the other employees were no longer his fellow servants.

The Court not only refused to apply the fellow servant rule in both cases, but it went out of its way to criticize it. The defense, at least as asserted in *McCue*, "was a narrow one, and in our opinion more technical than just."[113] In *Fort* the Court went further. Broad application of the rule, it declared, "would be subversive of all just ideas of the obligations" of the employer. "These corporations, instead of being required to conduct their business so as not to endanger life, would, so far as this class of persons were concerned, be relieved of all pecuniary responsibility" in the event they were injured. "A doctrine that leads to such results is unsupported by reason and cannot receive our sanction."[114]

Although the Court remained uncomfortable with the rule throughout the 1870s,[115] it began to change during the following decade. In 1883 in *Randall v. Baltimore & Ohio Railroad Co.*[116] it applied the fellow servant doctrine to deny recovery to a brakeman, working at night in a switchyard where he had never worked before, who had been hit by a locomotive driven by an engineer who had failed to sound a whistle. The Court showed no sympathy, remarking casually that the worker had a lantern that could have led him to a safe place.[117] Further, *Randall* stated the rule with surprising broadness, suggesting that workers were fellow servants when they were employed by the same master and shared the same inclusive "common object, the moving of the trains."[118] Refusing "to weigh the conflicting views which have prevailed in the courts of the several States," the Court relied on "the very great preponderance of judicial authority in this country."[119] It cited decisions from eleven states.

The very next year, however, in *Chicago, Milwaukee & St. Paul Railway Co. v. Ross*[120] the Court refused to apply the fellow servant rule to an engineer and a conductor on the same train. Instead, it applied the so-called vice-principal doctrine, an exception to the fellow servant rule that held that workers were not fellow servants if one was supervising or directing the other. The Court again criticized the fellow servant rule, though more obliquely than it had in the 1870s, and suggested that properly applied it should have only a narrow scope.[121] Affirming a verdict for plaintiff, *Ross* did not even cite *Randall*.

The rationale of the fellow servant rule was based in part on the nature of local, face-to-face societies.[122] It was a fundamental principle of master–servant law that workers assumed the ordinary and known risks of an occupation, and in a local society workers could know their fellow employees well and guard against their recognized carelessness. Only five years before *Ross* the Court had explained the fellow servant rule on that basis, including among the risks that a worker could guard against

> the carelessness of those, at least in the same work or employment, with whose habits, conduct, and capacity he has, in the course of his duties, an opportunity to become acquainted, and against whose neglect or incompetency he may himself take such precautions as his inclinations or judgment may suggest.[123]

Such a rationale seemed to support only a narrow fellow servant rule, one that would be of limited use to large national corporations.

Ross, however, while retaining in part the older values of *Fort* and *McCue,* also reflected the Court's changing social attitudes. The local society rationale seemed increasingly less persuasive, and *Ross* stressed the rule's far broader alternative justification. "The obvious reason" why the worker was held to assume the ordinary risks of the employment, it declared, was that he "is supposed to have them in contemplation when he engages in the service, and that his compensation is arranged accordingly."[124] The true basis of the rule, in other words, was freedom of contract. *Ross,* decided in the mid-1880s, was the Janus of the Supreme Court's fellow servant cases, looking to the social sympathies of the past to guide its application of the rule but to the liberty-of-contract ideology of the future to supply its newly dominant rationale.

In justifying its rules of master–servant law in the 1880s, the Court began to give clear voice to a newly emerging social orientation. In 1887 it applied *Ross's* contractual rationale for the fellow servant rule to the doctrine of assumption of the risk, expressly endorsing the views of Thomas M. Cooley, the foremost laissez-faire legal theorist of the late nineteenth century. In *Tuttle v. Detroit, Grand Haven and Milwaukee Railway*[125] the Court upheld an assumption of risk defense to deny recovery to an employee, and it justified its acceptance of the rule and its contractual theory on the basis of "public policy." The three reasons of public policy that the Court sketched were revealing. The first reason was straightforward. To adopt the "opposite doctrine," the Court explained, would "subject employers to unreasonable and often ruinous responsibilities, thereby embarrassing all branches of business." The second reason assumed equally, though less overtly, that the paramount social goal was to protect the employer. Failure to enforce the terms of the contract, the Court explained, "would be an encouragement to the servant to omit that diligence and caution which he is in duty bound to exercise on behalf of the master, to protect him against the misconduct and negligence of others in the same service." Put bluntly, it was more important to protect the master from the possible derelictions of its servants than the servants from either the exactions of their masters or the negligence of other workers. The Court's third reason was addressed to the workers' welfare. "[I]n exercising such diligence and caution [that the law required, the employee] would have a better security against injury to himself than any recourse to the master for damages could afford."[126] The three policy reasons satisfied the Court. "This accurate summary of the law," it announced, "supersedes the necessity of quoting cases."[127]

While the reasoning in *Tuttle* accepted the idea that the protection of corporate employers was a matter of the highest priority, it also seemed to suggest some inchoate belief that industrial workers needed to be carefully controlled and disciplined. The Court's second reason hinted at this, and its third reason seemed to imply it directly. The latter was, after all, a non sequitur based on the truly arresting assumption that workers would not be careful to avoid personal injury if they thought they could recover money from their employers. Surely only a deep doubt about both the decency and intelligence of much of the industrial work force could explain such a scornful assumption. Given the shift that marked the Court's common law tort decisions after the mid-1880s, *Tuttle* suggests that those decisions may in some part have been the result of the Justices' growing anxieties about the nature and character of the rapidly expanding industrial labor force, anxieties that were perhaps heightened by the fact that a substantial part of that work force was made up of relatively recent immigrants from southern and eastern Europe. "Not every foreigner is a workingman," a Chicago clergyman declared the year *Tuttle* was decided, but "it may almost be said that every workingman is a foreigner."[128] Indeed, it was likely no accident that *Tuttle* came down in the immediate aftermath of the depression of 1885–86, the rapid rise and expansion of the Knights of Labor, and the infamous Haymarket riot that so alarmed and frightened many Americans across the nation.

Though the Court's master–servant decisions created federal common law, they usually did so without making that fact explicit. Whatever ambiguities there were about either the legal basis for its decisions or the scope of the Court's fellow servant rule were put to rest in 1893. *Baltimore & Ohio Railroad Co. v. Baugh*[129] resolved both. John Baugh, a fireman, was working on a locomotive with an engineer who was in charge of their work detail. Baugh was seriously injured when the engineer negligently drove the locomotive along a section of track that he was not authorized to use and collided with another train. Baugh, a citizen of Ohio, sued in his home state, and the railroad, incorporated in Maryland, removed. The lower federal court, following the common law of Ohio which accepted the vice-principal exception, instructed the jury that an employee "placed in authority"[130] over another was not a fellow servant. The jury returned a verdict for Baugh.

The Supreme Court, with Justice David J. Brewer writing for a majority of seven, settled the federal common law issue in the opinion's second paragraph. "This is not a question of local law" to be resolved by following Ohio decisions. Rather, it was "one of general law, to be determined by a reference to all the authorities, and a consideration of the principles underlying the relations of master and servant."[131] Relying on *Swift, Randall, Ross* and a dozen other cases, *Baugh* maintained that the Court had for many years rendered independent judgments on general law issues and that on a number of occasions, in *Ross* for example, it had refused to follow local common law. Practical considerations stemming from the multistate nature of railroad activity, it pointed out, confirmed that the issues involved were not "local."[132]

Turning next to the "vexed question" of the proper scope of the fellow servant rule, *Baugh* admitted that the courts were badly divided. "[P]erhaps there is no one matter upon which there are more conflicting and irreconcilable decisions in the various courts of the land," it stated, "than the one as to what is the test of a common service."[133] The Court did not hesitate, however, to reject the vice-principal doctrine and to define the fellow servant rule in nearly all-encompassing terms. "*Prima facie*, all who enter into the employ of a single master are engaged in a common service, and are fellow-servants."[134]

Baugh dealt with *Ross* at length, using the discussion to emphasize the breadth of the rule it was laying down. First, it readily adopted *Ross*'s narrow contract rationale, quoting the earlier opinion's pivotal language about known risk and adjusted compensation. It then showed the illimitable reach of such a rationale. The worker assumed the risk of a vice-principal's negligence, the Court explained, for the same reason that he assumed the risk of a coworker's negligence. "If he is paid for the one, he is paid for the other; if he assumes the one, he assumes the other."[135] Second, *Baugh* boldly reversed *Ross*'s narrow rule of liability. The prior decision, *Baugh* stated, was based on the principle that employees were not fellow servants if one of them had "the control and management *of a distinct department.*" When *Ross* concluded that a conductor had control of a "distinct department," it had simply misapplied its own correct principle. "But this rule can only be fairly applied when the different branches or departments of service are in and of themselves separate and distinct." To make clear the comprehensive sweep of its rule, *Baugh* gave a critical example. "Thus, between the law department of a railway corporation and the operating department, there is a natural and distinct separation."[136] Excluding the heads of such departments, all other employees in the departments were fellow servants. By identifying "the operating department" as a single and legally significant division, *Baugh* meant that all railway employees involved in operating trains were fellow servants. For workers in mining, transporting, and manufacturing, the definition in effect wiped out both of the major common law exceptions to the fellow servant rule, the distinct division rule and the vice-principal doctrine.

After that, the decision itself was easy. Contrary to the common law of Ohio, Baugh and the engineer were fellow servants. The company, therefore, was not liable. The Court reversed Baugh's jury verdict.

Justice Brewer, who wrote the opinion in *Baugh*, was perhaps the Court's most determined proponent of the federal fellow servant rule, its most outspoken defender of private property, and its most fervent advocate of an activist federal judiciary. In the 1890s he repeatedly warned against the dangers of "coercion" from "the mere force of numbers" and proclaimed that "under no form of government, is a firm, strong, stable judiciary more needed than in a 'government of, by, and for the people'."[137] Two years before *Baugh* Brewer attacked the "timid judges" who feared to denounce social wrongs, such as "the spoliation and destruction of private property through the agency of that undefined and perhaps undefinable power, the police power of the State."[138] Between the oral argument and the decision in *Baugh*, while he was preparing to deliver his opinion in the case, Brewer addressed the New York State Bar Association, denouncing for himself a number of social wrongs, including the oppression and violence of labor unions. "It is the unvarying law," he declared, "that the wealth of a community will be in the hands of a few."[139] Then, reflecting his own deeply felt and intertwined attitudes toward law, progress, religion, society, and private property, Brewer turned to the railroads:

> The property of a great railroad corporation stretches far away from the domicile of its owner, through State after State, from ocean to ocean; the rain and the snow may cover it; the winds and the storms may wreck it; but no man or multitude dare touch a car or move a rail. It stands as secure in the eye and in the custody of the law, as the purposes of justice in the thought of God.[140]

How, Brewer asked rhetorically, can the nation preserve justice and order from the threats of the discontented? "My reply is, strengthen the judiciary."[141]

Reflecting Brewer's social views, *Baugh* was characteristic of many of the Court's federal common law decisions in the decades around the turn of the century. In substance, it announced baldly the right of the federal courts to make general rules of common law in the face of contrary rulings in the state courts, and it gave corporations a highly favorable rule that severely limited their liability. In theory, like *Northern Assurance,* it made assumptions about freedom of contract and equality of bargaining the basis for a rule that harshly disadvantaged weaker and less sophisticated parties. In method, it discussed the practical impact of its rule only briefly and then—again like *Northern Assurance*—only in terms of protecting corporate business and facilitating interstate commerce. The practical problems that injured workers faced did not appear. Indeed, the Court essentially assumed that the interests of the workers were the same as those of their employers. In its brief reference to social context, *Baugh* did little but faintly echo Brewer's contemporaneous speech to the New York State Bar Association. "The lines of this very plaintiff in error extend into half a dozen or more States, and its trains are largely employed in interstate commerce," the opinion announced. "As it passes from State to State, must the rights, obligations and duties subsisting between it and its employees change at every state line?"[142] The question in Brewer's mind, if not in the thought of God, answered itself.

Two Justices dissented. Chief Justice Melville W. Fuller stated his view that *Ross* controlled and that the decision "unreasonably enlarges" the employer's exemption from liability.[143] Justice Stephen J. Field, Brewer's uncle and the author of the Court's opinion in *Ross,* dissented at length. He argued that "justice and humanity" required that Baugh retain his judgment[144] and that the federal courts follow the law of Ohio because it was "neither uncertain nor doubtful."[145] Field then raised the stakes and launched a frontal attack on the doctrine of *Swift* itself. He charged that it encouraged forum shopping and thereby favored corporations[146] and that it led the federal courts into an unconstitutional invasion of the power reserved to the states by the Tenth Amendment. Apologizing for having himself "erroneously" applied the doctrine on numerous occasions, he admitted but decried the fact that the doctrine had "often been advanced in judicial opinions of this court to control a conflicting law of a State."[147] The mere fact that the Court had applied the doctrine in the past, however, was no reason to continue its use. "[T]here stands, as a perpetual protest against its repetition, the Constitution of the United States."[148] Field concluded by bemoaning the majority's treatment of *Ross* which, he predicted, would "destroy its usefulness as a protection to employees in the service of large corporations."[149]

A landmark decision twice over, *Baugh* inspired a confident expansion of the federal common law of torts and established the broadest possible application of the fellow servant rule in the federal courts. The Supreme Court repeatedly reaffirmed both of the principles for which it stood,[150] and the lower courts faithfully enforced them. Six years after *Baugh* came down, Judge William Howard Taft of the Sixth Circuit emphasized the sweep of its fellow servant rule. "The Baugh Case has set such limits to the vice-principal doctrine that it is exceedingly difficult to suggest a position, outside of the superintendent or acting superintendent of the various great departments of the road, which will not be filled by fellow servants of all the other employees."[151] Though *Ross* was not "expressly overruled," Taft noted, it has "no force of authority" beyond its own exact facts. Less than a year after Taft wrote, the Supreme Court finished the job. *Ross,* it declared in 1899, "must be deemed to have been overruled, in effect if not in terms, in the subsequent case of *Baltimore & Ohio Railroad v. Baugh.*"[152]

Although the Court enforced *Baugh* rigorously into the second decade of the twentieth century, its fellow servant decisions often pushed one or more of the Justices into dissent. The sharpest split occurred in 1904. *Northern Pacific Railway Co. v. Dixon*[153] presented a case in which the employee could have neither known the fellow servant whose negligence caused his injury nor protected himself from it. He was killed in a head-on collision because a telegraph operator fell asleep and failed to send ahead the proper signal. Brewer, writing for a bare majority, followed *Baugh* and held that the telegraph operator was a fellow servant of the deceased worker and ruled that the railroad was not liable. In a rare, and rarely acrimonious, dissent written by Justice Edward D. White, four Justices protested *Baugh*'s all-encompassing reach and seemed to charge the majority with acting on the basis of social bias. The Court, they maintained, refused to follow the trend toward judicial modification of the fellow servant rule and instead enforced its own "contradictory propositions" that systematically found against the employee.

"The result being," the dissenters charged bluntly, "that recovery cannot be had in any event."[154]

Internal opposition to *Baugh* remained, but it was seldom as outspoken as in *Dixon*. State and federal legislation would increasingly shrink its field after 1906, but the sweeping fellow servant rule laid down in *Baugh* remained alive in the federal courts in all its rigor.[155] Whenever the defense might apply, employers wanted their cases heard in federal courts. "As the federal decisions on the subject differ widely from those of some states," a commentator noted in 1913, "this makes the selection of the forum a very important step in many of these cases."[156] The four dissenters in *Dixon* agreed. "It is undoubtedly true," they upbraided the majority, "that in many decisions of state courts of last resort the rigor of the rule of fellow servant has been assuaged."[157] At a time when state courts were severely modifying the fellow servant rule and when jury verdicts were running as high as ten to one in favor of injured workers, the federal fellow servant rule—which allowed judges to direct verdicts and thereby effectively eliminate the jury in many cases—was a legal instrument of ruthless effectiveness.[158]

Doctrinal Leverage: Freedom of Contract and the Tort Liability of Common Carriers

The federal courts further narrowed corporate tort liability when they expanded the areas in which one party could agree to limit or waive the liability of another. The change was marked in the law of "common carriers" which for centuries had imposed the highest standards on those who offered transportation to the public. The common law held common carriers strictly liable for injuries to goods, and it held them to the utmost degree of care in safeguarding their passengers.[159]

In *Railroad Company v. Lockwood*,[160] handed down in 1873, the Court refused to allow a common carrier to contract out of liability for the negligence of its employees. The issue was whether a railroad company was liable for injuries suffered by a drover who was traveling with his stock, and the railroad claimed that its agreement with the drover was a complete defense. The signed agreement provided that the drover was shipping enough stock to merit a "free" pass, that in exchange for the pass the drover waived all claims for injury against the railroad, and that in consideration of the agreement the railroad agreed to carry the drover's stock at reduced rates.[161] The Court ruled that the issue was one of "general commercial law" and, contrary to what appeared to be the applicable state law,[162] held that the drover was actually a "passenger for hire" and that the agreement did not relieve the railroad of its liability as a common carrier.[163]

Lockwood, decided in the same term as *McCue* and *Fort* and a year after *Wilkinson*, reflected the values of a Court deeply concerned about the social impact of the nation's emerging industrial society, particularly the size and power of national corporations. Rejecting arguments about freedom of contract, the Court insisted that the "carrier and his customer do not stand on a footing of equality" and that the customer lacked "any real freedom of choice."[164] The transportation business was "mostly concentrated in a few powerful corporations, whose position in the body politic enables them to control it," the Court declared. "They do, in fact, control it, and impose such conditions upon travel and transportation as they see fit, which the public is compelled to accept."[165] If permitted to impose contracts limiting their liability for employee negligence, their de facto power would enable them "to change the law of common carriers in effect, by introducing new rules of obligation."[166] To allow a common carrier to contract out of such liability, "as the business is now carried on, would be subversive of the very object of the law." And the subversion would be total in the case of corporations, the Court noted, "where the carrier is an artificial being, incapable of acting except by agents and servants."[167]

Although *Lockwood* echoed the past and warned against the future, it carried the seeds of its own limiting doctrines. It expressly left open the question of a railroad's liability to a person on a "free" pass; and it reaffirmed the principle that, where limitations of liability would be fair and economically advantageous to both parties, a common carrier might properly agree to modify the normal rule of strict responsibility for injuries to goods.[168] *Lockwood* remained a leading case throughout the period,[169] but federal common law developed by limiting, not expanding, its rule.

In subsequent years the Court approved broader contractual limitations on common carrier liability for goods shipped,[170] and in the early twentieth century it recognized as a basic principle of interstate transportation the ability of common carriers to limit that liability. In 1906 Congress amended the Interstate Commerce Act in the Hepburn Act, and Section 20 of the new statute—the so-called Carmack amendment—gave shippers a cause of action against their initial carrier regardless of whether the initial carrier controlled their goods at the time of injury. The amendment improved shippers' chances of recovering for damaged freight, but the Court construed it to restrict the amounts they might receive. In a series of decisions before World War I, it held that the Carmack amendment preempted state law, which was often more favorable to the shippers, and that it allowed carriers to impose substantial limitations on the amounts for which they would be liable.[171]

By the first decade of the twentieth century the Court was also ready to take a more drastic step. It upheld limitations on common carrier liability for personal injuries. In doing so, it denied the protection of the law to two classes of individuals that seemed to evoke relatively little sympathy from the federal courts at the turn of the century, industrial workers and those who did not pay their way.

In 1904 the Court decided the question expressly left open in *Lockwood*. In *Northern Pacific Railway Co. v. Adams*[172] it held that a person riding on a free pass was not a "passenger for hire" within the meaning of *Lockwood* and hence that a provision in a pass exempting the railroad from liability for injury was valid. In reaching its decision, the Court narrowly construed an Idaho wrongful death statute that was open to a broader construction and, noting that the states were widely divided on the issue,[173] based its decision on federal common law grounds. The railroad had "waived its right as a common carrier to exact compensation," the Court decided, and in exchange it was freed from the duties of a common carrier. The parties "stood on an equal footing," and "no public policy was violated thereby."[174]

Adams, of course, left the states free to maintain the contrary rule, and many of them did.[175] The Court, however, eventually closed off that state law option for all passes used in interstate commerce. Two years after *Adams* Congress passed the Hepburn Act[176] and made it unlawful for a common carrier to issue free passes "except to its employees and their families." In construing the statute the Georgia Court of Appeals held that, because passes were limited to employees and their families, they were issued in consideration for employment and were therefore not "free." Accordingly, the Georgia court ruled that an exemption from liability in such passes was not valid. On appeal in 1914, the United States Supreme Court reversed, ruling that a "free pass" was a "free pass" and that its provisions exempting a carrier from liability for personal injury were valid and enforceable.[177] In *Lockwood,* of course, the Court had held that a "free pass" was not necessarily a "free pass," but under *Adams* and the Hepburn Act it refused to follow such an analysis. Nine years later the Court closed the circle and made the rule of *Adams* binding across the nation. It held that the Hepburn Act preempted state law in interstate commerce and made provisions in free passes exempting carriers from liability valid and enforceable regardless of any and all contrary state rules.[178]

If the nationalized *Adams*–Hepburn Act rule prevented one group of workers from relying on the protection of *Lockwood,* the Court's decision in *Baltimore & Ohio Southwestern Railway Co. v. Voigt*[179] did the same thing to another group. Antedating *Adams* by four years, and providing the principal federal common law authority on which *Adams* relied,[180] *Voigt* came to the Court on the single certified question whether a railroad was liable as a common carrier to the employee of an express company who was traveling on a train under special contractual arrangements. Two contracts were involved. In the first, between the two companies, the railroad agreed to provide and transport special cars for the United States Express Company, and the express company agreed to pay the railroad and hold it harmless for any injuries to the express company's employees. In the second, between the express company and its employee, the company agreed to hire the employee, and the employee agreed to assume all risk of injury from his employment and to hold both the express company and the railroad harmless for any injury he might receive. The Supreme Court held that the contracts relieved the railroad of its duties as a common carrier and that the express company employee was not a "passenger for hire" under *Lockwood.*

The Court answered the question presented under the law of common carriers, but its application of *Lockwood* finessed the social issues raised by the special three-party relationship embedded in the case. *Lockwood* had voided contracts exempting common carriers from liability for two reasons, *Voigt* explained, to ensure "personal safety" and to counter the "position of [bargaining] advantage" that common carriers enjoyed.[181] *Voigt* held that neither reason applied to the facts presented. "We have here to consider not the case of an individual shipper or passenger, dealing, at a disadvantage, with a powerful corporation," the Court explained, "but that of a permanent arrangement between two corporations embracing within its sphere of operation a large part of the transportation business of the entire country."[182] The only contract to be judged by the standards of *Lockwood,* in other words, was the contract to which the common carrier was a formal party. The Court described at length the nature of the "partnership relation" between the railroad and the express company, and it concluded that the railway express business "requires the participation of both companies on terms agreed upon in special contracts."[183] Because the companies were bargaining equals and their agreement was reasonable, *Lockwood* did not invalidate their contract.

Having decided that the contract between the express company and the railroad was valid, the Court then considered the employee's situation. Ignoring questions of both "personal safety" and unequal bargaining power and assuming the validity of the terms of the employment contract, the Court noted that "these agreements" created "a very different relation" between the employee and the railroad from "the usual one between passengers and railroad company."[184] The relationship seemed "to more nearly resemble that of an employe than that of a passenger." Given his "employee" status and the Court's previous observation that the two companies were engaged in "a joint business," one legal conclusion seemed logical. "And, of course, if his position was that of a common employe of both companies, he could not recover for injuries caused, as would appear to have been the present case, by the negligence of fellow-servants."[185] The Court did not, however, rest its decision on an implied fellow servant status. Rather, it denied liability on the ground that the employee had signed a contract and expressly agreed to assume all risk of injury. He "was not constrained to enter into the contract whereby the railroad company was exonerated from liability to him," the Court declared. Because he had "entered into the same freely and voluntarily," he was properly bound by it.[186]

Voigt was the *Northern Assurance* of federal tort law. It not only established a rule of common law favorable to employers, but it also confirmed the power of contract in general to narrow the limits of liability that the law would impose. The case was not a traditional common carrier case, one between a railroad and a shipper or passenger. Rather, it was essentially an employment case, one in which two companies made their businesses mutually less costly and less risky to themselves by successfully narrowing the common law rights of an employee. The railroad avoided its liability as a common carrier, and the express company narrowed its duty to provide a safe workplace. At no point did the Court allude to that social and economic reality.

As with *Northern Assurance,* corporations learned from *Voigt,* and they were in many cases able to utilize contractual methods of limiting their liability. The federal courts applied *Voigt,* for example, not only to uphold contractual arrangements that exempted railroads from liability to the employees of companies doing a regular business with them[187] but also to uphold agreements that exempted them from liability to certain kinds of "special" passengers, usually the employees of companies that did occasional or *ad hoc* business with the roads.[188] Perhaps even more important, *Voigt* and similar cases suggested ways in which companies could arrange or divide their work with other companies, with subsidiaries or affiliated companies, or with special "independent contractors" in order to limit their liability even further. Such efforts did not always work, but companies repeatedly tried them and in some cases succeeded.[189]

Voigt, like both *Baugh* and *Northern Assurance,* gave another important practical advantage to corporations. It created a powerful legal defense that could be established with a bare minimum of evidence, often merely a single contract. If the plaintiff introduced the relevant contract or testified to his employment and the circumstances of his injury, the company might have no need to present its own evidence. Frequently, in fact, employers simply moved for dismissal before the plaintiff's case or for a directed verdict at its end. "From 1888 to 1906, 244 railway cases were removed on motion of the railways from state courts to the Federal courts in Kansas City, Missouri," one attorney reported in 1912. "Two hundred and fourteen of these cases against the railways were dismissed by the Federal judges."[190]

Although *Voigt* followed the form of *Lockwood*'s analysis, its tone and values were those of *Baugh* and *Northern Assurance. Lockwood*—like *Fort, McCue,* and *Wilkinson*—regarded freedom of contract as a subsidiary value. *Voigt* made it central:

> [I]t must not be forgotten that the right of private contract is no small part of the liberty of the citizen, and that the usual and most important function of courts of justice is rather to maintain and enforce contracts, than to enable parties thereto to escape from their obligation on the pretext of public policy.[191]

That was the express premise of *Northern Assurance* and the implicit premise of *Baugh,* which—though not formally a contract case—helped free the fellow servant rule from a restrictive social rationale and placed it squarely on a market-contract basis.

Further, whereas *Lockwood* expressed deep concern over the rise of "powerful corporations" with unfair bargaining leverage, *Voigt* showed no concern with the possibility that the common carrier had used its position to force the express company to bargain away the rights and safety of its employees. Just as *Northern Assurance* permitted insurance companies to protect themselves from liability for the "faithless agent" by placing the risk on their policyholders, *Voigt* allowed the railroads and their corporate business partners in effect to expand the *Baugh* rule to protect all of them from liability to the employees of the other companies. *Voigt* revealed, too, as had both *Baugh* and *Northern Assurance,* the Court's often selective method of dealing with social facts. In contrast with *Lockwood, Fort, McCue,* and *Wilkinson,* the turn-of-the-century cases ignored the conditions that severely limited the freedom of individuals and expressly assumed a nonexistent bargaining equality between the parties. They discussed only those social considerations that supported their assumptions of equality and reflected what they conceived of as the demands of the new national economy.

Voigt, Baugh, and *Northern Assurance* were pillars of the federal common law. They favored national corporations, and they laid down legal rules that many states either qualified or rejected. Their policies, too, went far beyond the more general procommercial policies of *Swift* and *Gelpcke* by directly imposing the risks of business on those least able to bear them. They contributed to making the federal courts forums that innumerable private plaintiffs wished to avoid. The gulf, too, that separated the values articulated in *Lockwood, Fort, McCue,* and *Wilkinson* in the 1870s from those given voice in *Voigt, Baugh, Northern Assurance,* and their numerous turn-of-the-century companions—*Coos County, Lewis, Adams, Patton,* and *Dixon* among others—helped measure the extent to which the federal common law changed between the 1870s, when the system of corporate diversity litigation was beginning to take shape, and the turn of the century, when it flourished in its most expansive and—for plaintiffs—oppressive phase. The latter decisions cast their shadows far beyond the confines of the written law reports into the vast recesses of the informal legal process. In that process they immeasurably strengthened the hand of the corporations, undoubtedly helping discourage, discount, or defeat far more claims than ever reached final legal judgment or appeared in the law reports.

Chapter 4

The Battle for Forum Control, I:
The Jurisdictional Amount and the
Limits of Corporate Liability

Although most individuals who had claims against corporations never brought them to court, hundreds of thousands did. As the system of corporate diversity litigation formed in the 1870s and early 1880s, plaintiffs quickly recognized the disadvantages that removal imposed. The burdens of distance and delay were immediately obvious; the procedural and institutional disadvantages of removal quickly became apparent; and by the late 1880s and early 1890s the federal common law grew noticeably unfavorable in an increasing number of states. Plaintiffs felt ever more keenly the desirability, and in many cases the necessity, of avoiding removal at all costs. "It is a well recognized fact in judicial history," wrote a Nebraska federal judge in 1912, "that plaintiffs, in actions brought by employees against railway companies for damages resulting from personal injuries, have quite generally and for many years sought to bring and retain their actions in the state courts." The judge acknowledged frankly the practical motives at work. "The expense of trials and appeals in the federal courts have been deterrents, and the variance in the rules of law in such cases has also been well understood."[1]

The threat of removal confronted every individual who sued a foreign corporation, and the dangers and burdens of a federal litigation often gave the threat compelling force. The pivotal legal issue in the system of corporate diversity litigation, then, was jurisdictional: Could plaintiffs somehow shape their actions to avoid federal jurisdiction and prevent removal? The system's archetypal battle for forum control, the Nebraska federal judge noted, was "well attested by the multitude of applications to remand such cases which have been constantly presented to the federal courts."[2] A review of more than seven hundred reported decisions in diversity cases in the circuit courts between 1903 and 1906 found that almost 20 percent dealt with challenges to the court's jurisdiction and more than 8 percent of the entire sample involved motions to remand.[3]

Corporate defendants removed frequently and, in many instances, as a matter of course. "[W]here the amount involved is sufficient to give jurisdiction," declared a federal judge in New Mexico in 1930, almost "all litigation between nonresidents and residents" in the state was taken to the local federal court.[4] Plaintiffs fought the tactic vigorously and with every device they could muster. Often they simply discontinued actions that their adversaries removed. Sometimes, when they had no other choice and the costs were acceptable, they moved for remands to state court. Most important, with increasing aggressiveness they sought to exploit procedural devices that would make their actions nonremovable. The use of nonremovable forms of action quickly became the crux of plaintiffs' counterstrategies.

Treatise writers on federal jurisdiction increasingly acknowledged, though often reluctantly and with disapproval, the centrality of the battle over removal. "The removal acts are so framed," explained the successor to Judge John F. Dillon's treatise in 1898, "that it is often possible for the plaintiff, by manipulation of the cause of action . . . to prevent the removal altogether."[5] By the early twentieth century a few bolder treatises incorporated sections bluntly titled "Devices to Prevent Removal."[6] Such antiremoval tactics, a 1913 text declared, "are frequently successful."[7] It was no accident that Dillon and his contemporaries who wrote for the practicing bar concentrated more intently on removal jurisdiction than any generation of American legal writers before or since.[8]

Removal: Patterns of Settlement and Resistance

By the 1890s more than half of all private federal civil suits were discontinued in one way or another, but the statistics in the American Law Institute (ALI) study of thirteen judicial districts revealed some of the telling differences that remained hidden in the gross numbers. Among actions at law between private parties, 6.7 percent were settled by "Stipulation, Consent, Confession, or Compromise," whereas 60.7 percent were settled by "Voluntary Dismissal, Discontinuance, Withdrawal or Nonsuit."[9] The first category suggested that most of the terminations in the second category were cases that were not settled by mutual agreement, though in some of them unrecorded or subsequent settlements probably occurred. It seems likely, in any event, that a high percentage of private civil plaintiffs in the federal courts abandoned their federal actions without a court decision and perhaps without reaching any kind of settlement agreement with their adversary.

The settlement pattern for all diversity actions at law was similar to the pattern of all private civil cases, but a sharp difference appeared in the pattern between original and removed diversity actions. In the former, 9.3 percent were in the compromise category and 52 percent in the voluntary discontinuance category. Among removed cases, however, only 5.7 percent were compromised and 64 percent voluntarily discontinued.[10] The differences highlighted characteristics of the system and the importance of forum control. They show that removal broadened the realm of the informal legal process by inducing a relatively high percentage of plaintiffs to terminate their actions voluntarily once defendants had forced them out of a state forum. They also show that removal altered the parties' views as to settlement value in converging ways: Both plaintiffs and defendants considered removal harmful to plaintiffs' chances. Defendants became less willing to compromise, and plaintiffs more willing to discontinue.

Although most removed diversity plaintiffs responded simply by discontinuing their actions, a small but still significant number sought to avoid federal jurisdiction by moving for remands. Among all varieties of civil suits, in fact, the most common conflicts over jurisdiction erupted in removed diversity actions. The ALI study found that objections to jurisdiction occurred two to three times more frequently in diversity actions than in cases brought under all other jurisdictional heads, and approximately 60 percent more frequently in removed than in original diversity actions. Challenges to jurisdiction occurred in 14.4 percent of all removed diversity cases, a far higher percentage than in any other jurisdictional category.[11]

The ALI study also found that plaintiffs who challenged removal were often successful. The federal courts sustained jurisdictional objections in removed diversity actions more frequently than in original diversity suits, 55 percent in the former compared with 36 percent in the latter. In more than half of the cases in which they sustained objections to jurisdiction, the federal courts ordered remands. The numbers suggest that it was more common for state court defendants to stretch to get into federal court than it was for plaintiffs to do so originally.[12]

Finally, other data show that remands were most common, in both absolute and relative terms, in tort and insurance contract cases, the core areas in which the system of corporate diversity litigation operated. The reports of the United States Attorney General for 1936 and 1937, the first years that report such statistics, show that remands in those two years occurred in 1.7 and 1.8 percent, respectively, of the private civil actions heard in the federal courts. Among categories most likely to contain all or mostly diversity cases, remands were ordered in 2 percent of real property actions, 1.9 percent of general contract cases, 0.3 percent of trademark and unfair competition cases, and 1.1 percent of "other private actions" not involving a federal statute. In contrast, remands occurred in tort and insurance contract actions in 3.7 and 5 percent, respectively, of the cases.[13] A study of state and federal courts in a California county from 1880 to 1900 found that remands in personal injury actions came even more frequently, occurring in almost 15 percent of all removals.[14]

The number and frequency of voluntary discontinuances and motions to remand show the determination of individual plaintiffs to avoid a federal forum and suggest equally the extent to which removal strengthened the position of defendants. As tactical devices, however, neither was a weapon of choice. The former was obviously self-defeating. The latter was burdensome and, judging by the data in the ALI study, not possible in most cases.

For plaintiffs in the system, then, the key to success was to file their actions in some form that promised to defeat defendants' right to remove. Indeed, the voluntary discontinuance was in large part an afterthought, the last-minute tool of plaintiffs who had failed to plan their strategy and properly shape their actions. Conversely, the motion to remand was for the most part the necessary, though reluctantly used, tool of plaintiffs who had made an effort to file their actions in a nonremovable form but who had made mistakes, decided to gamble on risky tactics that promised larger recoveries, or found themselves litigating against a corporation that was particularly determined to get the case into federal court and keep it there.

Although the law offered a variety of ways to defeat removal, at least in theory, individual plaintiffs were for the most part restricted by time, money, and knowledge as well as by the limited local practice and experience of most of their attorneys. In those circumstances the simplest and most obvious way to defeat removal, and probably the most common tactic by far that they used, was to assert a claim for less than the jurisdictional amount. It seems almost certain, in fact, that many of the removed actions that were voluntarily dismissed from the federal courts were subsequently refiled in the state courts for amounts less than the federal jurisdiction minimum.

The Jurisdictional Amount: Claim Discounting and Its Tactical Variations

The right to remove under diversity jurisdiction extended only to cases in which the "amount in controversy" or "matter in dispute" was in excess of a statutorily specified amount. Although in theory a device to keep small claims out of the national courts, the jurisdictional amount had been recognized early in the history of the federal courts as a method of forum control.[15] If plaintiffs sought federal jurisdiction, they could if necessary inflate their claims; if they sought to keep their suits in state court, they could attempt to mask the value of their claims or simply discount them.

Over the years the federal courts had been far more concerned with inflated and masked claims than with discounted ones. Inflated claims presented an obvious danger. They increased the federal caseload, frustrated the purpose of the statutory requirement, and extended federal jurisdiction to cases beyond its authorized limits. Masked claims, those that stated the amount sought either ambiguously or not at all, were also a problem. Whether stemming from some pleading difficulty or from tactical design, they could defeat the purpose of the jurisdictional statutes and deprive defendants of their right to remove. Unlike the other two, however, discounted claims posed none of those problems. They seemed unexceptionable and innocuous. Because the plaintiff was master of her suit, she should be able to set her claim at any reasonable amount she wished. If she sought less than she could have, the decision was properly hers alone. The choice transgressed no federal statute or interest, and surely her adversary had no just cause to complain that he might be liable for a smaller rather than a larger amount.

By the 1870s the courts had developed a series of rules to regulate use of the jurisdictional amount as a tool of forum control. They required that the amount in dispute appear on the face of the pleadings and held that in actions for money the sum demanded in the complaint established, with limited exceptions, the amount in controversy. Once federal jurisdiction attached, whether originally or by removal, it was not ousted either by an amendment lowering the amount demanded or by a final judgment for less than the jurisdictional minimum. To limit inflated claims, the courts refused to take jurisdiction if the amount pleaded was not reasonably supported by plaintiff's factual allegations and legal theories. That rule had almost no significance in tort cases where the amount of damages properly due could seldom be determined with precision and was generally left to the jury. Its use was limited for the most part either to actions based on notes or contracts, where legal rules or the written instruments at issue determined the damages available, or to disputes over property whose value could be readily determined. To counter masked claims, the courts allowed removal petitions to show that the matter in dispute was more than the jurisdictional amount or, in effect, to force plaintiffs to respond and expressly state their claim below the jurisdictional minimum.

The federal courts showed little concern with discounted claims. Although they refused to surrender jurisdiction when the plaintiff tried to discount his claim after removal, they nevertheless generally allowed the same plaintiff to escape by taking a voluntary dismissal. As the Supreme Court commented in 1863, "the plaintiff may seek a recovery for less than the sum to which he appears entitled by the allegations" of the pleadings.[16] Seventy-five years later, when the system of corporate diversity litigation was contracting, the Court again acknowledged the tactic. "If [the plaintiff] does not desire to try his case in the federal court," it noted, "he may resort to the expedient of suing for less than the jurisdictional amount."[17] It seems likely, in fact, that the practice commended itself to many federal judges, perhaps primarily as a method of docket control. In the 1930s, for example, the Fourth Circuit was widely recognized as both a dedicated proponent of the federal common law and a sympathetic forum for business interests, especially insurance companies. Yet it repeatedly upheld the right of plaintiffs in removed actions to discontinue voluntarily when the result would almost certainly be a refiled state court action with a discounted claim.[18]

Reported cases in the late nineteenth and early twentieth century seem to show a widespread and apparently increasing use of the jurisdictional amount as a device to avoid federal jurisdiction. In the Judiciary Act of 1887–88 Congress narrowed the jurisdiction of the national courts and attempted to slow their growing caseload, and as part of its effort it raised the jurisdictional amount from $500 to $2,000. By quadrupling the amount that plaintiffs could claim and still avoid removal, the statute encouraged use of the tactic by, in effect, drastically lowering the discount rate. Increasingly, plaintiffs in a wide variety of situations, including many business and commercial disputes involving relatively small amounts, resorted to the device.[19] The subsequent increase in the jurisdictional amount in 1911 from $2,000 to $3,000 had a similar though apparently smaller impact.

As the system of corporate diversity litigation formed, individuals suing national corporations adopted claim discounting as a standard tactic. Though employed less often in insurance cases before World War I, largely because the value of most policies was less than the jurisdictional amount,[20] its use in personal injury actions proliferated. "[T]he amount of damages sought to be recovered in tort cases," an Iowa state judge wrote in 1915, "is often limited, so that there may not be a removal to the federal court."[21] Stating personal injury claims slightly below the jurisdictional minimum, noted a federal judge in Alabama in 1902, was "the known practice of the profession in drawing such complaints."[22]

The widespread adoption of the tactic revealed the extreme importance that parties suing national corporations attached to the choice between state and federal courts. Unlike inflated claims, which could have been inspired by greed as much as anything else, discounted claims evidenced an intense forum preference. Because the law generally restricted a plaintiff's recovery to the amount pleaded,[23] avoiding federal jurisdiction by claiming less than the jurisdictional amount required sacrificing part of the claim from the very beginning of the action. The tactic not only capped the potential recovery but also, by doing that, weakened plaintiff's position in negotiating a settlement. Moreover, its use deprived plaintiffs of one of their major advantages, the right to have a jury—most likely sympathetic—determine the amount of damages free from the express limit they had placed on it. Finally, the tactic also required plaintiffs to forgo any attempt to win punitive damages. Although the Supreme Court had held that corporations could be liable in special circumstances for punitive damages, it also held that claims for punitive damages be included in computing the jurisdictional amount.[24]

The obverse side also held on the issue of forum preference. Corporate defendants were sometimes willing to risk larger potential liabilities in order to secure federal jurisdiction. Rejecting what would ordinarily have been in their clear self-interest, they frequently fought to keep or push claims above the jurisdictional amount in order to lock plaintiffs in the national courts.[25] It was "an abuse," bemoaned one corporate attorney in 1932, "where, in order to retain the state jurisdiction, litigants time without number reduce the amount of their claims below the jurisdictional amount for removal."[26]

Reported cases involving the jurisdictional amount almost certainly represent only a small fraction of the cases in which plaintiffs used the tactic to avoid removal. In tort actions for money damages, where the amount in controversy was the amount pleaded, plaintiffs could with ease and certainty plead nonremovable claims and obviate any jurisdictional dispute on the matter.[27] Moreover, plaintiffs deciding to discount their claims had every incentive to plead with absolute clarity, for the last thing they wanted was to waste additional time and money litigating a procedural issue that they were expressly conceding. Because such cases remained in state courts and because only a small percentage of state decisions were published, cases brought for less than the jurisdictional amount would either have gone unreported or, if reported, would not have presented issues involving the jurisdictional amount. Further, given the relatively small amounts of money at issue and the frequency with which cases were settled out of court, it seems likely that most of those cases were either settled without judgment or abandoned without result. In either event, they would almost certainly have disappeared from the historical record.

State cases involving discounted claims, therefore, constituted a major element of the informal legal process that characterized the system. Plaintiffs' attorneys repeatedly acknowledged using the tactic. "Only last term of the federal court in this state," recalled an Idaho attorney in 1928,

> I had a client who claimed damages from the railroad company for a defective crossing. The company asked for a transfer from the state court to the federal court, knowing my client had no money to carry through a case in the federal courts, as he would have had to do, even though he won in the lower court. So we were forced to dismiss and bring a new action in the state court for a sum less than $3,000 all because of diversity of citizenship.[28]

The next year a Nebraska lawyer gave similar reasons for adopting the same tactic. "I have another case pending now for a client, a comparatively poor man, where I have had to waive in the neighborhood of $800 sooner than put him to the expense of trying to carry a case through a Federal Court."[29] An Arizona lawyer considered the tactic as routine. "[I]t has been the experience of this office that when we have a claim against a nonresident exceeding the sum of $3,000," he explained in 1933, "that it is much more expedient to reduce our claim than to go into the Federal Court."[30] It seems highly unlikely that the law reports contain more than an occasional and faint echo of what was a widespread and everyday litigation tactic.

The reported cases involving the jurisdictional amount, themselves numerous, strengthen that conclusion. Individuals suing corporations for personal injuries tended to litigate questions about the amount in controversy in two types of situations. In one the plaintiff had made a mistake of some sort, and the defendant tried to exploit it in order to move the case into federal court. In the other, by far the more common, the plaintiff was on the prowl. Those in the latter group were usually willing to limit their claims, if necessary, to defeat federal jurisdiction, but they first wanted to see whether they could somehow trap the defendants in state court while retaining claims above the jurisdictional minimum. Some of those who used the jurisdictional amount for offensive purposes did so shrewdly but fairly. Others may have done so only shrewdly. Although it was not always clear in jurisdictional amount cases who, if anyone, was attempting to outwit whom, the importance of forum choice to both sides was apparent.

Many disputes over the jurisdictional amount arose directly from the pleadings. Sometimes plaintiffs attempted to split their claims into multiple causes of action, each seeking less than the jurisdictional minimum but together seeking an amount well above it. Sometimes they pleaded different theories of liability, leaving it unclear whether they were seeking multiple recoveries or were simply being overly cautious in ensuring that their pleadings would conform to their proof. Other pleading ambiguities occasionally raised questions about the exact amount that plaintiffs sought. In some of those cases defendants had strong grounds to attempt removal; in others they were probably more interested in attempting to get into federal court than they were in clarifying an allegedly ambiguous pleading.[31] For the most part such pleadings cases were straightforward, and the courts generally resolved them with relatively easy rulings of law.

The greater number of jurisdictional amount disputes arose not from ambiguous pleadings but from aggressive plaintiffs' tactics. As the system of corporate diversity litigation became established in the 1880s, plaintiffs began to develop tactics to counter the advantages that their opponents enjoyed. Often not content with mere passive and sacrificial claim discounting, they hoped to use the jurisdictional amount for offensive purposes. The Judiciary Act of 1887–88 opened new possibilities for them when it significantly shortened the time within which defendants were required to file their removal petitions. Under the Judiciary Act of 1875, a removal petition was timely if filed at the term of court when the case could have first been tried. Under the 1887–88 act, the petition had to be filed at the time when the defendant was required by state law "to answer or plead to" the complaint.[32] The Supreme Court, moreover, immediately emphasized that the intent of the statute was to restrict the jurisdiction of the national courts,[33] and it held that the timing requirement was to be strictly construed.[34]

New statutory language, ambiguities in state practice concerning defendants' time to "answer or plead," and an unquestionably shorter time period combined to encourage plaintiffs to gamble that they might be able to sue for an amount above the jurisdictional minimum but still manage to keep their action in the state court. There had always been the chance that for whatever reason a defendant might not remove or might fail to do so properly, and the Judiciary Act of 1887–88 increased markedly the likelihood that defendants would somehow blunder if they tried. As early as 1894 a South Carolina federal judge noted the large number of recent precedents concerning the timeliness of removal petitions under the new statute. "[N]early all of them," he noted, arose "in the eighth and ninth circuits."[35] Although the gamble was apparently more common in the West, where the geographical burdens of the corporate system weighed most heavily, plaintiffs in many states adopted it. They brought suits for amounts in excess of the jurisdictional minimum and, especially in the first decade after the statute's passage, succeeded in many cases in holding them in state court because defendants were late in filing their removal petitions.[36] Sometimes plaintiffs agreed to stipulations extending a defendant's time to file for removal and then won remands on the ground that the time for filing a removal petition was a nonwaivable statutory requirement and therefore that stipulations could not extend it.[37]

If the cases where defendants failed to file promptly for removal left any doubt that plaintiffs were adopting a timing gamble tactic, numerous cases in which defendants did attempt to remove promptly dispelled it. Frequently, plaintiffs rushed to amend their claims and drop them below the jurisdictional minimum.[38] It seems certain that they were taking a calculated risk, hoping to maintain a large claim past the removal deadline and gambling that they could, if defendant took action, amend their pleadings before the removal papers were filed in the state court. Often, in fact, plaintiffs seemed poised to act as soon as they learned that the defendant had set out for the courthouse. Amendments lowering the amount claimed were offered almost simultaneously with the removal petitions, and the defendant's right to remove often turned on which party had filed earlier on the same day.[39] Because the rewards for success on either side were substantial, the tactic almost inevitably created the appearance of impropriety. A Delaware case raised the possibility that the plaintiff's attorney enjoyed an understanding with the court that it would delay filing the removal petition until he arrived to amend,[40] and an Arkansas case presented an official record that conflicted with the sworn testimony of the court's clerk as to whether the amendment to the complaint or the removal petition had been filed first.[41]

Plaintiffs were also encouraged to gamble, of course, because they had a second chance to avoid removal. Even if the defendant filed first and removed, they were not out of hope. Although they could no longer secure a remand by amending, they could still escape by moving for a voluntary dismissal or nonsuit.[42] The federal courts would usually grant such motions unless a defendant could show that it would be legally prejudiced, a difficult standard that required more than a showing that plaintiff would subsequently refile the same action in state court.[43] If the court granted a nonsuit, the plaintiff was generally free to reinstitute the action in any form and forum he chose.[44] Thus, a gamble that the defendant would not or could not remove was relatively safe and, even if lost, unlikely to lock the plaintiff in the federal court.[45] It seems highly probable that a significant percentage of the voluntary discontinuances that marked the federal dockets each year were preliminaries to filing second actions in state courts with discounted claims.

By and large neither pleading ambiguities nor timing gambles posed serious problems for the courts. Doctrinally, they raised standard issues that fell within established guidelines. Practically, their results were so highly fact specific that no matter how unseemly the details they seldom appeared to implicate broader social or legal issues. By the turn of the century, too, fewer defendants seemed to blunder in filing their petitions. As long as defendants were kept in state courts only because they faced claims below the jurisdictional amount or because they were themselves responsible, by choice or by fault, for their presence in the state forum, the federal courts felt justified in tolerating the tactics and accepting their results.

In the late 1880s, the inventiveness of plaintiffs' attorneys and their intensifying battle with foreign corporations inspired a new and exceptionally powerful method of turning the jurisdictional amount into an offensive weapon. Assisted by the short filing period introduced by the Judiciary Act of 1887–88, the new tactic found its principal legal support in a series of Supreme Court decisions in the mid-1880s. The Court held repeatedly that the statutory time limit for filing a removal petition was to be rigidly enforced and, more particularly, that once the right to remove had lapsed "it is not restored by an amendment of the pleadings afterwards so as to present different issues."[46] The rule quickly spawned a particularly sharp tactic, the delayed upward amendment of the amount claimed after defendant's time to remove had elapsed. With surprising suddenness the tactic came into use, and in 1890 a test case arrived before the Court.

In *Northern Pacific Railroad Co. v. Austin,*[47] plaintiff sued in state court for fire damage caused by the railroad's locomotive. He sought an amount slightly under the jurisdictional minimum, and defendant made no attempt to remove. Immediately prior to trial, however, the plaintiff moved to amend his complaint by raising his claim above the jurisdictional amount. Over the railroad's objection, the court proceeded with trial and, when the evidence supported the higher claim, granted the plaintiff's motion to amend. The jury awarded a verdict above the minimum, and the railroad appealed on the ground that the trial court had allowed plaintiff to defeat its federal right to remove. The Supreme Court stated the railroad's argument directly. Defendant maintained "that the plaintiff had purposely laid his damages in the first instance at a sum which did not permit a removal, and then sought to increase the *ad damnum* after the trial commenced and when it was assumed to be too late to remove."[48]

Although defendant's argument was both fair and forceful, the Court sidestepped it and affirmed plaintiff's judgment below. In spite of the bald facts and the railroad's persistence in raising the removal issue from the moment that plaintiff had moved to amend all the way to its final appeal, the Court denied relief on the most technical of rationales. Because defendant had not made a formal application to remove after plaintiff's amendment, the Justices decided, the state court had not technically denied a federal right. Hence, the Court was without jurisdiction to review the matter. The opinion scarcely touched on the railroad's argument, much less the justice of its cause, and it commented on the legal status of the plaintiff's tactic in only half a page.

The Court's reasoning in *Austin* revealed that in 1890 the Justices were either unable or unwilling to recognize the sharpening litigation tactics that would shortly throw federal procedural law into turmoil. First, the opinion sketched three possible and apparently equally plausible ways that the Court might, if forced, eventually decide the issue of the legitimacy of the delayed upward amendment tactic. Only one of the three—that a plaintiff who raised the amount of his claim might be estopped from relying on the time limit—would block the tactic. The other two would, in effect, sanction it. One of those possibilities was that plaintiff's motive "could not be inquired into," the Court announced, and the other was that a motive to prevent removal "would not affect the result." Second, and even more surprising, in support of the tactic the Court cited cases that upheld a plaintiff's right to avoid the Court's appellate jurisdiction by voluntarily giving up the part of her judgment that was above the Court's own appellate jurisdictional minimum. Those cases, obviously analogous to instances where plaintiffs avoided federal court by seeking less than the jurisdictional amount, seemed wholly inapposite to the upward amendment tactic. The Court's citations, however, ignored the drastic difference between the two tactics. Finally, confirming that the Court simply did not see the new tactic as a serious or pressing problem, it concluded with an equanimity that bordered on the callous. If defendants could not remove when faced with the delayed upward amendment tactic, the Court remarked, they "would simply suffer for want of comprehensiveness in the [removal] statute."[49]

The Court's curiously aloof opinion in *Austin* marked the last years of the first stage in the system's evolution. On one hand *Austin* addressed something quite new, a seemingly unfair and obviously powerful tactic that defeated removal and at the same time allowed claims in state courts to soar beyond the jurisdictional minimum. On the other hand the Court did not, or at least would not, recognize the potential legal and social significance of such a tactic. Its understanding of the social context still reflected the years that preceded the Judiciary Act of 1887–88 when federal jurisdiction appeared too broad and the principal jurisdictional abuse seemed to be collusive attempts by parties to commercial disputes to gain access to federal courts, not the calculated efforts of individual plaintiffs to avoid them.[50] Although *Austin* stood near the threshhold of the system's harshest and most wide-reaching middle phase, it remained rooted in the initial period when the system's social patterns remained somewhat blurred, when its characteristic cases were relatively few and scattered, and when its standard tactics had not yet grown hard and sharp. It came, too, before the intensifying social turmoil of the 1890s.

Although the hesitancy that marked *Austin* would vanish from the Court before the decade was out, it seemed scarcely to affect the lower federal judiciary. Not only did the delayed upward amendment tactic appear clearly improper, but its uses quickly became apparent. By the 1890s, the legal battles that characterized the system were growing more bitter and their social significance more obvious and explosive. A single type of litigation—personal injury plaintiffs suing corporations that were frequently their employers—emerged as the system's paradigmatic case. Increasingly, plaintiffs used the jurisdictional amount to avoid the federal courts and, if possible, to trap defendants in state courts while maintaining large claims against them. Although plaintiffs were usually successful in the numerous cases where they were willing ultimately to amend their claims downward, they met with little success when they attempted the reverse. Unlike the Supreme Court in *Austin,* the lower courts quickly rejected the delayed upward amendment tactic. A federal judge in Indiana denounced a variation in 1893, insisting emphatically that removal "cannot be defeated by any artifice, evasion, or omission."[51] A post-*Austin* edition of Dillon's treatise on removal probably spoke for most federal judges in the 1890s when it declared the tactic intolerable. Time limitations on removal, the treatise proclaimed, "can have no application to cases where the plaintiff's filing one pleading and then substituting another, after the time for removal has gone by, was a mere trick or device to keep the defendant in the state court."[52]

The strong opposition to the *Austin* tactic in the lower courts discouraged most plaintiffs from using it to assert and hold large claims in the state courts, and the other methods of using the jurisdictional amount for that purpose remained risky and increasingly unavailing. By the late 1890s the overwhelming majority of plaintiffs who were willing to discount their claims decided simply to file below the minimum amount and to avoid the risk of removal and the burden of a costly remand fight.

The Social Role of the Jurisdictional Amount

In the context of the system, the jurisdictional amount served to limit the size of claims that large numbers of plaintiffs brought against corporations. It thereby enforced a partial but nevertheless effective limitation on corporate liability. It was perhaps no accident that a study of railroad compensation practices regarding injured employees in the 1870s, when the jurisdictional amount stood at $500, found that "[s]ettlements for less than $500 were made routinely without consulting central office executives."[53] During the period when the system of corporate diversity litigation was in operation, the jurisdictional amount served as a distributive economic force that impinged seriously on individual plaintiffs.

Although the social function of the jurisdictional amount was clear, the scope of its impact was not. It would be impossible to gauge that scope in any terms that could approach quantitative precision. Several general conclusions, however, seem warranted.

The most obvious conclusion is that the principal social impact of the jurisdictional amount occurred not in the federal cases where the discounting tactic was most visibly litigated but in the presumably far more numerous state cases where discounted claims were used without ever becoming disputed issues. In overwhelming numbers individual plaintiffs sued in their local courts, and it was in those local courts that discounted claims abounded. Although there seems to be no way, absent detailed local studies, to estimate how many state cases involved discounted claims, a comparison of the federal and state caseloads suggests the probable magnitude of the practice.

The basic fact was that the state courts carried well over 90 percent of the cases brought in the United States. In 1933, Leon Marshall, one of the earliest students of judicial statistics, estimated that state courts of general jurisdiction handled approximately a million civil cases per year. His estimate excluded approximately 300,000 divorce actions and "many millions" of cases in local courts of limited jurisdiction.[54] Studies of local courts made Marshall's estimate plausible. As early as 1873 the state trial courts in Ohio decided more than 15,000 civil actions, and in 1876 New Hampshire's courts of general jurisdiction had more than 10,000 cases pending. In 1903 the local courts in Kansas City had 5,100 cases pending, approximately 60 percent of them suits against businesses.[55] California's Alameda County received more than 3,300 civil filings in 1910.[56] The general caseloads of the states continued to swell into the 1930s before the Depression sharply decreased new filings.[57]

By comparison, the federal caseload was miniscule. Pending private civil cases rose from approximately 12,000 in the early 1870s to 40,000 by 1900, hit a peak of around 45,000 before World War I, and declined to 25,000 shortly after the war.[58] More specifically, when Marshall estimated that state courts of general jurisdiction heard a million civil cases a year, the federal courts had a little over 60,000 civil cases pending, barely half of which were private actions.[59] In the years when New Hampshire's courts had 10,000 cases pending and Kansas City's 5,100, the New Hampshire federal court had 79 and the Western District of Missouri, which covered not just Kansas City but half the state, had 255. Compared with the approximately 3,000 actions against businesses pending in the Kansas City courts in 1903, a mere 196 private civil actions were on the docket of the Western District of Missouri. While Ohio's courts were disposing of 15,000 civil suits in 1873, the two federal districts in the state terminated a combined total of 325.[60] Alameda County's 3,320 civil filings in 1910 far outnumbered the 696 private civil actions filed that year in the whole of the Northern District of California, a district that included other heavily populated counties around San Francisco Bay.[61]

However inexact the numbers and however much they varied by time and place, the state dockets across the nation dwarfed their federal counterparts. Most of those cases were in the state courts, writers have often stated, because they involved only small amounts of money. Recognition of the ways in which the system of corporate diversity litigation operated supports a different causal hypothesis. Many of those cases in the state courts were brought for relatively small amounts of money because plaintiffs were intentionally holding down their claims in order to avoid removal. Even if the percentage of state court cases attributable to a claim-discounting strategy was small, the huge number of cases in the state courts would make the absolute number of discounted claims cases bulk large. Indeed, if only a small percentage of the state cases involved discounted claims, their total number could easily equal or surpass the total number of private diversity cases on the entire federal docket. The specter of potential removal, after all, hung over every tort and contract action filed in the state courts by a resident against a foreign corporation.

A second conclusion is that the social impact of the jurisdictional amount varied over time as prevailing economic conditions, particularly wage and price levels, changed. During the period from the 1870s through the 1930s, workers' wages rose substantially though erratically in both real and nominal terms. In general, wages rose steadily in the 1880s and during the long period from 1897 to 1920. They stagnated or fell most broadly in the depressions of the 1870s, the 1890s, and the 1930s.[62] There were, of course, vast differences in wages according to sex, race, region, occupation, industry, and employer. Blacks, women, farm workers, southerners, and the unskilled were among the lower-paid groups, and conversely, males, whites, skilled craftsmen, industrial workers, and those in the Northeast and industrial Midwest were among the higher. In the 1870s, for example, unskilled railroad workers earned $200 to $300 a year, whereas the highest-paid workers—locomotive engineers, iron puddlers, and conductors—could make from $600 to $900.[63]

In spite of such variations, average income figures provide a useful method of charting economic change. Specifically, the average annual earnings of nonfarm labor rose from around $300 before the Civil War to near $500 in the early 1870s, dropped back to around $425 in the later 1870s, and then rebounded to approximately $500 in the late 1880s. The 1890s forced a drop to around $450, but a slow climb began from about $470 in 1897 to $574 in 1910, and then to $633 in 1915. World War I forced up average wages rapidly, and they surged above $1,400 in 1920. After falling slightly in the brief postwar recession, they stayed in the $1,400 to $1,500 range for the rest of the decade, before dropping in the 1930s to a Depression low of just above $1,000 in 1933.[64]

A comparison with average annual income levels translates the jurisdictional amount into more specific and meaningful human terms. Most striking, the comparison shows the extreme practical impact of the increase that the Judiciary Act of 1887–88 made in the jurisdictional amount. Since the Civil War, inflation and rising wage levels had pushed yearly incomes upward toward and then, by the mid-1880s, near or above the jurisdictional minimum, a process that in effect forced extreme discounts on plaintiffs who sought to avoid federal jurisdiction by claiming less than the minimum. The ratio between the jurisdictional minimum and average annual income dropped from more than one and a half to around one for much of the period between 1870 and 1887. To avoid the federal courts by discounting a claim, in other words, workers or their families had to limit their formal demand to amounts that were near or, in some cases, less than a single year's wages. Whether considered as the maximum amount that they had a chance to recover at law or the outside limit from which they negotiated downward toward a settlement, the amount promised niggardly compensation. The increase made by the act of 1887–88, then, was dramatic. Immediately their maximum discounted claim jumped to approximately four times the average single year's wages.

For the next three decades the ratio of the jurisdictional amount to average annual income remained comparatively high. It stayed near or above four past the turn of the century before beginning gently to drop to just over three in 1910. The next year, when Congress raised the minimum to $3,000, the ratio jumped to more than four and a half. By 1916, immediately before the United States' entry into World War I, it still stood at almost four. Wartime inflation quickly pressed the ratio downward, forcing it to two by 1920. For the next decade it fluctuated slightly above that number until the Depression of the 1930s reversed the trend. The ratio climbed to near three in 1933 before beginning to drop back toward two and a half by the late 1930s.

The ratio provides a rough measure of the human meaning of the jurisdictional amount in the context of the system of corporate diversity litigation. The requirement pressed most harshly by far on plaintiffs in the earlier years. In contrast, from 1887 to World War I, it allowed plaintiffs to escape the federal courts while retaining the opportunity to win not only larger but relatively more meaningful awards. From 1917 to about 1930, however, the discount that it forced on plaintiffs grew increasingly sharp before easing again in the 1930s.

The congressional increases in 1887 and 1911 must have encouraged claims discounting for much of the rest of the period. The fact that the radical increase in the ratio after 1887 coincided with the onset of the system's harshest phase in the early 1890s suggests that claims discounting probably rose abruptly and steeply after 1887 and most likely remained at comparatively high levels into the second decade of the twentieth century. In contrast, the practice probably declined in importance after World War I, as the fall in the ratio from the war through the end of the 1920s dampened the incentive to discount. More important, by the time the United States entered the war federal and state employers' liability and workmen's compensation statutes had substantially reduced the pool of potential plaintiffs who might need to use the discounting device. In spite of its probable decline, however, claim discounting remained in use throughout the remainder of the period. The ratio never approached the lows that it had reached in the 1870s and 1880s, and average wages remained throughout at a level at least twice the jurisdictional amount.

A third general conclusion is that the jurisdictional amount had its greatest impact on those who had suffered more severe injuries and had relatively large claims to assert. Although the minimum posed no problem for plaintiffs with small claims that required little or no discounting, its impact became proportionally harsher as the seriousness of plaintiffs' injuries grew and as the larger amounts potentially at issue sharpened the incentives for injured parties to bring suit. Several criteria demonstrate that the discount it could impose on those with large claims was steep.[65]

The actual discounts that plaintiffs evidenced in their pleadings and the amounts that juries awarded and courts approved gave some indication of the extent of the discounts that the jurisdictional miminim required. Although the former came in all sizes, most seemed to be steep, often ranging from 50 to 80 percent or more of the damages initially pleaded.[66] Similarly, jury verdicts, although unpredictable and often erratic, frequently ran from two to five times the jurisdictional amount and, especially after World War I, sometimes as high as ten times the federal minimum.[67] In 1893 in *Baugh,* for example, where the plaintiff was seriously injured but not killed, the verdict approved by the state court was almost three and a half times the jurisdictional minimum. In personal injury actions in Alameda County, California, between 1880 and 1900, the average award was $3,651, seven times the jurisdictional amount before the Judiciary Act of 1887–88 and almost double that amount after it.[68]

Two congressional studies of judgments won by railroad workers confirm the availability of recoveries well above the jurisdictional amount. The first, covering the years from 1908 to 1910 when the federal minimum was $2,000, found that judgments in all courts averaged $2,536 in cases involving deaths, $11,272 in cases involving permanent total disability, and $3,515 in cases involving permanent partial disability. Because the study did not exclude state court judgments in suits brought with discounted claims, the numbers most likely understate the size of the judgments that were available.[69] The second congressional study, covering 1932 when the jurisdictional amount stood at $3,000, found that judgments averaged $5,854 in cases of death and $3,491 in cases of major disability.[70]

The 1932 study did more, however, than show the availability of recoveries in excess of the jurisdictional minimum. It provided an additional breakdown that suggested more specifically the practical significance of removal and the jurisdictional amount. In actions brought under state law—many of which would have been removable unless brought for less than the jurisdictional amount—judgments averaged $3,122 in death cases and $2,413 in major disability actions. In suits brought under the Federal Employers' Liability Act—all of which were by special statutory provision nonremovable irrespective of the amount sought—the judgments were three to four times larger, averaging $13,159 in the former and $7,419 in the latter.[71] Although numerous factors probably contributed to the variation, it seems most likely that claims discounting in the state courts was particularly significant.

Others studies revealed a similar pattern. An analysis of state and federal actions in California's Alameda County showed that state court tort plaintiffs sought on average only about two-thirds of the amount that comparable federal plaintiffs sought. State court judgments in the county were also lower than were federal judgments, especially between 1901 and 1910.[72] Another study of 435 state and federal appellate opinions in tort actions from 1875 to 1905 found that recoveries in federal court averaged $6,450 in death cases and $5,983 in bodily injury cases, whereas recoveries in state courts averaged $4,704 and $3,471 in the same categories. The state recoveries averaged only 73 percent and 58 percent, respectively, of the federal recoveries. Only a small percentage of the federal judgments were for amounts below the jurisdictional minimum, but between a quarter and a half of the state court judgments fell below it. Given the fact that the judgments involved similar types of cases from the same time period, it seems probable that the prevalence of claim discounting was a major factor in such striking discrepancies.[73]

Finally, workmen's compensation statutes offer another touchstone. Widely adopted between about 1911 and 1917, the statutes generally provided for compensation to injured workers without regard to negligence, and they established schedules of payments for various kinds of injuries. For the most part they set compensation rates at relatively low levels, often providing for payments equal to approximately half of an employee's wages for specified periods of time that varied according to the severity of the injury. Their relatively low rates reflected the theory that the acts created a new and more reasonable social balance. Workers lost the opportunity to seek large recoveries in exchange for the certainty of receiving compensation. Employers lost their powerful common law defenses in exchange for limitations on their maximum potential liability.[74] "Upon a rough estimate," concluded one early student of the workmen's compensation statutes in 1914, the injured worker "often receives about half damages."[75]

Comparing the statutes' compensation rates for serious injuries with the jurisdictional amount, two conclusions leap forward. First, the initial schedules established before World War I clustered around the jurisdictional minimum. Injuries that were serious but not totally disabling could commonly bring awards of $1,500 to $2,500. Those that were permanently disabling were capped at around $3,500 to $4,000, though an occasional state allowed awards up to $5,000 or $6,000.[76] If those award limits equalled half of the damages otherwise proper, the workmen's compensation statutes show that the jurisdictional amount imposed substantial discounts on more seriously injured workers. Second, the legislatures gradually increased the maximum awards to amounts well above the jurisdictional minimum. By the early 1920s, in fact, maximum awards commonly ranged from $5,000 to $8,000,[77] and in states with generous provisions the maximum awards available for widows with young children could rise above $10,000.[78] By 1932 the average awards made under the District of Columbia workmen's compensation law and the federal Longshoremen and Harbor Workers Compensation Act were double the jurisdictional minimum, $6,709 for the former and $5,875 for the latter.[79] In the years after World War I, then, the jurisdictional amount apparently forced severe discounts on plaintiffs who used it to avoid federal jurisdiction.

A fourth general conclusion is that the de facto limitation on liability that the jurisdictional amount created was probably of far greater economic benefit to the railroads than to most other corporations. Most of the roads had relatively narrow operating margins or shaky financial positions, and the industry's most pressing and general economic problem—raising income sufficiently above variable operating costs to allow coverage of unusually high fixed costs—forcefully pressed the roads to make every effort to cut variable costs. Though potential liability for personal injuries constituted only a small part of the railroads' total overhead, it was a more significant part of their variable operating costs and thus a particularly inviting target for cost cutting. Moreover, of course, the railroads were particularly dangerous to both consumers and workers, and they witnessed consistently high numbers of injuries over the years, especially during the forty years from the mid-1880s through the 1920s. Given their distinctive combination of persistent economic problems and massive claims exposure, the railroads probably derived significant benefits from the jurisdictional amount.[80]

More broadly, there seems to be no way to quantify the general economic impact attributable to the jurisdictional amount. Much, and probably most, of its impact resonated in the informal legal process, in plaintiffs' unrecorded decisions to discount and file in state court or to settle their claims with or without filing suit. How, for example, could one measure the consequences of the railroads' practice in the 1870s of generally paying claims for less than the jurisdictional amount but resisting claims above it? The likely impact of the practice seems as clear as it seems beyond the possibility of calculating. Again, how could one measure the response that juries would have made to the higher claims that the jurisdictional amount eliminated? Unlike the damages available in contract actions that were limited and often narrowly determined by legal rules, the amount of damages awarded in tort suits was relatively flexible and *ad hoc*. Given the tragic and horrible nature of so many of the injuries and the sympathy exhibited by most juries, larger claims would probably have led often to larger recoveries. Such speculations, however, are beyond quantification. Moreover, there are too many unknown and unknowable factors—including the yearly number of potential diversity cases involving reasonable damages above the jurisdictional minimum and the availability to plaintiffs of alternative methods of avoiding federal jurisdiction—to make macroeconomic estimates anything other than wild guesses.

The general economic impact of the jurisdictional amount may, in fact, have been most important to corporations not in terms of specific dollars saved but, rather, in terms of the legal and practical support the limit gave to the common belief in the late nineteenth and early twentieth centuries that liability for the injuries caused by economic enterprise should be relatively low. In the context of the system of corporate diversity litigation, the broadest and most important de facto social function of the jurisdictional amount may have been to symbolize, legitimize, and institutionalize the relatively low valuation that both the society and the law placed on the life and health of injured persons.[81]

Recognition of the social function that the jurisdictional amount played in the system of corporate diversity litigation casts further light on both the subsidy and efficiency theses. It isolates a specific area in which the legal system operated methodically and regularly to induce plaintiffs to discount their claims, and it thereby identifies a continuous de facto subsidy that the legal system offered to corporate enterprise. Further, by tracing the ways in which institutional and procedural arrangements combined to induce widespread claim discounting, recognition of the social function of the jurisdictional amount points to a major flaw in the efficiency thesis. Claims discounting in the system of corporate diversity litigation meant that the courts regularly awarded damages below the amounts that plaintiffs might otherwise have won under the applicable rules of the common law of the states. In economic terms, the jurisdictional amount in the system operated to push damages to artificially low levels and thereby prevented the rules of the common law from imposing on corporate defendants the "true" costs of accidents. The result, in economic terms, was that those common law rules could not achieve socially efficient results.

Finally, the social function of the jurisdictional amount suggests one last conclusion. There is little or no necessary correspondence between the doctrinal prominence of a rule and its social significance or, more importantly, between its theoretical complexity or intellectual magnetism and its practical impact. Doctrinally, the jurisdictional amount seems insignificant and uninteresting, a simple, mechanical, and intellectually trivial detail. In fact, for half a century it may have been one of the most effective, if indirect, distributive rules in the American legal system. It kept many small cases out of the federal courts, but it also transformed into "small" cases untold numbers of claims that were crucial to aggrieved individuals and whose proper value was by no means small. In the system of corporate diversity litigation, the jurisdictional amount did not just reroute small claims, it created them.

Chapter 5

The Battle for Forum Control, II:
Joinder and the Limits of the System

Since 1806, when Chief Justice John Marshall wrote the Supreme Court's opinion in *Strawbridge v. Curtis*,[1] the federal courts had held that jurisdiction based on citizenship required "complete" diversity between the adversary parties. Complete diversity meant that the citizenship of each of the plaintiffs in an action had to be different from the citizenship of each of the defendants; common citizenship between any plaintiff and any defendant destroyed diversity and deprived the federal court of jurisdiction.[2] If a plaintiff could sue a resident and a nonresident defendant together, she could destroy complete diversity and thereby prevent removal.[3]

Unlike claim discounting, however, joining multiple defendants as a device to defeat removal could be complicated and perilous. The former tactic was available in any action for damages and, if pleaded clearly, was certain to defeat federal jurisdiction. The latter was less widely available and much less certain in result. Although defendants had no recourse when plaintiffs sought less than the jurisdictional amount, they could often challenge joinders successfully.

Most important, the joinder of nondiverse defendants in order to block removal magnified the incentives on both sides. Unlike suits brought for less than the jurisdictional minimum, the joinder tactic enabled plaintiffs to achieve both of their primary procedural goals, defeating removal and still asserting a large claim. Although corporate defendants were often reconciled to the use of discounted claims, they fought joinders with tenacity and determination. Regardless of the outcome in individual cases, their persistent opposition gave notice that the joinder tactic promised only increased risks and higher costs. Their repeated challenges to the tactic probably dissuaded many plaintiffs, especially those with smaller claims, from even attempting joinders. In the 1890s, joinder cases emerged as the system's high-stakes litigation form, and corporate defendants had powerful incentives to fight the tactic.

The law gave nonresident defendants two principal ways to counter a joinder. They could negate it by showing that it was "sham" or fraudulent, or they could avoid it by showing that their dispute with the plaintiff constituted a "separable controversy." The former approach relied essentially on court-made rules, whereas the latter was based on a statutory provision that originated in the "separable controversy" act of 1866.[4] To prevail on a claim of sham or fraudulent joinder, the defendant had to allege that the joinder was made for the sole purpose of defeating the jurisdiction of the federal court. That allegation, however, was essentially formal, for the plaintiff's actual motive in choosing his adversaries was not the issue. Rather, although variously stated, the standard for fraudulent or sham joinder was regarded as "objective." The defendant had to show that the joinder was based on untrue allegations or that it relied on a claim that, for clear legal or factual reasons, could not be brought against one or more of the defendants. To establish the existence of a separable controversy, a nonresident defendant had to show that the plaintiff pleaded a cause of action against it that was legally separate from the causes asserted against any resident defendant and that the separate dispute could be "fully determined" by the court without the presence of the other defendants. A variation allowed courts to find that a party was merely "nominal," one against whom no "real" claim was asserted or who had no tangible interest in the action. If complete diversity existed when sham, nominal, or fraudulently joined parties were disregarded or when the parties to a separable controversy were considered alone, a nonresident defendant could remove.

Through the early 1880s the law of joinder developed in relative tranquillity, free from the pressures that corporate diversity litigation would later place on it. Perhaps most important, the rule requiring complete diversity, the doctrinal prerequisite for joinder as an antiremoval device, received powerful reaffirmation in the years around 1880. The Judiciary Act of 1875 and the forces of nationalism unleashed by the Civil War spurred a challenge to the long-established complete diversity doctrine. The 1875 act broadly expanded the jurisdiction of the lower federal courts to include cases arising under federal law, and it enlarged their jurisdiction based on citizenship. In its provisions concerning diversity, the statute tracked the language of the Constitution when it conferred jurisdiction over cases "in which there shall be a controversy between citizens of different states." That choice of language, together with the statute's clear purpose to expand federal jurisdiction, gave rise to the argument that Congress had intended to stretch federal diversity jurisdiction to its broadest constitutional reach and that the Constitution required only "minimum" diversity, that is, diversity between any one plaintiff and any one defendant regardless of the citizenship of other parties.[5]

Lawyers and judges debated the question, and the dispute flared most visibly in 1879 in a series of decisions that the Supreme Court handed down under the easy-to-remember title of the *Removal Cases*.[6] Writing for the majority, Chief Justice Morrison Waite ignored the constitutional question and, though not necessary to the decision, stated that the act of 1875 retained the established requirement of complete diversity.[7] Two Justices, though concurring in the judgment, took exception to the majority's statement. In a separate opinion Justice Joseph P. Bradley—a Republican, a nationalist, and a railroad lawyer—wrote what amounted to a plea for minimum diversity and what he considered "the fair and proper jurisdiction of the Federal courts."[8] Minimum diversity, Bradley argued, was essential to allow the federal courts to deal with important interstate commercial matters such as "those which relate to the foreclosure and sale of railroads extending into two or more States."[9] Pointing to the likely bias of state courts in favor of their own citizens and the value of the federal courts as instruments of nationalism, he quickly dismissed the "only objection" he saw to minimum diversity, the possibility that it would cause the federal courts to be "overwhelmed with business."[10] That objection, Bradley contended, was an insufficient basis for maintaining the complete diversity rule. The controlling issue was not the state of the docket but the proper construction of the statute and the essential institutional role of the national courts. "If the [federal] judicial force is not sufficient to meet the exigency," Bradley proclaimed, "let it be increased."[11]

In spite of Bradley's plea, the Chief Justice's dictum in the *Removal Cases* prevailed. Although the Court refrained throughout the period from deciding whether the Constitution itself mandated complete diversity, it settled the statutory issue conclusively in a stream of decisions over the next several years.[12] Successive editions of Judge John F. Dillon's treatise charted the development. In 1877 and 1881 it made the case for minimum diversity, downplaying in the latter edition the import of Waite's contrary dictum in the *Removal Cases*. "But the latest rulings of the Supreme Court," the 1889 edition acknowledged, "manifest a very decided intention" to restrict diversity jurisdiction to actions "between plaintiffs and defendants not one of whom possesses a common citizenship with any of the parties on the other side."[13] Because the Judiciary Act of 1887–88 retained the same language regarding diversity jurisdiction that the 1875 act used, complete diversity continued after its passage as the unquestioned rule.

During the 1870s and 1880s the Court also construed the separable controversy statute, reenacted and broadened in the Judiciary Act of 1875,[14] in ways that limited its reach.[15] The leading Supreme Court cases that construed it arose from a variety of factual contexts that had been familiar to the early nineteenth century. They frequently involved multiple claims to real property or relatively complex disputes over corporate or commercial matters. Their factual situations suggested no particular social pattern, and the Court decided them free from general political or social pressures. Aside from eliminating the provision that allowed removal by plaintiffs, the Judiciary Act of 1887–88 left unchanged the language of the separable controversy act.

In construing the separable controversy statute, the Court generally regarded plaintiffs as masters of their suits and allowed them to frame their complaints in any legally proper manner they chose. If a plaintiff asserted a joint claim—one that alleged some type of shared liability—against multiple defendants, it was irrelevant that he could have sued one or more of them severally, or sued them on different claims, or sued other or additional parties in their place. "A defendant has no right to say that an action shall be several which a plaintiff elects to make joint," the Court declared in *Louisville and Nashville Railroad Co. v. Ide*[16] in 1885. Moreover, the plaintiff's claim was to be judged by his pleadings. "The cause of action is the subject matter of the controversy," *Ide* explained, "and that is for all the purposes of the suit whatever the plaintiff declares it to be in his pleadings."[17] In a series of decisions in the early and mid-1880s the Court repeatedly applied those rules and held that a joint cause of action did not present a separable controversy, that the joint cause of action rule applied to both contract and tort suits, and that separate answers or defenses presented by different defendants did not alter the nature of a cause of action that a plaintiff had pleaded as joint.[18]

Defendants' other doctrinal countermeasure, fraudulent joinder, was litigated less often. The Supreme Court held that defendants had the burden of alleging and proving fraud, and its few decisions suggested that proving fraud in such cases would be difficult. An 1886 decision, for example, seemed to imply that fraud might not be provable under any circumstances if the joinder itself were technically proper.[19] Through the early 1880s the more common problem of jurisdictional abuse remained the effort of parties to create, not defeat, federal jurisdiction,[20] and the standard applicable to fraudulent joinders remained undeveloped.

Emergence of the Tort Joinder Tactic

The Court's decisions in the early 1880s on both separable controversies and complete diversity prepared the way for, and probably helped inspire, the emergence of joinder as a primary antiremoval tactic. As the system of corporate diversity litigation took shape and the number of suits by individuals against corporations began to rise sharply in the 1880s,[21] the tactic began coming into noticeable use. Joinder of a resident defendant in an action against a foreign corporation was an obvious way to defeat diversity and avoid federal jurisdiction, and those injured by the machinery owned or used by large corporations began to recognize that candidates for joinder were frequently available. Typically, plaintiffs brought their actions against the foreign corporations and joined as codefendants either small local companies that had some legal or business relation with the foreign corporation or, by far the more common, resident employees of the corporation who had some involvement with the injury.

The lower federal courts responded with suspicion and often found grounds on which to uphold contested removals. Even though the complete diversity requirement was unquestioned, there still was leeway in dealing with separable controversies and fraudulent joinders.[22] A federal judge in Iowa probably spoke for many of his colleagues when he denied a motion to remand in 1885. Removal, he declared, was a "sacred" right that the federal courts were required to protect.[23] Through the 1880s and into the 1890s the lower courts—without Supreme Court precedent dealing expressly with such tactically motivated joinders—struggled with the problem of defining removal jurisdiction in a new and explosive social context and with received doctrine that seemed inadequate.

By the early 1890s tort litigation was growing more rapidly than the number of industrial accidents, and use of the joinder tactic became increasingly common. The number of railroad tort cases alone may have tripled between 1885 and 1895, growing especially rapidly in the West and South, perhaps in part as a result of the roads' expanding efforts to cut operating costs and the downward pressure their efforts placed on the amounts that companies offered in order to settle claims out of court.[24] The states also expanded the pool of removable actions by adopting foreign corporation statutes that allowed local courts to assert personal jurisdiction over nonresidents who did business within their borders. In 1885 fewer than twenty states had adopted such statutes, but in the next ten years that number jumped to thirty-five.[25] By the 1890s, too, the procorporate image of the federal courts was hardening, spurring more determined efforts by many plaintiffs to remain in the state courts.[26] When *Baugh* established the sweeping federal fellow servant rule in 1893, it seemed to confirm dramatically the growing belief that the federal courts favored business. More specifically, for injured workers with common law claims, *Baugh* frequently made avoiding the federal courts an imperative. "In recent years," noted a treatise on removal published in 1901, "there has been much bitter litigation as to the right to remove suits."[27]

Equally important, sharpening social, political, and cultural conflict highlighted the growing use of joinder and cast it in the minds of many lawyers and

judges as part of the more general threat to social stability and established interests that erupted in the 1890s. The very fact that industrial injuries began generating an escalation in tort litigation suggested deepening social conflict and growing
worker militance. Two decades of intensifying labor turmoil seemed to reach a
crescendo in the early 1890s as violent strikes in Homestead, Pennsylvania, in the
East and Coeur d'Alene, Idaho, in the West followed in rapid succession. The
fierce depression that began in 1893 brought widespread hardship and intensified
the sense of social conflict. More specifically, the depression compounded the
financial problems that injured workers faced and made companies even less
willing and able to compensate them. With one-quarter of the nation's total
railroad assets in receivership by 1895,[28] for example, the pressure on the roads to
slice variable costs—including payouts for personal injuries—became particularly
acute. Class antagonisms flared, compounded by a growing hostility toward the
multiplying numbers of immigrants from southern and eastern Europe who made
up an increasingly large part of the new industrial working class. By the late
nineteenth century, in fact, immigrants and their children constituted a majority of
the American industrial work force. Justice David J. Brewer, a forceful critic of
the decade's social protest movements, warned in 1895 that such movements were
particularly dangerous when their strength lay "with the rabble and in the city."[29]
Many in the well-to-do classes looked with anxiety at any attempt, apparent or
real, to attack established interests, especially when recent and disfavored immigrant groups were involved; and for their part, industrial workers in the late
nineteenth century showed a new willingness to organize and to strike.[30]

Widespread rural-based protests reinforced the challenges that urban workers
began to raise. Beginning in the late 1880s the nation's farm population suffered
from increasing deflation and a regional economic recession. In Kansas alone, for
example, by 1890 60 percent of the taxable land in the state was mortgaged, and
between 1889 and 1893 mortgage companies foreclosed on eleven thousand
farms.[31] Political agitation against banks, railroads, and corporations in general
intensified throughout the Midwest, South, and West. In 1891 the spreading dis-
content spurred the founding of the Populist party, an agrarian-based third party
that advocated a number of radical proposals, including government ownership of
the railroads, a graduated personal income tax, and an eight-hour day for labor.
The new party's rhetoric stressed the growing chasm between individual citizens
and the power and wealth of national corporations. Its platform in 1892 envisioned "our homes covered with mortgages; labor impoverished; and the land
concentrating in the hands of the capitalists."[32] For a half-dozen years in mid-
decade the Populist party constituted a major force in American politics, electing
hundreds of local officials and a handful of senators, governors, and state supreme
court justices.

While the decade seemed to bristle with conflict and hardship, the year 1894
was particularly cruel, the first full year of depression following a relentless winter. Opening with an unprecedented 2 million to 3 million workers unemployed,
the year witnessed almost fourteen hundred strikes supported by an equally unprecedented half-million workers. In the spring unemployed marchers in "Coxey's
army" set out for Washington, DC, from seventeen gathering points, and in April
125,000 members of the United Mine Workers went out on a strike that was
quickly broken. In May the Pullman strike began. Centered in Chicago, it spread

to 150,000 members of the American Railway Union in more than a dozen states and eventually erupted in mob riots, widespread property destruction, and armed intervention by federal troops.[33] "Certainly during all those dark days of the Pullman strike, the growth of class bitterness was most obvious," wrote Jane Addams of Chicago's Hull House. "The fact that the Settlement maintained avenues of intercourse with both sides seemed to give it opportunity for nothing but a realization of the bitterness and division along class lines."[34]

In that harsh and strife-filled context, as the flow of post-*Baugh* tort joinder cases swelled to a stream, the Sixth Circuit took the lead in broadening the doctrinal access channel into the federal courts. The circuit boasted two of the most respected and conservative lower court judges in the nation, William Howard Taft and Horace H. Lurton, both of whom would eventually sit on the United States Supreme Court, the former appointing the latter in 1909 shortly after his election to the presidency. When Taft heard a rumor that federal troops had killed thirty of the Pullman strikers, he remarked optimistically that "everybody hopes that it is true." When he subsequently learned that only six had been killed, he complained that it was "hardly enough to make an impression."[35] In August 1894 Taft expressed his views publicly, warning that workers, socialists, and legislatures were endangering the developing aggregations of corporate capital that served as the engines of social progress. The duty of protecting those necessary and beneficial aggregations fell on the courts, he maintained, and the duty fell with particular gravity on the federal courts.[36]

Late in the year Taft, sitting with a district judge, heard two typical tort joinder cases. In each the plaintiff was an injured railroad worker who sued his employer, a railroad corporation chartered out of state, and joined with it other employees whose citizenship was the same as plaintiff's. In *Hukill v. Chesapeake & Ohio Railway Co.*[37] the plaintiff's attorney stated that he had joined the other employees to avoid federal jurisdiction,[38] and in *Powers v. Chesapeake & Ohio Railway Co.*[39] the plaintiff had previously dismissed a prior suit after removal and subsequently refiled with resident employees joined as codefendants. In each case the plaintiff voluntarily dismissed the other employees before trial, and the railroads immediately petitioned for removal. Plaintiffs, relying on *Austin* and the Supreme Court's construction of the timing provisions of the Judiciary Act of 1887–88, moved to remand on the ground that the railroad's time to remove had elapsed prior to the dismissal of the employee-defendants.

Using *Powers* as the major opinion, Taft wrote angrily and broadly. The plaintiffs, he charged, had created "a device to deprive the Chesapeake & Ohio Railway Company of its constitutional and statutory right to come into this court."[40] He passed over technical flaws in the removal petitions and refused to rest with the fact that each plaintiff had properly pleaded a joint cause of action. He focused, instead, on the nature of the plaintiffs' tactics: in *Hukill* the acknowledgment of intent, in *Powers* the dismissal and refiling of the suit, and in both the eventual dismissal of the resident defendants. Taft took particular notice of a most practical consideration. "The joinder of a fireman or an engineer or a conductor as defendants in an action to recover $25,000 against a railroad company, without explanation," he charged, "of itself raises a suspicion that it is not done merely to recover judgment against the employes [*sic*]."[41] In each case he held that the plaintiff's tactic was legally fraudulent and that the fraud precluded him from raising the issue of time. Taft ruled both removals proper and denied the motions to remand.

Legally, Taft's opinions in *Powers* and *Hukill* were unsatisfactory. Although there seemed no question about the actual motive of either plaintiff, their motive was not the proper test for fraudulent joinder. Taft's opinions failed to articulate a clear reason why the plaintiffs' actions constituted legal fraud. Both the voluntary dismissal of an action and the voluntary dismissal of some defendants prior to trial were proper and ordinary, and in each case the dismissals had been made with the approval of the trial court. Moreover, there was no question that the plaintiff in *Powers* had a right to file a second action after the voluntary dismissal of his first suit. Finally, the reference to the employee-defendants' likely inability to pay was legally irrelevant.

For the purpose of blocking the joinder tactic, however, Taft's decisions were even less satisfactory. Future plaintiffs could readily avoid their strictures by refusing to admit their reasons for acting and refusing to dismiss the resident defendants. Even worse, both decisions assumed that the plaintiffs had properly pleaded joint causes of action that would not ordinarily have been removable. "So, in the case at bar, had the plaintiff retained the resident defendants as parties until judgment, however clear it was that his intent in so doing was to defeat removal," Taft wrote in *Powers,* "the case could not have been removed, because, in his petition, he stated a good cause of action against the defendants so joined."[42] Because Taft repeated essentially the same statement at two other points in his opinion, injured employees could hardly fail to learn from and rely on *Powers* to help them avoid federal jurisdiction.

Lurton had responded similarly in his first major effort to deal with the joinder tactic. A year and a half before *Powers* he confronted a variation of the tactic in a case brought on behalf of a government employee killed while riding on a train as a United States mail clerk. In *Arrowsmith v. Nashville & Ducatur Railroad Co.*[43] the administrator of the deceased employee's estate, who had discontinued a prior suit after removal, sued the operating railroad and joined as codefendant the resident railroad company that had leased the track and rolling stock to the operating company. Stressing the importance of defendant's right to remove, Lurton declared that the federal courts must "be astute not to permit devices to become successful which are used for the very purpose of destroying" that right.[44] He denied plaintiff's motion to remand on the ground that under local law and the lease between the roads the lessor railroad was not liable on the merits. The lessor was, therefore, a "sham" defendant whose presence did not destroy diversity.

Despite his desire to protect removal, Lurton's approach in *Arrowsmith* was no more designed to achieve that end broadly than was Taft's approach in *Powers.* Because the decision was based on the language of the lease between the companies, *Arrowsmith* could not provide a general rule that would defeat the joinder tactic. Lurton, like Taft in *Powers,* had apparently not yet recognized the importance that the joinder tactic would assume after *Baugh,* or decided what if anything could be done about it. In *Arrowsmith* he even remarked thoughtlessly that remand would be required if the lessor railroad were "jointly or separably liable."[45] From the point of view of cutting off the joinder tactic, that statement was as harmful as Taft's comment that a claim against a master and his servant was properly a joint cause of action.

The following year, as the plaintiff in *Powers* began the long process of appealing to the Supreme Court and employee joinder cases poured into the federal courts, Taft and Lurton had the opportunity to consider the situation more fully. Both believed that it was essential for the federal courts to maintain broadly the right to remove diversity actions. Their opinions in *Arrowsmith* and *Powers* had agreed, after all, on one exceptionally dubious legal proposition that only the most unrestrained defenders of removal advanced. As Lurton announced flatly in the former, "[t]he right to remove is a constitutional right."[46] If one wished to protect a broad right to remove from the threat of employee joinders, however, neither fraud nor actual motive—both difficult to prove—would serve, nor would such a specific ground as the language of a particular lease. If joinders were to be effectively stopped, it would be necessary to find a sweeping and easily applicable legal theory. In the "joint cause of action" doctrine, Taft and Lurton concluded, lay the Achilles heel of the joinder tactic.

In late 1895 the two sat together to hear a motion to remand in *Warax v. Cincinnati, New Orleans & Texas Pacific Railway Co.*,[47] a case that presented what had become the standard fact pattern. Plaintiff, an injured employee, had dismissed a previous suit after his employer removed and had then refiled with a resident employee added as a second defendant. The railroad again removed, and plaintiff moved to remand. This time Taft and Lurton seized the opportunity, avoided specifics, and struck broadly.

With Taft writing, *Warax* held that the plaintiff had failed to state a joint cause of action against the employer and the fellow employee because each was potentially liable on a different legal theory. The employee would be liable because he was personally negligent, but the railroad would be liable only on the "public policy" ground of *respondeat superior.* "Liabilities created on two such wholly different grounds cannot and ought not to be joint."[48] Since there was no joint cause of action, a separable controversy existed and the nonresident defendant could remove. On that ground *Warax* denied plaintiff's motion to remand.

In the guise of an afterthought, embarrassing but nevertheless necessary, Taft scuttled his own earlier opinions in *Powers* and *Hukill.* The rule laid down, he observed casually at the end of his opinion in *Warax,* "may be somewhat at variance with some remarks which were made incidentally" in the two earlier decisions. If so, the incidental remarks had no weight. They were "not necessary" to the cases and were "little considered" in them. More important, insofar as the earlier cases discussed a joint cause of action against master and servant, Taft announced, the matter had been "assumed rather than decided."[49]

Warax was clean, simple, and sweeping. In import and method it was the procedural analogue of *Baugh.* It was, like *Baugh,* based on the federal common law, premising its rule on the implicit assumption that the federal courts had authority to decide—independent of state decisions—whether a common law cause of action was joint or several.[50] Further, in effect it expanded *Baugh*'s reach. By making it more difficult for plaintiffs to avoid federal jurisdiction, *Warax* made *Baugh*'s fellow servant rule more widely applicable. Finally, the breadth of its holding matched *Baugh*'s sweeping rule that made almost all corporate employees fellow servants. A company could not be directly liable to an injured employee, *Warax* stated, unless it had been "present by any corporate or superintending officer."[51] Because industrial accidents would almost never involve a superintending corporate officer, a corporation would almost never be directly liable to an injured person. Accordingly, almost never would a joint cause of action in tort lie against the corporation and one of its employees. Hence, as *Baugh* made almost all corporate employees into fellow servants and thereby ensured that the fellow servant defense would be available in almost all tort actions brought by employees, so *Warax* prevented plaintiffs—whether employees or third parties—from asserting a joint cause of action against employers and their employees in almost all cases and thereby ensured that the separable controversy act would almost always be available to enable corporate defendants to remove tort actions to the federal courts.

Were *Warax* widely followed, it would render the employee joinder tactic useless. Taft and Lurton designed it to be a leading case, and they relied on it almost immediately to deny another motion to remand in *Hukill,* which had been discontinued after Taft's first decision and then refiled again and again removed.[52] Further, the principle of *Warax* was not necessarily limited to suits involving fellow servants or even to suits involving employer–employee codefendants. It could be generalized to any situation where the alleged joint liability of codefendants rested on different legal theories. Shortly after announcing *Warax,* in fact, Taft applied it to deny a joint cause of action that attempted to defeat removal by joining an employee and the receiver appointed for his employer.[53]

Although the federal courts divided over the tort joinder tactic, most were apparently opposed to its widespread use, especially in suits between employers and employees. A federal judge in Kentucky denied a remand in 1899 on the authority of *Warax* and alluded to the growing problem that the joinder tactic presented. A court could not "ignore its own knowledge of the surrounding situation" that was a "matter of public current history."[54] Another federal judge, acknowledging that the facts before him "cannot come literally within the principles established" by *Warax* and *Hukill,* denied a motion to remand because the facts came "within the spirit of the principles announced in those cases, and with the evil they were meant to remedy."[55] By the late 1890s *Warax* had established itself as a leading if controversial federal authority that negated the joinder tactic.[56]

Resolution and Irresolution: The Federal Courts Divided

For two days in December 1897 the Supreme Court heard argument on the appeal of Taft's decision in the *Powers* case. It was, after more than a decade of intensifying litigation, the Court's first employee joinder case. The decision, announced the following month, revealed both the Court's unwillingness to confront the issue and the extent to which it had changed since 1890. In early 1898, in *Powers v. Chesapeake and Ohio Railway Co.,*[57] it affirmed Taft's denial of the motion to remand, refused to resolve the joinder question, and decided instead—broadly and authoritatively—the timing issue it had avoided eight years earlier in *Austin.*

The Court's opinion in *Powers* stressed the simple fact pattern presented. The plaintiff had been able to keep his action in state court because the resident defendants destroyed diversity of citizenship, but when he voluntarily dismissed them before trial he destroyed diversity. "[T]he case then for the first time became one in its nature removable."[58] Quoting at length from *Austin,* but leaving out its language about the possible "want of comprehensiveness in the [removal] statute,"[59] the Court stated the broad issue that it was ready to decide: "whether a defendant may file, in the state court in which the suit was commenced, a petition for removal, after the time mentioned in the act of Congress has elapsed, in a case which was not removable when that time expired."[60] *Powers* answered the question in the affirmative. The basic principle it established was that whenever a case that had initially been nonremovable became removable by virtue of some voluntary action by plaintiff, a defendant could remove. The Court thus chose to lay down a comprehensive principle of removal law, one that covered issues involving the jurisdictional amount as well as joinder.

The depression of the 1890s and seven years of corporate diversity litigation moved the Court from *Austin* to *Powers*. In the latter decision, the Court relied on no new legal principles. It pointed to no newly discovered significance in the words of the removal statute. It adduced no new evidence regarding legislative history or congressional intent. In the few places where it cited precedents it invariably included cases that antedated *Austin*. Its reasoning rested, instead, on a simple fact that it had evidently not understood or not regarded as significant a mere seven years earlier. To construe the statute any differently, the Court explained, "would utterly defeat all right of removal in many cases."[61] That conclusion rested on one foundation only, the increasingly aggressive plaintiffs' tactics of the 1890s.

Although Taft's decision below had turned on fraud, the Court refused to deal with that issue. It was establishing a clean, comprehensive, and easily applicable rule to safeguard removal, and implicating fraud in any way would only weaken the new rule. Moreover, though it was responding to the procedural battles of corporate diversity litigation, the Court was nevertheless determined to deny that fact and to sanitize its analysis. *Powers* explained its rule by invoking two examples that were both hypothetical and disingenuous. A different rule would "utterly defeat" removal, the Court explained, because state courts would generally allow plaintiffs to amend their pleadings in reasonable situations: where, "for instance," a defendant had been joined by "an honest mistake" not discovered until after another defendant's time to remove had passed, or where a plaintiff brought suit for what he believed to be a "comparatively trifling" injury that he "afterwards discovered to be so much graver."[62] In *Powers* the Court relied on imaginary examples to deny by implication the social reality that was compelling its hand. Finally, although neither *Warax* nor the point it decided was at issue in *Powers*, the Court made a special effort to take note of Taft's later decision. It seemed to chide the lower court for changing positions between its decisions in *Powers* and *Warax* and to imply that the rule laid down in *Warax* was dubious. The Court emphasized that its own cases had repeatedly held that a cause of action in tort was "whatever the plaintiff declares it to be in his pleadings." It was the lower court's decision in *Powers*, not in *Warax*, that applied "this rule."[63] Still, the Court expressly stated, it was not considering or deciding whether the *Warax* rule was "the correct one."[64]

With the Court's decision in *Powers*, the relative importance of joinder and the jurisdictional amount as antiremoval devices became radically unequal. Burying the delayed upward amendment tactic that *Austin* had let pass, *Powers* ensured that plaintiffs who used the jurisdictional amount to defeat removal would, without extraordinary good fortune, be forced to discount their claims. Conversely, in choosing to establish a broad timing rule and restricting its holding to that single issue, *Powers* allowed the joinder tactic to stand. Even more important, by implying that the *Warax* rule was incorrect, it raised the hope that joinder might be available in tort actions against employers and their employees. The single limitation that *Powers* placed on joinders, that the resident defendant could not be dismissed prior to trial, could be avoided. Although personal or social reasons could still constrain employees from suing coworkers or job foremen, the legal obstacle it posed would generally be slight.[65]

Personal injury plaintiffs continued throughout the life of the system to use the jurisdictional amount to avoid the federal courts, and the tactic retained its advantages of universal applicability and certainty of result. For plaintiffs who had smaller claims or who wanted to avoid additional costs and delays, suing below the jurisdictional minimum remained attractive. For those who were unable to join resident defendants, it remained the principal alternative to avoid removal. After *Powers*, however, the law was basically settled, and the practice of discounting claims, though standard, became largely invisible. When parties litigated the issue, it tended to be in the standard ambiguous pleading or timing gamble cases.[66]

The potentially powerful but now repudiated *Austin* tactic still appeared on occasion and sometimes even succeeded when protesting defendants failed to petition formally for removal.[67] Generally, however, it survived only in fringe forms. Some plaintiffs continued to allege large damages in the body of their complaints while limiting their formal demands to amounts under the jurisdictional minimum. The courts usually held that the demand prevailed over the damages alleged, assuming that *Powers* would prevent late upward amendments to the formal demands.[68] Other plaintiffs relied on procedural techniques that might induce defendants to file late. The use of stipulations extending defendant's time to answer continued, with plaintiffs occasionally gaining remands on the ground that such agreements could not extend the congressionally mandated time limit available to petition for removal.[69] A scattering of other ploys and near ploys, causing defendants to file their removal petitions late, surfaced randomly. When plaintiffs appeared culpable, the courts generally upheld the late petitions and allowed removals on one or another ground.[70] One plaintiff tried perhaps the baldest variation, amending his claim upward while arranging constructive but not actual notice to the defendant. The Supreme Court of Iowa, suggesting that the tactic smacked of fraud, held that the petition was timely and the action was removable.[71]

If *Powers* settled major issues about timing and the jurisdictional amount, however, it left the matter of joinder—now the most critical procedural question in the system—wide open. The Court did not act hastily on it. It was two years before it again decided another employee joinder case, and then it once more refused to confront *Warax* directly.

In *Chesapeake & Ohio Railway Co. v. Dixon*[72] the plaintiff sued the railroad and two of its resident employees for the death of her husband who had been run over at a street crossing. The railroad claimed that its controversy with the plaintiff was separable because its alleged liability "rested on a wholly different basis from that of the liability of its servants." The Court noted the railroad's specific reliance on *Warax* which, it stated, "held that there were separable controversies in such cases."[73] After discussing the issue, the Court remarked that the authorities were split and that, in any case, it need not decide whether *Warax* was correct.

Instead, it affirmed the state court's refusal to order removal on the tortured, double-negative formulation that "it cannot properly be held that it appeared on the face of this pleading, as a matter of law, that the cause of action was not entire."[74]

Warax and the tort joinder tactic clearly split the Court. If the broad but careful holding in *Powers* seemed apt, the uncertain holding in *Dixon* did not. The opinion directly acknowledged the *Warax* issue but then avoided it. It seemed to suggest, but refused to say, that *Warax* was incorrect. It cited at one point "the principle of the identification of the master with the servant"[75] but then noted that such a principle was unnecessary to its decision. It suggested that an allegation of "concurrent negligence" might not be necessary to state a joint cause of action but then stretched noticeably to read such an allegation into the complaint. "Other grounds of concurring negligence," the Court added with unusual generosity, "may be imagined."[76] On that point of pleading *Dixon* seemed to rest. "And where concurrent negligence is charged the controversy is not separable."[77] Doctrinal uncertainty and some unspoken but uneasy internal truce constrained the Court. Only six Justices joined the majority, while the two dissenters—Justices John M. Harlan and Edward D. White, neither of whom was noticeably reticent—did not write.[78]

In spite of the uncertainties, *Dixon* encouraged use of employee joinders to defeat removal. The decision, declared the *Virginia Law Register* in 1901, "will doubtless revolutionize the practice in tort actions against foreign corporations in the State courts."[79] *Dixon* seemed to approve the principle of joint liability between masters and servants, and it seemed to place in plaintiffs' hands the power to prevent removal by pleading concurrent negligence. Contemporaneous decisions of the Court in related areas also seemed to support those conclusions,[80] and the Court's repeated reliance on its early tort joinder cases from the 1880s[81] seemed to confirm that the formal allegations of a joint cause of action and concurrent negligence were, absent proof of fraud, sufficient to defeat removal.

Although plaintiffs' attorneys across the nation read *Dixon* that way, corporate attorneys did not. The Court's opinion had not, at least arguably, decided what law determined whether a joint cause of action existed, whether a formally proper pleading would prevent removal if controlling substantive law did not allow a joint cause of action, what test determined whether a fraudulent joinder had been made, or how far into the merits of a case a court could inquire in order to settle any of those issues. It had also allowed *Warax* to stand.

The results were predictable. Legions of plaintiffs adopted the joinder tactic, and corporate defendants fought it vigorously on all fronts. Joining a resident defendant, particularly an employee, had become the "almost universal practice in vogue of late years," complained a federal judge in Kansas in 1904.[82] Such joinders had "become a common practice," a South Carolina federal judge agreed disapprovingly the same year. It "taxes the credulity of the court to believe that in suits of that character there is any bona fide expectation of recovering damages from any other than the railway companies." His conclusion was probably shared widely, though not usually voiced, by the lower courts. "There is, in consequence, a strong presumption in every such case that the employe [sic] defendants are joined for no other purpose than to defeat the right of a nonresident defendant to remove."[83]

Another result was also predictable. The decisions in the lower federal courts split wildly. Some applied *Powers* and *Dixon* to uphold employee joinders,[84] though a few judges seemed to reach that conclusion only reluctantly. A federal judge in Washington made it clear, for example, that he thought a corporate defendant was entitled to remove but that *Powers* "constrains me to hold otherwise."[85] Others avoided *Dixon* and denied motions to remand. Some expressly limited *Dixon,* most persuasively on the ground that it reached only cases pleading "concurrent negligence,"[86] while others rested on findings of fraud or essentially ignored *Dixon.*[87] In a split decision the Fourth Circuit offered five separate constructions of *Dixon.* One judge maintained that *Dixon* supported removal, and two judges ordered a remand on the ground that no separable controversy existed under any one of four other theories for which they thought the case might be taken to stand.[88]

Although *Dixon* was ambiguous, some lower court decisions seemed to turn more on the judge's desire to protect removals than on either the plaintiff's pleadings or the Court's guidelines. *Warax,* for example, retained surprising vitality. Lurton himself admitted that *Powers* and *Dixon* had "shaken" its authority,[89] but many lower courts continued confidently to cite and follow it.[90] A few expressly utilized the federal common law, as Taft had done implicitly in *Warax,* and denied motions to remand on the ground that federal common law controlled and, contrary to established state law, did not recognize the cause of action pleaded as being joint.[91]

A South Carolina federal judge exemplified the attitudes of those federal judges who seemed determined to defeat the joinder tactic. In *Bryce v. Southern Railway Co.,* decided in 1903, a United States railway mail clerk, badly injured in a derailment, sued the company and two of its resident employees, the train's engineer and conductor. The judge stated that "the right of removal must be tested by the allegations of the complaint" and noted that Bryce pleaded "the joint negligence" of the railroad and its two employees. Moreover, the judge admitted, it was "not possible to distinguish this case" from *Dixon.*[92] Repeatedly alluding to plaintiff's possible motive in joining the resident employees, he insisted that motive was "immaterial."[93] He quoted both *Warax* and *Hukill* but refused to base his decision on either. Finally, resting on the pleading requirements of the South Carolina Code, he concluded that plaintiff had not alleged sufficient facts to apprise the two employees of the precise acts of negligence for which they might be held liable. There were, he decided, "no facts stated connecting these defendants with that derailment."[94] Holding that "no actionable charge of negligence has been made against these two defendants,"[95] the judge denied the motion to remand.

Bryce refused to give up. He moved for a rehearing, insistently pressing *Dixon* and other Supreme Court cases on the judge. "[T]he arguments of counsel upon the motion," the judge assured the parties on rehearing, "demand and have received most careful consideration."[96] Essentially repeating his earlier analysis, however, he again refused to remand the action. To keep the employees in the action, he announced, "something more than the charge of negligence or joint negligence with the railway company must be made."[97]

Bryce's persistence accomplished nothing beyond demonstrating that the judge was simply not going to order a remand. Most obviously, the judge simply refused—in spite of *Dixon*—to accept the significance of the fact that Bryce pleaded joint negligence. Further, he ignored the fact that Bryce also pleaded that the engineer and conductor were in charge of operating the train when it derailed, an allegation of fact that asserted a critical and undeniable connection between the employee defendants and the derailment. Finally, and perhaps most revealing, the judge reached his decision by imposing on Bryce a wholly unreasonable pleading burden. He required him to plead specific acts of negligence at a time when the plaintiff could not have known what specific actions the engineer or conductor took in connection with the derailment.

The two opinions in *Bryce* illustrated not only a widely shared judicial hostility toward the joinder tactic but also the basic legal technique that many federal judges used to defeat remand motions. Probing from the pleadings to the ultimate merits of a plaintiff's claim, they explored every factual allegation and legal theory raised until they found some ground on which they could deny that the cause of action was truly "joint." Sometimes their task was relatively easy, but sometimes it required ingenuity.[98]

Sometimes, too, the effort seemed wholly *ad hoc*. A 1903 case from the Southern District of Iowa represented an apparently arbitrary method of upholding a removal. While inspecting track, a railroad employee was run down from behind and killed by an unscheduled train. The administratrix of his estate jointly sued the nonresident railroad company and the resident engineer who had been operating the locomotive. Seeking to plead within the *Dixon* rule, the complaint carefully alleged the "joint and concurrent negligence of both." On motion to remand, the court concluded that the employee had been contributorily negligent in not making "diligent inquiry" about "irregular trains" and that different evidence would be required to show negligence on the part of each of the defendants. Those factors, the judge stated without further analysis, somehow meant that the claims were separable.[99] The court denied the motion to remand.

The Tort Joinder Tactic Upheld

For six years the Supreme Court failed to resolve the tort joinder issue, though it continued to drop hints that supported a broad reading of *Dixon*.[100] Then in 1906 it accepted certified questions from the Sixth Circuit that posed the issue squarely. In *Alabama Great Southern Railway Co. v. Thompson*[101] the Court ruled that a railroad could be sued jointly with its operating employees even though the only negligence alleged was against the employees, no allegation of concurrent negligence was made against the company, and *respondeat superior* was the sole basis of the company's liability. Such a cause of action, *Thompson* held, could not be removed on the ground that it contained a separable controversy.

The Court quickly disposed of the railroad's argument, offered with "much earnestness," that joinder denied it a right to be heard in federal court and to have the federal common law applied to its case. "The Federal courts in some States," the Court acknowledged, "hold a different rule as to the doctrine of fellow-servants from that administered in the state courts, and in other ways administer the common law according to their own views."[102] Those differences were irrelevant to the law of joinder, however, and common law rules did not control the separable controversy question. Rather, the question was one of federal statutory construction, and, properly construed, the statute made the existence of a separable controversy turn on the pleadings.

In *Thompson,* the Court tried to place the separable controversy issue on a clear and simple basis, and its statements seemed to guarantee that plaintiffs would enjoy a wide latitude in avoiding the federal courts. The issue turned quite literally, *Thompson* stressed, on "the cause of action stated in the complaint." If the pleadings termed it "joint," that would settle the matter. The decision seemed to obviate questions about the source of the controlling substantive law and the appropriate standard of review. A cause of action pleaded as joint was sufficient to defeat removal on the grounds of separable controversy, the Court insisted in language that appeared to settle the matter beyond cavil, even if "the plaintiff has misconceived his cause of action and had no right to prosecute the defendants jointly."[103]

In spite of its strong language, *Thompson* left loose ends, at least for those determined to find them. One was *Warax* which, the Court explained, "has been much cited and sometimes followed in the Federal courts."[104] Although *Thompson* was clearly inconsistent with *Warax,* the Court still refused to make that conclusion explicit. A second loose end was the question of what law determined whether a joint cause of action existed. On a broad reading of *Thompson*—that as a matter of federal statutory construction the pleadings controlled regardless of whether the plaintiff had "misconceived" his claim under state law—the source of the controlling law appeared to be settled. The Court, however, in *Thompson*'s companion case, *Cincinnati, New Orleans and Texas Pacific Railway Co. v. Bohon,*[105] upheld a state court's denial of a removal petition on state law grounds. Because state law controlled negligence matters and conferred a joint cause of action on the plaintiff, the Court declared, there could be no separable controversy and hence no right to remove. Even though *Bohon* addressed the sensitive context of state court denials of removal petitions, its stress on the significance of state law did not seem entirely consistent with *Thompson*'s exclusive reliance on the form, mistaken or not, of the pleadings. A third loose end was the matter of fraud. The certified questions in *Thompson* did not raise the issue, and the Court passed it off with the most sweeping of asides. "In such cases entirely different questions arise," it commented, "and the Federal courts may and should take such action as will defeat attempts to wrongfully deprive parties entitled to sue in the Federal courts of the protection of their rights in those tribunals."[106]

The following year, in *Wecker v. National Enameling and Stamping Co.,*[107] the Court clarified the fraud issue. Assuming under *Thompson* that the pleadings precluded the presence of a separable controversy, the Court examined affidavits submitted on the motion to remand and concluded that the plaintiff's allegations about the resident employee-defendant were without factual basis. Defendants' affidavits showed that the resident employee had no connection with the injury and no duties that related to it. Plaintiff's affidavit failed to contradict defendants' testimony and relied essentially on speculation to implicate the resident. Such a factual showing, *Wecker* held, justified the conclusion that the resident "was joined for the purpose of defeating the right of the corporation to remove." To the claim that the plaintiff had not known the resident defendant's true relation to the company, the Court declared that "knowledge may be imputed where one willfully closes his eyes to information within his reach."[108] *Wecker* affirmed the denial of plaintiff's motion to remand.

Over the next several years, the Court also clarified the source of law issue. Following *Bohon,* it repeatedly upheld state court denials of removal petitions on the ground that state law determined whether a joint cause of action existed.[109] In 1911 it applied the same rule to a case arising from the lower federal courts, holding that even in the absence of a motion to remand jurisdiction over an action removed on the ground of separable controversy was lacking when the cause of action pleaded was joint under state law.[110] Together, the decisions seemed to establish that in all cases state law determined whether a joint cause of action existed.

With *Thompson, Bohon,* and *Wecker* the Court established the main lines of federal joinder law that continued through the 1940s. Though it heard a dozen more tort joinder cases in the following decade and several more in the 1920s, the later cases broke little new ground. In the following three decades, on only the rarest of occasions did the Court find for a defendant who had been denied the right to remove.[111] Instead, its decisions almost uniformly upheld contested joinders, and in practice their cumulative impact expanded the ability of plaintiffs to join resident defendants and defeat federal jurisdiction.[112]

After *Thompson* the lower federal courts granted remand motions on joinder disputes more readily than they had previously.[113] A number did so, too, even though they harbored grave doubts about the nature of the employee joinder tactic. "[S]ince the decision of the Supreme Court in the Alabama Southern case, supra," noted a Montana federal judge only months after *Thompson* came down, "this court has been called upon to consider a large number of motions to remand."[114] Clearly struggling with the problem of articulating a coherent doctrine on joinders, the judge noted in particular his own concern about the use of the tactic. "[W]here an action is brought by a resident against a nonresident corporation and a subordinate servant who is a citizen of the state, and it is made to appear that the servant is not responsible financially," he explained, "it is difficult to avoid a suspicion that the real and only object of joining the two in the suit is to evade the jurisdiction of the federal court."[115] A federal judge in Minnesota shared that view. "It is probably true," he wrote in 1910, "that in these cases the employes [*sic*] are always joined for the purpose of keeping the actions out of the federal courts."[116] Nevertheless, recognizing that the joinders before them passed muster under *Thompson,* both judges granted the motions to remand. Such overt expressions of skepticism, in fact, were not uncommon when federal judges decided, reluctantly but obediently, to remand actions involving employee joinders.[117]

What *Thompson* did for plaintiffs on remand motions in the federal courts, *Bohon* and its progeny did for them on removal petitions in the state courts. By upholding a state court's right to deny a removal petition and by stressing that state law determined whether a joint cause of action existed, the Court's decisions increased substantially the number of cases in which state courts could safely deny removal petitions. The result was to encourage the state courts to use their authority more frequently, preventing many defendants from forcing plaintiffs to fight remand motions in the federal courts.[118]

In spite of the increased strength of the joinder tactic, however, a number of federal judges continued to pose obstacles to its use in tort actions. The spirit of

Warax, if not its name, continued to roam some of the lower courts. On the one hand, most federal judges apparently believed that *Thompson* had in effect over-ruled *Warax.* Although they did not generally record that conclusion or attempt to draw inferences from it,[119] they did abruptly stop citing Taft's opinion. The dubi-ous distinction that one federal judge drew in 1908, that *Warax* continued to control "in nondeath cases,"[120] proved singular. On the other hand, a number of the decisions that refused to order remands after *Thompson* seemed to apply in various altered forms the broad principle of *Warax*—that causes of action based on different theories of liability could not, regardless of the pleadings, be joint. Some distinguished overtly among the theories of liability involved, and others delved into the legal or factual merits to the point where they identified some basis on which they could either split the plaintiff's cause of action or find that it did not truly assert a claim against the resident defendant.[121] Seven years after *Thompson* the Supreme Court, implicitly noting the extent to which some of the lower courts were defeating the joinder tactic, found it necessary to instruct them that on a motion to remand they were "not to decide whether a flaw could be picked in the declaration on special demurrer."[122]

In one way or another, then, a number of federal judges effectively limited *Thompson.* A few expressly denied that the Supreme Court had meant what it said about "misconceived" pleadings,[123] and without such bluntness others imple-mented that view. The "true rule," a Missouri federal judge stated blandly some six years after *Thompson,* "is that the federal court upon a proper petition for removal may examine into the merits" of a plaintiff's claim.[124] After the Supreme Court repeatedly reaffirmed the *Bohon* rule, the lower courts began consistently to apply state law, not federal common law, to determine whether a joint cause of action existed, but many of them examined pleadings closely and, if state law did not recognize the joint action pleaded, denied remands.[125] An Oregon judge in 1911 probably summarized a widely shared view. The "temptation" to join a resident defendant to prevent removal was "so great," he declared, that the practice "invite[d] the closest scrutiny."[126] Although the chances of a successful joinder were much better after *Thompson* than before it, lower court scrutiny often went far beyond the guidelines announced in the Court's "leading" case on the subject and continued to pose risks for tort plaintiffs who used the tactic.

Although doctrinal changes after *Thompson* made joinder to defeat diversity more reliable and promising, plaintiffs continued to face practical obstacles in using it. Resident defendants were not always readily available, and in many cases those available were friends or neighbors, fellow employees, or job superiors. And *Powers,* of course, prevented plaintiffs from using the socially less divisive tactic of dismissing resident defendants prior to trial. For injured employees, joining such defendants could create tense personal or job-related problems, especially in the common but dangerous situation where a necessary resident defendant was the injured plaintiff's work gang boss, foreman, or supervisor. Further, joinders provoked corporate defendants into particularly vigorous legal, if not job-related, countermeasures. In cases brought for claims below the jurisdic-tional minimum, there was usually little that a defendant could do to move the action into federal court and relatively little incentive to try. Joinder cases, how-ever, were legally more vulnerable and economically more important. As a result, corporate defendants were more likely to remove them and compel plaintiffs to conduct remand fights. If the company were determined and the claim large, it could put on evidence and submit briefs that could require expensive and time-consuming responses. Between arguments that the joinder was fraudulent and the controversy separable—especially when the issue was before one of the lower court judges known to give joinder matters "the closest scrutiny"—plaintiff's remand motion could well be lost.

While the tactical use of the jurisdictional amount represented a surrender to the corporate system, however, a successful joinder allowed the plaintiff to escape. For individuals litigating against national corporations, joinder carried both the risks and the rewards of high-stakes litigation, and cumulatively the successes and failures of joinders helped define the system's operative scope.

The Tension Between Substance and Procedure

The Supreme Court's joinder decisions after 1900 gradually formed one area of federal law into a strong, if not guaranteed, tool for tort plaintiffs who were suing national corporations. From that perspective the joinder cases seemed inconsistent with the social results of many of the Court's common law decisions in the decades around the turn of the century. It was striking, for example, that the same nine Justices who in 1900 paved the way for *Thompson* with the important if ambiguous decision in *Dixon* would also hand down within a few months before and after that case the harsh decisions in *Voigt* and *Patton,* both of which imposed severe burdens on precisely the same type of plaintiffs whom *Dixon* most benefited. Further, *Dixon* arguably and *Thompson* certainly were far more important to such plaintiffs than was either *Voigt* or *Patton*—or, for that matter, than was *Baugh* itself. As long as tort plaintiffs could stay out of the federal courts on jurisdictional grounds, the common law rules applied there were irrelevant to them. And further, as long as the joinder device was available, plaintiffs could anchor themselves in the state courts and at the same time assert damages claims well above the jurisdictional amount.

The joinder tactic confronted the Court with a critical choice, one that aroused conflicting concerns and stirred opposing values. The conflicts helped explain the Court's delay in addressing the employee joinder issue, its awkward hesitations in *Powers* and *Dixon,* its ambivalence about *Warax,* and the thin and sometimes deeply buried fault lines that ran through its post-*Thompson* opinions.[127] The Court's separable controversy precedents, on which *Dixon* and *Thompson* relied so heavily, were not fully determinative. They provided support for the results in those cases, but the Court could have distinguished them. Indeed, the Court's precedents from the 1870s on the fellow servant and parol evidence rules had posed no insurmountable problem when its views on those issues began shifting in the 1880s and 1890s.

Powerful considerations pushed the Court to curtail the joinder tactic. The Justices recognized its social significance as well as the results that the *Warax* rule promised. Moreover, regardless of their varying social sympathies, the Justices knew that joinder had become a tool of widespread jurisdictional manipulation that undoubtedly caused abuses. The tactic frustrated the announced purposes of diversity jurisdiction and often negated the right to remove, and its success represented a triumph of the lawyer's cleverness over the law's intent. Certainly there was support in the business community—and vigorous institutional support in the lower courts—for an authoritative and forceful effort to curtail or eliminate the tactic.

Indeed, the lower courts often strained to defeat joinders. Many federal judges seemed to resent deeply the fact that plaintiffs were purposely avoiding them and negating what they regarded as their rightful jurisdiction. There was, after all, no doubt in anyone's mind, at least in cases where the codefendants were resident employees, why plaintiffs were suing multiple parties. In some cases the lower courts may have reacted to particularly egregious facts that made the plaintiff's purpose gratingly obvious or his methods nakedly manipulative. In other cases they may have reacted to the power of a defendant's more personal plea that the federal judge alone stood between it and consignment to a state court where the dangers of local prejudice threatened. To some extent, too, they were probably reacting to what they perceived as a surge in unfair and unethical litigation tactics in tort actions. Around the turn of the century many elite lawyers associated such tactics with the emergence of a new and specialized plaintiffs' personal injury bar, a bar that in the professional opinion of the day included a large number of "ambulance chasers" and other unethical practitioners.[128]

Because ensuring a broad jurisdiction for the federal courts and protecting the interests of national corporations were generally compatible in the system of corporate diversity litigation, it would be impossible to determine the precise extent to which either of the two distinct purposes motivated federal judges. In some judges' minds the two attitudes may well have been almost indistinguishable. Nevertheless, it still seems likely that in some joinder cases—*Warax,* for example—specific social values favoring corporate enterprise were important considerations in leading federal judges to strain to uphold removals.

Judge John W. Philips of the Western District of Missouri was one of the federal judges who consistently opposed the joinder tactic and found ways to avoid both *Dixon* and *Thompson.* Philips announced his views in 1904. Use of the joinder device was becoming "so universal," he declared, that every case required the "closest scrutiny" from the courts. Otherwise, "the practical result is to be a denial to nonresident corporations of the right of removal."[129] Philips made it clear that he would not allow such a result. In cases where controlling doctrine could easily have allowed employee joinders to block removal, he regularly found ways to defeat the tactic and uphold federal jurisdiction.[130]

Philips's joinder decisions were particularly suspicious because he carried a reputation as one of the most procorporate judges on the federal bench. "In fourteen years," declared an article in *Everybody's Magazine,* "only one final verdict against a railway in a personal injury case was secured before Judge Philips."[131] Critics accused Philips of favoring corporate interests and of operating under the influence of a "kitchen cabinet" headed by the local attorney for the Standard Oil Company. Further, they charged him with repeatedly accepting free transportation and other favors from the railroads, including the use of the Rock Island Railroad's "directors' car" whenever he traveled.[132] Philips himself made his general social views apparent in 1905 when he accused legislatures of being "inconsiderate, rash, and reckless" and sweepingly denounced ambulance chasers, political reformers, and those who attempted "to promote pernicious litigation by abrogating long-established rules of law."[133] His views on tort litigation seemed equally clear. Personal injury actions were increasing, he explained in 1904, "because lawyer and client stand as full partners in the spoil."[134] Given Philips's personal social views, his reputation as a procorporate judge, and the apparently consistent lack of success that tort plaintiffs suing railroads had in his court, it seems likely that his decisions defeating the joinder tactic were written at least in part from a sympathy for corporate enterprise and for the specific purpose of ensuring a favorable federal forum for corporate defendants.

Although Philips's sympathies toward corporate enterprise were probably shared by a number of federal judges, it seems equally likely that others who opposed the joinder tactic did so primarily because it offended their ideas of the proper scope of federal jurisdiction, not because they specifically wished to help corporations. In that regard two typical employee joinder decisions by federal Judge Charles F. Amidon of North Dakota, one of the most ardent political progressives on the federal bench, are particularly instructive.[135] In 1903, after *Dixon* and before *Thompson,* Amidon frustrated the joinder tactic and upheld a removal in *Helms v. Northern Pacific Railway Co.*[136] Distinguishing *Dixon* and following Taft's analysis in *Warax,* Amidon canvassed treatises and cases from a variety of jurisdictions to establish the principle that causes of action based on different grounds of liability were separate and not joint. Eight years later, and five years after *Thompson,* Amidon again upheld a removal, even though plaintiff joined a resident employee as a codefendant. In *Floyt v. Shenango Furnace Co.*[137] he abandoned any reference to *Warax* and the theory that causes of action based on different grounds of liability were separable controversies. Instead, he rested on the entirely different ground that the plaintiff charged the employee only with "nonfeasance" and that under "well-established principles of the common law" such an employee "was not liable to third parties or coemployes for nonfeasance." Because the "plaintiff has no cause of action against the employe,"[138] Amidon reasoned, the complaint evidenced a fraudulent joinder and did not, therefore, prevent removal.

Amidon's opinions in *Helms* and *Floyt* were devoid of references to social context, and the decisions seemed inconsistent with his progressive political views. Neither his sympathies for injured workers nor his suspicion of corporate size and wealth induced him to accept the joinder tactic. If he had been so inclined, too, he could easily have made and supported decisions to remand in both cases.

In spite of the careful doctrinal analyses in the two cases, they suggest that Amidon was led to his decisions neither by the force of logic nor by the command of precedent. Although *Thompson* forced him to abandon *Warax* and the distinct "ground of liability" theory he had developed so fully in *Helms,* in *Floyt* he turned to an alternative approach that again allowed him to reach the same result. His reasoning seemed arbitrary and purposeful. Amidon failed to distinguish, discuss, or even cite *Thompson* or any of the Supreme Court's subsequent decisions that construed the separable controversy act and consistently denied removals. In addition, he ignored Minnesota law which, under *Bohon* and its progeny, should have determined whether plaintiff stated a cause of action against the employee. Instead, Amidon denied the cause of action on "well-established principles of the common law." Finally, relying on *Wecker* to support his conclusion about fraudulent joinder, he ignored important differences between the cases that made *Wecker* easily and persuasively distinguishable.[139]

Together, Amidon's opinions and his progressive political views suggest that he was animated by a desire to keep control over federal jurisdiction in the hands of the national courts and by a concern over the dangers of allowing plaintiffs to manipulate jurisdiction so easily. Although his progressivism was hardly typical of the federal bench, his suspicion of the joinder tactic surely was. His response suggests that at least much of the determined opposition to the joinder tactic among lower court judges arose not so much from any specific sympathy for corporate enterprise but from the desire to protect what they regarded as the integrity of their jurisdiction.[140] Indeed, Amidon's political atypicality strengthens that conclusion. If a dedicated progressive resented such jurisdictional manipulation even though it brought results that he most likely regarded as socially desirable, it would seem even more likely that those who did not share his political values would also scorn such manipulation.

Regardless of the forces that pushed the lower judiciary to restrict joinders, however, other considerations ultimately moved the Supreme Court in the opposite direction. It is possible, even, that one or more of the Justices may have been induced to tolerate the joinder tactic at least in part as a means of limiting the federal common law of master and servant. If any of the Justices were so moved, Harlan and to a lesser extent White seemed the most likely candidates. In 1900 both had dissented in the *Dixon* joinder case. Although neither wrote, their dissents were almost certainly rooted in a wish to protect the jurisdiction of the national courts and not in any special sympathy for corporate interests.[141] Subsequently, both cast aside their doubts and accepted in *Thompson* a rule that was far more sweeping and forceful than the one they had rejected six years earlier in *Dixon.* One intervening factor that might have helped alter their views was the Court's 1904 decision in *Northern Pacific Railway Co. v. Dixon.*[142] Outraged by the Court's application of the fellow servant rule where it seemed wholly unjustified, the moderately conservative White wrote a scathing dissent in which Harlan and two others joined.[143] Reacting harshly and angrily, White accused the majority of giving the fellow servant rule "contradictory" applications for the apparent purpose of denying recovery "in any event." The decision, he concluded bluntly, made the railroad "a licensed wrongdoer as respects its employees."[144] The year after *Thompson,* moreover, both White and Harlan exhibited their strong interest in limiting the employers' defenses when they voted in another close five-to-four split to construe a federal statute to restrict both assumption of risk and contributory negligence.[145] Of the two, Harlan was the more likely to have joined *Thompson* on instrumentalist grounds. Compared with White, he was more result oriented; he dissented more commonly from the Court's harshest decisions under the federal common law; and he had consistently opposed the federal fellow servant rule.[146]

Whether Harlan, White, or any of the other Justices leaned toward a broad joinder rule in some part to limit the federal common law, it seems extremely unlikely that a majority of the Court shared that view. Justices Rufus W. Peckham, Henry B. Brown, William R. Day, and particularly David J. Brewer, the author of *Baugh,* consistently supported a broad fellow servant rule, and Justices Oliver Wendell Holmes, Jr., and Joseph McKenna did so on occasion.[147] All six, however, joined *Thompson.* Indeed, Peckham, Brewer, and Brown were with the majority in the 1900 *Dixon* joinder case, where they were joined by two other adherents to the federal fellow servant rule, Justices George Shiras, Jr., and Horace Gray. It was apparent, then, that the Court adopted the broad joinder doctrines of *Dixon* and *Thompson* with the full approval of *Baugh*'s staunchest supporters.

The considerations that led Brewer and the supporters of the federal fellow servant rule to adopt a broad joinder policy were thus essential to the Court's decisions in *Dixon* and *Thompson*. One, surely, was the potentially expansive nature of the separable controversy statute. If not cabined sharply, it could throw federal procedural law into confusion and flood the national courts with cases. The Court had guarded against that danger long before the tort joinder tactic came into widespread use. During the preceding thirty-five years, one federal judge noted in 1910, the Supreme Court had reversed findings that a separable controversy existed in thirty-three of the thirty-seven cases that had come before it.[148] Taft's reasoning, in point of fact, was too powerful. *Warax* not only conflicted with established doctrine, but its application also threatened to inundate the federal courts with separable controversies drawn not just from tort suits against corporations but from all areas of the law. *Warax* stood for a principle of fragmentation, one that would create separable controversies in all employee joinder suits and, once adopted, could not easily be restricted—assuming even that such restriction was desirable—to that single class of actions.

A second consideration was more technical, the simplicity and utility of a "face of the pleadings" rule. Such a rule—determining the issue by reference to the allegations stated in the complaint—was relatively easy to apply and eliminated for the most part any need to inquire into difficult issues of fact. The latter was an especially important advantage in a rule designed to regulate a frequently recurring but nevertheless preliminary issue of jurisdiction. Moreover, such a rule was consistent with the general approach of federal procedural law. The jurisdictional amount was determined, with narrow exceptions, by the face of the complaint,[149] and similarly a federal question sufficient to confer jurisdiction had to appear on the face of the complaint, not by way of counterclaim, defense, or reply.[150] In both instances a face of the pleadings rule served to simplify determinations of jurisdiction and, at least in the latter case, to help control the expanding federal caseload.[151]

Perhaps most important, the Court's liberal–individualist, freedom-of-contract ideology that contributed to the results in *Voigt* and *Northern Assurance* as well as *Baugh* was only obliquely relevant to the joinder issue. Unlike a direct commitment to protect business interests, which would have disposed the Justices against the rules announced in *Dixon* and *Thompson,* the more complicated values of the Court's liberal individualism may have seen the joinder tactic as only a minor threat in practice and an unimportant detail in theory.[152] It may have been decisive, in fact, that in *Dixon* and *Thompson* the Court was not required to address explicitly social issues or lay down a rule that directly implicated the Court's fundamental values. Regardless of how many plaintiffs avoided the federal courts by using the joinder tactic, the principles and values for which the fellow servant rule and the federal common law stood remained officially and prominently in place.

Those considerations, however, are partial and preliminary. The shifting tensions between joinder doctrine and the federal common law, and more widely among all of the critical procedural and substantive rules applied in the system of corporate diversity litigation, are parts of a broad and complicated story. *Powers, Dixon,* and *Thompson,* as we shall see, were not unusual. They were, instead, characteristic of the Court's changing attitudes in the decades around the turn of the century. A more considered and complete assessment of their significance and of the Court's other related substantive and procedural decisions must await an examination of the whole history of the system of corporate diversity jurisdiction.

Chapter 6

Removal and the Problems of Local Prejudice: Three Perspectives on the System

Individual plaintiffs and corporate defendants fought persistently and tenaciously over removal for a simple but compelling reason. The nature of the forum helped determine both the likelihood that plaintiffs might win and, if they did, the amounts they would receive. Even more important, in the far broader informal legal process, the nature of the forum substantially raised or lowered the litigation value of plaintiffs' claims and therefore the amounts at which the parties would ultimately agree to settle their disputes. The reasons why forum selection had that impact were many, but two of them operated widely and forcefully. Social and institutional factors made the federal courts particularly burdensome forums for many individual plaintiffs, and in critical areas the federal common law provided corporations with highly favorable substantive law.

Corporations, however, painted a different picture. They minimized or denied the importance of the practical burdens that federal jurisdiction imposed on individuals, and they ignored the substance of the federal common law in favor of heralding its ostensibly nonpartisan "uniformity." Ultimately, they defended their use of removal on the ground that the federal courts protected them from "local prejudice." Although there seems little doubt about the pervasive role that both practical burdens and the federal common law played in corporate diversity litigation, the role that local prejudice played was much less clear.

The significance of local prejudice presents an unavoidable problem for any attempt to estimate the overall calculus of advantage in the system of corporate diversity litigation. If local prejudice deprived corporations of fair trials in the state courts with any regularity or frequency, that fact would constitute a major counterbalance to the practical and legal advantages that corporate defendants reaped from the availability of federal jurisdiction. Conversely, if local prejudice deprived corporate defendants of fair trials only rarely or in unusual circumstances, then it would provide little counterweight to those advantages. The more that federal jurisdiction protected corporate defendants from biased forums, in other words, the less was the unfairness of imposing on individual plaintiffs the disadvantages that came with removal. Conversely, the less that federal jurisdiction protected against biased forums, the greater was the unfairness of imposing those burdens on individual litigants.

According to orthodox legal thought, the purpose of diversity jurisdiction was to protect nonresidents from local prejudice by giving them a fair and impartial forum in which to try their claims or defenses. From the 1870s when the system of corporate diversity litigation began taking shape to the 1940s when it disintegrated, judges, scholars, politicians, and practitioners argued continuously over the extent to which local prejudice against foreign corporations existed or influenced judicial proceedings. Defenders of diversity jurisdiction warned that the threat was real and substantial, stressing its special force in parts of the South and West. Critics of the jurisdiction denied its existence, at least as anything more than a rare, isolated, and disappearing phenomenon.

Most scholars would surely agree that at various times there was prejudice, and sometimes open hostility, toward foreign corporations in many states, that those community attitudes probably had some influence on the courts, and that the state courts seemed more susceptible to such influence than did the federal courts.[1] There seems to be no way, however, to measure either the extent to which local prejudice in fact influenced the state courts or the extent to which the federal courts were in fact "fairer" forums. Indeed, the terms "prejudice" and "fairer" are themselves conclusory, problematic, and value laden. Ostensibly "anticorporate" attitudes could be based on legitimate views as to what was "reasonable," what was "due care," or what a party "should have known." Some of the rules and procedures in the federal courts, too, could be seen as "biased" toward corporate defendants in practice or intent. Not surprisingly, the comparative evaluation of state and federal courts has for two hundred years constituted a persistently recurring and highly controversial political issue in the American judicial system. One scholar concluded, in fact, that efforts to assess the comparative virtues and defects of the parallel state and federal court systems are "futile" because the project raises "an empirical question for which no empirical measure is possible."[2]

Although precise or quantified answers seem unobtainable, the history of two specific removal statutes furnishes some perspective on both the system of corporate diversity litigation and the significance of local prejudice in that system. The Reconstruction Congresses enacted two statutes that were specifically addressed to the problem. Both the "prejudice and local influence act" of 1867 and the Civil Rights Act of 1866 sought to protect blacks and northern whites working in the South by broadening their access to the national courts. The former expanded the right to remove under general diversity jurisdiction, and the latter extended both original and removal jurisdiction to cases involving certain new federal civil rights. An examination of litigation under the two statutes provides three useful perspectives on the system.

First, decisions under the former, commonly referred to simply as the "local prejudice act," show that the Supreme Court construed the statute in a manner that paralleled the way that it interpreted the quite different language of the separable controversy act. Until the early 1890s the Court construed the local prejudice act narrowly to limit removals; then for the next dozen years it stretched the act and broadened the right of national corporations to remove; finally, in 1905, it again reversed course and drastically narrowed the scope of removal under the statute. The cases under the local prejudice act thus strengthen the conclusion that the nature and sequence of the Court's decisions under the separable controversy act were neither random and accidental nor dictated by doctrinal logic or statutory language. They show, instead, that the decisions under both statutes reflected the Court's calculated and changing responses to the system of corporate diversity litigation.

Second, the history of the local prejudice act also suggests that the dangers corporations faced from local prejudice may, in fact, have been considerably less than has often been claimed. Although the record is far from complete or unambiguous, the reported cases indicate that corporate defendants found it extremely difficult to produce evidence of local prejudice and that they were not, at least generally, able to persuade the federal courts that local prejudice endangered their rights in the state courts. The history of the act, in short, suggests that the influence of local prejudice on the state courts may have been overstated and that its dangers may have justified removal in only a relatively small number of unusual cases.

Third, the history of the Civil Rights Act illuminates the role of local prejudice in the system of corporate diversity litigation by offering a revealing contrast. It establishes the fact that there was an almost complete disregard for the problem of local prejudice when the dangers of unfairness affected a different area of law and a different social group. The legitimate concern in the federal system with the dangers of local prejudice, in other words, was in practice sharply limited, and it did not imply solicitude for all litigants, even those able to show that they were victims of unconstitutional state actions. Further, the history of the Civil Rights Act highlights the fact that diversity jurisdiction and removal—irrespective of whether local prejudice operated against corporate defendants often, sometimes, or not at all—conferred on those corporations a truly exceptional procedural benefit. The right to remove gave corporate defendants legal advantages that many other defendants did not possess; it conferred those advantages free from the burden of making any kind of showing that some real prejudice actually threatened them; and it bestowed those advantages even though federal removal law compelled another well-known class of defendants—which suffered from extreme, systematic, and widely recognized forms of local prejudice—to take their chances in the very state courts that so often abused them. To defend the existence of diversity jurisdiction on the basis of the protection it supposedly provided against local prejudice, in other words, raises fundamental questions of social and legal policy but does not begin to resolve them.

The Local Prejudice Act and the System

The original local prejudice act[3] allowed nonresidents to remove regardless of whether they were plaintiffs or defendants and to do so "at any time before the final hearing or trial." To remove under the act, parties had only to submit affidavits stating that they had reason to believe that from "prejudice or local influence" they would be unable to obtain justice in the state courts. For twenty years the act had relatively little significance for corporate diversity litigation. Although the minimal requirement of a simple affidavit made removal for local prejudice easy, the statute offered little incentive for corporate use. Its plaintiff removal provision was irrelevant to the system, and its extended time provision was a minor consideration. In the 1870s and early 1880s the system was still taking shape, and neither corporate removal practices nor plaintiffs' countertactics were fully developed.[4] More important, the basic restrictions that applied to general diversity jurisdiction also limited removals under the local prejudice act. The statute expressly imposed the standard jurisdictional amount requirement, and beginning in the early 1870s the Supreme Court ruled in a series of cases that removal for local prejudice required complete diversity between the adversary parties.[5]

The statute suddenly took on new importance in the late 1880s, however, when the full development of the system coincided with the enactment of the Judiciary Act of 1887–88. In its second section the act consolidated the removal provisions for general diversity and federal question cases with the provisions for removal under the separable controversy act and the local prejudice act. It made a number of substantial changes in the law and generally narrowed the scope of federal jurisdiction.[6] Its language, however, was in many places ambiguous.[7]

Four changes in the local prejudice provision immediately raised questions that pertained to the system's operation. One was whether the defendant's time for filing the removal petition had been shortened. The 1867 act allowed removal "at any time before the final hearing or trial," and the Supreme Court had established that this meant that defendants could remove even after one or more trials on the merits if, for whatever reason, a full retrial were ordered.[8] The 1887–88 act deleted the word "final" and allowed defendants to remove "at any time before the trial." A second question concerned the procedure for removal and the nature of the showing required to establish the existence of local prejudice. Whereas the original act required only a good faith affidavit, the 1887–88 act required that local prejudice "shall be made to appear" to the court. The statute offered no indication of how that showing was to be made.[9] A third question was whether the jurisdictional amount was required. Unlike the original act, the version enacted in the 1887–88 statute did not include any reference to a jurisdictional minimum.

The fourth issue was whether removal for local prejudice required complete diversity of citizenship. Although the language of the Judiciary Act was spare, it did provide a basis for arguing that Congress had made a substantial change in prior law. Referring to suits "in which there is controversy between a citizen of the State in which the suit is brought and a citizen of another State," the original act had provided that "such citizen of another State" could remove. Using identical introductory language, the Judiciary Act of 1887–88 provided that "any defendant, being such citizen of another State," could remove. Insertion of the phrase "any defendant" arguably singled out one of several defendants and suggested that the statute eliminated the complete diversity requirement. But the language was, at best, ambiguous. The statute could also be construed far more narrowly to mean that unlike the general diversity provision, the local prejudice clause did not require that all defendants join in the removal petition itself.[10] According to that construction, insertion of the phrase "any defendant" would simply mean that one nonresident defendant with diverse citizenship could not be forced to stay in state court by the refusal of other nonresident defendants with diverse citizenship to join in a petition for removal.

Although the Judiciary Act of 1887–88 was uniformly recognized as an effort to restrict federal jurisdiction, in its immediate wake the lower federal courts threatened to construe its local prejudice clause to enlarge that jurisdiction drastically. The statute's ambiguities gave them some justification but could hardly explain their apparent enthusiasm for construing the statute so broadly. Sound principles of statutory construction did not support the use of bare and ambiguous language in an admittedly badly drafted statute—whose general purpose the Supreme Court repeatedly identified as the restriction of federal jurisdiction—to expand the jurisdiction of the national courts. Even less could sound principles of statutory construction lend support when expansive readings required such radical doctrinal changes as eliminating the jurisdictional amount or abandoning the doctrine of complete diversity. In moving in those directions, at least some of the lower courts were apparently driven more by sectional, economic, or ideological motives than by the compulsion of the statutory language. The Judiciary Act of 1887–88, an Oregon federal judge noted, might be termed a "confederate" measure.[11] Judge John F. Dillon, a fervent unionist who advocated broad federal jurisdiction, declared it "reactionary" legislation that damaged the national courts.[12]

By the late 1880s, too, removal had clearly emerged as a major corporate litigation tool, and the countertactics of claim discounting and joinder were coming into common use. Few federal judges could have failed to recognize that expanded jurisdiction under the amended local prejudice act would be a boon to corporate defendants. Whatever the motives of the judges who decided the cases, there was little question who would benefit from a broadly conceived jurisdiction under the new local prejudice provision.

An 1888 decision by federal Circuit Judge Howell E. Jackson, later a United States Supreme Court Justice, illustrated the possibilities that the clause offered for expanding corporate access to the national courts. Both the claim and the party alignment in *Whelan v. New York, Lake Erie & Western Railroad Co.*[13] were standard. A street railway passenger, injured when the streetcar he was riding in collided with a railroad locomotive, brought suit in an Ohio state court. He alleged a joint cause of action against the railroad, the street railway company, and two other railroads that had leased the tracks to the operating road. The plaintiff and three of the corporate defendants were citizens of Ohio, and the operating railroad was a citizen of New York. All the defendants demurred, in effect a motion to dismiss, and the state court overruled the demurrers. At that point, the nonresident railroad filed a petition to remove on the ground of local prejudice. In an elaborate opinion, Jackson upheld the removal.

On each of the four issues raised by the amendments to the local prejudice act *Whelan* adopted the construction that expanded the statute's reach.[14] On the timing issue, it held that a demurrer was not a "trial" and that removal was still proper, as it had been under the original local prejudice act, "at any time before the (final) trial."[15] Thus, *Whelan* extended the time that defendants had to file their petitions and expanded the actions that they could take in state court before deciding to remove. On the procedural–evidentiary issue, the decision held that removal was authorized on the simple basis of defendant's affidavit, that plaintiff could not dispute the affidavit's statements, and that the court was not to make any further inquiry into the matter.[16] In short, it placed defendant's right to remove for local prejudice almost beyond challenge. Concerning the jurisdictional amount, both *Whelan*'s reasoning and its statements implied, though they did not decide, that suits for less than the jurisdictional amount could be removed for local prejudice.[17] Finally, on the issue of complete diversity, *Whelan* held that the statute established an exception to the general rule and that minimum diversity sufficed to allow a federal court to hear the case.[18] The latter two conclusions—

combined with the right to automatic removal on the basis of an affidavit that could not be challenged—made the new local prejudice act an overpowering tactical tool for corporations. It would enable them to negate both claim discounting and joinder, plaintiffs' most important and widely used antiremoval tactics.

Whelan quickly became a leading if controversial case. In separate decisions on circuit in 1888 two Supreme Court Justices, John M. Harlan and David J. Brewer, rejected its holding on the procedural–evidentiary issue, and Harlan expressed further disagreement with its dictum about the jurisdictional amount.[19] Nevertheless, a number of the lower courts agreed with its conclusions, and only on the procedural–evidentiary issue did a clear majority of decisions seem to reject it.[20] On the complete diversity question, *Whelan* seemed to win general approval, especially after Jackson qualified its holding the following year. In *Thouron v. East Tennessee, Virginia, & Georgia Railway Co.*,[21] he held that nonresident defendants could remove for local prejudice only when all of the plaintiffs were residents of the forum state. The *Whelan–Thouron* rule, that minimum diversity was sufficient to allow removal if all the plaintiffs were residents of the forum, quickly picked up support in the lower courts.[22]

Although the Supreme Court eventually rejected *Whelan* on every point, its decisions over the next fifteen years reflected the pressures of the system's most intense phase. Quickly, and before the political and social pressures of the 1890s began to intensify, the Court resolved the jurisdictional amount and timing issues and a significant part of the procedural–evidentiary question, in each instance doing so in ways that restricted federal jurisdiction. The social conflicts of the 1890s, however, led the Court to reverse direction. For more than a decade it allowed and encouraged an extended federal jurisdiction by refusing to settle the complete diversity question, the most critical legal issue in the system. Only in late 1905, after it had resolved its views on the more general role of joinder in the system, did it finally decide that issue. Its decisive decision on the scope of the local prejudice act came barely two months before its major decision in *Thompson* which similarly limited the separable controversy act as an antijoinder device.

The Court's first major decision under the local prejudice act came in 1890, the same year it handed down its opinion in *Austin* refusing to bar the delayed upward amendment tactic. *In re Pennsylvania Co.*[23] quickly answered the jurisdictional amount question, rejecting *Whalen*'s comments and holding that the standard monetary requirement applied to suits under the new clause. The Court relied heavily on Harlan's two-year-old circuit decision to that effect,[24] and its reasoning suggested that it regarded the question as a relatively simple one. First, the Court explained, "we should bear in mind the history of the law, and read the whole of the two [original and amended] sections together." Because the jurisdictional minimum was required in the original, "we naturally expect to find the same amount required" in the amended version.[25] Second, the language and structure of the Judiciary Act's second section, which consolidated general removal provisions with special ones, showed that the local prejudice clause "describes only a special case comprised in the preceding [general removal] clauses."[26] Thus, because the general removal clause required the jurisdictional amount, the local prejudice act necessarily did also.

Even though the Court's second reason was persuasive, its first was not. There was, after all, no basis for reading the old and new statutes as consistent when the latter changed the former. And regardless of whatever one might "naturally expect," the fact remained that the amended statute dropped the jurisdictional amount requirement that the earlier statute had expressly mandated. If reading the two versions together supported any proposition, it was surely that the new statute had eliminated the jurisdictional minimum.

The Court's willingness to adopt its unconvincing first reason as a basis for continuing the jurisdictional amount requirement was significant, then, not for any light it cast on issues of statutory construction, but for the way it illuminated the attitudes of the Justices. In 1890 they were simply determined to cut federal jurisdiction. The Justices were not particularly demanding of whatever reasoning permitted them to reach that end, and they were not affected by the fact that the construction they adopted would harm the litigation interests of corporate defendants. *Pennsylvania* rested on the same social attitudes and outlook that had led the Justices to their comparable decision earlier that same year in *Austin*.

Pennsylvania also settled part of the procedural–evidentiary question and in doing so rejected *Whelan*'s automatic removal rule. The language "it shall be made to appear" was significantly different from the original act's requirement of a simple affidavit. "Our opinion is that the Circuit Court must be legally (not merely morally) satisfied of the truth of the allegation" concerning local prejudice.[27] That required "some proof suitable to the nature of the case," which meant at least "an affidavit of a credible person" and "a statement of facts in such affidavit, which sufficiently evince the truth of the allegation."[28] The Court did not, however, resolve the whole issue. It refused to specify "[t]he amount and manner of proof required in each case,"[29] and it failed to decide whether plaintiffs had a right to be heard and to submit counteraffidavits on the issue. Those matters, *Pennsylvania* concluded, "must be left to the discretion of the court."[30]

Barely a year later, in January 1892, the Court rejected *Whelan*'s broad timing rule. In *Fisk v. Henarie*[31] it stressed the fact that the Judiciary Act of 1887–88 struck the word "final" from the phrase in the original act that had allowed removal at "any time before the final trial." The change, the Court explained, "was manifestly to restrain the volume of litigation pouring into the Federal courts" and was consistent with the purpose of the Judiciary Act of 1887–88 "to restrict the jurisdiction" of those courts.[32] Relying on decisions construing similar language in the Judiciary Act of 1875, *Fisk* held that the new wording meant that the removal petition had to be filed at any time "before or at the term at which the cause could first be tried."[33] Although the time during which parties could remove for local prejudice remained longer than under the general removal statute, *Fisk* established a shorter removal period than *Whelan* had recognized, and it eliminated the possibility of removing under a new trial order after a first trial.[34]

Thus by the beginning of 1892, less than five years after passage of the amended local prejudice act, the Court had settled two of the four issues that the amendments raised and established at least general guidelines for dealing with the third. On each of the three the Court rejected *Whelan*. On each of the three, too, its ruling served to narrow federal jurisdiction, fully consistent with the Court's recognition of the purpose of the Judiciary Act of 1887–88 and, for the most part, inconsistent with the litigation advantage of corporate defendants. Together, *Fisk* and *Pennsylvania* blocked numerous removal attempts and undoubtedly discouraged many others.[35]

On the fourth issue, whether the statute required complete diversity, the Court temporized. In separate circuit opinions in 1891 both Chief Justice Melville W. Fuller and Justice L. Q. C. Lamar seemed to accept the minimum diversity rule, though each avoided the issue by remanding on the ground taken in *Thouron* that some of the plaintiffs were nonresidents.[36] The following year in *Fisk* the full Court avoided the issue. Ordering a remand on the ground that the removal petition was filed too late, *Fisk* ignored the holding of the court below that the statute did not require complete diversity.[37] Then, in 1894 a unanimous Court expressly declared the issue unsettled. "Whether this act permits one of two or more defendants to remove any case which he could not have removed under earlier statutes," it stated in *Hanrick v. Hanrick,*[38] "is a question upon which there have been conflicting decisions in the Circuit Courts, and upon which we are not now required to express a definitive opinion."

The Court's treatment of the complete diversity issue paralleled its handling of *Warax* and the general joinder question. The two issues, of course, reflected the same problem of litigation tactics. Because joinder negated removal and still allowed large damage claims to remain in the state courts, it was plaintiffs' most powerful procedural tool. As it came into widespread use in the 1890s, corporate defendants pressed vigorously to establish doctrines to defeat or limit it. Fraudulent joinder was one; the separable controversy statute, especially as construed by *Warax,* was another. So, too, was the local prejudice act—if, but only if, it authorized removal in the absence of complete diversity.

Without further guidance from the Supreme Court, the lower judiciary responded favorably to the argument that "any" nonresident defendant could remove for local prejudice. By the mid-1890s the *Whelan–Thouron* minimum diversity rule prevailed.[39] Though corporations did not use the local prejudice clause nearly as often as they did the separable controversy statute, most likely because of the former's evidentiary requirement, they found it a burdensome but nonetheless effective way to parry the joinder tactic.[40]

The Supreme Court avoided the complete diversity question under the local prejudice act for the same reasons that it temporized on *Warax* and the general joinder issue. The Justices were divided, under pressure, and operating in a period of escalating social tensions. When opponents quickly challenged the federal income tax law of 1894, for example, some of the most prominent lawyers in the nation—William D. Guthrie, James C. Carter, Joseph H. Choate, and Attorney General Richard Olney among others—appeared before the Court to attack and defend it in elaborate and sometimes extreme terms. In March 1895 the Court devoted a week to oral argument in the case. Carter, himself one of the leaders of the conservative bar, defended the tax as a method of moderating a sharpening class conflict "in which the poor always go to the wall." He urged the Court to accept "the voice of the majority" because "the opposing forces of sixty millions of people have become arrayed in hostile ranks upon a question which all men feel is not a question of law, but of legislation."[41] On the other side Choate, one of the great advocates of the nineteenth century, charged that the tax was "communistic" and that its attack on property would destroy "the very keystone of the arch upon which all civilized government rests." Responding aggressively to Carter's plea, he urged the Court to defy the "mighty army of sixty million citizens" who supported the tax and to uphold the Constitution "no matter what the threatened consequences of popular or populistic wrath may be."[42]

After a preliminary opinion and an additional day for reargument, later that same year the Court finally declared the tax unconstitutional. The Justices split five to four. In a series of opinions they echoed the emotions and accusations of counsel. Elections were becoming "a war of the poor against the rich," Justice Stephen J. Field declared, concurring separately in the Court's decision. "The present assault on capital is but the beginning."[43] Dissenting, Justice Henry B. Brown warned of a "national calamity" and the coming "submergence of the liberties of the people in a sordid despotism of wealth."[44]

The next year the decade's conflicts reached frenzied proportions when both the Populists and the Democrats nominated William Jennings Bryan of Nebraska to run for president on a platform that directly attacked the Supreme Court. Senator Benjamin R. Tillman of South Carolina—"Pitchfork Ben" Tillman—led the way, bluntly accusing the Court of ruling "in the interest of monopolies and corporations."[45] Governor John Peter Altgeld of Illinois charged the federal courts with "astounding pretension and usurpation of power" and sounded the partisan refrain that federal judges "have the same passions and prejudices that other men have."[46] Defenders of the federal courts responded in kind. When the governor of Pennsylvania joined the attack on the Supreme Court's decisions, a lawyers' magazine labeled his remarks "ridiculous" as well as "incendiary and foolish." The governor, the journal declared, was "a crazy and dangerous creature" who was "no better than an anarchist."[47] The Bryan–Populist threat engendered deep fears and enabled the Republicans to raise lavish and unprecedented amounts of money from business interests. They reported spending the staggering sum of $4 million in the presidential campaign and in fact may have spent three or four times that amount. The New York Life Insurance Company alone contributed $50,000 to their effort. Suggesting the depth of the threat that many business groups perceived in the decade, the directors of the Metropolitan Life Insurance Company made a contribution against Bryan and Populism that they regarded as being "more a matter of morals than it was of policy."[48]

In the ominous and uncertain context of the 1890s the Supreme Court was unable or unwilling to decide a major procedural issue in the system against the litigation interests of national corporations. The social tensions of the 1890s and the Court's resulting desire to expand corporate access to the federal courts seemed a particularly convincing explanation for the Court's indecision, too, because on doctrinal grounds the minimum diversity issue was an easy one. The 1887–88 amendments were at most ambiguous, and to abandon the long-established and universally adopted statutory construction requiring complete diversity on the basis of the scant phrase "any defendant" seemed reckless, especially when alternative constructions could give the words effect and at the same time retain the complete diversity requirement. The recklessness also would have been unwarranted because many lawyers believed, with considerable support from Supreme Court dicta and practice, that complete diversity was a requirement of the Constitution itself.[49] Moreover, all the other changes made in the local prejudice clause tended in one way or another to narrow its scope, and the overriding purpose of the Judiciary Act of 1887–88 was to restrict federal jurisdiction. In the years immediately following the act's passage the Court repeatedly acknowledged that purpose and, more important, used it in other areas as a guide in construing the statute's ambiguities.[50] There seemed no plausible reason why the acknowledged statutory purpose should not have provided similar guidance on the question of complete diversity under the local prejudice clause. Further, allowing suits to be removed in the absence of complete diversity seemed to violate the provision of the Judiciary Act of 1887–88 that limited removals to suits that were within the "original" jurisdiction of the federal courts. Such original jurisdiction, of course, required complete diversity.[51]

Perhaps most immediately compelling, the Court's own reasoning in the *Pennsylvania* case seemed to require it to uphold the complete diversity rule. In holding that the amended local prejudice clause was subject to the jurisdictional amount, the Court stated that the clause should be read in light of the original version. In a series of cases in the 1870s and 1880s the Court had repeatedly ruled that the original act—which had also been silent on the issue—required complete diversity.[52] Further, *Pennsylvania* held that the amended local prejudice clause required the jurisdictional amount because it "describes only a special case" within the general removal provisions of the statute and hence was subject to all the limitations imposed on the general removal jurisdiction.[53] On that analysis, the amended local prejudice clause equally required complete diversity.

Regardless of the compelling legal arguments at hand, only after the turn of the century, when prosperity returned, optimistic middle-class reform emerged, and the general sense of imminent class conflict waned, did the Justices reach a consensus and settle the issue. It was no accident that they did so in a decision that came down barely two months before *Thompson*. In late 1905 in *Cochran v. Montgomery County*[54] the Court held that complete diversity was required under the local prejudice act. Most revealing, it disposed of the issue easily and on doctrinal grounds that had been available for at least fifteen years. Complete diversity was required, *Cochran* explained, because the local prejudice clause was not a "separate and independent ground" for removal, because complete diversity was required under the original 1867 act, because the purpose of the Judiciary Act of 1887–88 was to restrict federal jurisdiction, because the contrary conclusion would violate the rule that only suits within the original jurisdiction could be removed, and because the phrase "any defendant" meant only that the clause did not require all defendants to join in the removal petition. For authority it relied on Harlan's 1888 circuit opinion and on its own 1890 decision in *Pennsylvania*.[55]

If the reasoning in *Cochran* contained no surprises, neither did its practical results. The decision destroyed the utility of the local prejudice clause as a method of defeating the joinder tactic and pushed the clause to the system's periphery.[56] After *Cochran*, removal for local prejudice offered corporate defendants only minor advantages of little general use. It provided a longer time in which to file the removal petition, and it allowed a defendant to remove without the agreement of its nonresident codefendants.[57] Corporations could obviate the need for the former by filing promptly or as a matter of course, and they generally had little need of the latter because single defendants also could petition for removal without their codefendants under the separable controversy act. With so little to gain from its use after 1905, corporations seldom felt the need to take on the evidentiary burden of attempting to show local prejudice. In the years after *Cochran* the local prejudice clause tumbled into near oblivion.

The decisions construing the local prejudice clause reflected the sharp struggles that marked corporate diversity litigation and mirrored the pattern of decisions under the separable controversy act. They showed that at least many of the lower federal courts held more expansive views of their jurisdiction than did the Supreme Court and suggested that at least some of them may have been more favorably disposed toward corporate enterprise than were the Justices in Washington. Further, they suggested strongly that the Court's delay in deciding the pivotal complete diversity issue—both its careful and long-term avoidance of the issue and the doctrinal ease with which it disposed of the matter in 1905 on the basis of time-worn agruments—was the result of factors other than doctrinal uncertainty. Reacting to the social conflicts of the 1890s, the Court could not during that strident decade decide major procedural issues in the system against the litigation interests of national corporations.

Local Prejudice: The Corporate Failure of Proof

Until *Cochran* imposed the complete diversity requirement, the local prejudice act remained available to corporate defendants as a method of defeating the joinder tactic. The reported cases under the act, however, suggest that corporations used the statute relatively infrequently. Although there were undoubtedly a number of reasons for that sparing use, one might well have been the fact that local prejudice in the state courts was considerably less common and influential than corporate attorneys often claimed.

Despite the accepted rationale of diversity jurisdiction, in fact, there seem to be several reasons to doubt whether local prejudice constituted a major and pervasive threat to corporate defendants in the system. Indeed, perhaps most of the historical evidence supporting the existence of such prejudice comes from interested parties, corporate spokespersons and those disposed on political and ideological grounds to favor a broad jurisdiction for the national courts.[58] In the absence of independent confirmatory evidence, such testimony is as suspect for interest as is the contrary testimony of populists, progressives, states' righters, and plaintiffs' attorneys who often denied without qualification that local prejudice affected state court adjudications.[59] In some instances, too, the allegations of prejudice advanced by corporate spokespersons seemed facially dubious. In defending the need for diversity jurisdiction before the House Judiciary Committee in 1932, for example, an attorney for a Maryland bank illustrated the existence of local prejudice by citing a case that had occurred "some years ago in the *federal* court."[60] One could plausibly speculate that if prejudicial conduct in the state courts had been at all common—or if the bank's attorney had known or heard of even a single instance of it—he would almost certainly have cited that example in preference to the one he used.

Some corporate spokespersons, moreover, denied that corporations were often or regularly threatened by local prejudice in the state courts. The general solicitor of one southern railroad, for example, was quite emphatic when he appeared before a congressional committee in 1911. "We get very fair treatment from the courts in the States where the Norfolk & Western operates, with exceptions which are sufficiently exceptional to be peculiar," he declared.[61] Similarly, the general counsel of the National Board of Fire Underwriters, who stressed the danger of "a deep-seated prejudice against corporations," nevertheless informed Congress in 1932 that "[w]e remove very few cases to the Federal courts."[62] Thus, even corporate spokespersons who believed that local prejudice could present a grave danger to corporations nevertheless described the threat as limited to only a small minority of cases.

Further, to the extent that evidence supports the claim that local prejudice was a danger, it locates that danger most clearly in the context of public policy issues that directly affected major state and local interests, most noticeably in instances of debt repudiation.[63] Throughout the latter half of the nineteenth century, the efforts of state and local governments to repudiate their bonds posed a constant and highly charged problem. Beginning with the landmark case of *Gelpcke v. Dubuque*[64] in 1864, the Supreme Court and the lower federal courts frequently blocked repudiation and quickly came to be regarded as the great protectors of eastern capital against southern and western depredation. The long and bitter battles over repudiation fixed in the minds of many a powerful image of both the dangers of local prejudice and the unreliability of the state courts.[65] That image, in turn, helped color general attitudes toward the state and federal courts. Cases dealing with state and local bond repudiations, or similar cases affecting important state or local interests, however, involved profoundly different social, political, and economic factors than did the mine-run of private tort or insurance actions. To whatever extent the state courts were influenced by local prejudice in the former, there is little or no reason to assume that they were similarly influenced in the latter.[66]

Perhaps of greatest importance, there is also reason to believe that to whatever extent prejudicial factors did affect the state courts, they often benefited corporations rather than victimizing them. Union officials and their attorneys, for example, often complained of the influence that large corporations and local employers held over state courts. It was to the workers' disadvantage, declared an attorney who represented railroad employees, to try their actions "in rural communities or small towns where the railroad company has the upper hand."[67] In 1892 the attorney general of the United States charged that such corporate influence extended even to jurors. "In many localities," he cautioned, "these great corporations have an unwarranted influence among the people who are summoned as jurors in the State courts."[68] To the extent that it existed, in other words, prejudice affecting the state courts was probably a two-edged sword.[69]

Those various considerations do not, of course, disprove the allegation that the state courts were influenced by prejudice against foreign corporations. They do suggest, however, that there are reasons to be skeptical of the claim that such local prejudice constituted either a significant and common danger or one that worked only against the interests of corporate defendants. They also suggest that the actual situation was probably far more complex than the standard corporate charge of local prejudice would imply and that corporate defendants had numerous ways aside from removal to defend themselves or to turn local conditions to their advantage. With those considerations in mind, an examination of the decisions under the local prejudice act provides an additional ground for questioning whether local prejudice was a major and widespread danger for corporate defendants.

The express language of the act forced the federal courts to deal with the problem in individual cases. In *Pennsylvania* the Supreme Court laid down only general guidelines and left the rest "to the discretion of the court."[70] For their part, the circuit courts of appeals seemed satisfied to allow the lower courts ample room to exercise that discretion. In 1902 the Sixth Circuit considered the issue of procedure and proof under the clause, and it noted that *Pennsylvania* and a single 1893 decision of the Eighth Circuit were the only federal appellate cases that it could find on the subject.[71] In spite of the apparent lack of close oversight, however, the lower courts had by the mid-1890s generally agreed to require some proof of the facts on which defendants based their allegations and to give plaintiffs notice and an opportunity to be heard in opposition.[72] Both the appellate decisions reported up to 1902 reversed removals that had been ordered on the basis of *ex parte* applications. "The question [of local prejudice] should be determined by the court as it would determine any other issue of fact," the Eighth Circuit had declared in 1893,[73] and nine years later the Sixth Circuit instructed the lower courts to allow plaintiffs a hearing and to give the factual record "careful scrutiny."[74]

Under those standards, the reported decisions of the federal courts between 1887 and 1905 show that corporate defendants failed to produce evidence of local prejudice in any significant number of cases and thereby support the proposition that local prejudice may well have been considerably less prevalent and serious than corporate spokespersons often claimed. First, corporate defendants apparently attempted removal under the local prejudice act in relatively few cases, and they attempted to use it much less often than they did the separable controversy act or the fraudulent joinder doctrine. If the separable controversy act was simpler to use because it seldom raised complicated factual issues, that was not necessarily true for the claim of fraudulent joinder, which could also turn on difficult-to-prove factual allegations.[75] In contrast with their infrequent use of the local prejudice act, however, corporate defendants continued regularly throughout the period to plead fraud as a method of defeating joinders.

Second, corporate defendants apparently sought removal for local prejudice less frequently in the years after 1891 than they had from 1887 to 1891, and by the turn of the century they attempted to use the act only rarely. That trend suggested that the evidentiary requirements established in *Pennsylvania* in 1890—although relatively loose—erected an imposing obstacle to removals under the act. The decline in usage was especially noteworthy because, even after *Pennsylvania*, the lower federal courts did not seem to impose particularly demanding requirements for proving local prejudice. Affidavit evidence generally sufficed, and some courts continued to limit plaintiffs' right to contest defendants' allegations and occasionally even refused to accept opposing affidavits. In upholding a removal for local prejudice in 1893, Judge William Howard Taft—who warned throughout his life against the dangers of bias and prejudice in the state courts—expressed the view that "if [local prejudice] exists, it can be easily shown."[76]

Third, the absence of removals under the local prejudice act seems particularly probative given the powerful incentive that corporate defendants had to exploit the opportunity the statute created. The system's removal battles were at their most intense in the decades around the turn of the century, and in *Fisk* and *Hanrick* the Supreme Court had in effect sanctioned the adoption of the minimum diversity standard by the lower courts. From 1887 to *Cochran* in 1905 the local prejudice act stood as a potentially powerful weapon to defeat the joinder tactic.

The fact that corporate defendants increasingly ignored the act after *Pennsylvania* suggests that in most cases they could not produce credible evidence that local prejudice posed a threat to them.

Fourth, the absence of removals under the statute also seems significant because the federal courts were acutely sensitive to their duty to protect nonresidents and would surely have given fair and sympathetic consideration to any facts regarding local prejudice that corporate defendants presented.[77] As innumerable cases under the separable controversy act showed, for example, many of the lower federal courts wished to maintain a broad removal jurisdiction, and some seemed determined to protect the right of corporations to have their cases heard in a federal forum. Further, the minimal standards of proof imposed by *Pennsylvania,* the wide scope left to the lower courts' discretion, and the apparent reluctance of the appellate courts to review decisions involving proof of local prejudice all point to the conclusion that the lower courts were free to grant relief to any corporate defendant that made a credible showing. Indeed, the Supreme Court's decisions in the 1890s holding the door open for removals with minimum diversity sounded an unmistakable call to the lower courts to use the local prejudice act to safeguard corporate defendants from biased state forums. Had those defendants been able to present any credible evidence of local prejudice, it is difficult to believe that the lower federal courts would not have allowed them to remove.

Finally, of course, the significance of the corporate failure to utilize the local prejudice act is further accentuated by the fact that it occurred during the 1890s. In that decade, social tensions and hostilities were unusually intense, and whatever local prejudices existed against large corporations must have been at their peak. The Supreme Court's removal decisions after the early 1890s apparently reflected that precise fear. And yet even in that strife-filled decade—compelled by powerful practical incentives, granted a decisive counter to the joinder tactic, offered the opportunity to make their case in a sympathetic federal forum, and operating in a period of bitter social conflict—they still failed to make the case that local prejudice capable of influencing the state courts was anything more than a rare and isolated phenomenon.

Indeed, the significance of the corporate failure to use the local prejudice clause was compounded by two additional factors. One was that on at least a few occasions corporate defendants were allowed to remove on apparently thin evidence.[78] Another was that plaintiffs sometimes failed to present counter affidavits and contented themselves with denying the sufficiency of defendants' allegations and proof. In some instances the failure to submit opposing affidavits probably reflected the economic necessity that forced many plaintiffs to minimize their litigation costs.[79] To the extent that federal courts accepted minimal evidence as sufficient to establish local prejudice or plaintiffs failed with any frequency to produce substantial counter affidavits, defendants would have had a much better chance of prevailing—if, again, they had possessed any credible evidence to support an allegation of prejudice.

After 1890, however, the lower federal courts allowed relatively few removals under the local prejudice act.[80] As early as 1889 a federal judge in Missouri held that an allegation of general prejudice against foreign corporations was insufficient to support removal. It was improbable, he declared, that a state court could not deal impartially with "a business controversy between an ordinary foreign business corporation and a citizen of Macon county." If the facts were to the contrary, "the petitioner ought to be able to show with more clearness the cause of the prejudice that exists against it."[81] The Eighth Circuit declared in 1893 that claims of local prejudice were often groundless.

> [A]ffidavits like the one under consideration are filed when it is perfectly obvious that the only prejudice that has any existence in fact is the prejudice of the affiant against the people of the county, of whom he knows nothing, and whose impartiality and fairness he impeaches without the slightest foundation of fact.[82]

Although the cases under the act suggest that corporations exaggerated the dangers of local prejudice, any conclusions must necessarily remain tentative and limited. The probative value of the cases, after all, rests in the first instance on their small numbers, and a variety of factors other than the absence of local prejudice undoubtedly helped minimize those numbers. It is possible, for example, that for reasons of federalism or personal tact federal judges might have refrained from publishing decisions in which they found local prejudice or that they might even have been unwilling to make the necessary finding in the first place. Similarly, local attorneys may often have been reluctant to produce unflattering evidence that impugned either the courts of their states or a particular judge before whom they expected to appear in the future. Finally, of course, there was the substantive evidentiary problem itself. Proof of something as amorphous and often covert as "prejudice" could be particularly difficult to develop, and the showing required was heavy. Defendant had to establish not only that it might not be able to obtain justice in the particular state court where the action was filed but also that it would not be able to obtain justice in any other court of the state to which it had a right under state venue law to transfer the case. These considerations impose serious limitations on the evidentiary value of the cases under the local prejudice act, and they require that any conclusions be tentative and guarded.

Recognizing those limitations, however, at least three conclusions seem warranted. First, the cases decided under the local prejudice act support the proposition that as a shield against local prejudice diversity jurisdiction was substantially overbroad. For eighteen years from 1887 to the Supreme Court's *Cochran* decision in 1905, corporate defendants had powerful incentives to use the local prejudice act but failed to do so. The nature and number of the cases between 1891 and 1905 suggest that local prejudice may have been a relatively minor and occasional factor in diversity cases and therefore that the burdens that the jurisdiction imposed on many individuals were not warranted by concomitant increases in fairness to corporate defendants.

Second, to the extent that general diversity jurisdiction was created to protect nonresidents against local prejudice, the cases under the local prejudice clause highlight the critical fact that the general jurisdiction was based only on a series of presumptions. On the basis of little or no organized empirical evidence the law simply presumed that prejudice against nonresidents existed, that it would likely influence the state courts, and that the need to protect against it outweighed whatever burdens the removal to a federal forum imposed on resident plaintiffs.

Third, practice under the local prejudice act also shows that there was no institutional necessity that diversity jurisdiction be based on a presumption. The jurisdiction, as a matter of practice, could have operated on an actual prejudice standard. Enforcing the local prejudice act from 1887 to 1905, the federal courts applied just such a standard. The cases suggest that they did so fairly and reasonably. The local prejudice clause did not fall into disuse because the federal courts were unable to evaluate evidence concerning the existence and significance of local prejudice. Rather, it fell into disuse because corporations failed to produce evidence of its presence in any but a handful of cases and because *Cochran* subsequently terminated the only significant tactical utility the act possessed.[83]

Local Prejudice: Removal as Substantive Social Policy

The extraordinary nature of removal based on diversity of citizenship—and the law's highly selective concern with the threat of local prejudice—appears stark when compared with the removal jurisdiction created by the Civil Rights Act of 1866.[84] Emerging from the same Reconstruction policies that created the local prejudice and separable controversy acts, civil rights removal was intended to protect freedmen and Unionists by allowing them to remove suits when they were unable to enforce their federal rights in southern state courts.[85]

Until 1879, when the Supreme Court first ruled on the subject, the leading case construing the scope of civil rights removal was *Texas v. Gaines,*[86] an 1874 decision by Supreme Court Justice Joseph P. Bradley on circuit. There, Bradley faced the question "whether local prejudice against a colored person, by reason of his race and color, alleged to be so great that he cannot have a fair trial in the state courts" was sufficient to support removal of a criminal prosecution.[87] Reasoning prudentially, Bradley concluded that allowing removal in such a case would flood the federal courts and force him to consider the constitutionality of the removal statute. Both results should be avoided. "We think [the act] is intended to protect against legal disabilities and legal impediments to the free exercise of the rights secured," he ruled, "and not to private infringements of those rights by prejudice or otherwise."[88]

Bradley's 1874 opinion in *Gaines* stands as a kind of symbolic pivot for his changing views which, in turn, seemed to reflect the changing attitudes that the 1870s brought to both the Supreme Court and the nation as a whole. Three years before *Gaines,* Bradley had dissented from one of the Court's first decisions under the Civil Rights Act, *Blyew v. United States,* and there gave voice to the Reconstruction desire to protect the freed slaves. Considering the practical situation in the southern states and the need to make the statute effective, Bradley argued that the Civil Rights Act provided remedies against a state's failure to protect black citizens from extralegal prejudice and abuse. Failure to construe the statute liberally, he insisted in *Blyew,* "is to expose [black citizens] to wanton insults and fiendish assaults; is to leave their lives, their families, and their property unprotected by law."[89] Three years later in *Gaines,* Bradley seemed to have lost both his awareness of the legal impact of extralegal prejudice as well as his desire to make the statute effective. In 1879, eight years after *Blyew* and five years after *Gaines,* Bradley dissented in the *Removal Cases.* There, his earlier concern with the dangers of local prejudice reappeared, focused this time, however, not on the threat to blacks but on the threat to interstate railroads. "[L]ocal tribunals in such [interstate railroad] cases, however upright and pure," he warned, "are naturally more or less favorably affected towards the interests of their own citizens." To counter such prejudice, he argued, federal jurisdiction should be expanded by abandoning the doctrine of complete diversity. When Bradley dealt with the efforts of the railroads to remove, he did not—contrary to his approach in *Gaines* when he dealt with the removal rights of blacks—either shrink from deciding a difficult constitutional issue or surrender to the fear of crowded dockets. Rather, he boldly announced his views on the former and cavalierly dismissed the significance of the latter. "If the judicial force is not sufficient to meet the exigency," he demanded with apparent fervor, "let it be increased."[90]

When the 1870s began, memories of the triumphant war still inspired much of the North, and the goals of Radical Reconstruction remained vibrant. Republican governments were established in the ex-Confederate states; the Black Codes and other racially biased laws were repealed; and the Union army was on call where it did not remain in occupation. Federal officials often worked hard to protect the rights of freedmen and white Unionists, and the national courts provided relatively hospitable forums for the enforcement of Reconstruction legislation. By the end of the decade, however, Reconstruction was dead. New civil rights legislation ceased, and the federal government lost interest in enforcing the laws already on the books. Two hundred civil rights prosecutions in 1875 withered to only twenty-five in 1878.[91] The Union army was withdrawn from the last southern states it occupied, and white "redeemers" gained power across the entire sweep of the ex-Confederacy from Virginia to Texas. Ensconced once more in the nation's capitol, Democratic delegations from the South again formed a powerful and determined bloc in Congress. Throughout the ex-slave states new laws designed to control and exploit free blacks, somewhat milder and more cleverly drawn than their predecessors, were being put in force.[92]

If the 1870s witnessed a massive shift in social and political attitudes toward black Americans, the Supreme Court ratified and strengthened those changes in a series of decisions during the decade.[93] Then, in the 1879–80 Term it handed down its first decisions construing the removal provisions of the Civil Rights Act. With Bradley joining the majority in a series of four decisions,[94] the Court established the basic law of civil rights removal that would remain in force for more than eighty years. Upholding the statute's constitutionality, the Court gave it a narrow and formal construction that made the existence of local prejudice and extralegal civil rights violations irrelevant to the right to remove.

Virginia v. Rives was the decisive opinion. A state court had denied the removal petitions of two black defendants who claimed that they could not get a fair trial because of racial prejudice and because blacks were systematically kept off juries in their county. The local federal judge, Alexander Rives, issued a writ of habeas corpus and placed the blacks in the custody of the United States marshal. Virginia sought a writ of mandamus from the Supreme Court ordering Judge Rives to release the defendants to state authorities. The dispositive issue, the Supreme Court explained, was whether the state court had acted properly in denying defendants' removal petition. Because Virginia had no written law excluding blacks from juries, the Court held that the removal petition had been properly denied.

Rives seemed to exclude all de facto abuses in the state judicial process from the grounds that would support removal. It underscored the proposition that the

Fourteenth Amendment reached only state action and that the Civil Rights Act, passed under the amendment's authority, was directed "against that [state action] alone."[95] The Court held, however, that the statute was even narrower than the amendment and "clearly" did not cover all discriminatory state action.[96] Specifically, *Rives* explained, the statute did not reach state judicial actions. In a revealing passage the opinion explained—indeed, spotlighted with fanfare—the minimal significance that the Court was attributing to the civil rights removal statute:

> The statute authorizes a removal of the case only before trial, not after a trial has commenced. It does not, therefore, embrace many cases in which a colored man's right may be denied. It does not embrace a case in which a right may be denied by judicial action during the trial, or by discrimination against him in the sentence, or in the mode of executing the sentence. But the violation of the constitutional provisions, when made by the judicial tribunals of a State, may be, and generally will be, after the trial has commenced. It is then, during or after the trial, that denials of a defendant's right by judicial tribunal occur. Not often until then.[97]

Rives restricted civil rights removal to cases where state law expressly rejected a defendant's federal rights. Even if state officials had purposely excluded blacks from the jury, as the defendant alleged but did not attempt to prove, their actions—though "a gross violation" of state and federal law—would still not give defendant a right to remove.[98] Rather, the law presumed that the state courts would rectify the wrong, either at trial or on appeal. If not, the defendant's sole federal remedy was, after final judgment in the state courts, a writ of error to the United States Supreme Court under Section 25 of the Judiciary Act.[99] Removal, in any event, was not available.

Rives reduced civil rights removal to a trivial remedy. It limited the statute to cases involving formal state enactments that contravened federal rights, and it expressly excluded from its coverage most if not all actions that were taken as part of a state's judicial process, actions that the Court acknowledged could be reached under the Fourteenth Amendment. Moreover, by dismissing defendant's claim that the state purposely though informally excluded blacks from its juries, it supported the proposition that no amount of evidence showing de facto racial prejudice and discrimination could warrant removal. Indeed, its insistence on the statute's particularly narrow scope, its focus on the formal written law, and its disregard for the claim of de facto discrimination could easily have helped point the way for those who were, as the opinion came down, in the process of restoring white supremacy to the South.

Although the legislative materials are scarce and the statutory language unclear, *Rives* seemed far more a product of the social views of the Supreme Court in 1879 than of the Reconstruction Congresses. The eye-of-the-needle scope that *Rives* gave to removal seemed inconsistent with the purposes of the Reconstruction legislation and surely inconsistent with the effective protection of the rights of black Americans. Moreover, the Court's reading of the statutory language was, at best, merely plausible.[100] Still, whether Congress passed an exceptionally narrow statute or whether the Court misconstrued it in a transformed social context, after 1879 the civil rights removal statute offered no remedy for blacks against extralegal local prejudice, no matter how virulent and oppressive or how effective that prejudice was in denying their legal rights.[101]

The timing of *Rives* was ironic. While the Justices were hearing argument in the case and drafting their opinions, the nation's capital was in an uproar over the precise issues that *Rives* would hold beyond the reach of the removal statute. In early 1879 thousands of blacks began migrating from several southern states, principally North Carolina, into Indiana and Kansas. By spring large numbers had reached St. Louis, where many residents were horrified at the descriptions they heard of conditions in the South. A group of the city's prominent citizens petitioned Congress on their behalf. The overwhelming and consistent testimony of the freedman, the petition stated, "proves conclusively" that egregious abuses were common in the southern states, including threats of personal violence, general terror tactics, and murder.[102] Democrats and white southerners responded angrily, blaming the migration and publicity on unscrupulous black politicians, northern troublemakers, and passenger-hungry railroads.

Quickly the migration burst into national politics, and in December the Senate established a select committee to investigate the whole affair. The five-member committee heard 153 witnesses from nine states in nineteen days of testimony in January and February 1880, and it then wrote two of the most profoundly conflicting reports that any congressional committee has ever produced. Voting in effect on the guilt or innocence of the white South, three senators explained the migration as the result of politics and cupidity, while two described it as "wretched, miserable people flying from oppression and wrong."[103] Although their conclusions were contradictory, both reports agreed that blacks complained, in the words of the majority, about "their mistreatment in the courts of justice."[104] The majority dismissed the complaints as "ignorant,"[105] while the minority concluded that "the negro has but little hope of justice."[106]

The black migration, the extensive debate and hearings, and the report of the Senate Select Committee highlighted the national context within which the Court decided *Rives*. The Justices were keenly aware of the allegations of extralegal discrimination and of ruthless local prejudice in the South, and they knew equally well the attitude of the white South and of the two political parties. All seven Justices in the majority were Republicans, and the two dissenters who protested the breadth of the removal statute were Democrats. It seems likely that at least some of the majority Justices—many of whom had ties to the antislavery movement or congressional Reconstruction—believed or at least suspected that the minority report of the Senate Select Committee was far closer to the truth than was the majority report. Whether they decided *Rives* as they did because they felt the compulsion of the statutory language or because they were influenced by the massive shift in the nation's political attitudes, however, the resulting law failed to protect blacks from the most blatant, virulent, and implacable form of local prejudice that existed anywhere in the nation.[107]

During the quarter-century after *Rives,* the Court heard at least a dozen similar cases, and it consistently hardened the preclusive language of *Rives.* Succeeding decisions established that removal was justified only when a state statute or constitution denied federal rights and that proof of actual prejudice in the administration of the laws was simply not relevant.[108] Not once in the period did the Court authorize a removal under the Civil Rights Act.

Neal v. Delaware,[109] decided in the Term after *Rives,* illustrated the legal situation that resulted. A black criminal defendant petitioned for removal and moved to quash his indictment on the ground of affidavit evidence that blacks had been purposely excluded from both the grand and petit juries that heard his case.[110] The state submitted no contradictory evidence. "Nor does it appear," the United States Supreme Court noted, "that, on the hearing of the motions, the State controverted, in any form, the allegation, made with the utmost directness, that her officers had purposely excluded from the juries, because of their color, citizens of the African race, qualified to perform jury service."[111] The state trial court nevertheless denied defendant's motions on the ground that there was no evidence in the record to support his claims, and it then denied his further motion to subpoena the appropriate officials to provide the necessary evidence. On appeal in the Delaware Supreme Court, the Chief Justice dismissed defendant's argument against the state's practice of excluding blacks from juries by declaring that the exclusion was "in nowise remarkable" because "the great body of black men residing in this State are utterly unqualified by want of intelligence, experience, or moral integrity to sit on juries."[112] On those facts, the United States Supreme Court reversed defendant's conviction and ordered his indictment quashed, but it also upheld the denial of his removal petition.

Neal illustrated the difference between the remedy of removal and the remedy of ultimate appeal to the Supreme Court. Unrefuted evidence of purposeful and systematic discriminatory practices, tantamount to an admission of unconstitutional behavior by the state, was insufficient to justify the former, even though it required the Court to grant relief on the latter. Indeed, *Neal* provided powerful authority for the conclusion that no amount of evidence showing de facto unconstitutional behavior could merit a federal court in allowing a removal under the Civil Rights Act. Although the Court held that racially prejudiced administration of the law violated the Constitution, it also decided that it would be the sole federal court to make that judgment.

The result was to preserve the ideal of law and constitutional supremacy in a procedural framework that left blacks almost wholly bereft of legal remedies capable of translating the abstract ideals into social realities. Relatively few individuals, and even fewer blacks in the turn-of-the-century South, could take appeals to the United States Supreme Court. Over the next decades a few such cases trickled up to the Court. In contrast, during the same decades both formal and informal practices of racial discrimination and abuse spread widely and grew in intensity. Daily and in the most fundamental ways, relentless discrimination backed by both random and methodical violence pressed into the lives of millions of blacks. Whereas the ability to remove might have given at least many of them access to impartial forums, the necessity of appealing to the Supreme Court stringently confined that possibility to a handful. An appeal to the Supreme Court under Section 25 was a remedy for civil rights violations in the same way that a lottery ticket is a remedy for poverty.[113]

The fate of an Alabama surety statute, racially neutral on its face, illustrated the ineffectuality of the Section 25 remedy in such a context. Enacted in 1883 and upheld by the state's supreme court the same year, the statute helped establish and enforce the state's elaborate system of forced black labor. The United States Supreme Court eventually declared it unconstitutional as a form of involuntary servitude in violation of the Thirteenth Amendment. The declaration of unconstitutionality came in 1914, however, after the statute and its system of forced labor had been in operation for thirty-one years and after the Alabama Supreme Court had upheld its constutitionality at least sixteen times. The large number of cases that the state supreme court heard indicated that the statute was repeatedly and widely used at the local level.[114]

By the 1890s the Court faced mounting evidence of racial discrimination and increasingly closed its eyes to the process. Legalized segregation was spreading across the South; racial violence was exploding; and the rhetoric of white racism was reaching new heights.[115] In 1896 the Court decided *Plessy v. Ferguson,*[116] upholding legalized racial segregation in railroad cars, and in a series of contemporaneous decisions it continued to negate the civil rights removal statute.[117] The 1898 edition of Dillon's treatise spelled out the results. Civil rights removal, it stated, did not protect against "personal or class prejudice or political feeling, and the like." Indeed, it had nothing to do with de facto local prejudice. The treatise concluded:

> Hence the fact that, in the locality where a suit is brought or an indictment found against a negro, there exists a sentiment and prejudice hostile to him because of his race and color, *although it may be so strong as to prevent him from enjoying a fair trial,* is not a case, under this statute, for the removal of the case into the federal court.[118]

Doctrinally, of course, civil rights removal and the *Rives* line of cases had nothing to do with removal under general diversity jurisdiction. Together, however, they illustrated one simple but fundamental point. The removal jurisdiction of the federal courts did not exist to protect generally against local prejudice, nor did it exist even to protect generally against local prejudice so extreme as to cause systematic and ruthless denials of the most basic constitutional guarantees. Rather, removal jurisdiction existed only to protect certain particularly favored classes of litigants in certain special types of situations. Removal on the grounds of diversity of citizenship protected nonresident litigants, and when the law—on the mere presumption that such litigants might encounter local prejudice—conferred on them the right to remove, it granted a most extraordinary procedural benefit. If an appeal under Section 25 was an adequate remedy for black Americans, it would surely have been an adequate remedy for nonresidents in general or for foreign corporations in particular.

Whether and to what extent prejudice existed in the general run of diversity cases is not known. That it existed in the post-Reconstruction South and helped create abusive and—even under the Supreme Court's narrow decisions at the time—unconstitutional practices was clear. In diversity cases federal law was willing simply to presume the existence of prejudice and to grant a broadly effective remedy; in civil rights cases it was content to ignore the prejudice and to offer only a paper remedy. In both areas the extent to which local prejudice actually affected defendants was ultimately beside the point. The respective jurisdictions were created and construed not on the basis of any showing about the dangers of "local prejudice" or any considered evaluation of the need for various carefully tailored remedies but, rather, on a desire to accomplish divergent and ulterior social goals. For its part, diversity jurisdiction was simply designed to favor nonresidents who engaged in interstate commerce. In a variety of ways, some intended and others not, it did just that.

Chapter 7

Contraction and Evolution:
The System After 1910

As the system of corporate diversity litigation began to take shape in the 1870s and reached its harshest phase after 1890, so it began to contract in the years after 1910 while at the same time acquiring dynamic new characteristics. The overall scope of the system shrank; many of its major legal and nonlegal elements became less unfavorable to plaintiffs; and the tactics of its adversaries escalated sharply.

The system's fundamental dynamic remained in operation. Corporate defendants continued to remove regularly, and plaintiffs continued to use both joinder and claim discounting to avoid the federal courts. The latter tactic remained uniformly available in tort actions and in the early 1920s came into more common use in contract and insurance actions.[1] For the most part, however, the practice of claim discounting remained part of the informal legal process and seldom surfaced in the law reports unless a plaintiff had been careless or contriving.

Largely because it served as a high-stakes avoidance technique, joinder remained both more visible and more controversial. Although it declined in importance in industrial injury cases with the enactment of the Federal Employers' Liability Act and state workmen's compensations statutes, the tactic spread more widely into other types of suits, including automobile accident and consumer product cases. Joinder disputes were no longer concentrated in cases involving employers and employees. If the number of joinder disputes remained large, the more varied social patterns they presented seemed to diffuse much of the emotional intensity that marked the use of the tactic in industrial injury cases in the decades around the turn of the century.[2]

The law of joinder continued largely as it had in the decade after *Thompson*. Although the Supreme Court heard fewer tort joinder cases after 1915, its later cases provided additional support for the proposition that *Thompson* did not mean that "misconceived" pleadings were dispositive. The Court upheld a series of decisions that denied removal but often stressed the fact that the cause of action at issue was joint under controlling state law.[3] Only once did it uphold the denial of a motion to remand on grounds of fraud, and its opinion retained the fraudulent joinder doctrine within narrow confines by resting on the fact that the plaintiff had not challenged defendant's detailed factual allegations of fraud.[4]

In the lower courts joinder decisions remained diverse, constituting in the words of a 1928 law review note an "exceedingly complex and confused body of law."[5] Similar facts not uncommonly led to different results, sometimes of course because local procedural rules differed.[6] Some courts still seemed to strain to uphold removals and in effect negated, with the Supreme Court's apparent approval, *Thompson*'s statement that the pleadings controlled even when mistaken about the existence of a joint cause of action.[7] Most of the lower courts, however, seemed less hostile to the joinder tactic and more ready to grant remands than they had been in the three decades before the war.[8] Some even stated that *Thompson* and its progeny had overruled *Warax*.[9] The change in attitude reflected a reduction of the social tensions that surrounded the tactic, the force of two decades of liberal joinder decisions by the Supreme Court, and the fact that by the 1920s and 1930s the pleading rules of the states generally allowed more causes of action to be pleaded as joint than they had at the turn of the century.[10] One survey in the mid-1930s, for example, found that the procedural rules of twenty-three states allowed the joinder of master and servant in suits charging negligence on the part of the servant and that only nine blocked such joinders.[11]

In spite of basic continuities, however, the system changed noticeably after 1910. Technological and institutional developments ameliorated the problems of distance and delay that had helped structure the system. Similarly, Congress restricted removals, and increasingly both federal and state legislation circumscribed the area in which the federal common law held sway. Crosscurrents, however, were also at work. In the years after 1910 the Supreme Court expanded both the corporate right to remove and the scope of the federal common law, opening new areas where the system could operate. Although the Court's expansions were noteworthy, they were quite minor compared with the far broader restrictions that Congress and the state legislatures placed on the system's operation.

The types of cases that were litigated in the system also changed. Personal injury actions continued to dominate the tort docket, but suits involving railroads and streetcars began to lose their relative importance, though still remaining the largest single source of work-related injuries. Increased efficiency, the Depression of the 1930s, and the general economic decline of the railroads after 1920 reduced the number of railroad employees from the peak of more than 2 million immediately after World War I to barely 1 million in the 1930s. Even during World War II railroad employment never topped 1.5 million. The lower employment levels combined with improved safety equipment to reduce the number of injuries dramatically after 1926. Railroad deaths fell from more than 10,000 a year between 1904 and 1917 to around 5,000 a year during the 1930s, while nonfatal accidents plummeted from close to 200,000 annually before World War I to around 30,000 in the 1930s. Even with the frenetic activity that came with World War II fatal injuries to employees increased only slightly and nonfatal injuries rose to only 60,000 per year, less than a third of the total three decades earlier.[12]

In spite of the decline in railroad and streetcar accidents, the total amount of tort litigation grew steadily. Actions involving other industrial and workplace injuries increased, and manufacturers' product liability cases became more noticeable, though they remained only a small part of the tort docket. Motor vehicles emerged as the major new source of tort litigation. A minor docket factor in 1910, automobiles probably accounted for a quarter of the total tort litigation in the 1920s and 1930s and a third or more by the 1940s. On the federal docket they made up a smaller but still large and growing category of tort suits, accounting for 15 percent of all diversity cases by 1941 and 27 percent by 1948.[13]

Insurance actions changed, too. The amount of insurance in force multiplied rapidly, and the number of suits grew. Although the major life insurance companies tended after the early years of the twentieth century to litigate less frequently and settle somewhat more readily, the number of insurance suits probably doubled between the late nineteenth century and the interwar years. Marine and fire insurance litigation seemed to decline in relative importance, but actions based on health and disability policies became more common. The latter suggested a significant shift in the class basis of insurance plaintiffs, as more working-class claimants apparently bought insurance and eventually litigated a growing number of cases that involved relatively small amounts of money.[14] Although the system as a whole contracted after 1910, during the 1920s and 1930s it expanded in the area of insurance litigation.

Perhaps most striking, inspired by the changing social and legal landscape of the twentieth century, individual plaintiffs and corporate defendants created a range of new tactics in the quest for litigation advantage. Of greatest significance, plaintiffs in small but nevertheless significant numbers began to bring their suits outside their home states, while corporations introduced federal equity as a major force in the system. If plaintiffs improved their tactical position in tort litigations after 1910, companies did the same in insurance cases.

The Emergence of a Plaintiffs' Personal Injury Bar

The escalation in litigation tactics, already visible during the 1890s in the appearance of the delayed upward amendment tactic and the proliferating use of joinder, was rooted in the social and professional transformation of the American legal profession in the decades around the turn of the century. Increasingly stratified in the late nineteenth century, the bar fell under the leadership of corporate lawyers in relatively large urban law firms and under the domination of the legal–cultural world view of prosperous Anglo-Saxon Protestants. By the turn of the century, however, a new type was emerging, the socially unconnected urban attorney who specialized in personal injury actions or other noncorporate work, represented poorer individuals, lived on contingent fees, and regularly sued businesses of every size. Frequently a product of the allegedly inferior night law schools that began to spread rapidly in the 1890s, the new urban personal injury attorney was often Catholic or Jewish and a product of the new immigration from southern or eastern Europe that had marked the decades since the 1880s. By the first decade of the twentieth century the emerging plaintiffs' personal injury bar was well established.[15]

Although white Protestant personal injury attorneys also flourished, the partisan gulf that opened between the established bar and the personal injury bar grew as much from ethnic and social differences, real and perceived, as from their professional ones. The Dean of the Yale Law School captured the complex cultural attitudes of the elite bar in 1904 when he addressed a symposium entitled "The Ideals of the American Advocate." "[P]ersonal honor is the distinguishing badge of the legal profession," he insisted. The attorney "cannot do, as a lawyer, anything which dishonors him as a Christian gentleman and a law-abiding member of society."[16] A decade later John W. Davis, a distinguished leader of the corporate bar, identified himself bluntly as one of those "who resent all immigration in general and that of the Russian Jew in particular."[17] At the 1914 annual meeting of the Association of American Law Schools Professor Joseph Beale of Harvard sounded the alarm bluntly. "As long as our doors were entered chiefly by immigrants of cognate blood," he declared, "the common law as it was studied by Story and Langdell" had remained safe. "But within the last twenty years a horde of alien races from Eastern Europe and from Asia has been pouring in on us." Those immigrants were "accustomed to hate the law" and were "hostile above all to all wealth and power." Their presence, Beale warned ominously, "must in the long run determine the nature of the law."[18]

The elite bar placed its hostility to personal injury attorneys on the level of ethics, professional and otherwise. "A growing multitude is crowding in who are not fit to be lawyers, who disgrace the profession after they are in it," Justice David J. Brewer charged in 1895.[19] Four years later the *Virginia Law Register* denounced the "blood-sucking generation" of new personal injury lawyers who had become "a stench in the nostrils" of honest members of the bar.[20] The often-implicit connection between ethics and ethnicity, however, occasionally poked through to the surface. The "class rolls of the night schools in our great cities" have "a very large proportion of foreign names," declared the Dean of the University of Wisconsin Law School in 1915. "The result is a host of shrewd young men, imperfectly educated, crammed so they can pass the bar examinations, all deeply impressed with the philosophy of getting on, but viewing the Code of Ethics with uncomprehending eyes." It was "this class of lawyers," he charged, that caused "Grievance Committees of Bar Associations the most trouble."[21]

The standards of practice, many lawyers warned, were declining drastically. "Most cases which are wholly without merit," charged another critic after the turn of the century, "are started with the expectation that the defendant will settle for at least the amount which it would cost him to try the case,—a species of blackmail."[22] Established attorneys repeatedly accused the personal injury bar of using improper or blatantly unlawful tactics, including the use of paid witnesses to strengthen or even create a client's case and the manipulation of settlement accounts to cheat the attorney's own client.[23] "So common has perjury become," one critic exclaimed, "that jurors are inclined almost to applaud a clever lie well told."[24]

Whatever else they did or did not do, many of the new personal injury attorneys aggressively sought business—quickly dubbed "ambulance chasing"—and in some cases organized elaborately to get it. "Let me tell you frankly, gentlemen, that if you don't solicit them you won't get them," a Chicago personal injury attorney told students at Northwestern University Law School in 1906. "[Y]ou will not get these injury cases unless you look for them, because they are being looked for by others."[25] Around the turn of the century the first law firm "chasers" or "runners" began attracting attention in the larger cities, and the practice of organized solicitation was widely recognized. "There was a notorious case not long ago in one of our larger cities," noted another law writer, "where the day after a street car collision, thirty-four suits were brought from the office in favor of passengers."[26] The next year the *Yale Law Journal* reported that a young attorney in Tennessee had "rushed to the scene of [a mine] disaster" and "secured some forty cases."[27]

Chasing tactics varied from the relatively reasonable to the outrageous. "Drug stores and bar rooms are subsidized," one critic explained; "it is carefully noised abroad that so and so is good for twenty-five dollars if a safe case is sent him."[28] At its most elaborate levels the practice included full or part-time solicitors who literally tracked down potential clients and sometimes exploited ethnic or religious ties, cultivated police and medical contacts for paid referrals, and pressured injury victims and their families to sign large contingent fee agreements in dubious circumstances. Sometimes, attorneys apparently filed suit without even securing the agreement of their alleged clients. "There have come to my attention cases wherein attorneys have begun an action in the name of an injured man, without any acquaintance with, or authority from, the injured party," declared a Detroit lawyer. Sometime after he had filed suit the attorney would try to have the injured person "persuaded that the court had appointed the attorney in question." The problem was exacerbated, the critic pointed out, because such injured persons were often "ignorant of our legal procedure, as well as of our language."[29]

In the social and economic context of the turn of the century, the emergence of the new urban personal injury bar began to alter the nature of tort and insurance litigation. Increasingly, corporate defendants confronted a new breed of legal adversaries who were often skillful, tenacious, and unusually bold. Although some personal injury attorneys undoubtedly used tactics that were questionable or illegal, many others were simply more shrewd, specialized, and perhaps driven than were the attorneys that corporations and their counsel had faced only a decade or two earlier. When the *Virginia Law Register* denounced the ambulance chaser in 1899, it included in its indictment the arresting and particularly revealing charge—intended, of course, to deprecate—that he "knows by style and volume all the accident case-law of his State."[30]

The drastic change in the nature of both practice and the profession helped persuade many lawyers that the very integrity of the judicial system was at stake. The "intensity of practice," observed a Michigan judge in 1904, "has led a host of lawyers to the verge of abuse."[31] Two years later a leading lawyers' magazine sponsored a symposium on "The Abuse of Personal Injury Litigation"[32] and introduced the topic with an article entitled "Employers' Liability as an Industrial Problem."[33] To some corporate attorneys the two topics were synonymous. Personal injury litigation, the introductory article explained, "has developed a brood of abuses" that were "common to all phases of that enormous docket." The abuses, however, were "peculiarly obnoxious in the field of employers' liability."[34] The participants, of course, disagreed with the reasons for the abuses. The fault lay with "the cold-blooded rule of gain, born of corporate greed," declared one participant, while another blamed the low ethical standards of the personal injury bar. Abusive litigation, the latter maintained, was due to the "skillful and unscrupulous lawyer" who could always maneuver to "frame a theory and distort testimony" to get any case to the jury.[35]

The emergence of the personal injury bar and the questionable practices associated with it spurred both corporations and the profession to take action. One response was organizational. Shortly after the turn of the century a number of insurance, railway, construction, and other companies organized the Alliance Against Accident Fraud. Its purpose, explained an attorney for a group of street railway companies, was "publicity and prosecution for the crooks, including professional litigants, 'fakirs,' false witnesses, shyster lawyers, tricky doctors, ambulance-chasers, and runners."[36] Another response was to urge the profession to reform the procedures and administration of the courts. The use and abuse of procedural technicalities, declared a distinguished New York attorney, capturing the mood of much of the corporate bar, was turning litigation "into a game, in which the keen and crafty on the whole have the advantage."[37] A third response was rhetorical. The leaders of the organized bar proclaimed widely and repeatedly the idealistic nature of their profession. It was "the profession of those who contend for the rights of others," Simeon E. Baldwin, a founder of the American Bar Association (ABA), announced in 1904. "Altruism and personal sacrifice are its foundations."[38] A final response was the effort of the bar associations to adopt written codes of professional ethics. In 1908 the elite bar pushed the American Bar Association to adopt for the first time a code of professional ethics, and in the next few years numerous state and local bar associations followed suit. Although the codes were narrow and in part unexceptionable, their strictures on solicitation, contingent fees, and related practices seemed to favor the established corporate attorney, ignore the economic realities of a socially stratified profession, and restrict the tools of the new urban practitioner regardless of the integrity of his practice or the condition of his potential clients.[39] It required another nine years before the ABA formally recognized the legitimate and unmet need of the poor for legal services by urging support for the legal aid societies that had begun appearing in a few larger cities.[40]

Although members of the elite bar reacted with growing hostility to the new urban personal injury attorney, workers and their representatives were more sympathetic. "I am not one of those who set up a hue and cry against so-called 'ambulance chasers'," announced the acting president of the Order of Railway Conductors in 1911. Rather, "an attorney who furnishes both money and brains to fight for those who otherwise can not fight for themselves," he declared, "is entitled to rich compensation, as many men could not even get into court except for them." In spite of their shortcomings, "under the present system this class of attorneys is the natural concomitant of the system."[41] The president of the Brotherhood of Railroad Trainmen went even further, though his compliment, too, remained backhanded. "The ambulance chaser is damned in good legal society," he told a congressional committee, "but he is an angel of goodness and purity compared to the railway claim agent."[42]

The emergence of a plaintiffs' personal injury bar around the turn of the century helped turn the system of corporate diversity litigation in a new direction. Sophisticated and in some cases sharp tactics became increasingly available to plaintiffs, and the corporate defense bar was forced to develop its own new countertactics. The accelerating process of innovation and response began to generate a continuing escalation of litigation tactics that characterized the third phase of the system. Though surely victimizing some poor and unfortunate individuals, the rise and spread of the plaintiffs' personal injury bar also helped in some part to redress the imbalance in the legal representation generally available to individual and corporate litigants and thereby helped ameliorate for many claimants the system's harsh operation.

Even though the emerging personal injury bar developed new and more powerful litigation tactics, its major economic impact probably occurred in the informal legal process. Able and experienced attorneys had, after all, often been available to those with legal claims. Before the turn of the century, however, large numbers

of potential tort plaintiffs failed to seek legal representation on their own. Ignorance, loyalty, pressure, fear, or the bar created by hastily signed releases prevented huge numbers of injured persons from consulting an attorney, much less
from bringing suit. By the turn of the century, however, when personal injury
attorneys began searching out potential plaintiffs, they began to draw more and
more injured persons out of that inactive reservoir and into the claims-asserting
process. Although some ambulance chasers undoubtedly asserted unfounded or
dishonest claims, the major economic impact of the emerging personal injury bar
was almost certainly due to its success in raising the "conversion" rate of potential
claims into actual claims. Indeed, the competitive pressures that forced many
personal injury attorneys to solicit potential claimants as quickly as possible after
an accident in order to beat out their professional rivals also allowed them to
frustrate the efforts of the companies to secure immediate releases from the same
injured persons. By substantially increasing the numbers of persons who asserted
some type of claim, by negating the efforts of corporate claim agents to obtain
releases immediately after accidents, and by credibly raising the threat of formal
legal action, the new personal injury bar almost certainly raised the total amounts
that companies paid in out-of-court settlements, even if the amounts paid in
individual cases remained relatively small. Regardless of the ethics of claims
solicitation, then, so-called ambulance chasing probably increased markedly the
overall settlement costs that companies incurred. It created a growing economic
problem for corporations and helped generate the deep hostility of their attorneys
toward the new personal injury bar.

As the personal injury bar developed and began to moderate the balance of
inequality, other changes were also operating to restrict the advantages that
corporations enjoyed in the system of corporate diversity litigation. In particular,
the burdens imposed by both distance and delay began to decline in importance,
and legislation on both the national and state levels began to restrict or eliminate
some of the system's more unfavorable legal elements. Although many of the
changes were gradual and long term, by the 1920s and 1930s the system was
affecting fewer claimants and imposing less unfavorable conditions on those it
did affect.

Decline in the Burdens of Distance and Delay

Geography and demographic patterns helped create some of the defining social
conditions that characterized the system in the late nineteenth century. The relative distance of the federal courts was a common and often severe problem for
individual litigants, and it imposed large extralegal costs on them. By the early
twentieth century, however, three interrelated developments were significantly
reducing that burden.

The first was the steady increase that Congress made in the number of locations where the federal courts sat. On the trial court level, where litigants were
most immediately and directly affected, Congress added terms in a hundred new
cities and towns between 1910 and 1937, expanding them from 276 to 376 locations.[43] Additional locations for the appellate courts contributed to the same
result. Beginning in 1902, Congress sporadically authorized additional appellate
terms in a few larger cities, and in 1929 it created a new Tenth Circuit by dividing

the huge Eighth Circuit into two relatively equal parts and establishing additional locations in which each would sit. The new circuit, the Senate and House reports stated, would "reliev[e] the litigants and judges of the strain and the great amount of travel now required."[44]

As Congress brought more federal courts to the people, the seemingly inexorable process of urbanization also brought more people to the federal courts. From 28 percent of the total population in 1880, the nation's urban population rose to 40 percent in 1900 and to 46 percent in 1910. Sometime in the next decade, urban residents became a majority, and by 1930, 56 percent of the population lived in urban areas.[45] The growth, of course, came not merely in the large cities but also in the medium and smaller cities and towns that burgeoned throughout the country. The number of cities with populations greater than 100,000 grew from 38 in 1900 to 92 in 1940, and those with populations between 25,000 and 100,000 grew during the same years from 122 to 320.

Urbanization, combined with the increased number of locations where the federal courts held terms, meant that a growing percentage of the population lived in cities where the federal courts sat. Until the 1880s less than 20 percent of the population probably did so. The number jumped to around a quarter by 1900 and to more than a third by 1920. By 1930 approximately 40 percent of the population lived in cities where the federal courts sat. In addition, the percentages for the latter years were in reality much higher, as spreading suburbanization meant that growing numbers of people lived quite close to cities even though not within their official limits. In the late nineteenth century about a third of the nation's population lived in counties where the federal courts sat, and by 1910 about half did so. By 1930, however, close to two-thirds of the population probably lived in urbanized counties that hosted terms of the federal courts.[46]

It was the concentration of population in the cities that was key to decreasing the general burden of distance. The increase in new court locations kept up with neither the growth in general population nor the multiplying number of middle-sized cities and towns, and the rural and small town population continued to grow in absolute terms throughout the period. There was a federal court location for every 300,000 residents in the 1880s, one for every 330,000 in 1910, and one for every 350,000 in 1930. Similarly, the percentage of census-designated "urban areas" that hosted the federal courts declined throughout the period. From approximately 18 percent in 1880, the number dropped to about 14 percent in 1900 and to less than 11 percent in 1930. Still, the higher relative concentration of people meant that between 1880 and 1930 the percentage of the population living in cities that hosted a federal court more than doubled.

Although the combination of urban concentration and additional court locations lightened the burden of distance, the federal courts continued to be less accessible than the state courts. As late as 1940 about a third of the population still lived outside counties that hosted federal trial terms, and the demographic changes that lightened the burden of distance on the trial level had less effect on the appellate level. In 1891 approximately 5 percent of the population probably lived in counties where the federal appellate courts sat, and by the 1930s only about 20 percent did so. A majority of the people, then, remained at some distance from the federal appellate courts. In 1948 the ten circuit courts of appeals convened in only twenty of the forty-eight states, and the average distance from the farthest point in the nonsitting states to the nearest federal appellate court was more than 375 miles.[47]

It was thus the third factor, the development of the automobile, that probably had the widest impact on reducing the burden of distance. For those who still lived some distance from a federal court, the automobile cut the time and cost of travel, lessened its inconvenience, and freed them from the necessity of conforming to the timetables, depots, and routes of the railroads. Moreover, by allowing several people to travel as cheaply as one, it helped minimize the additional costs of transporting the trial entourage of lawyer, plaintiff, and witnesses. As the automobile came into common use, its advantages became available to most plaintiffs; and as it crystallized into the classic symbol of American freedom conceived in terms of spatial mobility, its use became both an adventure and a pleasure.[48]

The automobile was a rare item in 1900, and the embryonic automobile industry did not experience its first real growth until after the brief financial panic of 1907. The following year Henry Ford produced the first Model T, and William C. Durant founded General Motors.[49] Total automobile production jumped from 33,000 in 1906 to 181,000 in 1910. In 1914 it surpassed the production of animal-drawn wagons, and by 1916 it reached 1.5 million. After a brief slowdown during the war, the automobile industry boomed in the 1920s, producing 1.9 million cars in 1920, more than 3 million in 1923, and more than 4 million in 1929. Although the industry made fewer than 3 million cars between 1900 and 1915, it produced almost 40 million in the next fifteen years and, in the Depression decade of the 1930s, another 26 million.[50]

The industry's success and its massive social impact came not merely from the number of cars it made but from its efficient assembly line production methods that allowed it to manufacture and sell at relatively low prices. Ford specifically aimed his production strategy at the mass manufacture of a single type of relatively inexpensive automobile, and General Motors included an equivalent model in its varied line of cars designed to fit different income levels. The result was to make the automobile accessible to millions of Americans whose enthusiastic demand for cars supported the industry's expanding productive capacity. Automobile registration skyrocketed. In 1900 there were only 8,000 registered motor vehicles in the United States and in 1910 less than half a million. Widespread ownership came in the following two decades. By 1920 total motor vehicle registration stood at 9.2 million and by 1930 at 26.7 million. Although there was 1 automobile registered for every 201 persons in the country in 1910, there was 1 for every 13 in 1920 and 1 for every 5 by 1930.[51] By the mid-1920s approximately half of all American families had a car. If a plaintiff did not own one, his attorney probably did.[52]

Road and highway construction kept pace. In the late nineteenth century an enthusiasm for bicycles inspired a "good roads" movement in the Northeast, and the railroads began to support road construction to provide feeders for rail transportation. Before 1900 the results were minimal. In the forty years since 1860, the nation's surfaced roads had grown only slightly, inching from a little less than 100,000 to barely 125,000 miles. By the turn of the century, however, political and economic support began coalescing around the goal of road improvement, and after 1910 the presence of the automobile galvanized the effort. State funds for road building grew exponentially. Total outstanding state debt for road construction, which stood at $12.7 billion in 1900, leapt to $225.4 billion in 1920 and to more than $1.5 trillion by 1930. The federal government joined the effort, appropriating funds and attempting to improve standards in the Federal-Aid Road Act of 1916 and then the Federal Highway Act of 1921. Results quickly followed, especially after the latter. In the first decade of the twentieth century paved mileage almost doubled to 200,000 miles, and in the next decade it almost doubled again. By the time nation entered World War II, Americans could travel on more than 1.5 million miles of paved roads and highways.[53]

As massive as the road improvements were, until the mid-1920s they were concentrated in the cities. As late as 1924 only 160,000 miles of rural roads, approximately 5 percent of the nation's total, had any kind of hard surface. During that decade, however, the state and federal governments began surfacing almost 40,000 miles each year, and in the 1930s, for the first time, they began funneling more of their highway funds to rural areas than to urban ones. By the late 1940s more than half of all rural roads had been surfaced, about 200,000 miles with high-quality coverings.

If the developments were uneven, they were also sweeping and dramatic. In 1900 almost three-quarters of all Americans lived many miles from the nearest federal trial court, and travel to it imposed heavy burdens and costs on them. But by 1940 only about half lived any significant distance from a federal court, and for most of them the automobile and the highway had lightened—and in many cases essentially eliminated—the burdens and costs of travel as a significant litigation factor. Some geographical pockets remained disadvantaged, and many individuals were unable to buy or otherwise use a car, but by the late 1940s the burdens of distance no longer operated commonly and generally to handicap a significant percentage of plaintiffs who litigated against national corporations.

As the years after 1910 witnessed the decline of distance as a critical factor in corporate diversity litigation, they saw a similar if somewhat more problematic decline in delay in the federal system. The average duration of civil cases in the national courts plunged from its peak of approximately four years in 1912 to less than one year by 1938. The decline was problematic because the statistical averages masked differences among districts and kinds of actions and because unlike the minimization of distance as a problem, the reduction of delay seemed a gain that could be lost in the future. Regardless of qualifications, however, delay declined substantially as a factor in federal litigation during the three decades after World War I.[54]

The federal caseload, which had grown steadily if somewhat erratically since the late nineteenth century, expanded enormously in the years after World War I. Increasing economic activity, progressive regulatory legislation, and commercial disputes engendered by massive war production and its sudden postwar termination all contributed. Prohibition, initiated during the war, by itself poured tens of thousands of criminal prosecutions into the national courts. In 1915 35,000 new cases were filed in the federal courts, of which about 20,000 were criminal prosecutions. By 1925, with Prohibition in full force, 115,000 new cases came in, and criminal prosecutions accounted for two-thirds of the total. The peak came in 1932, when 152,000 new actions were filed, almost 97,000 of them criminal suits. The Depression cut the amount of civil litigation, however, and the end of Prohibition in 1933 more than halved the number of federal criminal prosecutions. Only

70,000 new federal cases were filed in 1934, less than half of them criminal. For the next decade, the number of new cases ranged between 70,000 and 80,000, before rising in the late 1940s toward 90,000.[55]

More striking than the rise and fall of the federal caseload, however, was the steady and precipitous drop in the ratio of pending to new cases. In 1915, for example, 35,000 new cases were filed, but 79,000 remained pending at the end of the year. In contrast, the peak filing year of 1932 saw 152,000 cases added but at year's end, only 86,000 pending.[56] During the 1920s and 1930s, in other words, the federal courts terminated cases far more quickly and in far greater numbers than they had ever done previously. Although they apparently disposed of thousands of Prohibition cases with the greatest expedition, they also treated civil suits with a new dispatch. In several years between World War I and the Depression, civil terminations exceeded new civil filings, and from 1930 to 1942, civil terminations exceeded civil filings in every year but one.[57]

As a result, the average duration of federal civil suits fell sharply throughout the period. From a high of slightly over four years in 1912, the average duration dropped below three years in 1917. After erratic fluctuation in the war and imme-diate postwar years, the average duration dropped below two years in 1922 and gradually declined to one year in the late 1930s. It remained there throughout the 1940s.[58]

Much of the initial impetus for accelerating the federal judicial process came from the growing movement for professional procedural reform that began to crystallize after the turn of the century. In part the movement was a response to the obvious problems posed by increasingly crowded dockets. The rapid growth in the nation's population and a sharp upswing in business activity following the depression of the 1890s poured ever-growing numbers of cases into the courts. In part, too, the movement stemmed from the rising concern over the types of cases that were occupying the courts. Some legal reformers hoped to improve the judicial process in order to counter the questionable tactics they associated with the plaintiffs' personal injury bar, and others sought to find more effective ways to deal generally with the industrial injury cases that were swamping the courts.[59] Finally, the movement for procedural reform reflected the growing interest in efficiency and administration that progressivism inspired after the turn of the century. If scientific research and professional expertise could improve human institutions generally, many lawyers reasoned, they could surely do the same for the judicial system.

Minimizing delay was widely recognized as desirable and necessary, and im-proved judicial efficiency seemed to be the kind of achievement that science and social engineering could effect. In 1902 New York established a Commission on Law's Delays to determine the extent of the backlog in the state's courts and to make recommendations for expediting their work. The commission focused, among other things, on the desirability of collecting statistics to measure the activities of the courts and the need to improve procedural rules and administra-tive practices.[60] In 1903 a leader of the St. Louis bar hailed the profession's recognition of "the need for a rational system of procedure" as central to the "progressive development of our jurisprudence,"[61] and two years later another attorney charged more simply that the law still operated on a "medieval time-table."[62] Moreover, at least in the abstract, the goal of increased judicial efficiency readily commanded nearly unanimous support. It appealed to political progressives as a method of aiding poorer litigants and to political conservatives as a means of ensuring respect for the courts and established law. President William Howard Taft, a fervent believer in increasing judicial efficiency as a means of preserving social stability, made judicial reform one of his principal goals. Improved judicial procedure that would reduce the costs and delays of litigation, he announced in 1909, was "the greatest need in our American institutions."[63]

In the decade after 1910 the reformers began to have some impact. The Judicial Code of 1911 abolished the old circuit courts and simplified some elements of federal practice, and a slight increase in the number of judges after 1914 provided some relief from growing dockets.[64] In 1919 Congress abolished the fee system and placed federal court clerks on a salary basis, a reform that helped professionalize the clerks' offices and eliminated one minor cost grievance.[65] Even more important, federal judges responded to the expanding backlog of cases and the protests against delay in the courts by processing actions more swiftly. Between 1900 and 1912, individual federal trial judges terminated an average of approximately 250 cases per year, but during the following ten years they terminated more than 450 per year.[66]

More significant changes came in the 1920s. The flood of postwar civil suits and Prohibition prosecutions forced Congress to do something to relieve the congestion, and Taft, now Chief Justice of the United States, was ready with a series of proposals. He urged on Congress the ideas he had been espousing for the past fifteen years, especially the need for a more centralized administrative system for the federal courts. In 1922 Congress gave him much of what he asked for. It authorized an additional twenty-four district judges, gave the Chief Justice limited power to transfer judges temporarily to busier districts, and created the Conference of Senior Circuit Judges, later called the Judicial Conference, to be presided over by the Chief Justice of the United States.[67] The interdistrict transfer provision proved to be of only minor use, but the new judgeships increased the size of the lower judiciary by more than 20 percent. Of greatest long-range importance, the Judicial Conference provided the first formal institutional mechanism through which the Chief Justice and Senior Circuit Judges could exert administrative authority over the lower judiciary. Taft and his successor, Charles Evans Hughes, forged the conference into a major force in judicial politics and administration. The establishment of the Administrative Office of the United States Courts in 1939, under the direction of the Judicial Conference, further extended the power of the judiciary to control its own business.[68]

Although the Judicial Conference worked on a range of matters affecting the federal judiciary, it focused much of its effort on accelerating the disposition of cases and clearing the federal dockets. Through its annual report and the lobbying efforts of Taft and others, the conference incessantly asked for additional judges and sought expanded funding for better libraries, additional court personnel, and law secretaries and clerks for the judges. The number of district court judges rose from 138 after the act of 1922 to 162 in 1930 and then to 199 by 1940.[69] By the 1940s, law clerks were available for all federal judges, not just those on the appellate courts.[70] Further, the conference repeatedly pressed the district judges to clear their dockets and move cases along quickly. Among its first efforts it recommended that trial judges expedite litigation as much as possible, disallow continuances by agreement of counsel, notice annually the dismissal of inactive cases, and submit periodic reports on the state of their dockets. Although the rule against continuances by agreement met considerable opposition in the lower courts, the other recommendations of the conference were apparently in general effect by the late 1920s.

The growth in the number of district judges was important in cutting the average duration of federal civil actions, but the administrative centralization and increased pressure to expedite cases was equally critical. Case terminations per judge, which had already jumped from 351 in 1915 to 618 in 1921, moved even higher after the conference came into existence. Terminations per judge peaked at 948 in 1932 and averaged 850 cases per year between 1924 and 1933 before declining when the total caseload began its steep Depression-born, post-Prohibition descent.[71]

Although the average duration of federal civil actions fell sharply in the years after World War I, the problem of delay continued to affect some litigants. The Judicial Conference repeatedly noted that congestion plagued some districts, principally those in a few large cities, and it reiterated its plea for additional judges.[72] In 1936 the Attorney General found that dockets were "current" in fifty-one of eighty-five federal judicial districts. By current, he meant that cases could be tried at the next succeeding term of court after the parties notified the court that they were ready. In sixteen districts there was an additional delay amounting to less than six months, and in eighteen others a delay that exceeded six months.[73] Noting that much of the delay occurred before a case was ready for trial, the Attorney General found in 1938 that 32 percent of the cases on the docket had been pending for at least two years and 22 percent for at least three.[74] Thus, even though average duration dropped to about one year, almost a quarter of the cases on the federal dockets still remained untried and unresolved after three years.

Despite the problem areas, however, delay in the federal courts declined significantly during the three decades from World War I to the late 1940s. By 1925 the average duration of a case had dropped to about eighteen months, and throughout the 1930s and 1940s it fluctuated around one year, approximately one-quarter of the average duration in 1912.[75] Although delay was much higher in a few major urban centers and somewhat higher in another ten to fifteen districts, the burden of delay was substantially less in the three decades after World War I than it had been in the three preceding decades.

Legislative Encroachments

Within the broad limits set by the Constitution, the legal foundations of the system were vulnerable to legislation. State statutes could oust the federal common law and impose at least indirect restraints on the ability of corporations to remove. Congress, too, could override rules of the federal common law, and it enjoyed almost complete authority to alter or terminate the jurisdiction of the lower federal courts. Although statutory law had grown throughout the late nineteenth century, after 1910 it came to occupy most of the industrial tort law field and, on a smaller and more varied scale, encroached further into the areas of contract and insurance law. As legislative efforts expanded, the realm of the federal common law contracted. Jurisdictional legislation also narrowed the scope of the corporate system. Although Congress left the basic structure of federal jurisdiction unchanged, it limited the right to remove in several important areas and forced corporate defendants to litigate more of their cases in the state courts.

The increasing sweep of legislation resulted from a variety of factors. The growing size and complexity of the national economy led state legislatures to try to protect their local interests and in turn forced the federal government to assert a national interest. The rise of science, professional associations, and faith in administrative expertise convinced Americans that they could and should use governmental agencies to control their social environment.[76] Suspicion and fear of large corporations and a growing compassion for the victims of industrialization spurred many to support ameliorative legislation, while a desire to stabilize a rapidly changing social order, to protect one's market position, or to secure other special legislative favors drove others. As the early years of the twentieth century inspired the movement for efficiency and administrative expertise in the federal judicial system, so they gave birth to a range of similar movements for legislative reform of the society at large. Whatever their agendas, the various groups proposed legislative solutions that usually threatened the realm of the common law and pushed, gently or not, against the boundaries of the system of corporate diversity jurisdiction.[77] Some of the solutions directly attacked those boundaries and the system itself.

By the 1890s insurance regulation was growing more widespread and detailed, and between 1895 and 1903 a large number of states, especially in the West and South, passed statutes controlling the licensing of insurance agents, establishing more rigorous deposit and liability requirements, and attempting to improve the position of policyholders in litigating their claims against the companies. State statutes established mandatory terms and provisions for policies sold locally, limiting in the process both the contractual options of the companies and the reach of the common law. Half or more of the states adopted statutes aimed at discouraging or preventing insurance companies from removing suits to the federal courts.[78]

For the system of corporate diversity litigation, however, state and federal legislation altering the law of torts caused the more important and far-reaching changes. Not until the 1890s did any number of states begin to limit the employers' defenses by statute, and as late as 1906 the common law remained the predominant source of rules in industrial tort cases. Although half the states had made some effort to moderate the fellow servant rule by statute, only seven had abolished it entirely. Similarly, some twenty states had qualified the assumption of the risk defense, but the doctrine still remained viable in most and powerful in many. Contributory negligence was virtually free of legislative modification. Only three states had altered it by statute in any way.[79] Moreover, some of the statutes that modified the common law defenses were themselves quite narrow and for the most part left the defenses in force.[80]

Between the turn of the century and World War I the Supreme Court upheld the constitutionality of state employers' liability and safety appliance statutes. It affirmed the right of the states to regulate hazardous business activities[81] and to enact special legislation protecting railroad workers.[82] In 1910 it sanctioned state authority to make the fact of a railroading injury prima facie evidence of a company's negligence as applied to both passengers and employees, thereby allowing the states to apply a presumptive evidentiary rule that rejected the federal rule that the Court had announced a decade earlier in *Patton*.[83] A year later it upheld a state statute that prohibited companies from defending on the ground that an injured employee had accepted benefits from a company's relief department.[84] By World War I it was clear that the states had broad constitutional authority to remake the law of industrial accidents. It was "indisputable," the Court declared in 1917, that state employers' liability statutes could provide that "the doctrines of contributory negligence, assumption of risk and fellow servant shall not bar recovery, and that the burden of proof shall be upon the defendant to show a compliance with" relevant safety appliance statutes.[85]

In the first decade of the twentieth century, however, more and more Americans were growing dissatisfied with the common law of industrial accidents, even as modified by employers' liability laws. The system of common law adjudication was, they argued, wasteful and inefficient in the context of modern industry and the massive number of injuries it caused. Recovery remained a matter of chance; jury awards were erratic and often unrelated to the severity of the injury; and ever-growing multitudes of claims seemed to be swamping the courts. Moreover, the system frequently required protracted litigation, imposed long delays on injured workers, and forced them to pay a large percentage of any recovery to their lawyers. Further, because the system retained the negligence principle, however seriously modified, workers who were themselves at fault or who were unable to prove either causality or their employers' negligence were left without compensation. Quickly after the turn of the century the idea grew that industrial injuries should be considered an unavoidable part of the productive process and that compensation should be awarded automatically as a normal cost of doing business.

The rise of the new personal injury bar probably contributed significantly to the growing dissatisfaction with the common law system. By altering the balance of inequality, especially in the huge and murky informal legal process, personal injury specialists steadily drove up the total costs that accidents imposed on corporations. Further, by raising the specter of perjury, dishonest claims, and unethical tactics—which, regardless of their frequency, corporate attorneys seemed to fear deeply—they raised the threat of persistent and unfairly imposed liabilities. Perhaps too, by forcing companies and their attorneys to deal professionally with "lower" elements of the bar, they may also have made handling tort claims particularly distasteful to some corporate representatives. Although the growing demands for reform of the law of industrial compensation stemmed from a variety of factors, it seemed no accident that fundamental change followed by little more than a decade the full emergence of the new personal injury bar.[86]

So, too, the Supreme Court's decisions restricting removal jurisdiction after 1900 probably helped fuel the spreading dissatisfaction among corporations with common law litigation. By broadening substantially the opportunities for plaintiffs to defeat removal and ensure themselves a state forum, the Court altered the calculus of litigation advantage in the system and forced higher settlement costs on corporate defendants. As litigation became less promising and more costly, the alternatives seemed ever more attractive.

The sweeping reform to which many groups turned was workmen's compensation. Although compensation laws came in a number of varieties, their basic theory was simple. Workers would be relieved of the burden of litigation and guaranteed compensation for injury irrespective of fault. Formal payment schedules would determine the amount of compensation due according to the worker's wage level and the severity of his injury. A state board or commission would administer the plan, and employers would fund it. In return for the funding, the compensation programs would relieve employers of liability for industrial injuries, free them from the costs of litigation and claims administration, and enable them to predict rationally their costs of doing business. In addition, because the scheduled compensation levels would be set at about half of the workers' actual losses, the programs were not expected to raise significantly the employers' overall costs.[87]

After a decade of increasingly serious discussion, the workmen's compensation movement swept the United States in the years after 1910. A growing body of statistical information seemed to confirm the inefficiency of the fault system and the apparent inevitability of industrial accidents, while political pressure mounted in favor of substantial reform. Presidents Theodore Roosevelt, William Howard Taft, and Woodrow Wilson successively endorsed the idea, and many business, labor and reform organizations lent their support. Although there were sharp disagreements over procedures, time restrictions on recovery, and the amounts to be paid, few opposed the basic idea of workmen's compensation. In a rush, twelve states enacted workmen's compensation laws in 1911, and within the next seven years another twenty joined them.[88]

In a series of cases between 1915 and 1919 the Supreme Court upheld several varieties of workmen's compensation acts against a range of constitutional challenges. "The scheme of the act is so wide a departure from common-law standards respecting the responsibility of employer to employee," it declared in the first major test case, "that doubts naturally have been raised respecting its constitutional validity."[89] In spite of intimations that the statutes came close to constitutional limits, the Court let them stand as reasonable exercises of the police power. Two years later, in its most closely divided decision on workmen's compensation, the Court upheld an Arizona law that was particularly favorable to injured workers because it allowed them to choose between a guaranteed compensation system and a jury action under a broad employers' liability law. In 1919, a year and a half after argument on the Arizona statute and after repeated false starts, five Justices finally voted to uphold it.[90]

Thus, by the beginning of the 1920s, workmen's compensation had spread across the nation and survived constitutional scrutiny. Most of the remaining states quickly fell into line. By 1923 forty-two states had enacted workmen's compensation statutes, and in 1948 the last holdout made it unanimous.[91] Under the new statutes administrative determinations, often quick and simple, annually awarded compensation for hundreds of thousands of industrial injuries and cut deeply into the number of cases that would otherwise have been drawn into the system of corporate diversity litigation. Moreover, even when awards under the statutes were contested in court, as they were far more frequently than workmen's compensation advocates had anticipated, the statutory law of the states—not the federal common law—generally controlled the outcome. The workmen's compensation movement virtually eliminated the federal common law in what had been one of the largest classes of cases in the system.[92]

On the federal level Congress, too, was narrowing the bounds of the system of corporate diversity litigation. The federal Safety Appliance Act of 1893 began the process.[93] The act mandated a variety of mechanical improvements on interstate railroads, including improved braking and coupling equipment, and it abolished the assumption of risk defense when an injury was caused by a violation of the statutory requirements. Not until the early twentieth century, however, did the act begin to have an impact on tort litigation. Congress gave the railroads until 1898 to meet most of its safety requirements, and the railroads succeeded in delaying the statute's effective date. In December 1897 294 carriers petitioned the Interstate Commerce Commission (ICC) for a five-year extension, claiming economic hardship as a result of the depression. The ICC granted a two-year extension. Subsequently, the roads petitioned again, claiming an inability to repair cars because of the rush of business that followed the depression's end. The commission extended the statute's effective date for another seven months.[94] Technical problems and a narrow scope also lessened the statute's immediate effectiveness. Arguably, at least, it applied to only some railroad cars and reached them only when they were actually moving in interstate commerce. Further, the statute did not expressly create a private cause of action on behalf of injured workers. Instead, it provided for enforcement upon complaint by local United States Attorneys and imposed a mild penalty of $100 for each violation.

After the turn of the century the situation began to change. In late 1901 the act finally went into full effect, and in 1903 Congress passed an amendment[95] that eliminated much of the act's arguable narrowness. The following year the Supreme Court reversed a strained and narrow construction that the Eighth Circuit had placed on it. The statute, the Court declared in *Johnson v. Southern Pacific Co.*, should be construed liberally to achieve "the plain intention of Congress" to "promote the public welfare by securing the safety of employes [*sic*] and travelers."[96] In his annual report for 1905 the Attorney General hailed the decision for "sustaining the law and placing it upon a firm foundation," and he announced that "the Government is determined upon a strict enforcement." Although United States Attorneys received only 11 reported violations of the Safety Appliance Act in 1903, in the next two years they received almost 300 and initiated 110 prosecutions.[97]

Both Congress and the Court continued to extend the reach of federal railroad safety legislation during the next decade. Congress expanded the Safety Appliance Act again in 1910[98] and imposed additional safety requirements in the Hours of Service Act in 1907[99] and the Boiler Inspection Act of 1911,[100] establishing in the latter an elaborate system of federal safety inspections and company reporting requirements. Beginning in 1908 the Court put a more muscular construction on the Safety Appliance Act. "The obvious purpose of the legislature," it declared, "was to supplant the qualified duty of the common law with an absolute duty deemed by it more just."[101] During the following decade it held that the statute imposed liability for violations even when a railroad was free of negligence.[102]

Congress encroached further on the system of corporate diversity litigation when it repeatedly nibbled at the jurisdiction of the lower courts in the years after 1910. In 1911 it raised the jurisdictional amount to $3,000,[103] and in 1915 it deprived federally chartered railroads of the right to remove.[104] During the war, too, when Congress authorized the federal government to operate the railroads, it expressly provided that federal involvement would not enlarge the ability of any railroad to remove suits to the national courts.[105] Finally, it trimmed the right of removal again in 1925 when it extended the ban on removal by federally chartered railroads to include other federally chartered corporations.[106]

The single most direct limitation that Congress placed on the operation of the system was the Federal Employers' Liability Act (FELA). The first FELA,[107] enacted in 1906, fell victim to the Supreme Court two years later on the ground that its provisions reached beyond interstate commerce.[108] Within months of the decision Congress responded by passing a second FELA, carefully narrowed to meet the Court's view of interstate commerce.[109] The new act applied only to a "common carrier by railroad" operating in interstate commerce, and it covered only injuries that occurred to employees "while engaging in interstate commerce." In 1912 the Court upheld the constitutionality of the narrowed act.[110]

The FELA reoriented the federal law of industrial accidents and abrogated critical parts of the federal common law. In the cases it reached the act abolished the fellow servant rule, substituted a "comparative negligence" standard for the defense of contributory negligence, and eliminated both the assumption of risk and the contributory negligence defenses whenever a violation of any federal safety act contributed to the injury. Another provision voided contracts that exempted common carriers from any liability that the statute created, and a 1910 amendment authorized a new cause of action for the heirs of workers killed in the course of employment.[111] Each provision passed constitutional muster. No one, the Supreme Court declared in upholding the second FELA, had a "vested" right to "any rule of the common law."[112]

In general the federal courts construed the FELA reasonably, though they emphasized that it did not remove every obstacle to recovery.[113] Contributory negligence and assumption of the risk, though limited, remained viable defenses, and the latter seemed to expand in significance outside the context of the Safety Appliance Act.[114] Most important, plaintiffs still had to prove fault on the part of their employers.[115] Those obstacles barred recovery for many workers. In 1914 the Supreme Court ruled that whatever common law issues arose under the statute were federal issues and hence that federal law controlled their determination.[116]

In addition to changing the substance of interstate railroad tort law, Congress passed an amendment to the FELA in 1910 that added two significant procedural changes.[117] One was an expanded choice of venue that allowed plaintiffs to bring suit in any district where the cause of action arose or where the railroad was resident or doing business.[118] The other was an express antiremoval clause. The latter amendment provided that state and federal courts had concurrent jurisdiction over FELA actions and that "no case arising under this Act and brought in any state court of competent jurisdiction shall be removed to any court of the United States."[119]

In spite of the seemingly clear wording of the antiremoval amendment, employers sought to avoid it. They argued that the 1910 amendment merely prevented removal of FELA actions when jurisdiction rested solely on the federal question that arose under the statutory claim itself. If diversity of citizenship existed, they contended, an employer should still be able to remove. The lower federal courts rejected the contention almost unanimously, though sometimes reluctantly. "If this court had the power to amend the proviso to the removal statute, it would speedily do so," a New York federal judge announced in 1915. "It is a harsh rule to deprive carriers engaged in interstate commerce of the privilege of removing."[120] The Supreme Court settled the issue between 1915 and 1917. In three separate cases it held that the 1910 amendment meant literally that "no case" brought under the FELA could be removed.[121]

The FELA scheme apparently appealed to many congressmen. When the workmen's compensation movement began to sweep across the nation, a range of reform groups began pushing for a federal compensation act. In 1910 Congress appointed a special joint congressional Employers' Liability and Workmen's Compensation Commission that held extensive hearings and recommended a federal workmen's compensation bill.[122] President Taft supported the proposal, and the Judiciary Committees of both the Senate and the House reported it favorably. Progressives and some labor groups criticized it, however, claiming that the bill was too restrictive and niggardly in its treatment of injured workers and that it unfairly relieved the railroads of the liabilities created under the FELA and the Safety Appliance Act. The five dissenters on the House Judiciary Committee specifically protested a provision of the bill that, they maintained, would make it difficult for claimants to bring suits under the proposed act in the state courts. The provision, the dissenters charged, would "operate to the benefit of the railroads by enabling them to have these cases tried in the Federal courts."[123] Although the Senate passed the bill in 1912, it died in the House. Subsequent efforts failed to revive it.[124]

Not only did Congress choose to stay with the FELA scheme in 1912, but it later decided to reuse it. In 1915 it passed a far-reaching act intended to protect American seamen, probably the most disadvantaged group of workers in the country. The act was designed to end a variety of abuses and to improve the health, safety, and living conditions under which they worked.[125] In the Jones Act of 1920 Congress amended the statute and extended all the substantive and procedural provisions of the FELA to seamen, including the absolute ban on the removal of personal injury actions against employers.[126] In the mid-1920s the Supreme Court ruled that the fellow servant rule no longer barred recovery for injured seamen and that their actions for damages in state courts could not be removed.[127]

In the years after 1910, then, the system was both contracting in scope and evolving in form. State employers' liability and workmen's compensation laws combined with the FELA and federal safety and jurisdictional legislation to compress sharply the boundaries of the federal common law and to allow more plaintiffs to negate the threat of removal. The scope of the system, like the burdens of distance and delay, was shrinking. At the same time, the system continued to function and developed new characteristic patterns of litigation, in large part, of course, because of the tactical sophistication of the new plaintiffs' personal injury bar. The most immediate changes occurred in tort litigation under the FELA. As a class, railroad tort claims had spurred fiercely contested litigations prior to passage of the FELA, and they continued to do so after it. Indeed, litigation under the FELA and related safety acts exploded in the years after 1910, and within five years they accounted for almost 10 percent of the appeals that reached the Supreme Court's docket.[128]

The System Curbed: Litigation Under the FELA

The FELA struck at the system of corporate diversity litigation on two levels, limiting as a matter of substantive law the defenses available to employers and conferring on employees as a matter of procedural law a broad choice of venue and an absolute choice between state and federal forums. Although in actions under the statute there would be no formal difference in the applicable rules of substantive law that state and federal courts would apply, the special procedural characteristics of the FELA nevertheless gave employees powerful advantages, including choice among judges, procedural rules, geographical locations, and jury systems. Equally important, they allowed plaintiffs to avoid federal court without risking a remand battle over joinder and without having to discount their claims.[129]

Not surprisingly, employees took advantage of their absolute forum choice under the FELA to bring the great majority of their claims in the state courts. A study of three federal circuits found that railroad tort actions fell off sharply in both the Fifth and Ninth Circuits after 1910 and that maritime tort suits dropped noticeably in the Second Circuit after the passage of the Jones Act.[130] The American Law Institute (ALI) study of thirteen federal judicial districts during the year 1929–30 found that seven of the districts did not terminate a single FELA case during the entire year and that three others—all with relatively large populations and dockets—terminated a mere two, three, and four FELA actions respectively. It seems clear that the great majority of FELA plaintiffs strongly preferred a state to a federal forum.[131] As a general matter, the federal courts probably heard no more than a fifth of all FELA actions, and likely less.[132] Moreover, a review of 182 applications for certiorari in FELA cases between 1926 and 1931 suggested that their choice was wise and that FELA plaintiffs often fared quite well in the state courts.[133] In both its substantive and procedural provisions, then, the FELA significantly altered the balance of tactical advantage in the system.

The most troubling and illuminating litigation problems that the statute created arose from its interstate commerce requirement. In an abundance of caution after the Supreme Court struck down the first FELA, Congress framed the second act in terms of a double restriction. First, it reached only "common carriers by railroad while engaging in commerce between any of the several states or territories." Second, it covered the employee only "while he is employed by such carrier in such [interstate] commerce." Thus, the act required both the railroad and the injured employee to be operating in interstate commerce at the time of injury. An unending stream of difficult and in many cases essentially arbitrary fact decisions seemed unavoidable.

The Supreme Court struggled awkwardly to draw a line that would identify the kinds of situations that fell within the statute. "The true test," it stated in one of its earliest decisions, was whether "the work in question [was] a part of the interstate commerce in which the carrier is engaged."[134] That "test," of course, was not the least bit helpful, and by 1914 the Court admitted that "it is difficult to define the line which divides the State from interstate business." Among the reasons for the difficulty was the fact that the railroads did not divide their business along those lines. "[D]uring the same day, railroad employes [*sic*] often and rapidly pass from one class of employment to another."[135] The early decisions of the Court seemed to construe the statute broadly,[136] but those after mid-1914 began to restrict its reach to injuries "closely" related to interstate commerce. By 1917 it was clear that the FELA did not cover a large number of railroad activities and that many injuries would fall outside its scope. In general, employees would be covered if at the time of their injury, they were working on a train moving or about to move on a run that would cross state lines or if they were servicing equipment immediately involved in interstate traffic. Conversely, they would be outside the statute if they were working on trains moving intrastate or with supplies or equipment that would not be immediately used on interstate trains.[137] Thus, although the FELA withdrew many railroad tort cases from the system, it left many others untouched.[138] And those actions that were not within the FELA, including those that challenged state workmen's compensation awards, remained removable under diversity jurisdiction even if they were controlled by state statutory law.

The FELA's interstate commerce requirement caused problems, however, not merely because it imposed an artificial distinction on the railroads' operations but also because litigants quickly learned the importance and utility of manipulating it. The requirement had a double significance. First, it determined whether federal or state substantive law would apply, a determination that became critical after the Supreme Court's 1917 decision in *New York Central Railroad Co. v. Winfield*.[139] There, the Court held that the FELA preempted the field of compensation for railroad injuries in interstate commerce and that it consequently provided the exclusive remedy for those within its coverage. Specifically, *Winfield* ruled that state workmen's compensation statutes could not be applied to railroad workers injured in interstate commerce, and it thereby prevented plaintiffs covered by the federal statute from obtaining recovery under state law when the latter was more favorable for them than the former. More important, *Winfield* meant that railroad workers in interstate commerce, unlike intrastate railroad employees and most other industrial workers, would be without a legal remedy if they failed to prove fault on the part of their employers or if their employers established what remained of the assumption of risk defense. Second, and independent of whatever substantive rules would be applicable, the FELA's interstate commerce requirement also determined whether a plaintiff could rely on the procedural rights that accompanied a cause of action under the statute, particularly the guarantee against removal. Corporations and their employees litigated the interstate commerce requirement for both of those reasons.

They litigated the issue, too, with ferocity. Barred by *Winfield* from falling back on state workmen's compensation remedies, interstate railroad workers faced the prospect of being left entirely without compensation if their FELA claims failed. At the same time, FELA claims promised a guaranteed antiremoval device and vastly more generous recoveries than were available under workmen's compensation. FELA plaintiffs, in fact, often sought particularly large amounts, commonly pleading claims for $25,000 to $50,000. After 1910, FELA actions became, like joinder cases, another high-stakes litigation form for tort plaintiffs.

Given *Winfield* and the large difference in the amounts recoverable under the FELA and workmen's compensation acts, the parties quickly learned to turn the uncertain scope of the FELA's commerce requirement into a tactical lever. Here, of course, the sophistication of the tort specialists in the personal injury bar was particularly valuable to injured workers. Plaintiffs with strong cases on the merits stretched for an interstate commerce allegation to avoid a small workmen's compensation award; those with weak claims denied that they were working in interstate commerce, preferring the certainty of workmen's compensation to the unacceptably high risks of an unpromising lawsuit. Employers followed the converse strategy. Pushing a weak claim within the ambit of interstate commerce could force a plaintiff to settle cheaply or abandon his suit, whereas establishing that a meritorious claim arose in intrastate commerce could push liability onto the state's workmen's compensation system, reduce the worker's recovery drastically, and save the employer many thousands of dollars.

Further, regardless of the potential recoveries, employees recognized that sometimes they could also use the FELA to prevent an undesired removal even if they most likely did not have a meritorious claim under the federal statute.[140] When they could protect themselves on the merits by pleading an alternative cause of action under state law, they could use the FELA largely or solely as an antiremoval device by alleging that their injury may have occurred in interstate commerce.[141] Plaintiffs were, of course, limited by the requirement that their pleading be in "good faith," but the murky nature of the Supreme Court's line between interstate and intrastate activities often furnished ample leeway. Because the Court had termed the line "difficult" to draw and declared that each case "must be decided in the light of the particular facts,"[142] the "good faith" pleading requirement probably deterred few aggressive plaintiffs' attorneys anxious to avoid federal court. When faced with the issue of unfounded allegations of interstate commerce, the Supreme Court applied the established rule that, absent "a fraudulent purpose to prevent removal,"[143] plaintiff's allegations determined whether a case could be removed. Just as plaintiffs used other jurisdictional tactics to avoid federal court, so they succeeded in preventing removals by pleading claims under the FELA even when their interstate commerce allegations appeared weak and the courts eventually rejected them on their merits.[144]

If employees could exploit the uncertainty of the interstate commerce requirement to defeat removals, employers could exploit it to seek more favorable substantive law, whether state or federal, and to drive up their employees' litigation costs. Whether a plaintiff opted for an FELA claim, a state law claim, or both in the alternative, the amorphous interstate reach of the FELA—exclusive within its domain—often gave employers an additional ground on which to challenge the pleadings. Because the issue was highly fact specific, its resolution could require considerable time and effort. Further, even when there was no significant difference in the substantive law that would be applicable but the employee asserted an FELA claim in the alternative primarily to block an anticipated removal, the interstate commerce allegation remained critical and subject to the same attack by an employer who wanted to remove. In any of those situations, the interstate commerce requirement meant that employers could raise additional and complex issues that would increase both the costs of litigation and the uncertainty of its outcome.[145]

The interstate commerce requirement thus expanded the opportunities for tactical maneuvering and magnified the pressures of the informal legal process. By imposing an additional burden of proof on plaintiffs and compounding the uncertainties they faced, it often strengthened the railroads' bargaining position. "The facts that go to prove the nature of the commerce," the vice-president of the Order of Railway Conductors told Congress in 1916, "are peculiarly within the knowledge of the carrier."[146] A congressional study of railroad injuries in 1932 suggested the practical significance of that jurisdictional uncertainty. It found a large discrepancy between the amounts of both judgments and settlements for train-related as compared with non–train-related injuries. In death and serious injury cases, train-related disabilities received two to three times the amount of compensation that comparable non–train-related disabilities received, whether by settlement or judgment.[147] A central difference between train-related and non–train-related injuries was that the former were far more likely to involve interstate commerce and far more likely to do so in a way that was beyond reasonable challenge.[148] There was "more uncertainty as to whether a nontrain accident comes under Federal or State jurisdiction," the study concluded, "and the employee injured in a nontrain accident is more likely to accept a settlement at a lower figure rather than risk the outcome of a suit."[149]

If the FELA's interstate commerce requirement augmented the influence of the informal legal process, its provision nullifying employers' devices to avoid statutory liability attempted to constrain that same process. Section 5 of the act declared void "any contract, rule, regulation, or device whatsoever, the purpose or intent of which shall be to enable any common carrier to exempt itself from any liability created by this Act."[150] In large part the section was directed at the railroad relief departments that compelled employees to waive their rights to bring legal actions for injury in order to receive their benefits. In *Philadelphia, Baltimore and Washington Railroad Co. v. Schubert*,[151] decided in 1912, the injured employee had accepted $79 in benefits, and his employer raised the standard relief association release clause as a defense to his subsequent suit. The Supreme Court rejected a variety of company arguments, applied Section 5 to void the release, and affirmed the employee's judgment for $7,500.[152]

Although Section 5 unquestionably covered the relief department contract in *Schubert*, it was less clear whether it reached the kind of contract that had been at issue in *Voigt*. The case that would provide the answer, *Robinson v. Baltimore & Ohio Railroad Co.*,[153] reached the Court in 1915. The plaintiff, injured in a collision, was a porter on a Pullman sleeping car carried on an interstate train. The railroad relied on the porter's contract with the Pullman Company, in which the porter agreed to assume all risk of injury from his employment and released from any claims for injury all railroads over which he might travel. Technically, of course, the issue in *Robinson* was one of statutory construction, but it drove to the heart of both the social values and doctrinal ambiguity that had marked *Voigt*. Indeed, both parties relied on *Voigt* to support their position.

The parties agreed that the pivotal question was whether the porter was "employed" by the railroad within the meaning of the FELA. Plaintiff relied principally on *Voigt*'s statements that the railroad and the express company were operating a "joint business" and that they had created "a sort of partnership relation."[154] In addition, he relied on cases declaring that the Pullman Company itself was not a common carrier independent of the railroad and, in particular, on the Court's 1880 decision in *Pennsylvania v. Roy*[155] which held that with respect to the safety of passengers, a Pullman porter was "in law" the employee of the railroad. For its part, the railroad, perhaps anticipating the *Roy* argument, refrained from introducing into evidence whatever contract existed between it and the Pullman Company. Instead, relying on *Voigt* and other cases, it denied that the porter was its employee and maintained that his contract with the Pullman Company was valid and enforceable. *Voigt* had, of course, noted that the injured messenger's presence on the train "was not in pursuance of any contract directly between him and the railroad company."[156]

Affirming *Voigt's* continued validity, *Robinson* announced "that, unless condemned by statute, the contract was a valid one and a bar to recovery."[157] Then, confining *Roy* to cases involving the railroad's strict duty as a common carrier to safeguard passengers, the Court denied that any joint business or agency relation existed between the two companies and concluded that the services performed by the porter for the railroad were nothing more than "an incidental matter."[158] Stating that the statutory term "employed" should be taken in its "natural sense" and pointing out that Congress used no words to indicate that it intended to reach the *Voigt* situation, *Robinson* held that the statutory term was limited to "the conventional relation of employer and employe [sic]."[159] Section 5, therefore, did not apply, and the porter was barred by his contract with Pullman from recovering from the railroad for his injuries.

One obvious potential loophole in the *Voigt–Robinson* rule remained. For almost forty years both state and federal courts had tended to deny common carrier status to sleeping car, railway express, and similar companies that worked regularly with the railroads. Those cases rested in part on tradition and in part on a concern that treating the other companies as common carriers might somehow dilute the strict standard of care that the railroads owed to their passengers.[160] But given the clear purpose of the FELA, there seemed no reason why the statutory category "common carrier by railroad" could not be construed to include those other types of companies.

In a fiery opinion in 1918 the Fifth Circuit did just that.[161] Emphasizing the close business and contractual relations between the railroad and the express company, the Fifth Circuit avoided *Robinson* and cited *Voigt* for the proposition that an express company messenger could fairly be considered an employee of both companies. Primarily, however, it relied on the purpose and scope of the FELA. "It was the purpose of Congress to provide special protection to persons subject to the hazards incident to the operation of railroads," the court explained. "There could have been no reason for giving the protection to a railroad conductor, and refusing it to an express messenger."[162] Then, seeming to address and challenge the Supreme Court directly, the Fifth Circuit declared that "[n]o court ought at this time, in the face of the unequivocal language of the Congress, to make a ruling which would differentiate" between the employees of railway express companies and those of the railroads themselves.[163] The court held that Wells Fargo & Company was a common carrier by railroad within the meaning of the FELA and that Section 5 voided its employee's contract that released the railroad from liability.

If the Fifth Circuit intended its opinion as a challenge, the Supreme Court did not flinch. It reversed. In *Wells Fargo & Co. v. Taylor*,[164] decided in early 1920, the Court stated flatly that *Robinson* controlled and that the statute did not apply. The statutory category "common carrier by railroad" meant only "a railroad company acting as a common carrier."[165] It supported the construction by citing "the ordinary acceptation of the words" and the fact that the statute referred in other sections to railroad equipment. Under *Voigt,* it concluded, the employee's contract was valid and the railroad was free from liability.

Robinson and *Taylor* limited the reach of the FELA and kept *Voigt* alive as a principle of the federal common law. Even more, they again confirmed the power of the informal legal process and the utility of contract as methods of restricting employer liability. The decisions allowed the railroads to continue to avoid liability to third-party employees under the FELA or the common law,[166] and they raised new possibilities for cutting back the liabilities imposed by the new statute. Increasingly integrated operations between two or more companies promised greater efficiency, and as an incident they also offered methods of avoiding liability to employees under the FELA.[167] Further, companies could commit certain parts of their operations to small "independent contractors" who, because they were by legal definition not employees, would also be unable to claim under the FELA.[168] The railroads, in conjunction with other carriers and related companies, tried all of those tactics. Again, they showed that the companies enjoyed advantages not just in litigation tactics but also in their ability to structure and arrange their most basic affairs in ways that would be most likely to insulate them from liability and impose the risks of injuries on inexpert, unorganized, and unsuspecting individuals.

Although the FELA reached only interstate railroad workers, its impact on the system of corporate diversity litigation was nevertheless significant. Railroad workers constituted the most visible, organized, and determined plaintiffs' group in the system. The FELA's antiremoval provision allowed a large number of them to avoid the federal courts, and its substantive provisions offered them relatively favorable rules on which to rely. Even though the FELA did not guarantee recovery, as workmen's compensation acts did, it was a huge improvement over *Baugh.* The undeniable risk of FELA litigation, too, was in large part balanced by the statute's procedural advantages and its promise of recoveries far in excess of those available under workmen's compensation.

Some evidence, too, suggested that the act helped improve the general position of railroad workers. First, and most important, it apparently helped convince the railroads to expand their efforts to improve safety standards and practices, and it may have eventually contributed to the decline in railroad injuries that began in the mid-1920s.[169] Second, it also apparently encouraged more plaintiffs to carry their claims to final judgment and helped raise the average settlement value of their claims. In 1908–10, just as Congress was passing the FELA and its initial amendments, final legal judgments involving injured railroad workers were rendered in 4.6 percent of death claims and 5.4 percent of total permanent disability claims.[170] In comparable cases in 1938–40 final judgments occurred in 8 percent of the former and 16 percent of the latter. Although the percentage of final judgments remained approximately the same in partial permanent disability cases, it almost doubled in claims for temporary disability.[171] Further, in 1932 both settlements and judgments in FELA cases were much higher than they were in non-FELA cases during the same year or than they had been in all cases in 1908–10. Adjusting for differences in income levels between 1908–10 and 1932, the FELA seemed in particular to have helped raise both settlement amounts and judgments in death cases.[172]

The Changing Contours of Federal Judge-made Law

For most of the Justices on the Supreme Court, and probably for the majority of federal judges, the proliferation of state and national legislation threatened more than the domain of the federal common law. On the state level legislation threatened the ideal of uniform national laws, and on both state and federal levels it frequently threatened the values associated with liberty of contract. Finally, it also threatened the relative independence that the federal judiciary had so long enjoyed. For most of the nineteenth century the federal courts had been free to develop the federal common law and, far more generally, to supervise the growing national economy with relatively little legislative interference. By the first decade of the twentieth century the rising tide of legislation seemed to place all of those values and interests under siege.

The Supreme Court responded in complex and sometimes inconsistent ways as the Justices tried to reconcile their views of the Constitution and the society with those of the legislative and executive branches of the state and federal governments. In general they found ways to approve most of the new legislation, as the decisions upholding the various provisions of the FELA, the Safety Appliance Act, and state employers' liability and workmen's compensation statutes attested. As the Court's decision in the Arizona workmen's compensation case attested, however, they sometimes upheld them by only the narrowest of margins; and as the first FELA decision showed, they sometimes failed to uphold them at all. In a small but growing and often particularly important number of cases, the Court invalidated reform statutes and erected constitutional barriers to certain kinds of social and economic legislation.

Crystallizing in the 1890s, the doctrine of substantive due process emerged in the years after 1900 as a powerful constitutional limit on government action, prohibiting state and federal legislation or administrative actions that unreasonably deprived individuals of their rights to liberty and property under the Fifth and Fourteenth Amendments. The Supreme Court, of course, was the ultimate arbiter of what was "reasonable" as well as what constituted protected "liberty" and "property." Laws aimed at eliminating child labor, improving the position of labor unions, and regulating hours of work and levels of pay proved especially vulnerable.

Substantive due process became critical to the federal common law because it stood constitutional guard over the latter's realm. To the extent that it created areas into which legislatures could not intrude, it ensured that the federal common law would remain vital and untouched. When the Supreme Court ruled in 1908 and 1915 that federal and then state statutes outlawing the "yellow-dog" labor contract were unconstitutional, for example, it secured at least part of the field of employment contracts for the federal common law.[173] In 1917, when the Court subsequently held in *Hitchman Coal & Coke Co. v. Mitchell*[174] that yellow-dog contracts were valid and enforceable in the federal courts, it created federal common law in the newly secured area.

Hitchman was not unique. Beyond the use of substantive due process, in the years before World War I the Supreme Court found other ways to preserve and enhance the lawmaking powers of the national courts. In 1905 it decided that federal law, not the common law of the states, controlled the scope and meaning of contracts when an issue arose under the Constitution's contract clause. "And we determine for ourselves the existence and extent of such contract," the Court emphasized in *Muhlker v. Harlem Railroad Co.*[175] Two years later it announced in *Kansas v. Colorado*[176] that the federal common law controlled disputes between states and that neither the states nor the other branches of the federal government could establish law in such cases. In 1909, in *Siler v. Louisville and Nashville*

Railroad Co.,[177] the Court expanded the jurisdiction of the federal courts to hear and decide state law claims when there was no diverse citizenship. The federal courts could decide state law issues if they were joined with federal claims, and they could pass over the federal claims and "decide the local questions only, and omit to decide the Federal questions."[178] The following year, in *Kuhn v. Fairmont Coal Co.*,[179] the Court extended the federal common law into matters of local property law, an area that had previously been regarded as beyond the reach of the *Swift* doctrine.

Similarly, the Court expanded its use of the commerce clause to widen the area of federal supremacy. It continued to invoke the "dormant" commerce power to invalidate state legislation that intruded excessively on interstate commerce even in the absence of a federal statute; and in a series of decisions under the Carmack Amendment, other sections of the Hepburn Act, and the Safety Appliance Act, it used the doctrine of preemption to exclude state laws entirely from major areas of interstate commerce. When Congress regulated interstate commerce, the Court repeatedly held in the years before World War I, its legislation was exclusive. The states could not validly enact supplementary laws, let alone inconsistent ones. The problem was that in none of those statutes had Congress expressed its intent to preempt all relevant state legislation. Traditional doctrine held that in the absence of such congressional intent, the states enjoyed some constitutional authority to supplement national legislation. However desirable uniformity might have been, and the case for uniformity seemed dubious in some of the decisions, it was the Court that determined on its own that preemption was necessary. Although it was technically construing federal statutes rather than making common law, its decisions barred state legislative authority from important areas of commerce and established the federal courts—within the general guidelines of the congressional statutes—as in effect the principal legal authority in those areas.[180]

The Court used the same preemption argument when it construed the FELA in *Winfield,* and with the same results. In each instance the Court's decisions attempted to enforce uniform national rules and at the same time enhanced the lawmaking authority of the federal courts. For the most part, too, the decisions seemed to protect the interests of the carriers at the expense of both shippers and workers. There was more than irony involved when *Winfield* supported its contention that "the controlling law should be uniform and not change at every state line" by citing only a single authority, the Court's 1893 decision in *Baugh.*[181]

Perhaps the most striking area where the Court demanded uniformity and expanded the lawmaking powers of the federal judiciary was in admiralty. In *Southern Pacific Co. v. Jensen,*[182] decided the same year as *Winfield,* the Court held that a state workmen's compensation statute could not provide a remedy for a fatally injured maritime worker. The Constitution conferred the admiralty jurisdiction exclusively on the federal courts, *Jensen* explained, and it did so to preserve the "essential" characteristics of that jurisdiction and to maintain the "uniformity" of its law. Allowing state workmen's compensation statutes to intrude would frustrate both purposes. Unless and until Congress exercised its legislative authority over the field, the maritime law—construed authoritatively by the federal courts alone—remained in force and beyond the power of the states to alter.[183]

Jensen gave rise to a rather remarkable sequence of lawmaking that demonstrated the extent to which the Court was committed to uniform laws. Twice, in

1917 and again in 1922, Congress tried to amend the law to allow state workmen's compensation statutes to provide remedies for injured maritime workers. Both times the Court held the acts unconstitutional.[184] The requirement of uniformity in the maritime law, it declared, meant that Congress could provide workmen's compensation remedies for maritime workers only by enacting a uniform national statute. In 1927, a full decade after *Jensen*, Congress provided such a national statutory remedy for injured maritime workers in the Longshoremen's and Harbor Workers' Compensation Act.[185] Five years later the Court upheld its constitutionality.[186]

Complementing its various techniques that freed the federal judiciary from state law, the Court also gave narrow constructions to some federal statutory provisions and thereby allowed parts of the federal common law to survive and even thrive. It narrowed the reach of the Safety Appliance Act and expanded, in effect as a matter of federal common law, the employer's right contractually to limit its liability.[187] More important, by holding that the FELA both preempted state law and left assumption of risk and contributory negligence as valid defenses, the Court preserved much of the federal common law of master and servant. During the 1920s and 1930s, in fact, it often construed the two defenses broadly and seemed to expand their scope in FELA cases.[188] "The rights and obligations of the petitioner," the Court noted explicitly in 1926, "depend upon [the FELA] and applicable principles of common law as interpreted by the federal courts."[189] Finally, by regularly reviewing the sufficiency of evidence on which the judgments of state courts rested in FELA actions, the Court attempted sporadically but repeatedly to force on the states a federal common law standard of proof.[190]

Although the Court created alternative areas of judicial independence as legislation encroached, the overall significance of the federal common law in the system of corporate diversity litigation nonetheless declined sharply. The new areas of judicial independence were more limited than the old. Some of them did not apply to diversity actions, and others did not survive. Litigation between the states was rare, and the authority to construe federal statutes, though critical, remained a restricted and ultimately dependent power. The Longshoremen's and Harbor Workers' Compensation Act deprived *Jensen* of much of its practical significance in 1927, and in 1932 the Norris–LaGuardia Anti-Injunction Act interred *Hitchman* by declaring yellow-dog contracts unenforceable in the national courts.[181] In 1939 Congress in effect wiped out a long series of federal common law decisions when it amended the FELA and sharply restricted the defenses of assumption of risk and contributory negligence.[192] Even *Kuhn*, which pushed the *Swift* doctrine into local property law, proved to be a limited expansion. More to the point, whatever its general impact, it had only a minor role in the system of corporate diversity litigation. Relatively few individuals, at least from the working classes, found themselves litigating real property claims against national corporations.

Further, at least some of the doctrines of the federal common law became less burdensome to plaintiffs. Shortly after the first FELA was passed, for example, a few federal courts began moderating *Patton's* rigorous evidentiary standards. In 1908, though framing its opinion in narrow and cautious language, the Sixth Circuit applied the doctrine of *res ipsa loquitur* in an employee's personal injury action.[193] After 1910 other courts followed, and in decisions in 1914 and 1917 the Supreme Court seemed to recognize that the Safety Appliance Act and the FELA together called for less exacting standards of proof than *Patton* seemed to demand.[194] By the 1920s most federal courts treated *Patton* as the product of a bygone era, and they generally allowed injured workers to rely on *res ipsa*. "Since the Patton Case," noted the Second Circuit in 1923, the courts have increasingly "recognized the practical difficulties which arise in a case of injury or death because of defective appliances or equipment." They recognized, in short, that the "plaintiff, in such circumstances, has either no means or no adequate means of ascertaining" exactly what happened and why it happened. Consequently, *res ipsa* should be available.[195]

Thus, if *Voigt* and *Northern Assurance* still stood as vital principles of federal law in the 1920s and 1930s, *Baugh* and *Patton* had been largely negated. Although the federal common law still disadvantaged many individuals, especially insurance claimants, it reached fewer tort plaintiffs and treated them less unfavorably than it had in the years before 1910. The federal common law remained alive after World War I, but legislation confined its scope and the federal courts themselves softened some of its harshness.

In the years after 1910 the system changed in three principal ways. First, and by far most broadly, its scope contracted and its harshness toward plaintiffs moderated. A specialized personal injury bar provided plaintiffs with more widespread representation and more sophisticated tactics. The extralegal burdens of distance and delay lightened. The domain of the federal common law shrank. State and federal legislation gave plaintiffs more favorable substantive and procedural law, and Congress specifically narrowed removal jurisdiction. Finally, the FELA and workmen's compensation acts withdrew huge numbers of industrial injury cases from the system's operations.

Second, but on a far narrower scale, the Supreme Court partially offset those developments by bringing new areas into the realm of the federal common law and, as we shall see, by expanding the right of insurance companies to remove. Further, the Court countered the legislation that shrank the domain of the federal common law by enhancing the ability of the federal judiciary to control statutes, to enforce national standards, and especially to limit the laws of the states. In doing so it used the doctrine of preemption, the dormant commerce clause, substantive due process, and the "implicit" lawmaking powers that it found in the grants of jurisdiction over suits between states and suits in admiralty.

Third, and perhaps less obvious, in both tort and insurance actions the system's litigation tactics grew more complex. Attorneys for both individuals and corporations developed a range of new tools, and litigation in the system began to spread onto the interstate level and into federal equity courts. That last change in the system, exemplified by the uses that the parties learned to make of the FELA's interstate commerce requirement, requires separate and more extended discussion.

Chapter 8

The Rise of Interstate Forum Shopping

From early in the nation's history Americans recognized the opportunities that the geographical breadth and federal structure of the United States offered to the bold and imaginative. In the years after the Civil War national corporations began methodically to utilize those opportunities, and the uses they made of diversity jurisdiction exemplified some of the advantages that the enterprising could create from the materials of geography and federalism.[1] Individuals who sued national corporations, and more particularly the plaintiffs' personal injury bar, eventually proved no exception.

One of the fundamental conditions that formed and sustained the system of corporate diversity litigation was the practical necessity for individuals to bring suit near their homes. When changes in transportation and social organization freed more individuals from that condition and alterations in jurisdictional rules expanded their legal opportunities to litigate in out-of-state forums, the system gained a new and dynamic quality. Although the great majority of individual plaintiffs continued to sue near their homes, after 1910 sizable numbers began for the first time to bring their suits in out-of-state forums that offered them special advantages. Interstate forum shopping was hardly new, but the number and especially the type of plaintiffs who began to adopt the tactic were.

The changes that the twentieth century wrought in American society guaranteed that growing numbers of plaintiffs would attempt to exploit the advantages of interstate litigation tactics. With the advent of progressivism, the general political climate changed profoundly, generating a strong sympathy for individuals who were injured by corporations and a new admiration for those who fought back. The political rhetoric of progressivism etched the image of injured workers and consumers as corporate victims, and it exhorted them to use every legal weapon at hand to force corporations to do justice. The Federal Employers' Liability Act (FELA) and states' workmen's compensation statutes—both of which offered new opportunities and incentives for interstate forum shopping—were major accomplishments of progressivism, and it seemed only proper that their intended beneficiaries take full advantage of the rights they conferred.

Improvements in interstate transportation and communications were essential to the process, as was the ability of growing numbers of Americans in the early years of the twentieth century to put them to use. Ethnic and immigrant aid societies, settlement houses, and labor unions grew in significance and sophistication, and they provided wider social contacts for workers and their families, spread information about the legal system, and guided those with potential claims to legal specialists who would represent them.[2] After 1910, for example, the railroad brotherhoods expanded their efforts to help members and their families when injury or death forced them to seek compensation. They recognized that the problem was twofold: Their members needed protection against both the companies and the dishonest chasers.[3] The unions began to assist injured workers or their families in attempting to settle claims, and they began more actively to investigate personal injury attorneys to identify those who were both able and honest and who were also willing to give "assurances against overcharging."[4]

Two of the unions, the huge Brotherhood of Railroad Trainmen and the much smaller Brotherhood of Railroad Signalmen, took even stronger measures. In the early 1920s, reported an attorney for the trainmen, complaints grew that the roads were exacting "ridiculously low settlements" through "dismissals and economic pressure" and that "ambulance-chasing lawyers" were inducing union members to sign "unconscionable contracts for 50 or 60 percent of the recoveries."[5] Investigations confirmed many of the reports, he explained, and in 1930 the Trainmen established their own legal aid department. The Signalmen soon did the same.[6] The Trainmen required locals to report all injuries to the national headquarters, and they sent out their own investigators to examine the facts and provide information and advice to injured workers or their families. In addition, they appointed as regional counsel eighteen law firms across the nation that agreed to represent members for a maximum contingent fee of only 25 percent.[7] The Brotherhood's investigators informed injured members and their families about the regional counsel, and the organization regularly published their names and addresses in its magazine, the *Railroad Trainman,* which circulated to nearly 220,000 members.[8] By the late 1940s the Trainmen's regional counsel were concluding more than six hundred cases a year on behalf of injured railroad workers and obtaining settlements that averaged more than five times the amounts paid to those who settled without legal representation.[9]

The personal injury bar, too, developed its own entrepreneurs. Successful urban tort specialists developed reputations and contacts that brought them out-of-state business, and some attorneys and firms began to expand their soliciting operations beyond the limits of their city and state.[10] By the beginning of the 1920s, ambulance chasing, especially in serious tort cases where damage claims ranged from $10,000 up to $50,000 or more, had become the newest form of interstate commerce.

The Legal Foundations of Interstate Forum Use

The legal right of Americans to sue in out-of-state forums rested largely on two long-established doctrines, one rooted in common law ideas and the other in the Constitution. The first was the rule that any otherwise proper judicial forum that could validly exercise personal jurisdiction over a defendant could adjudicate a "transitory" cause of action. Essentially, the law regarded a cause of action as transitory if it would impose personal liability on one individual in favor of another, as opposed to determining rights to real property, enforcing a criminal or penal sanction, or adjudicating an issue of status, such as marriage. The idea was that transitory causes of action accompanied the parties wherever they went, and considerations of prudence and justice required that an aggrieved person be able to obtain her remedy wherever she was able to locate the wrongdoer. "Wherever, by either the commor law or the statute law of a State, a right of action has become fixed and a legal liability incurred," the Supreme Court declared in 1880, "that liability may be enforced and the right of action pursued in any court which has jurisdiction of such matters and can obtain jurisdiction of the parties."[11]

The second fundamental doctrine that underwrote interstate forum shopping rested on Article IV, Section 1 of the Constitution: "The citizens of each state shall be entitled to all privileges and immunities of the citizens in the several states." Although the scope of the clause was far from settled in the nineteenth century, several Supreme Court decisions stated that access to the courts of the states was one of the privileges that the clause guaranteed.[12] Thus, not only did American courts of general jurisdiction have the right to enforce transitory causes of action, but plaintiffs who were United States citizens also had a right, largely undemarcated in scope but unquestionably constitutional in nature, to sue on those claims in the courts of every state in the nation.

Two relatively technical legal doctrines, in turn, helped shape and limit the strictly legal advantages that plaintiffs could gain by suing in out-of-state forums. The first was called "conflict of laws" or "choice of law," and it determined which state's laws properly applied to a case. The law conceived a cause of action as "arising" under the laws of a particular state or nation and held that the laws of that place should be applied to determine the validity of the cause, regardless of the forum where it was heard. Commonly followed "conflicts" rules, for example, held that tort claims were controlled by the laws of the place where the injury occurred and that contract claims were controlled by the laws of the place where the contract was entered into or where it was to be performed.[13] The second doctrine that determined what legal advantages would be available from interstate forum shopping was based on the distinction between substance and procedure, and it determined how much of the foreign state's law was to be applied. Basically, the forum applied only the "substantive" law of the foreign state—the specific rules that determined the validity and scope of the cause of action—and then followed its own procedural or "remedial" law to determine how the cause was adjudicated and what the results would be.[14]

Thus, when plaintiffs brought out-of-state suits on transitory causes of action— at least when they did so to obtain the advantages of more favorable law—they were usually, though not always, seeking advantages that were formally matters of "procedure." The category of procedure, however, had a broad and often uncertain scope. It generally determined, for example, the burden of proof, the scope of the pleadings, the possibilities of discovery, the range of available remedies, the applicable statute of limitations, and the role and nature of the jury. "[A]s a practical matter," the Supreme Court of Utah noted, "the number of jurors required, the rules of procedure, the manner of selecting jurors, the geographic location of the court and other circumstances materially influence the trial of cases."[15] So-called procedural rules were sufficient, in short, to create a multitude of potentially significant differences between the courts of various states and the judgments that they might render. When the "conflicts" rules applied in out-of-state forums also offered the possibility of selecting a more favorable substantive law, the legal incentive for interstate forum shopping was even more compelling.

Interstate forum shopping was driven, however, as much or more by a search for extralegal advantages than it was by the search for more favorable legal rules, whether substantive or procedural. The tactic gave plaintiffs added flexibility in choosing the kind of judge they wanted as well as the opportunity to select a court where the docket was relatively current. It also enabled them to avoid courts in areas where defendant corporations were thought to exert particularly strong influence. Further, suing out of state allowed plaintiffs in some cases to turn the burden of geography in their favor. Selecting distant locations sometimes forced their corporate adversaries to transport their usually more numerous witnesses a thousand miles or more and to bear the cost and inconvenience of replacing employee-witnesses on their jobs for several days or even weeks. The tactic could, in short, give plaintiffs their own leverage in the informal legal process. Finally, and perhaps most important, interstate forum shopping enabled plaintiffs to bring their suits in locations where they could retain a seasoned personal injury specialist and, especially, where the juries tended to award the largest verdicts. In some states, a representative of the Brotherhood of Locomotive Engineers told Congress in 1913, "the juries are rendering verdicts that upon an average are perhaps not more than one-third of what they are rendering in these other states."[16] Three decades later an attorney defended his interstate forum shopping before the House Judiciary Committee. "The way I look at it is I owe a duty to my client, and that is to obtain as large an amount as possible," he explained. "From my experience of 33 years I felt there were certain jurisdictions where the verdicts were larger, where they stand up."[17]

Sometimes, a distant federal court would be as effective as a state court in giving a plaintiff the advantages she sought. Usually, however, only the state court would serve, especially when the plaintiff sought benefits from state procedures—such as a nonunanimous jury verdict—that were not followed in the federal courts. For the most part the standard tactics to prevent removal retained their importance in interstate forum shopping cases, and plaintiffs continued generally though perhaps somewhat less consistently to prefer the state courts.

While conflict-of-laws rules and the substance–procedure distinction shaped the strictly legal advantages that plaintiffs could reap from interstate forum shopping, other doctrines set limits to the general availability of out-of-state forums. The first limit, of course, was the necessity of obtaining personal jurisdiction over the defendant. State service of process statutes established various ways in which plaintiffs could obtain personal jurisdiction over defendants, and the Constitution set limits to their reach. Generally, individuals could be sued in any jurisdiction where they were physically present, where they resided, or where they consented to suit. Corporations were subject to suit in their incorporating states, wherever they had consented to be sued, and wherever they were "present" in a state by virtue of "doing business" there. The latter two were terms of high art. The mere fact that a corporation's officers or employees were physically present in a state or that it solicited business there did not necessarily mean that it would be subject to suit in the state, but the use of in-state agents to conduct continuous activities other than mere solicitation would likely subject the corporation to a state's jurisdiction.[18]

A second limit arose from a range of restrictions that states put on the causes of action that they created and on the kinds of cases that they allowed their courts to hear. In general, the Supreme Court denied states the power to restrict to their own courts those causes of action they created that were "truly" transitory, but it permitted them to close their courts to certain kinds of claims that arose under the laws of other states.[19] If the states chose to limit interstate forum shopping, in other words, they could do so more effectively by narrowing access to their own courts by means of reasonable domestic procedural rules than by attempting to block access to the courts of other states by creating "nontransitory" causes of action for personal liability.

Equity constituted a third limit on interstate forum shopping. Generally, state equity courts held that they had jurisdiction to enjoin their own citizens from conducting out-of-state litigations when those actions were oppressive, vexatious, or inequitable. Past the turn of the century, the courts regarded equitable restraints on foreign litigations as exceptional decrees that were justified only by "grave reasons."[20] When the foreign suit would allow a citizen to evade an established policy of his home state or take unconscionable advantage of an adversary, however, equity would restrain its prosecution.

Until the first decade of the twentieth century, the doctrines supporting and restricting interstate forum shopping had little relevance to the system of corporate diversity litigation. Indeed, most of those doctrines were relatively undeveloped, and the conflicts and inconsistencies among them were unresolved and largely unexplored.[21] That situation began changing after 1910, and by the 1920s the doctrines supporting and limiting the right of plaintiffs to sue out of state became the focus of sharp conflict.

In part the change resulted from the efforts of Congress, the Supreme Court, and the states to ensure that foreign corporations would be answerable for their actions. Generally, the courts and the legislatures agreed that it was fair and reasonable to subject corporations to suit in any jurisdiction where the corporations carried on significant business activities. Gradually if erratically in the decades around the turn of the century they expanded the jurisdictional reach of the states and allowed the broader exercise of personal jurisdiction over foreign corporations.[22] In 1870, for example, only a half-dozen states had enacted laws that required foreign corporations to consent to jurisdiction in order to do business within their borders. By 1900, however, forty states had adopted such laws, and by 1910 virtually every state in the nation had done so.[23] Most immediately relevant, the statutes often authorized jurisdiction over corporations on causes of action that arose in other states, thus allowing nonresident plaintiffs asserting claims that arose in their home states to secure personal jurisdiction over corporations in the enacting states.

The Supreme Court unintentionally created a new incentive for interstate forum shopping when it ruled on a technical matter of federal venue law in 1906. In actions based solely on diversity jurisdiction, venue was proper under the Judiciary Act of 1887–88 only in a federal judicial district where the plaintiff or defendant resided. In 1892 the Court decided in *Shaw v. Quincy Mining Co.*[24] that, aside from the district of plaintiff's residence, a corporation could not be sued originally in a federal court under diversity jurisdiction in any district other than the district of its incorporation—the district of its "residence" within the meaning of the venue statute. Two years later it held in *Tennessee v. Union & Planters' Bank*[25] that no action could be removed unless it could have been brought as an original suit in the same federal court. The logical conclusion seemed to be that no corporation could remove an action brought in any district other than the ones where the plaintiff or defendant resided. In 1906 *Ex parte Wisner*[26] held that conclusion to be the law.

Prior to *Wisner,* however, and in spite of the apparent logic of *Shaw* and *Union & Planters' Bank,* the federal courts had generally held that suits could be removed regardless of venue restrictions.[27] In 1895 the Supreme Court sanctioned that practice. In *Mexican National Railroad Co. v. Davidson* it ruled that the second section of the Judiciary Act of 1887–88, which limited removals to suits within the original jurisdiction of the federal courts, referred only to the requirements for subject matter jurisdiction "and not to the clause relating to the district in which suit may be brought."[28] The resulting rule gave corporations a distinct advantage, allowing them to remove suits brought in districts where federal venue was improper but preventing plaintiffs from suing them originally in a federal court located in the same districts. Where federal venue was improper, in other words, corporate defendants had the choice between federal or state forums, but plaintiffs had none. In *Wisner* the Court ignored the reasoning in *Davidson* and based its decision primarily on the need to enforce the purpose of the Judiciary Act of 1887–88 to contract the jurisdiction of the federal courts.[29]

In addition to terminating the forum advantage that the *Shaw–Davidson* rule gave corporate defendants, *Wisner* also provided plaintiffs with a new interstate antiremoval tool. If they brought suit in the court of a state where neither of the parties resided, where federal venue would be improper, *Wisner* would block removal. The tactic was as powerful as joinder, defeating federal jurisdiction without requiring claim discounting.

Wisner was a classic case in the system of corporate diversity litigation. Given its reasoning and practical results, it was no surprise that it came down the same year as *Thompson* and a year after *Cochran.* All three of those decisions conferred important procedural advantages on plaintiffs suing foreign corporations, and together they substantially moderated the social impact of the system of corporate diversity litigation. Nor was it any surprise that the 1890s witnessed *Shaw* and *Davidson,* whereas *Wisner* awaited the following decade. From a different perspective, too, *Wisner* was reminiscent of *Austin,* marking the Court's apparent inability to anticipate the tactical escalations that the system would shortly generate. As *Austin* suggested that in 1890 the Court had not yet realized the aggressiveness with which plaintiffs in the system would press for tactical advantages, so *Wisner* suggested that in 1906 the Court did not yet anticipate that any appreciable number of plaintiffs would or could escalate their tactics to an interstate level.

Congress also contributed to the rise of interstate forum shopping when it amended the FELA in 1910. Not only did it make actions under the FELA nonremovable, but it also added a special venue provision and a section that expressly conferred on state courts concurrent jurisdiction to hear FELA suits.[30] Together, the three amendments gave powerful evidence of a statutory policy to confer on plaintiffs the right to an unusually wide and untrammeled choice of forums to assist them in enforcing their statutory remedies. The antiremoval provision, of course, gave them an absolute choice between state and federal forums. The special venue provision gave them a wide choice among federal judicial districts by freeing them from the strict limitations of the general federal venue statute that limited causes of action based on federal law to the district of defendant's residence. In contrast, the special venue provision allowed FELA plaintiffs to sue in any district where the defendant resided, where the cause of action arose, or where "the defendant shall be doing business at the time of commencing such action."[31] Finally, the provision that expressly granted concurrent jurisdiction to the states seemed to give FELA plaintiffs the right to bring their actions in any otherwise appropriate state court and to require those state courts to honor the plaintiff's choice of forum.[32]

FELA plaintiffs, unlike those who relied on *Wisner,* did not sue out of state to prevent removal. The statute's antiremoval provision eliminated that threat. Rather, they brought their suits out of state solely in an effort to obtain the most advantageous forum available. Interstate forum shopping under the FELA showed the way that plaintiffs, freed from some of the system's legal and social constraints, were able to exploit aggressively the new litigation opportunities that the twentieth century opened up.

In 1916 the Supreme Court increased the incentives for FELA plaintiffs to use their broad venue rights. A few states had begun to experiment with their jury systems, and by 1910 several allowed nonunanimous jury verdicts, usually providing that a majority of only nine or ten of twelve was sufficient. Employers protested the changes, particularly their use in tort actions where juries were already regarded as heavily proplaintiff. Appealing to the Seventh Amendment, they fought vigorously to have the practice prohibited in actions under the FELA. In 1916 the Supreme Court settled the issue in *Minneapolis & St. Louis Railroad Co. v. Bombolis.*[33] Consolidating appeals from five states, the Court rejected the Seventh Amendment argument and ruled that nonunanimous verdicts were allowed in state court actions brought under the FELA. The decision relieved the nonunanimous verdict of its uncertain constitutional status and probably made defendants sued in states that allowed nonunanimous verdicts more willing to raise their settlement offers.[34]

State workmen's compensation statutes added another, though more limited, opportunity and incentive for interstate forum shopping. Most of the statutes contained two types of provisions that led to overlapping coverages between the laws of different states. On one hand, the statutes provided for compensation to workers injured within the enacting states. On the other hand, most also allowed recovery for injuries suffered out of state when the injured employee was a resident or citizen of the enacting state or when his employment originated in that state.[35] As worker mobility increased in the early twentieth century, accelerated by the new and drastic demands of war mobilization, more and more injured workers had the opportunity to choose among the compensation systems of the state where they were injured, the state where they resided, and—if different from the other two—the state where they entered into their employment contracts. Although workmen's compensation statutes had many similarities, they often differed widely in their specific provisions and especially in their schedules of benefits. Increasingly after about 1915 the courts heard suits arising from workmen's compensation disputes involving nonresident employees who were seeking longer statutes of limitations, narrower exceptions to coverage, higher compensation rates, or longer compensable periods.

Torts and the Emergence of Interstate Forum Shopping

Interstate forum shopping by individual tort plaintiffs began coming into common use around 1915 and received one of its earliest official recognitions during World War I. On April 9, 1918, the Director General of Railroads, the newly created federal officer in charge of wartime transportation, issued General Order 18 under the statutory powers that Congress had given him less than a month earlier. The order in effect suspended the FELA's broad venue provision and limited suits against carriers under federal control to two districts, those where the cause of action occurred and those where the plaintiff resided. The order spelled out its justification. "[I]t appears that suits against the carriers for personal injuries, freight and damage claims, are being brought in States and jurisdictions far remote from the place where plaintiffs reside or where the cause of action arose." Such suits required railroad workers and officials to "travel sometimes for hundreds of miles" and to miss "a week or more" of their work. Their cumulative result was the disruption of the nation's rail system. The protection of injured workers, the Director General declared, did not warrant or require the "practice of suing in remote jurisdictions."[36]

Suggesting the aggressiveness with which plaintiffs and their attorneys had begun to use interstate forum shopping, the Director General had to amend his order after only nine days. Actions brought in the district of a plaintiff's residence, supplementary General Order 18A provided, could be brought only "where the plaintiff resided at the time of the accrual of the cause of action." In only nine days, apparently, some plaintiffs had already moved their residence to new states and filed their actions there.[37]

Several states seemed particularly attractive forums. New York was known for awarding particularly large verdicts, and Texas for allowing juries unusually wide latitude.[38] Several states, including Kentucky, Virginia, and Oklahoma, offered nonunanimous jury verdicts.[39] Missouri was a strong favorite, offering not only a reputation for hostility toward insurance companies but also a nonunanimous jury verdict, relatively handsome damage awards, and a local law that gave forceful recognition to the rights of nonresidents to sue in the state courts.[40] In special situations, too, other states could have a desirable statute of limitations, measure of damages, pretrial discovery practice, or any of dozens of other substantive or procedural rules that would furnish critical assistance.[41] In every situation the structure and attitudes of the local bar—especially the sophistication, interstate contacts, and ethical standards of its personal injury attorneys—were paramount considerations.

Of all the states that offered attractive forums, however, none rivaled Minnesota in its combination of both favorable law and an enterprising plaintiffs' bar. When the Director General's orders lapsed in 1920, interstate forum shopping jumped. By February 1923 a count of cases docketed in Minnesota state courts identified more than a thousand personal injury cases brought by nonresident plaintiffs against foreign railroad corporations that did not even operate lines in the state. The suits sought an average of approximately $25,000 in damages.[42] The count, moreover, understated the number of suits in Minnesota that involved interstate forum shopping: It was based on a survey of only sixty-seven of the state's eighty-seven counties; it did not count any suits that had been removed;

and it did not include any cases against foreign corporations that were not railroads. Perhaps most important, it did not include cases that were brought by out-of-state plaintiffs on out-of-state causes of action against railroads that did operate lines in the state. Similarly, by the late 1920s, the federal District of Minnesota had become one of the most heavily burdened federal courts in the country.[43] "It is more or less an open secret," noted the *Minnesota Law Review* in 1929, "that a plaintiff who has a cause of action against a railway company, no matter where he resides, may find it to his advantage to try the case in Minnesota."[44]

The legal system in Minnesota was distinctly favorable to plaintiffs. It recognized a far-reaching rule of personal jurisdiction over foreign corporations, placed the burden of proving contributory negligence on the defendant, provided that plaintiffs were not subject to examination before trial, and applied a generous employer–employee joinder rule, thus making a critical antiremoval device readily available.[45] Its supreme court, too, construed remedial statutes liberally.[46] The Minnesota jury was especially attractive. State law provided for a nonunanimous verdict by ten of twelve jurors and gave its juries considerable latitude in fixing the amount of damages.[47] Equally or more important, its juries had a reputation for bringing in handsome verdicts for plaintiffs. Lawyers throughout the country, reported one law review, knew of "the notorious liberality of Minnesota jurors."[48]

The Minnesota Supreme Court, moreover, was committed to basic legal propositions that protected interstate forum shopping. It propounded a muscular construction of the privileges and immunities clause that seemed to give citizens a constitutional right to sue on transitory causes of action in any locality they chose, even when the defendant was a nonresident and the cause of action arose outside the forum state.[49] In 1916 the state's supreme court held that any foreign corporation that could be lawfully served in Minnesota could be sued there on any transitory cause of action regardless of where it arose and, further, that a foreign corporation was subject to service in the state if it had a local agent transacting business, regardless of the nature or amount of the business transacted.[50] Equally critical in the battles that erupted over interstate forum shopping, beginning in 1916 the Minnesota Supreme Court adopted the rule that nonresident plaintiffs could maintain suits in Minnesota even if equity courts in their home states enjoined them from prosecuting those actions.[51]

As favorable as the local law appeared, it was probably not as important in making Minnesota such a widely sought forum as was the entrepreneurial spirit of some of the state's personal injury firms. A number of them actively solicited "imported" business. They organized multistate operations that scanned out-of-state newspapers for notices of accidents and employed drummers or local agents to identify potential plaintiffs and induce them to sign retainers. Some of the importers advanced funds to support their clients, and a few apparently engaged in even more blatantly unethical practices. Their operations ranged across a dozen or more states, and during the 1920s they brought suits to Minnesota from as far east as Indiana, as far south as Kentucky, and as far west as Washington.[52]

In 1924 in *Weinard v. Chicago, Milwaukee & St. Paul Railway Co.*,[53] a tort suit brought in Minnesota by a Washington State plaintiff, the defendant railroad submitted an affidavit concerning the soliciting operations of Minnesota attorneys. The court found the railroad's allegations, including specific charges of organized solicitation made against the plaintiff's attorneys, to be supported by the evidence and, in essence, not even disputed by the brief and delicately drawn reply papers that plaintiff's attorneys submitted.[54] The affidavit stated on information and belief that more than fifteen Minnesota law firms solicited out-of-state cases on a systematic and widespread basis. On personal knowledge, it gave specific figures about its own experiences. In the four years since the expiration of General Order 18, the affidavit stated, nonresident plaintiffs had brought numerous freight-related cases and 224 personal injury or death suits against it in Minnesota on causes of action that arose outside the state. The plaintiffs resided in at least ten different states, with fourteen coming from Washington and thirty-one from Montana.

In particular, the railroad decried the burden of distance that the suits cast on it, for in some cases it had to transport its witnesses for more than a thousand miles to the trial site. The result, it affirmed, was that plaintiffs had an unfair advantage and the company often had to pay larger amounts to settle. Protesting the way that interstate forum shopping shifted the balance in the informal legal process, the railroad stated that "a considerable number of such imported actions against the defendant have been settled, and that in the settlement thereof the defendant has been induced to pay sums larger than would be otherwise warranted, on account of the difficulties of defending such actions under the circumstances above set forth."[55] The railroad's affidavit also suggested the extent to which geographical burdens on a defendant might enhance a plaintiff's claim and raise its settlement value. The 191 personal injury actions brought against it by those residing in Minnesota at the time of injury or filing sought an average of less than $16,000 each; the 224 personal injury suits brought by out-of-state residents sought damages that averaged in excess of $40,000 each.[56]

During the late 1920s, soliciting operations in Minnesota grew increasingly elaborate and methodical. Five years after *Weinard* the same railroad asked the Wisconsin courts to enjoin a citizen of that state from bringing suit against it in Minnesota. One of the same attorneys who had been involved in the *Weinard* case represented the Wisconsin citizen and would-be Minnesota plaintiff, and over the years the railroad had "labored industriously" to compile evidence on his soliciting operations. The road took the opportunity to lay out what it had learned, and the trial court made a series of detailed findings, including the finding that the attorney's law firm maintained a formal "Soliciting Department" and spent more than $100,000 a year on its operations. At a time when average nonfarm income in the United States was approximately $125 a month, the court found that the firm's attorneys

> employ one E. L. Harrigan as Superintendent of said Soliciting Department at a salary of $10,000 per year; that said Jacob J. Stahl and four other persons, similarly engaged, are employed by said law firm at salaries of $300.00 a month, and that all of said employees are also provided with allowances for all their traveling, hotel and other expenses amounting to considerable sums of money each month.[57]

Reviewing the record on appeal, the Wisconsin Supreme Court concluded that "the findings of fact were fully sustained."[58] In its own summary it noted specially that one of the firm's members "traveled about the country soliciting business," that "the firm maintains a slush fund and entertainment fund" as well as "a corps of expert witnesses," and that it "annually loans to clients $50,000."[59]

Although as late as 1948 a spokesman for the Illinois Central Railroad still regarded Minnesota as "the most outrageous example" of an importing state,[60] during the 1930s and 1940s personal injury attorneys in New York, California, and Illinois transformed their states into major importing centers. A survey conducted by the railroads for the years 1941 to 1946 showed that those three states, together with Minnesota and Missouri, accounted for 2,319 suits that the roads classified as imported, 92.3 percent of the cases they identified.[61] By World War II the importing was concentrated in five cities, New York, Chicago, Oakland, St. Louis, and Minneapolis–St. Paul. Each was a rail center; each was home to one of the more successful regional counsel of the Brotherhood of Railroad Trainmen; and each provided the kind of jurors and size of verdicts that personal injury victims and their attorneys avidly sought.[62]

By the 1930s and 1940s, in fact, representatives of the railroads and the brotherhoods agreed on two issues. Large verdicts generally came in large cities, and interstate forum shopping was costly to the railroads.[63] "In the 18 years the legal aid department of the brotherhood has been in existence," explained a representative of the Brotherhood of Railroad Trainmen, "the average amount paid to victims of railroad negligence in settlement out of court has substantially increased and the average amount of the verdicts recovered has risen."[64]

Defense and Counterthrust

Expanding use of interstate forum shopping and the active involvement of the railroad brotherhoods combined with mounting evidence of abuses in personal injury litigation to spur direct and vigorous attacks on solicitation and its associated evils. The altered political tone of the postwar decade gave further encouragement to corporations, insurance companies, bar associations, and civic groups to strike back forcefully. Investigations in a number of cities and states publicized the excesses of organized ambulance chasing, and in 1927 the National Bureau of Casualty and Surety Underwriters organized its Claims Bureau to help orchestrate the fight against abusive and fraudulent practices. In Boston at least eighteen attorneys were disbarred; the licenses of dozens of doctors were suspended or revoked; and several hundred fake claimants were convicted. New Jersey, New York, Illinois, Georgia, Ohio and Wisconsin were among the states that uncovered unethical practices and brought indictments and disbarrment proceedings. On a related track, many lawyers and bar groups fought to raise educational requirements and other admission standards in an effort to improve the quality and "character" of the profession. Although abuses were real, anti-Semitism and other nativist strains frequently helped drive the improvement campaigns, as did the desire of some to help curb the number of personal injury actions brought against businesses.[65]

Some states responded directly to the interstate forum shopping problem. New York and South Carolina were among those that tried limiting the access of nonresidents to their courts, especially in tort suits when the cause of action arose elsewhere.[66] Other states, such as Michigan and Indiana, took a different approach, enacting legislation designed to ensure that their own residents would sue at home.[67] Ohio tried both methods.[68] Iowa and Nebraska, sandwiched vulnerably between Minnesota and Missouri, were particularly determined. They responded to their neighbors' attorneys by making it unlawful to solicit certain classes of cases for out-of-state prosecution.[69]

The American Bar Association (ABA) joined the effort. In 1927 its Committee on Jurisprudence and Law Reform proposed federal legislation that would make state court injunctions prohibiting citizens from prosecuting out-of-state actions binding on all other state courts under the full faith and credit clause. The statute would have overthrown the rule followed in such popular interstate forums as Minnesota and Missouri that such injunctions were not binding under the constitutional provision.[70] The following year the ABA adopted a new Canon of Ethics in its Code of Professional Responsibility that prohibited attorneys from representing "any organization, such as an association, club or trade organization" and at the same time representing any of the group's individual members.[71] The canon was subsequently used to condemn the regional counsel system that the Brotherhood of Railroad Trainmen established.[72]

Corporations, particularly the railroads, fought interstate forum shopping with every tool they could muster, and their interests frequently coincided with those of the bar associations anxious to eliminate ambulance chasing and to stop the loss of relatively lucrative local business to out-of-state attorneys. Like the railroad in *Weinard,* they tried to expose and discredit those involved in importing legal business as well as those who solicited suits against corporations and other business interests.[73] They pressed for investigations of the alleged abuses and urged the enactment of legislation designed to restrict the practice.

As litigants, corporations also adopted their own special tactics. Sometimes, for example, they engaged in their own counter–forum shopping. If injured workers threatened to bring out-of-state suits or if they had particularly strong cases or large claims, corporations could attempt to preempt them by initiating proceedings under local workmen's compensation acts. They could thereby limit their potential liability or at least force on the claimants the burden of litigating two separate proceedings in two different states.[74] Another tactic was to offer injured workers negotiation agreements—dubbed "Rock Island releases" by the brotherhoods[75]— whereby the parties agreed to try to settle their disputes out of court, and in exchange for a small payment the worker agreed to limit any subsequent suit he might bring to the courts sitting in one specific state.[76] The Rock Island release was, in effect, a buyout of the claimant's right to use the interstate forum shopping tactic. If the company reached the worker before he had spoken with counsel, the injured person would likely have been unaware of the true market value of his venue right and would have seen the offer as a windfall.[77]

Most visible to the legal process, corporations responded in court to the plaintiffs who selected out-of-state forums. They sought direct relief in the courts to which nonresident plaintiffs brought their suits, seeking discretionary or other nonfinal dismissals on the ground that it was unfair and unduly burdensome for a defendant to be forced to litigate in an inconvenient forum unnecessarily distant from the place of injury. The courts began haltingly to respond. Prior to 1910 the doctrine of *forum non conveniens* was largely unknown to American courts outside admiralty, but after World War I a few state courts began to discuss the doctrine and to give it effect.[78] The federal courts declined to do so, however, and in FELA cases they held that they had no discretion to refuse to hear a case over which they had jurisdiction.[79]

Corporations also sought collateral relief in the courts of plaintiffs' home states, filing bills for equitable relief to enjoin them from prosecuting their out-of-state suits. If the courts found that the out-of-state suit was filed to avoid a policy of the home state or that it imposed serious and unnecessary burdens on the defendant, they would grant the injunctions.[80] The latter tactic succeeded in many cases, and its regular use—even if frequently unsuccessful—served as a significant practical deterrent to interstate forum shopping. Its use increased the costs for both plaintiffs and out-of-state importers, and it created for the latter the additional risk that they might incur substantial costs and still not be able to try the action on the merits in their chosen forums. Although injunctions probably convinced many plaintiffs to abandon their foreign ventures, they failed to dissuade many others. Often, in fact, even when they were granted, injunctions had little effect. Some states—Minnesota and Missouri, for example—refused to close their courts to nonresident plaintiffs whose home courts had enjoined them from prosecuting their out-of-state suits, and plaintiffs could usually avoid sanctions for violating injunctions if they were willing to leave home and take up new residence in the forum state.[81]

The injunction tactic was particularly important and controversial in FELA suits. Much if not most interstate forum shopping was done under the act's aegis, but injunctions against FELA plaintiffs raised a series of complicated questions concerning the scope of the statute, the limits of equity, and the relations between state and federal courts. Although both federal and state courts split on the issues, the federal courts seemed to be more protective of plaintiffs' rights under the FELA, generally unwilling to grant injunctions, and in agreement that state courts—whether or not they could enjoin FELA actions in other state courts— could not enjoin them when the actions were in federal court.[82] Though courts were often reluctant to enjoin FELA plaintiffs, in many cases corporations succeeded in obtaining injunctions.

In their efforts to establish a doctrine of *forum non conveniens* and to have out-of-state suits enjoined, corporations exhibited a keen awareness of the burdens that distance imposed on litigants. Like the defendant railroad in *Weinard,* they began regularly to stress the multiplied expenses and inconveniences that trials in distant forums caused. Although the added distance could run to a thousand miles or more, in most cases it was less. Indeed, in a good many imported cases the distance was less than the additional distance that removal imposed on numerous individual plaintiffs.[83] Nevertheless, when distance became a plaintiffs' tool, corporate defendants loudly proclaimed its unfairness and vigorously sought relief from its oppression. Sometimes they succeeded. In a case decided in 1927 under the equal protection clause, the United States Supreme Court protected a foreign corporation from an allegedly discriminatory venue by finding that an added seventy-five miles "of course tended to increase materially the burden otherwise incident to presenting a defense."[84] The corporations did not, of course, discuss the different relative burdens that distance could place on national corporations and individuals, nor did they comment on the different relative burdens that an out-of-state suit would place on a corporation compared with what an in-state removal would impose on an individual.[85]

A pivotal 1930 Minnesota case illustrated the lines of battle over interstate forum shopping. The previous year the United States Supreme Court had construed the privileges and immunities clause narrowly in a suit involving interstate forum shopping under the FELA, and the decision provided a new basis to attack the relatively open-ended practices that Minnesota allowed.[86] When the issue came before the state's high court in *Boright v. Chicago, Rock Island & Pacific Railroad Co.,*[87] the defendant railroad was joined by five other roads as amici arguing that the Supreme Court's recent opinion required or at least prompted the Minnesota courts to dismiss the action of the nonresident plaintiff. Opposing the defendant's effort as amici were four of the railroad brotherhoods and the lawyers who had represented the nonresident plaintiffs in *Weinard.* The Minnesota court distinguished the decision of the United States Supreme Court, held to its earlier position, and refused to dismiss the suit.

The Expansion of Federal Judicial Forum Control

A variety of considerations made the federal courts sensitive to the problems created by interstate forum shopping. In some instances, federal judges probably reacted on the basis of a sympathy with national business or resentment at the calculated efforts made to avoid their jurisdiction. Some of the tactics that plaintiffs used, although clearly lawful, were overtly manipulative. Further, in some instances at least, it appeared that out-of-state suits were used primarily to impose heavy burdens of distance on corporations or to bring apparently lucrative and unethically solicited out-of-state business to organized importers. The unflattering professional aura that surrounded the importers and the more general professional movement against ambulance chasing that gained momentum in the 1920s combined to make much interstate forum shopping look particularly dubious. After the decision of the Minnesota Supreme Court in *Boright,* one law review critic charged simply that the "victory was for the personal injury racket."[88]

Another factor was the powerful interest in docket control and case management that developed out of the Judicial Conference and the burdens of a growing caseload. As judges, lawyers, scholars, and government officials sought methods of dealing with the flood of new cases by streamlining and rationalizing the nation's legal system, interstate forum shopping cases, though relatively small in numbers, often jumped out as examples of particularly "unreasonable" forum use. "Among the cases discussed above as examples of litigation instituted in an inappropriate forum," explained one commentator in 1929, "the type most frequently occurring exhibits a foreign corporation sued in a jurisdiction which is alien alike to its domicile, to the plaintiff's residence, and to the place where the cause of action arose."[89] The law reviews gave considerable attention to the issue, although the articles in the 1920s and early 1930s that initially stressed the problems of interstate forum shopping seemed to reflect a desire to protect corporate interests as much as to reform the legal system.[90] As the profession came increasingly to think of state and federal courts not simply as the separate judicial arms of independent sovereignties but as interrelated parts of a national judicial system, the propriety of establishing rational and comprehensive rules of forum choice seemed more and more obvious and necessary.

The federal courts had two tools immediately available, statutory construction and constitutional interpretation. During the 1920s they used both to restrict interstate forum shopping, though at no point did they attempt to do more than moderate the practice. Although the corporations enjoyed successes, they were limited ones.

One success came in the construction of the federal removal statute. In *Wisner* the Supreme Court had held that a state court action brought in a federal judicial district in which neither party resided could not be removed under diversity jurisdiction because original venue was improper in such district. Before about 1910, plaintiffs had not used the *Wisner* rule as a method of avoiding removal in suits against national corporations. Apparently neither plaintiffs nor the personal injury bar had yet developed any significant interstate contacts, and few attorneys had recognized the antiremoval potential of the tactic.[91] Around 1910, however, perhaps related to the interstate forum shopping practices that the FELA amendments inspired, plaintiffs' attorneys began to incorporate *Wisner* into their armory. Unlike the use of FELA venue, however, the *Wisner* tactic was available to any plaintiff, and corporations and other legal entities used it as commonly as did individuals suing national corporations.[92] Generally, the tactic proved successful, though plaintiffs had to avoid any action that could be construed as a waiver and raise their venue objection as soon as the defendant removed.[93] "A surging increase in the number of such removal cases," declared one treatise writer, "makes the problem one of great practical importance."[94]

Some plaintiffs cleverly managed to refine the tactic and lighten the burden of distance it imposed. The venue statute was framed in terms of the federal judicial district, not the state, in which the parties resided, and almost half the states were divided into two or more such districts. Although *Wisner* had involved an action brought in a state in which neither party resided, its logic and the language of the venue statute suggested that an action should be nonremovable if it were brought in a judicial district where neither of the parties was a resident, even if one or both lived in another district in the same state. The argument met with some success.[95]

Similarly, plaintiffs won a second minor victory on the venue issue when the courts refused to sanction one of the boldest counters to the *Wisner* tactic that defendants attempted. A few defendants argued that improper venue in the federal district to which the case would ordinarily be removed should not defeat federal jurisdiction. If the case were otherwise properly removable, they proposed, the federal court to which the suit would ordinarily have been removed should order the action transferred to a second federal court in a district where venue was proper. Without statutory basis or support in precedent or practice for interdistrict transfers, the proposal did not commend itself to the courts.[96]

Although the lower courts followed *Wisner* when they felt that they had no choice, they subjected it to unusually frank criticism and often found ways to avoid it.[97] They focused on its weak reasoning, its inconsistency with prior law under *Davidson,* and on its questionable status after the Supreme Court itself criticized and modified the opinion. *Wisner* seemed to confuse the issues of subject matter jurisdiction and venue, and two years after it came down the Court "overruled" certain "unnecessary" language in the opinion.[98] The Supreme Court did not, however, question *Wisner's* basic holding that improper venue, if objected to, would prevent removal.

Although the language of the federal venue statute was imprecise and subject to diverse interpretations, almost uniformly the critics of *Wisner* in the lower federal courts rested their arguments on the construction of that language, not on the obvious and growing practice of interstate forum shopping that had converted *Wisner* from a relatively trivial technicality into a significant tactical tool. A federal judge in California held that the Supreme Court had overruled *Wisner* on the venue issue;[99] a New York federal judge declared that the Court had meant to overrule *Wisner* but had failed to make its intent clear;[100] and a Georgia federal judge declared that the Court had not yet overruled *Wisner* but would do so in the near future.[101] A Kentucky federal judge took the most aggressive stance. "I am confident in the belief that the Supreme court will overrule [*Wisner*] directly the first opportunity it gets," he announced in 1914 at the conclusion of a powerful and extended critique of the case, "and, so believing, I think I am justified in refusing to follow it."[102] The major point on which most of the lower courts agreed was that the cases construing *Wisner* were, as Judge Learned Hand declared in 1918, "in entire conflict."[103]

The Supreme Court made the Kentucky federal judge wait almost a decade before proving him right. For years it allowed *Wisner* to stand, refusing to settle the confusion and satisfy the decision's critics. Then, as interstate forum shopping escalated rapidly after 1920 and three new conservative Justices arrived in the next two years, the Court suddenly and unanimously took action. In a federal question case decided in November 1922, it seemed to overthrow *Wisner,*[104] and two months later it did so formally in *Lee v. Chesapeake & Ohio Railway Co.*[105] Treating *Wisner* as an aberration and the issue as one determined simply by the language of the venue statute, *Lee* declared *Wisner* "essentially unsound" and formally overruled it.[106] If a plaintiff brought a state court suit in a federal judicial district where both parties were nonresidents, *Lee* held, an action otherwise removable under diversity jurisdiction could be removed to the federal court in that district without regard to original venue requirements. The "exercise of the right of removal," the Court stated, "rests entirely with the defendant and is in no sense dependent on the will or acquiescence of the plaintiff."[107]

Although the Court purported merely to construe statutory language, its construction was hardly the result of any newly discovered clarity in the standing words of Congress. Rather, *Lee* was the product of a range of converging pressures. Broadly, the decision reflected the increasingly nationalistic outlook that marked the Supreme Court in the 1920s and its greater willingness to limit the role of the state courts while expanding the sway of the national judiciary. Doctrinally, it marked the Court's recognition that federal venue law was confused and ambiguous and that the relevant procedural doctrines required clarification. Practically, it was part of the Court's general efforts in the 1920s both to protect removal jurisdiction and to cut back on interstate forum shopping.[108] Finally, *Lee* was also consistent with the interest of some of the Justices in protecting the legal position of foreign corporations. In practical terms, it restored the advantage that corporations had enjoyed prior to *Wisner,* allowing them to remove in every foreign federal district if they were subject to state suit there while at the same time allowing them to remain immune in those districts from original federal actions.[109] In *Lee* the importance of those various attitudes outweighed the doctrine of *stare decisis* as well as one of the Court's most prominently heralded goals of the 1920s, restricting the rapidly growing caseload of the federal courts. Although *Lee* affected only a relatively small number of cases, it tilted toward increasing rather than decreasing the federal docket.

Lee also illustrated the anomalous quality of diversity jurisdiction. If the purpose of the jurisdiction was to protect nonresidents from local prejudice, it furnished no basis for allowing removal of suits that involved exclusively nonresident parties. On the local prejudice theory *Wisner* construed the venue statute properly, limiting removals to suits involving resident plaintiffs and nonresident defendants. But the real issue in *Wisner* suits, after all, was not local prejudice but forum choice and tactical litigation advantage; and when plaintiffs sought benefits by bringing out-of-state suits, they were utilizing the opportunities that the established rules created. When the lower courts opposed *Wisner* and the Supreme Court overruled it, they were not protecting nonresidents from local prejudice. They were, rather, supporting other policies.

Though *Lee* favored corporations litigating diversity cases against individuals, it did not confer a major advantage on them. The *Wisner* tactic was relatively sophisticated and expensive, and plaintiffs did not use it nearly as widely or easily as, for example, they used joinder. Moreover, unlike the rules that exclusively or primarily helped individuals who sued corporations, such as joinder and the procedural provisions of the FELA, *Wisner* was also available to corporations and other business groups when they chose to bring suits. Indeed, given the greater financial and legal resources that corporations enjoyed, they were able to use the *Wisner* tactic more readily than individuals were and, considering the entire range of civil litigations, probably did so as or more often than individuals did. In short, although a variety of considerations induced the Court to overrule *Wisner,* including no doubt the widespread and persistent criticism that emanated from the lower courts, the desire to control interstate forum shopping and to clarify federal venue law was more important[110]—and certainly important to more of the Justices—than was any wish to protect corporate interests.[111]

Only four months after *Lee* came down, the Court struck against interstate forum shopping a second time, giving birth to one of its more unusual constitutional doctrines, commerce clause venue. In *Davis v. Farmers Co-Operative Equity Co.*[112] the Court struck not only at interstate forum shopping but at its practice in Minnesota. The issue was one of personal jurisdiction, whether it was constitutional for the state to compel foreign corporations to consent to suit in Minnesota as a condition for maintaining a soliciting agent in the state. The Court, however, refused to decide *Davis* on the issue of personal jurisdiction or under the due process clause.[113] Instead, it invoked the commerce clause and announced a new constitutional limitation on forum choice. Stressing the importance of "matters of common knowledge" about proliferating personal injury and freight damage claims brought in "remote" jurisdictions, *Davis* gave voice to the growing belief that the business of the nation's courts should be systematized and rationalized.[114] In dealing with interstate operations and foreign corporations, it declared, the "requirements of orderly, effective administration of justice are paramount."[115] When corporations were forced to defend suits in states that had no significant connection with the dispute, interstate commerce was unduly burdened and the rational allocation of judicial business frustrated. The "orderly, effective administration of justice," *Davis* stated,

> does not require that a foreign carrier shall submit to a suit in a State in which the cause of action did not arise, in which the transaction giving rise to it was not entered upon, in which the carrier neither owns nor operates a railroad, and in which the plaintiff does not reside.[116]

The Court ruled that the Minnesota statute as applied imposed an unconstitutional burden on interstate commerce and reversed the judgment for plaintiff.[117]

Justice Louis D. Brandeis, the leading progressive on the Court, wrote the unanimous opinion in *Davis*. Appointed by President Woodrow Wilson in 1916, Brandeis worked for two decades to moderate the political and social orientation of the Court's conservative majority while at the same time trying to elaborate a coherent approach to questions of the proper role of the federal courts.[118] Hostile to the federal common law and substantive due process, and sympathetic to labor and legislative reforms, Brandeis dissented forcefully from many of the Court's antiprogressive decisions. Seeking to reshape the role of the federal judiciary, he hoped to limit their jurisdiction, especially in diversity of citizenship cases. Narrowing federal jurisdiction, Brandeis thought, would focus the work of federal judges more appropriately on issues of national law, alleviate docket problems and thereby help preserve the quality of the national judiciary, and enable the state courts to play a broader role in the nation's judicial system. His progressivism and his views about federal jurisdiction overlapped, too. Limiting diversity jurisdiction, he believed, would deny to corporations many of the tactical advantages that they derived from their access to the national courts.

Although sympathetic to the plight of injured workers and deeply suspicious of the size and power of national corporations, Brandeis also placed a high value on social and administrative efficiency. In *Davis* his progressive attitudes toward injured workers and large corporations—as well as his deep commitment to the rights of the states—gave way to another characteristic goal, rationalizing and systematizing jurisdiction in a newly emerging national judicial system. Interstate forum shopping, Brandeis concluded in the early 1920s, was legally abusive and socially wasteful. In stressing that the "orderly, effective administration of justice" was "paramount," he gave voice to one of his deepest beliefs and at the same time introduced into the discussion of federal venue law—as the Court had failed to do in *Lee*—an express recognition that the seemingly abstract rules of venue in fact implicated basic social and institutional concerns. Thus, while the commerce clause venue doctrine alleviated the litigation burdens on national corporations, perhaps appealing to some of the antiprogressive Justices for that reason, Brandeis favored it as a device that would allow the federal courts to regulate nationwide forum use and to do so on what he regarded as the appropriate rational basis, a practical analysis of litigation costs and convenience.

As the state and lower federal courts began to grapple with the problems of applying the *Davis* rule,[119] they immediately confronted the question of its applicability in FELA actions. Although their decisions were not unanimous, many reasoned that the specific rights of forum choice that Congress granted to FELA plaintiffs trumped any countervailing practical considerations that might otherwise make a forum choice an unreasonable burden on interstate commerce. Some simply ruled the *Davis* doctrine inapplicable to FELA suits,[120] and others held that a suit brought in the state of plaintiff's residence did not constitute an unreasonable burden on interstate commerce.[121]

In 1927 the Supreme Court heard its first case under the FELA that raised the commerce clause question, and it held in *Hoffman v. Foraker* that the venue did not impose an unreasonable burden on interstate commerce. Although a nonresident plaintiff had brought the suit on a cause of action that arose outside the forum state, the Court held that venue was proper because the defendant railroad was sufficiently connected to the forum state to make suit there reasonable. The railroad was a local corporation; it operated lines in the state; and it had an office and agent in the county where the suit was filed.[122] The "orderly, effective administration of justice," the Court explained, required that suit be allowed on such facts even though "interstate commerce is incidentally burdened."[123]

Two years later, however, the Court ended any belief that FELA actions were immune from the *Davis* doctrine. In *Michigan Central Railroad Co. v. Mix*,[124] with Brandeis again writing for a unanimous bench, the Court reversed a Missouri judgment in an FELA action where the defendant railroad was a foreign corporation, operated no rail lines in the state, had given no consent to be sued there, and did no business in the state other than soliciting interstate shipments. The facts, the Court explained, were identical to those in *Davis* with one exception. "There, the plaintiff was a nonresident," it stated. "Here, the plaintiff had become a resident in Missouri after the injury complained of, but before instituting the action."[125] The Court held that the difference was not sufficient to bring a different result.

In 1932, in *Denver & Rio Grande Western Railroad Co. v. Terte*,[126] the Court heard another FELA action where the plaintiff had become "a bona fide resident and citizen" of the forum state prior to instituting his action."[127] Two defendant railroads raised commerce clause objections to the forum. The Court applied *Mix* to hold venue improper as to one and *Hoffman* to hold it proper as to the other. Regarding the first defendant, the Court noted that the only factual difference with *Mix* was that the railroad owned and used property in the forum. That added fact was not sufficient to make venue proper.[128] Regarding the second defendant, it differed from the railroad in *Hoffman* in that it was a foreign corporation. That difference the Court also held irrelevant. The second railroad owned and operated lines in the forum, and it was licensed to do business there. Those contacts were sufficient, the Court ruled, to make venue proper.[129]

By the early 1930s the outlines of the commerce clause venue doctrine seemed relatively clear. It applied to FELA suits, and it held that venue might be improper even where the plaintiff brought suit in his home state, at least if he had taken up his residence there after being injured. The logic of the doctrine, moreover, seemed to suggest that a suit would impose the same burden on interstate commerce even if the plaintiff had resided in the forum state prior to his injury.[130] The critical issue seemed to be the extent of the corporation's contacts with the forum state. Proper venue under the commerce clause apparently required that a railroad operate lines in the forum and have some additional connection with that state, such as an office or a license to do business there.

The commerce clause venue doctrine was, like *Lee*'s construction of the general venue statute, an effort to restrict interstate forum shopping. Although its purpose was to promote social efficiency, it was manifestly a defendant's doctrine. Beyond its obvious tactical value—permitting defendants to deny plaintiffs their choice of forum—commerce clause venue seemed to turn primarily or perhaps exclusively on the nature of the burdens that the corporate defendant suffered. Because its applicability was based on transportation and service efficiency, conditions that raised railroad expenses or took employees away from their jobs seemed the relevant factors. Moreover, the doctrine gave relatively little weight to plaintiff's residence. Although *Davis* suggested that plaintiff's residence within the forum might have significance,[131] *Mix* and *Terte* established that such residence taken up after the injury—even though "bona fide" and established prior to suit—did not. The doctrine's lessened regard for plaintiff's residence was clearly designed to prevent circumvention of its restriction on venue, but the result was still more limiting than was the general federal rule that governed change of citizenship for purposes of diversity jurisdiction. In diversity cases, the federal courts had long held that a new permanent residence, even if arranged solely for jurisdictional purposes after a cause of action had arisen, was effective in altering the party's citizenship.[132] *Mix* and *Terte* imposed a more rigorous restriction.

The Court's use of the commerce clause to restrict interstate forum shopping was only one of numerous efforts that it made in the 1920s and early 1930s to develop constitutional doctrines of judicial forum control. In 1929, for example, the Court construed the privileges and immunitites clause narrowly in order to strike indirectly at the practice. In *Douglas v. New York, New Haven & Hartford Railroad Co.*[133] a Connecticut citizen sued a Connecticut corporation on an FELA claim that arose in Connecticut. He filed his action in New York. Pursuant to statutory authorization, the New York state court exercised its discretion and refused to hear the suit. The plaintiff appealed on the ground that the privileges and immunities clause and the FELA compelled the state court to take jurisdiction. The Supreme Court rejected the constitutional argument by relying on a logical, though exceptionally thin, distinction. The privileges and immunities clause protected only "citizens," and the New York statute allowed its courts to dismiss suits brought by "nonresidents," not by "noncitizens." The two categories, though overlapping at approximately the 99 percent level, were nevertheless distinct, as citizens of one state could and did reside in other states. The Court upheld the statute on the ground that the Constitution allowed reasonable discriminations between residents and nonresidents and that the discrimination at issue was reasonable.[134] The Court disposed of the argument based on the provision of the FELA that conferred concurrent jurisdiction on the state courts by holding that the statute did not require states to hear cases when their refusal was based on some reasonable and nondiscriminatory general policy. "[T]here is nothing in the Act of Congress that purports to force a duty upon such Courts as against an otherwise valid excuse."[135]

Similarly, in the years after World War I the Court began invoking the full faith and credit clause to regulate the reach of state legislation and thereby limit the opportunities plaintiffs had to choose between different substantive laws. Applying the clause initially to cases involving insurance and corporate governance,[136] the Court ruled in 1932 in *Bradford Electric Light Co. Inc. v. Clapper*[137] that the clause required the enforcement of Vermont's workmen's compensation law in an action brought in New Hampshire. The plaintiff was seeking more favorable substantive law in New Hampshire, and she had a plausible claim that its law should be applied. Her deceased husband was often sent to work in New Hampshire by his employer, and the injury that caused his death occurred there. The Supreme Court, however, ruled that those facts were not sufficient to allow New Hampshire to apply its own substantive law when both the employer and employee were residents of Vermont, when they entered into their employment agreement in Vermont, and when both had accepted the Vermont workmen's compensation statute as a term of employment. New Hampshire's refusal to apply the Vermont statute was a denial of full faith and credit.[138]

Finally, the Court shaped both the equal protection and due process clauses in order to accomplish similar results.[139] The latter, of course, had long served to control venue indirectly by limiting the power of the states to exercise personal jurisdiction over nonresident defendants. And although the gradual relaxation of due process limits on personal jurisdiction was one of the major legal factors that spurred the rise of interstate forum shopping, the Court began gradually in the early twentieth century to use it specifically to restrict the opportunities for interstate forum shopping.[140] In one series of cases it relied on the due process clause to narrow the construction given to state statutes that required corporations to consent to suit as a condition of doing business, holding that such consent did not ordinarily extend to causes of action that arose outside the forum state.[141] In another series, mainly insurance cases, it used the due process clause to prevent forum states from applying their own law to govern contracts that were, in the Supreme Court's view, properly controlled by the laws of other states. The decisions limited the ability of plaintiffs to seek out favorable substantive law, and they also assisted insurance companies in their efforts to select the state law that would be applied to their contracts.[142]

In spite of its varied efforts, however, the Court enjoyed little success in using the Constitution to control interstate forum shopping. In part the difficulty was due to the seemingly endless variety of issues that the cases presented and in part to the countervailing values that so frequently prompted against enforcing tight limits on the practice. Moreover, given the conflicts among the states and the tensions between the constitutional clauses, any broad rule raised the danger of potential abuses that could be worse than mere random individual forum shopping. The great clauses of the Constitution seemed too broad and balanced in their reach to be less than cumbersome when applied to many of the practical kinds of problems that interstate forum shopping raised.

The conflicting jurisdiction of the states compounded the Court's difficulty in using the Constitution to control venue. Some states continued to hear the claims of nonresident plaintiffs and refused to restrict access to their courts beyond the narrowest compulsion of the Constitution. Minnesota and Missouri, for example, continued to welcome suits by nonresidents. The supreme courts of both states construed *Davis* narrowly, allowing nonresidents to sue on out-of-state claims as long as the defendant operated lines in the state and maintained agents there.[143] Similarly, they avoided *Douglas* easily, construing it to mean only that a state court with statutory discretion similar to New York's could choose not to hear certain kinds of suits. "We have no statute similar to that of New York," the Minnesota court announced promptly only a month after *Douglas* came down.[144]

To some extent, too, older ideas and doctrines limited the Court's options. Despite the clear tendency of its cases limiting interstate forum shopping, traditional federal practice and the lack of statutory authorization prevented it during the 1920s and 1930s from developing an express doctrine of *forum non conveniens*. Further, an apparent belief that courts could not "ascertain in advance of trial the number and importance of probable witnesses within and without the State" raised an additional obstacle to the acceptance of such an overtly discretionary doctrine.[145] Finally, in an age of growing and widespread geographical mobility,

the established rules of federal jurisdiction seemed increasingly to provide opportunities to forum shop and to defeat removal. Plaintiffs had long been free to
change their citizenship for diversity purposes, and after the war a still small but
increasingly noticeable number seemed ready to do so.

The Court's 1931 decision in *Mecom v. Fitzsimmons Drilling Co., Inc.*[146] symbolized the complexity of the Court's task. The case presented the overt use of a
potentially powerful interstate antiremoval device, the appointment in a wrongful
death action of an out-of-state administrator who was a citizen of the defendant's
chartering state. The facts in *Mecom* made the nature of the tactic obvious. Before
the administrator's appointment, the original plaintiff, the wife of the decedent,
had filed three separate actions and dismissed each one after the defendant removed. The Supreme Court, however, faced a long-established rule that an administrator's citizenship controlled for diversity purposes, regardless of the citizenship
of the deceased or his beneficiaries. Applying that rule, the Court held that the
action was not removable. Thus, in spite of its efforts to curb interstate forum
shopping, the Court in *Mecom* felt compelled to follow established doctrine and in
effect to sanction the use of a simple and overt interstate antiremoval device.[147]

By the mid-1930s, in fact, the Court apparently sensed more fully the complexity of the issues and seemed to back off from its effort to control interstate forum
shopping through the Constitution. In 1934 in *International Milling Co. v. Columbia Transportation Co.*[148] it substantially qualified its commerce clause venue doctrine. It declared that the plaintiff's residence, "even though not controlling, is a
fact of high significance" and pointedly announced that *Davis* was "confined
narrowly within the bounds of its own facts."[149] When another state court closed
its doors to a nonresident FELA plaintiff, the Court demonstrated that *Douglas*
had clear limits and held the denial of access unconstitutional.[150] When practical
reasons suggested that a state should be able to assert personal jurisdiction over a
foreign corporation even when its activities in the state were minimal and the
cause of action arose elsewhere, the Court found leeway in the due process
clause.[151] When a forum state applied its own workmen's compensation statute to
an injury that occurred elsewhere, the Court stressed the practical social facts that
made the decision reasonable. In *Alaska Packers Association v. Industrial Accident Commission of California* in 1935 it rejected any "automatic" application of
the full faith and credit clause, and—claiming somewhat unconvincingly to be
consistent with *Clapper*—set forth a flexible test that would choose between
potentially controlling state laws by comparing the "governmental interests" of
the various states whose laws might reasonably be taken to control.[152]

Throughout the 1930s, then, interstate forum shopping remained in common
use despite the varied efforts to restrict it. In *Lee* the Supreme Court used federal
venue law to deprive plaintiffs of one incentive for bringing their suits out of state,
and state equity courts proved to be important tools in deterring or blocking many
other such actions. The improved interstate transportation and increasingly sophisticated organization that marked twentieth-century life, however, made interstate
forum shopping too attractive and available to be easily cabined, especially in the
face of the FELA, workmen's compensation acts, and the traditional legal doctrines that supported the tactic. As the Court's other approaches were proving
unsatisfactory, it suggested in the mid-1930s that it might someday embrace a
more direct and overtly flexible approach to the problem. A broad and discretion-

ary doctrine of *forum non conveniens,* it hinted in 1935, might be proper "in appropriate cases."[153] Nonetheless, the Court in the 1930s was not prepared to take such a step. The seemingly inexorable escalation of litigation tactics represented by the growth of interstate forum shopping continued throughout the interwar years and into the 1940s.

Chapter 9

Tactical Escalation in Insurance Litigation

Although state statutes continued to encroach incrementally on the common law of insurance contracts, no legislation, state or federal, altered the law relevant to insurance actions in the system to the extent that the Federal Employers' Liability Act (FELA) and workmen's compensation statutes did for tort suits. Congress continued to leave insurance regulation to the states, and the Supreme Court continued to give the states broad but not unlimited regulatory freedom. For their part, the states maintained their general efforts to foster the private insurance system while protecting policyholders from harsh provisions.

If substantive insurance law changed relatively little after 1910, however, insurance litigation in the federal courts changed drastically. Beginning in the early 1920s, it increased in volume, sharpened its tactics, and pressed hard against the limits of established procedures. The tactical escalation that began to transform tort litigation in the 1890s hit insurance litigation in the 1920s.

By the late 1920s life insurance companies alone were litigating several thousand cases a year. Although the great majority were in the state courts, most of those actions were for amounts below the jurisdictional minimum. In 1932, when the jurisdictional amount stood at $3,000, the average value of all life insurance policies in the United States was only $2,400.[1] When removal was available, however, the companies used it. "I venture the thought," declared an Iowa attorney in 1933, "that just one hundred per cent of those [actions that are] removable are removed."[2] An attorney for the Association of Life Insurance Presidents confirmed that estimate when he informed Congress in 1932 that the companies removed "the important cases" to the federal courts. Asked to define an important case, he responded with precision. "I believe that the law has fixed what we call a major case, by fixing the limit at $3,000."[3]

Before World War I the characteristic private insurance litigation was a straightforward policyholder's action at law against the insuring company for payment of the amount due under a policy, an action usually heard in a state court.[4] Although the small face amounts of most policies held the bulk of those actions in the state courts, two other factors contributed to the relatively static nature and comparatively small amount of insurance litigation in the federal courts. One was the proliferation in the late nineteenth century of state statutes that effectively restricted the ability of insurance companies to use the federal courts, and the other was the relatively few opportunities the law gave companies to invoke federal equity jurisdiction. The early 1920s witnessed the end of both of those limiting conditions.

Federal Equity and the Insurers' Right to Remove

In 1869 the Supreme Court held in *Paul v. Virginia*[5] that corporations were not "citizens" within the meaning of the "privileges and immunities" clause. The decision, reflecting the deep suspicion of corporate enterprise that characterized many of the Court's decisions from the Civil War into the 1880s, was designed to ensure that the states could retain firm control over the activities of foreign corporations.[6] *Paul* meant that corporations chartered in one state did not have a constitutional right to enter and carry on an intrastate business in other states. Shortly after the decision came down, a number of states, driven by the twin forces of states' rights ideology and the desire to control the local operations of national corporations, began to use their authority to exclude foreign corporations from conducting local business as a method of pressuring them to litigate their disputes in the state courts. In 1874 in *Home Insurance Co. v. Morse*[7] the Supreme Court struck down such a restrictive statute, holding that a state could not compel foreign corporations to agree not to remove as a condition of obtaining licenses to do business in the state. Two years later, however, in *Doyle v. Continental Insurance Co.*[8] the Court held that a state had the right to exclude foreign corporations on any ground it chose. On that basis, it ruled that a state could provide that a foreign corporation's license to do local business would be revoked if the company removed. The two decisions appeared inconsistent in result if not in theory, but many of the states seized on *Doyle* to justify statutes that restricted corporate removals.

Although the Court refused to disavow either precedent, increasingly *Morse* seemed to stand for the governing rule. Repeatedly the Court stated the general rule that federal jurisdiction was controlled by the Constitution and by acts of Congress and that the states could not restrict it.[9] More important, in *Barron v. Burnside*[10] in 1887 it voided another state statute that required foreign corporations to agree not to remove actions, and in 1892 in *Southern Pacific Co. v. Denton*[11] it overturned a statute that provided for revocation of a foreign corporation's right to do business if it removed. The language of the cases seemed to overrule *Doyle,* and most lawyers and judges assumed that the Court had in effect done so.

Many states refused, however, to abandon their antiremoval statutes, and in 1906—within months of *Cochran, Thompson,* and *Wisner*—the Court sanctioned their efforts and infused new life into *Doyle.* In *Security Mutual Life Insurance Co. v. Prewitt*[12] it upheld a Kentucky statute that required the state's insurance commissioner to revoke the business license of any foreign insurance corporation that removed a state action to federal court. The Court reaffirmed the right of the states to exclude foreign corporations and, after reviewing all its prior decisions on the point, announced the basic principle that governed the removal issue. "As a State has power to refuse permission to a foreign insurance company to do business at all within its confines, and as it has power to withdraw that permission when once given, without stating any reason for its action," *Prewitt* explained, "the fact that it may give what some may think a poor reason or none for a valid act is immaterial."[13] The resulting rule seemed to be that although the states could not secure or enforce a company's agreement not to remove, they could prevent the company from operating within their borders if it actually removed a suit.

Insurance companies were especially vulnerable to the *Prewitt* rule. *Paul v. Virginia* had not only placed corporations outside the privileges and immunities clause, but it had also held that the business of insurance was not "commerce" within the meaning of the commerce clause. The Supreme Court followed that principle consistently in a long series of decisions.[14] Thus, unlike railroads and other national corporations, insurance companies did not engage in a business that was protected by the commerce clause.[15] Hence, although the commerce clause protected most other industries by guaranteeing them the right to conduct interstate business in all the states, it offered no such protection to insurance companies. If a state revoked an insurance company's license, then, the company would simply be out of business in that state. After *Prewitt*, insurance companies coexisted uneasily with antiremoval statutes in half or more of the states while fearing that additional states might adopt similar legislation.[16]

At the same time that state antiremoval laws restricted the insurance companies, prevailing law gave them little opportunity to take advantage of federal equity, a potentially powerful tool for them. Equity offered an ideal remedy against questionable policyholder claims since it—unlike the common law—could cancel or rescind written agreements on the ground of fraud or mistake. Equally important, equity offered the companies major procedural advantages, including a less demanding standard of proof for fraud,[17] the opportunity to preempt the policyholder's choice of forum, and a way to avoid generally propolicyholder juries. The problem was that federal equity jurisdiction was seldom available to the companies. Limited by statute and precedent, it did not extend to cases where there was an "adequate remedy at law."[18] The federal courts held that the companies had an adequate remedy at law when they could raise fraud as a defense to an action on a policy or initiate their own action at law for deceit against the policyholder. Because in most cases companies could do one or the other, they were generally unable to obtain relief in federal equity courts.

In 1870 Judge John F. Dillon, then a federal circuit judge, heard a suit in equity to cancel an insurance policy for fraud. It was, Dillon believed, a case of first impression since "the American reports do not show that any similar bill has been filed."[19] Although he upheld the principle that the federal courts had equity jurisdiction over suits to cancel or rescind written agreements, Dillon applied traditional principles to deny relief. Equity would not act because the company's fraud claim could be asserted as a defense to an action at law on the policy and the policyholder was obliged by the policy to bring an action within a year.

Dillon recognized the purpose of the suit and spelled out his views clearly. The company was attempting to preempt the policyholder's choice of forum, and it was trying to avoid facing a jury. "From the supposed sympathy of jurors in favor of the assured as against the insurance company, and from the supposed even-handed impartiality of the judge," he explained, "it is not difficult to see that companies, having the choice of courts, would prefer the equitable to the legal forum." The preference was understandable because the fears of the insurance companies "have, by far, too much foundation."[20] Nevertheless, Dillon concluded, federal equity would not give relief. Not only was the legal remedy adequate, but allowing equity to afford relief in such a case "would be to transfer the great bulk of all litigation arising out of losses under policies, from the courts of law into the courts of equity."[21] Further, it would deprive policyholders of trial by jury which, whatever its imperfections, was a constitutional right that equity was bound to respect.[22] Jury bias, Dillon pointed out, was to be remedied not by increased use of equity but by "the more liberal exercise by the common law courts of the power to grant new trials."[23]

The following year the Supreme Court confirmed the narrow scope of federal equity jurisdiction in such suits. In *Insurance Company v. Bailey*[24] the company brought suit to cancel two policies allegedly procured by fraud, and the beneficiary subsequently filed an action at law to recover on them. Although the Court made clear its view that the evidence supported the company's claim of fraud, it ruled that equity jurisdiction was lacking "upon grounds wholly disconnected from the merits."[25] Stressing as Dillon had the fact that equity deprived the defendant of a trial by jury, the Court emphasized that it had no jurisdiction where an adequate remedy at law existed. Without proof of "special circumstances," *Bailey* held, an adequate remedy at law existed when the company's obligation to pay had become "fixed" as "a purely legal demand" for money due and the beneficiary had filed an action at law where the company's fraud claim could be raised as a defense.[26]

Bailey remained the leading federal case on suits to cancel insurance policies for half a century, and in 1903 the Court reaffirmed it in a decision that brought together both the scope of federal equity in insurance suits and the power of the states to block removals to the federal courts. *Cable v. United States Life Insurance Co.*[27] presented a standard suit to cancel for fraud, and *Bailey* seemed to control. The obligation to pay had become fixed, and the beneficiary had brought an action at law in an Illinois state court. The company, however, contended that federal equity jurisdiction existed because its situation fell within *Bailey*'s "special circumstances" exception. The two special circumstances that it alleged went to the core of the system of corporate diversity litigation. First, the company pointed to an Illinois statute that provided for revoking the license of any insurance company that attempted to remove an action to a federal court. Because that statute forced it to abandon its right to remove, the company argued, the statute denied it an adequate remedy at law. Second, the company contended that it would suffer "irreparable injury" if forced to remain in the state court because "the [common] law is more favorable to insurance companies as administered in the Federal than in the state court."[28]

The Court ruled against the company on both issues. It had little difficulty with the second argument. Although there were differences between state and federal common law, the Court refused to transform that fact into a premise that would extend equity jurisdiction. The company's contention, it stated peremptorily, "cannot be regarded for a moment."[29] Regarding the impact of the antiremoval statute, the Court sidestepped. *Prewitt* lay three years in the future. Although the scope of a state's authority to revoke business licenses was not settled, the Court acknowledged, one principle was "entirely clear." However broad a state's power to exclude foreign corporations, it could not prevent any party from exercising its federal right to remove. Thus, regardless of whether Illinois could constitutionally impose penalties on the company if it removed, the Court explained, it could not bar the company from removing. The company's failure to remove, therefore, was due to its own decision to accede to the state statute rather than to challenge it by asserting its federal right. "The embarrassment attaching to the complainant

herein" was "one of its own creation," the Court held, and the company's awkward position "furnishes no ground for appealing to a Federal court of equity."[30]
Because there were no special circumstances under *Bailey,* the suit should be
dismissed.

Cable offered a clear view of the tensions that marked corporate diversity
litigation and of the Court's willingness in 1903 to accept state limitations on
removal jurisdiction that assisted policyholders. The insurance company was being squeezed. The antiremoval statute pressured it to stay in the state court where
the Illinois common law, contrary to federal common law, was unfavorable on the
controlling issues. "This court and the Supreme Court of Illinois appear to differ
radically" on the common law, the company's attorneys insisted. "One or the
other must be wrong, and if the Illinois Supreme Court is wrong, then [the
company] could have had no remedy at all in the state court from the standpoint
of this court."[31] The United States Supreme Court showed no sympathy. It may
simply have seen no doctrinal way out given the established precedents and the
views of the sitting Justices, or it may have meant the freedom of contract language that animated its contemporaneous common law decisions to such an extent
that it was prepared to ignore not only practical restraints on that freedom but
even a formal legal one. More likely, the Court simply regarded the company's
strategy as too clever. Refusing to challenge the statute directly, the company tried
to use its state-law disability as leverage to pry open the door to federal equity. In
Cable the Court made it clear that it was unwilling to allow such corporate tactics
to stretch the limits of federal equity jurisdiction.

The company's theory of federal equity jurisdiction carried the same expansive potential that marked Taft's theory of joinder in *Warax,* and across doctrinal
fields *Cable* joined *Thompson* in affirming strict limits on corporate access to the
federal courts. In each case the Court confronted a critical issue in the procedural
law of the system of corporate diversity litigation, and in each it refused to aid
corporations at the price of making significant changes in fundamental rules of
procedure that would markedly expand the jurisdiction of the federal courts. In
their social consequences, *Cable* and *Thompson* were of a piece with the Court's
other major decisions—*Dixon, Wisner, Cochran,* and *Prewitt*—that sharply
cabined the system during the critical years from 1900 to 1906.

The *Bailey–Cable* rule and the Court's toleration of state antiremoval statutes continued for two decades.[32] The *Bailey–Cable* rule itself was restrictive,
holding that federal equity would not—absent "special circumstances"—assert
jurisdiction over a company's suit to cancel a policy if a loss had occurred and
the beneficiary was suing or about to sue. In such circumstances the company
had an adequate remedy at law. The rule was particularly restrictive, too, because it applied in practice to the great majority of fraud or mistake cases.
Insurance companies seldom discovered fraud or mistake prior to loss. For the
most part it was only after a loss, when the beneficiary demanded payment and
the company investigated, that problems emerged. That seemed particularly true
with life, health, and disability policies. Individuals were invariably tempted to
insure when they learned that they had medical problems, and the companies
were particularly suspicious of claims made on recently issued policies.[33] The
Bailey–Cable rule kept most of those disputes beyond the reach of federal equity, and *Prewitt,* upholding the constitutionality of state antiremoval statutes,

helped ensure that most of the resulting actions at law would be restricted to the courts of the states.

The Jazz Age in Insurance Litigation

The 1920s transformed the nature of the system's insurance litigation. Of greatest importance, in 1922 the Supreme Court finally settled the issue of state authority that it had avoided in *Cable* and upheld, at least with respect to insurance companies, in *Prewitt.* In *Terral v. Burke Construction Co.*[34] the Court declared that its earlier decisions "can not be reconciled," and it expressly overruled both *Doyle* and *Prewitt.*[35] It held that foreign corporations had a federal right to bring or remove actions to the national courts and that the states could not constitutionally penalize them or withdraw their right to do local business because they exercised that right.

Terral invalidated restrictive statutes in approximately half the states and eliminated the insurance industry's fear that others might also adopt them. For the first time since the corporate system developed in the 1870s, and especially since *Prewitt,* insurers had unrestricted and unproblematic access to federal courts across the nation. They wasted no time in taking advantage of the opportunity. "These insurance companies are the worst offenders in the matter of resorting to the Federal Courts," complained a California attorney a decade later.[36] Since *Terral,* a Texas attorney agreed, "practically all suits brought against foreign corporations, involving more than $3,000.00, have been and are being removed."[37] The results were the same in Nebraska. "[N]ow all the big foreign insurance companies are removing every possible case to the federal court and appealing to the higher federal courts if they lose," protested a plaintiffs' attorney in Lincoln. "The result is that people with just claims against insurance companies are compromising and settling for half of what is due them, rather than run the gauntlet of the federal courts."[38] The threat of removal was so useful in helping to force low settlements that some companies reportedly served formal notice on claimants that in the event they filed actions on their policies, the companies would remove them to federal court.[39] In the years after *Terral* well over a thousand private insurance cases per year poured into the federal courts, accounting for 10 to 15 percent of the diversity docket. The companies were responsible for more than 90 percent of the total, bringing approximately half as original suits and half as removals. Although most insurance cases remained in the state courts, the great bulk of those were for amounts below the jurisdictional minimum.[40]

With unhampered access to the federal courts, the companies quickly exploited developments in insurance law to expand at long last the availability of federal equity jurisdiction. Central to their success was the "incontestability" clause that had become common after the turn of the century.[41] Although drafted in various forms, incontestability clauses generally provided that the insurer could not contest the validity, as opposed to the scope or meaning, of a policy after it had been in effect for a period of time, usually one or two years. By the 1920s many states required the inclusion of incontestability clauses in locally sold policies, and the popularity of the clauses combined with competitive pressures to induce most companies to offer them in their policies.[42]

Widespread use of incontestability clauses, however, created a critical problem for the companies. If a loss occurred before the contestable period had run, the insured or her beneficiary could delay bringing suit until after the period expired and thereby deprive the company of its ability to defend. The difficulty the companies faced was particularly acute since by the mid-1920s the courts had generally agreed that the only way a company could "contest" a policy was in a judicial forum.[43] Some type of equitable relief seemed necessary.

In late 1923 the Supreme Court increased the risk of insurance companies in incontestability cases but strengthened their claim on federal equity. In *Mutual Life Insurance Co. of New York v. Hurni Packing Co.*,[44] an action at law to collect under a life insurance policy, the Court ruled that the contestable period continued to run after the insured's death and that the company, having failed to contest the policy within the period, could no longer question its validity. *Hurni* was important because of the argument on behalf of the company that the Court rejected. "The rule that death of the insured stops the running of the contestability period is a necessary implication of" the *Bailey–Cable* rule, the company's attorneys argued.[45] "If the insurance company must wait until the action at law is commenced, and assert its defense of fraud in that action," then that rule must be based on the premise that "the rights of both insurance company and beneficiary are fixed by the maturing of the policy through the death of the insured."[46] On the ground that the language of the clause at issue controlled and seemed clear, the Court dismissed the company's argument.[47]

Although limited to the specific language of the clause at issue, *Hurni* lent support to the proposition that a loss under a policy did not ordinarily suspend the running of the contestability period. That conclusion, in turn, implied that a company's plight in such situations should be recognized as a special circumstance under the *Bailey–Cable* rule. Otherwise, an insurance beneficiary, by delaying her legal action on the policy until the contestability period had run, could leave the insurer with neither a legal nor an equitable remedy.

Hurni, in a sense, did what *Cable* had refused to do. It construed the federal common law in a way that led to the expansion of federal equity jurisdiction.[48] Rejecting the common law rule of some states—for which the company had contended—that a loss fixed the rights of the parties,[49] *Hurni* provided a premise that forced open the doors of federal equity courts for the insurance companies. By the late 1920s, company suits to cancel policies, especially those with incontestability clauses, had become a staple of the federal diversity docket.

In addition to *Hurni*, other factors also helped accelerate the rush of insurance companies into the federal courts after *Terral*. First, not only did the federal courts often apply a more favorable substantive law than did the state courts, but in the 1920s it seemed likely that they would become even more favorably disposed toward the companies. In 1921 and 1922 three new Justices, one of them William Howard Taft, the new Chief Justice, took their seats on the United States Supreme Court. All three were widely regarded as highly property conscious and sympathetic to business, and the Court's major decisions seemed immediately to reflect their new influence.[50] *Terral*, like the Court's contemporaneous decision in *Lee* overruling *Wisner*, was consistent with the new Court's heightened solicitude for national business interests.

As with *Lee*, of course, *Terral* did not represent a simple attempt to assist business. In deciding the case the Taft Court was driven by a commitment to the supremacy of federal law and the federal courts. Indeed, Taft himself was so intent on negating the idea that the states could restrict the jurisdiction of the national courts that he took it upon himself to write the Court's opinion in *Terral* and to include in it language that echoed the views that he and Lurton had expressed while on the Sixth Circuit in the 1890s. Removal, the new Chief Justice declared in *Terral*, was not merely a federal right but a constitutional right.[51] Taft's constitutional language was so clearly unfounded and misleading, however, that the Court felt compelled later the same year to restate accepted doctrine and in effect to repudiate *Terral*'s reference to the constitutional nature of removal.[52] Regardless of both the repudiation and the fact that *Terral*'s immediate practical significance was to assist insurance companies, the Court nevertheless sought in the decision to implement a fundamental constitutional principle. Holding that the states could not use their powers to limit or defeat a federal right created by Congress, it reaffirmed the supremacy of federal law and federal rights in the American constitutional system.

Second, the insurance companies avidly sought federal jurisdiction because the number and importance of insurance disputes grew as the total value of insurance in force skyrocketed. The value of life insurance in force stood near $25 billion in 1917, but it doubled twice in the next dozen years and by 1929 exceeded $100 billion. Coverage, moreover, was spread more widely. In 1928 seven million workers held more than $25 billion in industrial and group policies.[53] As the amount of insurance in force grew, the percentage of policies that came within the jurisdictional amount also increased. And as litigations multiplied and the cumulative amounts at stake compounded, companies felt ever more keenly the need to develop more effective litigation tactics and to seek more favorable forums whenever possible.

Third, as the companies invoked federal jurisdiction more commonly in the 1920s, they began to recognize and exploit the procedural advantages that federal equity offered, particularly the opportunity to avoid jury trials.[54] They came to see the possibilities, for example, in the Law and Equity Act of 1915, a procedural reform that allowed defendants to plead equitable defenses and seek equitable relief in actions at law.[55] Drafted and sponsored by the American Bar Association (ABA), the statute was hailed as a step toward simplifying federal procedure and minimizing the inconveniences caused by the division between law and equity.[56] Whatever its general utility, the act created procedural uncertainties and the consequent opportunity to narrow the jury's role in "merged" cases. Taft, a strong advocate of both procedural reform and the merger of law and equity, admitted as much when he addressed the ABA at its annual meeting in 1914. The consolidated procedure would not disadvantage plaintiffs, however, Taft explained, as it would save them the delay and expense of defending a separate suit in equity.[57]

If the Law and Equity Act itself had not initially inspired parties who preferred to avoid juries, the Supreme Court's 1922 decision in *Liberty Oil Co. v. Condon National Bank*[58] surely did. The Court granted certiorari in the case to settle "the important question of practice"[59] that the statute raised, and Chief Justice Taft again took the opportunity to write the Court's opinion. The statute, he wrote for a unanimous bench, "is an important step toward a consolidation in the federal courts of law and equity."[60] To the question of the procedures applicable in "merged" cases *Condon* gave a sweeping answer. When the defendant interposed an equitable defense, it transformed the legal action into a suit in equity. Because equitable proceedings had traditionally enjoyed a priority over those at law, the equitable issues should be tried first without a jury, and the legal issues—if any remained—would then be tried to a jury. When *Condon* relied on equity's traditional priority, it blinked the central problem that the statute raised. Traditional equity, at least in the federal courts, was available only if a party had no adequate remedy at law. *Condon* seemed to mean that the statute's equitable defenses provision enabled a defendant to transform an action at law into a suit in equity and thereby to preempt, in whole or in part, a plaintiff's right to a jury trial even when federal equity would not have granted relief if the defendant had brought an original suit in equity.[61]

In the summer of 1923, in the immediate wake of *Terral* and *Condon,* the Fourth Circuit helped inaugurate the new phase in the system's insurance litigation. In *Jefferson Standard Life Insurance Co. v. Keeton*[62] it ruled that the court below had jurisdiction over several suits seeking cancellation of insurance policies on the ground that the beneficiaries could delay in bringing actions for payment until after the contestable periods had expired. That much seemed fair. *Keeton,* however, went further and, over a strong dissent, helped lay the foundation for a radically expanded federal equity practice. First, it held that federal equity jurisdiction should be exercised even though the beneficiaries had brought actions at law after the company filed its suits and before the expiration of the contestable period. It expressly held the *Bailey–Cable* rule inapplicable and ignored the fact that in *Bailey* itself the beneficiary's state court action had also been filed after the company's federal equity suit. Second, relying in part on *Condon,* it held that the equity suits should not be stayed in favor of the legal actions. *Keeton* declared, in fact, that the judge below could not as a matter of discretion postpone the former until the latter were tried. The company's equity claims must be tried before the claimants' actions at law. Third, the court added emphatic dicta to the effect that, had the companies not removed the beneficiaries' actions at law, the federal court could properly have enjoined their prosecution pending disposition of the federal equity suits.

Keeton quickly became a leading case, cited by most courts and followed by many. The Fourth Circuit repeatedly reaffirmed it,[63] and other circuits similarly narrowed *Bailey* and ruled that a policyholder's action at law did not oust federal equity.[64] The Sixth, Seventh, and Eighth Circuits extended the principle by declaring that a policyholder's action could not give the insurer an adequate remedy at law so long as the policyholder could take a voluntary dismissal.[65] By the 1930s the federal courts were exercising their equity jurisdiction more broadly and granting relief to insurance companies in a much wider range of cases than they had previously.[66] By 1934 the Seventh Circuit concluded that the right of an insurance company to invoke federal equity jurisdiction, even if the company could raise its defense in a claimant's action at law, was recognized in "by far the majority of cases in the federal courts."[67]

The companies methodically used their new access to federal equity to develop a number of tactics that enabled them to avoid jury trials. When policyholders or their beneficiaries brought actions in the state courts, the companies could remove them and then seek stays while their own suits in equity to cancel the policies proceeded to judgment.[68] If a stay were not available, they could attempt to utilize the Law and Equity Act. In several circuits the courts allowed equitable pleas in policyholder actions at law to preempt jury determination of critical issues of fact.[69] When removal was not available or a company wanted to prevent a policyholder from even initiating a state action, it could sometimes obtain an injunction to block state proceedings.[70]

It seems likely that the expanded use of federal equity to cancel policies and the companies' successes in exploiting the jurisdiction, obtaining stays and injunctions, and generally reducing the use of juries in insurance litigation had a cumulative and pervasive effect. Some policyholders and beneficiaries were likely dissuaded from even bringing their own independent actions at law.[71] It seems equally likely that the general social result was fewer policyholder victories in court, a wider scope for the informal legal process, and more settlements for smaller amounts of money.

Although *Terral, Condon, Hurni* and the more aggressive tactics of some companies reshaped insurance litigation in the 1920s, they did not invariably bring success to the industry. Frequently companies ran into strong opposition. Some federal courts refused to follow the lead of *Keeton* and other decisions that broadened equity practice, and they continued to dismiss company suits on the ground that adequate remedies at law existed.[72]

The insurance plaintiffs' bar, too, adapted to the new environment and developed its own new tactics. One was interstate forum shopping which insurance claimants also began to adopt after 1910. If Missouri took second place to Minnesota in importing tort actions, it may have ranked first in insurance suits. Missouri carried a reputation as a state particularly hostile to insurance companies, and it offered relatively favorable procedural law. By 1910 or 1915, explained the general counsel of the National Board of Fire Underwriters, it had become "quite customary" for plaintiffs to sue "in the western part of Missouri."[73] The state became a readily available forum because it required foreign insurance companies, as a condition of doing local business, to authorize appointment of an agent for receipt of process in any action against the company regardless of where the cause arose or where the parties resided. In 1917 the United States Supreme Court upheld the constitutionality of the statute,[74] and the state's position as a popular forum for out-of-state insurance plaintiffs was secured.

Another claimants' tactic, similar to the administrator device approved in *Mecom*, was the use of assignees to prevent removal. A Missouri attorney confided in 1933 that in several cases he had successfully avoided removal by having his clients assign their claims to a person whose citizenship was the same as the insurer's. The main problem, he noted, was that the tactic was "a little bit expensive."[75] An Iowa attorney relied on *Mecom* in recommending the same tactic. "[L]awyers are more and more realizing," he wrote, "that Federal removal can be prevented by means of an assignment and are making such assignments to avoid Federal jurisdiction."[76] Apparently at least a few legal entrepreneurs attempted to serve policyholders and turn a profit from the assignment tactic by making themselves regularly available to defeat removal. Residing in the home states of insurance companies, they took an interest in policies by assignment and thereby destroyed diversity.[77]

A third tactic was to adapt standard antiremoval devices to insurance litigation. Variations on claim discounting, for example, became increasingly visible.

Some claimants who had two or more separate policies were able to split their claims and sue on each of them separately for an amount below the jurisdictional minimum. In such cases it was not clear whether policyholders were taking advantage of particularly keen foresight or simply enjoying good fortune because they had not originally purchased, or perhaps had not been able to afford, a single policy with a larger face value. The tactic was generally successful. The federal courts held that claims based on different policies presented distinct causes of action and that the amounts claimed on each could not be aggregated for jurisdictional purposes.[78] Policyholders, too, were more visible in discounting their claims and bringing suits for amounts below the jurisdictional minimum as well as below the face value of their policies. On established theory, though not without some struggling, the federal courts accepted the tactic and refused jurisdiction.[79] A policyholder in South Dakota even revived the delayed upward amendment tactic and, when the insurer failed to remove after a posttrial motion to increase the claim, succeeded in raising his state court recovery to double the jurisdictional minimum.[80]

Insurance plaintiffs also tried to borrow the joinder tactic but, in contrast with their growing use of claim discounting, had little success with it. The formal two-party nature of most insurance contracts made it difficult to allege joint liability against a third party.[81] Most of the attempts to use the joinder tactic arose from the growing number of automobile accident suits that began to proliferate in the 1920s. Injury victims tried to bring joint claims against the other drivers and their insurance companies, hoping to reach directly into the deep pockets of the insurer and also to prevent removals. A few states provided assistance with "direct action" statutes that authorized suits by injured parties directly against the insurer of the alleged tortfeasor.[82] In a number of states, however, local procedural rules blocked the tactic by, for example, barring joinder of causes of action based on contract with those based on tort.[83] More important, the companies increasingly drafted their insurance contracts to avoid such joinders. Sometimes, too, the courts were hostile to the tactic. When the South Carolina legislature created a joint cause of action for tort victims against alleged tortfeasors and their insurers, the local federal court avoided its provisions and allowed removal by discovering special limitations in the statute. "[W]here the damages sought are for wilfulness and negligence or in an amount greater than the policy limits," he ruled, "the action is not joint and a separable controversy is presented."[84] Although joinder became a noticeable factor in insurance litigation, it was available in only a relative handful of cases.[85]

Insurance claimants also forged their own special tactics.[86] In the early twentieth century policies offering monthly benefits, especially accident and disability policies, became common. Disputes concerning such policies usually arose when the company claimed either fraud or termination of the disability and then refused to make further payments. To avoid removal, plaintiffs began to bring actions solely for the amount of the accrued and unpaid monthly benefits, an amount invariably under the jurisdictional minimum.[87] Settled doctrine supported them, holding that the amount in controversy "is determined by the amount involved in the particular case, and not by any contingent loss either of the parties may sustain by the probative effect of the judgment, however certain it may be that such loss will occur."[88] In 1928 the Supreme Court upheld the doctrine and seemed to guarantee the claimants' tactic when it affirmed the rule that the amount in controversy was properly limited to the value of the payments that had already accrued.[89]

The companies quickly adopted countermeasures, exploiting as much as possible the availability of federal equity. As the railroads and other corporations fought interstate forum shopping by seeking injunctions against out-of-state suits, so the insurance companies tried to exploit the opportunities that federal equity offered to defeat claimants' newly aggressive antiremoval and related tactics. One target was the use of assignments to parties whose citizenship was the same as the company's. "The insurance companies," complained one attorney in 1933, "are now attempting to frustrate such assignments by injunctions against assignees in the home state of the insurance company, where the insurance company may have influence."[90]

Another target was policyholder attempts to sue below the jurisdictional minimum. By utilizing their newly expanded access to federal equity and seizing the initiative, insurance companies could preemptively force controversies into the federal courts by filing suits to cancel and claiming that the amount in controversy was the total face value of all disputed policies or, especially in disability cases, the total amount for which they might ultimately be liable.[91] The efforts succeeded in numerous cases. Federal courts exercised equity jurisdiction in such preemptive suits, and they did so even where the insured had claims only for disability payments totalling less than the jurisdictional minimum.[92] Again, the Fourth Circuit was in the forefront. In 1933, for example, it upheld federal equity jurisdiction over an action to cancel where the insured had filed a state action at law for $450 in accrued disability payments prior to being served in the company's federal equity suit. Vigorously enforcing its broadened equity jurisdiction, the Fourth Circuit upheld an order enjoining the policyholder from proceeding with his state action.[93]

In the 1930s the tactics on both sides, particularly in disability claims, became even more aggressive. Some claimants, encouraged by a 1926 decision of the Sixth Circuit,[94] attempted to turn the tables on the companies. Assuming that the amount in controversy was the company's total potential liability, they brought actions for nonpayment on the theory of "anticipatory" breach of contract by the insurer and claimed as damages large lump-sum amounts. The courts, however, usually rejected the theory and consigned them to a recovery of accrued benefits only.[95] The inventiveness of the companies proved somewhat more fruitful. Borrowing from the equity precedents that held the amount in controversy to be a company's total potential liability, some pressed to expand federal jurisdiction in actions at law. The jurisdictional minimum in policyholder actions for accrued payments, they argued, should be measured not by the amount sought but by the size of the reserve fund that a company would have to maintain in order to fund the payments. In the mid-1930s a few federal courts accepted the argument and ruled that companies could remove actions at law for accrued benefits when the amount that plaintiffs actually sought was less than the jurisdictional minimum.[96] An Arizona attorney protested in 1933 that the federal court had denied his motion to remand an action for disability benefits "although we only demanded judgment in a sum less than $500.00." The court, however, adopted the theory "that the liability of the company under the policy might exceed at some time $3,000."[97]

The depression helped drive the tactical escalation. Massive unemployment and economic hardship led policyholders to file disability claims whenever they possibly could, and many companies began to face the prospect of mounting deficits. As late as 1931, for example, the income of one company from its disability policies exceeded its losses paid by almost $20 million. But only two years later its losses paid exceeded its income by almost $30 million.[98]

Legislation, too, contributed to the tactical escalation. Interpleader was a traditional equitable remedy available to "stakeholders" who were faced with the inconsistent claims of two or more parties to the same property or fund. Its use, however, was restricted by the limited ability of courts to obtain personal jurisdiction over all the claimants. In 1917, 1925, and 1926 Congress passed federal interpleader acts[99] that made the remedy more readily available by allowing nationwide service of process. The statutes gave the federal courts jurisdiction over equity suits for interpleader brought by insurance companies, and they authorized the courts to enjoin other state or federal actions involving the same controversy. Although a useful reform, the federal interpleader acts gave insurance companies one more tool that allowed them to shape litigations in their favor and limit the access of claimants to a trial by jury.[100]

Of far greater importance, the years after World War I witnessed the arrival and spread of a new remedy termed a declaratory judgment. Virtually unknown to American law before 1915, the "declaration of rights" was a judgment without an accompanying order granting coercive relief or awarding damages. In theory, it provided a simple method of settling disputes when they first arose and before parties took irrevocable actions or incurred avoidable costs and liabilities. Unlike equitable remedies, such as injunctions, it required no special or onerous conditions precedent to its use. In 1915 New Jersey authorized its courts to grant declaratory judgments; a few states followed in the early 1920s; and by the mid-1930s almost three-quarters of the states had adopted the device.[101] In 1934 Congress passed a federal Declaratory Judgment Act, giving the federal courts jurisdiction to grant declaratory relief.[102]

Like interpleader, the declaratory judgment was particularly useful to the insurance industry. "Experience," explained its foremost academic proponent, "indicates that insurance companies themselves frequently have occasion to move as actors to disavow a policy or a liability before loss."[103] Unlike interpleader, however, the declaratory judgment was not confined to one specific situation. It was a far more powerful device since it could be used in any dispute. It was generally available where parties could seek other legal or equitable remedies, and it was equally available when no other remedy yet existed.[104]

In particular, the declaratory judgment opened several new possibilities for the industry's litigation. First, by allowing for a declaration of rights prior to actual claim or loss, the remedy enabled insurance companies to take the initiative in bringing suit, thereby giving them control of timing and the choice of forum. The latter benefit was especially critical, of course, in states where the federal common law differed from the state law. Second, by eliminating the procedural requirements for equitable relief, the declaratory judgment allowed companies to take the initiative in more cases and with less difficulty when they wished to control timing or forum selection. Third, because the remedy was vaguely regarded as equitable, it raised the possibility that the trial of an action for declaratory relief would be to the court rather than to a jury. A number of courts, in fact, held or at least implied that there was no right to a jury in a suit for declaratory relief.[105] Thus, the availability of the new remedy meant that companies could more frequently seize the initiative and thereby control the suit's timing, probably determine its forum, secure whatever advantages existed under the federal common law, and perhaps deprive the claimant of a trial by jury.

In addition, the declaratory judgment offered the companies a new method to satisfy the jurisdictional amount. The general rule was that the amount in controversy in a declaratory action was the value of the right or liability at issue.[106] By striking quickly and bringing suit for a declaration concerning the validity of an entire policy, companies could ensure that the amount in controversy would be above the jurisdictional minimum. Suits for declaratory judgment, in other words, served as a device to counter two of the principal tactics that claimants used to avoid federal jurisdiction, discounting claims and suing only for accrued benefits.

The Supreme Court: Searching for Middle Ground in the Mid-Thirties

The growth of insurance cases in the national courts and the procedural innovations they spawned pressed a relentless stream of critical issues toward the Supreme Court. In the mid 1930s the Court heard more than a dozen important insurance cases, and it struggled to clarify doctrine and to impose greater order on the law of insurance litigation. Its initial reaction to the mounting turmoil, in fact, was to try to reduce the companies' incentives to use the federal courts by urging the lower courts to restrain their independent judgment of the common law in insurance disputes. In separate decisions in 1933 and 1934 the Court began to emphasize the desirability of subordinating the federal common law to "a benign and prudent comity" when state common law was clear, the issue lacked national importance, and the correct rule was "balanced with doubt."[107]

In 1935, as part of a more general effort to cabin the corporate use of the Law and Equity Act,[108] the Court curbed some of the companies' most creative tactics. In *Enelow v. New York Life Insurance Co.*[109] and a companion case[110] it reversed two decisions of the Third Circuit and ruled that the statute did not allow companies to force an action at law into an equity court and thereby deprive plaintiffs of their right to jury trials. "The test under [the statute]," the Court announced, "is whether the defendant could have maintained a bill in equity on the same averments.[111] Insofar as plaintiff's action for damages gave the company an adequate remedy at law, in other words, the statute did not open an alternative route into equity. Further, citing *Bailey* and *Cable,* the Court reached out to warn against another of the companies' new tools. If an action at law provided an adequate remedy, it cautioned, "a bill in equity would not lie to stay proceedings in that action in order to have the defense heard and determined in equity."[112]

Later the same year *Di Giovanni v. Camden Fire Insurance Association*[113] continued the process of restraining the companies' new tactics, reversing a decision of the Eighth Circuit that upheld federal equity jurisdiction over a company's suit to cancel two policies. The company alleged that the jurisdictional amount was satisfied by the combined face value of the policies and that it had no adequate remedy at law because the policyholder planned to initiate separate actions on each policy, thereby forcing on the insurer the burden of defending multiple suits. The Supreme Court rested its decision on the latter point, ruling that the inconvenience of defending two suits was insufficient to warrant the exercise of federal equity jurisdiction. Although the Court narrowly restricted its holding, it set down several seemingly weighty dicta. It noted that in an action at law the jurisdictional amount could not be met by combining the face values of separate policies,[114] and it cited *Enelow* for the proposition that federal equity would not cancel a policy if the policyholder's action at law were "threatened" or "imminent."[115] Perhaps most significant, *Di Giovanni* stressed the importance of restricting federal equity in order to preserve two fundamental rights, the policyholder's right to a jury trial and the state's right to jurisdiction over actions at law involving amounts less than the jurisdictional minimum. "Congress, by its legislation," the Court emphasized, "has declared its policy that cases involving less than the jurisdictional amount be left exclusively to the state courts."[116]

Although the Court curtailed some of the companies' most aggressive uses of federal equity, it agreed with them in other areas. In 1935 it limited the efforts of policyholders to win large recoveries on the theory of anticipatory breach of contract by providing insurers with a good faith defense,[117] and the following year it essentially terminated the theory's utility in insurance litigation. The latter case, *New York Life Insurance Co. v. Viglas,*[118] reversed a First Circuit decision and held that in an action for breach of contract to pay periodic benefits the beneficiary's damages were ordinarily limited to the amount of the unpaid installments. Similarly, although the Court did not directly address the question of the jurisdictional amount in company suits to cancel, its related decisions seemed to confirm that in such suits the face value of the policy was properly the amount in controversy.[119]

In 1937 the Court made its most comprehensive attempt to untangle the procedural issues raised by the new insurance litigation. *American Life Insurance Co. v. Stewart*[120] was a standard company suit to cancel two policies, where the beneficiaries had brought a state court action after the company's suit but well before the contestable period expired. It included one unusual, not to say bewildering, fact. The beneficiaries had signed a stipulation providing that the equity suit would proceed to trial prior to their action at law. The Tenth Circuit ruled that the stipulation could not control a determination of federal equity jurisdiction and ordered the suit dismissed on the ground that the company had an adequate remedy at law. On rehearing, with one judge dissenting, it affirmed its decision on the authority of *Enelow* and *Di Giovanni.*[121]

The case was obviously critical. It raised a major issue of federal procedure and equitable remedies, and the insurance industry vigorously pressed its concern. The Tenth Circuit had granted the rehearing because numerous insurance companies requested it and sought permission to submit amicus briefs.[122] The industry was anxious about the extent to which some of the lower courts were beginning to deny equitable relief under *Enelow* and *Di Giovanni.*[123] The Court, too, may have been sensitive to the criticism that the two decisions provoked. The First Circuit, for example, expressly criticized the Court for ignoring the danger that a policyholder could defeat an insurer's adequate remedy at law by discontinuing her action at law after the contestable period had run. "In other words," the First Circuit stated with extreme clarity, "the Supreme Court erred in reaching the conclusion that it did in the Enelow Case."[124]

The companies had a strong argument. In spite of *Bailey,* the Court had declared in other areas that a subsequently available remedy at law did not oust federal equity,[125] and there were by 1937 numerous lower court decisions upholding the right of an insurance company to equitable relief in such circumstances. The lower courts had allowed the remedy, *Stewart* stated, "with impressive uniformity."[126] There was, too, the fact that an incontestability clause put an insurance company in a particularly vulnerable position and that, as *Stewart* also noted, "the possibility of bad faith, perhaps concealed and hardly provable, accentuates the [company's] difficulty."[127] The dissent below ably stated the case, distinguishing the Court's prior rulings and stressing the practical danger to a company when the timing and continuation of its supposedly adequate remedy at law remained in the hands of the adverse party.[128]

The Court responded deftly in *Stewart* with a classic opinion by Justice Benjamin N. Cardozo that reversed the Tenth Circuit. On the one hand, it rejected the dicta in *Enelow* and *Di Giovanni* that a policyholder's action was necessarily an adequate remedy at law and upheld the availability of equitable relief. The advantages of incontestability clauses, *Stewart* declared, should not be turned into "weapons of oppression."[129] On the other hand, the opinion emphasized the importance to its decision of the policyholders' unusual and inexplicable stipulation that the company's equity suit should proceed first. "There is, indeed, a possibility that the bringing of actions at law might have been used by the [policyholders] to their advantage," it commented drily, "if they had not chosen by a stipulation to throw the possibility away."[130] *Stewart* implied that the beneficiaries had thrown away more than a possibility, and it suggested in broad terms the proper procedures that the lower courts should follow in such cases. A court had discretion to "hold one lawsuit in abeyance" while another proceeded. Because equitable relief was "exceptional and the outcome of necessity," the filing of an action at law by the policyholder called for the exercise of that discretion.[131] Although *Stewart* did not attempt to set forth a rule, the considerations it advanced and the cases it cited pointed toward a proposed general practice. If policyholders acted with reasonable promptness, they should have priority in trying their claims at law; if insurers wanted protection, they should be able to file in equity and at least have their defense preserved there pending final judgment in the policyholder's action at law.

Stewart, of course, could do little more than attempt to balance *Enelow* and *Di Giovanni* in sketching general guidelines for the uses of equity in insurance litigation. Complex and weighty doctrinal problems remained. How, for instance, would the new federal Declaratory Judgment Act affect the conduct of insurance litigation? Little was clear in 1937 beyond the fact that the tactical uses of the remedy, if not carefully cabined, could add immeasurably to the volatility of insurance litigation. A month after it decided *Stewart* the Court upheld the constitutionality of the Declaratory Judgment Act in *Aetna Life Insurance Co. v. Haworth,* and its decision approved the aggressive use of the device by an insurance company to obtain a judgment of nonliability, a type of action that the insurer could not have brought without the new declaratory remedy.[132] When and under what circumstances the federal courts would grant declaratory relief remained to be decided. So, too, did the question whether and when an action for a declaratory judgment was to be tried to a jury. So, finally, did the question of what substantive law was to be applied in suits for declaratory relief. If the act authorized the federal courts to grant a remedy in actions that would not have been cognizable in the federal courts prior to 1934, as was the case in *Haworth,* did that in effect open up a new way for companies to seize the initiative and ensure themselves a federal forum and the application of federal common law?[133]

As practical and doctrinal questions mushroomed, insurance companies expanded their efforts to exploit the new procedural rules.[134] Policyholders' attorneys responded with unorganized and sporadic efforts to counter the companies, but increasingly in the mid-1930s they seemed on the defensive. The overall context of insurance litigation, however, was about to change dramatically. Within a year the federal common law would be abolished, and within a decade the system of corporate diversity litigation would be largely a memory.

Chapter 10

Disintegration

The system of corporate diversity litigation, shrunken though still operative in the 1930s, disintegrated in the decade after 1937. Year by year the automobile and then the airplane continued steadily to lighten the burden of distance while the federal courts maintained their ability to minimize the burden of delay. As the turmoil of depression and war disrupted the established order, the New Deal effectively transformed the political and social values of the federal judiciary. The Supreme Court, altered profoundly after 1937 by President Franklin D. Roosevelt's new appointments, restructured American constitutional law, expanded the power of government to regulate the economy, and began to view labor and minorities with greater sympathy. By the late 1940s the national courts no longer seemed the special protectors of corporate interests, and in increasing numbers of cases individual plaintiffs began to regard them as desirable forums.

More directly, in 1938 the new "Roosevelt Court" toppled one of the pillars of the system. In *Erie Railroad Co. v. Tompkins*[1] it repudiated *Swift v. Tyson* and ended the reign of the independent federal common law. Equally important, it then began a decade-long campaign to eradicate the differences between the legal rules followed in state and federal courts that could induce defendants to remove.

By the end of the 1940s the historically specific system of corporate diversity litigation that had emerged in the 1870s and peaked in the decades around the turn of the century had largely disappeared. Although de facto social inequality continued to handicap individuals who sued large corporations and the formal law of diversity jurisdiction stood essentially unmodified, changes in both society and doctrine altered the practical significance of the jurisdiction. Social and legal pressures no longer drove plaintiffs to avoid the federal courts, and many of the advantages that national corporations had found in removal no longer existed.

The New Deal and the Political Transformation
of the Federal Courts

Protests against the federal courts and their perceived favoritism toward business had been heard since the 1870s, and the political conflicts of the 1890s had made them staples of American politics. The widespread belief that the federal courts were biased in favor of corporate interests became an integral part of the political-cultural attitudes that helped shape the system. If not measurable, as was the distance to the nearest federal court, the belief was nevertheless a general conditioning presumption that strengthened the contrasting views of the parties regarding the desirability of a federal forum.

In the 1920s the protests against the federal courts intensified. The Supreme Court invalidated numerous social reform statutes, including two successive federal child labor laws,[2] and struck forcefully at organized labor.[3] Checking the powers of both federal and state governments, the Court became to business interests a tower of strength and to most progressives a conservative partisan. During the business- and Republican-dominated 1920s, however, the protests against the federal courts had little effect. By 1933, when President Herbert Hoover left office, conservatives were securely in control of the national judiciary. A majority of the Justices on the Supreme Court were wedded to substantive due process and the federal common law, and three-quarters of the judges in the lower courts were Republican appointees.[4]

The depression of the 1930s and the attempts of the state and federal governments to meet its challenge drove the political conflict over the federal courts toward a crisis. The Court invalidated critical New Deal legislation,[5] and Roosevelt and his supporters attacked its "horse and buggy" attitude. The lower courts, too, seemed hostile to the New Deal. From 1933 through early 1936 they issued almost two thousand injunctions against various government agencies, most involving taxes under the New Deal's farm program, and deprived the government of some $180 million in revenues. A federal statute prohibited injunctions restraining the collection of federal taxes, Attorney General Homer Cummings informed Roosevelt in exasperation, but the federal courts nevertheless "seem to have found a way of declaring it inapplicable." Indeed, Cummings complained, they "permitted the use of injunctions rather freely."[6] The administration's adversaries rushed to defend the federal courts as the bulwarks of American freedom, but New Dealers never doubted that the majority of Justices on the Supreme Court and a large number of lower federal judges were driven by conservative and probusiness biases.

Triumphantly reelected in 1936 with staggering majorities in both houses of Congress, Roosevelt introduced in the following February his plan to "pack" the Supreme Court and immediately set off what became one of the great political–constitutional debates in American history.[7] Bitter opposition erupted, led by disaffected Democrats and the bar associations. Republicans and business groups purposely stayed on the sidelines, privately providing support and encouragement. A combination of factors, including the symbolic power of the Constitution and the Court, ultimately forced Roosevelt to admit defeat and withdraw his proposal in exchange for two minor procedural reform bills.[8] By August it was all over.

If the Court-packing plan went down to defeat, however, so did substantive due process and the "old" Supreme Court. In the spring, while the fate of the Court-packing bill was still in doubt, two Justices seemed to alter their positions, giving the progressive wing of the Court a bare majority. Between March and May, in a series of identical five-to-four votes, the Court rejected the doctrine of liberty of contract and upheld two pivotal New Deal measures, the National Labor Relations Act and the Social Security Act.[9] Finally, in May Justice Willis Van Devanter, one of the staunch antiprogressives on the Court, announced his retirement. Roosevelt was able to make his first appointment, and few doubted that others would soon follow. The Court's pro–New Deal decisions and Van Devanter's announcement dissipated whatever support remained for the Court-packing bill and seemed to ensure its defeat.

During the next four years, Roosevelt reconstituted the Court. Within months of Van Devanter's retirement, a second anti–New Deal Justice resigned. By the beginning of 1938 the President had appointed two new Justices, and the progressive wing seemed to have a solid majority. Other resignations followed, and by 1941 Roosevelt had made seven appointments to the Court. Of the two holdovers, one had been in the Court's progressive wing, and the other was one of the two who seemed to alter their views and move toward the progressive position in the spring of 1937.

Although the Roosevelt Court soon developed its own fault lines, the new Justices were in substantial agreement on the social and economic issues that animated the New Deal. By the late 1940s they had reshaped American constitutional law. Between 1938 and 1946 the "new" Court overruled thirty prior Supreme Court decisions and qualified or restricted many more.[10] It buried the doctrine of liberty of contract, interpreted federal law more favorably for organized labor, and expanded the reach of federal authority under the commerce clause. At the same time, it often showed a particular concern for the rights and prerogatives of the states and their courts, and it allowed a wider range of state economic regulation, including statutes that affected interstate commerce. To a lesser extent, too, the new Court explored relatively undeveloped areas of the Constitution. It began haltingly to strengthen the individual protections offered by the Bill of Rights and showed an increased sensitivity to the values implied in the First Amendment.[11]

The new Court rejected what the Roosevelt Justices regarded as the "activism" of the old Court and proclaimed the propriety of "judicial restraint," the idea that courts should generally defer to the legislative authority of Congress and the states. The Court repeatedly emphasized that its role was to treat statutes sympathetically and, if at all possible, favorably and that it should construe them to achieve the purpose of the underlying social policies that they embodied. Although personal and ideological differences would wrack the Court beginning in the early 1940s, especially in cases involving the Bill of Rights, throughout its existence the Roosevelt Court never questioned the "plenary powers" of Congress in matters of economic regulation. Its members agreed, at least in theory, that they ought not interpret the Constitution as they believed that the old Court had done, by reading into it their own social and economic values.[12]

The transformation of the Supreme Court both symbolized and helped effectuate a similar transformation in the entire federal judiciary. As its new decisions came down and the shape of federal constitutional and statutory law changed, the lower courts gradually if somewhat erratically adapted. Equally important, although the Republicans had controlled 75 percent of the federal bench in 1933, their numbers dwindled over the years. Increasingly the lower courts were filled with Roosevelt appointees, generally loyal New Dealers and often committed progressives. Especially after 1937 Roosevelt had candidates for judicial appointment screened carefully to determine their attitude toward the New Deal.[13] As the combination of a Roosevelt Court, new constitutional doctrines, and the increasingly progressive makeup of the lower judiciary reached a critical mass, the political and social orientation of the entire federal judiciary seemed to shift. The change, of course, was not absolute. Divergence and opposition continued to exist, just as they had before 1937. But still, by the late 1940s, both the law and the judges in the lower federal courts were radically different from what they had been little more than a decade earlier.

No longer did individuals suing national corporations have any general basis to believe that they were more likely to encounter a hostile judge in a federal court than in a state court. Statistics regarding Federal Employers' Liability Act (FELA) cases reveal the extent to which the views of tort plaintiffs changed. Prior to 1941 FELA plaintiffs has brought an average of fewer than 150 cases a year to the national courts. As the public image and social orientation of the federal courts shifted during the 1940s, however, the numbers began to rise. FELA plaintiffs filed 321 actions in the federal courts in 1944, 412 in 1945, and 661 in 1946. Although part of the increase was due to the larger number of railroad injuries that occurred during World War II, the number of federal FELA actions multiplied more rapidly than the injuries did. Even more revealing, when the number of railroad injuries fell significantly after 1944, federal FELA actions continued to rise steadily. In 1947 there were 799, and in 1948 more than 1,000.[14] Indeed, in the three years at mid-century, 1949 through 1951, FELA plaintiffs filed an average of 1,054 cases per year in the national courts, seven times the number they had filed in the federal courts during the late 1930s.[15]

On a parallel track, corporate defendants seemed generally less determined to secure a federal forum. Removals declined in frequency and importance. In spite of the judicial and legislative efforts to restrict removals after 1905, the American Law Institute (ALI) study found that they still exceeded original diversity suits as late as 1929–30. In the 1940s, however, removals dropped steadily as a percentage of the diversity docket. By 1941 they accounted for less than half of the total, and by the late 1940s, less than a third. The percentage of removals brought by corporations also fell, and the number of remands dropped sharply, suggesting that defendants stretched less often to gain access to the national courts.[16]

Although the Roosevelt Court was known primarily for its major constitutional decisions, it also dealt with issues that arose from corporate diversity litigation, and its new orientation began altering elements of the system. In 1941, for example, in *Toucey v. New York Life Insurance Co.*[17] the Court restricted the grounds on which federal courts could enjoin proceedings in state courts. Reflecting the Court's new sense of self-restraint and respect for state courts, *Toucey* prevented an insurance company from enjoining a second action on a policy brought in state court—in a nonremovable form—after the company had won a previous suit on the policy in federal court. The decision forced the company to make its defense in the state court rather than the federal court. Reflecting its new sympathy for injured workers, the Court refused to limit injured stevedores to recovery under a federal workmen's compensation statute and allowed them also to seek full legal damages from the owners of the ships on which they worked. In *Seas Shipping Co., Inc. v. Sieracki* the Court emphasized that its decision was designed to prevent a shipowner from avoiding his broad liability in admiralty by "parcelling out his operations to intermediary employers whose sole business is to take over portions of the ship's work" and thereby "strip the men performing its service of their historic protection" in admiralty.[18] Similarly, in 1945 the Court reconceptualized the law of personal jurisdiction in *International Shoe Co. v. State of Washington*[19] and, in doing so, expanded the constitutional authority of the states to assert jurisdiction over foreign corporations. The decision limited the ability of foreign corporations to structure their business so that they could carry on activities in a state but remain beyond the reach of its courts, and it made it easier for plaintiffs to sue foreign corporations in their home states.[20]

In 1939 the Roosevelt Court addressed one of the classic issues in the system. In *Neirbo Co. v. Bethlehem Shipbuilding Corp.*[21] it altered the construction of the federal venue statute to eliminate the advantage that corporate defendants had enjoyed since the Taft Court overruled *Wisner* in the *Lee* case. The plaintiff brought a federal diversity action against Bethlehem Shipbuilding in a district in which neither of the parties had a residence. Under the prevailing federal rule, venue was improper in such a district, and the defendant could force a dismissal by objecting. Bethlehem objected, and the courts below ordered the suit dismissed. The Supreme Court, however, construed the term "residence" in the venue statute to include any district in which a foreign corporation had designated an agent for service of process pursuant to state law. Filing such a designation, the Court reasoned, operated as a general consent to be sued in any court in the district, including a federal court. Because Bethlehem had designated an agent for receipt of process in the district, it had a residence in the district for federal venue purposes. Accordingly, plaintiff's suit was proper, and the Court reversed the dismissal below.

Although *Neirbo* was an artfully crafted opinion that purported to rely on a consistent series of cases back to *Harris* and *Schollenberger,* it in fact substantially restructured federal venue law and seemed primarily a result-oriented social decision designed to rectify one of the practical results of *Lee. Neirbo* deprived corporate defendants of a specific tactical advantage—the ability to avoid federal suits when they preferred a state forum while at the same time being able to remove when they wished to avoid a state forum. The Court's opinion noted specifically that the new rule prevented the law from "giving discriminatory freedom to foreign corporations."[22]

One of the most noticeable areas of change was in the Court's attitude toward the FELA. "[T]he Supreme Court is determined to permit recovery for the injured or deceased railroad employee and to place the responsibility for railroad accidents where it rightfully belongs," concluded one law review article in 1946. "It is evident that these late cases are in direct conflict with the earlier decisions."[23] Throughout the 1940s the Court construed the statute sympathetically, and several of the New Deal Justices were particularly interested in finding ways for FELA plaintiffs to recover. The Court gave the 1939 amendments to the FELA an emphatic and sweeping construction. It held "that every vestige of the doctrine of assumption of risk was obliterated from the law" and instructed the lower courts that "[n]o case is to be withheld from a jury on any theory of assumption of risk." The idea that any defense could bar a worker from recovery for an injury that resulted from his employer's negligence, the Court announced emphatically, "must not, contrary to the will of Congress, be allowed recrudescence under any other label in the common law lexicon."[24] The Court frequently reviewed FELA actions, regularly upholding jury verdicts for plaintiffs that state or federal appellate courts had overturned for lack of evidence[25] and broadly and forcefully construing the rights that the statute granted to plaintiffs.[26]

The Court gave a muscular construction to Section 5 of the statute, which voided contracts or other devices to defeat liability under the act. In *Duncan v.*

Thompson[27] it invalidated a post–injury negotiation agreement in which a worker accepted $600 in exchange for his agreement to try to settle his claim and, if he later chose to bring suit, to return the $600. The promise to return the money was a condition precedent to suit, the Court held, and under Section 5 it was unlawful. As in *Neirbo*, the decision seemed to turn more on the practicalities of the situation than on the words of the statute. The worker had signed the agreement while he "was still suffering from his injuries, his wife was in the hospital, and he needed money."[28] The condition precedent was unlawful because, given the social and economic realities, it operated not as a reasonable device to restore the status quo ante but as a device that would de facto prevent suit altogether. "[I]n view of Duncan's straitened circumstances," the Court explained, "the probability [that he could return the $600] would seem negligible."[29] Several years later the Court extended *Duncan* to invalidate "Rock Island releases," post–injury agreements in which workers received small payments in exchange for waiving their venue rights under the FELA. The right "to bring suit in any eligible forum," the Court declared, was "a right of sufficient substantiality" so that it could not be waived.[30]

The Court was acutely aware of just how substantial the right of venue choice under the FELA had proved to be. The most divisive FELA issues it faced in the 1940s arose from the extensive interstate forum shopping that the act encouraged and the persistent efforts of the railroads to find methods of defeating it. The most powerful method that the railroads used was the injunction ordering plaintiffs not to prosecute their suits in foreign jurisdictions, and in two split decisions in 1941 and 1942 the Roosevelt Court rejected the use of such injunctions. In the first, *Baltimore & Ohio Railroad Co. v. Kepner*,[31] the Court held that state courts could not, on the ground that the venue of an action was vexatious or unreasonable, enjoin their own citizens from prosecuting FELA actions filed in a federal court. The following year, in *Miles v. Illinois Central Railroad Co.*,[32] the Court applied the same bar to FELA suits filed in state courts.

The Justices in the majority—six in *Kepner* and four plus a concurrence in *Miles*—relied on the fact that Congress had specially granted to FELA plaintiffs the right to select their forum from a wide range of possible venues and, implicitly but realistically, on the fact that the right was in practice a highly valuable one. Expressly limiting the commerce clause venue cases from the 1920s, *Kepner* used a variation of the preemption doctrine and ruled that the FELA's venue provision "filled the entire field of venue in federal courts." The right granted to plaintiffs, the Court ruled, "cannot be frustrated for reasons of convenience or expense."[33] *Miles* stressed that the venue provision was an integral part of a federal right even when the plaintiff chose to sue in a state court. Because it arose from federal law, the plurality declared, "the right to sue in state courts of proper venue where their jurisdiction is adequate is of the same quality as the right to sue in federal courts."[34] Because Congress had determined "that the carriers must bear the incidental burden" of plaintiffs' venue choices, the states could not rule to the contrary.[35]

In contrast, the dissenters emphasized the traditional equity powers of the states to enjoin their own citizens and the emerging doctrine of *forum non conveniens*. Regarding the former, they argued that equity's right to prevent vexatious litigation was long established and beneficent and that nothing in the statute or its legislative history showed a congressional intent to limit it. Regarding the latter, they cited the commerce clause venue cases and stressed the need for the courts to impose reasonable restrictions on litigants' venue choices. Although in *Kepner* the dissenters repeatedly referred to *forum non conveniens* as "familiar," the authorities that they cited belied that contention.[36] The doctrine had been little known or used in American courts outside admiralty, and it began to emerge only in the 1920s and primarily as a result of the FELA, the very statute that the dissenters sought to limit by its use. In the early 1940s barely a half-dozen states formally recognized the doctrine, and the federal courts and more than forty other states did not.[37]

The most refreshing opinion in the two cases was Justice Robert H. Jackson's solo opinion concurring in *Miles*. "Realistically considered," Jackson wrote, "the issue is earthy and unprincipled," whether a plaintiff under the FELA "may go shopping for a judge or a jury believed to be more favorable than he would find in his home forum." Courts usually disfavored such forum shopping, but "with lawyerly indirection" they discussed the problem in artificial language about "vexatious" suits rather than in the language of orderly judicial administration. Although he agreed with the dissenters on the need for stronger control over forum choice, Jackson explained, the FELA nevertheless granted to plaintiffs a broad right to select their forum. And venue choice, an important method of obtaining a litigation advantage, was a valuable practical right. Given the country's "backward system of dealing with industrial accidents," he pointed out, it seemed likely that the FELA's venue provision was simply a method of "loading the dice a little in favor of the workman." He found that such a construction of the statute was particularly persuasive given the situation that would result from allowing injunctions. "It seems more probable that Congress intended to give the disadvantaged workman some leverage in the choice of venue," he concluded, "than that it intended to leave him in a position where the railroad could force him to try one lawsuit at home to find out whether he would be allowed to try his principal lawsuit elsewhere."[38]

Although the Roosevelt Court exhibited a new sympathy for those who sought to sue national corporations, it did not, of course, invariably rule in their favor. Manifesting the same reluctance to enjoin state courts that inspired *Toucey,* for example, the Court refused in 1941 to give special equitable protection to FELA plaintiffs.[39] It ruled that a federal court hearing an FELA suit could not enjoin a defendant from prosecuting a suit in the plaintiff's home state seeking to enjoin the plaintiff from prosecuting the federal FELA action. Similarly, two years later five Justices concluded that the full faith and credit clause barred an injured worker from obtaining the larger workmen's compensation payments provided by his home state after he had won a smaller compensation award in the state where he was injured.[40] Although there were strong legal arguments on both sides, the majority disregarded the practical social reasons that favored the worker and ruled instead for the employer.[41] In 1948 the Roosevelt Court even upheld the *Adams*–Hepburn Act rule that railroads could exempt themselves from liability for injuries suffered by passengers traveling on free passes. With three Justices dissenting, the Court deferred to "the long and well-settled construction" of the Hepburn Act and the fact that Congress had amended the act's free-pass section in 1940 without attempting to alter the *Adams* rule.[42] The sympathies of the Roosevelt Court were different from those that had marked the Court in the late nineteenth and early twentieth centuries, and they often made a difference in the way it analyzed and disposed of cases. No more than with earlier Courts, however, did those sympathies invariably affect the new Court or determine, apart from other considerations, the reasoning or results that it adopted.

Faced with the need to elaborate new constitutional doctrine in a new age, the Roosevelt Court increasingly encountered complexity. Its social values and sympathies, like its views of the commerce clause and the Fourteenth Amendment, remained distinctively a product of the New Deal, but after the early 1940s those attitudes seemed less and less able to guide the Court or to maintain unity among the Justices. In the early 1940s new and emotional issues began fragmenting the Court, but even relatively traditional "progressive" issues such as the proper scope of the FELA played an important role in dividing the Justices into opposing camps. The angry opinions that split the Court in *Kepner* and *Miles* reflected, and helped forge, those early divisions. The degree of solicitude that the Court should show for FELA plaintiffs, in fact, became a perennial flashpoint among the Justices in the late 1940s and early 1950s.[43]

In spite of its growing fragmentation, however, the Roosevelt Court remained remarkably united in one area that was central to the system of corporate diversity litigation. It uprooted the federal common law and then throughout its existence methodically sought to minimize or eliminate the differences in applicable legal rules applied in the state and federal courts.

The End of the General Federal Common Law

In April 1938, less than a year after the first of the Justices on the old Court resigned, the Supreme Court overruled *Swift v. Tyson* and ended the reign of the general federal common law. In *Erie Railroad Co. v. Tompkins*[44] the Court criticized the *Swift* doctrine on a variety of grounds, pointing out that it had failed to bring uniformity to the law and had spread from the commercial law into a wide range of common law fields. In particular, it stressed that *Swift* encouraged parties to forum shop between state and federal courts and that it discriminated against the citizens of a state in favor of noncitizens. "It made rights enjoyed under the unwritten 'general law' vary according to whether enforcement was sought in the state or in the federal court," *Erie* explained, "and the privilege of selecting the court in which the right should be determined was conferred upon the noncitizen."[45] The result was that "the doctrine rendered impossible equal protection of the law" and "prevented uniformity in the administration of the law of the State."[46]

Erie underscored the problems that *Swift* had created by focusing on a case that the Court had decided ten years earlier, *Black and White Taxicab and Transfer Co. v. Brown and Yellow Taxicab and Transfer Co.*[47] There, a railroad and a taxi company, both Kentucky corporations, wanted to confer an exclusive privilege on the latter to solicit business at the former's train station in Kentucky. Such an agreement, however, though valid under the federal common law, was contrary to the common law of Kentucky. The taxi company reincorporated in Tennessee and executed there an exclusive solicitation agreement with the railroad. It then brought suit in a Kentucky federal court to enjoin its rival, a taxi company chartered in Kentucky, from interfering with its exclusive privilege. In 1928 the Supreme Court affirmed the lower court's ruling that the reincorporation created a valid basis for federal diversity jurisdiction, that the federal common law properly controlled the case, and that the agreement was enforceable.

The *Taxicab* case quickly became notorious. The egregious nature of the jurisdictional manipulation involved made it a powerful symbol of the abuses that *Swift* and diversity jurisdiction allowed. Equally important, the dissent of Justice Oliver Wendell Holmes, Jr., struck a resounding blow at the basic concept of a federal common law by denying its theoretical and constitutional validity. Amplifying his own earlier dissents in *Kuhn* and *Jensen,* and supporting much of the argument that Justice Stephen J. Field had made thirty-five years earlier in his dissent in *Baugh,* Holmes charged that the idea of a general federal common law was based on a "fallacy." The only law was the law of a particular sovereign, he maintained, and a sovereign's courts made its law as much as its legislature did. In disregarding the common law of the states, the federal courts were ignoring the properly controlling state law and thereby invading the constitutional authority of the states. The independent federal common law, Holmes declared, represented "an unconstitutional assumption of powers by the Courts of the United States."[48]

Erie quoted extensively from the dissents of Field and Holmes, and it rested its decision on the Constitution. It denied that there was or could be any general federal common law because, beyond the areas governed by the Constitution and the statutes of Congress, the laws of the individual states were the only valid laws that could exist. As the courts of the states made laws as valid as those of their legislatures, the federal courts exceeded their constitutional powers when they disregarded state decisions and enforced their own common law. "[I]n applying the [*Swift*] doctrine," the Court concluded, "this Court and the lower courts have invaded rights which in our opinion are reserved by the Constitution to the several States."[49] When adjudicating issues of state law, *Erie* held, the federal courts were bound to follow the common law as well as the statutory law of the states.

Justice Louis D. Brandeis wrote the Court's opinion. Seizing on an otherwise wholly unremarkable common law tort suit, he persuaded a somewhat hesitant majority to use it as the vehicle to overrule *Swift.* His opinion for the Court, in turn, brought together most of the major themes of his judicial career. In broad constitutional terms, *Erie* expanded the power of the states to control their own common law and at the same time restricted the nonconstitutional lawmaking power of the federal judiciary to those areas over which Congress held the ultimate constitutional authority to legislate. With respect to limiting the scope of federal jurisdiction, *Erie* indirectly restricted both diversity and removal by eliminating one of the major incentives for their use. In terms of rationalizing the nation's judicial system, it sought to eliminate the arbitrariness inherent in a rule that made the applicable substantive law vary depending on the forum that heard an action and—as had Brandeis's opinion in *Davis* initiating the commerce clause venue doctrine—to discourage jurisdictional manipulation and bring greater order and predictability to litigation practice. In political and social terms, *Erie* deprived corporations of the favorable rules of the federal common law and remedied one of the major disadvantages that plaintiffs faced in the system of corporate diversity litigation. Finally, in quite personal terms, *Erie* allowed Brandeis to pay public homage to Holmes, his departed friend and colleague, who for more than a quarter-century had been recognized as the major intellectual and constitutional antagonist of *Swift* and the federal common law.

Erie was an unusually dramatic case, and its New Deal context and the fact that Brandeis wrote for the majority highlighted its political and intellectual origins. Since the late nineteenth century legal writers had criticized *Swift* on the various grounds that the Court discussed, and the dissents of Field and Holmes had convinced many that *Swift* was unsound in theory as well as in practice. Southerners and westerners, and political progressives generally, had charged for more than half a century that the federal common law favored business interests, encouraged corporate forum shopping, and denigrated the authority of the states. The context of the Court's decision in *Erie,* however, blending easily into the context of both earlier criticisms and the New Deal revolution, tended to obscure the extent to which the challenges of escalating litigation tactics helped move the Court toward abolishing the federal common law by forcing the Justices to recognize its anomalous and discordant nature.[50]

Litigation between individuals and corporations had become increasingly arbitrary and unstable after 1910. The growing arbitrariness—the fact that the value of a case could be determined largely by the tactical possibilities open to the parties, not by its merits—was apparent across the board. The arbitrariness no longer related merely to the basic questions of whether plaintiff lived in a town that was distant from the nearest federal court, or in an area where the federal court had a particularly heavy backlog, or in a state where the local and federal common law conflicted. Instead, litigation tactics had generated new and multiple levels on which arbitrary differences wholly unrelated to the merits of a suit could prove significant or even dispositive. Could the plaintiff join a resident codefendant? Could either of the parties exploit the interstate commerce requirement of the FELA or the Jones Act to force the other to litigate in an unfavorable forum? Could an insurance company seize the initiative by interpleading or seeking an equitable remedy or bringing a suit for a declaratory judgment? Was a plaintiff able to arrange for an out-of-state administrator or assignee, or was she willing to entrust her case to a distant importer? Could she avoid or, if necessary, defeat a preemptive equity suit designed to deprive her of a jury trial or to terminate her out-of-state suit?

The use of specialized procedural tactics and countertactics made litigation increasingly volatile and unpredictable. As parties and their attorneys grew more sophisticated, they created an ever-growing number of tactics to squeeze out an advantage. As the methods of transportation and communications improved, they yielded ready access to courts across the nation. As social subgroups organized and gained in experience and as the bar grew more specialized, they opened up for larger numbers of litigants the tactical possibilities that their predecessors had discovered. "For every weapon there is a counter weapon," an attorney for the Brotherhood of Railroad Trainmen explained. "For every form of attack a defense is developed."[51] Tactical inventiveness and organizational development combined to intensify the pressures that pushed against the limits of both doctrine and court structure.

Equally important, the arbitrariness and volatility were becoming more visible to the formal law. Until World War I the problem of distance had been irrelevant as a legal factor, and the problem of delay merely one of administration. The doctrines of the formal law ignored both. The new characteristics of the system, however, were different. The formal law could not ignore the persistence and frequency of certain types of jurisdictional disputes, the widening scope of inter-state forum shopping, the pressures for expanded equitable remedies in state and federal courts, and the need to answer increasingly complex questions about personal jurisdiction, choice of law, the full faith and credit clause, the role of *forum non conveniens,* the availability and conditions of declaratory relief, and the scope of the constitutional right to trial by jury.

Indeed, diversity litigation in the system and actions under the FELA were not the only areas where tactical escalation was developing or threatened. Diversity jurisdiction could offer advantages in other types of litigation as well. Given their greater resources and the much larger amounts at stake, corporations and wealthy individuals were likely to prove even more inventive in disputes involving real estate or commercial transactions. Intracorporate conflicts and shareholder deriva-tive suits could also spur the most determined and byzantine of litigations.

When Congress passed the Rules Enabling Act[52] in 1934, it symbolized and accelerated the changes that the twentieth century was bringing to litigation prac-tice. The act conferred on the Supreme Court the authority to prepare and promul-gate, subject to congressional approval, rules of procedure for the federal courts, and it provided for the repeal of the Conformity Act. The new Federal Rules of Civil Procedure were promulgated and went into effect in 1938. The enabling act and the new rules gave further institutional support to the idea that the federal courts constituted a national system of courts, and they in effect recognized that large corporations and a national economy were making twentieth-century corpo-rate legal practice into an interstate enterprise. Separating federal from state prac-tice, the new Federal Rules at once freed the national courts from state procedural rules, confirmed implicitly the higher professional status of federal practice, and facilitated the development by large urban law firms of a national practice in sup-port of the nationwide operations of their corporate clients.[53]

Those nationwide operations were visible in the 1930s when a number of corporations mounted elaborate legal campaigns to stall the New Deal. Compa-nies shopped across the country for the judges and circuits that were most willing to block government agencies, and they cleverly employed shareholder derivative suits to obtain injunctions prohibiting company compliance with the laws. The latter tactic allowed suspiciously "friendly" suits with minimal opposition or agreed-upon facts, and it often prevented the government from even participating in the defense of the challenged laws or administrative actions.[54] Justice Jackson, who had fought many of the New Deal's legal battles when he was Assistant Attorney General, noted the clever uses that the New Deal's opponents made of shareholder derivative suits. The "apparent adversaries were not in real contro-versy," he explained. "They framed the issues to suit themselves."[55] Small wonder, then, that in his concurrence in *Miles* Jackson readily appreciated the "realistic" significance of venue choice under the FELA. "There is nothing which requires a plaintiff to whom such a choice is given," Jackson had remarked, "to exercise it in a self-denying or large-hearted manner."[56]

It was, in short, up to Congress and the Court to regulate federal litigation, and since the 1920s the Court had made sporadic efforts to control many of the new litigation tactics. With few exceptions, the complexity of the issues and con-flicts within the Court had blocked any major advance. Commerce clause venue and the full faith and credit clause seemed of limited use at best, and the tensions

between the legal and equitable jurisdiction of the federal courts remained unresolved. In a legal world where sophisticated and complex litigation tactics were
growing common, simplicity and order seemed highly desirable. And with a large
scholarly and administrative contingent in the legal profession focused on judicial
efficiency and concerned with the federal courts as an integrated system, inconsistencies and conflicts stood out ever more sharply. In that context the federal
common law appeared increasingly discordant, a wild card that—whatever its
merits might otherwise have been—consistently exacerbated the problems of arbitrariness, instability, and tactical escalation that characterized twentieth-century
litigation.

As the Court tried to grapple with interstate forum shopping, the tactical
escalation in insurance litigation, and similar developments in other areas, so it
began gradually to moderate the federal common law in the 1930s. To the extent
that differences between the common law of the states and the federal courts
could be effectively minimized, the incentives for forum shopping and other tactical maneuvers could be lessened. In 1933 the Court limited the *Swift* doctrine in
insurance cases by introducing the principle that the federal courts should accept
state common law if the issue was "balanced with doubt."[57] In the mid-1930s it
applied the same principle to other common law areas[58] and seemed to defer more
often to state courts for the determination of local policies and laws.[59] The fact
that the Court itself continued on occasion to apply *Swift* only highlighted the
apparent unpredictability of the doctrine.[60]

A 1934 case illustrated both the extent to which the federal common law
contributed to instability and the Court's consequent effort to constrain its impact.
Pennsylvania and Florida, the two states whose law might have applied, had both
enacted the Uniform Negotiable Instruments Law, a widely adopted model statute
designed to unify commercial law. Instead of construing the statute in light of the
judicial decisions of either state, which were themselves in conflict on the point,
the Third Circuit exercised its independent judgment. "The construction given by
state courts of last resort to state statutes, which are merely declaratory of the
common law or of the law merchant," the Third Circuit reasoned, "does not bind
federal courts."[61] Instead of two possibly conflicting rules, then, the existence of
the federal common law meant that there would be three—all, of course, relating
to a statute drafted and enacted to make American commercial law uniform. In
Burns Mortgage Co. v. Fried[62] the Supreme Court held simply that there was "no
valid distinction" between a statute that altered or merely declared the common
law. In either situation the decisions of the state courts construing a statute were
binding on the federal court.

In addition to limiting the forum shopping incentive created by the federal
common law, the Court in the mid-1930s also tried to control litigation tactics by
placing more emphasis on the need to preserve the narrow limits of federal jurisdiction. "Due regard for the rightful independence of state government, which
should actuate federal courts," it declared in 1934, "requires that they scrupu-
lously confine their own jurisdiction to the precise limits which the statute has
defined."[63] In *Gay v. Ruff,*[64] for example, it resolved a significant split among the
lower courts by ruling that a tort action could not be removed on the ground that a
railroad's receiver, appointed to office by a federal court, was a federal officer
within the meaning of a congressional statute authorizing removal by federal

officials. Writing for the Court, Brandeis took the opportunity to stress the pattern he discerned in the FELA, the Jones Act, and similar legislation that had limited jurisdiction since the Judiciary Act of 1887–88. Construing the statute to deny removal, he cited the authority of "the established trend of legislation limiting the jurisdiction of the federal trial courts."[65]

Similarly, the Court cautiously explored the uses of discretionary dismissals as a device to control jurisdiction and limit the caseload.[66] In 1933, for example, it adopted the so-called internal affairs rule that required courts to dismiss actions involving the internal management and governance of corporations so that the courts of their chartering states could apply the local law that properly controlled.[67]. The decision reversed the prior practice of the federal courts which had generally accepted jurisdiction in such cases. More to the point, it eliminated opportunities for forum shopping and other sophisticated tactics in some particularly complex types of cases, such as shareholder derivative suits, where the incentives for using elaborate litigation tactics were particularly strong.[68]

If the old Supreme Court struggled with the federal common law and the challenges of tactical escalation, however, it still refused to abolish *Swift*. That drastic step required a new Court. When *Erie* came down, six Justices voted to overturn *Swift:* Brandeis and Justice Harlan F. Stone, members of the Court's so-called progressive wing who had joined Holmes's dissent in the *Taxicab* case; Chief Justice Charles Evans Hughes and Justice Owen J. Roberts, the two Justices who had apparently switched their positions in 1936–37; and Justices Hugo L. Black and Stanley Reed, the first two Roosevelt appointees who had recently joined the Court. The remaining Justices, members of the Court's anti–New Deal wing who had been with the majority in the *Taxicab* case, dissented.[69]

Although *Erie* eliminated the wild card of the federal common law, it arguably had some potential to increase incentives for interstate forum shopping. By abolishing the relative interstate uniformity of the federal common law, *Erie* raised the possibility that parties, knowing that the common law applied in the federal courts would no longer be uniform, might be encouraged to seek more favorable substantive law in distant states. The Roosevelt Court discounted that possibility for two reasons. First, it was more hypothetical than real. Choice-of-law rules and the full faith and credit clause restricted forum shopping for more favorable substantive state law. Indeed, interstate forum shopping was inspired in relatively few cases by differences in the states' substantive laws. Rather, it arose for the most part from the advantages offered by different procedural rules and judicial practices or by such extralegal factors as the specialized abilities of local importers, the lure of de facto larger verdicts, and the leverage gained by imposing practical burdens on adversaries. Second, and more important, the Roosevelt Court knowingly made a fundamental value choice. *Erie* protected the 95 percent of individual plaintiffs who sued, usually out of necessity, in their home states. For those plaintiffs intrastate uniformity between state and federal court was infinitely more important than whatever degree of uniformity *Swift* engendered in the common law applied nationally in the federal courts. Whatever instabilities and arbitrariness existed in the legal system, *Erie* would minimize them for the vast majority of individuals.

Although *Erie* was a product of the early Roosevelt Court, the later Roosevelt Court enforced it broadly.[70] The New Deal Justices who subsequently joined the

Court shared *Erie*'s hostility to forum shopping but doubted its constitutional language. Although the constitutional basis of the decision was not clear, many of them assumed that it rested on the Tenth Amendment. As good New Dealers, they were suspicious of the Tenth Amendment which, under the old Court, had served as a substantive limitation on the powers of Congress.[71] Accordingly, they simply ignored *Erie*'s constitutional language, embraced it as establishing a broad anti–forum shopping policy, and transformed that policy into a major principle of federal law.

In a series of cases handed down during the 1940s, the Court enforced *Erie* to minimize the legal incentives for intrastate forum shopping. In 1940 it held that the federal courts were bound not just by the decisions of a state's "highest court" but, in the absence of such decisions, also by the rulings of intermediate state appellate courts and even by the rulings of state trial courts.[72] The following year in *Klaxon v. Stentor Electric Manufacturing Co.*[73] it held that *Erie*'s "prohibition" against "independent determinations" of state laws by federal courts "extends to the field of conflict of laws," even though the field was traditionally classified as an area of "procedural" law. In diversity cases involving state law issues, *Klaxon* held, federal courts were bound to apply the choice-of-law rules of the state in which they sat.[74] In 1945 in *Guaranty Trust Co. v. York*[75] the Roosevelt Court handed down its most far-reaching elaboration of *Erie,* holding that it required federal courts to apply state "procedural" rules if they would "significantly affect the result of a litigation."[76] The "nub of the policy that underlies Erie," *York* declared, was that the "accident" of diverse citizenship should not lead to a different result in a federal court than would occur in a state court.

Together *Klaxon, York,* and the Court's other decisions in the 1940s implemented *Erie* broadly and reduced to a minimum the differences in the formal law that state and federal courts in the same state would apply.[77] By the end of the decade the federal courts applied not only the common law rules of the state in which they sat but also some of the "procedural" rules that the local state courts followed. Though differences in procedure and institutional structure between state and federal courts remained, the divergent general federal common law had been thoroughly rooted out and the law applied in state and federal courts sitting in the same state brought closely into line.

Toward Mid-Century: The Disintegration of the System

By the end of the 1940s, when the Roosevelt Court's forceful application of *Erie* had transformed the way in which the federal courts treated common law claims, the litigation patterns that formed the system of corporate diversity litigation had ceased to hold. The reason was clear. The compelling pressures that had so frequently and regularly driven individual plaintiffs to avoid the federal courts had either disappeared or declined drastically in force.[78]

First, nearly two decades of Democratic appointments to the federal judiciary, together with the political image that the New and Fair Deals projected, had eliminated the popular belief that the federal courts had a procorporate bias. Indeed, those changes had convinced many that the national courts had come to share a bias that favored, among others, labor unions and personal injury plaintiffs, especially those claiming under the FELA. No longer did individuals suing national corporations generally fear that the federal courts might be relatively unsympathetic to their claims. To the contrary, they sometimes assumed that the national courts would be particularly favorable to them.

Second, improvements in transportation had reduced the burdens of distance to a minor and often nonexistent consideration. By mid-century the widespread availability of automobiles and superhighways had brought the overwhelming majority of litigants within relatively easy reach of the federal courts. Moreover, to the extent that distance and geography remained significant, their effects were more random, varied, and diffuse than they had been several decades earlier.[79] Indeed, as the rise of interstate forum shopping demonstrated, in some cases distance had become an offensive weapon that individuals used against corporations.

Third, delay in the national courts had declined sharply in absolute terms. At a minimum, it was far less significant as a general factor in federal litigation than it had been in the late nineteenth and early twentieth centuries. In addition, the administrative reforms in the federal courts may well have made delay less of a problem in the federal system generally than it was in many or most of the states. Contemporaneous procedural reforms, too, made the federal courts more attractive forums for many plaintiffs. Simplifying pleading and expanding discovery, the new Federal Rules of Civil Procedure, first promulgated in 1938, lightened some of the practical and procedural burdens that often obstructed plaintiffs' efforts.

Fourth, legislation had largely withdrawn from the system its largest and most vulnerable plaintiff group, industrial workers with personal injury claims. State and federal workmen's compensation acts provided alternative administrative remedies that kept most claimants out of court, and the FELA placed interstate railroad workers beyond the reach of removal. Encouraged by the Roosevelt Court's more expansive view of the commerce power, Congress extended the reach of the FELA in 1939, bringing more than two-thirds of all injured railroad workers within its coverage. Moreover, by 1947 most American workers were covered by some type of statutory program. Of those not covered by some federal act, more than 70 percent came under the protection of state workmen's compensation laws.[80]

Finally, *Erie* extinguished the federal common law. No longer did removal mean that a corporate defendant could secure a different and quite possibly more favorable substantive law. Further, concerned deeply about the problem of forum shopping between state and federal courts, the Roosevelt Court had moved methodically to minimize the likelihood that even so-called procedural rules would bring different results in a federal, as compared with a state, court.

Although the conditions that created the system of corporate diversity litigation had disappeared or were rapidly dissipating in the 1940s, Congress and the Supreme Court also began to take steps to restrict the two principal new tactics that the parties in the system had developed after 1910, the preemptive use of equity and the declaratory judgment by insurers and the use of interstate forum shopping by plaintiffs. The courts gradually checked most of the advantages that insurance companies had obtained from their aggressive new tactics, and the Court and then Congress limited the ability of plaintiffs to shop among the states for more favorable forums.

When relief in federal equity or by way of declaratory judgment became available in the 1920s, insurance companies quickly recognized the tactical advantages presented (see Chapter 9). Using the devices to initiate suit, potential defendants could "invert" the party structure that would have existed in a standard action at law to enforce the policy. They could thereby gain for themselves the plaintiff's advantage of determining when and where an action would be filed. Further, by suing in equity or maintaining that a declaratory judgment was "essentially equitable," potential defendants could also prevent their adversaries from having their claims heard in an action at law where their constitutional right to trial by jury would apply.

In terms of their opportunity to initiate actions and control forum choice, the companies were successful in using equity and the declaratory judgment to limit use of the jurisdictional amount as an antiremoval device. In 1940 in *Stoner v. New York Life Insurance Co.*[81] the Supreme Court held that a federal court had jurisdiction over an insurer's action for a declaratory judgment if the total payments in dispute, not merely those that had already accrued, exceeded the jurisdictional minimum. Use of the new tactic thus allowed the companies to put at issue the value of the entire policy, pushing the amount in controversy above the jurisdictional minimum and thereby preventing plaintiffs from ensuring a state forum by suing for a lesser amount.[82]

At the same time, however, the Supreme Court also restricted the tactical advantages that the devices offered. Most important, by abolishing the federal common law, *Erie* deprived the companies of the single most obvious legal advantage they would have derived from controlling forum choice.[83] Indeed, the possibility that the Declaratory Judgment Act would have encouraged widespread efforts to manipulate jurisdiction in order to obtain the benefits of the federal common law may well have been one of the major if unstated factors that influenced the Court's decision in *Erie*.

Beyond that, the Court attempted to police the tactical uses of the declaratory judgment. It stressed the need for a real and immediate controversy between the parties[84] and declared expansively that a declaratory judgment was not appropriate where a federal court would have denied injunctive relief under traditional equitable principles.[85] In particular, it tried to set limits on the use of the declaratory judgment when the federal plaintiff was a defendant in a parallel state court action at law. In 1941 it held that a federal court in a declaratory judgment action could not enjoin a pending state proceeding raising the same issues,[86] and the following year in *Brillhart v. Excess Insurance Co.* it held that the lower courts had discretion to refuse to hear diversity suits seeking declaratory relief if there was a pending state court action that presented the same issues between the same parties.[87] The lower courts tended to use that discretion, often staying insurers' federal suits when claimants brought parallel state actions, sometimes even when the insurers had filed first.[88] Although it analyzed the problem in terms of maintaining comity between the state and federal courts, the Roosevelt Court was specially sensitive to the dangers of procedural manipulation that the declaratory judgment made possible.[89]

In regard to the effort to preempt claimants' right to trial by jury, the situation initially looked promising for the companies. Not only had they enjoyed some successes in the 1920s and 1930s, but the new Federal Rules of Civil Procedure further confused the status and availability of the right to a jury trial. Among their principal accomplishments, the Federal Rules went well beyond the Law and

Equity Act of 1915 and provided for the complete "merger" of law and equity in the national courts, substituting in the place of two theoretically separate "systems" a single form of action called a "civil action." The merger raised an immediate and obvious procedural question: To what extent did the right to trial by jury in actions at law apply in merged civil actions that contained both "legal" and "equitable" elements? By the late 1930s, then, the right to trial by jury seemed endangered by both the supposedly equitable nature of declaratory relief and the complete merger of law and equity in the federal system.

In spite of their efforts to exploit the promise, however, the companies were not in the long run able to limit the claimants' right to trial by jury. Although for two decades the Supreme Court failed to resolve the question of the scope of the constitutional right to trial by jury in the new procedural context,[90] by the early 1940s the lower federal courts had generally agreed on an approach that preserved the right by recurring to the traditional distinction between law and equity. In dealing with merged actions the lower courts looked for the underlying, "essential," or predominant nature of the cause of action that was presented. If it appeared similar to causes of action that had been cognizable at law before 1938, they considered it "legal" and held that the constitutional right to trial by jury applied. Similarly, in dealing with suits for declaratory relief the lower courts considered the type of action that would have been used to obtain judicial relief on the given facts in the absence of the declaratory remedy. If that type of premerger action were legal, then the right to trial by jury would apply in an action seeking declaratory relief.[91]

By the late 1940s, in fact, the lower federal courts were rigorously protecting the right to jury trials in declaratory judgment actions. There was "great judicial suspicion" of parties who claimed that their actions for declaratory judgments should not be tried to a jury, declared the *Harvard Law Review* in 1949 after a comprehensive survey of declaratory judgment actions during the decade. "This attitude pervades the cases, especially those in the insurance field," it concluded, "and is manifested by the singular lack of success of the reported attempts to avoid jury trial."[92]

Finally, between 1959 and 1962 the Supreme Court settled the question of the scope of the right to trial by jury in the new procedural context, and it did so in a way that considerably broadened that right. The Court abandoned the historical approach that the lower courts had been using and adopted in its place a dynamic approach that expanded the category of issues that warranted a jury and, further, ensured that any factual issue in a case that bore on a legal claim would be tried to a jury.[93] By the early 1960s neither the declaratory judgment nor the merged civil action offered insurance companies any way to prevent a jury trial when claimants sought monetary relief from insurers.

If the companies ultimately failed to limit claimants' right to trial by jury or to win approval for many of their tactical innovations, plaintiffs also lost much of the advantage they had gained from interstate forum shopping. Since the 1920s the railroads had sought to amend the FELA, and in the early 1940s they redoubled their efforts when three developments combined to intensify the economic pressures that interstate forum shopping imposed on them. First, the 1939 amendments to the FELA expanded the statute's coverage toward the limits of the federal commerce power while at the same time abolishing the defense of assumption of risk.[94] The amendment thus brought more employees within the FELA's protection and eliminated what had become the railroads' most important defense under the statute. Second, the onset of the World War II drove the costs of employee tort suits rapidly upward. The demands of wartime transportation inundated the railroads with business and forced them to expand their work force, in many cases by hiring young and inexperienced workers. Accidents began to multiply. By 1944, the wartime peak, the annual number of employee deaths had more than doubled compared with that of 1938, and the number of injuries had almost tripled.[95] Equally significant, wartime prosperity and inflation helped push the cost-of-living upward, and jury verdicts rose accordingly. Finally, the Supreme Court's rulings in *Kepner* and *Miles* in the early 1940s deprived the railroads of one of their most effective deterrents to interstate forum shopping, the ability to have out-of-state FELA actions enjoined.[96] Indeed, the language of the two decisions was so broad that the federal courts and many state courts began to regard an FELA plaintiff's choice of forum as unchallengeable. In 1945, for example, the California Supreme Court held that a state court could not refuse to hear an FELA case on *forum non conveniens* grounds and declared that the statute gave plaintiffs "an absolute right" to enforce their choice of forum.[97] During the next two years the Supreme Court of the United States appeared to agree.[98]

The railroads complained bitterly, and venue became increasingly visible as a legal and political issue.[99] In 1946, when the Republicans won control of Congress for the first time since 1930, the railroads prepared to launch a major campaign. Allied with bar associations condemning ambulance chasing and small-town lawyers who resented the loss of lucrative business to big-city tort specialists, the railroads threw their efforts behind a bill that made venue in FELA actions proper only in the districts where the cause of action arose and where the injured person lived at the time of his injury.[100] They reported to Congress that in the preceding five years more than 2,500 FELA suits had been filed outside the federal district where the injury occurred or where the injured party lived at the time of his accident. The bill, they insisted, was intended primarily to combat unethical solicitation practices and to protect injured workers from out-of-state ambulance chasers.[101]

The underlying economic issue, however, remained apparent. "The amount of money paid out by railroads for employee personal injuries has greatly increased in the last few years," the vice-president and general counsel of the Santa Fe Railway explained to Congress in 1948. Attributing much of the increase to claims solicitation and proplaintiff judicial decisions, he stated that on the Santa Fe line "personal-injury payments to employees rose from $351,329 in 1939 to $3,600,003 in 1946."[102] In the same years, he continued, industrywide payments for personal injuries jumped from about $22.6 million in 1939 to almost $67 million in 1946.[103]

The railroad brotherhoods fought the bill vigorously, receiving support from liberal and labor groups, including the American Federation of Labor and the National Farmers Union.[104] The bill, declared a representative of the Brotherhood of Railroad Trainmen, "is a railroad law supported by the American Association of Railroads and designed to save money for the railroad corporations at the expense of passengers or trainmen injured by them."[105] Under questioning from senators critical of the bill, its supporters acknowledged the impact that they expected it would have on the size of jury verdicts. "I think they would decrease," acknowledged one of the railroads' leading spokesmen.[106]

Although the bill passed the House by a narrow margin in 1947,[107] the Senate refused to act. Three factors stalled it. One was the determined opposition that the brotherhoods mounted together with the powerful case they made that, as one congressman charged, "the real purpose back of this legislation is to save the railroads hundreds of thousands of dollars."[108] The second was the fact that in 1947 the United States Supreme Court, responding to the general rise in interstate forum shopping, held for the first time that the federal courts could properly apply the doctrine of *forum non conveniens* in actions at law and dismiss those brought in inconvenient forums that had little connection with the underlying dispute.[109] The decision helped direct Congress away from the FELA amendment by casting federal law relating to interstate forum shopping in a more comprehensive context. The third and probably most important factor that killed the FELA amendment was the availability to Congress of an appealing alternative that readily led to compromise. A new Revised United States Judicial Code, long in the works, had been completed by mid-1947, and it contained in its Section 1404 an innovative venue provision that utilized the *forum non conveniens* concept.[110]

Congress had been working on the code since 1944. The goal of the revision was "the substitution of plain language for awkward terms, reconciliation of conflicting laws, repeal of superseded sections, and consolidation of related provisions."[111] Although there was "no purpose on the part of the Revision staff to effect any change in existing law," the Chief Reviser explained, inconsistencies and ambiguities in the law did require "a few such changes."[112]

The *forum non conveniens* provision contained in Section 1404 of the new code was far more than a technical amendment. It was, rather, a substantial change in federal procedural law that promised to have a major impact on the conduct of interstate litigation. Its somewhat surprising presence in a revision that allegedly had "no purpose" to change existing law illustrated the extent to which the twentieth century had fostered new attitudes toward federal procedure. The growing pressures of interstate forum shopping, decades of lobbying by railroads and bar associations, and the rationalizing drive of professional legal reformers seemed to have convinced both Congress and the legal profession that some such change was necessary. Reflecting mid-twentieth-century ideas of the practical and administrative nature of the judicial function, the new provision provided a mechanism that allowed federal judges to distribute judicial business throughout the nation according to their views of efficiency and justice. Section 1404 did not merely enact the doctrine of *forum non conveniens,* which was generally thought to require dismissal of an action brought in an inconvenient forum. Rather, it authorized the national courts to transfer cases to any other appropriate federal judicial district upon a showing that such a transfer would be in the interests of convenience and justice. Although the drafters did not stress the fact, the section was largely a response to interstate forum shopping under the FELA. The Reviser's notes, terse and technical, cited as the only "example of the need of such a provision" the Supreme Court's decision in *Kepner,* which held that state courts could not enjoin FELA actions in federal courts on the ground that they were brought in distant and burdensome forums.[113]

With passage of the Revised Judicial Code seeming certain, support for the railroad's bill to amend the FELA waned.[114] Section 1404 exerted a powerful appeal in the Eightieth Congress. It was a minor and ostensibly neutral technical element in a massive code drafted and revised by experts;[115] it would apparently give the railroads and bar associations much of what they wanted; it promised to limit many of the abuses in forum selection and claims solicitation; and it seemed to be a rational technical device that would utilize the national scope of the federal legal system and free its judges to dispose of disputes over forum choice on the specific facts of each case. Moreover, given the fact that the Supreme Court had already adopted the *forum non conveniens* doctrine and the further fact that the *Neirbo* rule—making venue in actions against corporations proper in any district where they were licensed to do business—was codified in the new revision,[116] the problem of interstate forum shopping clearly seemed to call for a remedy that transcended the single context of FELA suits. In 1948 Congress enacted the Revised Judicial Code with its new provision for the transfer of cases between federal judicial districts.

Immediately after its passage, the railroads began to use the new device. Within weeks a federal judge in Minnesota responded to a series of motions by transferring eight FELA cases to the districts where the injuries occurred.[117] Quickly the issue came before the Supreme Court, where a transferred FELA plaintiff argued that Section 1404 did not apply to actions under any statute, such as the FELA, that contained its own special venue provision. In *Ex parte Collett*,[118] decided expeditiously only a year after Congress enacted the new code, the Supreme Court held that Section 1404 covered "any civil action" and that it did not conflict with the FELA's provisions. Plaintiffs could still institute their FELA suits in a wide range of districts, but their court of choice could still transfer them to another district. Such transfers, of course, would usually negate the efforts of organized legal importers and deprive plaintiffs of much or all of the advantage, legal or extralegal, that they had sought in their chosen and now formally "inconvenient" forum.

Although Section 1404 and *Collett* imposed limits on interstate forum shopping, they did not block it completely. The Supreme Court ruled that the section did not apply to FELA suits brought in state courts and that *Miles* remained good law.[119] Thus, as long as the FELA retained its antiremoval and broad venue provisions, plaintiffs could still sue successfully in distant states if they confined their actions to state courts and selected states that did not themselves adopt some version of *forum non conveniens*. By the late 1940s, however, a small but growing number of states began adopting the doctrine,[120] and in 1950 the Court held that states were free within the limits of the privileges and immunities clause to apply their own *forum non conveniens* doctrines to FELA suits.[121]

By mid-century, then, some variation of *forum non conveniens* seemed to many an almost inevitable consequence of the escalation of litigation tactics in the age of interstate legal practice. The mobility of plaintiffs and the sophistication of the personal injury bar were simply too great not to be curbed. After some thirty years of experience with relatively widespread interstate forum shopping and a growing effort to fashion an American doctrine of *forum non conveniens,* Congress, the Court, and a growing number of states agreed that its time had come.

Still, however, the same developments in transportation and communications that gave rise to interstate forum shopping also made it easier for corporations to defend in distant locations, whether or not it was fair or wise to require them to do so. Indeed, if Section 1404 were desirable judged by the burdens that distance imposed on corporate defendants in the 1940s, substantial relief had surely been desirable a half-century earlier judged by the burdens that distance imposed on removed plaintiffs in those years. If it was unfair and unreasonably burdensome for the railroads in the 1940s to be forced to transport their witnesses and attorneys for a thousand miles to a distant forum, it was at least as unfair and unreasonably burdensome for individual plaintiffs at the turn of the century to be forced to transport theirs for the additional fifty to two hundred miles that removal often required.

The point here is not that Section 1404 was unwise or unfair. The point, rather, is that the practical burdens imposed by inconvenient forums could be extremely heavy and that those burdens helped determine the out-of-court settlement value of legal claims and defenses. The railroads' testimony regarding the impact of interstate forum shopping after World War I—that the burdens of practical inconvenience forced them to pay larger amounts in order to obtain settlements—is equally compelling if unintentional testimony about the impact of removal on plaintiffs in the decades around the turn of the century. The only difference, of course, was that in the earlier period the practical impact of inconvenience disadvantaged individual plaintiffs, and the companies were able to force settlements for smaller amounts than would otherwise have been acceptable.

Regardless of such comparisons, however, by mid-century the system of corporate diversity litigation had disappeared, and its two most important twentieth-century tactical extensions had been severely limited. Although equitable and declaratory remedies still offered aggressive parties numerous opportunities to seize the initiative in litigation, they did not allow them to choose between different substantive laws in the state and federal courts or enable them to deprive their adversaries of the right to trial by jury. Similarly, although parties continued to use interstate forum shopping, their efforts were subject to new constraints.[122] Although insurance claimants preserved their right to trial by jury, plaintiffs lost some of their advantage in forum choice. On the former issue the courts relied on a constitutional mandate and on traditional categories of legal analysis, and they showed a deep respect for the values associated with the jury. On the latter issue they were more responsive to social changes and the need for doctrinal flexibility, and they seemed newly enthusiastic about the opportunities for rationalizing the business of the federal courts as a national system. In both areas, the courts were unsympathetic to the efforts of parties who tried to manipulate procedural and jurisdictional rules to obtain tactical advantages that lay beyond the formal purposes of the doctrines they sought to use.

A New Age: Revisions of the
Federal Judicial Code, 1948–58

The Revised Judicial Code of 1948 marked the passing of the system of corporate diversity litigation. The new code ratified some of the system's legal elements and changed or modified others, but in every case—even the relatively major change wrought by Section 1404—it did so with little controversy and no significant partisan political conflict. In part, that was because the changes made were few and generally minor and because Congress placed the revision in the hands of a committee of experts that kept matters on the level of technical adjustments. It was, however, also because the issues growing out of diversity jurisdiction no longer had any major differential impact on large and socially identifiable groups of litigants. Arguably the new code slightly favored corporations when it altered the language of the venue section to make it fully consistent with *Lee*,[123] adopted the flexible rule on the timing of removal petitions established in *Powers*,[124] and expanded the authority of the federal courts to enjoin state actions by restoring "the basic law as generally understood and interpreted prior to the Toucey decision."[125] If so, the code similarly favored plaintiffs when it expanded the districts where venue was proper in suits against corporations by codifying the *Neirbo* rule[126] and when it narrowed the scope of removal under the separate controversy provision.[127] In simplifying removal procedures generally and in eliminating the awkward requirement that defendants first present their removal petitions to the state court, the Revised Code probably helped all parties.[128] In any event, the provisions—whether they modified the law or merely codified it—no longer evoked the images and passions of the social–legal conflict that had marked the preceding seven decades.

On one level, the most revealing change in the Revised Code was its outright repeal of the local prejudice act. The repeal showed the impact that *Cochran* had had on the act's use. As the official Reviser's notes stated, "the practice of removal for prejudice or local influence has not been employed much in recent years."[129] Indeed, its use had been exceptionally rare after *Cochran*. How rare was amply demonstrated by the fact that the code, purporting to make no significant changes in existing law, could dispose of an entire category of federal jurisdiction without protest, opposition, or apparently even much professional awareness.

More important, repeal of the local prejudice act dramatically captured the profound ambivalence and ambiguity that continued to underlie diversity jurisdiction. The local prejudice act, "born of the bitter sectional feelings engendered by the Civil War and Reconstruction period," the Reviser's notes proclaimed in richly patriotic terms, "can have no placc in the jurisprudence of a nation since united by three wars against foreign powers."[130] The act was allegedly repealed, in other words, because it was insulting and inappropriate to base a federal jurisdictional statute on the assumption that Americans from one part of the nation might need protection against the prejudice of other Americans from a different part of the nation. Yet, of course, the code retained general diversity jurisdiction, the jurisdiction that was based on the far broader—and therefore presumably far more insulting—assumption that prejudice against Americans who were not local citizens was so pervasive and dangerous that all out-of-staters should automatically be able to escape from the state to the federal courts.

If the Judicial Code of 1948 coincided with the passing of the system, congressional reconsideration of the code ten years later confirmed its disappearance. In seeking ways to limit the continually expanding dockets of the federal courts, Congress in the 1950s uncovered what was apparently the system's last vestige. Insurance companies defending suits that challenged workmen's compensation awards were using removal to impose the burden of distance on some plaintiffs. The telling fact, however, was that the practice was confined to only three or four states and may have operated on a significant scale only in Texas, which in geographical terms was easily the nation's largest state.[131] In amending the Judicial Code in 1958 Congress terminated the companies' practice by enacting another antiremoval provision. It extended to plaintiffs challenging workmen's compensation awards the same absolute choice of forum it had previously given plaintiffs under the FELA and the Jones Act.[132]

Further, the 1958 revision of the Judicial Code also altered the doctrine of corporate citizenship, providing that for jurisdictional purposes a corporation was to be treated as a citizen of both its chartering state and the state where it had its "principal place of business." It did so to combat the evil it saw reflected in the *Black & White Taxicab* case, where a local corporation had reincorporated out of state in order to obtain an advantage against a local rival. In 1958 Congress accepted the claim that scheming "local" corporations were the source of the only other significant abuse that plagued diversity jurisdiction. Those corporations, the House and Senate reports concluded, sought foreign charters to secure more favorable operating laws, special tax benefits, and access to the national courts. Their foreign charters, however, were "not intended for the prime purpose of doing business in the foreign State." Consequently their out-of-state incorporation tactic was "neither fair nor proper." Those harmed by the use of such foreign charters were local business rivals that were placed at a competitive disadvantage.[133]

The analysis that moved Congress to amend the doctrine of corporate citizenship in 1958 was revealing for two reasons. First, it showed that aside from the narrowly limited abuse in workmen's compensation cases, the local corporation problem was the only noteworthy social issue involving diversity that came to the attention of Congress. Insofar as the jurisdiction operated to the social detriment of any identifiable group, then, it disadvantaged local businesses. Furthermore, the culprits were not national corporations but only other authentically local companies. Insofar as Congress found that diversity jurisdiction had social resonance in the 1950s, then, the problems created and the social groups involved were entirely diferent from what they had been from the 1870s to the 1940s. Second, the repeated invocation of the *Black & White Taxicab* case seemed to carry the suggestion that its factual situation represented the major long-term social problem that diversity jurisdiction had fostered. In fact, of course, *Black & White Taxicab* represented only the relatively rare case of manipulative reincorporation that occasionally surfaced in the reports, not the multitudinous and standard types of cases in the system of corporate diversity litigation where the jurisdiction had brought its most widespread and long-term consequences. To the extent that Congress and much of the legal profession had by the 1950s come to remember the *Black & White Taxicab* case as exemplifying the social significance of diversity jurisdiction and the federal common law, they had lost contact with the social history of both.

The loss of historical understanding, however, was not surprising. By the 1950s the perception of diversity jurisdiction and of the federal courts generally had shifted from what it had been during the half-century from the 1880s to the 1930s. The practical litigation significance of diversity jurisdiction had not only changed, but fundamental alterations in American society had restructured the role and image of the federal courts and the basic politics of federal jurisdiction. No longer did populists, progressives, and New Dealers attack the federal courts for their alleged conservative social biases. To the contrary, their perceived political successors, termed "liberals" after World War II, admired and protected the national judiciary. The constitutional doctrines of the Roosevelt Court, the altered political orientation and Democratic tone of the federal bench, the rise of civil rights and civil liberties concerns, and, above all, the emergence of the Warren Court after 1954 combined to transform the political and social image of the federal courts from conservative guardians of private property to liberal guardians of individual rights. That transformation—replacing one fundamental political–judicial premise with another—established anew the broader social context in which Americans considered questions of the scope of federal jurisdiction.

By the mid-1950s, in fact, the national courts were under concerted political attack from those who called themselves conservatives. Most southerners and many Republicans were outraged at some or all of the Warren Court's decisions mandating racial desegregation and seeming to frustrate efforts to track down communist subversives. Many business groups, too, including the United States Chamber of Commerce and the National Association of Manufacturers, were angered at the Court's use of the preemption doctrine in the mid-1950s to restrict state right-to-work laws. Together, southerners, anticommunists, and some business groups launched a broad attack on the federal courts, seeking to limit or overthrow recent Supreme Court decisions and to restrict the Court's appellate jurisdiction in critical areas.[134] The attacks culminated in 1958, when the political pressures for Court-curbing legislation reached intense levels and members of Congress introduced dozens of bills seeking to limit the federal courts. The anti-Court forces joined to support several restrictive bills, eventually agreeing to concentrate their efforts on an omnibus proposal sponsored by Republican Senator William E. Jenner of Indiana. The Jenner bill sought to curtail the Supreme Court's appellate jurisdiction and prevent it from reviewing several categories of cases, including those involving federal or state antisubversive programs and similar programs enforced by local school boards. After a bruising political battle that lasted throughout the spring and summer, liberals in the Senate managed to defeat all of the restrictive bills. In August the Senate tabled Jenner's proposal by eight votes.

Out of the same political battle that drove the Jenner bill came a southern-sponsored bill to restrict diversity jurisdiction by denying corporations the status of "citizen." Although the bill's sponsor, Congressman William M. Tuck of Virginia, offered his measure as a method of eliminating "congestion" in the federal courts, his rhetoric belied his ostensible purpose. Tuck echoed some of the views that populists and progressives had expressed decades earlier, but in the immediate wake of the Warren Court's desegregation decisions and the resulting swarm of anti-Court bills his language suggested the driving force of profoundly different social attitudes and motives. A "greedy and Gargantuan Central Government in the last few years has usurped the powers of the States by expanding its activities into almost every phase of our existence," Tuck declared when he first introduced his bill in 1955, a year after *Brown v. Board of Education*.[135] "[W]e can feel its tentacles in all walks of life."[136]

Reacting, political liberals jumped to the defense of both the federal courts and diversity jurisdiction. Anxious to protect the national courts and no longer fearful of large national corporations in the way that many populists and progressives had been, they had no sympathy for the Tuck bill. To the extent that they remained suspicious of the power and politics of large corporations, in fact, they were quite content to keep those corporations in the federal courts where they and the national judiciary, perceived in the late 1950s to be relatively liberal, could more effectively police them.

It was illuminating, too, that Congress rejected the Tuck bill in favor of the proposal that would limit corporate access to the national courts by adopting the "principal place of business" amendment. In revising the Judicial Code the primary and repeatedly stated concern of Congress was to remedy the problems created by the continuously growing caseload of the national courts. The Tuck bill would have cut the diversity docket by almost two-thirds and sliced the entire federal civil docket by 25 percent.[137] In contrast, the "principal place of business" amendment promised to eliminate less than 4 percent of the diversity docket and less than 2 percent of the total federal civil caseload.[138] Testifying against the Tuck bill, Judge Albert B. Maris of the Third Circuit, representing the Judicial Conference of the United States, admitted that the southern proposal "would unquestionably effect a much greater reduction in the caseload of the Federal courts."[139] Congress, nevertheless, shelved the Tuck bill in favor of the "principal place of business" amendment, a change that promised to have no significant impact on the docket. The explanation, of course, was simple. However serious the problem of congestion was, and however abstruse or technical the specific legal issues were, Congress knew full well that questions of the scope and nature of federal jurisdiction remained ultimately issues of social values and political purposes.

The decision to reject the Tuck bill and adopt the "principal place of business" amendment reflected a commitment to two basic policies that Congress regarded as far more important than the goal of reducing docket problems. The first was to maintain the integrity of the national courts against an assault that attempted to use congressional power over federal jurisdiction as a direct political weapon. Some members of Congress were undoubtedly moved by the general principle that such legislative efforts were improper, but many—including the liberals— were also determined to defend the Warren Court and the whole federal judiciary against retaliation by anticommunists and prosegregationists. Whatever its merits in terms of docket problems, the Tuck bill was rooted in the same southern, states-rights drive that in the late 1950s pushed a number of different proposals to curb the national judiciary. In that political context liberals were in no mood to cut the jurisdiction of the federal courts by 25 percent, regardless of the subject matter involved. The second policy was to recognize the dominant role of large corporations in the nation's economy and to accord their activities the time and attention of the national courts. The distinction that Congress drew between local and national corporations—for which it cited no significant evidence—allowed it for the first time to give its formal blessing to the judicially developed doctrine of corporate citizenship and to confer on national businesses the statutory right of access to the federal courts. That policy judgment was profoundly if subtly different from the traditional premise that justified diversity jurisdiction. In 1958 Congress was not concerned with protecting corporations against the dangers of local prejudice but with keeping in the hands of the national courts what it regarded as in every realistic sense the basic affairs of the nation.

The hearings that the House Judiciary Committee held in 1957 on the Tuck bill and the other proposals to limit diversity jurisdiction differed strikingly from the hearings that the same committee had held a quarter-century earlier when Congress considered several similar bills to curtail the jurisdiction. In 1932 the hearings were part of a paradigmatic political battle over the system of corporate diversity litigation. Led by Senator George W. Norris of Nebraska, a long-time critic of the federal courts, progressives in Congress mounted a serious effort to limit diversity. Considering several restrictive bills, the Senate Judiciary Committee reported favorably on Norris's own radical proposal that would have abolished the jurisdiction. The only defenders of diversity were "extremely wealthy people or powerful corporations," the committee's report charged, and they used diversity to impose "extreme hardship" on their adversaries. The result was "injustice and discrimination."[140]

In the 1930s the confrontation over the various proposals to restrict diversity remained sharp and bitter. Defenders of the jurisdiction—business groups and bar associations—lobbied forcefully against all of the restrictive bills. Not without reason did the Senate Judiciary Committee call attention to the "nationwide propaganda" on the issue that came "mostly from large corporations, mainly through their attorneys."[141] In the hearings before the House Judiciary Committee the American Bar Association (ABA) coordinated a show of massive and extreme corporate support for diversity jurisdiction. The support was massive because representatives of the ABA and numerous major trade organizations testified against the bills and insisted that the jurisdiction was essential to the well-being of American business.[142] The support was extreme because many of the representatives maintained that diversity jurisdiction and the doctrine of corporate citizenship were of constitutional stature, and they insisted that Congress lacked the power to alter them. A bank attorney declared diversity jurisdiction "a mandate of the Constitution," and the general counsel of the National Association of Manufacturers proclaimed it a "fundamental constitutional right."[143] Indeed, one lawyer appeared in person to attack the bills, claiming that he was testifying "not for any client" but solely because of his long interest in and familiarity with the federal courts.[144] In a private letter written several years earlier Chief Justice William Howard Taft had identified the lawyer as a covert "lobbyist for the public utilities companies."[145]

In 1957, twenty-five years later, the hearings on the Tuck bill were entirely different in both tone and mood. Business groups were scarcely visible. Although they continued for the most part to support diversity and undoubtedly lobbied against restrictions, they avoided the frantic and public display of opposition that they had mounted in 1932. At the hearings only two witnesses appeared, Tuck and Judge Maris. With liberals and most nonsoutherners joining to support diversity jurisdiction, the Tuck bill had no chance.[146]

By the late 1950s, then, the system of corporate diversity litigation was a thing of the past. Its characteristic patterns of litigation behavior no longer held, and the social conflicts and political alignments that had surrounded it for more than half a century had dissolved. If slight vestiges remained in workmen's compensation cases in three or four states, Congress wiped them out in 1958 by extending to claimants an absolute choice of forum. If some of the system's structural elements remained, such as diversity jurisdiction and removal, they no longer induced the same patterns of litigation behavior or held the same practical significance. Rather, in a new social context they functioned in new and different ways. Diversity jurisdiction remained in common use, but plaintiffs suing national corporations were often the parties seeking to use it.

A law review note published in 1960 illustrated the reversal that had occurred in the assumptions underlying litigation tactics. Discussing recent statutory changes that allowed federal courts to assess costs against litigants, it explained that the "provisions reflect concern lest plaintiffs inflate their claims in order to bring themselves within federal jurisdiction." The practice of inflating claims for the purpose of creating federal jurisdiction was being used, it noted, in a "plethora of personal-injury cases."[147] Reversing the tactics of the earlier period, the practice constituted part of a new litigation pattern for a new sociolegal age.

Chapter 11

Retrospective: History, Procedure, and the Social Role of the Federal Courts

Industrialization, the westward movement, urbanization, immigration, the rail-roads—the composite of elements that transformed American society in the decades after the Civil War—created a social context that shaped anew the day-to-day significance of federal diversity jurisdiction. Those developments helped generate large national corporations that organized far-flung commercial and industrial operations; they spread the American population across vast ranges of the trans-Mississippi West; and they created hundreds of bustling towns and cities throughout the land. In the process they also generated new classes of grievances and multiplying numbers of injuries that forced millions of individuals to confront those corporations with claims for redress. Hundreds of thousands of those individuals eventually brought legal actions to seek relief. As they did so, they formed new patterns of litigation around the jurisdiction that the federal courts had exercised since 1789. The system of corporate diversity litigation emerged after 1870 and evolved through three major stages before disintegrating in a new mid-twentieth-century social context.

In the first stage, from the 1870s to the beginning of the 1890s, distinctive forms and patterns of litigation practice coalesced into a recognizable system. In the 1870s the Supreme Court helped create the system by adopting rules that allowed the federal courts to assert jurisdiction over corporations outside their chartering states. If it did so to assist plaintiffs who wanted to sue corporations in the federal courts of their own home states, as it reasoned in *Harris* and *Schollenberger,* its actions were consistent with the social orientation of many of its common law decisions in the decade. *Fort, McCue, Lockwood,* and *Wilkinson* revealed the Court's suspicion of the growing power of the new national corporations and its desire to protect those who brought suit against them. Those attitudes, too, seemed to influence the Court in many of its contemporaneous constitutional decisions.[1] In the 1880s the system crystallized. The burdens of distance, delay, and procedural complexity weighed heavily against growing numbers of individual plaintiffs. Certain types of insurance and tort claims multiplied and became standard; the litigation tactics of the parties fell into regular patterns; and the federal courts appeared to show a growing sympathy for the interests of national corporations. Uncertainly and haltingly, the Supreme Court began reorienting itself, losing some of its wariness about large corporations and some of its solicitude for those who sued them.

Austin and *In re Pennsylvania,* both decided in 1890, marked the last years of the first stage. In *Austin* the Court showed itself oblivious to the emergence of the potentially powerful and obviously unfair delayed upward amendment tactic, and in *Pennsylvania* it imposed serious restrictions on removals under the local prejudice act. Both strengthened the hands of plaintiffs. Moreover, on neither social nor doctrinal grounds did the Court seem to have any difficulties or qualms in reaching its decisions. A full decade would pass, however, before it again ameliorated the system's impact with a major jurisdictional ruling that assisted diversity plaintiffs.

The second stage, from the beginning of the 1890s into the first decade of the twentieth century, saw the system at its broadest and harshest. As the number of industrial tort suits continued to increase and Americans endured the most severe depression in their nation's history, the Supreme Court shaped federal law in ways that enhanced the litigation position of corporate defendants. In *James* it construed the doctrine of corporate citizenship to allow foreign corporations the greatest possible access to the national courts, and in *Powers* it allowed Taft's narrow joinder rule in *Warax* to stand while at the same time forcefully terminating the delayed upward amendment tactic it had allowed to pass only eight years earlier in *Austin.* In *Shaw* and *Davidson* the Court announced venue rules that favored corporate defendants; in *Hanrick* it expressly opened the door for the lower courts to defeat the joinder tactic by applying a minimum diversity standard in removals sought under the local prejudice act; and in *Denton* it seemed to invalidate state statutes that restricted the right of foreign corporations to remove. In substantive law areas its decisions followed a parallel track. The Court abandoned the social concerns that had marked its opinions in the 1870s and early 1880s and transformed critical areas of the federal common law into strong supports for corporate interests. *Baugh, Voigt, Patton,* and *Northern Assurance*—whether rooted in a commitment to the values of freedom of contract, a conservative impulse to secure the established order in a time of high social tensions, or the largely unconscious biases of class and privilege—erected a federal common law that often disadvantaged individual plaintiffs whose actions were removed to the federal courts.

The system's middle stage began drawing to a close during the first decade of the twentieth century, prompted initially by a striking series of decisions in which the court negated through procedural law the reach of its most probusiness common law doctrines. *Dixon* in 1900 and *Cable* in 1903 signaled the Court's willingness to moderate the system by allowing plaintiffs to escape its reach, and four major decisions in 1905–6 etched the pattern unmistakably. *Thompson, Wisner, Cochran,* and *Prewitt* opened gaping holes in the system that allowed countless plaintiffs to avoid federal jurisdiction. *Cochran* was soundly based on precedent and should have been announced a decade earlier. The Court's delay suggested the social pressures it felt in the tumultuous context of the 1890s. *Thompson, Prewitt,* and *Wisner,* however, were somewhat different. In those decisions the Court molded the law anew, and in each it laid down jurisdictional rules that favored individual plaintiffs. Like *Austin* and *Pennsylvania* fifteen years earlier, the three decisions contracted federal jurisdiction and conflicted with the litigation interests of national corporations. Moreover, like *Austin* in particular, *Prewitt* and *Wisner* did so on the basis of technical and dubious legal grounds.

The system's third stage, from its uneven contraction and evolution after 1910 to its disintegration during the 1940s, was the most complex and varied. Improvements in transportation and court administration steadily reduced the heavy burdens of distance and delay in federal litigation; legislation narrowed the scope of the federal common law and restricted the jurisdiction of the national courts; and the Federal Employers' Liability Act (FELA) and workmen's compensation acts removed from the system large numbers of potential plaintiffs. As the system contracted, however, it also evolved. A resourceful and specialized plaintiffs' personal injury bar increased the tactical options open to plaintiffs, and the system's litigation became more sophisticated and its patterns more varied. If its tort litigation declined in relative importance, its insurance litigation expanded.

The Supreme Court, watching the realm of the federal common law shrink, seemed to seek alternative areas to exert its lawmaking powers and then after 1920, with three new conservative Justices joining the Court in a business-dominated era, shifted from its 1905–6 position and closed off some of the escape routes from the system. It reversed two of its earlier decisions, *Prewitt* falling to *Terral* in 1922 and *Wisner* to *Lee* the following year. Further, the Court developed new doctrines to limit plaintiffs' choice of venue and allowed the lower courts to experiment for two decades with their equity jurisdiction as a device to restrict plaintiffs' tactics. Finally, as the pace and complexity of the new litigation tactics grew and the Court faced the social and political crises of the 1930s, it began to seek ways to limit the system's scope and, in particular, to reduce the growing arbitrariness and instability that had come to characterize much private civil litigation. A series of decisions between 1933 and 1937—*Gay, Fried, Trainor, Enelow, Di Giovanni, Alaska Packers,* and *International Milling* among others—signaled the stirrings of doctrinal shifts.

The decade after 1937 witnessed the disintegration of the system. Improvements in transportation and the nearly universal availability of the automobile greatly reduced the burdens of geography. The success that the federal courts enjoyed in administering their caseloads limited the general significance of delay and may well have dropped the average time from filing to judgment in the national courts below the comparable time required in most state courts. Further, the New Deal transformed the political image of the federal courts, and after 1937 the Roosevelt Court showed a marked sympathy for those who sued national corporations. In 1938 the Court announced in *Erie* the end of the general federal common law, and during the following decade it eliminated the differences in the substantive law applied in the state and federal courts and minimized at least many of the differences in procedural law. By the end of the 1940s the formal law offered relatively little incentive to choose between a state and a federal forum in a diversity action, and the federal courts were generally perceived as less favorably disposed toward corporations than were the state courts. Although inequality, tactical maneuvering, and the informal legal process all continued to exist—as did removal, diversity jurisdiction, and the doctrine of corporate citizenship—the patterns and dynamics of their use had changed profoundly.

Reviewing the evolution of the system of corporate diversity litigation, it seems certain that the American Law Institute (ALI) study, the single most comprehensive quantitative measure of the system, did not reflect the full scope of its operations in the decades around the turn of the century.[2] Because the ALI provided only a snapshot taken in the year 1929–30, its statistics incorporated the effects of the major legal restrictions on removal that came in the years between 1900 and 1920. In contrast with the situation revealed in the ALI study, the federal courts from the late 1880s to the first decade of the twentieth century almost certainly heard higher percentages of negligence cases, removed actions, and suits involving residents against foreign corporations. Most likely, remand motions and other challenges to federal jurisdiction were also much higher. In contrast, at least from *Prewitt* in 1906 to *Terral* in 1922, the federal courts almost certainly heard fewer insurance cases than the ALI study reflects.

The statistics compiled after 1940 by the Administrative Office of the United States Courts are not entirely comparable with those in the ALI study, but they indirectly support those conclusions by recording the further decline of the system between 1929–30 and the late 1940s. Compared with the numbers in 1929–30, the statistics for the 1940s show a drop in removals as a percentage of diversity cases and a drop in the percentage of removals effected by foreign corporations. They also show an apparently sharp drop in the number of remands in diversity actions.[3]

By the time the system disappeared at mid-century, the federal courts found themselves in a new era. The quarter-century before World War II was the seedbed of both modern litigation practice and a new administrative judicial style.[4] After 1910 an increasingly organized and hierarchical bar moved more fully toward specialization, and litigation began to lose its local flavor and take on national characteristics. The new Federal Rules of Civil Procedure, authorized in 1934 and promulgated in 1938, symbolized and accelerated much of the change. The availability of expanded discovery methods and more flexible and inclusive joinder rules as well as a sharpened competition among specialists combined with the higher stakes available in more types of actions to stimulate the use of sophisticated litigation tactics in an escalating search for advantage. Similarly, the pressures of a growing caseload merged with the ideals of expert administration to encourage federal judges to view their dockets as objects to be actively managed and cleared.[5] Further, and somewhat more subtly, in combination with the rise of interstate forum shopping and the spread of government administrative agencies, the same forces also helped induce the Supreme Court to expand judicial doctrines of forum control and to develop the uses of discretionary dismissals and stays as devices to allocate judicial business. Rather than simply assuming that the lower courts should decide the cases over which they had jurisdiction, the Court began to consider whether the courts could and should remit the parties before them to some other forum or remedy.

In that context, acceptance by the Supreme Court of the doctrine of *forum non conveniens* at the end of the 1940s symbolized the emergence of a distinctively twentieth-century style of thought about the federal judicial system. Reflecting a more general loss of faith in rigid legal rules, a confidence in professional expertise, a desire to increase the efficiency of the courts, and a commitment to the idea of an integrated national judicial system, the doctrine moved beyond the established rules of venue and traditional ideas about forum choice and committed to the discretion of federal judges the power to redistribute cases geographically on the basis of their individual judgments regarding "efficiency" and "convenience." "The doctrine leaves much to the discretion of the court to which plaintiff resorts," the Supreme Court acknowledged in 1947 when it approved the use of *forum non conveniens* in the federal courts. Indeed, it saw no point in even attempting to formulate a rule to govern the doctrine's application. "Wisely, it has not been attempted to catalogue the circumstances which will justify or require either grant or denial of [the *forum non conveniens*] remedy."[6]

The System of Corporate Diversity Litigation:
Method And Implications

For more than a century professional scholars in law, history, and the social sciences have sought to discover how the political and social worlds "really worked" and to explore the relationships between law and society. Following the lead of Roscoe Pound at the beginning of the twentieth century, American legal scholars came to refer to the distinction between "law in books" and "law in action." Much illuminating scholarship has resulted, and the past several decades have added many important works ranging from detailed statistical studies of judicial dockets to complex interpretations of the relationship between social change and the institutions and doctrines of the law.[7]

This book inquires further into the dynamics of the law in action, using a synthesizing, ecological approach to the study of law, society, and legal history. It explores the relationships between potential and actual legal claims on the one hand and, on the other, the social and legal factors that determined how parties disputed and disposed of those claims. The approach examines the ways in which the diverse relationships among those various elements combined and interacted over time to create and alter the rough patterns of behavior through which certain types of individuals and groups tended regularly to abandon, settle, and litigate certain specific types of claims.[8]

The book revolves around an analysis of what it calls a *social litigation system*. Such a "litigation" system is clearly narrower than a "claims disposition" system. It concentrates on "legal" patterns in the disputing process rather than on more sweeping "social" patterns of claims disposition. But the book nevertheless describes and examines a *social* litigation system. It attempts, in other words, to identify the ways in which more comprehensive claims-disputing and disposition patterns helped determine litigation practices. The book assumes that any understanding of litigation patterns requires some understanding of the broader claims-disputing and disposition system of which they are integral parts.

The concept of a social litigation system directs attention to the functional interrelationships among several factors. First, it begins with the basic social fact that drives the practices of both the formal and informal legal systems, human conflict. Its initial focus is not on doctrines or institutions but on the efforts of individuals and groups to achieve certain specific goals, and it accordingly underscores the pivotal importance of the social characteristics of adversary parties.[9] Second, it concentrates on social and historical context, recognizing that the influence of that context is complex, multiform, and often indirect. It is sensitive to the power of that context to alter the practical significance of legal rules and institutions, whether or not those rules and institutions themselves formally change. Third, it stresses the importance not just of cases but also of claims, not just of formal suits filed in the judicial system but also of actions taken anywhere that attempt to dispose of grievances that could give rise to legal claims. The formal law helps contour the informal legal process, but the latter is both more comprehensive and more vital. It surrounds, limits, and shapes the operation of the formal legal system. Fourth, the concept of a social litigation system emphasizes that the legal system is not merely an institution that maintains norms and enforces order but is also one that allows and to some extent encourages diverse results through the scope it gives to the opportunistic, methodical, creative, and ruthless efforts of private parties to exploit its every feature and nuance. It assumes that the formal purposes and theories that purport to explain rules or practices may well explain neither why or how parties in fact use them nor what actual social results they bring.

Finally, the concept of a social litigation system highlights the complex and unavoidable interplay among the formal elements of the legal system itself. It stresses the importance of forum options, for example, recognizing that for diverse types of litigants alternative courts are often far from equivalent, regardless of their formal standings as jurisdictional equals purportedly applying an identical substantive law. It also stresses the ways in which procedural rules modify, restrict, or even negate rules of substantive law. It assumes that substantive rules, despite their apparent clarity or breadth, may mean little or nothing, or perhaps something quite surprising, when seen in the functional litigation contexts where they are, or are supposed to be, controlling.

The concept of a social litigation system also highlights the changing dynamics between the formal elements of substance and procedure, the law's two classic internal divisions. The concept incorporates the assumption that we cannot begin to understand the practical significance of the former until we recognize the relevant circuity, flexibility, and multiformity created by the latter.[10] It also assumes, of course, that we cannot begin to understand the latter—procedure "in the abstract"—without understanding both the substantive rules to be enforced and the social context in which the enforcement would occur. The concept of a social litigation system, in fact, gives to procedure a special prominence and brings it more fully within the scholarly effort to study law as a social and cultural phenomenon.

Procedure offers a particularly rewarding subject to the legal historian because it constitutes the realm of irony in the law. As the practical consequences of the jurisdictional amount or of the FELA's special venue provision reveal, the apparently most trivial and mechanical of procedural rules can have an importance far beyond their ostensible purposes. Similarly, in qualifying, frustrating, or transforming the significance of substantive rules and rights, procedure can illuminate their practical human significance and spotlight the critical points where social factors impinge most sharply on the legal process. Indeed, procedural studies offer a particularly useful way to explore the actual operations of the legal process. Because procedure channels the movement of litigation that results in the reported cases that are taken to be the law, its frequently revealing indirections may, ironically, lead most directly from the law in books to the law in action.

Because procedural devices determine settlement values and systematically drain actions from the formal judicial system, the study of procedure as a social phenomenon—unlike a study of substantive law—points directly to the role and significance of the broader informal legal process. Surrounding the formal processes of law and litigation, the informal legal process filters to a trickle the number of cases that eventually go to judgment and receive the official application of legal rules to found facts. If at each point in that filtering process fair and reasonable legal criteria were applied to establish, evaluate, and discount claims, then the process would complement, indeed supersede, the formal law. The problem, of course, is that the informal legal process establishes, evaluates, and discounts claims not only on the basis or rules of law but on many other grounds as well. When the parties are unequal, the influence of legal criteria of evaluation tends to wither while the salience of nonlegal factors grows and often becomes determinative. Inequality thus tends to create greater and greater disparities between the actual results of the informal legal process and the ideally proper results required by the rules of the formal law. Procedure conceived as a social phenomenon can serve as a lens that helps us identify, if only partially, some parts of the often invisible informal legal process.

Although the significance of inequality and of the social pressures that shape the settlement process are generally recognized, it seems important to reiterate their role because we sometimes lose sight of them. The privacy of the informal legal process hides much of its operation from our view, and the ready availability of the law reports and statute books tempts us consciously or not to confine our gaze to the formal sources of law.[11] Indeed, this study is no more than a partial exception, based largely on those same formal sources. Still, however, we should push out from those sources and begin to explore the role and operation of the informal legal process more fully than we have, and our legal history will not tell its full story until we do.

The examination of the social system of corporate diversity litigation supports a number of conclusions. One is that scholars have probably overemphasized the extent to which the pressures of social change *directly* induced legal change.[12] In contrast, a consideration of the system of corporate diversity litigation shows how the creativity of litigation practice and the adaptive capacity of procedural devices helped generate alternative and unexpected ways by which the legal system opposed, channeled, or deflected the pressures that came with social change. Whereas labor unions and progressives attacked the fellow servant rule for a quarter of a century, for example, the law of joinder freed many tort plaintiffs from the generally fatal federal version of the rule adopted in *Baugh*. More broadly, *Dixon* and *Thompson* prevented the federal fellow servant rule from being applied to many employee tort actions several years before Congress abolished it officially in the FELA. Had the workmen's compensation movement not taken most employee injuries out of the court system, the changes in the federal procedural law of joinder would probably have affected far more individuals than were affected by the substantive abolition of the federal fellow servant rule in the FELA (limited as it was to interstate railroad workers).

Similarly, the railroads and insurance companies fought for more than three decades against the interstate forum shopping that developed after 1910 when changes in communication, social organization, and professional specialization gave new significance to traditional doctrines establishing the right of plaintiffs to choose their forum. The doctrine of *forum non conveniens,* crafted from a variety of litigation tactics and legal ideas, helped rationalize a national legal system while at the same time giving the companies much of what they wanted. Adoption of the doctrine required neither the formal repudiation of the constitutional theories and statutory rights that had given interstate forum shopping its legal standing nor any express recognition by Congress or the courts of what, in terms of political and social interests, they were in effect doing.

On an even broader level, the development of a collection of highly technical and apparently trivial federal procedural rules centering on the jurisdictional amount helped forge one of the great, if largely unspoken, social and legal compromises of the late nineteenth and early twentieth centuries. The operative rule was simple and well understood. If plaintiffs agreed to keep their claims reasonably small, they could guarantee themselves a state forum.

A consideration of the social system of corporate diversity litigation and the informal legal process also throws a somewhat different light on the significance of *Swift v. Tyson* and the federal common law. However important they were, it is clear that they constituted only one of the advantages that corporations enjoyed as a result of their ability to litigate in the federal courts. Other legal and nonlegal advantages were at least as important and, as a general matter, were probably more important. Further, it also appears likely that "uncertainty" about the law, a great evil according to *Swift's* corporate defenders, did not impose an unmitigated hardship on national businesses. Although corporations may well have wished to be able to rely on uniform and known (and, especially, favorable) law, uncertainties about the nature or source of the applicable substantive law could serve them well in the context of the system's litigation. Increased uncertainty added to the risks of litigation and tended to give additional leverage to parties with ample resources and the ability to spread their costs. In innumerable instances the heightened uncertainty and consequently magnified litigation risk that the specter of the federal common law engendered probably allowed corporate defendants to obtain steeper discounts from adversaries with few resources and but a single claim to pursue.

Conversely, the system's operations also illustrated some of the ways in which procedural rules limited or trumped the federal common law and showed that plaintiffs were increasingly able to exploit the legal opportunities that were available. Indeed, the innumerable procedural battles that marked the system revealed the extent to which many plaintiffs, though often at a serious disadvantage, fought back against their more powerful adversaries. Guided and encouraged by a personal injury bar that began developing at the end of the nineteenth century, they refused in many cases to succumb to the first blandishments of their adversaries or to the pressures that the informal legal process could impose. The system of corporate diversity litigation was one of the classic manifestations of the central social, political, and cultural confrontation that marked the age of industrial America, the struggle between individuals and the new national corporations. Sometimes the individuals won.

Recognizing the ways in which individual claimants in the system began to improve their litigation positions after the turn of the century expands our understanding of the origins and success of the workmen's compensation movement between 1900 and 1917. In particular, it helps explain why within a very few years some business groups became strong supporters of workmen's compensation on both the state and federal levels. The emergence of an aggressive plaintiffs' personal injury bar placed increasing social and economic pressures on corporations and drove up their overall costs for both settlements and litigations. Similarly, the Supreme Court's restrictive jurisdictional decisions between 1900 and 1906 altered the balance of litigation advantage in the system, and the proliferating use of the joinder tactic warned corporations that their overall settlement and litigation costs would rise even further in the future. Although corporate support for workmen's compensation grew from a number of sources, the altered dynamics of corporate diversity litigation was surely one of them.

Similarly, an awareness of the operation of the system of corporate diversity litigation suggests the need for qualifications in our understanding of the movement for "professional" judicial and procedural reform that began to gather momentum after the turn of the century. Although lawyers and bar associations have frequently and sometimes justifiably hailed the movement, numerous critics have disdained it. Focusing on its apparently conservative leadership and its concentration on abstruse and technical issues, critics have often pictured the movement as socially peripheral or worse: a form of inconsequential conscience salving, a self-serving effort to improve conditions for the bar itself, or even a sinister anti-progressive effort to distract people from more fundamental legal abuses. The history of the system of corporate diversity litigation suggests two qualifications. First, it shows that there was, indeed, a need for judicial and procedural reform in the late nineteenth century, and it shows further that technical and even apparently trivial procedural matters had a social significance that merited intensive reform efforts. Some of the problems that at least some professional legal reformers sought to remedy—litigation costs, delays in the courts, and abuses in appellate practice—constituted serious burdens that tended regularly and often to handicap the poor and less well-to-do. Second, the history of the system also suggests that professional legal reform did not primarily address those types of problems or confront the question of the extent to which social inequality and related practical issues undermined the ideal of the fair and equitable administration of justice. The burdens of geography, for example, were nearly invisible to professional legal reformers until FELA plaintiffs and others began methodically to use interstate forum shopping tactics in the 1920s. A central failing of the movement for professional procedural reform, then, was not that it dealt with technical and arcane issues but, rather, that it often focused on technical and arcane issues that were largely or wholly unrelated to the practical litigation problems that disproportionately burdened large numbers of ordinary Americans.

The history of corporate diversity litigation reminds us, too, of the complexity and variety in the American judicial system and the extent to which the written opinions of the Supreme Court may constitute a less than entirely reliable guide to the law and practices applied in the lower federal courts. The responses to *Austin, Wisner, Dixon,* and *Thompson,* for example, show that the lower courts may not only have their own ideas about what the law should be but may also press those views on the judicial system and the Supreme Court itself in various and sometimes quite effective ways. The cases also suggest that the "flexibility" that the lower courts enjoy is particularly extensive when dealing with such procedural issues. Those issues are less visible, less readily understood by laypersons, and less frequently reviewed by the Supreme Court. Perhaps most important, they are also less often dispositive in the formal legal process. The irony, however, is that those same decisions are often at least partially dispositive in the informal legal process. In many cases it is one or more preliminary procedural rulings that sufficiently narrow the upper and lower valuations of a case to induce the parties to terminate the action and settle. Thus, the divergence between the formal written rules of the Supreme Court and the practices applied in the lower courts may be most significant in those areas where judicial decisions are particularly influential in establishing the de facto value of suits and inducing the parties to settle.

A consideration of the system of corporate diversity litigation also contributes to our understanding of the "formalist" or "classical" era of American legal thought. Scholars have identified the period from the 1870s to the 1930s as a period in which large numbers of judges, lawyers, law professors, and legal writers tended to view the law as a set of pre-existing rules or principles and to consider judicial decisions as logical deductions from those premises. In spite of that general consensus, however, scholars have disagreed about a number of more specific issues, including whether and to what extent those jurisprudential attitudes characterized the period, molded the content of legal rules, and served as ideological screens that allowed or encouraged the judiciary to protect American business.[13] Although this study does not address developments in legal thought as such, judicial decisions involving corporate diversity litigation suggest at least three conclusions that relate to the discussion of formalism.

First, the procedural decisions in the system demonstrate that the sway of formalist jurisprudence was, at a minimum, limited. They show that federal judges were acutely sensitive to social contexts and consequences and, further, that they were fully aware of the manipulable and instrumental nature of legal rules. Federal judges often shaped their decisions in order to achieve a variety of identifiable social results that included—in degrees that varied by time, place, and individual judge—preventing jurisdictional manipulation, protecting corporate defendants, encouraging national economic growth, facilitating racial discrimination and abuse, countering the perceived shortcomings of the state courts, ensuring that the "correct" rules of the common law were applied, and securing the social and institutional authority of the national courts. The cases show, in short, that federal judges were inspired by a keen awareness of the social policies that their decisions served. Accordingly, the cases cast doubt on the proposition that those judges either conceived of law—or, at least, of procedural law—as a set of pre-existing principles or that they thought of judicial decisions as abstract logical deductions. Whatever the nature of the official reasoning that the judges offered or the variety of the public policies they favored, they often made their decisions on the basis of substantive value choices.

Second, the instrumentalism that marked those procedural decisions suggests the likelihood that a similar instrumentalism helped inform substantive law decisions as well. Although procedural and substantive issues present different types of problems and involve different kinds of considerations, they may nevertheless be closely related in terms of the social consequences that each tends to bring about. The history of the system of corporate diversity litigation shows that in one context, at least, federal judges were fully aware of the nature and existence of that functional relationship. Moreover, it seems doubtful that judges who so regularly considered procedural matters in instrumentalist terms would, when turning to substantive issues, abruptly and sharply limit themselves to such a radically dissimilar approach as formalism.[14] It is important to note, too, that in spite of their instrumentalist orientation in procedural cases, federal judges often cast their resulting opinions in formalist terms by refraining from express or detailed policy analysis. *Powers,* for example, was a coldly instrumentalist decision designed to remedy a specific and acute social-litigation problem. The Supreme Court, however, went to extreme lengths in order to avoid explaining or even acknowledging that fact. Its unwillingness to discuss the actual reason for its decision was particularly striking, in fact, because it could have convincingly relied on such traditional and undeniably legitimate policy grounds as the intent of Congress, the rights of litigants to fair procedures, and the need to protect the integrity of federal jurisdiction. The fact that *Powers* and numerous other procedural cases failed to engage in express or detailed policy analysis but were nevertheless pointedly instrumentalist suggests that the mere absence from many federal substantive law cases of detailed policy analysis is dubious evidence that they were decided on formalist rather than on instrumentalist grounds. Although the cases support the proposition that formalism was a recognizable style of official and public judicial behavior, they challenge the proposition that it was an operative judicial method that led judges to avoid the instrumentalist evaluation of conflicting policy alternatives.[15]

Third, and most generally, the cases also suggest that in studying formalism and classical legal thought scholars have overemphasized the importance of substantive legal rules and general jurisprudential thinking. Without in the least questioning the importance of either of those subjects, it nonetheless seems essential that scholars expand their field of relevant inquiry. In particular, they should probe the varieties of legal thought that have been lumped together as formalist, examine the development of legal thought in procedural areas, and explore attitudes toward legal practice, including the informal legal process.[16] Those approaches seem likely to deepen, if not alter significantly, our understanding of formalism and classical legal thought.

Beyond those matters, consideration of the system of corporate diversity litigation also raises three other issues that merit more extended discussion. One relates to the problem of local prejudice and the accepted rationale that diversity jurisdiction was a device to protect nonresidents. The second is the system's economic impact and the light it casts on the subsidy and efficiency theses concerning tort law in the late nineteenth and early twentieth centuries. The third concerns the political and social role that the federal courts played in the same years and the extent to which they did and did not show particular solicitude for the interests of national corporations.

Diversity Jurisdiction and "Local Prejudice"

An examination of the system of corporate diversity litigation establishes one fact beyond cavil. To whatever extent the fear or reality of local prejudice induced corporate defendants to prefer the federal courts, other powerful incentives also led them in the same direction. Corporate attorneys openly acknowledged the significance of the federal common law as a motive for removal, and all practitioners recognized the leverage to be gained by imposing on individual plaintiffs the heavy and varied burdens of distance, delay, and procedural complexity. Thus, whether or not corporate defendants were motivated by fear of prejudice, removal often gave them compelling litigation advantages that were unrelated to the jurisdiction's theoretical role as a device to ensure a "neutral" forum.

Recognition of the practical advantages that removal could bestow on corporate defendants also suggests that many of the corporate claims regarding local prejudice may warrant skepticism. Corporations would hardly have confessed to using federal jurisdiction in order to exploit the economic and social weaknesses of their adversaries. The idea of local prejudice, however, was readily available as an acceptable and sufficient explanation for removal. Indeed, history and practice had joined to make it a stock justification for any use of diversity jurisdiction. Further, the claim of local prejudice was an explanation that was almost impossible to disprove, especially since corporate spokespersons could emphasize their "fear" of local prejudice despite a lack of evidence of its actual existence.[17] Although corporate fears about local prejudice were undoubtedly real in some instances, it seems likely that such fears were often exaggerated or unfounded. Indeed, it also seems likely that much of whatever "prejudice" existed in state courts may well have benefited not individual plaintiffs but corporate defendants with special local influence. With those considerations in mind, it seems reasonable to hypothesize that much of the corporate rhetoric about local prejudice may, purposely or not, have been inflated to help deflect attention from other and less "proper" reasons that corporations had for removing their actions.[18]

That hypothesis, of course, does not deny that local prejudice existed, that it probably influenced the courts in some instances, and that the federal courts seemed to offer greater protections against such bias than did at least some state courts (see Chapter 1). The point, rather, is twofold. First, local prejudice may have been a much less serious problem for corporations in American state courts than has often been claimed, and in any event it was almost certainly a double-edged sword that often cut against their adversaries. Second, when corporations litigated against individual plaintiffs, removal gave them powerful de facto litigation advantages that were unrelated to either the theoretical purpose of diversity jurisdiction or the actual existence of local prejudice.

More broadly, this study supports those who have questioned whether the local prejudice theory provides a coherent foundation on which to explain the existence or scope of diversity jurisdiction.[19] Whatever reasons led the Framers to provide for diversity jurisdiction, two conclusions seem warranted regarding its existence in the late nineteenth and early twentieth centuries. First, as obvious as it is important, the jurisdiction did not—and was not designed to —protect all citizens against local prejudice. Rather, it offered some protection on only some occasions to only one category of citizen. Whatever its scope or effectiveness, the protection was directed at a value or values other than the desirability of guaranteeing an unbiased judicial forum to American citizens or, for that matter, even to all nonresident citizens. The cases under the Civil Rights Act of 1866 show that diversity jurisdiction was, in fact, based on a highly selective concern about the dangers of local prejudice, that it conferred special federal protection on only one of many categories of citizens, and that it did not confer that special protection on the group that most desperately needed it. Second, even if diversity jurisdiction had originally been designed as a method of protecting nonresidents from local prejudice, its elaboration over the years gave it an oblique relationship with that purpose. Rules regarding change of citizenship allowed manipulation; decisions such as *Lee* were simply unrelated to that purpose; and the doctrine of corporate citizenship radically transformed the social significance of the jurisdiction. Indeed, to the extent that nonresidents were actually threatened by local prejudice, the Supreme Court's decisions under the separable controversy and local prejudice acts would have deprived them in numerous cases of whatever protection a federal forum might have offered.

Perhaps a better explanation for the actual shape that the Supreme Court gave diversity jurisdiction over the years—or, at least, from the 1870s to the 1940s—was simply that the Justices generally if implicitly believed that they should maintain federal jurisdiction over issues and interests that they regarded as having national importance. Although jurisdiction over corporations was essential, jurisdiction over many issues involving corporations—including most run-of-the-mill tort and contract actions—was not. In 1905, when the Court was in the middle of its series of restrictive procedural decisions, for example, it rejected an opportunity to restrict diversity jurisdiction over corporate shareholder derivative suits. Such suits, of course, could put many millions of dollars at risk and determine fundamental issues of corporate control and governance that were central to the new national economy. In *Doctor v. Harrington*[20] the Court refused to accept a simple and quite logical application of the doctrine of corporate citizenship where the result would have been to destroy diversity of citizenship between corporations and their shareholders. Instead, it construed the doctrine to ensure that diversity jurisdiction would remain available in shareholder derivative suits. In doing so, the Court identified the underlying purpose that it saw animating the long and tortured history of the doctrine of corporate citizenship. "The reason of the presumption (we will so denominate it)," a unanimous Court explained, "was to establish the citizenship of the legal entity for the purpose of jurisdiction in the Federal courts."[21] The purpose of the doctrine, in other words, was to allow the federal courts to exercise jurisdiction over cases brought by and against corporations. Although imperfect, a generalized version of *Doctor*'s explanation—that the Supreme Court molded the rules of jurisdiction over the years to permit the federal courts to hear the types of cases it regarded as having national importance—probably makes more sense of the history of diversity jurisdiction than does the long-accepted local prejudice rationale.[22]

Of Subsidies and Efficiency: The Economic Significance of the System

Scholars have debated the extent to which nineteenth-century negligence law helped "subsidize" business enterprise by narrowing liability and allowing corporations to avoid much of the cost of industrial accidents.[23] To a large extent they have concentrated on the structure of substantive rules of law and on the formal legal process. Although the importance of such factors should not be minimized, an overall assessment of the economic impact of negligence law in the late nineteenth century requires a broader perspective. Substantive rules, whether they favored negligence plaintiffs or defendants, were not self-executing, and we can assess their actual social impact only in the context of litigation practice and the informal legal process.[24]

This study makes only a start at such a general assessment, but it shows that in one relatively large class of claims—those held by individuals against foreign corporations—late nineteenth- and early twentieth-century practice gave defendants advantages that enabled them to impose on others a substantial part of the costs of industrial injuries. The economic advantages of the right to remove appeared on three levels. First, the removal option meant that foreign corporations could sometimes obtain more favorable substantive law and win cases that they would otherwise have lost. Second, the removal option also meant that foreign corporations frequently could obtain a forum more favorable on procedural or institutional grounds, whether the advantage lay in a more sympathetic judge, a less suspicious jury, or more exploitable procedures. Again, the result in many cases was to allow corporations to win suits they would otherwise have lost or, at a minimum, to limit the amount of damages that they would otherwise have been assessed. Third, the removal option meant that corporations could impose heavy extralegal burdens that could drive up plaintiffs' litigation costs, handicap their efforts to put on evidence, and discourage them from prosecuting their suits to judgment. Removal or the threat of removal—usually, of course, working in combination with other informal pressures that companies could exert—frequently and regularly pressured plaintiffs to abandon their claims, to settle them for relatively small sums, or to discontinue and refile them for amounts under the jurisdictional minimum. Indeed, as we saw in Chapter 4, in the context of the system the jurisdictional amount by itself created a partial de facto ceiling on corporate liability. Given the creation each year of hundreds of thousands of potential new claims against foreign corporations, the aggregate result of the system's operation was to save them large sums of money.

The history of the system of corporate diversity litigation shows that the legal system as a whole—the operating, de facto system of claims disposition—gave numerous advantages to corporate defendants. Although subsidy may be a misleading term, the practical result of the system was nevertheless to confer economic benefits on corporate defendants. Perhaps a better approach would be to conceive of the operating system as a drastic and methodical, if somewhat erratic, process of discounting the overall amounts for which corporations were or should have been liable.

On a broader interpretive level, recognition of the role played by the system of corporate diversity litigation and the informal legal process seems to limit the utility of what has been called the strictly economic analysis of law. Operation of the system of corporate diversity litigation, of course, touches on only a small part of the general discussion about law and economics that scholars have carried on for the past three decades.[25] Still, that operation illustrates some of the ways that social conditions mold litigation practice and limit the de facto value of the rights that the formal law establishes. Indeed, the structure of the system may be seen as a complex set of transaction costs that burdened litigation against foreign corporations and thereby prevented the system from operating, in a strictly economic sense, with efficiency.

The system's economic significance may be judged to some extent by the light its operation casts on one of the earliest and most important examples of the economic analysis of law, Richard A. Posner's stimulating study of American negligence law during the years from 1875 to 1905.[26] Posner, a professor at the University of Chicago Law School and subsequently a judge on the United States Court of Appeals for the Seventh Circuit, has been one of the most prominent proponents of the economic analysis of law for the past two decades, and his study of late nineteenth-century negligence law remains both a valuable source of data and a classic statement of the law and economics approach.[27] Because his study analyzes negligence law in a period when the system of corporate diversity litigation operated at its peak, it provides a basis on which to compare his economic approach with the social and historical approach used to examine the system of corporate diversity litigation.

Posner's study directly challenges the subsidy thesis, which he terms the "orthodox view" of late nineteenth-century tort law.[28] Offering "a fresh look at the social function of liability for negligent acts," Posner posits the theory that negligence law fostered economic efficiency. Borrowing Judge Learned Hand's well-known formula, he identifies negligence as the failure to take precautions when the cost of such precautions is less than the cost of the harm that would likely result from such failure, discounted by the likelihood that such harm will occur. "If the cost of safety measures or of curtailment [of the economic activity]—whichever cost is lower—exceeds the benefit in accident avoidance to be gained by incurring that cost," he points out, "society would be better off, in economic terms, to forgo accident prevention."[29] And, of course, "a rational profit-maximizing enterprise will pay tort judgments to the accident victims rather than incur the larger cost of avoiding liability."[30] He then states his economic theory of common law negligence:

> Perhaps, then, the dominant function of the fault system is to generate rules of liability that if followed will bring about, at least approximately, the efficient—the cost-justified—level of accidents and safety. Under this view, damages are assessed against the defendant as a way of measuring the costs of accidents, and the damages so assessed are paid over to the plaintiff (to be divided with his lawyer) as the price of enlisting their participation in the operation of the system. Because we do not like to see resources squandered, a judgment of negligence has inescapable overtones of moral disapproval, for it implies that there was a cheaper alternative to the accident.[31]

On the basis of an extended examination of fifteen hundred appellate decisions handed down at ten-year intervals from 1875 to 1905, Posner concludes that the common law of negligence in the late nineteenth century was, with minor exceptions, consistent with his theory. It was "evenhanded in its treatment of the claims of victims and injurers" and "broadly designed to bring about the efficient (cost justified) level of accidents and safety."[32]

Putting aside the methodological difficulties of measuring "efficiency" and "cost" as Posner uses those terms, the operation of the system of corporate diversity litigation and the nature of the informal legal process from 1875 to 1905 help identify some of the limits of his analysis. First, it ignores the gap between formal legal rules and the informal social processes of claims disposition. Posner's theory pivots on the existence of an objective economic "cost of accidents" and specifies that legal damages are used as the measure of that cost. "For the negligence system to bring about an efficient level of accidents and safety," the theory holds, "the damage awards must be equal to the costs of accidents resulting from negligent conduct."[33] Yet, even assuming the existence of a true economic cost of accidents, examination of the informal legal process shows that the amounts of damages that defendants paid were generally not measures of any "objective" cost of the accidents involved. They were, rather, in large part the product of practical inequalities and of social factors related obliquely or not at all to the command of common law rules. The amounts paid varied not just with the "merits" of a case but also with the presence of intimidation, exploitation, and overreaching as well as the squeeze of economic exigency, the pressures of complex social relationships, the burdens of distance and delay, and the relative advantages for the respective parties of the state and federal judicial systems. As factors other than the legal merits of a case drove down the amounts of damages that negligent parties were forced to pay, damages failed to equal the "true" economic cost of negligent accidents, and the common law system failed to produce an efficient level of safety.[34] Indeed, to the extent that there were conflicting sets of state and federal common law rules, the very concept of the "legal merits" of a case was unavoidably relative, subjective, and—with respect to individual cases—essentially arbitrary.

Second, an examination of the system of corporate diversity litigation highlights the abstract nature of Posner's economic theory, its thin and formal empirical base, and the exceptionally narrow scope of its applicability. In spite of occasional language referring to "practice," the theory rests primarily on an analysis of the logical structure of legal rules.[35] And to the extent that the theory limits itself to describing the structure of doctrine alone, it cannot explain data that lie outside the formal legal process. Posner, for example, takes little account of statistics showing that settlement payments in industrial injury cases tended to be much lower than judgment amounts. He assumes, rather, that the difference merely reflects "rational" claim discounting. "[A]ll of these figures are misleading, because they must include numerous settlements of dubious claims drastically discounted to reflect the unlikelihood that the plaintiff can prove his case."[36] That assumption is both essential to Posner's argument and deeply flawed. It implies that the question of a plaintiff's ability to "prove his case" is simply a question of the weight of the objective evidence that bears on the "merits." It ignores the fact that "proving one's case" is in reality a complicated and risky process in which any number of social factors extraneous to the merits can weaken or defeat a party's efforts. Even more important, Posner's assumption also ignores the significance of the social pressures that operated—independent of any evaluation of the merits—to induce plaintiffs to settle their claims on a deeply discounted basis. Similarly, when Posner asks whether the damages that courts awarded were "adequate" to cover the costs of accidents, he confines his discussion to the amounts won in final appellate judgments. Acknowledging that his data allow only a "rough answer," he compares the present value of wages lost by a hypothetical injured worker with the average judgment awarded in cases of severe injury. The average judgment, he concludes, was sufficient to "compensate the injured employee for lost earnings and for the cost of medical treatment," with "some money left over for pain and suffering."[37] Thus Posner finds the theory confirmed, but only in the results of formal adjudications carried to final appellate judgment.

Third, the practice of corporate diversity litigation also suggests that even on the level of formal adjudications Posner's economic analysis is not convincing. His conclusion that common law damages were "adequate" requires severe qualification. To start with, the conclusion applies only to a relatively few tort claims. Appellate judgments, Posner himself estimates, probably represented only about 10 to 15 percent of the cases that reached judgment below,[38] an estimate that may well be too high.[39] Judgments below, in turn, represented less than half of all actions that were filed, and those actions that were filed constituted something less than 5 to 10 percent of the potential tort claims that injured workers could have brought but did not. Appellate judgments, in short, probably represented less than 5 percent of all tort actions filed and most likely something less than half of 1 percent of all assertable tort claims. Further, it seems likely that judgments in appellate cases were higher than those in cases not appealed. Defendants were more likely to appeal larger judgments than smaller ones, and the fact that a claim of "excessive" damages was itself a standard ground for appeal, especially in jury cases, suggests that large awards were particularly likely to be appealed. Statistics strengthen that hypothesis. The congressional Employers' Liability and Work-men's Compensation Commission found, for example, that in 1908–10 damages in appealed and nonappealed death cases together averaged $2,536, barely half of the $5,019 average that Posner found for appealed cases alone in 1905.[40] More-over, as Posner admits, judgment amounts do not take into account plaintiffs' litigation expenses. Including attorneys' fees, those expenses could easily con-sume half of a recovery. Although "adequacy" in this context is a particularly difficult concept to evaluate, let alone quantify, these considerations make it quite unlikely that by any reasonable standard the amounts of damages awards in the late nineteenth century provided adequate compensation to injured persons.

Posner's theory, however, tries to avoid the economic significance of plaintiffs' litigation costs. It is unlikely, he maintains, that litigation costs had any "serious economic consequences." His reason is simple. "The important point, viewing the negligence system as a system for bringing about an efficient quantum of safety and accidents," he explains, "is that the total costs of the accidents in which the defendant is negligent be made costs to the defendant."[41] From the systematic economic point of view, in other words, the fate of the plaintiffs is not relevant. That conclusion, of course, is implicit in Posner's basic premise that the "domi-nant function" of tort law is to bring about economic efficiency rather than to compensate injured persons.

The point is critical. The requirement for an efficient negligence law is not that plaintiffs receive "adequate" damages but that the "total costs" of accidents fall on negligent defendants. But here Posner's theory encounters a serious inconsistency. Although the "adequacy to plaintiffs" standard, if applied solely to appellate judgments, may be consistent with the theory's strict limitation to the analysis of formal legal rules, the "total costs to defendants" standard is not. The latter necessarily implicates all potential claims, not just those that ended in appellate decisions. For if the formal law imposed the total costs of all negligent accidents on defendants in only the less than 1 percent of injuries that went to a final appellate decision (or, for that matter, in only the less than 5 percent of injuries that ended in any kind of formal legal judgment), and if defendants paid plaintiffs less than the "total costs" in the remainder of the cases that were settled out of court, then defendants would never bear the full costs of negligent accidents and the system would not become efficient. Posner's theory, in other words, cannot limit itself to the analysis of formal law and appellate decisions on one side but invoke a total costs test on the other. Each is rooted in a different universe.

Further, in the actual operation of the negligence system, the importance of plaintiffs' litigation expenses was enormous. Even if, for the reason Posner gives, those costs could be ignored in the economic analysis of formal judgments, they could not be ignored in the economic analysis of settlements. Even in a wholly "rational" settlement, the litigation expenses that plaintiffs would avoid by settling provide part of the initial basis—in addition to whatever problems affect the merits of a claim—on which parties discount the amount of damages at issue and negotiate settlements. Given the burdens and expenses that the system of corporate diversity litigation imposed on plaintiffs, the discount in the late nineteenth century could be steep. In those common cases, probably the overwhelming majority of all nonlitigated claims, where plaintiffs did not retain an attorney, defendants could make discounts of 30 to 40 percent solely on that ground. Settlement offers invariably contain discounts for such expenses, and they would therefore have been far lower than rational assessments of the merits, by themselves, would have warranted. When plaintiffs—who settled at least 95 percent of their claims out of court—accepted such sharply discounted offers, they enabled defendants to avoid a significant part of the "total costs of the accidents." Thus, regardless of whatever happened in the courts, the informal legal process in the late nineteenth and early twentieth centuries assured defendants that they would not have to pay the total costs of industrial injuries. Again, on Posner's analysis, that result would have prevented the system from reaching an efficient level of safety.[42]

The historical operation of the system of corporate diversity litigation confronts the strictly economic theory with a dilemma. On the one hand, if the reach of the theory is limited to the impact of formal adjudications, it cannot explain the general economic significance of legal rules. The common law directly controlled only a small percentage of tort claims, and the informal legal process drove down the present value of claims sufficiently far below the present value of the costs of the accidents to defeat both the efficiency-allocation and compensation roles of tort law.[43] The theory neither describes the general economic interplay between the costs of accidents and of accident prevention nor attempts to identify the actual conditions under which an efficient level of safety would be reached. Conversely, if broadened to include all potential negligence claims, the theory must assume that out-of-court settlements generally approximated a "rational" discounting based solely on the legal merits of the claims. The argument of this book is that such an assumption is false.[44]

In light of the system of corporate diversity litigation and the informal legal process, then, the logic of Posner's economic theory of late nineteenth-century tort law supports three propositions. First, insofar as damage payments functioned to determine the level of safety, the entire tort law system in the late nineteenth and early twentieth centuries—formal and informal together—made it extremely unlikely that safety levels would even begin to approach efficiency. Second, insofar as the formal rules of tort liability did tend toward efficiency, whatever subsidy or discount the formal law itself granted to industrial enterprise came primarily from the matters that it excluded from its purview. As the formal law expanded the realm of freedom of contract and the informal legal process, in other words, the logic of Posner's economic theory of torts suggests that the law—operating in the context of the late nineteenth and early twentieth centuries—expanded the opportunities for corporations to use their social power, allowed them to extract larger discounts from larger numbers of injured persons, and thereby brought increasingly less efficient results. Illustrating the relationship between social power, the formal law of contract, and subsidies for business enterprise, *Voigt* stands as a paradigmatic example of that process. Throughout the period, in fact, the contract law of releases and waivers may have provided corporations far more economic benefits than did the tort law of negligence. Third, insofar as the courts applied an economic analysis to tort claims, as Posner argues they somehow did,[45] his theory establishes that corporations had compelling economic motives to exert whatever informal social pressures they could in order to minimize the costs of settling tort suits. According to Posner's economic theory, the courts were required to identify the true "costs" of accidents in order to determine whether defendants were negligent. To the extent that corporate defendants maintained a tight lid on settlements or other relief payments and drove those costs of accidents as low as possible, then, they would have been able both to minimize the damages properly due when they were found liable and at the same time—under the classic Learned Hand formula on which Posner relies—to increase their chances of avoiding liability altogether.[46]

Whether and to what extent the substantive rules of the formal law offered subsidies to business is for the most part beyond the scope of this study. It seems likely that they did provide some, particularly in limiting tort liability for employee injuries and in enforcing contracts in which individuals released, waived, or otherwise impaired their claims.[47] Whatever the size of the subsidies furnished directly by substantive rules of law, however, they were dwarfed by the continuous discounts that the law allowed corporations to exact in the informal legal process and the system of corporate diversity litigation.

The System and the Politics of the Federal Courts

Corporate attorneys maintained that they preferred the federal courts to obtain protection against local prejudice and to enjoy the benefits of a uniform national common law. As we have seen, those explanations were at best partial and misleading. The availability of the federal courts gave corporate defendants a number of practical advantages unrelated to either uniform national law or local prejudice.

Another explanation for the preference that corporations showed for the federal courts, offered persistently for more than half a century by populists, progressives, and New Dealers, was that the national judiciary simply favored property rights and shaped the law to protect national corporations. Focusing on the United States Supreme Court, historians and legal scholars tended for much of the twentieth century to accept and reiterate those charges. The "major value" that influenced the Supreme Court from Reconstruction to the New Deal, one distinguished scholar wrote in 1960, was "the protection of the business community against government."[48] The Court's "conservatism" after the 1890s, a widely used textbook in constitutional history declared in 1976, was "concerned primarily with protecting the property rights and vested interests of big business and with the defense of the prevailing economic and social order against agrarian and dissident reformers."[49]

In the past two decades students of the late nineteenth and early twentieth centuries have begun to qualify or reject such views. A number of scholars have come to agree that the courts in general and the Supreme Court in particular were animated to a large extent by traditional American values of liberty and equality, a commitment to the ideas of laissez-faire economics, and a Jacksonian hostility to legally created privilege and discriminatory "class" legislation. In particular, many of those scholars not only deny that judges were motivated by any desire to assist corporations but also maintain that many of them, at least until the end of the nineteenth century, were deeply worried by or even hostile to the growth of corporate enterprise.[50] Some scholars stress the evenhandedness and fairness of the Supreme Court's doctrines at the turn of the century,[51] although others continue to argue that irrespective of the Justices' motives their decisions often served to give property rights special protection and to increase the wealth and power of established interests.[52]

The debate over the political and social values of the Supreme Court is part of a more general reconsideration of late nineteenth- and early twentieth-century American law.[53] The problems raised are complex, and their difficulties are compounded by the seemingly endless variety to be found among different courts, judges, doctrines, and areas of law. Although the system of corporate diversity litigation encompasses only one part of the American legal system, it nevertheless casts some light on the question of whether and to what extent the federal courts, and the Supreme Court in particular, served as favorable forums for corporate interests in the long period from Reconstruction to the creation of the Roosevelt Court.[54]

Most obviously, the history of the system of corporate diversity litigation reveals the limited role that judicial values and legal doctrines of any kind played in the overall process of claims disputing and settlement. Corporations wielded extensive power in the informal legal process, and their ability to move their cases into the federal courts magnified that power. Indeed, that augmentation of the informal social power of national corporations was probably the single most significant practical consequence that resulted from the availability of federal jurisdiction. The operation of the informal legal process, then, shows that the federal courts had a considerable utility for corporate defendants but that much and likely most of that utility arose from sources other than the conscious intent, the informing social values, or the formal common law doctrines of federal judges. The greatest utility of the federal courts probably arose, instead, from social, institutional, and geographical factors wholly unrelated to the views of the judges. Indeed, the major practical significance of the federal common law in the decades around the turn of the century was that by shaping legal rules to conform to the values associated with freedom of contract, it helped expand the already sweeping scope of the informal legal process. Thus, although it is unquestionably true in one sense that the federal courts were favorable forums for corporate litigants, that sense had nothing to do with whether all, some, or no federal judges sought—consciously or unconsciously—to give special protection to corporate interests.

Further, a review of the system of corporate diversity litigation makes it clear that both the general significance of the federal common law and its relative importance as a functional element within the system varied markedly by both time and subject matter. In the 1870s and 1880s the Supreme Court was suspicious of large corporations and often sympathized with those who asserted claims against them. Its attitudes changed only slowly and erratically, and the Court did not announce its most strongly probusiness common law decisions until the turn of the century. *Baugh* and *Coos County* came down in 1893–94, while *Voigt, Lewis, Adams, Patton, Northern Assurance,* and the *Dixon* fellow servant case were all crowded together in the five years from 1900 to 1904. Some of those decisions, moreover, remained vibrant for only a relatively short time. Legislative action in Congress and the states after 1908 severely reduced the impact of *Baugh's* fellow servant rule, and largely on their own the lower federal courts abandoned *Patton* in the 1920s. Those two landmarks of the procorporate federal common law thus reigned for only about two decades each.

In tort actions, then, the federal common law was a major factor only from the mid 1880s to World War I, and it reached its peak of importance in the years between about 1893 and 1908. During those fifteen years it regularly confronted injured workers with fatal obstacles to recovery by giving sweeping defenses to employers and by imposing exacting evidentiary burdens on employees. The rules weighed heavily, too, because during those same years a number of the state courts developed innovative ways to ameliorate the harshness of their own common law rules and thereby widened the divergence between federal and state law. If the federal common law was the most important single element that made the federal courts favorable forums for corporate tort defendants during those fifteen years, however, it was still only one of several factors that contributed to the same result. For, throughout those years, the burdens of distance, delay, and procedural complexity also fell heavily on large numbers of plaintiffs.

In contrast, in insurance actions the federal common law was a major factor for a longer period of time, the entire half century before 1938, and reached its period of greatest relative importance later, in the 1920s and 1930s. Although at no time did the federal common law treat insurance claimants as unfavorably as it did industrial tort plaintiffs around the turn of the century, in the decades after World War I it became the dominant reason why insurance companies regarded the federal courts as desirable forums. In large part its magnified importance was due to the fact that the other elements that burdened plaintiffs in the system were declining steadily as litigation factors. As a consequence, the relative importance of the federal common law within the system inevitably grew. Its increased importance was also due to the fact that the rules governing insurance contracts that were applied in the federal and state courts may well have reached their point of greatest divergence during those same years. By 1930, for example, only two states accepted the restrictive federal parol evidence rule that *Northern Assurance* had established almost three decades earlier. Finally, the importance of the federal common law of insurance contracts enjoyed its peak of influence in the 1920s and 1930s because *Terral,* the extension of federal equity jurisdiction, the adoption of expansive definitions of the amount in controversy, and the introduction of the declaratory judgment device combined to make it applicable in a wider range of cases than it had been previously.

Although the extent to which the federal common law favored corporations thus varied by state, time period, and legal area, in cases dealing with insurance contracts and industrial torts it did come to favor business interests as the Court increasingly expounded and implemented an extreme freedom of contract ideology in common law fields. If the employment relation was the ideology's core area, the Court's insurance decisions from *Coos County* in 1894 to *Landress* in 1934 show that the values of freedom of contract enjoyed a long and influential life in other areas as well.[55] The changes in the late nineteenth century in the federal common law of insurance contracts and industrial torts paralleled the rise of substantive due process in constitutional law, and they demonstrated the breadth of the cultural orientation that underwrote the constitutional doctrine of "liberty of contract." They also suggest that in upholding much reform legislation that did not accord with that orientation the Court did, in a quite meaningful sense, "defer" to the legislature.[56] In spite of numerous necessary qualifications, from the 1890s to the 1930s—and especially in the decades around the turn of the century—the Court was imbued with a distinctive combination of cultural attitudes that included a commitment to the ideal of virile competition, a faith in the relative innocence of private social power, the acceptance of a morality that conceived of rectitude as the fulfillment of formally "bargained" promises, and a belief in the desirability of rationalizing and nationalizing the American economic system. That combination of attitudes and assumptions helped reorient the federal common law, just as it helped reorient constitutional law, and the resulting legal rules made it easier for the wealthy and more sophisticated to take advantage of the poor and less sophisticated.

Beyond those general considerations, an analysis of the system of corporate diversity litigation highlights two periods in which the Supreme Court's procedural decisions seemed strikingly to reflect important, if noticeably different, social orientations. In the first period, from the early 1890s to the end of the decade, the Court methodically and purposely expanded the jurisdiction of the lower courts over diversity actions. In the second period, immediately following the first, the Court abruptly reversed itself and in the first half-dozen years of the twentieth century sharply contracted that jurisdiction. Both periods were revealing.

Before considering the two periods in detail, however, it is important to emphasize that both should be understood in the first instance as parts of the same historical era in American law. The years essentially from the 1880s through World War I constituted the period when the American legal system began seriously and centrally to grapple with the challenges presented by massive industrialization, the rise of bureaucratic national corporations, and the whole complex of socio-economic change that accompanied and followed those developments. The courts, like the rest of the society, were often divided, confused, and uncertain as to how to deal with the changes and, in particular, how to treat the phenomenon of the new national corporation. State corporation law, federal antitrust law, and the developing field of administrative law—perhaps the three legal areas most directly concerned with the problems of regulating corporate behavior—were all in a state of flux throughout those years.[57] Although the Supreme Court in the most general sense protected and fostered national corporations, it also strove to ensure that the law would constrain them. Often, of course, the Court was uncertain as to the specific legal rules that should be applied to their activities. In such a period of change and uncertainty, then, it is not quite so surprising that the Court would, within little more than a single decade, twice reverse the course it had set in construing the jurisdictional rules that molded corporate diversity litigation.

Further, it is also useful to bear in mind the extent to which the Court's efforts in both the 1890s and the years after the turn of the century contrasted with its response in the 1920s and 1930s to the new tactics that developed in the system of corporate diversity litigation. In the latter period the two paramount innovations were methodical interstate forum shopping by plaintiffs and the aggressive use of federal equity by corporations. Although in the 1920s the Taft Court—seeking to restrain the former while encouraging the latter—leaned toward corporations, the Hughes Court in the 1930s appeared more neutral and, in fact, showed a particular sensitivity to the problems that federal equity presented to insurance claimants. In spite of the Court's different leanings in the two decades, however, the fact remains that under both Taft and Hughes its efforts were relatively discrete, small scale, and balanced. The idea of commerce clause venue, intended to restrict interstate forum shopping, was probably the most striking doctrinal innovation, yet the Court applied it sparingly and narrowly in the 1920s and then in effect abandoned it in the 1930s. Similarly, the Court struggled throughout the 1930s to find a workable balance that would give a reasonable scope to federal equity while preventing corporate litigants from using it for extraneous tactical purposes. In contrast, during both the 1890s and the years after the turn of the century the Court acted with greater breadth and more consistent purpose, and the coherent but contradictory patterns of its decisions in the two periods seemed to reflect more directly the acutely felt pressures of much broader and more immediate social and political considerations.

Politics and the System: The Court's First Reversal

In the first of the two critical periods, from about 1892 to the end of the decade, the Court's treatment of procedural–jurisdictional issues in the system revealed a wide and purposeful effort to protect and enlarge corporate removal rights. Its decisions swerved sharply from the approach it had taken in the years immediately following passage of the Judiciary Act of 1887–88. Recognizing and giving broad effect to the act's unquestioned purpose to limit federal jurisdiction, the Court from 1888 to the early 1890s repeatedly construed its provisions narrowly and invoked its purpose as a controlling guide when its language was ambiguous.[58] In 1890 both *Austin* and *Pennsylvania* followed that practice, allowing the delayed upward amendment tactic to stand and restricting removals under the local prejudice act. In that year the Court may have been unaware of the litigation significance of removal, or it may have considered the practical consequences of the jurisdiction to be of little importance, or it may even have seen no doctrinal basis for establishing any different rules. Whatever the explanation, within just a few years the Court came to recognize the litigation significance of removal, manifested a persistent concern with its scope, and found a variety of ways to expand it.

Austin the Court in effect overruled. Only eight years after it came down, *Powers* terminated the delayed upward amendment tactic by holding that the right to remove extended to a previously nonremovable case that became removable by virtue of some voluntary act of plaintiff. No longer seeing the possible "want of comprehensiveness" that *Austin* had noted in the removal statute, the Court concluded simply and quite accurately that any different construction of the statute "would utterly defeat all right of removal in many cases."[59]

Pennsylvania fared somewhat better. For more than a dozen years the Court merely ignored it. Although the decision—together with the Court's other opinions construing the Judiciary Act of 1887–88—seemed rather obviously to require complete diversity in removals under the local prejudice clause, after 1892 the Court suddenly began to portray that issue as being exceedingly difficult. It first avoided it and then in *Hanrick* in 1894 expressly declared it open and unsettled.

The result was to invite the lower courts to apply the increasingly accepted *Whelan–Thouron* minimum diversity rule that promised to broaden corporate removal rights. Indeed, when the Court finally held in 1905 that removal for local prejudice required complete diversity, every reason that it gave for its decision had been available and supported by authority for at least a decade. Principally, the Court revived and relied on *Pennsylvania*.

The same pattern appeared in the Court's treatment of joinders under the separable controversy act. Its decisions from the 1880s set out the principles on which it relied after 1900 when it narrowed removal rights under the act, and in *Dixon* and *Thompson* the Court insisted that those earlier decisions resolved the employee joinder question. If true, however, the Court failed in the 1890s to enforce those principles. Employee joinders had been in widespread use for well over a decade before the Court agreed to hear an appeal presenting the issue, and in its first two decisions on the question in 1898 and 1900 it temporized. In the face of *Warax* and widespread opposition to the joinder tactic in the lower courts, the Court refused to lay down a clear and specific rule and, though it seemed to regard *Warax* as dubious, refused to repudiate its expansive jurisdictional theory. By its refusal to act and then by its equivocation, the Court allowed the lower courts wide freedom in construing the separable controversy act and tolerated their frequent assertions of removal jurisdiction over actions raising claims that plaintiffs had pleaded as joint.

Similarly, the Court's venue decisions in the 1890s reflected the same pattern of expanding corporate removal rights. *Shaw* and *Davidson* made the federal courts available to corporations sued in states where neither party was a citizen. Not only did the two decisions allow corporate defendants to remove such suits to the local federal courts, but they also denied to plaintiffs the right to initiate their actions in those same courts. If the relevant language in the Judiciary Act of 1887–88 was ambiguous, it was nevertheless susceptible to a construction that would at least have given defendants and plaintiffs equal access to the national courts.[60]

The pattern was clear: In the early 1890s the Court suddenly stopped using the Judiciary Act of 1887–88 to restrict removal jurisdiction in diversity actions, and throughout the remainder of the decade it turned to the opposite course. It directly expanded removal jurisdiction in some areas and indirectly encouraged the lower courts to do so in others. For the most part, in fact, the Court achieved its results obliquely. It repeatedly failed to rule squarely on critical issues that affected the system and thereby allowed the lower judiciary to grant removals relatively freely. It refused to discuss or even refer to the practical problems that the procedural–jurisdictional questions raised, and in *Powers* it went out of its way to pretend that its repudiation of *Austin* was based on nothing but the possibility of innocent pleading mistakes. Indeed, the Court's techniques in the 1890s—largely delay, avoidance, and equivocation—support two separate propositions: that it knew exactly what it was doing and that, with the exception of its forthright decision to terminate the delayed upward amendment tactic, it recognized the dubious nature of its enterprise. Whatever the broader social values that inspired the Court at other times and in other areas, from the early 1890s to the end of the decade its procedural–jurisdictional decisions in the system of corporate diversity litigation were purposely and consistently, if somewhat surreptitiously, designed to protect the litigation interests of national corporations.

The Court's contemporaneous treatment of removal jurisdiction over federal questions highlights the extraordinary nature of its expansive decisions in diversity actions. In 1875 Congress for the first time conferred on the national courts general jurisdiction over cases presenting "federal questions"—issues that arose under the Constitution and laws of the United States. Federal question jurisdiction thus became the second of the two principal categories of jurisdiction that the national courts exercised. Between 1875 and 1887 actions presenting issues of federal law, regardless of which party raised them, could be maintained in the federal courts under the new federal question jurisdiction. In the absence of a federal law issue in the plaintiff's pleadings, the defendant could nevertheless remove on federal question grounds if she asserted a right, claim, or defense that arose under federal law.[61]

The Judiciary Act of 1887–88 limited removals to cases over which the lower courts were given "original" jurisdiction. Although it seems unlikely that Congress intended to restrict federal question removal,[62] the statutory change raised the question whether the term "original" meant that federal jurisdiction was limited only to cases that could be removed on the "original" pleadings, that is, on the plaintiff's statement of her cause of action. Could defendants still remove, in other words, if they were the ones who raised the federal question?

Initially, the Court answered the question in the affirmative. It construed the new statute to allow removal, absent a federal claim by plaintiff, on the basis of federal rights or defenses that defendant raised. It held that the original jurisdiction requirement referred only to cases that plaintiffs initiated in the federal courts, not to removals. In original cases so defined, then, jurisdiction existed only if plaintiffs themselves raised federal law issues. At the same time, however, because a removed action was not an original action, removal jurisdiction based on the presence of a federal question remained proper when the federal law issue was raised for the first time in defendant's responsive pleading.[63] For six years the Court retained that construction of the act.[64]

In 1894 it suddenly changed course.[65] In *Tennessee v. Union and Planters' Bank* the Court held that the judiciary act, by restricting federal question jurisdiction to cases over which the national courts had original jurisdiction, limited removals to cases in which the plaintiff and the plaintiff alone raised the federal law issue.[66] Regardless of the federal rights or defenses that defendants might claim, in other words, they could not remove unless the plaintiff had originally pleaded a federal law issue.

In the context of the Court's contemporaneous diversity decisions, *Union and Planters' Bank* was particularly revealing. First, although the Court's construction of the judiciary act was plausible, a more expansive construction was at least as reasonable—as the Court's earlier decisions held, as both Justices John M. Harlan and Stephen J. Field maintained in dissent, and as the legislative history of the Judiciary Act of 1887–88 seemed to indicate.[67] The statutory language hardly compelled the Court to restrict federal question jurisdiction to issues that appeared on the face of plaintiff's complaint. Second, by choosing to limit federal question removal to cases in which plaintiffs raised the federal law issues, the Justices chose to restrict the jurisdiction of the national courts. "Of course," Judge John F. Dillon's treatise on removal declared in 1898, "the effect of this rule is very greatly to narrow the jurisdiction of the federal courts in this class of cases."[68]

Third, the decision favored plaintiffs over defendants. If the former had federal claims, they were guaranteed the right to bring them before a federal court. But if the latter had federal rights or defenses, they enjoyed no such guarantee. The Court's decision denied defendants the equal opportunity to have their federal rights determined by a federal forum. Finally, in large part the Court based its restrictive interpretation on the general purpose of the Judiciary Act of 1887–88. The construction it adopted in *Union and Planters' Bank,* the Court explained, "is in accordance with the general policy of these [1887–88] acts, manifest upon their face, and often recognized by this court, to contract the jurisdiction of the Circuit Courts of the United States." For that guiding interpretative proposition it cited five of its recent cases, including *Pennsylvania.*[69]

The decision in *Union and Planters' Bank,* and the fact that the Court applied its restrictive rule regularly and often throughout the rest of the decade,[70] underscored the fact that the Court's expansion of diversity removal jurisdiction in the 1890s was both substantial and exceptional. In contrast, when dealing with federal question removals, the Court continued to use the language and guidelines of the Judiciary Act of 1887–88 to constrict the jurisdiction of the national courts. In doing so, too, it even cited as authority for its course *Pennsylvania* and other precedents from the late 1880s and early 1890s that restricted diversity removals—the very precedents that the Court refused to follow in dealing with diversity removals themselves. Further, in federal question cases it showed no particular concern for defendants and their rights, even though the defendants were asserting specifically federal rights. In his dissent in *Union and Planters' Bank* Harlan challenged the Court's conclusion that Congress had intended to deny defendants the same right that plaintiffs enjoyed to have specifically federal rights adjudicated in federal forums. "What possible reason could there have been?" he demanded.[71] Indeed, the construction of the judiciary act that *Union and Planters' Bank* adopted—that removals were strictly limited to cases over which the lower courts had original jurisdiction—was inconsistent with the *Whelan–Thouron* minimum diversity rule which expanded diversity removal jurisdiction under the local prejudice act. Given the reasoning in *Union and Planters' Bank,* the Court's de facto acceptance of the *Whelan–Thouron* rule in *Hanrick* the very same year—where it termed the minimum diversity issue unsettled—seemed indefensible on doctrinal grounds.

Although the Court's restriction of federal question removal in 1894 highlights the unusually expansive treatment that it gave to diversity removal, a striking twist the Court adopted in one area of federal question removal confirmed from another vantage point the specific social purpose that guided its procedural–jurisdictional decisions in the 1890s—providing federal forums for corporate tort defendants. The special doctrinal twist pertained to jurisdiction over cases involving corporate receivers appointed by federal equity courts. Although at common law a receiver could not be sued without permission of the court that appointed him, Section 3 of the Judiciary Act of 1887–88 abolished that rule.[72] In practical terms, Section 3 meant that tort plaintiffs who were forced to sue corporate receivers were no longer required to seek relief in the federal courts that had appointed the receivers. Instead, plaintiffs could sue them in the state courts. At the same time that Congress passed the judiciary act, the use of federal equity receiverships was becoming increasingly common and important in reorganizing weak and failing companies. Two hundred railroad companies were in federal receivership during the 1880s, and between 1891 and 1897 almost 350 more went through the same process.[73] The growth in receiverships inevitably meant that increasing numbers of tort plaintiffs were forced to sue receivers for their injuries. Because in diversity actions a corporate receiver's citizenship was determinative for purposes of jurisdiction,[74] the standard joinder tactic could prevent out-of-state receivers—just as it did foreign corporations themselves—from removing.

In 1892, as the use of federal equity receiverships swelled in importance, the Supreme Court held in *Texas and Pacific Railway Co. v. Cox* that a suit against a receiver appointed by a United States court was, by virtue of the receiver's federal appointment, a suit arising under the Constitution and laws of the United States. It was therefore cognizable in and removable to the federal courts on that basis.[75] *Cox* thus obviated the lack of diversity jurisdiction that resulted from a successful joinder by finding an alternative ground of federal jurisdiction, the presence of a federal question. In a series of decisions in the later 1890s the Supreme Court touched on but refused to disapprove the *Cox* doctrine and its use as a device to expand corporate removal rights.[76]

The *Cox* rule, however, soon confronted a serious doctrinal problem. Two years later *Union and Planters' Bank* restricted federal question removal by holding that a federal question sufficient to support a removal had to appear on the face of plaintiff's complaint. How, then, could a federally appointed receiver remove on the basis of a federal question if the plaintiff merely pleaded the elements of a common law tort action?

In establishing its plaintiff's pleading rule *Union and Planters' Bank* took care to answer that question and expressly to preserve the *Cox* rule. The Court explained that *Cox* relied on the fact that the judiciary act made special provisions for corporate receivers and gave them the legal capacity to sue and be sued. *Cox* thus meant that when suing federally appointed receivers plaintiffs had to plead, explicitly or by implication of law, the basis of defendants' capacity to be sued. In such cases plaintiffs necessarily pleaded a federal question on the face of their complaints.[77] Thus, *Union and Planters' Bank* not only restricted general federal question removal, but it also expressly carved out one special exception. Though involving a different jurisdictional basis than did the Court's contemporaneous decisions expanding diversity jurisdiction, the *Cox–Union and Planters' Bank* rule under federal question jurisdiction was consistent with the social orientation and purpose of the Court's diversity cases.

In spite of *Union and Planters' Bank*, however, *Cox* still remained dubious. Although the Court's reasoning in the two cases received some support from decisions that had announced that any federal "ingredient" in a cause of action was sufficient to support federal question jurisdiction,[78] the reasoning nevertheless seemed inconsistent with other decisions in which the Court declared that background or inconsequential federal elements were not sufficient to support jurisdiction. "A cause cannot be removed from a State court simply because, in the progress of the litigation, it may become necessary to give a construction to the Constitution or laws of the United States," the Court had stated in 1877 in its first decision construing the federal question provision of the Judiciary Act of 1875. "The decision of the case must depend upon that construction."[79] Similarly, three years after *Union and Planters' Bank* the Court held that a federal law issue did not support jurisdiction unless it presented "a real substantive question, on which the case may be made to turn."[80] In the equity receivership cases, regardless of whether plaintiff was formally required to plead the receiver's federal appointment, a standard tort claim seldom if ever raised any disputed question about the fact or significance of the federal appointment itself. Because the federal question that allowed jurisdiction in receivership cases was one that would not normally even be in dispute, *Cox* rested on a sweeping and particularly doubtful conception of a federal question. At bottom it simply reflected the Court's solicitude for receivers facing common law tort actions.[81]

In *Cox* the Court stretched to create a federal question sufficient to allow jurisdiction, and in *Union and Planters' Bank* it stretched a second time to pull the federal question that *Cox* created within the scope of the plaintiff's pleading rule. Together the two decisions allowed the Court to restrict general federal question removal while at the same time opening to corporate receivers seeking removal in common law actions their own special door into the federal courts. Indeed, the principal reason for the Court's abrupt decision to establish the plaintiff's pleading rule was most likely the belief that cutting federal question removal was a necessary trade-off to balance the swollen caseload that would result from the Court's contemporaneous decisions that expanded the opportunities of corporate tort defendants to remove diversity suits.[82]

Following *Cox* and *Union and Planters' Bank,* corporate tort defendants in receivership utilized their newly broadened removal rights. The lower courts upheld removals by federally appointed receivers in tort suits even in the absence of diversity of citizenship[83] and effectively negated the joinder tactic.[84] Further, the rationale of *Cox,* and perhaps the general signals that the Court was sending, inspired a few lower courts to stretch even further and to rule that federal receivers could remove tort actions that were "ancillary" to a receivership even though neither diversity of citizenship nor the jurisdictional amount was present.[85] At its broadest, then, *Cox* allowed tort defendants in receivership not only to negate the joinder tactic but to defeat claims discounting as well.

While *Union and Planters' Bank* illustrated the Court's relative lack of concern for defendants who asserted federal rights as well as a preference for diversity removal over federal question removal, *Cox* confirmed that the Court was purposely opening the federal courts to certain classes of defendants and identified the type of defendants that it intended to benefit. The receivership decisions tracked the familiar pattern that marked the Court's treatment of venue, the jurisdictional amount, the doctrine of corporate citizenship, and joinders under both the separable controversy and local prejudice acts. The common element was unmistakable: In each area the Court methodically and uniformly shaped its procedural–jurisdictional rules governing removal to strengthen the litigation position of corporations defending against common law tort actions.[86]

The Court's determination in the 1890s to expand the availability of removal to corporate tort defendants clearly reflected the presence of powerful social concerns among the Justices. The abrupt reversal of their earlier jurisdictionally restrictive course, the extent to which the decisions swerved from prior doctrine, the relatively oblique doctrinal methods that the Court employed, the concentration of so many related decisions within only a few years, and the consistency of the decisions in terms of their practical results all pointed to the controlling influence of pressing but unarticulated social concerns. After the 1880s, when the economy had boomed and Congress and the Court had joined to put aside Recon-struction and to narrow the jurisdiction of the lower courts, the political and social world began to grow increasingly ominous. The 1890s introduced a decade of turmoil marked by intensified labor unrest, sharpened class and ethnic hostilities, the rise of a seemingly radical populist political movement, and the most severe depression in the nation's history. In the federal courts the onset of the decade coincided with the influx of rapidly growing numbers of bitterly contested lawsuits—the result of escalating social militance rather than mounting industrial injuries[87]—brought overwhelmingly by members of an increasingly immigrant-based working class and marked by the rampant use of overt antiremoval tactics. After a half-dozen years spent limiting the jurisdiction of the federal courts in response to growing caseloads and the Judiciary Act of 1887–88, the Court sud-denly called a halt. Unnerved and undecided, it responded to the pressures of the 1890s by giving the lower courts broad leeway to counter the antiremoval tactics and to protect the removal rights of foreign corporations whenever they thought it necessary.[88]

Politics and the System: The Court's Second Reversal

Although the Court's jurisdictional decisions from 1892 to the end of the decade were striking in the extent to which they assisted corporate defendants, its compa-rable decisions in the half-dozen years after the turn of the century were equally striking in the contrary, proplaintiff results they brought. Indeed, as the new century dawned the Supreme Court again executed an about-face. In 1900 *Dixon,* although allowing *Warax* to stand, strengthened the joinder tactic and encouraged its use, and *Cable* three years later refused to allow a further expansion of removal jurisdiction. Then, in barely more than a year, between November 1905 and December 1906, the Court handed down four decisions—*Cochran, Wisner, Thompson,* and *Prewitt*—that drastically restricted the right of corporate defen-dants to remove.

   As it had in the 1890s, the Court's treatment of removal in the receivership context again confirmed the prevailing pattern.[89] In December 1900 it held in *Gableman v. Peoria, Decatur and Evansville Railway Co.*[90] that the "bare fact" that a federal court had appointed a receiver did not transform "all actions" brought against the receiver into cases arising under federal law. Consequently, in tort suits against corporate receivers, federal question jurisdiction was no longer regularly available as an alternative ground for removal. In *Gableman* itself, since diversity was the only other possible ground of federal jurisdiction, the plaintiff's joinder of a resident locomotive engineer with the out-of-state receiver was suffi-cient to defeat removal.[91] Although the Court attempted to claim—quite unper-suasively, not to say disingenuously—that its ruling was consistent with its previ-ous decisions in the 1890s, it acknowledged that *Gableman* "modified" certain "expressions" in three of its earlier decisions, including *Cox.*[92] After *Gableman,* federal question jurisdiction no longer served federal receivers as a method of defeating the joinder tactic.

   If the Court's expansion of corporate removal rights in the 1890s seemed a relatively direct response to the decade's bitter social conflicts, its general contrac-tion of those rights after the turn of the century was the result of more diverse and complicated considerations. Unlike the tactics it used in the 1890s, too, after 1900 the Court ruled squarely on the questions that removal raised and announced clear and broad rules. In the first decade of the twentieth century three kinds of general considerations moved the Court toward its second reversal. Technical concerns, relatively specific political and social considerations, and a fundamental constitutional–institutional reorientation all combined to switch the Court onto its new course.

On the technical and institutional level, several factors contributed to the about-face. First, the haunting and persistent tug of doctrine undoubtedly helped nudge the Court back to the approach it had taken in the years before the turmoil of the 1890s took hold. Several of its restrictive rulings from 1900 to 1906 were clearly rooted in the Court's prior precedents. *Gableman* and *Cochran,* at least, seemed to be overdue applications of traditional doctrine and the restrictive mandate of the Judiciary Act of 1887–88. The Court itself seemed to admit indirectly that the rules laid down in *Cochran* and perhaps *Wisner,* for example, should have been recognized a decade earlier. "The rule is now settled," it declared in 1905 in *Madisonville Traction Co. v. Saint Bernard Mining Co.,* "that, under the judiciary act of 1887, 1888, a suit cannot be removed from a state court, unless it could have been brought originally in the Circuit Court of the United States."[93] As authority for that "settled" proposition—which logically required the decision in *Cochran* and at least arguably in *Wisner*—the Court relied on four of its earlier decisions, all of which had been handed down between 1888 and 1895.

Second, by the turn of the century the Justices must have recognized both an institutional need to bring order and uniformity to the rulings of the lower courts and a professional and intellectual need to clarify basic federal jurisdictional doctrines. The combination of the social pressures of the 1890s, the widespread use of antiremoval tactics, and the Court's decade-long failure to resolve critical procedural issues had given new meaning to the phrase *diversity* jurisdiction. On joinder decisions in particular the lower federal courts were widely and even scandalously split. *Gableman, Cochran,* and *Thompson* seemed designed to put the major joinder issues to a final rest. The holdings in the first two were simple and straightforward, and *Thompson's* language concerning "misconceived" pleadings seemed an overstatement inspired by the desire to settle the issue sweepingly and definitively.

Third, pressures from the growing federal caseload pushed the Justices to find ways to control the swelling dockets, and restrictions on jurisdiction seemed an obvious and effective solution. Starting around 1903, in fact, the federal caseload began to rise. The number of actions filed jumped from 12,406 in 1903 to 15,986 in 1906, an increase of almost 30 percent. In the Court's decisions during the years immediately following the Judiciary Act of 1887–88, there was precedent for a jurisdictionally restrictive response to the problem of growing dockets.[94] Moreover, after the turn of the century the Court showed a strong interest in trimming the federal caseload by adopting narrow jurisdictional rules in diversity actions. In 1900 and again in 1904 it limited the availability of diversity jurisdiction in suits involving partnerships;[95] in 1907 it seemed to limit the removal rights of corporations consolidated in two or more states;[96] and in 1910 it construed the venue statutes to deny a federal forum to diversity plaintiffs who also pleaded federal claims.[97]

It seems likely, too, that special factors led the Court to its relatively early decision in *Gableman* in 1900. First, in 1898 Congress filled a twenty-year void by enacting a new national bankruptcy statute. The absence of such a law since 1878 had been a major factor in magnifying the importance of the federal equity receivership in the 1880s and 1890s. It seems likely that in 1900 the Justices assumed that the new bankruptcy provisions would largely supersede the equity receivership, that the latter would no longer affect a significant part of the economy, and, therefore, that their ruling in *Gableman* would influence only an inconsequential number of future tort actions. Second, the return of prosperity at the decade's end meant that fewer railroads, and fewer large ones, were in receivership. During the year from July 1, 1899, to June 30, 1900, for example, only sixteen railroads were added, whereas thirty-five were removed from receiverships. Further, as of June 30, 1900, only fifty-two roads remained in receivership, and they represented a total of only about four thousand miles of track, less than 3 percent of the nation's total.[98] By December 1900 the Justices most likely regarded the *Cox* rule as no longer significant for their earlier purposes.

Although such technical and institutional concerns were important factors in leading the Court to alter its course from the 1890s, they seem insufficient by themselves to explain the nature and scope of the Court's dramatic reversal. Neither the promptings of established doctrine nor the institutional need for consistent jurisdictional rules had, after all, been sufficient to induce the Court to act differently in the previous decade. Moreover, the need for doctrinal clarity and institutional consistency did not determine the nature and scope of the jurisdiction that the clear rules would establish. Rules that either broadened jurisdiction or restricted it less sharply would have satisfied those needs as easily as would have rules that narrowed it severely. Further, in its decisions in 1905–6 the Court not only limited federal jurisdiction but did so more sweepingly than its prior doctrine seemed to require. In stating that a "misconceived" pleading of a joint cause of action was sufficient to avoid removal under the separable controversy act, *Thompson* went well beyond the compulsion of the Court's precedents from the 1880s. *Prewitt,* moreover, represented a surprising break from previous doctrine, limiting or rejecting fundamental principles that had seemed established since the late 1880s.

Similarly, the pressures of a growing caseload also seem insufficient to explain the Court's about-face. The size of the federal caseload, after all, had been a perennial concern at least since the beginning of the 1880s.[99] The Judiciary Act of 1887–88 and the Court's subsequent restrictive decisions from 1888 to the early 1890s had failed to stop the growth, and the backlog continued to build until 1896 when the depression finally cut new filings. The number of pending federal civil cases then declined somewhat before again beginning to rise around 1904. By 1906, however, the total pending federal caseload was still some five thousand cases below the peak reached in the mid-1890s.[100] Thus, while the Court was surely concerned with docket problems, it seems unlikely that it regarded them as startling or grave enough to induce it to make major—and otherwise undesirable—alterations in federal jurisdiction.[101] In addition, almost all the increase in filings and pending cases came after 1903, too late to be a significant factor in the Court's earlier decisions in *Dixon, Gableman,* and *Cable.*[102] Unlike the situation at the end of the 1880s, too, Congress had not just enacted a more restrictive judiciary act that provided a new legislative mandate for the Court to cut jurisdiction. Finally, as *Doctor v. Harrington* and other contemporaneous decisions showed, the Court did not cut diversity jurisdiction in all areas.[103] Limitations on jurisdiction, like expansions, seemed to depend in some substantial part on who and what was being affected.[104]

Most compelling, however, the Court's reversal after 1900 was simply too broad, too abrupt, and too stark in its social and legal implications to be the result of technical concerns alone. The system's removal battles were bitterly contested and notorious, and neither a perennial desire to limit federal jurisdiction nor the logical and institutional demands of doctrine had determined the Court's decisions in the previous decade. The fact that the Court had methodically expanded diversity removal jurisdiction in the 1890s, in fact, made it clear that the Justices recognized the jurisdiction's social significance full well. Thus, when they embarked on their restrictive jurisdictional course after the turn of the century, the Justices necessarily recognized and accepted the practical anticorporate consequences that would result. They knew that plaintiffs would frequently and commonly deprive corporate defendants of their right to remove, that they would exploit whatever procedural advantages were available to them in the state courts, and that they would avoid and thereby in effect negate the substantive doctrines of the federal common law. They knew, too, that plaintiffs would also gain the benefit of whatever anticorporate local prejudice might influence the state courts.

Moreover, two of the Court's decisions in 1905–6, *Thompson* and *Prewitt,* established rules that were both doctrinally innovative and extremely favorable to plaintiffs. Both were also bound to affect large numbers of actions and enable plaintiffs to block removal in most tort actions against national corporations and perhaps half of the actions that policyholders would bring against insurers. Even more remarkable, both in effect withdrew from the federal courts the power to control the scope of their own jurisdiction. On a broad reading, *Thompson* placed the ability to defeat removal by pleading a joint cause of action solely in the hands of plaintiffs, and on a narrower reading it placed that ability—via *Bohon* and its progeny—in the hands of state courts or legislatures. *Prewitt* conferred on state legislatures the power to impose drastic de facto limits on the removal rights of foreign corporations, especially insurance companies. It seems extremely unlikely, then, that the Justices would have reversed themselves after 1900 in the way they did and to the extent they did if some broader consensus beyond issues of doctrinal logic and docket cutting had not helped unite and persuade them.

One fact, too, was undeniable. Whatever the nature of the new consensus in favor of restricting diversity jurisdiction, it enjoyed the full support of those "conservative" Justices who were most firmly committed to the freedom of contract values that the Court was enshrining in the federal common law. Indeed, the Court's restrictive jurisdictional decisions from 1900 to 1906 were contemporaneous with the Court's harshest common law rulings. *Voigt* came down in 1900, *Patton* in 1901, *Lewis* and *Northern Assurance* in 1902, and *Adams* and the *Dixon* fellow servant case in 1904. The Justices who voted with the majority in those federal common law cases stood equally with the majority in all of the restrictive jurisdictional cases. We have already seen that the Justices who supported *Baugh's* fellow servant rule were with the majority in *Dixon* and *Thompson* and that five of the six Justices who constituted the majority in the *Dixon* joinder case were consistent supporters of the federal fellow servant rule.[105] Those same allegedly "conservative" Justices—who were with the majorities in *Voigt, Patton, Lewis, Adams, Northern Assurance,* and the *Dixon* fellow servant case—also supported the Court's other restrictive jurisdictional decisions in *Gableman, Cable, Wisner, Cochran,* and *Prewitt.*[106]

The alignment of the Justices demonstrates that the Court's restrictive decisions cannot be explained as a result of "progressive" judges overcoming "conservative" or "procorporate" judges. Instead, the voting pattern raises a central question. Why did the Justices who seemed to favor corporations in their substantive common law decisions agree to a series of procedural decisions that greatly disadvantaged corporate litigants? Two relatively easy answers help explain their behavior. First, the Justices were not "procorporate" in any purposeful and direct way. They did not, that is, simply vote in favor of corporate parties or interests. Second, the substantive and procedural cases presented technically unrelated doctrinal issues, and there was no logical conflict between their decisions in the two areas. While those two observations are relevant, as answers to the question they are also insufficient. Given the widely recognized importance of removal to corporate litigants, the basic values and attitudes of the Justices who shaped the federal common law, and the Court's successive reversals in the 1890s and then again after 1900, both explanations seem facile and, at a minimum, incomplete.

Somewhat differently phrased, the hard questions remain. Why did Justices who apparently feared the dangers of local prejudice and saw diversity jurisdiction as a device to protect nonresidents suddenly decide to bar large numbers of those nonresidents from the national courts and abandon them to their fates in the state courts? Why did Justices who believed that their common law decisions laid down desirable legal rules and represented wise public policy stretch to sanction obvious antiremoval devices that would enable plaintiffs regularly and often to avoid application of those very substantive rules? How, more particularly, did the Justices who subscribed to the warning in *Northern Assurance* against the dangerous statutory revisions of the parol evidence rule that had been enacted "in most, if not all, of the States" find their way four years later to approve the ruling in *Prewitt* that in effect gave the states substantial power to control corporate access to the federal courts, deprived insurance companies in half the states of their right to remove, and consigned those companies to the rule of those same dangerous statutory revisions? The answer, in critical part, must be that the Justices as a group—and especially the majority "conservative" Justices—became convinced that there were fundamental policy reasons that necessitated sharp judicial limitations on the right to remove diversity actions.

The origin of such a consensus seems to lie, in the first instance, in the profoundly altered social context that marked the years after the 1890s. The depression ended, and the country entered a period of spreading prosperity. In particular, the half-dozen years after the turn of the century were highly prosperous for American railroads, and they gave rise to a confident optimism about the industry's strength.[107] The same years also witnessed the culmination of the so-called great merger movement. When it came to a close in 1904, almost two thousand firms had disappeared into large national corporations—seventy-two of which controlled at least 40 percent of their industries.[108] Both their new prosperity and their suddenly magnified size must have made corporations seem less vulnerable than they had seemed only a few years before and less in need of the special protection that the federal courts provided.[109] Similarly, the social and ethnic hostilities that had flared in the 1890s seemed to ease after the turn of the century, and Americans began talking of cooperation and progress. The fear of local prejudice must also have receded and seemed a less compelling reason to expand federal jurisdiction than it had in the 1890s.

The political context was equally transformed. On the city, state, and national levels American politics began to revolve around the growing and overlapping social reform movements that coalesced under the label of progressivism. Symbolized and dramatized in national politics by Theodore Roosevelt after he ascended to the presidency in 1901, progressivism surged across the nation, seeming to embody a renewed optimism about the future and a new confidence in the powers of both social sympathy and organized expertise to improve government, the economy, and social life in general.[110] Specifically, two distinct aspects of progressivism seemed salient to the Court's determination to restrict federal diversity jurisdiction. Progressivism spurred both a narrow movement within the legal profession to reform the courts and a broad attack in the political arena on the social biases of the Supreme Court. Both, in quite different ways, probably helped nourish the Supreme Court's new consensus.

The movement for professional procedural reform began to coalesce in the years after 1900, inspired in part by a growing concern over the numbers and conduct of personal injury actions brought against corporations. Some of that concern, too, was directed toward abuses in the system of corporate diversity litigation. In 1906, the year that *Wisner, Thompson,* and *Prewitt* came down, Roscoe Pound, then a relatively unknown law professor, addressed the annual meeting of the American Bar Association on "The Causes of Popular Dissatisfaction with the Administration of Justice."[111] Outlining a variety of weaknesses in the legal system, ranging from the general and perennial to the narrow and specific, Pound focused much of his criticism on what he termed the nation's "sporting theory of justice." American law had gone too far, he maintained, in accepting the idea that procedural rules were properly considered weapons of partisan maneuvering rather than rational methods for efficiently bringing the merits of an action before a court.

In stressing the need for efficiency in the courts, Pound saved some of his most critical comments for diversity jurisdiction and, in particular, for the battle over removal. "Even more archaic," he charged, "is our system of concurrent jurisdiction of state and federal courts in causes involving diversity of citizenship." The arrangement meant that "causes continually hang in the air between two courts" or that judgments were "liable to an ultimate overturning because they stuck in the wrong court." A study of decisions in diversity cases, he reported, showed that "in nineteen and three-tenths percent of the reported decisions of the circuit courts the question was whether those courts had jurisdiction."[112] Motions to remand, constituting more than 8 percent of the total, represented the largest single category of jurisdictional disputes. The law, Pound concluded bluntly, should not allow the "bandying of cases from one court to another on orders of removal and of remand."[113] The problem that struck him as most indefensible, in other words, was the extent to which the law allowed parties to litigate the issue of removal, the pivotal battleground in the system of corporate diversity litigation.

Although Pound's address provoked opposition as well as praise from the bar,[114] supporting words came from William Howard Taft, whose own changing views illustrated the gulf that separated the 1890s from the first decade of the twentieth century. The author of *Warax,* who had hoped in 1894 that more of the Pullman strikers would be shot, insisted in 1908 that true conservatives as well as progressives should strive "to remove real and just grounds for criticism in our present system."[115] Although he stressed the benevolence and rectitude of the courts, he noted that they were also slow, costly, and inefficient. Reform was necessary to preserve the judicial system from "popular condemnation" and to eliminate "the unequal burden which the delays and expenses of litigation under our system impose on the poor litigant."[116] Taft, in fact, acknowledged the power-ful role of the informal legal process. "The wealthy defendant," he declared, "can almost always secure a compromise or yielding of lawful rights because of the necessities of the poor plaintiff."[117]

Taft, like Pound, focused on problems created by diversity jurisdiction, espe-cially by "suits for damages for injuries to employees and passengers" and other third parties. "These are the cases which create most irritation against the courts among the poor," he acknowledged. "This is particularly true in such cases in the Federal courts."[118] Then, in an arresting passage, Taft spelled out his detailed and first-hand awareness of the existence and operation of the system of corporate diversity litigation:

> No one can have sat upon the Federal bench as I did for eight or nine years and not realize how defective the administration of justice in these cases must have seemed to the defeated plaintiff, whether he was the legless or armless employe himself or his personal representative. A non-resident railway corporation had removed the case which had been brought in the local court of the county in which the injured employe lived, to the Federal court, held, it may be, at a town forty or one hundred miles away. To this place at great expense the plaintiff was obliged to carry his witnesses. The case came on for trial, the evidence was produced and under the strict Federal rule as to contributory negligence or as to non-liability for the negli-gence of fellow servants, the judge was obliged to direct the jury to return a verdict for the defendant. Then the plaintiff's lawyer had to explain to him that if he had been able to remain in the State court, a different rule of liability of the company would have obtained, and he would have recovered a verdict. How could a litigant thus defeated, after incurring the heavy expenses incident to litigation in the Fed-eral court, with nothing to show for it, have any other feeling than that the Federal courts were instruments of injustice and not justice, and that they were organized to defend corporations and not to help the poor to their rights?[119]

The passage offered a vivid picture of the system of corporate diversity litigation and a candid acknowledgment of the way that legal and social conditions com-bined to transform removal into a tool of corporate litigation. It also confirmed, of course, that Taft knew quite well what he was doing in the 1890s when he crafted his opinion in *Warax.*

Taft's comments, of course, could be discounted. He made them in a speech given in August 1908 while he was running for President of the United States and, moreover, campaigning as the heir apparent of the charismatic and progressive Theodore Roosevelt. There were strong practical reasons why Taft would express sympathy for the plight of those who had been injured in industrial accidents and had found the law unresponsive. Moreover, the speech came after passage of the FELA when some of the evils he mentioned had at least been moderated. The speech, too, was a call for only mild reform, and Taft placed his comments in a safe and conservative context. Although he advocated some type of workmen's compensation scheme to move industrial accident cases into an administrative setting, he vigorously defended the integrity of the courts. More important, he attributed all the valid public dissatisfaction with the law and the courts to such technical and procedural problems as delayed opinion writing and excessive appeals. Although he alluded to the problems that the federal common law caused, for example, he refused to recommend that the doctrine be abolished. "The reform, if it is to come," Taft declared, "must be reached through the improvement in our judicial procedure."[120] His speech, packed with strong rhetorical statements about the poor and the victimized, submerged all substantive legal and social issues in the neutral call for more efficient administration and procedure.

In spite of discounts, however, Taft's speech was important for three reasons. First, it confirmed that the profession was well aware of the way that the system of corporate diversity litigation functioned and of the critical interconnections between the formal rules of law and the social context in which diversity jurisdiction operated. Second, to the extent that the speech was merely a calculated piece of political rhetoric, that very fact demonstrated the broad public and professional awareness of the system in the decades around the turn of the century. Third, the speech exemplified, as had Pound's address two years earlier, the thinking of a growing and important part of the legal elite, a part that included some of those who in the 1890s had appeared most sympathetic to corporate interests.

The lawyers who inspired and led the movement for professional procedural reform, generally moderate in their politics and practical in their orientation, saw a compelling need to simplify legal procedures in order to minimize the costs and delays of litigation. Their shared perceptions suggest that at least some of the Justices of the Supreme Court recognized the same problems and harbored the same concerns. Indeed, the operation of the system of corporate diversity litigation highlighted the significance of those burdens and the desirability of the reformers' goals. Forced repeatedly to confront the legal issues that the system made acute, the Justices could not have failed to recognize the important role played by distance, delay, and procedural complexity. In the spring of 1900, in fact, just as they were beginning their efforts to restrict diversity removals, seven of the Justices took notice of the problem of distance that plagued "some of the larger Western States." Denying the jurisdiction of the lower courts over certain miners' claims that arguably arose under a federal statute, the Court helped support its decision by pointing out that in the West "the Federal courts are often held only in the capital or chief city of the State, and at a great distance from certain parts of the mining regions therein."[121] The Court's restrictive jurisdictional decisions after 1900—especially the decisive four in 1905–6—were responsive in a patterned if limited way to the reformers' general concerns as well as to the more specific procedural problems that Pound and Taft discussed. In part the desire to minimize those practical burdens probably helped induce the Justices to restrict diversity removal in the confident and relatively tranquil days of a prosperous new century.[122]

A second salient characteristic of progressivism was the increasingly sharp political attacks that it seemed to inspire against the Supreme Court in particular and the federal courts in general. Politicians, journalists, labor leaders, settlement workers, and a variety of other social critics joined the critical chorus. As one scholar of popular attitudes toward the Court concluded:

> [T]he two decades that followed 1895 were unusual, not only because the Court ceased to be sacred—that had been the situation on several prior occasions—but because criticism occurred relentlessly, came from various sectors, and led eventually to questions, challenges and ultimately accusations being made against the U.S. Constitution and its authors. Only in the wake of Dred Scott had politicization of the Court been more severe, and polarization over constitutional issues more sharp.[123]

In 1905 the Court's decision in *Lochner v. New York*,[124] invalidating on due process grounds a state statute limiting the working hours of bakers, provoked particularly widespread criticism and was quickly transformed into a legal and political symbol of the Court's allegedly powerful procorporate bias. Not since the Court's bitterly controverted decision in 1895 declaring the federal income tax unconstitutional, noted another scholar, "had a case stirred as much protest in the popular press and professional journals."[125] Three years after *Lochner,* Woodrow Wilson, then the crusading president of Princeton University, declared that the whole federal common law was an illegitimate exercise of national judicial power and charged that the court system lacked "both simplicity and promptness" and was "unnecessarily expensive." The result, Wilson warned, sounding a refrain that became increasingly common in the years after 1900, "a rich litigant can almost always tire a poor one out and readily cheat him of his rights by simply leading him through an endless maze of appeals and technical delays."[126]

The Justices may have been unusually sensitive to such attacks. The charges of class bias came not merely from political agitators, or even from knowledgeable lawyers and prominent political figures, but also from the Court itself. Both in private letters and in his dissent in *Lochner* Justice Oliver Wendell Holmes, Jr. accused his colleagues of acting on the basis of class values,[127] and in 1904 in the *Dixon* fellow servant case four dissenters—led by the relatively conservative Justice Edward D. White and not including Holmes—bluntly indicted the majority for adopting "contradictory propositions" that enabled them to deny recovery to injured workers on any set of facts.[128] Further, the Justices may well have recognized that there was at least some basis for the political attack. Their removal decisions in the 1890s had, after all, purposely shaped federal procedural law to protect corporate defendants. And however pure their motives might have been, they knew that they had nonetheless warped doctrine to achieve a specific social goal. Indeed, if inferences from the oblique doctrinal methods that they used in the 1890s are sound, the Justices realized at the time that their efforts stemmed from social motives that they were unwilling to identify or explain publicly. Finally, some scholars have suggested that the structure of values and assumptions that underlay the dominant ideas of nineteenth-century legal thought began breaking down in the last two decades of the century and that the breakdown created, in the minds of many lawyers and judges, a "crisis of legitimacy."[129] To the extent that such a crisis existed and influenced the Justices, it may have pushed them—with the help of their memories of the Court's removal decisions in the 1890s—toward the series of restrictive jurisdictional rulings that would assist plaintiffs, demonstrate their own neutrality, and thereby confirm—if only in their own minds—the Court's institutional neutrality and legitimacy.

That hypothesis receives particular support from *Prewitt*. Of all the restrictive decisions, it was the most unexpected, surprising, and radical. It not only benefited insurance plaintiffs and subjected insurance companies to political pressure from the states, but it also transferred authority to exercise de facto control over the scope of federal jurisdiction from Congress and the federal courts to the legislatures of the states. Moreover, it represented an abrupt break with prior doctrine. Whereas the issues of joinder and of the proper construction of the Judiciary Act of 1887–88 had been bubbling for fifteen years, the Court's decisions in *Barron v. Burnside* in 1887 and *Southern Pacific Co. v. Denton* in 1892 had seemed to settle the law that states could not compel corporations to give up their right to remove. By 1898 the successor to Judge Dillon's treatise regarded the matter as closed, and in 1901 the major treatise on removal that sympathized with antiremoval statutes concluded similarly. "It is very doubtful," the latter declared, "if there is any way left in which to enforce most of these statutes of the various States which attempt to restrict removals."[130] When *Prewitt* suddenly upheld an antiremoval statute in the face of apparently well-established doctrine, it gave the Court's restriction on removal a relatively high degree of visibility among lawyers, politicians, and progressive activists.[131] It promised to draw the commendation of those who were most disposed to criticize the federal courts, and it prevented thousands of middle-class insurance claimants from being trapped in the system and fueling dissatisfaction with the national courts.[132] Most important, *Prewitt* preempted the immediate criticism and possible countermeasures that a contrary decision might have provoked from the legislatures of the twenty some states that continued to maintain antiremoval statutes.

Regardless of differences among the Justices, they moved in the new era to restrict diversity removal jurisdiction drastically. Those who shared the sympathies of progressivism, even if only in its narrowest professional incarnation as a movement for court reform, became newly sensitive to the practical problems of litigation and especially to the extralegal burdens that removal imposed on plaintiffs. Those who did not share those attitudes may have seen jurisdictional restriction as a way of deflecting the growing political criticism of the federal courts and of demonstrating to themselves or others the Court's institutional neutrality. For the former, the restrictive jurisdictional decisions helped eliminate the extralegal burdens that plagued the judicial system; for the latter, those same decisions allowed them to tack with the political wind and to moderate the impact of their substantive doctrine without compromising the integrity of their principles.

Progressivism and prosperity thus combined with narrower doctrinal and institutional considerations to foster among the Justices a willingness to limit the uses of removal in diversity actions. One final factor, however, perhaps the most important, also contributed to the Court's emerging consensus. On the broadest level, the restrictive decisions after the turn of the century were integral parts of the Court's fundamental reorientation of the role and focus of the federal judiciary.

The Reorientation of the Federal Judicial System

Central to the new consensus in favor of restricting removal jurisdiction in diversity actions was the Court's long-term, de facto, and only half-conscious reconsideration of the proper role of the federal courts in the age of a new national industrial economy. The reconsideration was rooted, of course, in the transforming social changes that marked the years after the Civil War and the rapidly mounting efforts of government on all levels to channel their course and ameliorate their impact. From the 1890s to World War I the Court reconceived and restructured the role of the national courts, to some extent in theory but even more so in practice, by remolding, sometimes broadly but more often in detail, both the law that the national courts applied and the jurisdiction that they exercised. Alternatively interpreting the Constitution, construing jurisdictional statutes, and molding the rules of pleading and practice, the Court reoriented its working concept of the federal judicial system as it determined across the range of cases that came before it where and how the limited resources of the national courts would be used. Essentially, the Court turned the lower federal courts away from state law issues and toward national ones. It expanded federal constitutional rights and the jurisdiction of the lower courts to enforce those rights, and as a practical institutional trade-off it curtailed federal efforts to adjudicate state law claims by restricting the jurisdiction of the lower courts over diversity actions.

In that long and complex process the years 1905–8 proved to be critical. Two monumental decisions, each foreshadowed in the Court's opinions for more than a decade, bracketed its major restrictive decisions on diversity removal in 1905–6. Together, the decisions concentrated in those four years reflected an altered view of the role of the national courts, and together they helped institute a fundamental reorientation in the federal judicial system.[133]

Lochner v. New York,[134] announced in early 1905, brought to fruition a line of cases beginning in the late 1880s that laid the foundations of substantive due process—the doctrine that the due process clause of the Fourteenth Amendment imposed substantive limits on state actions and that the judiciary was authorized to enforce those limits. Since the 1880s the Court had sporadically suggested that the Fourteenth Amendment gave it constitutional authority to determine the substantive fairness of state regulatory actions,[135] and in the 1890s it began scrutinizing the "reasonableness" of state rate-making efforts.[136] In 1897 for the first time it invalidated a state law on the express ground that it violated substantive limitations imposed by the due process clause.[137] *Lochner* blended those earlier decisions into a fundamental constitutional doctrine. Invalidating a New York statute that limited the number of hours that bakers could work each week, it announced in sweeping language that there were narrow constitutional limits within which states could restrict the "freedom of contract" of private parties. For more than three decades *Lochner* stood as a landmark decision construing the due process clause and symbolizing the reign of the constitutional doctrine of liberty of contract.

Three years later *Ex parte Young*[138] brought to culmination a parallel line of decisions. While the Court had been broadening the Fourteenth Amendment, it had also been narrowing the Eleventh, the constitutional amendment that denied the national courts jurisdiction to hear suits against states brought by individual citizens.[139] In 1897, for example, the Court held that the Eleventh Amendment did not preclude a federal suit against state officials for possession of real property allegedly owned by South Carolina.[140] Although doctrine remained unclear and frequently blocked suits against state officers,[141] under a variety of theories the lower federal courts heard a growing number of suits brought by individuals and corporations that sought to enjoin state actions alleged to be unconstitutional. Challenges to regulatory actions grew in number and variety on the Supreme Court's docket.[142] In 1903 the Court implied forcefully in *Prout v. Starr*[143] that the lower federal courts ought to and did have jurisdiction to protect citizens from state laws that contravened the Fourteenth Amendment.[144] Three years later it cited *Prout* as authority for the proposition that a suit against state officers to enjoin them from enforcing an allegedly unconstitutional tax was not a suit against a state within the meaning of the Eleventh Amendment.[145] In *Young,* then, the Court made those narrowing views the law. It held that the Eleventh Amendment did not deprive the national courts of jurisdiction over suits seeking to enjoin state officials from enforcing state statutes alleged to be unconstitutional under the Fourteenth Amendment. Because states could act only through their appropriate officials, *Young* in effect allowed the federal courts to block almost any action that a state might take.[146]

Between 1905 and 1908, then, *Lochner* enthroned substantive due process as a constitutional doctrine that authorized courts to invalidate state statutes and regulatory actions, and *Young* opened the doors of the lower federal courts officially and widely to those who sought to use the new doctrine.[147] Together, the two decisions gave the federal courts the constitutional authority—both the substantive law and the jurisdiction necessary to apply it—to serve as the frontline protectors of liberty and property against state interference. Both, too, provoked widespread criticism from progressive lawyers and politicians.[148]

Around those two landmarks a variety of other decisions clustered as the Court worked to establish the lines of a new federalism. *Lochner* and *Young* created, for example, what appeared to be a glaring constitutional anomaly. On the one hand, long-established construction held that the Fourteenth Amendment reached only "state action," that is, actions taken under the ostensible authority of state law. On the other hand, *Young* avoided the jurisdictional bar of the Eleventh Amendment by holding that when state officials acted in an unconstitutional manner their actions were stripped of their character as "state action." The decisions, then, seemed to create a dilemma: If allegedly unlawful acts constituted "state action" under the Fourteenth Amendment, did the Eleventh Amendment not bar the federal courts from hearing challenges to them? Conversely, if the Eleventh Amendment did not bar the federal courts from hearing challenges to those allegedly unlawful acts because they did not constitute "state action," were the acts not consequently beyond the reach of the Fourteenth Amendment? And further, what if the acts challenged on federal constitutional grounds were also unlawful under state law? Since acts that violated the federal Constitution were stripped of their character as "state action" under the Eleventh Amendment, should not acts that violated state law be stripped of their character as "state action" under the Fourteenth?

The Court struggled with those questions for a decade. In 1904 in *Barney v. City of New York* it seemed to hold that it was beyond a federal court's jurisdiction to hear a suit challenging the action of a state agency under the Fourteenth Amendment when the agency's action was clearly unlawful under state law.[149] Three years later the Court sharply distinguished *Barney*,[150] but two years after that it implied that *Barney* remained good law.[151] Only in 1913 did it finally settle the issue. Overruling *Barney* in effect, the Court resolved the dilemma by avoiding it. Ruling that actions of state officials that violated the federal constitution were "state action" for Fourteenth Amendment purposes but were not "state action" for Eleventh Amendment purposes, it held in *Home Telephone and Telegraph Co. v. City of Los Angeles* that the federal courts had jurisdiction to hear federal constitutional challenges to the acts of state officials regardless of the legality of those acts under state law.[152]

By the time it decided *Home Telephone*, five years after *Young*, the Court clearly saw the problem that *Barney* presented and decisively repudiated it. If followed, the Court declared, *Barney* would logically lead to restrictions on "the exercise of Federal judicial power under all circumstances" or "at least in every case where there was a coincidence between a national safeguard or prohibition and a state one." In every instance where state law guaranteed the right to due process, for example, any action by the federal courts "would depend on the ultimate determination of the state courts [of the state law issue] and would therefore require a stay of all action [in the federal court] to await such determination." The result would "render impossible the performance of the duty with which the Federal courts are charged under the Constitution," that is, "to afford protection to a claim of right under the Constitution of the United States, as against the action of a State or its officers." Indeed, *Home Telephone* stressed, the *Barney* doctrine "would in substance cause the state courts to become the primary source for applying and enforcing the Constitution of the United States."[153]

Just as *Lochner* and *Young* established much of the foundation for the reorientation of the federal judicial system, the *Barney–Home Telephone* line of cases exemplified both the doctrinal results and the basic institutional assumptions that followed in their wake. On the doctrinal level, the Court essentially nullified the Eleventh Amendment in suits challenging any action of a state agency or official, and it gave the Fourteenth Amendment a sweeping construction that stressed its "completeness" and "comprehensive inclusiveness."[154] The federal courts could apply the latter to any action that a state official might take, regardless of the action's status under local law. The Court refused to allow the Eleventh Amendment—the single constitutional amendment that expressly restricted the federal judicial power—to bar the federal courts from enjoining the actions of state officials, and it made the Fourteenth Amendment—the constitutional provision that most broadly constrained the authority of the states—a basis for the exercise of a far-reaching federal judicial power. On the level of institutional assumptions, the Court accepted the idea that the principal role of the national courts was to protect federal constitutional rights against interference by the states and the further idea that the federal courts were properly the "primary" protectors of those rights. Neither idea, of course, was wholly new, but the vigor and sweep that the Court gave to them, especially to the idea of the federal courts as the "primary" enforcers of the Constitution, announced the Court's reoriented view of the role of the national judicial system. Indeed, both unquestioned constitutional doctrine and the entire history of the national judiciary before 1875 contradicted the Court's declaration that "the Federal courts *are charged under the Constitution*" with the duty of protecting federal constitutional rights. It is perhaps not too great an exaggeration to say that in the interrelated decisions centering on *Lochner* and *Young* the Supreme Court created the twentieth-century federal judiciary.

The Court's new attitudes spread into other federal law areas as it attempted to balance its concern for the values of federalism with its new commitment to guarantee federal judicial protection for federal constitutional rights. In 1908 it held that, regardless of the administrative or judicial remedies that a state provided, a party seeking to challenge a state regulatory action on federal law grounds had the unquestionable right to do so ultimately in a federal court.[155] The following year it upheld a broad jurisdiction in the national courts to hear and decide challenges to state regulatory action based on state law, even in the absence of diversity of citizenship.[156] Finally, on the same day that it decided *Young,* the Court seemed to fill in any possible gap that might enable the states to avoid the compulsion of the Fourteenth Amendment. In *General Oil v. Crain* it declared that the Constitution—at least if there were any possibililty that the Eleventh Amendment might bar an action in the federal courts—compelled the states to provide a judicial forum to hear federal constitutional challenges to state regulatory actions.[157] The Court's anxiety about state regulatory policies was apparent. The decision in *Crain* was necessary, it explained, because the states might try to deny regulated parties any right to seek judicial review of regulatory actions in their own courts. "And it will not do to say that the argument is drawn from extremes," the Court announced dramatically. "Constitutional provisions are based on the possibility of extremes."[158]

The Court's sharpening focus on federal law problems after the turn of the century was not limited to constitutional matters. The rapid increase in federal legislation since the late 1880s, especially statutes regulating business activities, pushed a widening stream of federal questions into the national courts. When the Justices construed the federal Safety Appliance Act broadly in 1904,[159] for example, they expanded the scope of federal law that affected interstate railroads and guaranteed that actions under the statute would multiply rapidly. Similarly, their decision earlier the same year in the *Northern Securities* case,[160] extending the reach of the Sherman Antitrust Act to holding companies and supporting the enforcement efforts of the Roosevelt administration, seemed to ensure that the lower courts would hear a growing number of complicated antitrust prosecutions.[161] Indeed, the efforts of the states to limit corporate consolidations, which the Court had encouraged in the 1890s, had by the beginning of the twentieth century ended in frustration and failure. By 1904 it seemed clear that the major effort to regulate large-scale corporate enterprise in the United States would thereafter come at the national level and that most efforts to enforce as well as challenge those regulatory actions would be brought in the federal courts.[162]

On a parallel track, the Court's expansion of its substantive lawmaking power after the turn of the century was directed toward developing uniform national laws for a centralizing economy and ensuring that the federal courts would play a major role in the process.[163] *Muhlker* expanded the Court's ability vis-à-vis state law to control the application of the contract clause, and *Kansas v. Colorado* used the Court's constitutional jurisdiction over suits between states to raise the powers of the federal judiciary above those of Congress in dealing with interstate disputes. Similarly, *Jensen* and its progeny transformed the constitutional grant of admiralty jurisdiction into a mandate for a uniform national maritime law that both limited the powers of Congress and overrode the laws of the states. *Kuhn* introduced the federal common law into issues of local property law, and *Hitchman* expanded it to establish national rules for the law of labor employment contracts, a subject of growing national significance. Finally, the Court's widespread use of the dormant commerce clause and of preemption under a variety of new federal statutes constrained the lawmaking powers of the states and expanded the de facto power of the federal courts to shape the law in numerous areas critical to the national economy.

As the culmination of social, doctrinal, and institutional changes that had been in the making for at least two decades, the Court's intensifying commitment to issues of national law and to the central role of the federal courts in developing that national law suggests that the decisions restricting diversity jurisdiction from *Gableman* to *Prewitt* were ultimately and to a large extent simply corollaries of a fundamental shift in the Court's institutional orientation. That shift was away from common law issues, matters seen as having mere local importance, and the kinds of tort and contract actions that individuals brought against corporations; it was toward public law issues, matters of national importance, and the kinds of cases that pitted private citizens against government agencies. Because that reorientation meant that the federal courts would hear new and burgeoning classes of federal law actions, it generated a relentless pressure and an undeniable reason to trim their dockets of less important matters. The numbers of the new cases raising federal law claims might be large, and some of them—such as the increasingly common rate-making cases—were unusually onerous and time-consuming.[164] As *Doctor v. Harrington* suggested, too, the Court continued to believe that some diversity actions were particularly important and ought to remain in the national courts. The Court's reorientation thus not only directed it to limit diversity jurisdiction but also pointed somewhat selectively to the places where diversity jurisdiction should be restricted.

In retrospect, the years from 1905 to 1908 were critical in the evolution of the federal judicial system. *Lochner, Young,* and the Court's decisions that restricted removal of diversity actions were all of a piece. They constituted the collective pivot on which the Supreme Court began turning the federal courts from their past to their future. They marked the point when the orientation of the twentieth-century federal judiciary began taking form and when the focus of the national courts began shifting from diversity jurisdiction to federal question jurisdiction, from legal remedies to equitable remedies, from state-created common law rights to federally created statutory and constitutional rights, and from protecting against the wrongs committed by citizens to protecting against the wrongs committed by government.[165]

If the Court's new and sweeping restrictions on diversity removal symbolized and helped implement the Court's reorientation as much as did *Lochner* and *Young,* then *Union and Planters' Bank* in 1894 symbolized the Court's old orientation as much as did the late nineteenth-century cases that *Lochner* and *Young* distinguished or rejected. *Union and Planters' Bank* barred defendants who asserted federal rights from removing in the absence of diversity of citizenship at precisely the time when the Court was expanding the removal rights of defendants who did come within diversity jurisdiction. Symbolically and in effect the decision subordinated federal question jurisdiction to diversity jurisdiction. In doing so it reflected the traditional attitudes of the eighteenth and nineteenth centuries that the national courts were primarily forums for settling private disputes and that the state courts were appropriate and desirable tribunals to adjudicate federal law issues. Although the nineteenth-century Court recognized full well the key role it played in fostering a national market, it saw the lower federal courts as assisting mainly by adjudicating private law actions brought under diversity jurisdiction. Insofar as federal law issues were litigated and decided, whether in the lower federal courts or in the state courts, the Supreme Court had the authority to review and correct them. And though the role of the lower federal courts began to change after 1875 when Congress first conferred general federal question jurisdiction on them, three decades passed before the balance shifted and the Court fully reconceived and substantially restructured their role. In the context of the Court's contemporaneous diversity decisions, *Union and Planters' Bank* shows that as late as the 1890s the Court still saw the protection of defendants' federal rights as less central to the mission of the lower federal courts than the protection of their state-created, private law rights.[166]

That preference for diversity jurisdiction over federal question jurisdiction, of course, conflicted with the ideas about the proper allocation of federal judicial power that would come to dominance in the twentieth century. Judges and other legal writers would begin to focus more intently on the federal courts as instruments of sovereignty, as institutions designed to enforce both the rights and duties established by the Constitution and laws of the United States. Increasingly, legal writers would minimize the significance of private law issues and diversity jurisdiction while stressing the "essential" role of the national courts in deciding public law questions, construing and developing federal law, maintaining its nationwide uniformity, and vindicating specifically federal rights by ensuring their full and fair enforcement across the nation.[167]

Returning, then, to the question raised by the Court's contemporaneous decisions on common law and jurisdictional issues in the system of corporate diversity litigation, the answer emerges with some clarity. It was the Justices' changing attitude toward the nature and role of the national judicial system that was most instrumental in convincing them that jurisdictional restrictions were necessary and, more critically, that the restrictions had to be made in the mine-run of diversity cases. Ironically, in fact, the Court's commitment to freedom of contract may have contributed to its declining interest in common law diversity actions. Allowing parties extensive freedom to determine by private contract the rights they would have, the Court automatically restricted the role of the judiciary in supervising such agreements. The more capacious the realm of private contract, the less the need for judicial intervention; and the less the need for judicial intervention, the less the need to devote the limited resources of the federal courts to that purpose. The less that need, in turn, the less the need for diversity jurisdiction. Concomitantly, the same commitment to an expansive doctrine of freedom of contract made the Court increasingly wary of legislative actions that could interfere with private agreements. That wariness made the Court increasingly sensitive to the limits that the Constitution could impose on legislation, and that sensitivity, in turn, underscored the paramount importance of federal question jurisdiction.

Justice Brewer, the Court's most outspoken defender of individual rights and property interests, probably exemplified the thinking of the Justices who supported both substantive due process and the federal common law on the one hand and the Court's decisions restricting diversity jurisdiction after 1900 on the other. Brewer had long stressed the centrality of the judiciary in American society, and he advocated an exceptionally active role for the courts in protecting constitutional rights generally and the rights of private property in particular. At the same time, he recognized the growing problem of crowded dockets, the need to make practical compromises, and the types of legal issues that would prove critical to the newly emerging America of the twentieth century.[168] In 1895 Brewer announced his vision of the proper role of the Supreme Court: "a tribunal taking no cognizance of the minor disputes between individuals within the several States, but sitting in judgment upon the weightier controversies between States and citizens thereof, and determining the rights and liabilities of States to each other and to citizens."[169] In the social and political context of the new century, Brewer extended that vision to the role of the lower federal courts as well. It was necessary to expand their ability to control those "controversies between States and citizens thereof" and to limit their less important burden of deciding "minor disputes between individuals." In implementing that vision, he helped guide the Court in reconceiving the role of the national judiciary.

To the extent that there were contrasting views and distinctive wings on the turn-of-the-century Court, Brewer and Harlan were as far apart as any two Justices. Harlan dissented in *Baugh, Voigt, Adams, Northern Assurance,* and the *Dixon* fellow servant case as well as in both *Lochner* and *Young.* Brewer was with the majority in each.[170] The two agreed, however, on one central premise that characterized the turn-of-the-century Court. The Supreme Court possessed "vast powers" and properly played a central role in American government. "[T]he Supreme Court, whose organization and powers constitute the most striking and distinguishing feature of the Constitution," Brewer proclaimed in 1903, "has been a most potent factor in shaping the course of national events." It was, in fact, the pivotal institution of American government. "It stands to-day a quiet but confessedly mighty power, whose action all wait for, and whose decisions all abide."[171] Harlan agreed completely. "The power of the court, for good or evil," he declared the same year, "can scarcely be exaggerated." It was invested with "extraordinary authority" and constituted "the chief pillar of the national government."[172]

The premise that Brewer and Harlan shared projected a supreme confidence in both the Court's constitutional power and its ultimate authority in American government. That premise contrasted sharply with the far more tentative and restrained assumptions that had marked the thinking of most Justices from the nation's founding to the turn of the twentieth century, and it nurtured the consensus that lay behind the Court's reorientation of the national judicial system.[173] That shared premise helped lead the Justices to see the desirability and necessity of assigning to the lower federal courts a more prominent role in enforcing the truly national rules laid down by the "chief pillar of the national government." Unlike the state courts, the lower federal courts were directly and exclusively responsible to the Supreme Court. Compared with the state courts, they promised to enforce federal law more consistently, more uniformly, more reliably, and more readily. Conversely, that same shared premise minimized the importance of run-of-the-mill diversity cases that involved socially insignificant individual disputes over private law matters. In addition, even though the Court had authority to make rules of federal common law to govern such disputes, those rules nevertheless remained rules of "state" law. Any state legislature could, therefore, change or negate them, and by its own express admission the United States Supreme Court did not have the authority to make them binding on the courts of the states. The Court's mandate was fully authoritative only in matters of federal statutory or constitutional law, and only in those areas could the Court truly serve as the "chief pillar of the *national* government."

To a large extent, too, the attitudes that Harlan and Brewer exhibited were characteristic of much of the American legal profession, and certainly of its elite branch, in the first decade of the twentieth century. In spite of the doubts engendered by rapid social change and the challenges of political reformers, members of the legal elite presented a confident, complacent, and self-congratulatory public appearance. They believed that the law—and lawyers as its spokespersons and judges as its expositors—represented the summit of human wisdom. "The bar still maintains its rank for deep learning, high mental discipline and refined moral culture," declared an Oregon Supreme Court Justice in 1904. "The bench, drawn from its ranks, represents the best product of civilization and is the bulwark of constitutional freedom."[174] Responding to criticisms of the bar, Henry St. George Tucker announced in his presidential address to the American Bar Association in 1905 that the legal profession had "more potential for good than any other profession, excepting the Christian ministry" and that it was "in some respects more powerful for good than even that high profession."[175] Judge Dillon struck a similar note the same year when he addressed the twenty-fifth reunion of the Columbia Law School's graduating class of 1880. "The short period covered by your professional life has witnessed great changes in the conditions of society and government," he declared, and those changes threatened "to undermine the foundations and fabric of our social and political structures." To meet the challenge, Dillon proclaimed, "the services of our profession, services which only its members can render, are as necessary in the present as they have ever been found to be in the past, in this and all other free countries."[176]

In the first decade of the twentieth century no one articulated the reasons for reconsidering the role of the federal courts more forcefully than did Elihu Root, the preeminent representative of the nation's legal–political elite after the turn of the century. A successful New York corporation lawyer and one of the profession's most distinguished national leaders, Root served as Secretary of War from 1899 to 1905, Secretary of State from 1905 to 1909, and then United States Senator beginning in 1909. In 1904, when he addressed the Yale Law School's graduating class, Root exemplified the orientation that united the fundamental premise that Brewer and Harlan articulated with *Lochner, Young,* and the Court's restrictive jurisdictional decisions after 1900. "The features of our system of law which it is specially important to preserve inviolate are not to be found in the general body of municipal law which regulates the relation of members of the community to each other," Root announced.[177] That law was subject to "changing conditions and opinions," and much "that we deem essential now will doubtless become obsolete and be brushed aside by our successors."[178] Indeed, he admitted, in the area of private law "[w]e have no just ground for arrogating to ourselves any special superiority over the other civilized nations of the earth."[179] In contrast, however, Root proclaimed that American public law was a matter of national superiority and political absolutes. "When, however, we turn to the American law which regulates the relations of government and the agents of government to private citizens, we find a class of rules which it is essential to preserve inviolate in full force and vigor," he declared. "[A]s to these we cannot for a moment admit superiority or equality of merit in any system which does not embody them and make them effective."[180]

Particularly telling, Root did not identify the nation's superior and "essential" public law rules with those that embodied the substantive values of liberty and property. Rather, adopting a coldly pragmatic analysis, he underscored the importance of what he called the "secondary provisions"—procedural and remedial law—that enabled individuals to have their formal rights vindicated in the courts. "Spain professes as high a regard for the principles of liberty as we do," he explained. "Yet in 1899 we found hundreds of prisoners in the jails of Cuba who had been imprisoned for years without trial for want of some definite and certain way in which they could avail themselves practically" of their formal rights.[181] General declarations of principles or rights, Root continued, were "worthless" in the absence of "specific provisions enabling the individual citizen to bring [them] to the test of judicial determination."[182] Although such "secondary provisions" might seem "technical and contrary to the justice of the case," he admonished his audience, "unless [secondary] rules of law securing these specified rights are maintained inviolate, the general principles which we profess are not practically available for the protection of any citizen."[183] The essential element, and what made American law superior, in short, was the availability of effective judicial remedies against government actions. "This class of specific and definite provisions of a secondary nature," Root repeated emphatically, "is the sole protection of the individual citizen against the arbitrary exercise of the tremendous powers with which the agents of government are invested."[184] They were "the most invaluable part of our national inheritance."[185]

Root's speech tended to such extremes that it might have seemed heretical. It appeared to deny any special virtues to the common law and to dismiss "fundamental" principles as mere vague generalities. In identifying those important matters as inessential, however, Root threw his crucial dual point into clear relief. First, the major threat to liberty and property came from government, not from individuals. Second, effective procedural devices that placed the judiciary in a position of institutional primacy within the government—the availability of federal jurisdiction over, and equitable remedies against, other agencies of government—were of paramount importance. "There is," Root concluded, "one general characteristic of our system of government which is essential and which it is the special duty of lawyers to guard with care—that is, the observance of limitations of official power."[186]

Root's conviction that judicial checks on government were essential was widely shared in the legal profession, especially among the members of the legal elite. In his 1905 presidential address to the American Bar Association, for example, Henry St. George Tucker captured the same sense of change and challenge that animated Root:

What impresses one most deeply in an examination of the legislation of the states is the number and variety of subjects of legislation and the assumption (I will not say always improperly) by the state of functions which in our earlier history were unclaimed by it. We are a much-governed people, and there is nothing which affects the American citizen, from infancy to the grave, awake or asleep, in motion or at rest, at home or abroad, in his personal, social, political or property rights which is not the subject of regulation by the state.[187]

Government had vastly expanded, Tucker stressed, and as a result the need to maintain limits on its growth were becoming ever more critical. "[S]pecial care must be taken not to endanger any of those inalienable rights of 'life, liberty and property' guaranteed to every citizen under 'the law of the land'," he warned. "For it must be remembered that these are rights which do not proceed from government but are antecedent to government."[188]

If the legal profession, especially its elite branch, was confident of the wisdom and strength of the law and the legal profession, it was particularly confident of the federal judiciary. Its members saw the national courts as their special preserve, and they expected them to act broadly and forcefully.[189] The Supreme Court did so. In its decisions between the turn of the century and World War I, and especially in the pivotal rulings between 1905 and 1908, it reshaped federal constitutional and procedural law in ways that responded to the kinds of concerns that Root and Tucker articulated. Indeed, what separated the Court's predominant majority from its dissenters from the 1890s to the 1930s was precisely its faith in the wisdom and ability of the national judiciary to make law and to set limits to the lawmaking authority of Congress and the states. Substantive due process was the most visible and controversial area of the Court's lawmaking, but the federal common law, the expanded scope given to preemption and the dormant commerce clause, and the use of jurisdictional grants to claim substantive lawmaking power all reflected the same social values, the same activist lawmaking orientation, and the same faith in the wisdom and anointed role of the federal judiciary.

Growing more and more concerned about the dangers of legislative and administrative actions, the Supreme Court fashioned powerful doctrines to counter the threat while recognizing at the same time the declining relative significance of private tort and contract actions. After 1900 the Court moved from institutional necessity to clarify the jurisdictional doctrines that it had allowed to remain slack and unsettled in the 1890s and to restrict the growth of the overall federal caseload. In the process it recognized the desirability of restricting diversity jurisdiction as a way of alleviating some of the extralegal burdens on plaintiffs in the system, of answering at least to the satisfaction of the Justices themselves the political attacks of progressivism, and of compensating for the impact that its federal question decisions would have on the dockets of the lower courts. While the Court's federal common law decisions gave voice to its deepest social values, its restrictive procedural–jurisdictional rulings represented a compromise with the institutional requirements of the federal judiciary, the social sympathies and political challenges of progressivism, and the practical limitations imposed on the business of the lower courts by what the Justices perceived as a compelling need for a fundamental reorientation of the federal judicial system.

Notes

Introduction

1. The concept of a social system is often associated with the work of the sociologist Talcott Parsons. In order to avoid any possible misconceptions, therefore, it might be appropriate to state that my use of the term *social system* and the analysis in this study are not intended as applications of Parsons's elaborate theoretical approach. Rather, the kind of social litigation system that I discuss bears a much closer resemblance to the kinds of patterns suggested by a number of scholars who have more recently studied litigation trends in trial courts over time. See, for example, Marc Galanter, "Why the 'Haves' Come Out Ahead: Speculations on the Limits of Legal Change," *Law & Society Review* 9 (1974): 95; William L. F. Felstiner, "Influences of Social Organization on Dispute Processing," *Law & Society Review* 9 (1974): 63; Lawrence Friedman and Robert V. Percival, "A Tale of Two Courts: Litigation in Alameda and San Benito Counties," *Law & Society Review* 10 (1976): 267; Wayne McIntosh, "150 Years of Litigation and Dispute Settlement: A Court Tale," *Law & Society Review* 15 (1980–81): 823; Joel B. Grossman, Herbert M. Kritzer, Kristin Bumiller, Austin Sarat, Stephen McDougal, and Richard Miller, "Dimensions of Institutional Participation: Who Uses the Courts and How?" *Journal of Politics* 44 (1982): 86; David Engel, "Cases, Conflict, and Accommodation: Patterns of Legal Interaction in a Small Community," *American Bar Foundation Research Journal* (1983): 803; Stephen Daniels, "Ladders and Bushes: The Problem of Caseloads and Studying Court Activities over Time," *American Bar Foundation Research Journal* (1984): 751; Stephen Daniels, "Continuity and Change in Patterns of Case Handling: A Case Study of Two Rural Counties," *Law & Society Review* 19 (1985): 381; Wayne V. McIntosh, "A State Court's Clientele: Exploring the Strategy of Trial Litigation," *Law & Society Review* 19 (1985): 421; Lawrence M. Friedman, "Civil Wrongs: Personal Injury Law in the Late 19th Century," *American Bar Foundation Research Journal* (1987): 351; Lawrence M. Friedman and Thomas D. Russell, "More Civil Wrongs: Personal Injury Litigation, 1901–1910," *American Journal of Legal History* 34 (1990): 295; Charles R. Epp, "Connecting Litigation Levels and Legal Mobilization: Explaining Interstate Variation in Employment Civil Rights Litigation," *Law & Society Review* 24 (1990): 145.

For a series of helpful discussions of empirical research into specifically procedural issues, see the symposium entitled "Empirical Studies of Civil Procedure" published in successive issues (nos. 3 and 4) of *Law and Contemporary Problems* 51 (1988). In spite of its formalistic and rule-centered approach, the law and economics movement has also suggested some of the factors that influence the patterns that mark social litigation systems. See, for example, Richard A. Posner, "An Economic Approach to Legal Procedure and Judicial Administration," *Journal of Legal Studies* 2 (1973): 399; Note, "The Inefficient Common Law," *Yale Law Journal* 92 (1983): 862. Two law and economics analyses are of particular interest: George L. Priest, "Selective Characteristics of Litigation," *Journal of Legal Studies* 9 (1980): 399; George L. Priest and Benjamin Klein, "The Selection of Disputes for Litigation," *Journal of Legal Studies* 13 (1984): 13.

2. For many years scholars have examined the activities of interest groups in sponsoring and conducting litigation aimed at improving the general social and legal position of the groups they represent. See, for example, Clement E. Vose, *Caucasians Only* (Berkeley, CA, 1959); Clement E. Vose, *Constitutional Change: Amendment Politics and Supreme Court Litigation Since 1900* (Lexington, MA, 1972); Lee Epstein, *Conservatives in Court* (Knoxville, TN, 1985); Joseph F.

Kobylka, "A Court-created Context for Group Litigation: Libertarian Groups and Obscenity," *Journal of Politics* 49 (1987): 1061. The focus here is on a different type of litigation. Although corporate defendants in some ways did litigate methodically, individual plaintiffs did not.

3. It goes without saying that the cases in the system represented only a part of the civil litigation in the federal courts and only a part of their diversity docket. Numerous important classes of cases—equity receiverships, suits involving commercial transactions, and disputes over real property and corporate governance, to name only a few—are entirely absent. Each merits its own examination, and each is likely part of one or more other social litigation systems. Until such studies are made, we will not have an adequate picture of either those other systems or the overall social significance of federal diversity jurisdiction itself.

4. During the last decade scholars studying the work of the courts have come to emphasize the importance of local factors in explaining the changing characteristics of judicial workloads. This seems a wise and most helpful approach. See, for example, Stephen Daniels, "Caseload Dynamics and the Nature of Change: The Civil Business of Trial Courts in Four Illinois Counties," *Law & Society Review* 24 (1990): 299; Marc Galanter, "The Life and Times of the Big Six; or, The Federal Courts Since the Good Old Days," *Wisconsin Law Review* (1988): 921; Robert A. Kagan, Bobby D. Infelise, and Robert R. Detlefsen, "American State Supreme Court Justices, 1900–1970," *American Bar Foundation Research Journal* (1984): 371.

5. For example, Robert H. Mnookin and Lewis Kornhauser, "Bargaining in the Shadow of the Law: The Case of Divorce," *Yale Law Journal* 88 (1979): 950; Marc Galanter, "Justice in Many Rooms: Courts, Private Ordering, and Indigenous Law," *Journal of Legal Pluralism* 19 (1981): 1, 8, and n. 10, 11. I do not mean to suggest fault with either of these articles. Both, in fact, are particularly valuable discussions from which I have profited greatly. I cite them here only as illustrative.

6. See, for example, Stewart Macaulay, "Non-Contractual Relations in Business: A Preliminary Study," *American Sociological Review* 28 (1963): 55; William M. Even, "Comment," *American Sociological Review* 28 (1963): 67; Barbara Yngvesson, "Re-Examining Continuing Relations and the Law," *Wisconsin Law Review* (1985): 623. The excellent series of studies by Frank W. Munger, Jr., dealing with litigation in West Virginia, shows how cultural and social factors affect the frequency and ways in which parties seek to use the courts. See Munger, "Commercial Litigation in West Virginia State and Federal Courts 1870–1940," *American Journal of Legal History* 30 (1986): 322; Munger, "Social Change and Tort Litigation: Industrialization, Accidents, and Trial Courts in Southern West Virginia, 1872–1940," *Buffalo Law Review* 36 (1988): 75; Munger, "Law, Change, and Litigation: A Critical Examination of an Empirical Research Tradition," *Law & Society Review* 22 (1988): 57.

7. The subsidy thesis claims that nineteenth- and early twentieth-century common law imposed narrow rules of tort liability and thereby provided a de facto subsidy to business enterprise. The efficiency thesis maintains that those same common law tort rules imposed the costs of accidents on various parties—employers, employees, and consumers—in a way that maximized safety and minimized its costs—in a way, in other words, that was economically efficient. See Chapter 11.

8. This book argues, for example, that the subsidy or discount was for the most part, at least, not the result of intentional actions by the courts and that its existence was independent of whatever distributive effect the substantive rules of the common law might have had. The discount arose from a combination of social conditions and relations, procedural and jurisdictional rules, and the institutional organizations of the state and federal court systems. The book also contends that, insofar as the substantive rules of the common law contributed to the discount, they probably did so primarily by broadening, directly or indirectly, the scope allowed to the social processes of out-of-court settlements that marked the period. The importance of the substantive rules of tort liability in allowing potential defendants to discount their liability, in other words, may have been less important than the substantive rules of contract law that enabled them to obtain and use releases from liability. From those same arguments it follows that there are fundamental weaknesses in the broad claim that late nineteenth- and early twentieth-century common law tort rules brought "efficient" social results.

Chapter 1

1. Letter from Newton D. Baker to John J. Cornwell, November 28, 1934, Newton D. Baker Papers, Box 39, Folder "B&O—1934," Library of Congress.

2. Letter from H. L. Stires to Allen S. Bowie, November 10, 1934, Newton D. Baker Papers, Box 39, Folder "B&O—1934," Library of Congress.

3. Letter from Allen S. Bowie to John J. Cornwell, November 23, 1934, Newton D. Baker Papers, Box 39, Folder "B&O—1934," Library of Congress.

4. Letter from H. L. Stires to Allen S. Bowie, November 10, 1934, Newton D. Baker Papers, Box 39, Folder "B&O—1934,"; letter from John J. Cornwell to Newton D. Baker, November 20, 1934, and "The Baltimore & Ohio Railroad Company—Salaries in Excess of $4,800 per annum, January 1, 1930 Compared with July 1, 1933," Newton D. Baker Papers, Box 39, Folder "B&O—1934," Library of Congress.

5. Letter from John J. Cornwell to Newton D. Baker, November 27, 1934, Newton D. Baker Papers, Box 39, Folder "B&O—1934," Library of Congress.

6. United States Constitution, ARTICLE 3, SECTION 2.

7. 1 Stat. 73 (1789).

8. Thus, for example, in 1957 when Congress was considering limitations on diversity jurisdiction, the Judicial Conference of the United States—the administrative organization of the federal judiciary—strongly opposed any significant curtailment. Its report to Congress declared that it "sees no valid reason for the destruction of the ancient diversity jurisdiction of the Federal courts." See "Jurisdiction of Federal Courts Concerning Diversity of Citizenship," Hearing before Subcommittee No. 3 of the Committee on the Judiciary of the House of Representatives, 85 Cong., 1 Sess. (1957), p. 13.

9. There are grounds, beyond the concern of this study, that allow a party sued in a federal court to move, in effect, the trial of all or much of the case to a state court. In such cases the federal courts "abstain" from exercising their jurisdiction in order to serve some purpose thought to be of greater importance in the circumstances. Such cases are often controversial and implicate basic judgments of political and social policy. See Erwin Chemerinsky, *Federal Jurisdiction* (Boston, 1989), chaps. 12–14.

10. The statement in the text needs to be qualified. In February 1801, after the Federalists had lost the election of 1800 but before their terms expired, they pushed through Congress a judiciary act that granted general federal question jurisdiction to the national courts; see 2 Stat. 89, 92 (1801). When the new Congress convened, the Jeffersonian Republicans were in control, and they quickly repealed the Federalist act; see 2 Stat. 132 (1802). Thus, the federal courts were initially granted general federal question jurisdiction in 1801, but they exercised the jurisdiction for barely one year.

11. See generally Stanley I. Kutler, *Judicial Power and Reconstruction Politics* (Chicago, 1968); William M. Wiecek, "The Reconstruction of Federal Judicial Power, 1863–1875," *American Journal of Legal History* 13 (1969): 333; J. David Hoeveler, Jr., "Reconstruction and the Federal Courts: The Civil Rights Act of 1875," *Historian* 31 (1969): 604. For a contemporary summary of the Judiciary Act of 1875, 18 Stat. 470 (1875), by a strong supporter of expanded federal jurisdiction, see John F. Dillon, *Removal of Causes from State Courts to Federal Courts*, 3rd ed. (St. Louis, 1881), pp. 26–40.

12. 18 Stat. 470, 471–72 (1875).

13. Felix Frankfurter and James M. Landis, *The Business of the Supreme Court: A Study in the Federal Judicial System* (New York: 1928), pp. 89–102; Tony Freyer, "The Federal Courts, Localism, and the National Economy," *Business History Review* 53 (1970): 358–61.

14. The House of Representatives, which repeatedly pressed for jurisdictional restrictions, was apparently little concerned with restricting federal question jurisdiction in the later 1880s. Its primary, and almost exclusive, focus in pushing the Judiciary Act of 1887–88 was its desire to restrict diversity jurisdiction and to limit the ability of corporations to use it. See Michael G. Collins, "The Unhappy History of Federal Question Removal," *Iowa Law Review* 71 (1986): 717, 738–52.

15. 24 Stat. 552 (1887), as amended and corrected by 25 Stat. 433 (1888). The act narrowed federal jurisdiction, for example, by providing that national banks could no longer remove on the ground that suits brought against them arose under federal law. The law provided that for jurisdictional purposes national banks were to be considered citizens of the states in which they were located. See Dillon, *Removal of Causes*, 5th ed. (St. Louis, 1889), pp. 40–49.

16. Alfred D. Chandler, Jr., *The Visible Hand: The Managerial Revolution in American Business* (Cambridge, MA, 1977), pp. 90, 151, 168, 204; E. Merrick Dodd, "Statutory Developments in Business Corporation Law, 1886–1936," *Harvard Law Review* 50 (1936): 27; Martin J. Sklar, *The Corporate Reconstruction of American Capitalism, 1890–1916* (New York, 1988), esp. pp. 43–47 and citations.

17. Glenn Porter, *The Rise of Big Business* (New York, 1973), p. 79. See Sklar, *Corporate Reconstruction*, esp. pp. 154–66; Chandler, *Visible Hand*, esp. pt. 4; Naomi R. Lamoreaux, *The Great Merger Movement in American Business, 1895–1904* (New York, 1985); Vincent P. Carosso, *Investment Banking in America: A History* (Cambridge, MA, 1970), pp. 45–50; Peter George, *The Emergence of Industrial America: Strategic Factors in American Economic Growth Since 1870* (Albany, NY, 1982); James Livingston, "The Social Analysis of Economic History and Theory: Conjectures on Late Nineteenth-Century American Development," *American Historical Review* 92 (1987): 69.

18. Henry N. Butler, "Nineteenth-Century Jurisdictional Competition in the Granting of Corporate Privileges," *Journal of Legal Studies* 14 (1985): 129, 157; J. Willard Hurst, *The Legitimacy of the Business Corporation in the Law of the United States, 1780–1970* (Charlottesville, VA, 1970), chap. 1; Edward Q. Keasbey, "New Jersey and the Great Corporations," *Harvard Law Review* 13 (1899): 198, 264.

19. *Louisville Railroad Co. v. Letson*, 2 How. (43 U.S.) 497 (1844). For the development of the doctrine of corporate citizenship, see Gerard C. Henderson, *The Position of Foreign Corporations in American Constitutional Law* (Cambridge, MA, 1918), chap. 4; Dudley O. McGovney, "A Supreme Court Fiction: Corporations in the Diverse Citizenship Jurisdiction of the Federal Courts," *Harvard Law Review* 56 (1943): 853, 1090, 1225. In 1854 George Ticknor Curtis concluded that "the law on this subject [corporate citizenship] cannot at present be considered as settled." *Commentaries on the Jurisdiction, Practice and Peculiar Jurisprudence of the Courts of the United States* (Philadelphia, 1854), vol. 1, p. 89.

20. Henderson, *Position of Foreign Corporations*, chap. 5; Philip B. Kurland, "The Supreme Court, the Due Process Clause and the *In Personam* Jurisdiction of State Courts from *Pennoyer* to *Denckla*: A Review," *University of Chicago Law Review* 25 (1958): 569, 577–86; William Laurens Walker, "Foreign Corporation Laws: The Loss of Reason," *North Carolina Law Review* 47 (1968): 1.

21. 12 Wall. (79 U.S.) 65 (1870).

22. 6 Otto (96 U.S.) 369 (1878).

23. Frankfurter and Landis, *Business of the Supreme Court*, p. 90.

24. 161 U.S. 545, 563 (1896).

25. Ibid., p. 562.

26. The Court's decision in *James* was consistent with the rule that was being generally applied in the federal courts by the 1890s. See, for example, Henry Campbell Black, *A Treatise on the Laws and Practice Governing the Removal of Causes from State Courts to Federal Courts* (St. Paul 1898), pp. 160–63. Opposing: B. C. Moon, *The Removal of Causes from the Courts of the Several States to the Circuit Courts of the United States* (New York, 1901), p. 337, n. 9 on p. 338. In any event, *James* made the rule final and uniform, conferring on corporations the broadest removal right. See, for example, *St. Joseph and Grand Island Railroad Co. v. Steele*, 167 U.S. 659 (1897); *Louisville, New Albany & Chicago Railway Co. v. Louisville Trust Co.*, 174 U.S. 552 (1899); *Southern Railway Co. v. Allison*, 190 U.S. 326 (1903); *Hollingsworth v. Southern Railway Co.*, 86 F. 353 (C.C.D.S.C. 1898); *Taylor v. Illinois Central Railroad Co.*, 89 F. 119 (C.C.D.Ky. 1898); *Walters v. Chicago, Burlington & Quincy Railroad Co.*, 104 F. 377 (C.C.D.Neb. 1900).

27. *Harris*, 79 U.S. 83–84; *Schollenberger*, 96 U.S. 376–78. See Charles Warren, "Corporations and Diversity of Citizenship," *Virginia Law Review* 19 (1933): 661, 662–72; McGovney, "Supreme Court Fiction," pp. 1093–94.

28. The Court's rationale in *James* was unconvincing. Assuming, as the Court stated, that establishment of the doctrine of corporate citizenship went "to the very verge of judicial power," that proposition would not decide the issue. To the contrary, allowing incorporation by other states to expand a corporation's jurisdictional citizenship could be seen as withdrawing from the "verge" as easily as transgressing it. Indeed, insofar as most corporations had shareholders in many states, allowing multiple corporate citizenship would seem to have been more consistent with both social facts and the basic federal rule that diversity jurisdiction required "complete diversity" between the parties. See Chapter 5.

29. Venue requirements could impose additional restrictions on removals in states where neither plaintiff nor defendant was a resident. See Chapter 8.

30. Corporations that willingly accepted incorporation in more than one state or that resulted from the "consolidation" of two or more corporations chartered in different states presented a special and particularly confused problem. See Black, *Treatise*, pp. 167–72; Moon, *Removal of Causes*, pp. 332–39; Armistead M. Dobie, *Handbook of Federal Jurisdiction and Procedure* (St. Paul, 1928), pp. 199–204; Note, "Multiple Incorporation as a Form of Railroad Organization," *Yale Law Journal* 46 (1937): 1370.

31. Richard M. Abrams, *Conservatism in a Progressive Era: Massachusetts Politics, 1900–1912* (Cambridge, MA, 1964), p. 10, n. 24; Lawrence M. Friedman, *A History of American Law* (New York, 1973), p. 458; Charles W. McCurdy, "The *Knight* Sugar Decision of 1895 and the Modernization of American Corporation Law, 1869–1903," *Business History Review* 53 (1979): 304, 314–23; Hurst, *Legitimacy of the Business Corporation*, pp. 69–73. See generally Dodd, "Statutory Developments"; Henderson, *Position of Foreign Corporations*.

32. Robert A. Silverman, *Law and Urban Growth: Civil Litigation in the Boston Trial Courts, 1880–1900* (Princeton, NJ, 1981), pp. 101, 105. Agreeing: Wayne V. McIntosh, "A State Court's Clientele: Exploring the Strategy of Trial Litigation," *Law & Society Review* 19 (1985): 421, 427, 430, 436.

33. Lawrence M. Friedman and Jack Ladinsky, "Social Change and the Law of Industrial Accidents," *Columbia Law Review* 67 (1967): 50, 60. The state and federal governments did not begin to compile statistics on industrial injuries until the 1880s, and it was not until after the turn of the century that widespread and reliable numbers became generally available. See, for example, H.R. Doc. No. 380, 57 Cong., 1 Sess. (1902), pp. 895–941. James Willard Hurst illustrated the scope and speed of the transformation:

> [F]rom the first two central electric power stations of 1882, the number went to 3,600 by 1902 and to 4,700 by 1907; there were nine commercially operated electric street railways in this country in 1885, 789 by 1890, 987 by 1902 and 1,260 in 1912. [*Law and the Conditions of Freedom in the Nineteenth-Century United States* (Madison, WI, 1967), p. 88]

34. United States Bureau of the Census, *The Statistical History of the United States from Colonial Times to the Present* (Stamford, CT, 1965), p. 437; Friedman and Ladinsky, "Social Change," p. 60; Morton Keller, *Affairs of State: Public Life in Late Nineteenth-Century America* (Cambridge, MA, 1977), p. 402. See Friedman, *History of American Law*, pp. 409–27; Wex S. Malone, "The Formative Era of Contributory Negligence," *Illinois Law Review* 41 (1946): 151; Walter Licht, *Working for the Railroad: The Organization of Work in the Nineteenth Century* (Princeton, NJ, 1983), pp. 190–91; Robert S. Hunt, *Law and Locomotives: The Impact of the Railroad on Wisconsin Law in the Nineteenth Century* (Madison, WI, 1958), pp. 69, 155. For a superb discussion of the human and cultural factors that underlay the thousands of injuries and deaths that occurred at railroad crossings each year, see John R. Stilgoe, *Metropolitan Corridor: Railroads and the American Scene* (New Haven, CT, 1983), pp. 167–88.

35. Morton Keller, *The Life Insurance Enterprise, 1885–1910: A Study in the Limits of Corporate Power* (Cambridge, MA, 1963), p. 9.

36. William A. Fricke, *Insurance: "A Text Book"* (Milwaukee [?], 1898), p. 41.

37. Ibid., p. 43.

38. Keller, *Life Insurance Enterprise*, p. 187; Friedman, *History of American Law*, pp. 476–77.

39. "Limiting Jurisdiction of Federal Courts," Hearings before the Committee on the Judi-

ciary of the United States House of Representatives, 72 Cong., 1 Sess. (1932), p. 25 (statement of Hobart S. Weaver, attorney for the Association of Life Insurance Presidents).

40. H.R. Rep. No. 45, 44 Cong., 1 Sess. (1876), p. 2.

41. H.R. Rep. No. 1481, 53 Cong., 3 Sess. (1894), pp. 1–2.

42. Warren, "Corporations and Diversity of Citizenship," pp. 671–73.

43. 96 U.S. 378. See, for example, *Pomeroy v. New York & New Haven Railroad Co.*, 19 Fed. Cas. 965 (C.C.S.D.N.Y. 1857); *Hume v. Pittsburgh, Cincinnati and St. Louis Railroad Co.*, 12 Fed. Cas. 870 (C.C.D.Ind. 1877).

44. John Wilder May, *The Law of Insurance, as Applied to Fire, Life, Accident, Guarantee, and Other Non-Maritime Risks*, 2nd ed. (Boston, 1882), p. 886; 4th ed. (Boston, 1900), p. 1356.

45. H.R. Rep. No. 2028, 56 Cong., 2 Sess. (1900), p. 3.

46. Dobie, *Handbook of Federal Jurisdiction*, p. 364.

47. Letter from William H. Sawtelle to George W. Norris, June 7, 1930, George W. Norris Papers, Tray 78, Box 8, File: "Limiting Jurisdiction of Federal Courts, 1929–30," Library of Congress.

I used the Norris papers during two widely separated time periods, and in the interim they were reorganized and renumbered. The current organization identifies papers solely by box and file number, whereas the earlier organization also divided them by "Tray" number. I cite items from the collection by the system that was in effect at the time I used it. The index to the papers has a cross listing between the old and new numbering systems.

48. Lawrence M. Friedman, "Civil Wrongs: Personal Injury Law in the Late 19th Century," *American Bar Foundation Research Journal* (1987): 351, 359–60, 368–69.

49. There were 17,777 insurance actions in the total sample, but it is not known how many of those were removable. It is almost certain that the great majority, probably 80 to 90 percent, did not meet the jurisdictional minimum and were therefore not cognizable in federal court either originally or by removal. See Chapter 9.

50. The suits were almost certainly equitable actions seeking rescission or interpleader. The former were suits to cancel policies on such grounds as fraud or mistake, and the latter were suits to protect the companies from multiple payments when there were two or more claimants to the same payment due. The companies also used federal equity suits for tactical reasons to control timing and forum choice or to try to avoid a trial by jury. See Chapter 9.

51. "Limiting Jurisdiction of Federal Courts," Hearings before the Committee on the Judiciary of the United States House of Representatives, 72 Cong., 1 Sess. (1932), p. 25 (statement of Hobart S. Weaver, attorney for the Association of Life Insurance Presidents).

52. American Law Institute, *A Study of the Business of the Federal Courts: Part II, Civil Cases* (Philadelphia, 1934), pp. 56, 99–100. See Richard A. Posner, "A Theory of Negligence," *Journal of Legal Studies* 1 (1972): 29, 51.

53. American Law Institute, *Study of the Business of the Federal Courts*, p. 102 and Detailed Table 103.

54. The numbers on corporate removals are from Charles E. Clark, "Diversity of Citizenship Jurisdiction of the Federal Courts," *American Bar Foundation Research Journal* 19 (1933): 499. The numbers in this article are from the federal courts research project that the ALI published. Clark, the Dean of the Yale Law School, worked on the project, helped draft the report, and was instrumental in arranging its publication. There are minor discrepancies between the numbers in his article and those in the final published report, primarily because the latter is slightly more comprehensive.

55. Ibid., pp. 66, 103–4.

56. American Law Institute, *A Study of the Business of the Federal Courts*, p. 80 and Detailed Table 59.

57. The evidence seems reliable, but it is too thin, disparate, and imprecise to support any attempt at precise quantification. See J. Willard Hurst, *The Growth of American Law: The Lawmakers* (Boston, 1950), pp. 172–73; Charles E. Clark and Harry Shulman, *A Study of Law Administration in Connecticut* (New Haven, CT, 1937), p. 31; Francis W. Laurent, *The Business of a Trial Court: 100 Years of Cases* (Madison, WI, 1959), pp. 59–60; Gordon M. Bakken, *The Development of Law in Frontier California: Civil Law and Society, 1850–1890* (Westport, CT, 1985), p. 76; Lawrence M. Friedman and Robert V. Percival, "A Tale of Two Courts: Litigation in

Alameda and San Benito Counties," *Law & Society Review* 10 (1976): 267, 284–87; Gary T. Schwartz, "Tort Law and the Economy in Nineteenth-Century America: A Reinterpretation," *Yale Law Journal* 90 (1981): 1717, 1764; Frank W. Munger, Jr., "Commercial Litigation in West Virginia State and Federal Courts, 1870–1940," *American Journal of Legal History* 30 (1986): 322, 337, 342.

58. Friedman, "Civil Wrongs," p. 369. Some support for the same proposition appears in Morton Keller, "The Judicial System and the Law of Life Insurance, 1888–1910," *Business History Review* 35 (1961): 317, 323.

59. Lawrence M. Friedman and Thomas D. Russell, "More Civil Wrongs: Personal Injury Litigation, 1901–1910," *American Journal of Legal History* 34 (1990): 295, 308, 310.

60. Munger, "Commercial Litigation in West Virginia," pp. 337, 342.

61. Compare McIntosh, "State Court's Clientele," pp. 438, 441.

62. John C. Reed, *The Conduct of Lawsuits Out of and in Court: Practically Teaching, and Copiously Illustrating, the Preparation and Forensic Management of Litigated Cases of All Kinds* (Boston, 1885), pp. 121–22.

63. This attitude was unintentionally reflected, for example, by the general counsel of the National Board of Fire Underwriters when he testified before Congress in 1932. Contrasting the federal courts with the state courts, he referred to the latter as "the lower courts." "Limiting Jurisdiction of Federal Courts," Hearing before the Committee on the Judiciary of the United States House of Representatives, 72 Cong., 1 Sess. (1932), p. 31 (statement of J. H. Doyle). Compare Judith Resnik, "Housekeeping: The Nature and Allocation of Work in Federal Trial Courts," *Georgia Law Review* 24 (1990): 909.

64. This theme is developed at length in Chapter 2.

65. See, for example, Frank W. Munger, Jr., "Social Change and Tort Litigation: Industrialization, Accidents, and Trial Courts in Southern West Virginia, 1872–1940," *Buffalo Law Review* 36 (1987): 75, 108–9; Stanton Wheeler, Bliss Cartwright, Robert A. Kagan, and Lawrence M. Friedman, "Do the 'Haves' Come Out Ahead? Winning and Losing in State Supreme Courts, 1870–1970," *Law & Society Review* 21 (1987): 403, 432–37, 440–41.

66. 16 Pet. (41 U.S.) 1 (1842).

67. See, for example, Hessel E. Yntema and George H. Jaffin, "Preliminary Analysis of Concurrent Jurisdiction," *University of Pennsylvania Law Review* 79 (1931): 869. Supporters of the doctrine sometimes credited it with far more influence than it apparently merited. Alton B. Parker, a prominent lawyer and the Democratic presidential candidate in 1904, declared that "the student of the Common Law as administered in this country cannot but be impressed with the remarkable uniformity which has attended the application of its principles in forty-six different jurisdictions." See Alton B. Parker, "The Common Law Jurisdiction of the United States Courts," *Yale Law Journal* 17 (1907): 1, 7.

68. For the dominant view, at least within the legal profession, see Frederick Bausman, "Election of Federal Judges," *American Law Review* 37 (1903): 886. For a contrary view, see Walter Clark, "Law and Human Progress," *American Law Review* 37 (1903): 512, 517–18. Compare Kermit L. Hall, "Progressive Reform and the Decline of Democratic Accountability: The Popular Election of State Supreme Court Judges, 1850–1920," *American Bar Foundation Research Journal* (1984): 345.

69. It was commonly and widely assumed that juries tended to favor plaintiffs, especially when the defendant was a corporation. Byron K. Elliott and William F. Elliott, *The Work of the Advocate: A Practical Treatise* (Indianapolis, 1888), p. 117; Thomas M. Cooley, "The Uncertainty of the Law," *American Law Review* 22 (1888): 347, 364; Simeon E. Baldwin, *The American Judiciary* (New York, 1905), p. 371; Percy Werner, "The Abuse of Personal Injury Litigation," *Green Bag* 18 (1906): 201–3; Samuel S. Page, "The Defendant's Standpoint," *Illinois Law Review* 1 (1906): 27, 29–31.

There is some reason to think that jurors did not lean quite so frequently toward plaintiffs. See Friedman, "Civil Wrongs," pp. 364–65; Friedman and Russell, "More Civil Wrongs," pp. 305–10.

70. Warren, "Corporations and Diversity of Citizenship," p. 687; McGovney, "Supreme Court Fiction," pp. 1244–46. "Without the guidance of an intelligent judge, a jury would frequently come to unfortunate and even unjust conclusions. That there should be such guidance is

an essential part of the jury system, and it is generally given most effectually where the judges are the ablest and the most independent." Baldwin, *American Judiciary*, p. 187.

71. *United States v. Reading Railroad Co.*, 123 U.S. 113 (1887); *Herron v. Southern Pacific Co.*, 283 U.S. 91 (1931); Friedman, *History of American Law*, p. 424; Baldwin, *American Judiciary*, pp. 371–72. See, for example, *Southern Railway Co. v. Walters*, 284 U.S. 190 (1931); *Equitable Life Assurance Society v. McElroy*, 83 F. 631 (C.C.A. 8 1897); compare *Southern Railway Co. v. Priester*, 289 F. 945 (C.C.A. 4 1923) with *Priester v. Southern Railway Co.*, 149 S.E. 226 (Sup. Ct.S.C. 1929). On the rise of elective judgeships in the states, see Kermit L. Hall, "The Judiciary on Trial: State Constitutional Reform and the Rise of an Elected Judiciary, 1846–1860," *Historian* 45 (1983): 337–54; Hall, "Progressive Reform and the Decline of Democratic Accountability."

72. "Limiting Jurisdiction of Federal Courts," Hearings before the Committe on the Judiciary of the United States House of Representatives, 72 Cong., 1 Sess. (1932), p. 30 (statement of J. H. Doyle, general counsel, National Board of Fire Underwriters). See McGovney, "Supreme Court Fiction," pp. 1246–47; Warren, "Corporations and Diversity of Citizenship," p. 687. One study of the Boston state courts in the late nineteenth century, for example, found a relatively high percentage of foreign-born and blue-collar workers on the local juries. Silverman, *Law and Urban Growth*, pp. 41–43.

73. Andrew J. Hirschl, "Personal Injury Actions: The Plaintiff's Standpoint," *Illinois Law Review* 1 (1906): 16, 19.

Contemporary research on judicial behavior has confirmed the firsthand empirical observations of attorneys that the social backgrounds of judges tend to influence the ways in which they handle legal issues. See, for example, Stuart S. Nagel, "Judicial Backgrounds and Criminal Cases," *Journal of Criminal Law, Criminology and Police Science* 53 (1962): 333; Martha A. Levin, "Urban Politics and Judicial Behavior," *Journal of Legal Studies* 3 (1974): 339.

74. See, for example, *United States Mutual Accident Association v. Barry*, 131 U.S. 100, 120 (1889). On the differences between trial judges and their ability to shape and influence cases, see Kenneth M. Dolbeare, *Trial Courts in Urban Politics: State Court Policy Impact and Functions in a Local Political System* (New York, 1967); Jerome Frank, *Law and the Modern Mind* (New York, 1963), esp. chap. 12; Frank, *Courts on Trial: Myth and Reality in American Justice* (New York, 1963).

75. Woodrow Wilson, *The State: Elements of Historical and Practical Politics* (Boston, 1897), p. 508 (emphasis in original).

76. See, for example, Kermit L. Hall, "Constitutional Machinery and Judicial Professionalism: The Careers of Midwestern State Appellate Court Judges, 1861–1899," in Gerard W. Gawalt, ed., *The New High Priests: Lawyers in Post–Civil War America* (Westport, CT, 1984), pp. 29–49; Robert W. Gordon, " 'The Ideal and the Actual in the Law': Fantasies and Practices of New York City Lawyers, 1870–1910," in Gawalt, ed., *The New High Priests*, pp. 51–74; Robert W. Gordon, "Legal Thought and Legal Practice in the Age of American Enterprise, 1870–1920," in Gerald L. Geison, ed., *Professions and Professional Ideologies in America* (Chapel Hill, NC, 1983), pp. 70–110; Kermit L. Hall, "The Children of the Cabins: The Lower Federal Judiciary, Modernization, and the Political Culture, 1789–1899," *Northwestern University Law Review* 75 (1980): 423; Kermit L. Hall, "Social Backgrounds and Judicial Recruitment: A Nineteenth-Century Perspective on the Lower Federal Judiciary," *Western Political Quarterly* 29 (1976): 243; John R. Schmidhauser, "The Justices of the Supreme Court: A Collective Portrait," *Midwest Journal of Political Science* 3 (1959): 1; Munger, "Commercial Litigation in West Virginia," p. 342, n. 35. Compare Robert A. Kagan, Bobby D. Infelise, and Robert R. Detlefsen, "American State Supreme Court Justices, 1900–1970," *American Bar Foundation Research Journal* (1984): 371. See also Schmidhauser, *Judges and Justices: The Federal Appellate Judiciary* (Boston, 1979), esp. chap. 3; Stuart S. Nagel, "Political Party Affiliation and Judges' Decisions," *American Political Science Review* 55 (1961): 843; Robert A. Carp and C. K. Rowland, *Policymaking and Politics in the Federal District Courts* (Knoxville, TN, 1983).

77. For example, Freyer, "The Federal Courts, Localism, and the National Economy," *passim;* "Workmen's Compensation," Hearings before a Subcommittee of the Committee on Interstate and Foreign Commerce of the United States House of Representatives on H.R. 2944, 63

Cong., 2 Sess. (1914), pp. 16–17 (statement of Hon. Adolph J. Sabath, congressman from Illinois).

78. See, for example, Albro Martin, "Railroads and the Equity Receivership: An Essay on Institutional Change," *Journal of Economic History* 34 (1974): 685; Gordon, "Legal Thought and Practice," pp. 70, 101–7. William Howard Taft discussed the receivership issue in "Recent Criticisms of the Federal Judiciary," *American Bar Association Reports* 6 (1895): 262.

79. W. A. Coutts, "The Rule Forbidding Suits Against Receivers Without Leave, as Applied to Receivers Managing Railroad and Like Corporations," *American Law Review* 38 (1904): 516, 529.

80. Walter Clark, "Constitutional Changes Which Are Foreshadowed," *American Law Review* 30 (1896): 702, 705.

81. Editorial notes, *American Law Review* 37 (1903): 575, 576.

82. Herbert Croly, *The Promise of American Life* (Boston, 1909), p. 356.

83. C. P. Connolly, "Big Business and the Bench: The Federal Courts—Last Refuge of the 'Interests'," *Everybody's Magazine* 26 (1912): 827.

84. William Jennings Bryan, "Popular Versus State's Rights," *The Reader* 9 (1907): 461, 463.

85. Letter from Theodore Roosevelt to Henry Cabot Lodge, September 12, 1910, reprinted in Henry Cabot Lodge and Charles F. Redmond, eds. *Selections from the Correspondence of Theodore Roosevelt and Henry Cabot Lodge, 1884–1913* (New York, 1925), vol. 1, p. 391.

86. For Roosevelt's efforts on behalf of the recall of judicial decisions, see, for example, Theodore Roosevelt, "Judges and Progress," *The Outlook* 100 (1912): 40; Roosevelt, "Do You Believe in the Rule of the People?" *The Outlook* 100 (1912): 526; Roosevelt, "The Right of the People to Rule," *The Outlook* 100 (1912): 618.

87. Robert M. LaFollette, "Supreme Court Ruler of Nation," a speech before the American Federation of Labor, reprinted in the (Madison, WI) *Capitol Times,* June 29, 1922. A clipping is contained in the "LaFollette Family Papers," Series B, Box 226, Library of Congress.

88. Quoted in Leonard Baker, *Back to Back: The Duel Between F.D.R. and the Supreme Court* (New York, 1967), p. 108.

Chapter 2

1. See, for example, Marc Galanter, "Why the 'Haves' Come Out Ahead: Speculations on the Limits of Legal Change," *Law & Society Review* 9 (1974): 95. Galanter's "speculations," though difficult to test in broad and rigorous ways, have received some empirical support. See Marc Galanter, "Afterword: Explaining Litigation," *Law & Society Review* 9 (1975): 347, 357–60; George L. Priest and Benjamin Klein, "The Selection of Disputes for Litigation," *Journal of Legal Studies* 13 (1984): 1, 28; Stanton Wheeler, Bliss Cartwright, Robert A. Kagan, and Lawrence M. Friedman, "Do the 'Haves' Come Out Ahead? Winning and Losing in State Supreme Courts, 1870–1970," *Law & Society Review* 21 (1987): 403, 438–43; Lawrence M. Friedman, "Law, Lawyers, and Popular Culture," *Yale Law Journal* 98 (1989): 1579, 1593.

2. See, for example, Walter Licht, *Working for the Railroad: The Organization of Work in the Nineteenth Century* (Princeton, NJ, 1983), chap. 5; Paul V. Black, "Experiment in Bureaucratic Centralization: Employee Blacklisting on the Burlington Railroad, 1877–1892," *Business History Review* 51 (1977): 444.

3. Compare, for example, Clarence A. Lightner, "The Abuse of Personal Injury Litigation," *Green Bag* 18 (1906): 193, 915; Roger S. Warner, "Employers' Liability as an Industrial Problem," *Green Bag* 18 (1906): 185, 188; Crystal Eastman, *Work-Accidents and the Law* (New York, 1910), pp. 84–104; Carl Gersuny, *Work Hazards and Industrial Conflict* (Hanover, NH, 1981), pp. 55–67.

4. Alfred D. Chandler, Jr., *The Visible Hand: The Managerial Revolution in American Business* (Cambridge, MA, 1977), esp. chaps. 4–5; Morton Keller, *The Life Insurance Enterprise, 1885–1910* (Cambridge, MA: 1963), esp. chaps. 4–5; Peter George, *The Emergence of Industrial America: Strategic Factors in American Economic Growth Since 1870* (Albany, NY, 1982), chap. 5; Samuel P. Hays, *American Political History as Social Analysis* (Knoxville, TN, 1980), chap. 8.

5. Thomas C. Cochran, *Railroad Leaders, 1843–1899* (Cambridge, MA, 1953), p. 89; John

F. Stover, *Railroads of the South* (New York, 1961), pp. 86, 175. See Charles W. McCurdy, "American Law and the Marketing Structure of the Large Corporation, 1875–1890," *Journal of Economic History* 38 (1978): 631; Morton Keller, "The Judicial System and the Law of Life Insurance," *Business History Review* 35 (1961): 317.

6. Lawrence M. Friedman and Thomas D. Russell, "More Civil Wrongs: Personal Injury Litigation, 1901–1910," *American Journal of Legal History* 34 (1990): 295, 297–99.

7. Sen. Doc. No. 338, 62 Cong., 2 Sess. (1912), vol. 2, p. 1056.

8. Keller, *Life Insurance Enterprise,* pp. 217, 220–22. See Licht, *Working for the Railroad,* chap. 5; Francis W. Laurent, *The Business of a Trial Court: 100 Years of Cases* (Madison, WI, 1959), p. 62. Compare H. Laurence Ross, *Settled Out of Court: The Social Process of Insurance Claims Adjustments* (Chicago, 1970), pp. 21–22, 70–73, 96–106, 115, 140, 166–70, 211–15, 225.

9. See, for example, Gersuny, *Work Hazards,* pp. 55–97. Compare Ross, *Settled Out of Court,* pp. 211–15; Galanter, "Why the 'Haves' Come Out Ahead," pp. 97–104; Douglas E. Rosenthal, *Lawyer and Client: Who's in Charge?* (New York, 1974), pp. 70–93, 128–41. A plaintiff's personal injury lawyer has recently described his view of company practices as follows:

> The companies will seldom make a reasonable offer to settle small personal injury claims, especially those involving soft-tissue injuries. And when on occasion they move toward settlement, their offers demean the victims. They know that most people who are unrepresented by counsel will succumb to the "take it or leave it approach." Most individual claimants believe or are forced to believe that they must accept an adjuster's offer.
>
> The carriers also know that the majority of attorneys who represent the plaintiffs in these cases will usually settle claims rather than take the time, effort, and expense to go to trial. [Ellsworth T. Rundlett, 3rd, "Negotiating a Small Personal Injury Claim," *Trial* (Oct., 1991): pp. 55, 56]

10. Lawrence M. Friedman, *A History of American Law* (New York, 1973), p. 558.

11. "Limitation of Venue in Certain Actions Brought Under the Employers' Liability Act," Hearings before a Subcommittee of the Committee on the Judiciary of the United States Senate on S. 1567 and H.R. 1639, 80 Cong., 2 Sess. (1948), p. 32 (statement of John W. Freels, counsel to the Illinois Central Railroad).

12. "Limitation of Venue in Certain Actions Brought Under the Employers' Liability Act," Hearings before Subcommittee No. 4 of the Committee on the Judiciary of the United States House of Representatives on H.R. 1639, 80 Cong., 1 Sess. (1947), p. 65 (statement of Warren H. Atherton, Esq., member, Brotherhood of Railroad Trainmen).

13. Friedman, *History of American Law,* pp. 549–66; J. Willard Hurst, *The Growth of American Law: The Lawmakers* (Boston, 1950), pp. 342–52, 295–305; Stephen Botein, " 'What We Shall Meet Afterwards in Heaven': Judgeship as a Symbol for Modern American Lawyers," in Gerald L. Geison, ed., *Professions and Professional Ideologies in America* (Chapel Hill, NC, 1983), pp. 49–69; Robert W. Gordon, "Legal Thought and Legal Practice in the Age of American Enterprise, 1870–1920," in Geison, ed., *Professions and Professional Ideologies in America,* pp. 70–110; Gerard W. Gawalt, ed., *The New High Priests: Lawyers in Post–Civil War America* (Westport, CT, 1984), *passim;* John Phillip Reid, *An American Judge: Marmaduke Dent of West Virginia* (New York, 1968), pp. 129–30. For a more recent discussion of the relationship between lawyers and client base, see Donald D. Landon, "Lasalle Street and Main Street: The Role of Context in Structuring Law Practice," *Law & Society Review* 22 (1988): 213.

14. See, for example, Terry Thomason, "Are Attorneys Paid What They're Worth? Contingent Fees and the Settlement Process," *Journal of Legal Studies* 20 (1991): 187; Albert W. Alschuler, "Personal Failure, Institutional Failure, and the Sixth Amendment," *New York University Review of Law & Social Change* 14 (1986): 149. For an interesting examination in an analogous context, see Janet Cooper Alexander, "Do the Merits Matter? A Study of Settlements in Securities Class Actions," *Stanford Law Review* 43 (1991): 497.

15. Wayne K. Hobson, "Symbol of the New Profession: Emergence of the Large Law Firm, 1870–1915," in Gawalt, ed., *New High Priests,* pp. 3–27; Jerold S. Auerbach, " 'Born to an Era of Insecurity': Career Patterns of Law Review Editors, 1918–1941," *American Journal of Legal History* 17 (1973): 17; William O. Douglas, *Go East, Young Man: The Early Years* (New York,

1974), pp. 156–57; Emily P. Dodge, "Evolution of a City Law Office," *Wisconsin Law Review* (1955): 180, and *Wisconsin Law Review* (1956): 35; Friedman, "Law, Lawyers, and Popular Culture," p. 1601; Kermit L. Hall, *The Magic Mirror: Law In American History* (New York, 1989), pp. 212–14.

For suggestions that attorneys representing individual tort plaintiffs may have brought less training and fewer resources to their litigations than did corporate counsel, see Gawalt, ed., *New High Priests, passim;* Robert A. Silverman, *Law and Urban Growth: Civil Litigation in the Boston Trial Courts, 1880–1900* (Princeton, NJ, 1981), pp. 115–17, 137; Hurst, *Growth of American Law,* esp. pp. 301–13, 342–52; Jerold S. Auerbach, *Unequal Justice: Lawyers and Social Change in Modern America* (New York, 1976), chap. 1; William M. Wherry, "A Study of the Organization of Litigation and of the Jury Trial in the Supreme Court of New York County," *New York University Law Quarterly Review* 8 (1931): 640, 664–68; Wheeler et al., "Do the 'Haves' Come Out Ahead?" pp. 403, 432, n. 30, 437–41. Opposing: Richard A. Posner, "A Theory of Negligence," *Journal of Legal Studies* 1 (1972): 29, 91–92.

Studies of the bar in the twentieth century show the highly stratified nature of the legal profession, the dominance of the corporate attorney from the large firm, and some of the unequal social consequences that result. Many of those findings would most likely apply to the bar in the late nineteenth and early twentieth centuries. See, for example, Erwin O. Smigel, *The Wall Street Lawyer: Professional Organization Man?* (Bloomington, IN, 1969); Jerome E. Carlin, *Lawyers on Their Own: A Study of Individual Practitioners in Chicago* (New Brunswick, NJ, 1962); Joel F. Handler, *The Lawyer and His Community: The Practicing Bar in a Middle-sized City* (Madison, WI, 1967); Jack Ladinsky, "Careers of Lawyers, Law Practice, and Legal Institutions," *American Sociological Review* 8 (1963): 47; Jack Ladinsky, "The Impact of Social Backgrounds of Lawyers on Law Practice and the Law," *Journal of Legal Education* 16 (1963): 127; Hubert J. O'Gorman, *Lawyers and Matrimonial Cases* (Glencoe, IL, 1963); Ross, *Settled Out of Court,* pp. 73–86; John P. Heinz and Edward O. Laumann, *Chicago Lawyers: The Social Structure of the Bar* (New York, 1982). For an interesting study comparing the rural and urban bar that stresses the extent to which social factors shape the legal profession, see Donald D. Landon, *Country Lawyers: The Impact of Context on Professional Practice* (New York, 1990).

Similarly, studies of twentieth-century litigation support the proposition that sophisticated and economically strong institutions tend to do better in litigation than do individuals. Galanter, "Afterword: Explaining Litigation," pp. 357–60; Craig Wanner, "The Public Ordering of Private Relations, Part I: Initiating Civil Cases in Urban Trial Courts," *Law & Society Review* 8 (1974): 421, 437–38; Wanner, "The Public Ordering of Private Relations, Part II: Winning Civil Court Cases," *Law & Society Review* 9 (1975): 293, 305–6. Other scholars have shown that litigation correlates positively with relative wealth. See Leon Mayhew and Albert Reiss, "The Social Organization of Legal Contacts," *American Sociological Review* 34 (1969): 309; Joel B. Grossman and Austin Sarat, "Litigation in the Federal Courts: A Comparative Perspective," *Law & Society Review* 9 (1975): 321. Another study shows that the relative inexperience of counsel can have a significant effect on the outcome of litigations. Kevin C. McMunigal, "The Costs of Settlement: The Impact of Scarcity of Adjudication on Litigating Lawyers," *U.C.L.A. Law Review* 37 (1990): 833.

For a broad attempt to study lawyers across cultures, with considerable attention to American lawyers, see Richard L. Abel and Philip S. C. Lewis, eds., *Lawyers in Society,* 3 vols. (New York, 1988).

16. Wheeler et al., "Do the 'Haves' Come Out Ahead?" The conclusions summarized appear on p. 439 and the quotation on p. 440. See Frank W. Munger, Jr., "Social Change and Tort Litigation: Industrialization, Accidents, and Trial Courts in Southern West Virginia, 1872–1940," *Buffalo Law Review* 36 (1987): 75, 99, and n. 58.

17. For example, J. Willard Hurst, "The Functions of Courts in the United States, 1950–1980," *Law & Society Review* 15 (1980–81): 401, 428–30, 439–45; Galanter, "Why the 'Haves' Come Out Ahead," p. 95; Ross, *Settled Out of Court,* pp. 68–69, 141; Lawrence M. Friedman, "Civil Wrongs: Personal Injury Law in the Late 19th Century," *American Bar Foundation Research Journal* (1987): 351, 355; Wherry, "A Study of the Organization of Litigation and of the Jury Trial," pp. 400–9; United States Railroad Retirement Board, *Work Injuries in the Railroad*

Industry, 1938–40 (Chicago, 1947), vol. 1, *passim*. Social factors often prevent injured parties from even consulting an attorney or effectively considering the desirability of bringing an action. See Hurst, *Growth of American Law,* pp. 316–19; Ross, *Settled Out of Court,* pp. 68–69; Austin Sarat, "Studying American Legal Culture: An Assessment of Survey Evidence," *Law & Society Review* 11 (1977): 427, 436, 448–52, 464–72; David M. Engel, "The Oven Bird's Song: Insiders, Outsiders, and Personal Injuries in an American Community," *Law & Society Review* 18 (1984): 551, 565–66; Frank W. Munger, Jr., "Law, Economic Change and Litigation: A Critical Examination of an Empirical Research Tradition," *European Yearbook in the Sociology of Law* (1988): 141, 164–66.

18. H.R. Rep. No. 1078, 49 Cong., 1 Sess. (1886), p. 2. The report recommended a bill preventing corporations from removing in any state in which they did business, declaring that such removal "has given rise to much unnecessary expense and grave disadvantages to the citizens of States where corporations may be carrying on business" (p. 2).

19. Railroad Retirement Board, *Work Injuries,* vol. 1, p. 48. Also see vol. 1, p. 109; and Friedman and Russell, "More Civil Wrongs," pp. 310–13.

The formal law, of course, helped shape the invisible legal process. Sometimes, particularly when the adverse parties enjoyed relatively equal resources, it provided the basic structure for private settlements, and claim discounting represented an economically rational trade-off for eliminating risks of trial and costs of litigation. See, for example, Robert H. Mnookin and Lewis Kornhauser, "Bargaining in the Shadow of the Law: The Case of Divorce," *Yale Law Journal* 88 (1979): 950, 968. Sometimes, however, one of the parties was only dimly aware of his rights, and sometimes both parties' formal rights were largely if not totally irrelevant to the settlements. Indeed, in many cases the legal rules functioned in ways that were inconsistent with their own theory and purpose. See, for example, Note, "The Persecution and Intimidation of the Low-Income Litigant as Performed by the Small Claims Court in California," *Stanford Law Review* 21 (1969): 1657. On small claims courts generally, see Eric H. Steele, "The Historical Context of Small Claims Court," *American Bar Foundation Research Journal* (1981): 293.

20. Munger, "Social Change and Tort Litigation," p. 95.

21. Joseph F. Tripp, "An Instance of Labor and Business Cooperation: Workmen's Compensation in Washington State (1911)," *Labor History* 17 (1976): 530, 537.

22. Sen. Doc. No. 338, 62 Cong., 2 Sess. (1912), vol. 1, pp. 131, 135, 139, 143.

23. For the federal statistics, see the *Annual Report* of the Office of the Attorney General; Clark, "Adjudication to Administration." For the states, see Marc Galanter, "Reading the Landscape of Disputes: What We Know and Don't Know (and Think We Know) About Our Allegedly Contentious and Litigious Society," *U.C.L.A. Law Review* 31 (1983): 4, 36–47; Laurent, *Business of a Trial Court,* pp. 59–64,; Friedman and Percival, "Tale of Two Courts," pp. 286–89; Lawrence M. Friedman, "San Benito 1890: Legal Snapshot of a County," *Stanford Law Review* 27 (1975): 687, 695–96, 701; Charles E. Clark and Harry Shulman, *A Study of Law Administration in Connecticut: A Report of an Investigation of the Activities of Certain Trial Courts of the State* (New Haven, CT, 1937), pp. 7–29; Wherry, "Study of the Organization of Litigation," pp. 400–9, 640–48; Silverman, *Law and Urban Growth,* pp. 114–15, 136; Richard Lempert, "More Tales of Two Courts: Exploring Changes in the 'Dispute Settlement Function' of Trial Courts," *Law & Society Review* 13 (1978): 91, 111; Wayne McIntosh, "150 Years of Litigation and Dispute Settlement: A Court Tale," *Law & Society Review* 15 (1980–81): 823, 838–40, 847; Friedman and Russell, "More Civil Wrongs," p. 307. The expansion of the informal legal process may not have been as marked as the federal statistics imply. In some state courts the increase in settled or discontinued cases was relatively small. See Stephen Daniels, "Continuity and Change in Patterns of Case Handling: A Case Study of Two Rural Counties," *Law & Society Review* 19 (1985): 381, 400–2; Wayne V. McIntosh, "A State Court's Clientele: Exploring the Strategy of Trial Litigation," *Law & Society Review* 19 (1985): 421, 434–41.

24. There is a large and growing literature that discusses the advantages and disadvantages of litigation, as opposed to what has come to be called "alternate dispute resolution." For differing views on the negotiation process that occurs outside court, see, for example, Melvin Aron Eisenberg, "Private Ordering Through Negotiation: Dispute-Settlement and Rulemaking," *Harvard Law Review* 89 (1976): 637; Richard E. Miller and Austin Sarat, "Grievances, Claims, and

Disputes: Assessing the Adversary Culture," *Law & Society Review* 15 (1980–81): 525; Marc Galanter, "Justice in Many Rooms: Courts, Private Ordering, and Indigenous Law," *Journal of Legal Pluralism* 19 (1981): 1; David M. Engel, "Legal Pluralism in an American Community: Perspectives on a Civil Trial Court," *American Bar Foundation Research Journal* (1980): 425; Owen M. Fiss, "Against Settlement," *Yale Law Journal* 93 (1984): 1073; Samuel R. Gross, "The American Advantage: The Value of Inefficient Litigation," *Michigan Law Review* 85 (1987): 734.

25. For example, Carl Gersuny, "Work Injuries and Adversary Processes in Two New England Textile Mills," *Business History Review* 51 (1977): 326. There was, of course, considerable variation by geographical area, industry, type of claim, and individual corporation. See, for example, Frank W. Munger, Jr., "Commercial Litigation in West Virginia State and Federal Courts, 1870–1940," *American Journal of Legal History* 30 (1986): 322, 337–38; Munger, "Social Change and Tort Litigation," p. 102. Corporations in the late nineteenth century were often under acute pressure to cut their costs. See, for example, James Livingston, "The Social Analysis of Economic History and Theory: Conjectures on Late Nineteenth-Century American Development," *American Historical Review* 92 (1987): 69.

26. Licht, *Working for the Railroad*, p. 200.

27. Ibid., pp. 201–12.

28. Sen. Doc. No. 338, 62 Cong., 2 Sess. (1912), vol. 2, pp. 734–38. For Pittsburgh, see Crystal Eastman, *Work-Accidents and the Law* (New York, 1910), pp. 119–31, 153–64.

29. "Employers' Liability and Workmen's Compensation," Hearings before the Committee on the Judiciary of the United States House of Representatives on H.R. 20487, 62 Cong., 2 Sess. (1913), 6, 24 (statement of James Harrington Boyd, Chairman of the Employers' Liability Commission of the State of Ohio); Sen. Doc. No. 338, 62 Cong., 2 Sess. (1912), vol. 2, pp. 721–22, 734–36 (statement of J. Harrington Boyd, Chairman, Employers' Liability Commission of Ohio).

30. Sen. Doc. No. 338, 62 Cong., 2 Sess. (1912), vol. 2, pp. 756–57 (statement of Robert J. Cary, attorney, New York Central System). When Congress and the states began seriously considering workmen's compensation acts after 1908, many corporations and business groups favored them as devices to stabilize and limit the costs of industrial injuries. The critical issue was the amount that any such law would require them to pay. If compensation laws would be cost effective, at least many corporations favored their enactment. The desirability of a law that would limit costs and set compensation schedules at low rates was a consistent refrain of corporate spokesmen. Their goal was a law that would cost no more, and perhaps cost less, than did the common law system. Their hopes were based on the belief that by eliminating plaintiffs' attorney fees and other litigation and administrative costs, they could increase the amount of payments that actually went to injured workers while lowering their total costs. See Sen. Doc. No. 90, 62 Cong., 1 Sess. (1911), *passim;* Sen. Doc. No. 338, 62 Cong., 2 Sess. (1912), *passim;* James Weinstein, *The Corporate Ideal in the Liberal State: 1900–1918* (Boston, 1968), chap. 2; Roy Lubove, "Workmen's Compensation and the Prerogatives of Voluntarism," *Labor History* 8 (1967): 254; Lawrence M. Friedman and Jack Ladinsky, "Social Change and the Law of Industrial Accidents," *Columbia Law Review* 67 (1967): 50. For a provocative critique of the standard explanations for the rise of workmen's compensation, see Munger, "Social Change and Tort Litigation."

31. Quoted in Eastman, *Work-Accidents and the Law,* pp. 290–91.

32. Quoted in Gersuny, "Work Injuries and Adversary Processes," p. 329. For the emphasis on the "careless worker" theory that many corporate spokesmen espoused, see Anthony F. C. Wallace, *St. Clair: A Nineteenth-Century Coal Town's Experience with a Disaster-prone Industry* (New York, 1987), pp. 265–75; Gersuny, *Work Hazards and Industrial Conflict,* pp. 55–67.

33. George E. Clark to George W. Norris, February 6, 1933, George W. Norris Papers, Library of Congress, Box 198, File: "Limiting Jurisdiction of Federal Courts (71st & 72nd) Congress."

34. Sen. Doc. No. 338, 62 Cong., 2 Sess. (1912), vol. 1, p. 87. See Friedman, "Civil Wrongs," pp. 371–72.

35. Roger S. Warner, "Employers' Liability as an Industrial Problem," *Green Bag* 18 (1906): 185, 190.

36. Editorial note, *Virginia Law Register* 11 (1905): 843.

37. "Limitation of Venue in Certain Actions Brought Under the Employers' Liability Act,"

Hearings before Subcommittee No. 4 of the Committee on the Judiciary of the House of Representatives, 80 Cong., 1 Sess. (1947), p. 72 (testimony of Warren H. Atherton, member, Brotherhood of Railroad Trainmen).

38. Quoted in Lubove, "Workmen's Compensation," p. 260, n. 15.

39. "Employers' Liability and Workmen's Compensation," Hearings before the Committee on the Judiciary of the United States House of Representatives on H.R. 20487, 62 Cong., 2 Sess. (1913), vol. 2, p. 648 (statement of W. G. Lee, president of the Brotherhood of Railroad Trainmen). See "Limitation of Venue in Certain Actions Brought Under the Employers' Liability Act," Hearings Before Subcommittee No. 4 of the Committee on the Judiciary of the United States House of Representatives on H.R. 1639, 80 Cong., 1 Sess. (1947), pp. 156–57 (letter from Jno. F. Scott to Hon. John Jennings, Jr.), and p. 92 (statement of A. E. Lyon, executive secretary, Railway Labor Executives Association).

40. *Union Pacific Railroad Co. v. Whitney,* 198 F. 784, 793 (C.C.A. 8 1912).

41. *Bliss v. New York Central & Hudson River Railroad Co.,* 36 N.E. 65, 67 (Sup.Jud.Ct.Mass. 1894) (emphasis added).

42. See, for example, *Union Pacific Railway Co. v. Harris,* 158 U.S. 326 (1895); *Chesapeake and Ohio Railway Co. v. Howard,* 178 U.S. 153 (1900); *Wabash Railway Co. v. Lumley,* 96 F. 773 (C.C.A. 6 1899); *Great Northern Railway Co. v. Kasischke,* 104 F. 440 (C.C.A. 8 1900); *Great Northern Railway Co. v. Fowler,* 136 F. 118 (C.C.A. 9 1905); *Lion Oil Refining Co. v. Albritton,* 21 F. 2d 280 (C.C.A. 8 1927); *Kosztelnik v. Bethlehem Iron Co.,* 91 F. 606 (C.C.E.D.N.Y. 1898); *The Henry S. Grove,* 22 F.2d 444 (D.Md. 1927); *Jones v. Gulf, Colorado & Santa Fe Railway Co.,* 73 S.W. 1082 (Civ.Ct.App. Tx. 1903); *St. Louis, Iron Mountain & Southern Railway Co. v. Smith,* 100 S.W. 884 (Sup.Ct.Ark. 1907); *Pattison v. Seattle, Renton & Southern Railway Co.,* 104 P. 825 (Sup.Ct.Wash. 1909); *St. Louis, Iron Mountain & Southern Railway Co. v. Reilly,* 161 S.W. 1052 (Sup.Ct.Ark. 1913); *New Bell Jellico Coal Co. v. Oxendine,* 160 S.W. 737 (Ct.App.Ky. 1913); *Western Union Telegraph Co. v. Walck,* 161 S.W. 902 (Ct.Civ.App. Tx. 1913); *Connors v. Richards,* 119 N.E. 831 (Sup.Jud.Ct.Mass. 1918); Gary T. Schwartz, "Tort Law and the Economy in Nineteenth-Century America: A Reinterpretation," *Yale Law Journal* 90 (1981): 1717, 1752.

43. For example, *Wagner v. National Life Insurance Co.,* 90 F. 395 (C.C.A. 6 1898); *Gladish v. Pennsylvania Co.,* 107 F. 61 (C.C.A. 6 1901); *Chicago & Northwestern Railway Co. v. Wilcox,* 116 F. 913 (C.C.A. 8 1902); *Pacific Mutual Life Insurance Co. of California v. Webb,* 157 F. 155 (C.C.A. 8 1907); *Simpson v. Pennsylvania Railroad Co.,* 159 F. 423 (C.C.A. 3 1908); *Whitney Co. v. Johnson,* 14 F.2d 24 (C.C.A. 9 1926); *The Adonis,* 38 F.2d 743 (C.C.A. 3 1930); *Merwin v. New York, New Haven & Hartford Railroad Co.,* 62 F.2d 803 (C.C.A. 2 1933); *Barker v. Northern Pacific Railway Co.,* 65 F. 460 (C.C.E.D.Mo. 1895); *Heck v. Missouri Pacific Railway Co.,* 147 F. 775 (C.C.D.Colo. 1906); *Nelson v. Minneapolis Street Railway Co.,* 63 N.W. 486 (Sup.Ct.Minn. 1895); *Seeley v. Citizens' Traction Co.,* 36 A. 229 (Sup.Ct.Pa. 1897); *Houston & Texas Central Railroad Co. v. McCarty,* 60 S.W. 429 (Sup.Ct.Tx. 1901); *Alford v. Wabash Railway Co.,* 73 S.W.2d 277 (K.C.Ct.App.Mo. 1934).

44. The standard was described as requiring "clear, convincing, and unequivocal testimony." *Chicago & Northwestern Railway Co. v. Wilcox,* 116 F. 913, 917 (C.C.A. 8 1902). *Accord Chicago, St. Paul, Minneapolis & Omaha Railway Co. v. Belliwith,* 83 F. 437, 441 (C.C.A. 8 1897); *Merwin v. New York, New Haven & Hartford Railroad Co.,* 62 F.2d 803, 804 (C.C.A. 2 1933).

45. *Hill v. Northern Pacific Railway Co.,* 113 F. 914 (C.C.A. 9 1902); *Mahr v. Union Pacific Railroad Co.,* 170 F. 699 (C.C.A. 9 1909); *Johnson v. Merry Mount Granite Co.,* 53 F. 569 (C.C.D.Mass. 1892); *Vandervelden v. Chicago & Northwestern Railway Co.,* 61 F. 54 (C.C.N.D.Iowa 1894); *Barker v. Northern Pacific Railway Co.,* 65 F. 460 (C.C.E.D.Mo. 1895); *Heck v. Missouri Pacific Railway Co.,* 147 F. 775 (C.C.D.Colo. 1906). The prepayment requirement was not always enforced. See *Lumley v. Wabash Railroad Co.,* 76 F. 66 (C.C.A. 6 1896); *Johnson v. Chicago, Milwaukee & St. Paul Railway Co.,* 224 F. 196 (W.D.Wash. 1915).

46. The rule was based on *George v. Tate,* 102 U.S. 564 (1880). The Court identified the type of fraud that could be raised in an action at law as follows:

It is well settled that the only fraud permissible to be proved at law in these cases is fraud touching the execution of the instrument, such as misreading, the surreptitious substitution of one paper for another, or obtaining by some other trick or device an instrument which the party did not intend to give. [p. 570]

Essentially, fraud that led a party to sign an agreement that he did not intend to sign could be raised in an action at law, whereas fraud that induced a party to sign an agreement by misrepresenting facts or the terms and conditions stated in the agreement could not be. See *Shampeau v. Connecticut River Lumber Co.,* 42 F. 760 (C.C.D.Vt. 1890); *Johnson v. Merry Mount Granite Co.,* 53 F. 569 (C.C.D.Mass. 1892); *Messinger v. New England Mutual Life Insurance Co.,* 59 F. 529 (C.C.W.D.Pa. 1894); *Vandervelden v. Chicago & Northwestern Railway Co.,* 61 F. 54 (C.C.N.D.Iowa 1894). In 1898 the Sixth Circuit, with Judge William Howard Taft writing, attempted to avoid the rule and thereby allow plaintiffs to attack releases on the ground of fraud in their actions at law. *Wagner v. National Life Insurance Co. of Montpelier, Vt.,* 90 F. 395 (C.C.A. 6 1898). Taft explained that such a rule "avoids circuity of action, and thus facilitates the administration of justice" (p. 404). *Wagner,* however, was not widely followed, and the general rule remained the one based on *George v. Tate.* See *Pacific Mutual Life Insurance Co. of California v. Webb,* 157 F. 155 (C.C.A. 8 1907); *Simpson v. Pennsylvania Railroad Co.,* 159 F. 423 (C.C.A. 3 1908); *Hill v. Northern Pacific Railway Co.,* 104 F. 754 (C.C.D.Wash. 1900); *Stephenson v. Supreme Council A.L.H.,* 130 F. 491 (C.C.E.D.Pa. 1904); *Heck v. Missouri Pacific Railway Co.,* 147 F. 775 (C.C.D.Colo. 1906). But see *Union Pacific Railroad Co. v. Whitney,* 198 F. 784 (C.C.A. 8 1912). See generally Edwin H. Abbot, Jr., "Fraud as a Defense at Law in the Federal Courts," *Columbia Law Review* 15 (1915): 489.

47. Charles E. Clark, *Handbook of the Law of Code Pleading* (St. Paul, 1928), pp. 17–22, 44–51, 479–85; Philemon Bliss, *A Treatise upon the Law of Pleading Under the Codes of Civil Procedure,* 3rd ed. by E. F. Johnson (St. Paul, 1894), pp. 7–9, 602–7; George L. Phillips, *An Exposition of the Principles of Pleading Under the Codes of Civil Procedure (Chicago, 1896),* pp. 140–44, 248–51. See, for example, *Sanford v. Royal Insurance Co.,* 40 P. 609 (Sup.Ct.Wash. 1895); *St. Louis, Iron Mountain & Southern Railway Co. v. Smith,* 100 S.W. 884 (Sup.Ct.Ark. 1907).

48. See, for example, *Hill v. Northern Pacific Railway Co.,* 113 F. 914, 917 (C.C.A. 9 1902); *Johnson v. Merry Mount Granite Co.,* 53 F. 569, 571 (C.C.D.Mass. 1892); Clark, *Handbook of the Law of Code Pleading,* pp. 23–24.

49. *Lumley v. Wabash Railway Co.,* 71 F. 21, 23 (C.C.E.D.Mich. 1895).

50. *Wabash Railway Co. v. Lumley,* 96 F. 773, 774–75 (C.C.A. 6 1899).

51. Ibid., 71 F. 24.

52. *Lumley v. Wabash Railway Co.,* 76 F. 66 (C.C.A. 6 1896).

53. 68 P. 954 (Sup.Ct.Wash. 1902).

54. Ibid., pp. 954–55.

55. See *Spiess v. Sommarstrom Ship Building Co.,* 272 F. 109 (C.C.A. 9 1921); *Kirkland v. Ensign-Bickford Co.,* 267 F. 472 (D.Conn. 1920); *The Adour,* 21 F.2d 858 (D.Md. 1927); *Tompkins v. Clay-Street Hill Railroad Co.,* 4 P. 1165 (Dept. 1 Cal. 1884); *Seither v. Philadelphia Traction Co.,* 17 A. 338 (Sup.Ct.Pa. 1889); *Denver & Rio Grande Railroad Co. v. Sullivan,* 41 P. 501 (Sup.Ct.Colo. 1895); *Jackson v. Pennsylvania Railroad Co.,* 49 A. 730 (Ct.Err.& App.N.J. 1901); *Hubbard v. St. Louis & Meramec River Railroad Co.,* 72 S.W. 1073 (Sup.Ct.Mo. 1903); *Cleveland, Cincinnati & Chicago Railway Co. v. Hilligoss,* 86 N.E. 485 (Sup.Ct.Ind. 1908). Compare *Lindsay v. Acme Cement Plaster Co.,* 190 N.W. 275 (Sup.Ct.Mich. 1922).

For a general statement of the rule, see Thomas M. Cooley, *A Treatise on the Law of Torts, or the Wrongs Which Arise Independently of Contract,* ed. John Lewis (Chicago, 1907), pp. 102–4.

56. Hearings on H.R. 17036 before the Committee on the Judiciary of the United States House of Representatives, 60 Cong., 1 Sess. (1908), pp. 170–71 (statement of H. R. Fuller, representing the Brotherhood of Locomotive Engineers, Brotherhood of Locomotive Firemen and Enginemen, and Brotherhood of Trainmen); "Limitation of Venue in Certain Actions Brought Under the Employers' Liability Act," Hearings before Subcommittee No. 4 of the Committee on the Judiciary of the United States House of Representatives on H.R. 1639, 80 Cong., 1 Sess. (1947), pp. 65–66 (statement of Warren H. Atherton, Esq., member, Brotherhood of Railroad Trainmen); "Limitation of Venue in Certain Actions Brought Under the Employers'

Liability Act," Hearings before a Subcommittee of the Committee on the Judiciary of the United States Senate on S. 1567 and H.R. 1639, 80 Cong., 2 Sess. (1948), p. 230 (statement of Warren H. Atherton, representing the Brotherhood of Railroad Trainmen).

57. Gersuny, "Work Injuries and Adversary Processes," pp. 331–32.

58. The B & O denied that the rule worked in any "arbitrary manner against injured employees" because the company filed accident reports with the Interstate Commerce Commission and because the employees did not need to gather information about their injury. To support its claim, the railroad cited the fact that less than 1 percent of its injured employees prosecuted personal injury suits through to judgment and that 93 percent of them settled with the company without even retaining an attorney. "Amending the Employers' Liability Act," Hearings before a Subcommittee of the Committee on the Judiciary of the United States Senate on S. 3397 and S. 3398, 75 Cong., 3 Sess. (1938), p. 14 (statement of F. M. Rivinus, general counsel, Norfolk & Western Railroad Co.); p. 24 (statement of T. J. McGrath, general counsel, Brotherhood of Railroad Trainmen); pp. 30–32, 38–43 (statement of F. M. Rivinus, general counsel, Norfolk & Western Railroad Co.); "To Amend the Employers' Liability Act," Hearing before Subcommittee No. 4 of the Committee on the Judiciary of the United States House of Representatives on H.R. 5755, H.R. 7336, and H.R. 7621, 75 Cong., 1 Sess. (1937), pp. 13–14 (statement of Hon. Robert L. Ramsay, congressman from West Virginia). The B & O did not apparently recognize the extent to which its numbers were ambiguous.

59. Sen. Rep. No. 661, 76 Cong., 1 Sess. (1939), p. 5.

60. 53 Stat. 1404 (1939).

61. See, for example, Alan Dawley, *Class and Community: The Industrial Revolution in Lynn* (Cambridge, MA, 1976); Richard J. Oestreicher, *Solidarity and Fragmentation: Working People and Class Consciousness in Detroit, 1875–1900* (Urbana, IL, 1986); Bess Beatty, "Textile Labor in the North Carolina Piedmont: Mill Owner Images and Mill Worker Response, 1830–1900," *Labor History* 25 (1984): 485; James R. Barrett, "Work and Community in 'The Jungle': Chicago's Packing House Workers, 1894–1922" (Ph.D. Diss., University of Pittsburgh, 1981); David Alan Corbin, *Life, Work, and Rebellion in the Coal Fields: The Southern West Virginia Miners, 1880–1922* (Urbana, IL, 1981).

62. "Liability of Common Carriers," Hearing before the Committee on the Judiciary of the United States House of Representatives, 58 Cong., 2 Sess. (1904), p. 22 (statement of H. L. Fuller, legislative representative of the Brotherhood of Railroad Trainmen). The contract is reprinted on pp. 18–23.

63. H.R. Rep. No. 1386, 60 Cong., 1 Sess. (1908), pp. 6–7. If a worker executed a release after he became an employee, some states would refuse to enforce it on the theory that it was an agreement without consideration. See, for example, *Purdy v. Rome, Watertown & Ogdensburgh Railroad Co.,* 26 N.E. 255 (Ct. App. N.Y. 1891). Ordinarily such releases were made part of the employment contract so as to obviate the lack-of-consideration problem.

64. "Employers' Liability," Hearings before the Committee on Interstate Commerce of the United States Senate on S. 4092, 58 Cong., 2 Sess. (1905), p. 4 (statement of H. P. Fuller, legislative representative of the Brotherhood of Locomotive Firemen, Order of Railway Conductors, and Brotherhood of Railroad Trainmen); "Workmen's Compensation," Hearings before a Subcommittee of the Committee on Interstate and Foreign Commerce of the United States House of Representatives on H.R. 2944, 63 Cong., 2 Sess. (1914), p. 7 (statement of Hon. Adolph J. Sabath, congressman from Illinois); H.R. Doc. No. 380, 57 Cong., 1 Sess. (1902), pp. 934–35.

65. Licht, *Working for the Railroad,* p. 204; Gersuny, "Work Injuries and Adversary Processes," p. 331; Gersuny, *Work Hazards,* pp. 71, 78. While acknowledging the custom, some railroad officials also denigrated its significance. See Sen. Doc. No. 338, 62 Cong., 2 Sess. (1912), vol. 2, pp. 758–59 (statement of Robert J. Cary, attorney, New York Central System); pp. 1067–69 (statement of Frank V. Whiting, general claims attorney, New York Central Lines).

66. For example, *Quebe v. Gulf, Colorado & Santa Fe Railway Co.,* 81 S.W. 20 (Sup.Ct.Tx. 1904).

67. See, for example, "Limitation of Venue in Certain Actions Brought Under the Employers' Liability Act," Hearings before Subcommittee No. 4 of the Committee on the Judiciary of the United States House of Representatives, 80 Cong., 1 Sess. (1947), pp. 57–58, 72 (statement of

Warren H. Atherton, Esq., member, Brotherhood of Railroad Trainmen); p. 92 (statement of A. E. Lyon, executive secretary, Railway Labor Executives Association); pp. 156–58 (letter from Jno. F. Scott, Brotherhood of Railroad Trainmen, to Hon. John Jennings, United States House of Representatives, January 1, 1947); "Limitation of Venue in Certain Actions Brought Under the Employers' Liability Act," Hearings before a Subcommittee of the Committee on the Judiciary of the United States Senate on S. 1567 and H.R. 1639, 80 Cong., 2 Sess. (1948), p. 34 (remark of Sen. William Langer of North Dakota); pp. 241–43 (App. A to statement of Warren H. Atherton, representing the Brotherhood of Railroad Trainmen).

68. Releases obtained as a prerequisite for returning to work were enforced in *Hobbs v. Brush Electric Light Co.*, 42 N.W. 965 (Sup.Ct.Mich. 1889); *Forbs v. St. Louis, Iron Mountain & Southern Railway Co.*, 82 S.W. 562 (Ct.App.Mo. 1904); *Cleveland, Cincinnati, Chicago & St. Louis Railway Co. v. Hillegoss*, 86 N.E. 485 (Sup.Ct.Ind. 1908); *Genest v. Odell Manufacturing Co.*, 74 A. 593 (Sup.Ct.N.H. 1909); *Tindall v. Northern Pacific Railway Co.*, 107 P. 1045 (Sup.Ct.Wash. 1910); *Patton v. Atchison, Topeka & Santa Fe Railway Co.*, 158 P. 576 (Sup.Ct.Okla. 1916); *Carlson v. Northern Pacific Railway Co.*, 268 P. 549 (Sup.Ct.Mont. 1928).

Similar releases were voided in *Manchester Street Railway v. Barrett*, 265 F. 557 (C.C.A. 1 1920); *Missouri, Kansas & Texas Railway Co. v. Smith*, 81 S.W. 22 (Sup.Ct.Tx. 1904); *Louisville & Nashville Railroad Co. v. Winkler*, 173 S.W. 151 (Ct.App.Ky. 1915).

69. For example, *Houston & Texas Central Railroad Co. v. Brown*, 69 S.W. 651 (Ct.Civ.App.Tx. 1902); *Smith v. St. Louis & San Francisco Railroad Co.*, 148 P. 759 (Sup.Ct.Kan. 1915); *Ballenger v. Southern Railway Co.*, 90 S.E. 1019 (Sup.Ct.S.C. 1916). See *Pattison v. Seattle, Renton & Southern Railway Co.*, 104 P. 825 (Sup.Ct.Wash. 1909) (passenger).

70. Roger S. Warner, "Employers' Liability as an Industrial Problem," *Green Bag* 18 (1906): 185, 189.

71. The study cited does not argue that employer pressure explained the difference. Rather, it suggests that the differences can be explained in some part at least by the degree to which state common law treated nonemployees more favorably than it did employees. The study also shows, however, that the nature of the applicable law does not explain many characteristics of tort litigation in the state during these years. See Munger, "Social Change and Tort Litigation," p. 104.

72. The New Jersey study is quoted in Jerome Pollack, "Workmen's Compensation for Railroad Work Injuries and Diseases," *Cornell Law Quarterly* 36 (1951): 236, 260, and also pp. 243–44. For hostility to insurance claims agents as well as to personal injury attorneys, see Robert Asher, "Radicalism and Reform: State Insurance of Workmen's Compensation in Minnesota, 1910–1933," *Labor History* 14 (Winter, 1973): 19, 20; Tripp, "Workmen's Compensation," p. 531.

73. Railroad Retirement Board, *Work Injuries*, vol. 1, p. 9.

74. Ibid., vol 1, p. 38.

75. For the early history of employer relief associations, see Roy Lubove, *The Struggle for Social Security, 1900–1935* (Cambridge, MA, 1968), pp. 11–15; Stuart Brandes, *American Welfare Capitalism: 1880–1940* (Chicago, 1976), pp. 93–97.

76. Hearings before the Committee on the Judiciary of the United States House of Representatives on H.R. 17036, 60 Cong., 1 Sess. (1908), p. 87 (statement of Hugh L. Bond, Jr., second vice-president and general counsel of the Baltimore and Ohio Railway Co.); Emory R. Johnson, "Railway Departments for the Relief and Insurance of Employes," *Annals of the American Academy of Political and Social Science* 6 (1895): 424, 456.

During the same five years the companies contributed almost $2.6 million to cover various costs of the department. From 1903 to 1907, therefore, they apparently paid 12.6 percent of the cash funding of the departments. See Hearings before the Committee on the Judiciary of the United States House of Representatives on H.R. 17036, 60 Cong., 1 Sess. (1908), p. 87. The roads were generally unable to specify the amount of their departments' total costs that they paid (p. 85), but they sometimes stated that their total contributions to the relief departments were considerably higher than 12.6 percent. The actual amount and percentage of the total that the companies contributed was disputed (see, e.g., pp. 96–99) (statement of George B. Elliott, assistant general counsel of the Atlantic Coast Line Railway); pp. 134–40, 174 (statement of H. R. Fuller, representing the Brotherhood of Locomotive Engineers, Brotherhood of Locomotive

Firemen and Enginemen, and Brotherhood of Trainmen). For the B & O relief department reports from 1900 to 1907, see pp. 210–32.

One scholar concluded as follows:

> To a great extent, company contribution was quite small, averaging in 1907 only $1.81 per member each year. While the Public Health Service did find one company in a 1916 survey that paid the entire cost of its fund, it was the only one of 425 that did. Most companies simply bore the cost of administration—doing the paper-work and giving association officers time off for association tasks. [Brandes, *American Welfare Capitalism,* pp. 93–94]

A contemporary student concluded that the five major railroads paid one-fifth to one-sixth of the costs of their relief departments (see Johnson, "Railway Departments," p. 454).

77. Copies of the relief department contracts of the Baltimore & Ohio Railway Co., the Pennsylvania Railroad Co., and the Philadelphia and Reading Railroad Co., are reprinted in "Liability of Common Carriers," Hearing before the Judiciary Committee of the United States House of Representatives, 58 Cong., 2 Sess. (1904), pp. 27–31, and in Hearings before the Committee on the Judiciary of the United States House of Representatives on H.R. 17036, 60 Cong., 1 Sess. (1908), pp. 164–69. See Shelton Stromquist, *A Generation of Boomers: The Pattern of Railroad Labor Conflict in Nineteenth-Century America* (Urbana, IL, 1987), pp. 244–47.

78. Simeon E. Baldwin, *American Railroad Law* (New York, 1904), pp. 271–72. For decisions upholding the validity of the relief department releases, see Baldwin, *American Railroad Law,* p. 531; *Atlantic Coast Line Railroad Co. v. Dunning,* 166 F. 850 (C.C.A. 4 1908); *Day v. Atlantic Coast Line Railroad Co.,* 179 F. 26 (C.C.A. 4 1910); *Drobney v. Lukens Iron & Steel Co.,* 204 F. 11 (C.C.A. 2 1913); *State, to Use of Black v. Baltimore & Ohio Railroad Co.,* 36 F. 655 (C.C.D.Md. 1888). See Conrad Reno, *A Treatise on the Law of the Employers' Liability Acts of New York, Massachusetts, Indiana, Alabama, Colorado, and England,* 2nd ed. (Indianapolis, 1903), pp. 23–26.

79. Quoted in Hearings before the Committee on the Judiciary of the United States House of Representatives on H.R. 17036, 60 Cong., 1 Sess. (1908), p. 174 (statement of H. R. Fuller, representing the Brotherhood of Locomotive Engineers, Brotherhood of Locomotive Firemen and Enginemen, and Brotherhood of Trainmen).

In 1902 the *Yale Law Journal* concluded that the roads had established their employee relief departments "for the purpose of identifying the interests of employer and employe [*sic*], rendering [the employee] less likely to antagonize the company during labor difficulties, and of preventing a large percentage of damage suits brought by employes [*sic*] or their representatives" See Comment, *Yale Law Journal* 11 (1902): 161.

80. Sen. Doc. No. 338, 62 Cong., 2 Sess. (1912), vol. 1, pp. 131, 135, 139, 143; vol. 2, pp. 1029–33, 1068–69, 1361–62; Licht, *Working for the Railroad,* pp. 210–11.

81. Licht, *Working for the Railroad,* pp. 80–93, 98; Kurt Wetzel, "Railroad Management's Response to Operating Employees' Accidents, 1890–1913," *Labor History* 21 (1980): 351, 358–59, 364–65; "Workmen's Compensation," Hearings before the Committee on the Judiciary of the United States House of Representatives on H.R. 1, 61 Cong., 1 Sess. (1910), p. 19 (statement of Samuel Gompers, president of the American Federation of Labor).

82. Daunis McBride, *Richey's Federal Employers' Liability, Safety Appliance, and Hours of Service Acts* (Charlottesville, VA, 1916), p. 549. See Reno, *Treatise on the Law of the Employers' Liability Acts,* pp. 237–41.

83. *Southern Pacific Co. v. Allen,* 106 S.W. 441 (Ct.Civ.App.Tx. 1907); *Popular v. Minneapolis, St. Paul & Sault St. Marie Railway Co.,* 141 N.W. 798 (Sup.Ct.Minn. 1913); *Burho v. Minneapolis & St. Louis Railway Co.,* 141 N.W. 300 (Sup.Ct.Minn. 1913); Baldwin, *American Railroad Law,* pp. 222–31; H. G. Wood, *A Treatise on the Law of Railroads,* 2nd ed. by H. D. Minor (Boston, 1894), vol. 3, pp. 1759–61.

84. Sen. Doc. No. 338, 62 Cong., 2 Sess. (1912), vol. 2, p. 646 (statement of W. G. Lee, president of the Brotherhood of Railroad Trainmen).

85. Ibid., vol. 2, p. 648 (statement of W. G. Lee, president of the Brotherhood of Railroad Trainmen). See ibid., p. 653.

86. Eastman, *Work-Accidents and the Law,* p. 32, and see p. 94. See Gersuny, *Work Hazards*

and Industrial Conflict, p. 27; Christopher L. Tomlins, "A Mysterious Power: Industrial Accidents and the Legal Construction of Employment Relations in Massachusetts, 1800–1850," *Law and History Review* 6 (1988): 375, 386–93.

87. Reprinted in "Liability of Common Carriers," Hearing before the Committee on the Judiciary of the United States House of Representatives, 58 Cong., 2 Sess. (1904), p. 20 (statement of H. R. Fuller, legislative representative of the Brotherhood of Railroad Trainmen). Company pressure could have been as implied or overt as the situation required. For the movement after 1890 toward more subtle management techniques to impose discipline on railroad workers, see Stromquist, *Generation of Boomers,* pp. 240–42.

88. Sen. Doc. No. 338, 62 Cong., 2 Sess. (1912), vol. 2, p. 648 (statement of W. G. Lee, president of the Brotherhood of Railroad Trainmen).

89. A related tactic, for example, used by some of the national railroads, was the operation of special hospitals to care for injured workers. Like their relief departments, the railroads' hospitals were both benevolent to the workers and legally beneficial to the companies. They were probably highly effective in discouraging injured employees from bringing any legal action against the companies. As Lawrence M. Friedman wrote, "the railway hospital system reinforced a bargain that was at least implicit and sometimes quite open: people treated by railroad doctors do not sue" (Friedman, "Civil Wrongs," p. 373). Moreover, railroad doctors were in a position to help dissuade injured employees from bringing suit or even to minimize the extent of their injuries. How much they did so was unknown, but the operation of the railroad hospital system probably leaned in that direction (pp. 372–73). Further, even if the injured employee did bring suit, its hospital had given the railroad the advantage of knowing the exact extent of the plaintiff's injuries and of preparing its expert witness to testify. The railroad brotherhoods and their attorneys criticized the railroad hospitals on those and similar grounds. See, for example, "Limitation of Venue in Certain Actions Brought Under the Employers' Liability Act," Hearings before Subcommittee No. 4 of the Committee on the Judiciary of the House of Representatives, 80 Cong., 1 Sess. (1947), pp. 65–67 (testimony of Warren Atherton, member, Brotherhood of Railroad Trainmen); p. 151 (letter from A. F. Whitney, president, Brotherhood of Railroad Trainmen to Hon. Earl C. Michener, April 4, 1947); pp. 151–52 (letter from F. G. Pellett, state representative, Brotherhood of Railroad Trainmen, to Hon. Earl C. Michener, March 20, 1947); pp. 154–55 (letter from L. E. Monroe, district representative, Brotherhood of Railroad Trainmen, to Hon. Georgia L. Lusk, April 8, 1947); pp. 165–66 (letter from Marvin B. Simpson, Esq., to Hon. Lyndon B. Johnson, March 17, 1947).

90. New York Legislative Doc. No. 26, Message from the governor transmitting the final report of Jeremiah F. Connor (1920), p. 14.

91. Ibid., p. 34.

92. Sen. Doc. No. 338, 62 Cong., 2 Sess. (1912), vol. 2, p. 1056; Sen. Doc. No. 90, 62 Cong., 1 Sess. (1911), vol. 1, p. 97. Social as well as economic factors could dissuade workers from retaining counsel. See, for example, Engel, "The Oven Bird's Song," pp. 565–66; Sarat, "Studying American Legal Culture," pp. 427, 436, 448–52, 464–65, 466–72. Studies have repeatedly shown that unrepresented parties generally obtain lower settlements than do those with counsel. For example, Ross, *Settled Out of Court,* pp. 69–70, 116–21, 142–43, 167, 193–98; Marc A. Franklin, Robert H. Chanin, and Irving Mark, "Accidents, Money, and the Law: A Study of the Economics of Personal Injury Litigation," in *Dollars, Delay and the Automobile Victim: Studies in Reparation for Highway Injuries and Related Court Problems* (New York, 1968), pp. 27, 42–44, 46–47.

93. Joel Seidman, *The Brotherhood of Railroad Trainmen: The Internal Political Life of a National Union* (New York, 1962), p. 157.

94. Railroad Retirement Board, *Work Injuries,* vol. 1, p. 10.

95. Ibid., vol. 1, p. 50. Other factors in addition to representation probably help explain the discrepancies in amounts paid. For example, attorneys were presumably more willing to take cases that seemed relatively promising and more willing to file suit when their cases were strong (see vol. 1, pp. 50–51).

96. Ibid., vol. 1, p. 38.

97. Ibid., vol. 1, p. 43.

98. Ibid., vol. 1, pp. 39–43, 49–51, 123–25.

99. Ibid., vol. 1, p. 43.

100. Sen. Doc. No. 338, 62 Cong., 2 Sess. (1912), vol. 1, p. 139, and see pp. 131, 135, 143. The ratios held, too, when broken down by type and severity of injury. Among workers who lost one hand, those who settled received an average of $1,551, while those who went to final judgment received an average of $3,696. Among those who lost one foot, settlements averaged $1,497, while judgments averaged $3,492. For death claims, the comparable numbers were $1,157 and $2,536, and for permanent total disability, $3,838 and $11,272.

101. Apparently fees in the lower range were more common. See, for example, Sen. Doc. No. 338, 62 Cong., 2 Sess. (1912), vol. 2, pp. 734, 736, 738 (statement of J. Harrington Boyd, chairman, Employers' Liability Commission of Ohio); Railroad Retirement Board, *Work Injuries,* vol. 1, pp. 39–43, 49–51, 123–25.

102. Sen. Doc. No. 338, 62 Cong., 2 Sess. (1912), vol. 1, pp. 131, 139; vol. 2, p. 1029.

103. Sen. Doc. No. 338, 62 Cong., 2 Sess. (1912), vol. 2, p. 1029 (statement of H. L. Bond, Jr., general counsel, Baltimore & Ohio Railroad Co.).

104. The availability of funds from relief associations gave companies considerable leverage in making settlements. Because settlements of death and permanent injury claims averaged only about one-third of judgments, relief department funds covered a much higher percentage of the former than of the latter. Assuming workers with only medium-level relief association benefits, for example, companies would have had to pay approximately half of all settlement amounts from their own funds. In contrast, they would have had to use their own funds to pay more than 75 percent of judgments in permanent partial disability cases, about 80 percent in death cases, and well over 80 percent in permanent total disability cases. Settlements and relief departments thus allowed companies to pay smaller percentages of much smaller total amounts, and the combination was thus even more advantageous to corporations than the raw numbers indicated.

This assumes that relief association funds would and could be used by the company to help pay a legal judgment. See "Amendments to Federal Employers' Liability Act," Hearings before the Committee on the Judiciary of the United States House of Representatives on H.R. 14973, 64 Cong., 2 Sess. (1916), pp. 14–16 (statement of Val Fitzpatrick, vice-president of the Brotherhood of Railroad Trainmen). If they could not be so used, judgments would have been even costlier to the companies and settlements even more desirable and economical.

105. Sen. Doc. No. 338, 62 Cong., 2 Sess. (1912), vol. 1, p. 143.

106. Sen. Doc. No. 338, 62 Cong., 2 Sess. (1912), vol. 1, pp. 131, 135, 139, 143. See Nathaniel Richter and Lois G. Forer, "Federal Employers' Liability Act—A Real Compensatory Law for Railroad Workers," *Cornell Law Quarterly* 36 (1951): 203, 223–24 and works cited; Posner, "Theory of Negligence," pp. 83–85.

107. The discount factor used was the percentage obtained by subtracting the average number of days lost by those who settled from the average number of days lost by those who went to judgment and dividing the result by the total average days lost by those who settled.

108. Hearings before the Committee on the Judiciary of the United States House of Representatives on H.R. 17036, 60 Cong., 1 Sess. (1908), p. 80 (statement of Hugh L. Bond, Jr., second vice-president and general counsel of the Baltimore and Ohio Railroad Co.).

109. Walter Nugent, *Structures and American Social History* (Bloomington, IN, 1981), pp. 88–89, 103, 111.

110. United States Bureau of the Census, *The Statistical History of the United States from Colonial Times to the Present* (Stamford, CT, 1965), p. 14.

111. Quoted in John R. Stilgoe, *Metropolitan Corridor: Railroads and the American Scene* (New Haven, CT, 1983), p. 11.

112. Richard E. Sloan, *Memories of an Arizona Judge* (Stanford, CA, 1932), p. 80.

113. Office of the Attorney General of the United States, *Annual Report, 1885,* pp. 15–16.

114. Office of the Attorney General of the United States, *Annual Report, 1874,* pp. 20–21, *Annual Report, 1877,* pp. 18–19, *Annual Report,* 1887, pp. 272–75, *Annual Report, 1890,* p. xviii. See John D. W. Guice, *The Rocky Mountain Bench: The Territorial Supreme Courts of Colorado, Montana, and Wyoming, 1861–1890* (New Haven, CT, 1972), pp. 42, 45–46.

115. Rodman W. Paul, *The Far West and the Great Plains in Transition, 1859–1900* (New York, 1988), pp. 62, 195.

116. John F. Stover, *The Life and Decline of the American Railroad* (New York, 1970), pp. 100–2, 154–55. In addition to the "route" mileage referred to in the text, the railroads continued to build tens of thousands of miles of service and "second" mileage. See Albro Martin, *Enterprise Denied: Origins of the Decline of American Railroads, 1897–1917* (New York, 1971), pp. 55–61.

117. Passenger fares averaged around two to three cents a mile. In 1900 the average American worker earned $438 a year. See John F. Stover, *American Railroads* (Chicago, 1961), pp. 173–74, 177.

118. Letter from John Paul to Hatton W. Summers, February 2, 1938, John Paul Papers, Box 47, Folder: "1930–38," University of Virginia Library.

119. Kristin Bumiller, "Choice of Forum in Diversity Cases: Analysis of a Survey and Implications for Reform," *Law & Society Review* 15 (1980–81): 749, 771.

120. The number of counties in each state may be found in United States Bureau of the Census, *Thirteenth Census of the United States Taken in the Year 1910* (Washington, 1913), vols. 2, 3.

121. Office of the Attorney General of the United States, *Annual Report, 1895*, p. 4, *Annual Report, 1937*, p. 2; Felix Frankfurter and James M. Landis, *The Business of the Supreme Court: A Study in the Federal Judicial System* (New York, 1928), p. 131, n. 122.

122. 36 Stat. 1087 (1911). The itemization of counties and court locations by states appears on pp. 1105–30.

123. Illinois, Wisconsin, Kansas, Michigan, Minnesota, Nebraska, Mississippi, South Carolina, Utah, Georgia, Kentucky, Missouri, South Dakota, Tennessee, Texas, and Ohio.

124. In North Carolina the federal courts sat in eleven of ninety-eight counties, in Virginia ten of one hundred, in Oklahoma ten of seventy-six, in Iowa eleven of ninety-nine, in Louisiana seven of sixty-one, and in California six of fifty-eighty.

125. Wyoming, Colorado, Montana, Nevada, Oregon, Idaho, and Washington.

126. For population statistics, see Stromquist, *A Generation of Boomers*, pp. 159–61; for the locations of the federal courts in Iowa, see B. C. Moon, *The Removal of Causes from the Courts of the Several States to the Circuit Courts of the United States* (New York 1901), p. 512, n. 30.

127. For example, H.R. Rep. No. 118, 53 Cong., 1 Sess. (1893) (Michigan: create new division); H.R. Rep. No. 163, 53 Cong., 1 Sess. (1893) (Mississippi: shift counties); H.R. Rep. No. 357, 53 Cong., 2 Sess. (1894) (Kentucky: divide state into two districts); H.R. Rep. No. 1590, 54 Cong., 1 Sess. (1896) (Texas: add new location); H.R. Rep. No. 897, 56 Cong., 1 Sess. (1900) (Georgia: create new division); H.R. Rep. No. 1111, 56 Cong., 1 Sess. (1900) (Iowa: create new division); H.R. Rep. No. 2029, 56 Cong., 2 Sess. (1900) (Kentucky: divide state into two districts); H.R. Rep. No. 269, 57 Cong., 1 Sess. (1902) (Kentucky: add new location); H.R.Rep. No. 4269, 59 Cong., 1 Sess. (1906) (North Dakota: divide state into two districts); H.R. Rep. No. 2154, 60 Cong., 2 Sess. (1909) (Indiana: divide state into two districts). A large number of such congressional reports are collected in Bernard D. Reams, Jr. and Charles R. Haworth, eds., *Congress and the Courts: A Legislative History, 1787–1977: Documents and Materials Regarding the Creation, Structure and Organization of Federal Courts and the Federal Judiciary* (Buffalo, NY, 1978), vol. 4.

128. H.R. Rep. No. 1410, 54 Cong., 2 Sess. (1897), p. 2.

129. H.R. Rep. No. 771, 56 Cong., 1 Sess. (1900), p. 2.

130. H.R. Rep. No. 2935, 58 Cong., 2 Sess. (1904), p. 1.

131. H.R. Rep. No. 4404, 58 Cong., 3 Sess. (1905), p. 2.

132. H.R. Rep. No. 2324, 58 Cong., 2 Sess. (1904), p. 1.

133. H.R. Rep. No. 6602, 59 Cong., 2 Sess. (1907), p. 1.

134. H.R. Rep. No. 4967, 59 Cong., 1 Sess. (1906), pp. 1, 2.

135. *Duff v. Duff*, 31 F. 772, 775–76 (C.C.N.D.Cal. 1887).

136. Moon, *Removal of Causes*, p. 165.

137. Letter from Raymond N. Klass to George W. Norris, April 13, 1933, George W. Norris Papers, Tray 42, Box 8, File: "Limiting Jurisdiction of Federal Courts," Library of Congress.

138. *McIntyre v. Southern Railway Co.*, 131 F. 985, 986 (C.C.D.S.C. 1904). See Reid, *An*

American Judge, pp. 130–34. The problem of distance was repeatedly raised by those who argued for the restriction of diversity jurisdiction. See Tony A. Freyer, "The Federal Courts, Localism, and the National Economy, 1865–1900," *Business History Review* 53 (1979): 343, 346, 360.

139. The concept of "delay" masks any number of analytic difficulties and can refer to a number of very different situations. The text is concerned only with delay in the basic sense of the length of time necessary as a general matter to get an action to trial and judgment. For discussions of the problems of attempting to study and measure "delay," see, for example, Joseph A. Trotter, Jr., and Caroline S. Cooper, "State Trial Court Delay: Efforts at Reform," *American University Law Review* 31 (1982): 213; Joel B. Grossman, Herbert M. Kritzer, Kristin Bumiller, and Stephen McDougal, "Measuring the Pace of Civil Litigation," *Judicature* 65 (1981): 86.

140. Roy O. West, "The Abuse of Personal Injury Litigation," *Green Bag* 18 (1906): 200.

141. See Reginald Heber Smith, *Justice and the Poor* (New York, 1919), pp. 17–19; Hans Zeisel, Harry Kalven, Jr., and Bernard Buchholz, *Delay in the Court* (Boston, 1959), pp. 111–12, 114–19; Silverman, *Law and Urban Growth,* pp. 117, 139–40; Ross, *Settled Out of Court,* pp. 140, 224–29; Terence G. Ison, "The Therapeutic Significance of Compensation Structures," *Canadian Bar Review* 64 (1986): 605, 622–26. For an interesting effort to examine the subjective attitudes of tort plaintiffs toward the legal process, see E. Allan Lind, Robert J. Maccoun, Patricia A. Ebener, William L. F. Felstiner, Deborah R. Hensler, Judith Resnik, and Tom R. Tyler, "In the Eye of the Beholder: Tort Litigants' Evaluations of Their Experiences in the Civil Justice System," *Law & Society Review* 24 (1990): 953.

142. *New Bell Jellico Coal Co. v. Oxendine,* 160 S.W. 737, 740 (Ct.App.Ky. 1913).

143. Smith, *Justice and the Poor,* p. 84.

144. See the *Annual Reports* of the Office of the Attorney General of the United States; David S. Clark, "Adjudication to Administration: A Statistical Analysis of Federal District Courts in the Twentieth Century," *Southern California Law Review* 55 (1981): 65, 98, 104, 109; American Law Institute, *Study of the Business of the Federal Courts,* pp. 38–46.

145. Clark, "Adjudication to Administration," pp. 98, 102, 103, 108.

146. Office of the Attorney General of the United States, *Annual Report, 1905,* p. 130.

147. Office of the Attorney General of the United States, *Annual Report, 1905,* pp. 128–30.

148. Office of the Attorney General of the United States, *Annual Report, 1937,* pp. 1–3; Moon, *Removal of Causes,* 500–52, notes. Although the data included in the Attorney General's reports for 1937 and 1938 regarding delay seem reliable and are the only such data available, it should be noted that they were compiled in large part as ammunition for the New Deal's attack on delay in the federal courts which, in turn, was an important part of the rationale for the Court-packing plan of 1937. The Judicial Conference of the United States responded to the Attorney General's critique but did not dispute his basic data or most of his conclusions. See Office of the Attorney General of the United States, *Annual Report, 1937,* pp. 12–19, *Annual Report, 1938,* pp. 16–25.

149. See, for example, Editorial notes, *Central Law Journal* 38 (1894): 69; William Lambert Barnard, "A Summary of Conditions in the United States" in "The Law's Delay," *Green Bag* 17 (1905): 261.

150. Posner, "Theory of Negligence," pp. 50, 63, 72, n. 34.

151. Hurst, *Growth of American Law,* p. 173; Silverman, *Law and Urban Growth,* pp. 11–12, 112, 135.

152. Silverman, *Law and Urban Growth,* p. 117.

153. Friedman and Percival, "A Tale of Two Courts," p. 291.

154. Hiram W. Johnson to John McLaughlin, February 1, 1911, Hiram W. Johnson Papers, pt. 2, Box 1, Bancroft Library, University of California, Berkeley.

155. John F. Dillon, *Removal of Causes from State Courts to Federal Courts,* 3rd ed. (St. Louis, 1881), p. 66. In the subsequent edition, prepared by Dillon's successor, the quoted passage is retained but marked with a footnote stating that the increase in the jurisdictional amount from $500 to $2,000 in 1887 would "materially diminish" the problems previously noted. See Dillon, *Removal of Causes,* 5th ed. (St. Louis, 1889), p. 107.

156. Letter from Ronald C. Oldham to George W. Norris, April 26, 1928, George W. Norris Papers, Tray 42, Box 2 File: "S. 3151 (70th)," Library of Congress.

157. William Howard Taft, "The Delays of the Law," *Yale Law Journal* 18 (1908): 28, 35.

158. Henry P. Chandler, *Some Major Advances in the Federal Judicial System, 1922–1947* (St. Paul, 1963), pp. 3–5, 17 (reprinted from 31 F.R.D.); Office of the Attorney General of the United States, *Annual Report, 1895*, p. 14, *Annual Report, 1911*, p. 22, *Annual Report, 1915*, pp. 9, 47–50, *Annual Report, 1923*, p. 3. See Edwin C. Surrency, *History of the Federal Courts* (New York, 1987), pp. 376–78.

159. See, for example, Judicial Code of 1911, 36 Stat. 1087, 1094–99 (Secs. 28–39).

160. 36 Stat. 1095. See *National Steamship Co. v. Tugman*, 106 U.S. 118 (1882).

161. *Stone v. South Carolina*, 117 U.S. 430 (1886); *Carson v. Hyatt*, 118 U.S. 279 (1886); Black, *Treatise*, pp. 303–17; Moon, *Removal of Causes*, pp. 493–500.

162. Moon, *Removal of Causes*, pp. 565–67.

163. Since the enactment of Section 5 of the Judiciary Act of 1875, 18 Stat. 470, the federal courts had been required, on their own motion if necessary, to remand any action for which jurisdiction was lacking. The amending judicial acts of 1887–88 (24 Stat. 552 and 25 Stat. 433) and 1911 (36 Stat. 1087) retained the provision.

164. *Martin's Administrator v. Baltimore & Ohio Railraod Co.*, 151 U.S. 673 (1894).

165. See, for example, *Chicago & Northwestern Railway Co. v. Ohle*, 117 U.S. 123 (1886); *Johnson v. Accident Insurance Co. of North America*, 35 F. 374 (C.C.W.D.Mich. 1888); *Curnow v. Phoenix Insurance Co.*, 44 F. 805 (C.C.D.S.C. 1890); *Ross v. Erie Railroad Co.*, 120 F. 703 (C.C.E.D.N.Y. 1902); *Lewis v. Cincinnati, New Orleans & Texas Pacific Railway Co.*, 192 F. 654 (C.C.E.D.Tenn. 1910); Moon, *Removal of Causes*, pp. 564–67, 621–33; James Hamilton Lewis, *Removal of Causes from State to Federal Courts* (New York, 1923), pp. 489–94.

166. Consistent with this purpose to protect the federal right to remove, the statute made both denials of removal petitions by state courts and denials of remand motions by federal courts reviewable on appeal, but it made remand orders by the federal courts final and unreviewable. See Black, *Treatise*, pp. 363–65; Lewis, *Removal of Causes*, pp. 499–503. The statute allowed the courts to impose costs on the defendant for wrongful removal, and the payment of such costs was the purpose of the removal bond. *Mansfield, Coldwater & Lake Michigan Railway Co. v. Swan*, 111 U.S. 379 (1884). For corporate defendants, however, the costs were quite small and nothing more than an ordinary cost of litigation.

167. *Kern v. Huidekoper*, 103 U.S. 485 (1880); *Chesapeake & Ohio Railway Co. v. White*, 111 U.S. 134 (1884); Dobie, *Handbook of Federal Jurisdiction*, pp. 451–56; Moon, *Removal of Causes*, pp. 552–59; Black, *Treatise*, pp. 317–22; Lewis, *Removal of Causes*, pp. 450–65.

168. See, for example, Black, *Treatise*, 309–11, 317–18, 363–65; Note, "State–Federal Court Conflicts over the Removability of Causes: The Prospect Under the New Judicial Code," *University of Pennsylvania Law Review* 98 (1949): 80.

169. A state court's refusal to grant a removal petition could also, of course, cause problems for the defendant. Given the unequal resources of the parties and the relative value to each of what was at stake in the litigation, however, the problems were generally of much less consequence to the defendant.

170. Lewis, *Removal of Causes*, p. 8.

171. *Hagerla v. Mississippi River Power Co.*, 202 F. 771, 773 (D.Iowa 1912). See, for example, Milton R. Schlesinger and Joseph J. Strasburger, Jr., "Divestment of Federal Jurisdiction," *Columbia Law Review* 39 (1939): 595.

172. 17 Stat. 196 (1872).

173. *United States Mutual Accident Association v. Barry*, 131 U.S. 100, 120 (1889).

174. See Robert M. Hughes, *Handbook of Jurisdiction and Procedure in United States Courts* (St. Paul, 1913), pp. 389–417; Charles E. Clark and James W. Moore, "A New Federal Civil Procedure," *Yale Law Journal* 44 (1935): 387, 401–11; Surrency, *History of the Federal Courts*, pp. 138–41; Charles Warren, "Federal Process and State Legislation," *Virginia Law Review* 16 (1930): 546, 557–70.

175. Letter from Edwin A. Krauthoff to George W. Norris, October 18, 1927, George W. Norris Papers, Tray 42, Box 2, File: "S. 3151 (70th)," Library of Congress.

176. Letter from Matthew A. McCullough to George W. Norris, January 18, 1932, George W. Norris Papers, Library of Congress, Box 198, File: "Limiting Jurisdiction of Federal Courts (71st and 72nd) Congress."

177. Dobie, *Handbook of Federal Jurisdiction,* p. 580. See Thomas M. Boulware, *Guide to Removal and Its Prevention* (Allendale, SC, 1948), pp. 1–2. Compare Bumiller, "Choice of Forum in Diversity Cases," p. 772; David M. Trubek, Austin Sarat, William L. F. Felstiner, Herbert M. Kritzer, and Joel B. Grossman, "The Costs of Ordinary Litigation," *U.C.L.A. Law Review* 31 (1983): 72, 123.

178. Simeon E. Baldwin, *The American Judiciary* (New York, 1905), pp. 140–41.

179. Letter from C. W. Crossan to George W. Norris, December 10, 1931, George W. Norris Papers, Library of Congress, Box 198, File: "Limiting Jurisdiction of Federal Courts (71st & 72nd) Congress."

180. Letter from Raymond N. Klass to George W. Norris, February 15, 1933, George W. Norris Papers, Library of Congress, Box 198, File: "Limiting Jurisdiction of Federal Courts (71st & 72nd) Congress."

181. Frankfurter and Landis, *Business of the Supreme Court,* pp. 77–80 and n. 110, pp. 128–31 and n. 122; Surrency, *History of the Federal Courts,* chaps. 5–7.

182. H.R. Rep. No. 45, 44 Cong., 1 Sess. (1876), p. 4. The number in the text is an estimate based on the locations specified in Moon, *Removal of Causes,* p. 503, n. 19; Office of the Attorney General of the United States, *Annual Report, 1895,* p. 4; and Frankfurter and Landis, *Business of the Supreme Court,* p. 131, n. 122. Sometime after the turn of the century the discrepancy was apparently rectified. In 1910 both district and circuit courts were required to sit in the same number of locations. See Frankfurter and Landis, *Business of the Supreme Court,* p. 131, n. 122. The old circuit courts were abolished in the Judicial Code of 1911, 36 Stat. 1087 (1911).

183. Office of the Attorney General of the United States, *Annual Report, 1895,* p. 14.

184. *Bradford v. Southern Railway Co.,* 195 U.S. 243 (1904).

185. See 36 Stat. 866 (1910); Office of the Attorney General of the United States, *Annual Report, 1915,* pp. 9–10; *Kinney v. Plymouth Rock Squab Co.,* 236 U.S. 43 (1915).

186. The Court's appellate jurisdiction was limited to cases where the matter in controversy was at least $2,000, a jurisdictional minimum that Congress raised to $5,000 in 1875. See Benjamin Robbins Curtis, *Jurisdiction, Practice, and Peculiar Jurisprudence of the Courts of the United States,* 2nd ed. rev. by Henry Childs Merwin (Boston, 1896), p. 65. To avoid the costs of an appeal, plaintiffs with judgments in excess of those amounts could agree to waive their claim to the amount in excess of the appellate jurisdictional minimum.

187. Surrency, *History of the Federal Courts,* pp. 206–7.

188. Curtis, *Jurisdiction, Practice, and Peculiar Jurisprudence,* p. 65.

189. 26 Stat. 826 (1891).

190. Erwin C. Surrency, "A History of Federal Courts," *Missouri Law Review* 28 (1963): 214, 234.

191. H.R. Rep. No. 825, 64 Cong., 1 Sess. (1916), p. 3. Sometimes a court of appeals would help alleviate the problem by voluntarily holding court in an additional location. Such an arrangement offered no guarantee that alternative sites would continue in use, however, and many federal appellate judges strongly opposed sitting in more than one location. Between 1902 and 1911, for example, Congress improved matters in the six-state Fifth Circuit by requiring the court of appeals, which had previously convened only in New Orleans, to sit additionally in Atlanta, Montgomery, and Fort Worth. See Surrency, "History of the Federal Courts," pp. 234–35; 36 Stat. 1132 (1911). On the ground that the additional locations "imposed unnecessary hardship upon the judges of that court," the conference of senior circuit judges repeatedly called for Congress to restore the prior law and require the court to sit only in New Orleans. See Office of the Attorney General of the United States, *Annual Report, 1930,* p. 7, and see, *Annual Report, 1933,* p. 5, *Annual Report, 1934,* p. 6. Congress refused to comply.

192. H.R. Rep. No. 825, 64 Cong., 1 Sess. (1916), p. 3.

193. Office of the Attorney General of the United States, *Annual Report, 1915,* p. 84; H.R. Rep. No. 825, 64 Cong., 1 Sess. (1916), p. 2.

194. H.R. Rep. No. 825, 64 Cong., 1 Sess. (1916), p. 2.

195. Surrency, *History of the Federal Courts,* p. 206.

196. Posner, "Theory of Negligence," p. 95.

197. Friedman and Russell, "More Civil Wrongs," p. 308; American Law Institute, *A Study of the Business of the Federal Courts,* p. 94 (law docket only).

198. Henry Stockbridge, "The Applicability of English Methods to Conditions in the United States," *Green Bag* 17 (1905): 275, 281.

199. Werner, "The Abuse of Personal Injury Litigation," p. 203.

200. Letter from A. J. O'Melia to George W. Norris, March 25, 1932, George W. Norris Papers, Tray 42, Box 8, File: "Limiting Jurisdiction of Federal Courts," Library of Congress.

201. Letter from Donald Gallagher to George W. Norris, April 16, 1932, George W. Norris Papers, Tray 42, Box 8, File: "Limiting Jurisdiction of Federal Courts," Library of Congress. See Hearings before the Committee on the Judiciary of the United States Senate on S. 466, 79 Cong., 1 Sess. (1945), pp. 3–4, 6 (statement of Hon. William Denman of the United States Circuit Court of Appeals for the Ninth Circuit).

202. Alexander M. Bickel and Benno C. Schmidt, Jr., *The Judiciary and Responsible Government, 1910–21* (New York, 1984), p. 553, and also see pp. 563, 586, n. 128.

203. Trubek, et al., "The Costs of Ordinary Litigation," p. 122.

204. This assumes, of course, that the rules of the common law would have led to efficient results if applied. The "subsidy" and "efficiency" questions are discussed in more detail in Chapter 11.

Chapter 3

1. 16 Pet. (41 U.S.) 1 (1842).

2. One of the Court's most widely cited discussions of the nature of the federal common law appeared in *Western Union Telegraph Co. v. Call Publishing Co.,* 181 U.S. 92 (1901). There the Court said that there was "no body of Federal common laws separate and distinct from the common law existing in the several States in the sense that there is a body of statute law enacted by Congress separate and distinct from the body of statute law enacted by the several states" (p. 101). By that statement, however, the Court seemed to mean only that (in theory) the federal courts applied the common law of the states but that (in practice) they reached their decisions free from the control of state precedents. The idea was that they applied "the principles of the common law" (p. 102).

3. See, for example, *National City Bank v. National Security Co.,* 58 F. 2d 7 (C.C.A. 6 1932); *Peterson v. Metropolitan Life Insurance Co.,* 19 F.2d 74 (S.D.Iowa 1926); *Capitol City Bank, v. Swift,* 290 F. 505 (D.Okla. 1923).

4. *Burgess v. Seligman,* 107 U.S. 20 (1883).

5. Armistead M. Dobie, *Handbook of Federal Jurisdiction and Procedure* (St. Paul, 1928), pp. 563–64. For a general review of the nature of the federal common law, see pp. 557–78.

6. *Bouvier's Law Dictionary and Concise Encyclopedia,* 8th ed. by Francis Rawle (Kansas City, 1914), vol. 3, p. 3369.

7. When the federal courts chose to follow state common law, they often stressed in elaborate detail the extent to which state law was both clear and long settled. For example, *Bucher v. Cheshire Railroad Co.,* 125 U.S. 555 (1888); *Byrne v. Kansas City, Fort Smith & Memphis Railroad Co.,* 61 F. 605 (C.C.A. 6 1894). Often, however, they found that state decisions did not constitute such a settled course and that they were, accordingly, not required to follow them. See, for example, *Penman v. St. Paul Fire and Marine Insurance Co.,* 216 U.S. 311 (1910); *Aetna Life Insurance Co. v. Moore,* 231 U.S. 543 (1913).

8. *Bucher v. Cheshire Railroad Co.,* 125 U.S. 555, 583 (1888).

9. See Dobie, *Handbook of Federal Jurisdiction,* pp. 557–78; Edward Thompson Co., *The Federal Law of Contracts* (St. Paul, 1934), vol. 1, pp. 8–17; *Kuhn v. Fairmont Coal Co.,* 215 U.S. 349 (1910).

10. *Delmas v. Insurance Co.,* 14 Wall. (81 U.S.) 661 (1871); *Tidal Oil Co. v. Flanagan,* 263 U.S. 444 (1924).

11. George C. Holt, *The Concurrent Jurisdiction of Federal and State Courts* (New York, 1888), pp. 159–88; Mitchell Wendell, *Relations Between the Federal and State Courts* (New York, 1949), pp. 170–74, 185–86; H. Parker Sharp and Joseph B. Brennan, "The Application of the

Doctrine of Swift v. Tyson Since 1900," *Indiana Law Journal* 4 (1929): 367, 370; Edward Thompson Co., *Federal Law of Contracts*, vol. 2, p. 476; Note, *Harvard Law Review* 43 (1930): 926; *Salem Trust Co. v. Manufacturers' Finance Co.*, 264 U.S. 182, 191, n. 3–5 (1924); *Adams Express Co. v. Croninger*, 226 U.S. 491, 504–7 (1913). In his book *The Ages of American Law* (New Haven, CT, 1977) Grant Gilmore argues that the federal common law had a strongly unifying effect on the common law, at least in commercial areas and at least until the end of the nineteenth century. See pp. 30–35, 60–61, and 122, n. 24.

12. Some scholars argue that the Court specifically intended to assist a rising commercial class. For example, Morton J. Horwitz, *The Transformation of American Law, 1780–1860* (Cambridge, MA, 1977), pp. 245–52; Hessel E. Yntema and George H. Jaffin, "Preliminary Analysis of Concurrent Jurisdiction," *University of Pennsylvania Law Review* 79 (1931): 869. Other scholars stress the limited nature of the Court's decision in *Swift* and its close relationship to antebellum commercial law and practice. For example, Tony Freyer, *Harmony & Dissonance: The Swift and Erie Cases in American Federalism* (New York, 1981); Freyer, *Forums of Order: The Federal Courts and Business in American History* (Greenwich, CT, 1979); Herbert Hovenkamp, "Federalism Revisited," *Hastings Law Journal* 34 (1982): 201, 214–23. Another group of scholars emphasizes the extent to which *Swift* was the product of basic jurisprudential assumptions about the nature of law that were widely accepted in the first half of the nineteenth century. For example, Randolph Bridwell and Ralph U. Whitten, *The Constitution and the Common Law: The Decline of the Doctrines of Separation of Powers and Federalism* (Lexington, MA, 1977); William P. LaPiana, "*Swift v. Tyson* and the Brooding Omnipresence in the Sky: An Investigation of the Idea of Law in Antebellum America," *Suffolk University Law Review* 20 (1986): 771.

13. "Remarks," *American Law Review* 28 (1894): 146. For varieties of criticism of the federal common law, see William M. Meigs, "National Common Law," *Southern Law Review* 8 (1882): 414; George Wharton Pepper, *The Borderland of Federal and State Decisions* (Philadelphia, 1889). See generally Freyer, *Harmony & Dissonance*, pp. 75–122; Freyer, *Forums of Order*, pp. 121–36.

14. The relationships were only tendencies, of course, and there were exceptions. The person who became the most famous opponent of the federal common law, Justice Oliver Wendell Holmes, Jr., was a New England Republican with little sympathy for populist or progressive politics and a considerable if somewhat grudging admiration for large-scale corporate enterprise. See Chapter 10.

15. 1 Wall. (68 U.S.) 175 (1863).

16. See Charles Fairman, *Reconstruction and Reunion 1864–1888* (New York, 1971), pp. 910–1116; Charles Fairman, *Mr. Justice Miller and the Supreme Court, 1862–1890* (Cambridge, MA, 1939); Harold M. Hyman and William M. Wiecek, *Equal Justice Under Law: Constitutional Development, 1835–1875* (New York, 1982), pp. 365–70.

17. *Gordon v. Ware National Bank of Ware, Mass.*, 132 F. 444, 449 (C.C.A. 8 1904). Agreeing: *Hewlett v. Schadel*, 68 F.2d 502 (C.C.A. 4 1934).

18. Quoted in Felix Frankfurter and Harry Shulman, *Cases and Other Authorities on Federal Jurisdiction and Procedure* (Chicago, 1937), p. 198.

19. Classic examples of state courts vetoing reform legislation, for example, are *Ballard v. Oil Co.*, 34 So. 533 (Miss. 1903); *Hoxie v. New York, New Haven & Hartford Railroad Co.*, 73 A. 754 (Conn. 1909); *Ives v. South Buffalo Railway Co.*, 201 N.Y. 271 (1911).

Opinions varied as to whether the state or federal courts were less favorably disposed toward reform legislation. One analysis suggests that the states were no less favorable and perhaps, in general, more favorable to such legislation than were the federal courts: Melvin I. Urofsky, "State Courts and Protective Legislation During the Progressive Era: A Reevaluation," *Journal of American History* 72 (1985): 63. The state of Washington, for example, was known as a particularly progressive state. See Joseph F. Tripp, "Progressive Jurisprudence in the West: The Washington Supreme Court, Labor Law, and the Problem of Industrial Accidents," *Labor History* 24 (1983): 342. See generally Sidney Fine, *Laissez Faire and the General-Welfare State: A Study of Conflict in American Thought, 1865–1901* (Ann Arbor, MI, 1964), pp. 126–64.

20. Burden of proof on contributory negligence: *Inland and Seaboard Coasting Co. v. Tolson,*

139 U.S. 551 (1891); *Washington and Georgetown Railroad Co. v. Harmon's Administrator*, 147 U.S. 571 (1893); *Central Vermont Railway Co. v. White*, 238 U.S. 507 (1915).

Last clear chance: *Grand Trunk Railway Co. v. Ives*, 144 U.S. 408 (1892); *Chunn v. City and Suburban Railway of Washington*, 207 U.S. 302 (1907).

21. *Union Pacific Railway Co. v. Botsford*, 141 U.S. 250 (1891); H.R. Rep. 7587, 59 Cong., 2 Sess. (1907). See Andrew J. Hirschl, "Personal Injury Actions: The Plaintiff's Standpoint," *Illinois Law Review* 1 (1906): 16, 19–21.

22. See, for example, the sympathy shown to plaintiffs in *Force v. Standard Silk Co.*, 160 F. 992 (C.C.N.D.N.Y. 1908), aff'd 170 F. 184 (C.C.A. 2 1909); *Snare & Triest Co. v. Friedman*, 169 F. 1 (C.C.A. 3 1909); *Moss v. Gulf Compress Co.*, 202 F. 657 (C.C.A. 5 1913). Agreeing: Stephen B. Presser, *Studies in the History of the United States Courts of the Third Circuit* (Washington, DC, 1982), pp. 86–99.

23. Variations were innumerable. Compare, for example, *Miller v. Maryland Casualty Co.*, 193 F. 343 (C.C.A. 3 1912), with *Hawkeye Commercial Men's Association v. Christy*, 294 F. 208 (C.C.A. 8 1923). See Frank W. Munger, Jr., "Commercial Litigation in West Virginia State and Federal Courts, 1870–1940," *American Journal of Legal History* 30 (1986): 322; Munger, "Law, Change, and Litigation: A Critical Examination of an Empirical Research Tradition," *Law & Society Review* 22 (1988): 57.

24. Harry N. Scheiber makes an analogous point about the advantages to corporations of the "uncertainties" that stemmed from federalism in the late nineteenth century in "Federalism and the American Economic Order, 1789–1910," *Law & Society Review* 10 (1975): 57, 117. See Robert W. Gordon, "Critical Legal Histories," *Stanford Law Review* 36 (1984): 57, 78–80. See also William H. Simon, "The Ideology of Advocacy: Procedural Justice and Professional Ethics," *Wisconsin Law Review* (1978): 30; Robert M. Cover, "The Uses of Jurisdictional Redundancy: Interest, Ideology, and Innovation," *William and Mary Law Review* 22 (1981): 639.

25. *Carpenter v. Providence–Washington Insurance Co.*, 16 Pet. (41 U.S.) 495 (1842).

26. *Paul v. Virginia*, 8 Wall. (75 U.S.) 168 (1869).

27. For example, *Orient Insurance Co. v. Daggs*, 172 U.S. 557 (1899); *John Hancock Mutual Life Insurance Co. v. Warren*, 181 U.S. 73 (1901); *Carroll v. Greenwich Insurance Co. of New York*, 199 U.S. 401 (1905); *German Alliance Insurance Co. v. Lewis*, 233 U.S. 389 (1914); *National Union Fire Insurance Co. v. Wanberg*, 260 U.S. 71 (1922); *Merchants Mutual Automobile Liability Insurance Co. v. Smart*, 267 U.S. 126 (1925). For a discussion of the growth of regulatory legislation at the state level, see Spencer L. Kimball, *Insurance and Public Policy: A Study in the Legal Implementation of Social and Economic Public Policy, Based on Wisconsin Records, 1835–1959* (Madison, WI, 1960).

28. For example, *Equitable Life Assurance Society v. Pettus*, 140 U.S. 226 (1891); *New York Life Insurance Co. v. Cravens*, 178 U.S. 389 (1900); *McMaster v. New York Life Insurance Co.*, 183 U.S. 25 (1901); *Whitfield v. Aetna Life Insurance Co. of Hartford*, 205 U.S. 489 (1907).

29. *Mutual Life Insurance Co. of New York v. Cohen*, 179 U.S. 262 (1900); *New York Life Insurance Co. v. Dodge*, 246 U.S. 357 (1918); *Boseman v. Connecticut General Life Insurance Co.*, 301 U.S. 196 (1937).

30. Lawrence M. Friedman, *A History of American Law* (New York, 1973), pp. 477–80; Morton Keller, *The Life Insurance Enterprise, 1885–1910: A Study in the Limits of Corporate Power* (Cambridge, MA, 1963), pp. 187–93; Gordon M. Bakken, *The Development of Law on the Rocky Mountain Frontier: Civil Law and Society, 1850–1912* (Westport, CT, 1983), pp. 61–63.

31. George Richards, *A Treatise on the Law of Insurance*, 3rd ed. (New York, 1910), p. 213.

32. 151 U.S. 452 (1894). Some data support the proposition that insurance companies won their cases more frequently in federal courts than they did in state courts. See Morton Keller, "The Judicial System and the Law of Life Insurance, 1888–1910," *Business History Review* 35 (1961): 317, 323. Policyholders apparently also fared relatively well in state courts in the West; see Bakken, *Development of Law on the Rocky Mountain Frontier*, pp. 61–63.

33. 151 U.S. 453–54.

34. Ibid., p. 462.

35. Ibid., p. 464.

36. Ibid., pp. 463, 466.

37. Ibid., p. 464.

38. Ibid., p. 467.

39. *Hunt v. Springfield Fire & Marine Insurance Co.*, 196 U.S. 47 (1904); *Metropolitan Life Insurance Co. v. Foster*, 67 F.2d 264 (C.C.A. 5 1933).

40. *Bergholm v. Peoria Life Insurance Co.*, 284 U.S. 489 (1932); *Travelers Insurance Co. v. Thorne*, 180 F. 82 (C.C.A. 1 1910); *Bradley v. New York Life Insurance Co.*, 275 F. 657 (C.C.A. 8 1921); *Home Insurance Co. v. Currie*, 54 F.2d 203 (C.C.A. 5 1931); *Royal Indemnity Co. v. Watson*, 61 F.2d 614 (C.C.A. 5 1932); *Maryland Casualty Co. v. Nellis*, 75 F.2d 23 (C.C.A. 6 1935); *Meigs v. London Assurance Co.*, 126 F. 781 (C.C.E.D.Pa. 1904); *Lawson v. Twin City Fire Insurance Co.*, 2 F. Supp. 171 (E.D.Ky. 1932).

41. *Cable v. United States Life Insurance Co.*, 191 U.S. 288, 309 (1903). See *Prudential Ins. Co. of Am. v Stack*, 60 F. 2d 830 (C.C.A. 4 1932); *New York Life Insurance Co. v. Driggs*, 72 F.2d 833 (C.C.A. 4 1934).

42. *Reed v. Bankers Reserve Life Insurance Co.*, 192 F. 408, 411 (C.C.E.D.Wash. 1911). Agreeing: *Lincoln National Life Insurance Co. of Fort Wayne, Indiana v. Hammer*, 41 F.2d 12, 18 (C.C.A. 8 1930); *Donnelly v. Northwestern Life Insurance Co.*, 59 F.2d 46 (C.C.A. 5 1932). See William R. Vance, *Handbook of the Law of Insurance* (St. Paul, 1930), pp. 311–13.

43. 187 U.S. 335 (1902).

44. Ibid., p. 353.

45. *O'Brien v. Massachusetts Bonding & Insurance Co.*, 64 F.2d 33 (C.C.A. 8 1933); *Order of United Commercial Travelers of America v. Shane*, 64 F.2d 55 (C.C.A. 8 1933); *Davis v. Jefferson Standard Life Insurance Co.*, 73 F.2d 330 (C.C.A. 5 1934); *Metropolitan Life Insurance Co. v. Bukaty*, 92 F.2d 1 (C.C.A. 10 1937).

46. 291 U.S. 491 (1934).

47. Ibid., p. 497.

48. Ibid., p. 499.

49. Ibid., pp. 498–501.

50. Richards, *Treatise*, 3rd ed. p. 165, n. 4.

51. 13 Wall. (80 U.S.) 222 (1871).

52. When the equities presented a different situation, the Court in the 1870s could apply the parol evidence rule rigidly. *Insurance Co. v. Lyman*, 15 Wall. (82 U.S.) 664 (1872).

53. 13 Wall. (80 U.S.) 234.

54. Ibid., p. 235.

55. *Insurance Co. v. Mahone*, 21 Wall. (88 U.S.) 152 (1874); *Eames v. Home Insurance Co.*, 3 Otto (94 U.S.) 621 (1876). Compare *Miller v. Life Insurance Co.*, 12 Wall. (79 U.S.) 285 (1870); *Insurance Co. v. Wolff*, 5 Otto (95 U.S.) 326 (1877); *Phoenix Life Insurance Co. v. Raddin*, 120 U.S. 183 (1887).

56. 6 Otto (96 U.S.) 234 (1877).

57. Ibid., p. 244.

58. Ibid., p. 245.

59. *New York Insurance Co. v. Fletcher*, 117 U.S. 519 (1886).

60. 183 U.S. 308 (1902). On the erratic quality of the process, see *Continental Life Insurance Co. v. Chamberlain*, 132 U.S. 304 (1889) and *McMaster v. New York Life Insurance Co.* 183 U.S. 25 (1901). For the scope of the change and the general impact of *Northern Assurance*, compare Richards, *Treatise*, 2nd ed. (1893), pp. 68–102, with 3rd ed. (1910), pp. 158–220.

61. 183 U.S. 309, 315–16.

62. Ibid., p. 315.

63. Ibid., p. 361.

64. Richards, *Treatise*, 3rd ed., p. 208.

65. 183 U.S. 361.

66. The plaintiff in *Northern Assurance* brought and eventually prevailed on a suit to reform the policy. See 203 U.S. 106 (1906). It is noteworthy that the plaintiff was not a private individual but a building association.

67. 183 U.S. 364.

68. Ibid.

69. Ibid., pp. 328, 364. The Court did not attempt to reconcile its claim to "protect both parties" with either its statement that its rules were designed "to protect the companies" or its decision to protect the companies alone—at the expense of their policyholders—from "faithless agents."

70. Ibid., pp. 364–65. The 1893 edition of Richard's *Treatise* reflected the view that the federal courts were in the mainstream of insurance law with most states and that the courts generally were sympathetic to claimants (see, e.g., p. 73). The third edition in 1910 pointed out that many states rejected the rule of *Northern Assurance* (p. 206) and that most state courts followed more liberal rules than the federal courts did (pp. 161–62, 176–77, 206, 212).

71. Ibid., p. 321.

72. *Northern Assurance Co. of London v. Grand View Building Association,* 101 F. 77, 79 (C.C.A. 8 1900).

73. For example, *Penman v. St. Paul Fire & Marine Insurance Co.,* 216 U.S. 311 (1910); *Lumber Underwriters of New York v. Rife,* 237 U.S. 605 (1915).

74. For example, *Pennsylvania Casualty Co. v. Bacon,* 133 F. 907 (C.C.A. 2 1904); *MacKelvie v. Mutual Benefit Life Insurance Co. of Newark, N.J.,* 287 F. 660 (C.C.A. 2 1923); *Hartford Fire Insurance Co. v. Nance,* 12 F.2d 575 (C.C.A. 6 1926); *Aetna Life Insurance Co. v. Johnson,* 13 F.2d 824 (C.C.A. 8 1926); *Hartford Fire Insurance Co. v. Jones,* 15 F.2d 1 (C.C.A. 6 1926); *Odegard v. General Casualty & Surety Co.,* 44 F.2d 31 (C.C.A. 8 1930); *Eddy v. National Union Indemnity Co.,* 78 F.2d 545 (C.C.A. 9 1935); *Eddy v. National Union Indemnity Co.,* 80 F.2d 284 (C.C.A. 9 1935); *Schilling v. St. Paul Fire & Marine Insurance Co.,* 29 F.2d 607 (S.D.N.Y. 1927); *Lawson v. Twin City Fire Insurance Co.,* 2 F. Supp. 171 (E.D.Ky. 1932).

75. Richards, *Treatise,* 3rd ed., pp. 158–220, esp. pp. 161–62, 176–77, 206, 212.

76. Vance, *Handbook,* p. 493 and n. 38. See Charles B. Elliott, *An Outline of the Law of Insurance,* 2nd ed. (St. Paul, 1896), pp. 128–30. For example, *Jensen v. New York Life Insurance Co.,* 59 F. 2d 957 (C.C.A. 8 1932).

77. See, for example, *Newsom v. New York Life Insurance Co.,* 60 F.2d 241 (C.C.A. 6 1932); *Provident Mutual Life Insurance Co. of Philadelphia v. Parons,* 70 F. 2d 863, 867–68 (C.C.A. 4 1934).

78. Vance, *Handbook,* p. 508, and also see pp. 454–55; 502–14.

79. Office of the Attorney General of the United States, *Annual Report, 1937,* pp. 187–88. Two of the three categories of other contract actions are listed under "Private civil cases," as subcategories "National bank receivership cases" and "Other contracts" under the general category "Contract." The third category was created by combining the cases under "Contracts" in the sections headed "United States defendant" and "United States plaintiff." It is worth noting that the only other insurance contract category is "War Risk insurance" cases. In that category the courts directed jury verdicts in 35 percent of the cases. This year is the only year for which such statistics are available during the period in which the federal courts exercised their independent judgment under *Swift.*

80. 231 U.S. 543 (1913).

81. Ibid., p. 559.

82. *Mutual Life Insurance Co. of New York v. Phinney,* 178 U.S. 327 (1900); *Mutual Life Insurance Co. of New York v. Sears,* 178 U.S. 345 (1900); *Mutual Life Insurance Co. of New York v. Cohen,* 179 U.S. 262 (1900); *Mutual Life Insurance Co. of New York v. Hill,* 193 U.S. 551 (1904).

83. For example, *New York Life Insurance Co. v. Dodge,* 246 U.S. 357 (1918); *Boseman v. Connecticut General Life Insurance Co.,* 301 U.S. 196 (1937).

84. The companies learned, for example, from *Stipcich v. Metropolitan Life Insurance Co.,* 277 U.S. 311, 321 (1928). See, for example, *Subar v. New York Life Insurance Co.,* 60 F.2d 239 (C.C.A. 6 1932).

85. J. Willard Hurst, *The Growth of American Law: The Lawmakers* (Boston, 1950), p. 187; Timothy Brown, *Commentaries on the Jurisdiction of Courts,* 2nd ed. (Chicago, 1901), pp. 71–72.

86. Friedman, *History of American Law,* pp. 409–27; Wex S. Malone, "The Formative Era of Contributory Negligence," *Illinois Law Review* 41 (1946): 151; Grant Gilmore, *The Death of Contract* (Columbus, OH, 1974); G. Edward White, *Tort Law in America: An Intellectual History*

(New York, 1980), pp. 50, 60–62. Compare J. Willard Hurst, *Law and the Conditions of Freedom in the Nineteenth-Century United States* (Madison, WI, 1967), esp. pp. 20–23. Qualifying these views to some extent are Gary T. Schwartz, "Tort Law and the Economy in Nineteenth-Century America: A Reinterpretation," *Yale Law Journal* 90 (July 1981): 1717 (finding that the courts in California and New Hampshire were relatively favorably disposed toward tort plaintiffs other than employees); and Robert L. Rabin, "The Historical Development of the Fault Principle: A Reinterpretation," *Georgia Law Review* 15 (1981): 925 (finding that in many areas liability for negligence was expanding in the nineteenth century, though also confirming the generally narrow limits within which such liability existed).

87. 133 F. 485, cert. den. 201 U.S. 643 (1906).

88. Ibid., p. 485.

89. See, for example, *Union Pacific Railway Co. v. Daniels,* 152 U.S. 684 (1894); *Union Pacific Railway Co. v. O'Brien,* 161 U.S. 451 (1896); *Choctaw, Oklahoma and Gulf Railroad Co. v. McDade,* 191 U.S. 64 (1903); *Kreigh v. Westinghouse, Church, Kerr & Co.,* 214 U.S. 249 (1909); *Thomas v. Cincinnati, New Orleans & Texas Pacific Railway Co.,* 97 F. 245 (C.C.D.Ky. 1899) (Taft, J.); Simeon E. Baldwin, *American Railroad Law* (New York, 1904), pp. 247–73; H. G. Wood, *A Treatise on the Law of Railroads,* 2nd ed. (Boston, 1894), vol. 3, pp. 1724–35. Richard A. Posner, "A Theory of Negligence," *Journal of Legal Studies* 1 (1972): 29, 68, suggested that employees prevailed more frequently in federal appellate courts than they did in the state appellate courts. In a later work, however, he noted that "the common law rules created by federal courts tended to be more favorable to defendants than the counterpart rules in the states." Richard A. Posner, *The Federal Courts: Crisis and Reform* (Cambridge, MA, 1985), p. 54.

90. 179 U.S. 658 (1901).

91. For the Court's general acceptance of the *res ipsa* doctrine in tort cases beyond the master–servant area, see *San Juan Light Co. v. Raquena,* 224 U.S. 89 (1912).

92. Ibid., pp. 663–64. See *Texas and Pacific Railway Co. v. Barrett,* 166 U.S. 617 (1897); *Looney v. Metropolitan Railroad Co.,* 200 U.S. 480 (1906).

93. Sen. Doc. No. 338, 62 Cong., 2 Sess. (1912), vol. 1, p. 89; vol. 2, p. 221 (statement of F. W. Judson, representing the Brotherhood of Locomotive Engineers, Brotherhood of Locomotive Firemen and Enginemen, Order of Railroad Conductors, and Brotherhood of Railroad Trainmen).

94. *Final Report of the Industrial Commission,* H.R. Doc. No. 380, 57 Cong., 1 Sess. (1902), vol. 19, p. 933.

95. On the level of theory, the concept of causality was becoming increasingly problematic for late nineteenth-century thinkers even before the Court articulated the exacting requirements in *Patton.* See, for example, Morton J. Horwitz, "The Doctrine of Objective Causation," in David Kairys, ed., *The Politics of Law: A Progressive Critique* (New York, 1982), pp. 201–13; Thomas L. Haskell, *The Emergence of Professional Social Science: The American Social Science Association and the Nineteenth-Century Crisis of Authority* (Urbana, IL, 1977).

96. *O'Brien v. Chicago & Northwestern Railway Co.,* 116 F. 502 (C.C.N.D.Iowa 1902).

97. *Chicago & Northwestern Railway Co. v. O'Brien,* 132 F. 593 (C.C.A. 8 1904).

98. *Chicago & Northwestern Railway Co. v. O'Brien,* 153 F. 511 (C.C.A. 8 1907).

99. For example, *Mountain Copper Co., Ltd. v. Van Buren,* 123 F. 61 (C.C.A. 9 1903); *Northern Pacific Railway Co. v. Dixon,* 139 F. 737 (C.C.A. 8 1905); *Carnegie Steel Co. v. Byers,* 149 F. 667 (C.C.A. 6 1907); *Omaha Packing Co. v. Sanduski,* 155 F. 897 (C.C.A. 8 1907); *Missouri, Kansas & Texas Railway Co. v. Foreman,* 174 F. 377 (C.C.A. 8 1909); *Midland Valley Railroad Co. v. Fulgham,* 181 F. 91 (C.C.A. 8 1910); *Armour & Co. v. Harcrow,* 217 F. 224 (C.C.A. 8 1914); *Duree v. Wabash Railroad Co.,* 241 F. 454 (C.C.A. 8 1917); *Patton v. Illinois Central Railroad Co.,* 179 F. 530 (C.C.W.D.Ky. 1910); *Montbriand v. Chicago, St. Paul, Minneapolis & Omaha Railway Co.,* 191 F. 988 (C.C.D.Minn. 1911).

100. For example, *Bowes v. Hopkins,* 84 F. 767 (C.C.A. 7 1898); *Hodges v. Kimball,* 104 F. 745 (C.C.A. 4 1900); *Canadian Northern Railway Co. v. Senske,* 201 F. 637 (C.C.A. 8 1912).

101. For example, *Illinois Central Railroad Co. v. Coughlin,* 132 F. 801 (C.C.A. 6 1904); *Shandrew v. Chicago, St. Paul, Minneapolis & Omaha Railway Co.,* 142 F. 320 (C.C.A. 8 1905).

102. *Patton v. Illinois Central Railroad Co.,* 179 F. 530 (C.C.W.D.Ky. 1910); *Montbriand v.*

Chicago, St. Paul, Minneapolis & Omaha Railway Co., 191 F. 988 (C.C.D.Minn. 1911). In the first case, after denying recovery, the judge concluded on a personal note that emphasized the widespread effect that federal evidentiary requirements had on plaintiffs:

> My great sympathy for the unfortunate victim of this accident, who testified before me, has led me to an industrious re-examination of the questions involved. The result is that I find this case added to the long list of those where there was a failure of substantial evidence of actionable negligence. [179 F. 535]

103. One scholar concluded as follows:

> When it became necessary, for instance, to dull the edge of the fellow-servant rule, the [Wisconsin] Supreme Court adroitly used legal fictions, presumptions, constructive knowledge, and the burden of proof to carry deserving plaintiffs over doctrinal obstacles. By directing trial courts to submit crucial issues to the jury, it expanded the possibilities for recovery. [Robert S. Hunt, *Law and Locomotives: The Impact of the Railroad on Wisconsin Law in the Nineteenth Century* (Madison, WI, 1858), pp. 159–60]

Posner, "Theory of Negligence," p. 92, finds that the state courts widely applied the *res ipsa loquitur* doctrine, but he does not indicate whether or not they applied it in master–servant cases.

104. For example, *Armour v. Hahn*, 111 U.S. 313 (1884); *Kohn v. McNulta*, 147 U.S. 238 (1893); *Northern Pacific Railroad Co. v. Poirier*, 167 U.S. 48 (1897); *Chesapeake & Ohio Railroad Co. v. Hennessey*, 96 F. 713 (C.C.A. 6 1899); *Roymann v. Brown*, 105 F. 250 (C.C.A. 5 1900). On assumption of risk, see Francis H. Bohlen, "Voluntary Assumption of Risk," *Harvard Law Review* 20 (1906): 14, 91.

105. There was a gradual and growing effort in the late nineteenth century to modify or eliminate the employers' defenses, especially the fellow servant rule. By the 1890s the courts in a number of states, such as Wisconsin, had developed various exceptions and narrowing subrules that allowed worker recoveries, and they sometimes reached the same result by permitting juries enough leeway to find liability when a strict application of the rules might have required verdicts for defendants. See, for example, Lawrence M. Friedman and Jack Ladinsky, "Social Change and the Law of Industrial Accidents," *Columbia Law Review* 67 (1967): 50, 59–62; Friedman, *History of American Law* (1973), pp. 422–25; Hunt, *Law and Locomotives*, pp. 159–60; Robert M. Hughes, *Handbook of Federal Jurisdiction and Procedure in United States Courts* (St. Paul, 1913), pp. 18–19.

Although the tangles and inconsistencies of the law of fellow servants are legendary, it nevertheless seems that many, and perhaps most, states recognized exceptions to and qualifications of the doctrine that made their law relatively more attractive to tort plaintiffs than was the comparable federal law after *Baltimore & Ohio Railroad v. Baugh*, 149 U.S. 368 (1893). In 1896 one legal writer who surveyed the laws in numerous states concluded that "many of the American courts" had "adopted rulings appreciably diminishing the severity" of the fellow servant rule. See Speed Mosby, "The Fellow-Servant Doctrine," *American Law Review* 30 (1896): 840, 846. For examples of the ways that some of the states narrowed the fellow servant rule, see *Zintek v. Stimson Mill Co.*, 37 P. 340 (Sup. Ct.Wash. 1894) (person who supervised lumber yard is vice-principal; company liable); *Hankins v. New York, Lake Erie & Western Railroad Co.*, 37 N.E. 466 (Ct.App. N.Y. 1894) (train dispatcher is vice-principal to fireman on train; company liable); *Illinois Central Railroad Co. v. Hilliard*, 37 S.W. 75 (Sup.Ct.Ky 1896) (car inspector and conductor of freight train are not fellow servants; company liable); *Norfolk & Western Railroad Co. v. Ampey*, 25 S.E. 226 (Sup. Ct. Va. 1896) (master liable for unsafe equipment even if negligence of fellow servant contributed to injury); *Blomquist v. Great Northern Railway Co.*, 67 N.W. 804 (Sup.Ct.Minn. 1896) (a case arguably outside the scope of a state statute held to be within the reach of the statute; company liable for injury owing to negligence of a fellow servant).

In 1906 the Supreme Court itself acknowledged the divergence between the federal fellow servant rule and the rule as applied in a number of the states. See *Alabama Great Southern Railway Co. v. Thompson*, 200 U.S. 206, 219–20 (1906).

Even in states that rigidly retained the employers' defenses in their black letter law, the courts apparently applied them in ways that often allowed injured employees to recover. In

West Virginia, for example, the fellow servant rule remained in force, yet one study found that "nearly all of the employee cases going to trial were won by the railroad employee." The author notes that the "West Virginia Supreme Court of Appeals did not relax the doctrinal barriers to recovery by railroad employees, yet its decisions increasingly favored employees" (Munger, "Social Change and Tort Litigation," p. 88, n. 33, pp. 104–5). By the end of the nineteenth century the issue of the fellow servant rule split the judges on the state's supreme court. See John Phillip Reid, *An American Judge: Marmaduke Dent of West Virginia* (New York, 1968), pp. 51–54.

Similarly, the California Supreme Court applied the employers' defenses strictly, but it nevertheless also left room for jury verdicts that overwhelmingly favored plaintiffs. Compare Schwartz, "Tort Law and the Economy," pp. 1768–71, 1774–75; Bakken, *Development of Law in Frontier California,* pp. 76–83.

In some states there may have been little or no difference in the formal rules applied in the federal and state systems. New Hampshire, for example, rigorously enforced the employers' defenses. See Schwartz, "Tort Law and the Economy." The 1907 edition of Thomas M. Cooley's treatise on tort law stressed the extent to which the state courts in general accepted the fellow servant rule. It declared that the rule was supported by "an overwhelming weight of authority" in the states. The treatise stated that the "vice-principal" exception to the fellow servant rule was rejected by "the great weight of authority" and that the other major exception to the fellow servant rule, the "separate division" doctrine, was recognized only in Illinois, Nebraska, Kentucky, Utah, and Tennessee (in the last case where it was limited to railroad employees). The treatise probably masked a great deal of uncertainty and practical conflict in the state courts, however, when it acknowledged that "[s]ome disputes still remain which concern the proper limits of the doctrine, and what and how many are the exceptional cases." See Thomas M. Cooley, *A Treatise on the Law of Torts, or the Wrongs Which Arise Independently of Contract,* ed. John Lewis (Chicago, 1907), pp. 541–42, 545, 549–50.

106. For example, *Baltimore & Ohio Railroad Co. v. Doty,* 133 F. 866 (C.C.A. 6 1904); *Deye v. Lodge & Shipley Machine Tool Co.,* 137 F. 480 (C.C.A. 6 1905); *Carnegie Steel Co. v. Byers,* 149 F. 667 (C.C.A. 6 1907); *Morgan Construction Co. v. Frank,* 158 F. 964 (C.C.A. 6 1908); *Illinois Central Railroad Co. v. Hart,* 176 F. 245 (C.C.A. 6 1910); *Patton v. Illinois Central Railroad Co.,* 179 F. 530 (C.C.W.D.Ky. 1910). For earlier cases imposing rigorous evidentiary standards, see *Northern Pacific Railroad Co. v. Charless,* 162 U.S. 359 (1896); *Northern Pacific Railroad Co. v. Poirier,* 167 U.S. 48 (1897); *Dillon v. Union Pacific Railroad Co.,* 7 Fed. Cas. 718 (C.C.D.Neb. 1874).

107. Lester P. Schoene and Frank Watson, "Workmen's Compensation on Interstate Railways," *Harvard Law Review* 47 (1934): 389, 391–92.

108. *Hough v. Railway Co.,* 10 Otto (100 U.S.) 213, 216 (1870). See White, *Tort Law in America,* pp. 51–56; Comment, "The Creation of a Common Law Rule: The Fellow Servant Rule, 1837–1860," *University of Pennsylvania Law Review* 132 (1984): 579, 583, n. 21, 600–20. The Wisconsin Supreme Court, for example, seriously restricted the fellow servant rule in the 1870s, and the West Virginia Supreme Court of Appeals maintained a rigid adherence to the rule past the turn of the century. See Hunt, *Law and Locomotives,* p. 153 (Wisconsin); Reid, *American Judge,* pp. 51–54 (West Virginia).

109. 17 Wall. (84 U.S.) 553 (1873).

110. Ibid., p. 558.

111. Ibid., p. 559.

112. 17 Wall. (84 U.S.) 508 (1873).

113. 17 Wall. (84 U.S.) 514.

114. 17 Wall. (84 U.S.) 558.

115. *Hough v. Railway Co.,* 10 Otto (100 U.S.) 213 (1879), accepted the fellow servant rule but did so carefully, expressly noting four exceptions that limited its use.

116. 109 U.S. 478 (1883).

117. Ibid., p. 483.

118. Ibid., p. 484.

119. Ibid., p. 483.

120. 112 U.S. 377 (1884).

121. Ibid., pp. 383, 389–91. *Ross* apparently gave a narrower scope to the fellow servant rule than did the decisions of most states. See White, *Tort Law in America,* pp. 52–53.

122. For example, Edward L. Pierce, *A Treatise on the Law of Railroads* (Boston, 1881), pp. 358, 379.

123. *Hough v. Railway Co.,* 10 Otto (100 U.S.) 213, 217 (1879).

124. 112 U.S. 382–83. Contemporary evidence suggested that wages were not necessarily higher in the relatively more dangerous trades. Philip J. Doherty, *The Liability of Railroads to Interstate Employees* (Boston, 1911), p. 47; Crystal Eastman, *Work-Accidents and the Law* (New York, 1910), pp. 281–83; Gary T. Schwartz, "The Character of Early American Tort Law," *U.C.L.A. Law Review* 36 (1989): 641, 709. Both the "local society" and "freedom of contract" rationales had been spelled out in the mid-nineteenth-century fellow servant case that established the doctrine in the United States. See *Farwell v. Boston & Worcester Railroad,* 45 Mass. 49 (1842). On the court's reasoning in *Farwell,* see Alfred S. Konefsky, " 'As Best to Subserve Their Own Interests': Lemuel Shaw, Labor Conspiracy, and Fellow Servants," *Law and History Review* 7 (1989): 219.

125. 122 U.S. 189 (1887).

126. Ibid., p. 196.

127. Ibid., p. 196.

128. Quoted in Alan Trachtenberg, *The Incorporation of America: Culture and Society in the Gilded Age* (New York, 1982), p. 88.

129. 149 U.S. 368 (1893).

130. Ibid., p. 370.

131. Ibid.

132. Ibid., pp. 378–79.

133. Ibid., p. 379.

134. Ibid., p. 384.

135. Ibid. In his treatise on torts, Thomas M. Cooley made the same point:

> But it cannot be disputed that the negligence of a servant of one grade is as much one of the risks of the business as the negligence of a servant of any other; and it seems impossible, therefore, to hold that the servant contracts to run the risks of negligent acts or omissions on the part of one class of servants and not those of another class. [Cooley, *Treatise,* pp. 544–45]

136. 149 U.S., p. 383 (emphasis added).

137. David J. Brewer, "The Nation's Safeguard," *Proceedings of the New York State Bar Association, Sixteenth Annual Meeting* (New York, 1893), p. 39; Brewer, "The Federal Judiciary," *Twelfth Annual Meeting of the Bar Association of the State of Kansas* (Topeka, 1895), p. 83. The two speeches are available in the David J. Brewer Papers, Library of Congress, Washington, DC, vols. 1 and 2, respectively. For general and contrasting views of Brewer, see Arnold M. Paul, "David J. Brewer," in Leon Friedman and Fred L. Israel, eds., *The Justices of the Supreme Court, Their Lives and Major Opinions,* 4 vols. (New York, 1969), p. 1515; Robert E. Gamer, "Justice Brewer and Substantive Due Process: A Conservative Court Revisited," *Vanderbilt Law Review* 18 (1965): 615.

138. David J. Brewer, "Protection to Private Property from Public Attack," *New Englander and Yale Review* 55 (1891): 97, 107–8.

139. Brewer, "The Nation's Safeguard," p. 39.

140. Ibid.

141. Ibid., p. 44.

142. Ibid., p. 378.

143. Ibid., p. 411.

144. Ibid.

145. Ibid., p. 395.

146. Ibid., pp. 400–1.

147. Ibid., p. 401.

148. Ibid.

149. Ibid., pp. 408–9.

150. For example, *Northern Pacific Railroad v. Hambly*, 154 U.S. 349 (1894); *Northern Pacific Railroad Co. v. Charless*, 162 U.S. 359 (1896); *Northern Pacific Railroad Co. v. Peterson*, 162 U.S. 346 (1896); *Martin v. Atchison, Topeka and Santa Fe Railroad Co.*, 166 U.S. 399 (1897).

151. *Grady v. Southern Railway Co.*, 92 F. 491, 494 (C.C.A. 6 1899). Agreeing, for example, *Hunt v. Hurd*, 98 F. 683 (C.C.A. 7 1900). Often the lower courts did not even mention the local law issue; after *Baugh* the law was so clear that many or most plaintiffs apparently did not try to argue from state cases.

152. *New England Railroad Co. v. Conroy*, 175 U.S. 323, 343 (1899). See generally Albert Martin Kales, "The Fellow Servant Doctrine in the United States Supreme Court," *Michigan Law Review* 2 (1903): 79.

153. 194 U.S. 338 (1904).

154. Ibid., p. 352 (White, J., dissenting).

155. For continued application, see, for example, *Texas & Pacific Railway Co. v. Bourman*, 212 U.S. 536 (1909); *Beutler v. Grand Trunk Junction Railway Co.*, 224 U.S. 85 (1912); *Tweeten v. Tacoma Railway & Power Co.*, 210 F. 828 (C.C.A. 9 1914); *Union Pacific Railroad Co. v. Marone*, 246 F. 916 (C.C.A. 8 1917). The decisions in the lower courts before *Dixon* are numerous. See, for example, *Pennsylvania Co. v. Fishack*, 123 F. 465 (C.C.A. 6 1903). For statutory limitations on the employers' defenses, see Chapter 7. See the tepid statement of the rule at a much later date in Arthur B. Honnold, *Supreme Court Law* (Kansas City, 1933), vol. 2, pp. 1033–35.

156. Hughes, *Handbook*, pp. 18–19.

157. 194 U.S. 347.

158. See Morton Keller, *Affairs of State: Public Life in Late Nineteenth Century America* (Cambridge, MA, 1977), pp. 402–3 and works cited; Friedman, *History of American Law*, pp. 422–24; Bakken, *Development of Law on the Rocky Mountain Frontier*, pp. 108–9; Bakken, *Development of Law in Frontier California*, pp. 76–83.

159. See, for example, *New Jersey Stream Navigation Co. v. Merchants Bank*, 6 How. (47 U.S.) 383 (1848) (goods); *Stokes v. Saltonstall*, 13 Pet. (38 U.S.) 181 (1839) (passengers). I wish to thank Robert J. Kaczorowski for helping clarify for me some of the intricacies of common carrier tort law in the nineteenth century.

160. 17 Wall. (84 U.S.) 357 (1873).

161. Ibid., p. 358.

162. Ibid., pp. 367–68.

163. Ibid., p. 384.

164. Ibid., p. 379.

165. Ibid., p. 380.

166. Ibid., p. 379.

167. Ibid., p. 378.

168. Ibid., pp. 360, 377, 384.

169. *Norfolk Southern Railroad Co. v. Chatman*, 244 U.S. 276 (1917).

170. *Hart v. Pennsylvania Railroad Co.*, 112 U.S. 331 (1884); see *Express Co. v. Caldwell*, 21 Wall. (88 U.S.) 264 (1874). Compare *Myrick v. Michigan Central Railroad Co.*, 107 U.S. 102 (1882); *Hartford Fire Insurance Co. v. Chicago, Milwaukee & St. Paul Railway Co.*, 175 U.S. 91 (1899). But see *Liverpool and Great Western Steam Co. v. Phoenix Insurance Co.*, 129 U.S. 397 (1889).

171. *Atlantic Coast Line Railroad Co. v. Riverside Mills*, 219 U.S. 186 (1911); *Adams Express Co. v. Croninger*, 226 U.S. 491 (1913); *Boston & Maine Railroad v. Hooker*, 233 U.S. 97 (1914); *Kansas City Southern Railway v. Carl*, 227 U.S. 639 (1913). See Alexander M. Bickel and Benno C. Schmidt, Jr., *The Judiciary and Responsible Government, 1910–21* (New York, 1984), pp. 202–5, 415–18, and cases cited; Edwin C. Goddard, "The Liability of the Common Carrier as Determined by Recent Decisions of the United States Supreme Court," *Columbia Law Review* 15 (1915): 399, 475.

172. 192 U.S. 440 (1904).

173. Ibid., p. 452.

174. Ibid., pp. 453–54. See *Boering v. Chesapeake Beach Railway Co.*, 193 U.S. 442 (1904); *Smith v. Atchison, Topeka & Santa Fe Railway Co.*, 194 F. 79 (C.C.A. 8 1912).

175. See, for example, *Chicago, Milwaukee and St. Paul Railway Co. v. Solan*, 169 U.S. 133 (1898); *Southern Pacific Co. v. Schuyler*, 277 U.S. 601 (1913); *New York Central Railroad Co. v. Mohney*, 252 U.S. 152 (1920).

176. 34 Stat. 584 (1906).

177. *Charleston and Western Carolina Railway Co. v. Thompson*, 234 U.S. 576 (1914).

178. *Kansas City Southern Railway Co. v. Van Zant*, 260 U.S. 459, 469 (1923). See, for example, *Bush v. Bremner*, 29 F.2d 844 (D.Minn. 1928), aff'd 36 F.2d 189 (C.C.A. 8 1929).

179. 176 U.S. 498 (1900).

180. *Northern Pacific Railway Co. v. Adams*, 192 U.S. 452–53.

181. 176 U.S. 506.

182. Ibid., pp. 507–8.

183. Ibid., p. 511.

184. Ibid., p. 512.

185. Ibid., p. 513.

186. Ibid., p. 520.

187. *New York Central and Harlem River Railroad Co. v. Difendaffer*, 125 F. 893 (C.C.A. 7 1903); *Long v. Lehigh Valley Railroad Co.*, 130 F. 870 (C.C.A. 2 1904); *Kelly v. Malott*, 135 F. 74 (C.C.A. 7 1905); *McDermon v. Southern Pacific Co.*, 122 F. 669 (C.C.W.D.Mo. 1903).

188. *Clough v. Grand Trunk Western Railway Co.*, 155 F. 81 (C.C.A. 6 1907); *Allen v. Erie Railroad Co.*, 2 F.2d 712 (C.C.A. 6 1924); *Wilson v. Atlantic Coast Line Railroad Co.*, 129 F. 774 (C.C.N.D.Ga. 1904). Compare *Santa Fe, Prescott & Phoenix Railway Co. v. Grant Brothers Construction Co.*, 228 U.S. 177 (1913). See *Chicago, Rock Island & Pacific Railway Co. v. Maucher*, 248 U.S. 359 (1919) (Supreme Court holds state law, not federal law, controls and voids agreement between a circus and a railroad exempting the railroad from liability for injuries to employees of the circus). Before *Voigt*, some lower federal courts had ruled similarly. See, for example, *Chicago, Milwaukee & St. Paul Railroad Co. v. Wallace*, 66 F. 506 (C.C.A. 7 1895). When the employee had no knowledge of the agreements, the railroad could be liable. See *Sager v. Northern Pacific Railway Co.*, 166 F. 526 (C.C.D.Minn. 1908).

189. See discussion of FELA in Chapter 7. For an early example of the possibilities at common law, see *Hardy v. Shedden Co., Ltd.*, 78 F. 610 (C.C.A. 6 1897) (Taft, J.); for an example of the formidable problems of proof they could place on passengers see, for example, *Louisville & Nashville Railroad Co. v. Chatters*, 279 U.S. 320 (1929); for a later example of avoiding broad statutorily imposed duties, see *United States v. The Fruit Growers Express Co.*, 279 U.S. 363 (1929); for broad use by analogy, see *McCormick v. Shippy*, 124 F. 48 (C.C.A. 2 1903); for unsuccessful efforts, for example, see *The Standard Oil Co. v. Anderson*, 212 U.S. 215 (1909); *Woodward Iron Co. v. Limbaugh*, 276 F. 1 (C.C.A. 5 1921). Careful organization could also confer procedural advantages. For example, *McGuire v. Great Northern Railway Co.*, 153 F. 434 (C.C.N.D.Iowa 1907).

190. C. P. Connolly, "Big Business and the Bench: The Federal Courts—Last Refuge of the 'Interests,' " *Everybody's Magazine* 26 (1912): 827, 835. According to the author, of the thirty actions that survived motions to dismiss, only fourteen ended in verdicts for the plaintiff.

191. 176 U.S. 505.

Chapter 4

1. *Hulac v. Chicago and Northwestern Railway Co.*, 194 F. 747, 748 (D. Neb. 1912).

2. Ibid., p. 748.

3. Roscoe Pound, "The Causes of Popular Dissatisfaction with the Administration of Justice," *American Bar Association Reports* (1906): 395, 410–11.

4. Letter from Colin Neblett to George W. Norris, June 6, 1930, George W. Norris Papers, Tray 78, Box 8, File: "Limiting Jurisdiction of Federal Courts, 1929–30," Library of Congress.

5. Henry Campbell Black, *A Treatise on the Laws and Practice Governing the Removal of Causes from State Courts to Federal Courts* (St. Paul, 1898), p. 21.

6. For example, Robert M. Hughes, *Handbook of Jurisdiction and Procedure in United States Courts,* 2nd ed. (St. Paul, 1913), pp. 322–24; Armistead M. Dobie, *Handbook of Federal Jurisdiction and Procedure* (St. Paul, 1928), pp. 405–11.

7. Hughes, *Handbook of Jurisdiction and Procedure,* 2nd ed., p. 323.

8. For example, John F. Dillon, *Removal of Causes from State Courts to Federal Courts* (5 eds.) (St. Louis, 1875, 1877, 1881, 1887, 1889); W. F. Cooper, *Removal of Causes from State to Federal Courts* (St. Louis, 1877); Robert Desty, *Removal of Causes from State to Federal Courts* (4 eds.) (San Francisco, 1882, 1886, 1888, 1893); Emory Speer, *Removal of Causes from the State to Federal Courts* (Boston, 1888); Henry Campbell Black, *A Treatise on the Laws and Practice Governing the Removal of Causes from State to Federal Courts* (St. Paul, 1898) (successor to Dillon's treatise); B. C. Moon, *Removal of Causes from the Courts of the Several States to the Circuit Courts of the United States* (New York, 1901); James Hamilton Lewis, *Removal of Causes from State to Federal Courts* (New York, 1923).

9. American Law Institute, *A Study of the Business of the Federal Courts: Part II, Civil Cases* (Philadelphia, 1934), p. 66. The percentages were derived by subtracting the number of cases in which the United States was a party.

10. Ibid., pp. 66, 103. The numbers for original diversity actions were derived by subtracting the numbers for removed cases from those for all diversity actions.

11. The preceding calculations were drawn or derived from the tables on pp. 47, 56, 60–61, and 102–3.

12. The calculations are based on data given on the pages listed in n. 11. Successful remands occurred in 4.6 percent of all removed diversity cases (p. 103).

13. The tort cases do not include employers' or seamen's liability cases, in which the defendants did not have the right to remove. National bank receivership and antitrust cases also were excluded. See Office of the Attorney General of the United States, *Annual Report, 1936,* p. 179, *Annual Report, 1937,* pp. 188–89.

14. Lawrence M. Friedman, "Civil Wrongs: Personal Injury Law in the Late 19th Century," *American Bar Foundation Research Journal* (1987): 351, 368–69.

15. For example, *Wright v. Waters,* 30 Fed. Cas. 716 (C.C.D.C.1822); *Ladd v. Tudor,* 14 Fed. Cas. 923 (C.C.D. Mass. 1847); *Zinkeisen v. Hufschmidt,* 30 Fed. Cas. 933 (C.C.E.D. Wisc. 1874).

16. *Lee v. Watson,* 1 Wall. (68 U.S.) 337, 339–40. See *Kanouse v. Martin,* 15 How. (56 U.S.) 198 (1853); Black, *Treatise,* pp. 21–22, 64–89; Lewis, *Removal of Causes,* pp. 178–201.

17. *Saint Paul Mercury Indemnity Co. v. Red Cab Co.,* 303 U.S. 283, 294 (1938).

18. For example, *Prudential Insurance Co. of America v. Stack,* 60 F.2d 830 (C.C.A. 4 1932); *New York Life Insurance Co. v. Driggs,* 72 F.2d 833 (C.C.A. 4 1934); *Travelers' Protective Association of America v. Smith,* 71 F.2d 511 (C.C.A. 4 1934); *Aetna Life Insurance Co. of Hartford v. Wilson,* 84 F.2d 330 (C.C.A. 4 1936). Compare *Pilot Life Insurance Co. v. Habis,* 90 F.2d 842 (C.C.A. 4 1937) (note qualification on p. 844).

19. *Hayward v. Nordberg Manufacturing Co.,* 85 F. 4 (C.C.A. 6 1898); *Hampton Stave Co. v. Gardner,* 154 F. 805 (C.C.A. 8 1907); *Heffner v. Gwynne-Treadwell Cotton Co.,* 160 F. 635 (C.C.A. 8 1908); *Bateman v. Southern Oregon Co.,* 217 F. 933 (C.C.A. 9 1914); *Yates v. Whyel Coke Co.,* 221 F. 603 (C.C.A. 6 1915); *Sturgeon River Boom Co. v. W. H. Sawyer Lumber Co.,* 89 F. 113 (C.C.W.D. Mich. 1898); *W. T. Hughes & Co. v. Peper Tobacco Warehouse Co.,* 126 F. 687 (C.C.E.D.N.C. 1903); *Southern Cash Register Co. v. Montgomery,* 143 F. 700 (C.C.N.D. Ga. 1906); *Harley v. Firemen's Fund Insurance Co.,* 245 F. 471 (D.C.W.D. Wash. 1913); *Jellison v. Krell Piano Co.,* 246 F. 509 (D.C.E.D. Ky. 1917); *Bancroft Drainage District v. Chicago, St. Paul, Minneapolis & Omaha Railway Co.,* 167 N.W. 731 (Sup. Ct. Neb. 1918); *Southern Railway Co. v. Clarke,* 82 So. 516 (Sup. Ct. Ala. 1919); *Lesh v. Bailey,* 95 N.E. 341 (App. Ct. Ind. 1911); *Skelton & Wear v. Wolfe,* 200 S.W. 901 (Ct. Civ. App. Tx. 1918).

20. For the average size of insurance policies see Chapter 9. There was some claim discounting in insurance actions around the turn of the century. See *Waite v. Phoenix Insurance Co.,* 62 F. 769 (C.C.M.D. Tenn. 1894); *Simmons v. Mutual Reserve Fund Life Association,* 114 F. 785 (C.C.N.D. Ga. 1902); *Swann v. Mutual Reserve Fund Life Association,* 116 F. 232 (C.C.W.D. Ky. 1902); *E. A. Holmes & Co. v. United States Fire Insurance Co.,* 142 F. 863 (C.C.W.D. Tenn. 1906).

In addition to the reason suggested in the text, other factors held down the practice of claim discounting in insurance litigation. Perhaps most important, legislation in half or more of the states inhibited removals by insurance companies and thereby relieved much of the pressure on claimants to discount their claims. The states exercised particularly broad regulatory authority over insurance companies, and a number of them passed statutes limiting the ability of foreign insurance corporations to remove. Although the states did not have constitutional authority to prevent insurance companies from removing, until 1922 the Supreme Court upheld statutes allowing them to revoke an insurance company's license to do business in the state if the company actually exercised its right to remove. Accordingly, until 1922 insurance companies did not use removal as often or as commonly as did the railroads and other large national corporations. The situation changed after 1922; see Chapter 9. Claims discounting may also have been less common in insurance than in tort suits because in relative terms, federal judges and the federal common law were not as unfavorably disposed toward insurance claimants as they were toward tort plaintiffs, especially in master–servant cases. In addition, the fact that policies carried face amounts that readily set the value of a policyholder's claim may have dissuaded some claimants and courts from adopting the tactic.

21. *Markey v. Chicago, Milwaukee & St. Paul Railway,* 153 N.W. 1053, 1058 (Sup. Ct. Iowa 1915).

22. *Thompson v. Southern Railway Co.,* 116 F. 890, 892 (C.C.N.D. Ala. 1902). See, for example, a series of cases involving corporate receivers: *Carpenter v. Northern Pacific Railroad Co.,* 75 F. 850 (C.C.D.Wash. 1896); *Ray v. Peirce,* 81 F. 881 (C.C.D.Ind. 1897); *Gilmore v. Herrick,* 93 F. 525 (C.C.N.D.Ohio 1899).

23. "As a general rule, judgments must conform to the pleadings, and the relief granted is limited by that demanded in the complaint, both as to character and amount." *In re Kehl's Estate,* 254 N.W. 639, 640 (Sup.Ct.Wisc. 1934). Agreeing, for example, *Sweet v. Excelsior Electric Co.,* 31 A. 721 (Ct.Err.& App.N.J. 1895); *Davis v. Hall,* 97 N.W. 1023 (Sup.Ct.Neb. 1904); *Harbolt v. Hensen,* 253 P. 257 (Sup.Ct.Mont. 1927); *Woods–Hoskins–Young Co. v. Stone & Baker Construction Co.,* 114 So. 366 (Sup.Ct.Fla. 1927); *Donohue v. Pioche Mines Co.,* 277 P. 980 (Sup.Ct.Nev. 1929); *Haberly v. Farmers' Mutual Fire Relief Association,* 293 P. 590 (Sup.Ct.Oreg. 1930); *Watkins v. Blass,* 145 So. 348 (Sup.Ct.Miss. 1933); *Carolina Veneer & Lumber Co. v. American Mutual Liability Insurance Co.,* 24 S.E.2d 153 (Sup.Ct.S.C. 1943); *Houston & T.C. Railway Co. v. Shults,* 90 S.W. 506 (Ct.Civ.App.Tx. 1904); *Huff v. Fitzsimmons,* 132 So. 257 (Ct.App.La. 1st Cir. 1931).

24. *Barry v. Edmunds,* 116 U.S. 550, 562 (1886); *Scott v. Donald,* 165 U.S. 58, 90 (1897). See, for example, *Missouri, Kansas & Texas Railway Co. v. Chappell,* 206 F. 688 (W.D.Okla. 1913).

25. For example, *Simmons v. Mutual Reserve Fund Life Association,* 114 F. 785 (C.C.N.D. Ga. 1902); *Peters v. Queen Insurance Co. of America,* 182 F. 113 (C.C.S.D. Ga. 1910); *New York Life Insurance Co. v. Johnson,* 255 F. 958 (C.C.A. 8 1919); *Holt v. Bergevin,* 60 F. 1 (C.C.N.D. Idaho 1894).

26. Paul Howland, "Shall Federal Jurisdiction of Controversies Between Citizens of Different States Be Preserved?" *American Bar Association Journal,* 18 (1932): 499, 502.

27. For example, *Kaufman v. I. Rheinstrom Sons Co.,* 188 F. 544 (C.C.S.D.N.Y. 1911).

28. Letter from Chas. E. Harris to George W. Norris, April 21, 1928, George W. Norris Papers, Tray 42, Box 2, File: "S. 3151 (70th)," Library of Congress.

29. Letter from M. F. Harrington to George W. Norris, July 11, 1929, George W. Norris Papers, Tray 42, Box 2, File: "S. 3151 (70th)," Library of Congress.

30. Letter from William H. Westover to George W. Norris, April 20, 1933, George W. Norris Papers, Library of Congress, Box 198, File: "Limiting Jurisdiction of Federal Courts (71st & 72nd) Congress." See also letter from Walter J. Gex to George W. Norris, April 4, 1932.

31. *Western Union Telegraph Co. v. White,* 102 F. 705 (C.C.W.D. Va. 1900); *Simmons v. Mutual Reserve Fund Life Association,* 114 F. 785 (C.C.N.D.Ga. 1902); *Thompson v. Southern Railway Co.,* 116 F. 890 (C.C.N.D. Ala. 1902); *Coffin v. Philadelphia, W. & B.R. Railroad Co.,* 118 F. 688 (C.C.S.D.N.Y. 1902); *Swofford v. Cornucopia Mines of Oregon,* 140 F. 957 (C.C.D. Oreg. 1905); *E.A. Holmes & Co. v. United States Fire Insurance Co.,* 142 F. 863 (C.C.W.D. Tenn. 1906); *Taylor v. Midland Valley Railroad Co.,* 197 F. 323 (E.D. Okla. 1912); *Collins v. Twin Falls*

North Side Land & Water Co., 204 F. 134 (D. Idaho 1913); *Nashville, Chattanooga & St. Louis Railway Co. v. Hill*, 40 So. 612 (Sup. Ct. Ala. 1906); *Baltimore & Ohio Railroad Co. v. Worman*, 40 N.E. 751 (App. Ct. Ind. 1895); *Texas & Pacific Railway Co. v. Cushny*, 64 S.W. 795 (Ct. Civ. App. Tx. 1901); *Baltimore & Ohio Railroad Co. v. Ryan*, 68 N.E. 923 (App. Ct. Ind. 1903).

32. Compare Section 2, 18 Stat.470 (1875), with Section 3, 24 Stat.552 (1887), as corrected by 25 Stat.433 (1888). The main change that the act made in removal jurisdiction was to eliminate the provision that allowed plaintiffs to remove, a provision that was irrelevant to the system.

33. See, for example, *Smith v. Lyon*, 133 U.S. 315 (1890); *In re Pennsylvania Co.*, 137 U.S. 451 (1890).

34. *Kansas City, Fort Scott and Memphis Railroad Co. v. Daughtry*, 138 U.S. 298 (1891).

35. *Wilcox & Gibbs Guano Co. v. Phoenix Insurance Co. of Brooklyn*, 60 F. 929, 931 (C.C.D.S.C. 1894).

36. *Seager v. New York & Cuba Mail Steamship Co.*, 55 F. 880 (C.C.A. 2 1893); *Wedekind v. Southern Pacific Co.*, 36 F. 279 (C.C.D.Nev. 1888); *Dixon v. Western Union Telegraph Co.*, 38 F. 377 (C.C.N.D.Cal. 1889); *Delbanco v. Singletary*, 40 F. 177 (C.C.D. Nev. 1889); *McDonald v. Hope Mining Co.*, 48 F. 593 (C.C.D. Mont. 1891); *Turner v. Illinois Central Railroad Co.*, 55 F. 689 (C.C.W.D. Tenn. 1893); *Frisbie v. Chesapeake & Ohio Railway Co.*, 59 F. 369 (C.C.D. Ky. 1894); *Daugherty v. Western Union Telegraph Co.*, 61 F. 138 (C.C.D.Ind. 1894); *Gregory v. Boston Safe-Deposit & Transit Co.*, 88 F. 3 (C.C.D. Mass. 1898); *Williams v. Southern Bell Telephone & Telegraph Co.*, 21 S.E. 298 (Sup. Ct.N.C. 1895). The court denied plaintiff's motion to remand in, for example, *Lockhart v. Memphis & Louisville Railroad Co.*, 38 F. 274 (C.C.W.D. Tenn. 1889); *Allmark v. Platte Steamship Co.*, 76 F. 615 (C.C.E.D.N.Y. 1896); *Wilson v. Winchester & P. Railroad Co.*, 82 F. 15 (C.C.D.W.Va. 1897).

37. *Velie v. Manufacturers' Accident Indemnity Co. of the United States*, 40 F. 545 (C.C.E.D. Wisc. 1889); *Price v. Lehigh Valley Railroad Co.*, 65 F. 825 (C.C.N.D.N.Y. 1895); *Schipper v. Consumer Cordage Co.*, 72 F. 803 (C.C.S.D.N.Y. 1895); *Fox v. Southern Railway Co.*, 80 F. 945 (C.C.W.D.N.C. 1897). Sometimes defendants prevailed: for example, *Mayer v. Forth Worth & D.C. Railroad Co.*, 93 F. 601 (C.C.S.D.N.Y.1899).

38. *Smith v. Western Union Telegraph Co.*, 79 F. 132 (C.C.D. Ind. 1897); *Peterson v. Chicago, Milwaukee & St. Paul Railway Co.*, 108 F. 561 (C.C.W.D. Mo. 1901); *Western Union Telegraph Co. v. Campbell*, 91 S.W. 312 (Ct.Civ.App. Tx. 1905); *Stark v. Port Blakely Mill Co.*, 87 P. 339 (Sup.Ct.Wash. 1906); *Munnss v. American Agricultural Chemical Co.*, 103 N.E. 859 (Sup.Jud.Ct.Mass. 1914).

39. *Waite v. Phoenix Insurance Co.*, 62 F. 769 (C.C.M.D.Tenn. 1894); *Anderson v. Western Union Telegraph Co.*, 218 F. 78 (E.D.Ark. 1914); *Winslow v. Collins*, 14 S.E. 512 (Sup.Ct.N.C. 1892); *Cumberland Gap Building & Loan Association v. Wells*, 25 S.E. 246 (Sup.Ct. Ga.1896).

40. *Mullin v. Blumenthal*, 39 A. 991 (Super.Ct. Del. 1898).

41. *Stephens v. St. Louis & San Francisco Railroad Co.*, 47 F. 530 (C.C.W.D.Ark. 1891).

42. *Iowa Central Railway Co. v. Bacon*, 236 U.S. 305 (1915); *Cybur Lumber Co. v. Erkhart*, 247 F. 284 (C.C.A. 5 1918) (discontinue only); *Huskins v. Cincinnati, New Orleans & Texas Pacific Railroad Co.*, 37 F. 504 (C.C.N.D. Tenn. 1889); *McCabe v. Southern Railway Co.*, 107 F. 213 (C.C.D.S.C.1901) (discontinue only). Once the action had been removed, however, plaintiff could not then reduce the amount sought and thereby compel a remand. See, for example, *Donovan v. Dixieland Amusement Co.*, 152 F. 661 (C.C.E.D.N.Y. 1907).

43. In *Barrett v. Virginian Railway Co.*, 250 U.S. 473 (1919), the Court held that the right to take a nonsuit was controlled by state law under the Conformity Act. Most states allowed nonsuits at any time before trial, and some allowed them after trial but before verdict.

44. The Supreme Court settled the issue in *Southern Railway Co. v. Miller*, 217 U.S. 209 (1910). Before that time the general practice was the one described in the text. See, for example, James McCabe, "Federal or State Jurisdiction—A Criticism," *Albany Law Journal* 60 (1899): 171; Comment, *Virginia Law Register* 6 (1900): 577; Note, *Harvard Law Review* 17 (1904): 574.

45. A prudent plaintiff, however, would not start her new action before the formal dismissal of the removed one. *Iowa Central Railway Co. v. Bacon*, 236 U.S. 305 (1915); *Palmer v. Delaware, Lackawanna & Western Railroad Co.*, 222 F. 461 (N.D.N.Y. 1915).

46. *Phoenix Life Insurance Co. v. Walrath*, 117 U.S. 365, 366 (1886). See *Edrington v. Jeffer-*

son, 111 U.S. 770 (1884); *Fletcher v. Hamlet,* 116 U.S. 408 (1886); *Baltimore & Ohio Railroad Co. v. Burns,* 124 U.S. 165 (1888).

47. 135 U.S. 315 (1890).

48. Ibid., p. 316–17.

49. Ibid., p. 318.

50. See, for example, *Nashua and Lowell Railroad Corp. v. Boston and Lowell Railroad Corp.,* 136 U.S. 356, 374 (1890).

51. *Yarde v. Baltimore & Ohio Railroad Co.,* 57 F. 913, 915 (C.C.D. Ind. 1893).

52. Black, *Treatise,* p. 265, and also see pp. 261–62; *Langdon v. Hillside Coal & Iron Co.,* 41 F. 609 (C.C.S.D.N.Y. 1890); *Evans v. Dillingham,* 43 F. 177 (C.C.N.D.Tx. 1890); *Yarde v. Baltimore & Ohio Railroad Co.,* 57 F. 913 (C.C.D. Ind. 1893); *Mattoon v. Reynolds,* 62 F. 417 (C.C.D.Conn.1894). Plaintiffs may have been attempting to set up the tactic in other cases: *Smith v. Northern Pacific Railroad Co.,* 53 N.W. 173 (Sup. Ct. N.D. 1892); *Lake Erie & Western Railroad Co. v. Juday,* 49 N.E.843 (App. Ct. Ind. 1898).

53. Walter Licht, *Working for the Railroad: The Organization of Work in the Nineteenth Century* (Princeton, NJ, 1983), p. 205.

54. J. Willard Hurst, *The Growth of American Law: The Lawmakers* (Boston, 1950), pp. 172–73.

55. Morton Keller, *Affairs of State: Public Life in Late Nineteenth Century America* (Cambridge, MA, 1977), p. 355.

56. Lawrence M. Friedman and Robert V. Percival, "A Tale of Two Courts: Litigation in Alameda and San Benito Counties," *Law & Society Review* 10 (1976): 267, 277.

57. Hurst, *Growth of American Law,* p. 173.

58. David S. Clark, "Adjudication to Administration: A Statistical Analysis of Federal District Courts in the Twentieth Century," *Southern California Law Review* 55 (1981): 65.

59. Office of the Attorney General of the United States, *Annual Report, 1932,* p. 140. The number includes 26,240 cases in which the United States was a party, 5,270 admiralty suits, and 31,787 private civil actions. It does not include 72,970 bankruptcy cases.

60. Office of the Attorney General of the United States, *Annual Report, 1873,* pp. 22, 32, *Annual Report, 1876,* pp. 14, 18, 22, *Annual Report, 1903,* pp. 142, 145, 159, *Annual Report, 1932,* p. 140. Bankruptcies are not included in any of the numbers.

61. Office of the Attorney General of the United States, *Annual Report, 1910,* p. 108. The results of one study indicate that federal courts heard about 6 percent of the railroad accident cases that were decided by appellate courts between 1875 and 1905. Richard A. Posner, "A Theory of Negligence," *Journal of Legal Studies* 1 (1972): 29, 53.

62. Peter George, *The Emergence of Industrial America: Strategic Factors in American Economic Growth Since 1870* (Albany, NY, 1982), pp. 147–50 and works cited; Irving Bernstein, *The Lean Years: A History of the American Worker, 1920–1933* (Baltimore, 1966), pp. 66–67; United States Bureau of the Census, *The Statistical History of the United States from Colonial Times to the Present* (Stamford, CT, 1965), pp. 90–95.

63. Licht, *Working for the Railroad,* p. 126.

64. U.S. Bureau of the Census, *The Statistical History of the United States,* pp. 90–95.

65. One such measure is the capitalized present value of future earnings, a principal element of the damages allowed in tort suits for personal injury. For almost the whole of the period, the jurisdictional minimum was set at levels that ranged from approximately one-half to one-fifth or less of the present value of the future earnings of industrial workers with yearly incomes around the national average. See Louis I. Dublin and Alfred J. Lotka, *The Money Value of a Man* (New York, 1930), p. 177. That capitalized value should have been recoverable. Simeon E. Baldwin, *American Railroad Law* (New York, 1904), pp. 528–29; 347–49, 353–58, 414–26; Charles T. McCormick, *Handbook on the Law of Damages* (St. Paul, 1935), pp. 299–374.

Further, plaintiffs who suffered personal injury could also recover for lost past earnings, for pain and suffering, for medical and related costs, and for other special losses that could be proved. Recovery for those injuries could further widen the gulf between the jurisdictional amount and allowable damages. See Joseph A. Joyce and Howard C. Joyce, *A Treatise on Damages* (New York, 1903), vol. 1, pp. 205–319; 557–855; McCormick, *Handbook on the Law of*

Damages, pp. 299–327; William B. Hale, *Handbook on the Law of Damages,* 2nd ed. by Roger W. Cooley (St. Paul, 1912), pp. 115–73. For the growing acceptance in the late nineteenth century of the idea that damages could be recovered for psychological and emotional injuries, see Edward M. Brown, "Regulating Damage Claims for Emotional Injuries Before the First World War," *Behavioral Sciences & The Law* 8 (1990): 421.

Another such measure is the statutory limit that many states imposed on the wrongful death actions they created. In 1912, for example, when the jurisdictional amount had just reached $3,000, seventeen jurisdictions imposed limits: Four set the maximum at $5,000, one at $7,000, two at $7,500, and ten at $10,000. Five other states had recently abolished all limitations on recovery; see Hale, *Handbook on the Law of Damages,* pp. 427–28 and n. 25. See also Mc-Cormick, *Handbook on the Law of Damages,* pp. 358–59.

66. A random sampling for illustrative purposes shows the following: *Stephens v. St. Louis & San Francisco Railroad Co.,* 47 F. 530 (C.C. W.D. Ark. 1891) ($4,999 to $1,999); *Waite v. Phoenix Insurance Co.,* 62 F. 769 (C.C. M.D. Tenn. 1894) ($3,000 to $1,999); *Peterson v. Chicago, Milwaukee & St. Paul Railway Co.,* 108 F. 561 (C.C.W.D. Mo. 1901) ($10,000 to $1,999); *Donovan v. Dixieland Amusement Co.,* 152 F. 661 (C.C.E.D.N.Y. 1907) ($13,375 to $1,999); *Bacon v. Iowa Central Railway Co.,* 137 N.W. 1011 (S.C. Iowa 1912), aff'd 236 U.S. 305 (1915) ($10,000 to $1,990); *Munnss v. American Agricultural Chemical Co.,* 103 N.E. 859 (Sup.Jud.Ct. Mass. 1914) ($10,000 to $3,000); *Palmer v. Delaware, Lackawanna & Western Railroad Co.,* 222 F. 461 (D.C. N.D. N.Y. 1915) ($5,000 to $2,950); *Barber v. Atlantic Coast Line Railroad Co.,* 94 S.E. 280 (Ct. App. Ga. 1917) ($25,000 to $3,000).

67. See, for example, Dublin and Lotka, *Money Value of a Man,* pp. 81–85; Joyce and Joyce, *Treatise on Damages,* vol. 1, pp. 617–27 and cases noted.

68. Friedman, "Civil Wrongs," p. 365.

69. Sen. Doc. No. 338, 62 Cong., 2 Sess. (1913), vol. 2, pp. 131, 135, 139.

70. Sen. Doc. No. 68, 74 Cong., 1 Sess. (1935), p. 10.

71. Ibid.

72. Lawrence M. Friedman and Thomas D. Russell, "More Civil Wrongs: Personal Injury Litigation, 1901–1910," *American Journal of Legal History* 34 (1990): 295, 303–6.

73. Posner, "A Theory of Negligence," pp. 79–80. Unfortunately, the number of federal cases in the sample is small, and the critical dollar amount category that the article uses ($500 to $2,500) mixes recoveries above and below the jurisdictional amount. The last sentence in the text is thus an estimate, assuming that most but not all of the cases in the merged category were for amounts less than $2,000.

74. See, for example, Ralph S. Bauer, *Essentials of the Law of Damages* (Chicago, 1919), pp. 435–43.

75. Jeremiah Smith, "Sequel to Workmen's Compensation Acts," *Harvard Law Review* 27 (1914): 235, 240–41.

76. For statutes within the prevailing range see, for example, Mich. Stat. Ann. (Howell 1912), title 15, chap. 63, sec. 3939 et seq. (esp. sec. 3951–56); 1911 New Jersey Laws, chap. 95 (esp. sec. 11–12); South Dakota Rev. Code (1919), title 6, pt. 19, chap. 5, art. 4, sec. 9436 et seq. (esp. sec. 9459) (1917). Massachusetts allowed a maximum award of approximately $6,000, and California allowed $5,000. Sen. Doc. No. 338, 62 Cong., 2 Sess. (1912), vol. 1, pp. 1244, 1249, and see also pp. 1244–52.

77. See, for example, Tex. Rev. Civ. Stat. (Jenkins 1925), title 130, pt. 1, art. 8306 (1923); Ga. Code Ann. (Michie 1926), title 3, chap. 4, sec. 3154 (1) et seq. (1922); Ohio Ann. Gen. Code (p. 1926), title 3, div. 2, chap. 28b, sec. 1465–37 et seq. (1924).

78. See, for example, Oreg. Code (1930), title 49, chap. 18, sec. 49–1801 et seq. (esp. sec. 49–1827) (1921); Wash. Comp. Stat. (Remington 1922), title 50, chap. 7, sec. 7673 et seq. (esp. sec. 7679) (1919).

79. Sen. Doc. No. 68, 74 Cong., 1 Sess. (1935), p. 23.

80. Most of the railroads suffered from financial instability throughout much of the period. Bankruptcies, receiverships, and reorganizations were common. See, for example, Albro Martin, *Enterprise Denied: Origins of the Decline of American Railroads, 1897–1917* (New York, 1971); Herbert Hovenkamp, "Regulatory Conflict in the Gilded Age: Federalism and the Railroad

Problem," *Yale Law Journal* 97 (1988): 1017. Insofar as American corporations in general were pressed by declining profits and a narrowing return on capital, they may also have benefited significantly. See generally James Livingston, "The Social Analysis of Economic History and Theory: Conjectures on Late Nineteenth-Century American Development," *American Historical Review* 92 (1987): 69.

81. In his study of Alameda County, Friedman makes a similar point. See "Civil Wrongs," p. 373.

Chapter 5

1. 3 Cranch (7 U.S.) 267 (1806). See George Lee Haskins and Herbert A. Johnson, *Foundations of Power: John Marshall, 1801–15* (New York, 1971), pp. 616–18.

2. See, for example, *Coal Co. v. Blatchford*, 11 Wall (78 U.S.) 172 (1870).

3. Joinder was seldom used in insurance cases. Policyholders normally brought actions on their policies to recover promised benefits, and those carefully drafted agreements seldom provided any legal basis on which to claim that additional defendants could be jointly liable with the company. On special facts the tactic could occasionally be used. See *Mutual Reserve Fund Life Association v. Farmer*, 77 F. 929 (C.C.A. 8 1896); *McNulty v. Connecticut Mutual Life Insurance Co.*, 46 F. 305 (C.C.N.D. Iowa 1891). The general rule limiting a plaintiff's cause of action on a contract to the other party to the agreement was stated in *Hamilton v. Empire Gas & Fuel Co.*, 297 F. 422, 426 (C.C.A. 8 1924) (lease).

Although joinder under the separable controversy act presented a question of federal statutory construction, it also implicated the question of what parties could be properly joined in common law actions, an issue generally regarded in legal analysis as "procedural." On nineteenth-century state pleading practices and reforms, see Mitchell G. Williams, "Pleading Reform in Nineteenth Century America: The Joinder of Actions at Common Law and Under the Codes," *The Journal of Legal History* 6 (1986): 299; Stephen N. Subrin, "David Dudley Field and the Field Code: A Historical Analysis of an Earlier Procedural Vision," *Law and History Review* 6 (1988): 311.

4. 14 Stat. 306 (1866). The name separable controversy was commonly used for the statute, though the phrase did not appear in the title or text of the act.

5. See John F. Dillon, *Removal of Causes from State Courts to Federal Courts,* 3rd ed. (St. Louis, 1881), pp. 26–34.

6. 100 U.S. 457 (1879).

7. Ibid., pp. 468–69.

8. Ibid., p. 480 (Bradley, J., concurring). Justice Noah H. Swayne joined Bradley's opinion. Justice William Strong, who concurred in the judgment only, neither wrote for himself nor joined Bradley.

9. Ibid., p. 480.

10. Ibid., p. 481.

11. Ibid., p. 482.

12. For example, *Blake v. McKim*, 103 U.S. 336 (1880); *Barney v. Latham*, 103 U.S. 205 (1880); *Hyde v. Ruble*, 104 U.S. 407 (1881); *Fraser v. Jennison*, 106 U.S. 191 (1882); *Peninsular Iron Co. v. Stone*, 121 U.S. 631 (1887).

13. Dillon, *Removal of Causes*, 5th ed. (St. Louis, 1889), p. 115. Compare Dillon, *Removal of Causes*, 3rd ed. (1881), pp. 31–36. See Robert Desty, *The Removal of Causes from State to Federal Courts* (San Francisco, 1882), pp. 63–65, 125–28.

14. The amended version provided that the whole suit, not just the separate controversy, was removable. See Dillon, *Removal of Causes*, 5th ed. (1889), pp. 19–21. That conclusion was based on the fact that the 1875 act eliminated the language from the original act of 1866 that the courts had construed to mean that the separable suit between nondiverse parties was to remain in the state court.

This aspect of the amended separable controversy act—that the presence of a separable controversy allowed removal of the entire case—raised a fundamental constitutional issue. The removal of the entire case, including the claims against nondiverse parties, allowed the federal courts to take jurisdiction over actions in which complete diversity of citizenship did not exist, even though the action was removed under the courts' diversity jurisdiction and that jurisdiction, at least generally, required complete diversity. When faced with this issue in 1880, the Court in *Barney v. Latham,* 103 U.S. 205 (1880), upheld removal of the entire case under the separable controversy act on the statutory ground that Congress had so intended. The Court ignored the constitutional issue, though its decision arguably meant that it had implicitly concluded that complete diversity was a requirement only of the general diversity statute and not of the Constitution itself. The Court never ruled explicitly on the constitutionality of this aspect of the separable controversy act, and it did not rule on the nature of the general constitutional requirement until 1967 when it held in *State Farm Fire & Casualty Co. v. Tashire,* 386 U.S. 523 (1967), that the Constitution itself required only minimum diversity.

It is intriguing that such an obvious and widely recognized constitutional question remained unanswered for a century. See, for example, Note, "The Constitutionality of Federal Removal Jurisdiction over Separable Controversies Involving Citizens of the Same State," *University of Pennsylvania Law Review* 94 (1946): 239. In the context of the system of corporate diversity litigation, however, the failure to resolve the question seems understandable. Given the fact that the courts enforced the statute, corporate defendants had no desire to have it overturned. If it were to be challenged, plaintiffs would have to carry the issue. Two powerful disincentives, however, made plaintiffs unwilling to raise the constitutional problem. One was that a constitutional challenge would likely have increased both the cost of the litigation and the determination of the defendant to use every resource available to defeat the effort. A second was that such a challenge promised plaintiffs no worthwhile result. If such a challenge were successful and the lower courts were barred from hearing the entire case in separable controversy removals, plaintiffs would still have been faced with removals by nonresident defendants of their separable controversies. The only practical result would have been that plaintiffs would also have been left with a second suit against the resident defendants in the state court, a suit that in most cases they had no interest in pursuing. Plaintiffs' interest, then, was in seeing the concept of a "separable controversy" construed as narrowly as possible, not in challenging the constitutionality of the act.

15. *Blake v. McKim,* 103 U.S. 336 (1880); *Hyde v. Ruble,* 104 U.S. 407 (1881); *Fraser v. Jennison,* 106 U.S. 191 (1882); *Thayer v. Life Association of America,* 112 U.S. 717 (1885).

16. 114 U.S. 52, 56 (1885).

17. Ibid., p. 56.

18. *Barney v. Latham,* 103 U.S. 205 (1880); *Hyde v. Ruble,* 104 U.S. 407 (1881); *Ayres v. Wiswall,* 112 U.S. 187 (1884); *Pirie v. Tvedt,* 115 U.S. 41 (1885); *Sloane v. Anderson,* 117 U.S. 275 (1886).

19. *Plymouth Gold Mining Co. v. Amador,* 118 U.S. 264 (1886).

20. For example, *Williams v. Nottawa,* 104 U.S. 209 (1881); *Little v. Giles,* 118 U.S. 596 (1886).

21. Gordon M. Bakken, *The Development of Law on the Rocky Mountain Frontier: Civil Law and Society, 1850–1912* (Westport, CT, 1983), pp. 100–8; Bakken, *The Development of Law in Frontier California: Civil Law and Society, 1850–1890* (Westport, CT, 1985), pp. 73–79.

22. The joinder tactic failed to prevent removal in the following: *Clark v. Chicago, Milwaukee & St. Paul Railway Co.,* 11 F. 355 (C.C.D.Minn. 1882); *Beuttel v. Chicago, Milwaukee & St. Paul Railway Co.,* 26 F. 50 (C.C.N.D. Iowa 1885); *Spangler v. Atchison, Topeka & Santa Fe Railroad Co.,* 42 F. 305 (C.C.W.D.Mo. 1890) (finding removal proper on the ground of a separable controversy but nevertheless ordering remand on the ground that the petition for removal was not timely); *Rivers v. Bradley,* 53 F. 305 (C.C.D.S.C. 1892); *Fergason v. Chicago, Milwaukee & St. Paul Railway Co.,* 63 F. 177 (C.C.N.D.Iowa 1894); *Cookerly v. Great Northern Railway Co.,* 70 F. 277 (C.C.D.Wash. 1895); *Chamberlain v. New York, Lake Erie & Western Railroad Co.,* 71 F. 636 (C.C.N.D.Ohio 1895).

23. *Clarkhuff v. Wisconsin, Iowa & Nebraska Railroad Co.,* 26 F. 465, 467 (C.C.S.D.Iowa 1885).

24. Richard A. Posner, "A Theory of Negligence," *Journal of Legal Studies* 1 (1972): 29, 85–91; Shelton Stromquist, *A Generation of Boomers: The Pattern of Railroad Labor Conflict in Nineteenth-Century America* (Urbana, IL, 1987), pp. 122–30, 227–28, 261–62, 273–74; James Livingston, "The Social Analysis of Economic History and Theory: Conjectures on Late

Nineteenth-Century American Development," *American Historical Review* 92 (1987): 69; Frank W. Munger, Jr., "Social Change and Tort Litigation: Industrialization, Accidents, and Trial Courts in Southern West Virginia, 1872–1940," *Buffalo Law Review* 36 (1987): 75, 81, 89.

25. William Laurens Walker, "Foreign Corporation Laws: The Loss of Reason," *North Carolina Law Review* 47 (1968): 1, 13.

26. For the attack on the federal courts as probusiness, see, for example, John W. Akin, "Aggressions of the Federal Courts," *American Law Review* 32 (1898): 669; for the defense, see William Howard Taft, "Criticisms of the Federal Judiciary," *American Law Review* 29 (1895): 41.

27. B. C. Moon, *The Removal of Causes from the Courts of the Several States to the Circuit Courts of the United States* (New York, 1901), p. 553.

28. Herbert Hovenkamp, "Regulatory Conflict in the Gilded Age: Federalism and the Railroad Problem," *Yale Law Journal* 97 (1988): 1017, 1043.

29. David J. Brewer, "Some Thoughts About Kansas," *Twelfth Annual Meeting of the Bar Association of the State of Kansas* (Topeka, 1895), pp. 64–65. A copy of the speech is contained in the David J. Brewer Papers, vol. 2, Library of Congress.

30. See, for example, John Higham, *Strangers in the Land: Patterns of American Nativism, 1860–1925* (New York, 1963), pp. 68–105; Alan M. Kraut, *The Huddled Masses: The Immigrant in American Society, 1880–1921* (Arlington Heights, IL, 1982), pp. 86–87; Herbert Gutman, *Work, Culture, and Society in Industrializing America: Essays in American Working-Class and Social History* (New York, 1976), pp. 71–73; Herbert Gutman, *Power & Culture: Essays on the American Working Class,* ed. Ira Berlin (New York, 1982), chap. 11. Nativism and hostility to immigrants characterized many American workers and much of the union movement, especially after the depression of the 1890s. See, for example, Robert Asher, "Union Nativism and the Immigrant Response," *Labor History* 23 (1982): 325; A. T. Lane, "American Trade Unions, Mass Immigration and the Literacy Test: 1900–1917," *Labor History* 25 (1984): 5; John J. Bukowczyk, "The Transformation of Working-Class Ethnicity: Corporate Control, Americanization, and the Polish Immigrant Middle Class in Bayonne, New Jersey, 1915–1925," *Labor History* 25 (1984): 53; Catherine Collomp, "Unions, Civics, and National Identity: Organized Labor's Reaction to Immigration, 1881–1897," *Labor History* 29 (1988): 450.

31. Morton Keller, *Affairs of State: Public Life in Late Nineteenth Century America* (Cambridge, MA, 1977); Samuel Eliot Morison and Henry Steele Commager, *The Growth of the American Republic,* vol. 2 (New York, 1962), p. 335.

32. Quoted in Morison and Commager, *Growth of the American Republic,* vol. 2, pp. 337–38. For populism in general, see John D. Hicks, *The Populist Revolt* (Minneapolis, 1931); Lawrence Goodwyn, *Democratic Promise: The Populist Movement in America* (New York, 1976); Bruce Palmer, *Man over Money: The Populist Critique of American Capitalism* (Chapel Hill, NC, 1980); Norman Pollock, *The Just Polity: Populism, Law, and Human Welfare* (Urbana, IL, 1987).

33. Harold U. Faulkner, *Politics, Reform and Expansion* (New York, 1959), pp. 163–86. For a broader view of the social tensions culminating in the 1890s, see Robert H. Wiebe, *The Search for Order, 1877–1920* (New York, 1967), chap. 4.

34. Jane Adams, *Twenty Years at Hull-House* (New York, 1960) (originally published 1910), p. 158. See Trachtenberg, *Incorporation of America,* pp. 86–100.

35. Quoted in Henry F. Pringle, *Life and Times of William Howard Taft* (New York, 1939), vol. 1, p. 128.

36. William Howard Taft, "The Right of Private Property," *Michigan Law Journal* 3 (1894): 215.

37. 65 F. 138 (C.C.D.Ky. 1895).

38. Ibid., p. 140.

39. 65 F. 129 (C.C.D.Ky. 1895).

40. Ibid., p. 138.

41. Ibid., p. 131.

42. Ibid., p. 136.

43. 57 F. 165 (C.C.N.D.Tenn. 1893).

44. Ibid., p. 169.

45. Ibid., p. 171.

46. Ibid., p. 170.

47. 72 F. 637 (C.C.D.Ky. undated [circa 1895]).

48. Ibid., p. 643.

49. Ibid., p. 647.

50. Note that the joinder issue under the separable controversy act did present an issue of federal law, the proper construction to be given the language of the statute. *Warax* and many of the other joinder decisions of the federal courts, however, did not focus on the question as one requiring the construction of a federal jurisdictional statute. Rather, they considered the issue in terms of the nature of the common law action presented, a "state law" issue. Their approach to the jurisdictional question was shaped by the existence of the federal common law.

51. Ibid., p. 641.

52. *Hukill v. Maysville & Big Sandy Railroad Co.*, 72 F. 745 (C.C.D.Ky. undated [circa 1895]).

53. *Landers v. Felton*, 73 F. 311 (C.C.D.Ky. 1896).

54. *Prince v. Illinois Central Railroad Co.*, 98 F. 1, 2–3 (C.C.D.Ky. 1899).

55. *McCormick v. Illinois Central Railroad Co.*, 100 F. 250, 251 (C.C.D.Ky. 1900).

56. *Warax* was followed, for example, in *Hartshorn v. Atchison Topeka & Santa Fe Railroad Co.*, 77 F. 9 (C.C.W.D.Mo. 1896). Other courts denied remands on alternative grounds; for example, *Durkee v. Illinois Central Railroad Co.*, 81 F. 1 (C.C.N.D.Iowa 1897); *Burch v. Caden Stone Co.*, 93 F. 181 (C.C.D.Ky. 1899); *Batey v. Nashville, Chattanooga & St. Louis Railway*, 95 F. 368 (C.C.M.D.Tenn. 1899). Some lower court decisions, however, ignored *Warax* and ordered remands; for example, *Brown & Coxe Bros. & Co.*, 75 F. 689 (C.C.E.D.Wisc. 1896); *Kane v. City of Indianapolis, Ind.*, 82 F. 770 (C.C.D.Ind. 1897); *Deere, Wells & Co. v. Chicago, Milwaukee & St. Paul Railway Co.*, 85 F. 876 (C.C.S.D.Iowa 1898); *Marrs v. Felton*, 102 F. 775 (C.C.D.Ky. 1900).

57. 169 U.S. 92 (1898).

58. Ibid., p. 98.

59. Compare *Powers*, 169 U.S. 99, with *Austin*, 135 U.S. 318.

60. 169 U.S. 99.

61. Ibid., p. 100.

62. Ibid.

63. Ibid., p. 97.

64. Ibid.

65. See, for example, *Berry v. St. Louis & San Francisco Railroad Co.*, 118 F. 911 (C.C.D.Kan. 1902) (plaintiff refused to serve resident defendant; court allowed removal before trial).

66. For example, *Collins v. Twin Falls North Side Land & Water Co.*, 204 F. 134 (D.Idaho 1913).

67. The tactic was successful in *Enders v. Lake Erie and Western Railroad Co.*, 101 F. 202 (C.C.D.Ind. 1900) (late amendment increased the amount claimed above the jurisdictional minimum; removal defeated by failure to file petition promptly); *Martin v. Richmond Cotton Oil Co.*, 184 S.W. 127 (Ct. App. Mo. 1916) (late amendment raised amount claimed above jurisdictional minimum; removal defeated by failure to file petition promptly). The tactic failed in *Fort Smith & Western Railroad Co. v. Blevins*, 130 P. 525 (Sup.Ct. Okla. 1913) (late amendment raising amount sought, and defendant promptly sought leave to file removal petition; removal allowed). Compare *Murphy v. Stone & Webster Engineering Corp.*, 119 P. 717 (Sup. Ct. Mont. 1911) (late de facto dismissal of nonserved resident defendant; removal granted).

68. *Swann v. Mutual Reserve Fund Life Association*, 116 F. 232 (C.C.W.D.Ky. 1902); *Barber v. Boston & Maine Railroad Co.*, 145 F. 52 (C.C.D.Vt. 1906); *Springer v. Bricker*, 76 N.E. 114 (Sup. Ct. Ind. 1905); *Bacon v. Iowa Central Railway Co.*, 137 N.W. 1011 (Sup. Ct. Iowa 1912), aff'd 236 U.S. 305 (1915); *Barber v. Atlantic Coast Line Railroad Co.*, 94 S.E. 280 (Ct. App. Ga. 1917).

69. See, for example, *Bryson v. Southern Railway Co.*, 54 S.E. 434 (Sup. Ct.N.C. 1906). Compare *Hansford v. Stone-Ordean-Wells Co.*, 201 F. 185 (D. Mont. 1912) with *Heller v. Ilwaco Mill & Lumber Co.*, 178 F. 111 (C.C.D.Oreg. 1910) and *Williams v. Wilson Fruit Co.*, 222 F. 467 (D. Idaho 1915).

70. Plaintiffs may or may not have been attempting to confuse or mislead defendants in the following: *Oliver v. Iowa Central Railway Co.*, 102 F. 371 (C.C.S.D.Iowa 1900); *Fogarty v. Southern Pacific Co.*, 121 F. 941 (C.C.S.D.Cal. 1903); *Robinson v. Parker-Washington Co.*, 170 F. 850 (C.C.W.D.Mo 1909); *Bagenas v. Southern Pacific Co.*, 180 F. 887 (C.C.N.D.Cal. 1910); *Hoyt v. Ogden Portland Cement Co.*, 185 F. 889 (C.C.N.D.N.Y. 1911); *Adams v. Puget Sound Traction, Light & Power Co.*, 207 F. 205 (W.D.Wash. 1913); *Johnson v. Butte Alex Scott Copper Co.*, 213 F. 910 (D. Mont. 1914).

71. *Markey v. Chicago, Milwaukee & St. Paul Railway Co.*, 153 N.W. 1053 (Sup. Ct. Iowa 1915).

72. 179 U.S. 131 (1900).

73. Ibid., p. 136.

74. Ibid., p. 140.

75. Ibid., p. 139, and see p. 137.

76. Ibid., p. 139.

77. Ibid.

78. Justice McKenna did not participate. Harlan and White also dissented without opinion in a nearly contemporaneous decision that dealt with central issues concerning corporate diversity litigation in the insurance area. The decision also went against the companies and in effect narrowed the scope of federal jurisdiction. See *Cable v. United States Life Insurance Co.*, 191 U.S. 288 (1903). It seems likely that Harlan and White were motivated by the second concern, not the first. See n. 141 and Chapter 9.

79. Comment, *Virginia Law Register* 6 (1901): 645.

80. *Whitcomb v. Smithson*, 175 U.S. 635 (1900); *Chicago, Rock Island and Pacific Railway Co. v. Martin*, 178 U.S. 245 (1900); *Gableman v. Peoria, Decatur and Evansville Railway Co.*, 179 U.S. 335 (1900); *Kansas City Suburban Belt Railway Co. v. Herman*, 187 U.S. 63 (1902); *Southern Railway Co. v. Carson*, 194 U.S. 136 (1904).

81. For example, *Louisville and Nashville Railroad Co. v. Ide*, 114 U.S. 52 (1885); *Pirie v. Tvedt*, 115 U.S. 41 (1885); *Sloane v. Anderson*, 117 U.S. 275 (1886).

82. *Shaffer v. Union Brick Co.*, 128 F. 97, 99 (C.C.D.Kan. 1904). The popularity of the joinder tactic was clear from the frequent discussions it provoked, for example, in the *Central Law Journal*. See, for example, Rublee A. Cole, "Separable Controversy," *Central Law Journal* 53 (1901): 169; Cyrus J. Wood, "Joint or Severable Liability of Master and Servant for Negligence as Affecting Removal of Causes," *Central Law Journal* 54 (1902): 404; Editorial notes, *Central Law Journal* 58 (1904): 461; John J. McSwain, "Right of Removal of Causes on Behalf of Non-Resident Master Defendant," *Central Law Journal* 60 (1905): 303.

83. *McIntyre v. Southern Railway Co.*, 131 F. 985, 985–86 (C.C.D.S.C. 1904).

84. For example, *Dougherty v. Yazoo & Mississippi Valley Railroad Co.*, 122 F. 205 (C.C.A. 5 1903); *Moore v. Los Angeles Iron & Steel Co.*, 89 F. 73 (C.C.S.D.Cal. 1898); *Charman v. Lake Erie & Western Railroad Co.*, 105 F. 449 (C.C.D.Ind. 1900); *Riser v. Southern Railway Co.*, 116 F. 215 (C.C.D.S.C. 1902); *Knuth v. Butte Electric Railway Co.*, 148 F. 73 (C.C.D.Mont. 1906).

85. *Doremus v. Root*, 94 F. 760, 761 (C.C.D.Wash. 1899).

86. *Helms v. Northern Pacific Railway Co.*, 120 F. 389 (C.C.D. Minn. 1903); *Sessions v. Southern Pacific Co.*, 134 F. 313 (C.C.N.D.Cal. 1904). The language in *Dixon* supported that interpretation, as did the Court's further language in *Gableman v. Peoria, Decatur and Evansville Railway Co.*, 179 U.S. 337. State courts also followed the narrow construction; for example, *Southern Railway Co. v. Edwards*, 42 S.E. 375 (Sup.Ct.Ga. 1902).

87. *Dishon v. Cincinnati, New Orleans & Texas Pacific Railway Co.*, 133 F. 471 (C.C.A. 6 1904); *Diday v. New York, Pennsylvania & Ohio Railroad Co.*, 107 F. 565 (C.C.N.D.Ohio 1901); *Ross v. Erie Railroad Co.*, 120 F. 703 (C.C.E.D.N.Y. 1902); *Crawford v. Illinois Central Railroad Co.*, 130 F. 395 (C.C.W.D.Ky. 1904).

88. *Davenport v. Southern Railway Co.*, 135 F. 960, 963–64 (C.C.A. 4 1905).

89. *American Bridge Co. v. Hunt*, 130 F. 302, 304 (C.C.A. 6 1904). The Sixth Circuit enforced *Dixon* when concurrent negligence was pleaded and supported by factual allegations. *American Bridge Co. v. Hunt*, 130 F. 302 (C.C.A. 6 1904); *Roberts v. Shelby Steel Tube Co.*, 131 F. 729 (C.C.A. 6 1904).

90. For example, *Ross v. Erie Railroad Co.*, 120 F. 703 (C.C.E.D.N.Y. 1902); *Helms v. Northern Pacific Railway Co.*, 120 F. 389 (C.C.D.Minn. 1903); *Shaffer v. Union Brick Co.*, 128 F. 97 (C.C.D.Kan. 1904); *Crawford v. Illinois Central Railroad Co.*, 130 F. 395 (C.C.W.D.Ky. 1904); *Sessions v. Southern Pacific Co.*, 134 F. 313 (C.C.N.D.Cal. 1904); *Beltz v. Baltimore & Ohio Railroad Co.*, 137 F. 1016 (C.C.N.D.Ohio 1905).

91. *Yeates v. Illinois Central Railroad Co.*, 137 F. 943 (C.C.N.D.Ill. 1905); *Curtis v. Cleveland, Cincinnati, Chicago & St. Louis Railway Co.*, 140 F. 777 (C.C.E.D.Ill. 1905).

Most states apparently allowed a joint cause of action against a master and its servant: "The master and servant are in general jointly and severally liable for the tortious act of the servant committed in the course of the master's business." The result was that "the law permits all the wrong-doers to be proceeded against jointly." Thomas M. Cooley, *A Treatise on the Law of Torts, or the Wrongs Which Arise Independently of Contract*, ed. John Lewis (Chicago, 1907), p. 96 (citing cases from twelve states), pp. 98–99.

92. *Bryce v. Southern Railway Co.*, 122 F. 709, 710, 711 (C.C.D.S.C. 1903).

93. Ibid., p. 712.

94. Ibid., p. 713.

95. Ibid., p. 714.

96. *Bryce v. Southern Railway Co.*, 125 F. 958, 959 (C.C.D.S.C. 1903).

97. Ibid., p. 962.

98. *Kelly v. Chicago & Alton Railway Co.*, 122 F. 286 (C.C.W.D.Mo. 1903); *Davenport v. Southern Railway Co.*, 124 F. 983 (C.C.D.S.C. 1903); *Williard v. Spartanburg, Union & Columbia Railroad Co.*, 124 F. 796 (C.C.D.S.C 1903); *Gustafson v. Chicago, Rock Island & Pacific Railway Co.*, 128 F. 85 (C.C.W.D.Mo. 1904); *Crawford v. Illinois Central Railroad Co.*, 130 F. 395 (C.C.W.D.Ky. 1904); *McIntyre v. Southern Railway Co.*, 131 F. 985 (C.C.D.S.C. 1904); *Sessions v. Southern Pacific Co.*, 134 F. 313 (C.C.N.D.Cal. 1904); *Beltz v. Baltimore & Ohio Railroad Co.*, 137 F. 1016 (C.C.N.D.Ohio 1905); *Axline v. Toledo, Walhonding Valley & Ohio Railraod Co.*, 138 F. 169 (C.C.S.D.Ohio 1903). In general, many federal judges seemed reluctant to see their jurisdiction narrowed. See Armistead M. Dobie, *Handbook of Federal Jurisdiction and Procedure* (St. Paul, 1928), p. 348.

99. *Henry v. Illinois Central Railroad Co.*, 132 F. 715 (C.C.S.D.Iowa 1903).

100. *Gableman v. Peoria, Decatur and Evansville Railway Co.*, 179 U.S. 335 (1900); *Kansas City Suburban Belt Railway Co. v. Herman*, 187 U.S. 63 (1902); *Southern Railway Co. v. Carson*, 194 U.S. 136 (1904). But see *Geer v. Mathieson Alkali Works*, 190 U.S. 428 (1903).

101. 200 U.S. 206 (1906).

102. Ibid., pp. 219–20.

103. Ibid., pp. 220, 218.

104. Ibid., p. 214.

105. 200 U.S. 221 (1906).

106. 200 U.S. 218.

107. 204 U.S. 176 (1907).

108. Ibid., p. 185.

109. *Illinois Central Railroad Co. v. Sheegog*, 215 U.S. 308 (1909); *Southern Railway Co. v. Miller*, 217 U.S. 209 (1910); *Chicago, Rock Island and Pacific Railway Co. v. Schwyhart*, 227 U.S. 184 (1913); *Chicago, Rock Island & Pacific Railway Co. v. Dowell*, 229 U.S. 102 (1913); *Chesapeake & Ohio Railway Co. v. Cockrell*, 232 U.S. 146 (1914).

110. *Chicago, Burlington and Quincy Railway Co. v. Willard*, 220 U.S. 413 (1911).

111. See *Wilson v. Republic Iron & Steel Co.*, 257 U.S. 92 (1921) (fraudulent joinder); *Lee v. Central of Georgia Railway Co.*, 252 U.S. 109 (1920).

112. A subsidiary line of cases limited removals under *Powers* strictly to situations where plaintiffs voluntarily dismissed resident defendants, holding that neither directed verdicts dismissing such defendants nor failures to present evidence against them would justify removal. *Whitcomb v. Smithson*, 175 U.S. 635 (1900); *Kansas City Suburban Belt Railway Co. v. Herman*, 187 U.S. 63 (1902); *American Car & Foundry Co. v. Kettelhake*, 236 U.S. 311 (1915). The decisions made it possible to defeat removal with thin factual allegations implicating a resident defendant.

A second subsidiary line of cases held that a plaintiff could recover on a joint cause of action against a party proven liable even if he failed to prove that all of the joint defendants were liable. *Atlantic and Pacific Railroad Co. v. Laird,* 164 U.S. 393 (1896); *Southern Railway Co. v. Carson,* 194 U.S. 136 (1904).

113. For example, *Thomas v. Great Northern Railway Co.,* 147 F. 83 (C.C.A. 9 1906); *Enos v. Kentucky Distilleries & Warehouse Co.,* 189 F. 342 (C.C.A. 6 1911); *Buchanan v. W.M. Ritter Lumber Co.,* 210 F. 144 (C.C.A. 4 1913); *Russell v. Champion Fibre Co.,* 214 F. 963 (C.C.A. 4 1914); *Welch v. Cincinnati, New Orleans & Texas Pacific Railway Co.,* 177 F. 760 (C.C.E.D. Tenn. 1908); *Taylor v. Southern Railway Co.,* 178 F. 380 (C.C.N.D.Ga. 1910); *Foster v. Coos Bay Gas & Electric Co.,* 185 F. 979 (C.C.D. Oreg. 1911); *Lewis v. Cincinnati, New Orleans & Texas Pacific Railway Co.,* 192 F. 654 (C.C.E.D.Tenn. 1910); *Stevenson v. Illinois Central Railroad Co.,* 192 F. 956 (C.C.W.D.Ky. 1911); *McGarvey v. Butte Miner Co.,* 199 F. 671 (D.Mont. 1912); *Price v. Southern Power Co.,* 206 F. 496 (W.D.S.C. 1913); *Richardson v. Southern Idaho Water Power Co.,* 209 F. 949 (D.Idaho 1913); *Jones v. Casey-Hedges Co.,* 213 F. 43 (E.D.Tenn. 1913); *Case v. Atlanta & Charlotte Air Line Railway Co.,* 225 F. 862 (W.D.S.C. 1915); *Rountree v. Mount Hood Railroad Co.,* 228 F. 1010 (D.Oreg. 1916); *Key v. West Kentucky Coal Co.,* 237 F. 258 (W.D.Ky. 1916); *Martin v. New York, New Haven & Hartford Railroad Co.,* 241 F. 696 (S.D.N.Y. 1917); *Poorman v. Cleveland, Cincinnati, Chicago & St. Louis Railway Co.,* 255 F. 985 (E.D.Ill. 1918); *Atlantic Coast Line Railroad Co. v. Feaster,* 260 F. 881 (E.D.S.C. 1919).

114. *Shane v. Butte Electric Railway Co.,* 150 F. 801, 810 (C.C.D.Mont. 1906).

115. Ibid.

116. *Jacobson v. Chicago, Rock Island & Pacific Railway Co.,* 176 F. 1004, 1005 (C.C.D.Minn. 1910).

117. See, for example, *Galeotti v. Diamond Match Co.,* 178 F. 127 (C.C.N.D.Cal. 1910); *Clark v. Chicago, Rock Island & Pacific Railway Co.,* 194 F. 505 (W.D.Mo. 1912); *Springer v. American Tobacco Co.,* 208 F. 199 (W.D.Ky. 1913).

118. See, for example, *Cincinnati, New Orleans & Texas Pacific Railway Co. v. Evans' Administrator,* 110 S.W. 844 (Ct. App. Ky. 1908); *Gordon v. Northern Pacific Railway Co.,* 104 P. 549 (Sup. Ct. Mont. 1909); *Broadway Coal Mining Co. v. Robinson,* 150 S.W. 1000 (Ct. App. Ky. 1912); *Morgan's Louisiana & Texas Railroad and Steamship Co. v. Street,* 122 S.W. 270 (Ct. Civ. App. Tx. 1909). Compare Moon, *The Removal of Causes,* p. 553 (stating that in 1901, before *Bohon,* "the cases are legion in which State courts have refused to order removals").

119. Prior to World War I, *Stevenson v. Illinois Central Railroad Co.,* 192 F. 956, 959 (C.C.W.D.Ky. 1911), appears to be a rare exception.

120. *Evansberg v. Insurance Stove, Range & Foundry Co.,* 168 F. 1001, 1002 (C.C.E.D.Ky. 1908).

121. For example, *Nichols v. Chesapeake & Ohio Railway Co.,* 195 F. 913 (C.C.A. 6 1912); *Trivette v. Chesapeake & Ohio Railway Co.,* 212 F. 641 (C.C.A. 6 1914); *Atlantic Coast Line Railroad Co. v. Bailey,* 151 F. 891 (C.C.E.D.Ga. 1907); *Chicago, Rock Island & Pacific Railway Co.,* 151 F. 908 (C.C.W.D.Mo. 1907); *Lockard v. St. Louis & San Francisco Railroad Co.,* 167 F. 675 (C.C.W.D.Ark. 1909); *Evansberg v. Insurance Stove, Range & Foundry Co.,* 168 F. 1001 (C.C.E.D.Ky. 1908); *Reinartson v. Chicago Great Western Railway Co.,* 174 F. 707 (C.C.N.D.Iowa 1909); *Marach v. Columbia Box Co.,* 179 F. 412 (C.C.E.D.Mo. 1910); *Shaver v. Pacific Coast Condensed Milk Co.,* 185 F. 316 (C.C.D.Oreg. 1911); *Floyt v. Shenango Furnace Co.,* 186 F. 539 (C.C.D.Minn. 1911); *Macutis v. Cudahy Packing Co.,* 203 F. 291 (D.Neb. 1913); *Richardson v. Southern Idaho Water Power Co.,* 209 F. 949 (D.Idaho 1913) (remanding, however, for the failure of all necessary defendants to join the petition for removal); *Trana v. Chicago, Milwaukee & Puget Sound Railway Co.,* 228 F. 824 (W.D.Wash. 1915); *Martin v. Matson Navigation Co.,* 239 F. 188 (W.D.Wash. 1917).

An allegation of fraudulent joinder, of course, also remained available to defendants. For example, *Nelson v. Black Diamond Mining Co.,* 237 F. 264 (W.D.Ky. 1916).

Many of the decisions of the lower courts were reviewed in *McAllister v. Chesapeake & Ohio Railway Co.,* 198 F. 660 (E.D.Ky. 1912), where the district court had denied a motion to remand and then granted reargument on the basis of plaintiff's apparently quite strenuous insistence that remand was proper under the Supreme Court's decisions in *Illinois Central Railroad Co. v.*

Sheegog, 215 U.S. 308 (1909), and *Chicago, Burlington and Quincy Railway Co. v. Willard,* 220 U.S. 413 (1911). The district court again denied the motion to remand, essentially on the ground that the codefendants would be liable, if at all, on different theories. Eventually, the Supreme Court reversed, apparently holding that as long as the complaint pleaded a joint cause of action and the defendants could be liable for the same injury, there was no separable controversy and the action could not be removed. *McAllister v. Chesapeake & Ohio Railway Co.,* 243 U.S. 302, 310–11 (1917).

122. *Chicago, Rock Island & Pacific Railway Co. v. Schwyhart,* 227 U.S. 184, 194 (1913).

123. *Atlantic Coast Line Railroad Co. v. Bailey,* 151 F. 891, 894–95 (C.C.E.D.Ga. 1907); *Lockard v. St. Louis & San Francisco Railroad Co.,* 167 F. 675, 678–79 (C.C.W.D.Ark. 1909). In a breach of contract action unrelated to the social context of the employee joinder cases, Judge Learned Hand made the same point in *Hough v. Societé Electrique Westinghouse De Russie,* 232 F. 635, 636 (S.D.N.Y. 1916).

124. *Clark v. Chicago, Rock Island & Pacific Railway Co.,* 194 F. 505, 510–11 (W.D.Mo. 1912).

125. For example, *Jackson v. Chicago, Rock Island & Pacific Railway Co.,* 178 F. 432 (C.C.A. 8 1910); *Adderson v. Southern Railway Co.,* 177 F. 571 (C.C.N.D.Ga. 1910); *Cayce v. Southern Railway Co.,* 195 F. 786 (N.D.Ga. 1912); *Veariel v. United Engineering & Foundry Co.,* 197 F. 877 (N.D.Ohio 1912); *Puckett v. Columbus Power Co.,* 248 F. 353 (N.D.Ga. 1918).

126. *Shaver v. Pacific Coast Condensed Milk Co.,* 185 F. 316, 317 (C.C.D.Oreg. 1911).

127. Regardless of consistent results, the language of the Court's joinder opinions remained less than wholly consistent. The opinions failed to delineate the relationship between separable controversy and fraud, and they suggested that, if state law did not authorize a joint cause of action, a separable controversy might exist regardless of the allegations in the complaint. Language was available to support the latter result on two separate grounds, either that state law simply determined the matter or that assertion of a joint cause of action not authorized by state law could evidence fraudulent intent. Compare the cases cited in n. 86–87, 90–91, and 98 and the following: *Chicago, Rock Island & Pacific Railway Co. v. Whiteaker,* 239 U.S. 421 (1915); *McAllister v. Chesapeake & Ohio Railway Co.,* 243 U.S. 302 (1917); *Chicago & Alton Railroad Co. v. McWhirt,* 243 U.S. 422 (1917).

The fault lines that ran through the Court's opinions seemed to mirror differences among the individual Justices who wrote the successive opinions. Some made the pleadings seem determinative, whereas others implied that additional criteria were applicable. Compare the opinions of Holmes (*Sheegog,* 215 U.S. 308, and *Schwyhart,* 227 U.S. 184) and John H. Clarke (*McAlister,* 243 U.S. 302) on one side with the opinions of Lurton (*Dowell,* 229 U.S. 102) and Willis Van Devanter (*Cockrell,* 232 U.S. 146; *McWhirt,* 243 U.S. 422; and *Wilson,* 257 U.S. 92) on the other. Day, with Harlan joining, wrote an important dissent in *Sheegog* (215 U.S. 319), one of the cases that seemed to give the pleadings their broadest scope. Harlan had dissented in *Dixon.*

128. The emergence of the plaintiff's personal injury bar in the nineties and the profession's reaction is discussed at length in Chapter 7.

129. *Gustafson v. Chicago, Rock Island & Pacific Railway Co.,* 128 F. 85, 87–88 (C.C.W.D.Mo. 1904).

130. *Shephard v. Bradstreet,* 65 F. 142 (W.D.Mo. 1895) (Philips, J.); *Kelly v. Chicago & Alton Railway Co.,* 12 F. 286 (W.D.Mo. 1903) (Philips, J.); *Gustafson v. Chicago, Rock Island & Pacific Railway Co.,* 128 F. 85, 87–88 (C.C.W.D.Mo 1904) (Philips, J.); and *Chicago, Rock Island & Pacific Railway Co. v. Stepp,* 151 F. 908 (W.D. Mo. 1907) (Philips, J.). Compare *Robinson v. Parker-Washington Co.,* 170 F. 850 (W.D.Mo. 1909) (Philips, J.).

131. C. P. Connolly, "Big Business and the Bench: The Federal Courts—Last Refuge of the Interests," *Everybody's Magazine* 26 (1912): 827, 835.

132. In 1910 Philips left the federal bench, allegedly under the threat of a congressional investigation. He did not, in any event, retire. Rather, he practiced law until his death in 1919, including among his clients the Missouri Pacific Railway. See C. P. Connolly, "Big Business and the Bench: The Part the Railways Play in Corrupting Our Courts," *Everybody's Magazine* 26 (1912): 291, 306; Connolly, "Big Business and the Bench: The Federal Courts," pp. 827, 828, 830, 835–36. Philips's resignation was noted in *Green Bag* 22 (1910): 328, 372.

The threatened investigation apparently arose at least in part from allegedly improper expenses that Philips claimed from the government for his time spent sitting in other districts. There may have been some substance to the allegations. The *Annual Report* of the Attorney General for 1911 stated that its Bureau of Investigation had examined the finances of eighty-nine clerks' offices in the federal courts and found "gross irregularities" in eighteen. Some involved "actual dishonesty." Seven clerks were removed or resigned, and the Department of Justice ordered the initiation of four civil suits for restitution and five criminal prosecutions. Although the report did not mention any federal judge by name, it did state that "the judges have not always cooperated with the department in its efforts to correct irregularities in the conduct of these offices." See United States Attorney General, *Annual Report, 1911,* pp. 22–23. The year that Philips resigned, the *Central Law Journal* noted that a socialist magazine in Kansas had begun an attack on several unnamed federal judges and that its charges seemed to have substance:

> In most cases of assaults of this character upon the judiciary it is usually the most dignified thing to ignore them. But where such charges take the form of a recitation of particular instances and evidence is offered to prove them, and they thus become definite enough to challenge the attention of more respectable newspapers and even of members of the bar, it becomes the duty of the judges thus attacked, or of Congress to demand an investigation and refute the imputations thus made. [Comment, *Central Law Journal* 70 (1910): 231] Also see p. 248.

It is worth noting that federal Judge John C. Pollock of the District of Kansas, apparently a friend of Philips, was also charged with both dubious conduct and favoritism toward corporations. See Connolly, "Big Business and the Bench: The Federal Courts," pp. 827, 828–30. In 1904 Pollack also rejected the joinder tactic in an opinion that warned against "dangerous" doctrines that were "utterly destructive" of the right to remove. In essence Pollack avoided *Dixon* by adopting the *Warax* approach: *Shaffer v. Union Brick Co.,* 128 F. 97 (C.C.D.Kan. 1904). Pollock's opinion literally followed Philips's opinion in *Gustafson v. Chicago, Rock Island & Pacific Railroad Co.,* 128 F. 85 (C.C.W.D.Mo. 1904), which insisted on the need for the federal courts to give joinders the closest scrutiny.

133. John F. Philips, "The Law and Lawyers," *Green Bag* 17 (1905): 433, 438, 435. "No business man, or association of men, can venture upon any business enterprise under an existing statute, without apprehended danger of its early change or modification, or some new regulation or burden imposed upon it" (p. 437).

For a brief biographical sketch, see "Philips, John Finis," *Dictionary of American Biography,* vol. 14 (New York, 1934), p. 536. The author states: "As a judge, Philips was essentially conservative in his economic and social point of view" (p. 537).

134. John F. Philips, "The Ideals of the American Advocate—A Symposium," *Central Law Journal* 58 (1904): 426.

135. For biographical information about Amidon, see Kenneth Smemo, *Against the Tide: The Life and Times of Federal Judge Charles F. Amidon, North Dakota Progressive* (New York, 1986), esp. pp. 19–25, 33–67, 86–93; and Beulah Amidon Ratliff, "Charles Fremont Amidon, 1856–1937," *North Dakota Historical Quarterly* 8 (1940): 83. Amidon's biographer-daughter described the judge's social values in classic progressive terms: "Judge Amidon was as firm in seeking to prevent encroachment on the rights of the public by the impersonal corporation as he was to help safeguard the rights of the employee" (p. 90).

136. 120 F. 389 (C.C.D.Minn. 1903).

137. 186 F. 539 (C.C.D.Minn. 1911).

138. Ibid., p. 540.

139. In *Wecker,* for example, the Court relied on the defendant's contention that the complaint contained false allegations of material fact as well as the fact established by the record that the plaintiff had been unable or unwilling to contest the specific charge of fraud that the defendant supported by affidavit. In contrast, in *Floyt* Amidon relied solely on his statement of a common law rule to show that the complaint, merely by pleading an inconsistent theory of liability, was thereby evidence of plaintiff's fraud.

In addition, Amidon's new theory in *Floyt* seemed to contradict his reasoning in *Helms.* In the earlier decision he had declared that the critical question was "whether there are or are not two causes of action presented by the complaint." If there were only a "single" cause of action that was proper against only one of the defendants, there would be no separable controversy. In such a case the objection to joinder "goes to the merits," Amidon had explained in *Helms,* and defendant's "only redress is to defeat a recovery in the state court [on the merits]" (120 F. 395). Applied to *Floyt,* where Amidon found that plaintiff stated a good cause of action against only one of the two defendants, that reasoning seemed to call for a remand.

In fairness, it should be noted that the relevant passage in *Helms* is less than clear. Amidon's language could reasonably be construed to require remand only when the party requesting removal was the party against whom the single cause of action did not lie. According to that construction *Helms* and *Floyt* can be seen as consistent. But even if they are consistent on this point, they still suggest that Amidon was straining to avoid ordering a remand.

140. Amidon ruled against another injured railroad employee on procedural grounds when the plaintiff argued that state law made certain evidence inadmissible and that the state rule was binding on the federal court. Amidon, sitting by designation on the Eighth Circuit, held that the state rule did not bind the federal court and that the evidence was admissible. In spite of his sympathy for injured workers, Amidon sought to maintain what he regarded as the independence and integrity of the federal courts. *Chicago and Northwestern Railway Co. v. Kendall,* 167 F. 62 (C.C.A. 8 1909). Also see Smemo, *Against the Tide,* pp. 88–89.

The conclusion that Amidon's views were the result of a dislike for jurisdictional manipulation and a desire to maintain control over federal jurisdiction in the hands of the national courts is strengthened by the parallel views of another progressive on the federal bench, Judge Learned Hand of the Southern District of New York. Hand favored limiting *Thompson* because he believed that a broad reading of its language gave plaintiffs too much freedom to manipulate their causes of action in order to defeat removal. See *Hough v. Societé Electrique Westinghouse de Russie,* 232 F. 635, 636 (S.D.N.Y. 1916).

141. Both, particularly Harlan, tended to support the broad jurisdiction of the national courts in private law matters. See, for example, *Rosenbaum v. Bauer,* 120 U.S. 450, 459 (1887) (Bradley, Harlan, and Matthews, J.J., dissenting); *Fisk v. Henarie,* 142 U.S. 459, 469 (1892) (Harlan, J., dissenting); *Tennessee v. Union and Planters' Bank,* 152 U.S. 454, 464 (1894) (Harlan, J., dissenting); *Cable v. United States Life Insurance Co.,* 191 U.S. 288, 310 (1903) (Harlan and White, J.J., dissenting without opinion); *Illinois Central Railroad Co. v. Sheegog,* 215 U.S. 308 (1909) (Day and Harlan, J.J., dissenting); *Macon Grocery Co. v. Atlantic Coast Line Railroad Co.,* 215 U.S. 501, 511 (1910) (Harlan, J., dissenting).

Harlan did not vote to uphold broad federal jurisdiction in some cases involving the scope of the Eleventh Amendment. See, for example, *Fitts v. McGhee,* 172 U.S. 516 (1899) (per Harlan, J.); *Ex parte Young,* 209 U.S. 123, 168 (1908) (Harlan, J., dissenting).

142. 194 U.S. 338 (1904). The case was not related to the 1900 *Dixon* joinder case.

143. The two others were Chief Justice Melville W. Fuller and Justice McKenna. It is possible, though it seems unlikely, that either or both of those two could also have been moved in some part by this consideration. Both, especially Fuller, had dissented from some of the Court's fellow servant cases. Fuller, for example, had dissented in *Baugh.* See John E. Semonche, *Charting the Future: The Supreme Court Responds to a Changing Society, 1890–1920* (Westport, CT, 1978), p. 165. Both were with the majority in the 1900 *Dixon* joinder case.

144. Ibid., pp. 352, 356.

145. The 1907 decision was *Schlemmer v. Buffalo, Rochester and Pittsburg Railway Co.,* 205 U.S. 1 (1907).

146. Harlan repeatedly dissented from the Court's fellow servant rule, often alone. See *Northern Pacific Railroad Co. v. Peterson,* 162 U.S. 346 (1896); *Northern Pacific Railroad Co. v. Charless,* 359 U.S. 359 (1896); *Martin v. Atchison, Topeka and Santa Fe Railroad Co.,* 166 U.S. 399 (1897); *New England Railroad Co. v. Conroy,* 175 U.S. 323 (1899).

Harlan also dissented from the Court's federal common law decisions in *Voigt, Adams,* and *Northern Assurance.* White joined the majority in all three. On Harlan's result orientation, see G. Edward White, *The American Judicial Tradition: Profiles of Leading American Judges* (New York, 1976), pp. 129–45.

147. Both had joined the majority in applying the federal fellow servant rule, Holmes in the *Dixon* case, 194 U.S. 338 (1904), and McKenna in *Conroy,* 175 U.S. 323 (1899).

148. *Regis v. United Drug Co.,* 180 F. 201, 208 (C.C.D.Mass. 1910). See *Tolbert v. Jackson,* 99 F. 2d 513, 515–16 (C.C.A. 5 1938).

149. *Kanouse v. Martin,* 15 How. (56 U.S.) 198 (1854); *Kirby v. American Soda Fountain Co.,* 194 U.S. 141 (1904).

150. *Tennessee v. Union & Planters' Bank,* 152 U.S. 454 (1894); *Louisville & Nashville Railroad Co. v. Mottley,* 211 U.S. 149 (1908).

151. Another somewhat technical consideration arose from two fundamental principles of federal jurisdiction, that the jurisdiction of the United States courts was limited and that the party seeking jurisdiction had the burden of establishing its existence. See, for example, *Carson v. Dunham,* 121 U.S. 421 (1887). The basic decision that the Court implemented in its *Thompson–Wecker* complement was to abandon the separable controversy statute as a primary device to limit the employee joinder tactic and to countenance as a lesser evil its widespread use without proof of some type of actual fraud. Such a course relieved the judiciary of the major burden of preventing abuse and placed the burden where it belonged, on the party seeking removal and best able to identify and establish instances of actual fraud. As the Court commented in 1909, affirming a state court's denial of a removal petition, some methods of judicial screening "would be going too far in an effort to counteract evasions of Federal jurisdiction." *Illinois Central Railroad Co. v. Sheegog,* 215 U.S. 318.

152. Les Benedict, "Laissez-Faire and Liberty: A Re-Evaluation of the Meaning and Origins of Laissez-Faire Constitutionalism," *Law & History Review* 3 (1985): 293; Charles W. McCurdy, "Justice Field and the Jurisprudence of Government–Business Relations: Some Parameters of Laissez-Faire Constitutionalism, 1863–1897," *Journal of American History* 61 (1975): 970; William E. Nelson, *The Roots of American Bureaucracy, 1830–1900* (Cambridge, MA, 1982), esp. pp. 148–55; Herbert Hovenkamp, "The Political Economy of Substantive Due Process," *Stanford Law Review* 40 (1988): 379.

Chapter 6

1. See Chapter 1. The impact of elections on state judges may have been less substantial than has often been maintained. See Kermit L. Hall, "Progressive Reform and the Decline of Democratic Accountability: The Popular Election of State Supreme Court Judges, 1850–1920," *American Bar Foundation Research Journal* (1984): 345.

2. Erwin Chemerinsky, "Parity Reconsidered: Defining a Role for the Federal Judiciary," *U.C.L.A. Law Review* 36 (1988): 233, 256.

3. 14 Stat. 558 (1867). The statute subsequently appeared as Section 639 (3) of the Revised Statutes of the United States (1874). The initial draft of the act limited its operation to states that had joined the Confederacy. It is possible that some of those who supported broadening the bill to include the whole nation did so to assist corporate defendants. See Stanley I. Kutler, *Judicial Power and Reconstruction Politics* (Chicago, 1968), pp. 152–54, 157–58.

4. The few early cases pitting individuals against railroads that the Court did decide under the statute presented a variety of tactical situations, including two cases in which the individual plaintiff was the removing party. *Railway Co. v. Whitton's Administrator,* 13 Wall. (80 U.S.) 270 (1871); *Hurst v. Western and Atlantic Railroad Co.,* 2 Otto (93 U.S.) 71 (1876). The Court faced what was to become the standard situation in 1878 in *Railroad Co. v. McKinley,* 9 Otto (99 U.S.) 147 (1878).

5. *Case of the Sewing Machine Companies,* 18 Wall. (85 U.S.) 553 (1873); *Vannevar v. Bryant,* 21 Wall. (88 U.S.) 41 (1874); *Myers v. Swann,* 107 U.S. 546 (1882); *American Bible Society v. Price,* 110 U.S. 61 (1884); *Jefferson v. Driver,* 117 U.S. 272 (1886); *Cambria Iron Co. v. Ashburn,* 118 U.S. 54 (1886).

6. John F. Dillon, *Removal of Causes from State Courts to Federal Courts,* 5th ed. (St. Louis, 1889), pp. 57–72, provides a useful view of the law after passage of the act.

7. "Perspicuity is not a characteristic of the act," one federal judge commented in *Lookout Mountain Railroad Co. v. Houston,* 32 F. 711, 712 (C.C.E.D.Tenn. 1887). Another judge abjured

understatement and termed it "a very unskillful and slovenly piece of legislation." *Fisk v. Henarie*, 32 F. 417, 420 (C.C.D.Oreg. 1887). See B. C. Moon, *The Removal of Causes from the Courts of the Several States to the Circuit Courts of the United States* (New York, 1901), p. 568; Dillon, *Removal of Causes*, 5th ed., pp. 40–41, 57–72.

8. *Vannevar v. Bryant*, 21 Wall. (88 U.S.) 41 (1874); *Baltimore & Ohio Railroad Co. v. Bates*, 119 U.S. 464 (1886).

9. This problem may have been created by careless drafting. See Armistead M. Dobie, *Handbook of Federal Jurisdiction and Procedure* (St. Paul, 1928), p. 382.

10. Ibid., pp. 364–65.

11. *Fisk v. Henarie*, 32 F. 417, 422 (C.C.D.Oreg. 1887).

12. Dillon, *Removal of Causes*, 5th ed. (1889), p. 4; also see pp. 40–45.

13. 35 F. 849 (C.C.N.D.Ohio 1888).

14. A somewhat unorthodox figure, Jackson was an antisecessionist from Tennessee who held office under the Confederacy and later served as a Democratic senator from Tennessee elected as the result of a Republican stratagem. In 1886 he resigned from the Senate to accept appointment as a United States circuit judge, and in 1893 he was appointed to the Supreme Court. His most famous vote in a very brief tenure was cast in dissent from the Court's invalidation of the first federal income tax. See Willard L. King, *Melville Weston Fuller: Chief Justice of the United States, 1888–1910* (Chicago, 1967), pp. 180–81, 207–16.

15. 35 F. 849, 858 (C.C.N.D.Ohio 1888).

16. Ibid., pp. 860–66.

17. Ibid., pp. 854, 856.

18. Ibid., pp. 854.

19. *Short v. Chicago, Milwaukee & St. Paul Railway Co.*, 34 F. 225 (C.C.D.Minn. 1888) (Brewer, J.); *Malone v. Richmond & Danville Railroad Co.*, 35 F. 625 (C.C.E.D.N.C. 1888) (Harlan, J.).

20. Supporting *Whelan* on the jurisdictional amount: *Fales v. Chicago, Milwaukee & St. Paul Railway Co.*, 32 F. 673 (C.C.N.D.Iowa 1887) (dictum); *Huskins v. Cincinnati, New Orleans & Texas Pacific Railway Co.*, 37 F. 504 (C.C.N.D.Tenn. 1889); *McDermott v. Chicago & Northwestern Railway Co.*, 38 F. 529 (C.C.N.D.Iowa 1889); *Frishman v. Insurance Cos.*, 41 F. 449 (C.C.D.Kan. 1890). Opposing: *Tod v. Cleveland & Mahoning Valley Railroad Co.*, 65 F. 145 (C.C.A. 6 1894); *Carson & Rand Lumber Co. v. Holtzclaw, 39 F. 578 (C.C.E.D.Mo. 1889)*; *Roraback v Pennsylvania Co.*, 42 F. 420 (C.C.D.Conn. 1890).

On the timing issue: *Fisk v. Henarie*, 32 F. 417 (C.C.D.Oreg. 1887). Opposing: *Davis v. Chicago & Northwestern Railway Co.*, 46 F. 307 (C.C.N.D.Iowa 1891).

On the procedural–evidentiary issue: *Fisk v. Henarie*, 35 F. 230 (C.C.D.Oreg. 1888); *Hilis v. Richmond & Danville Railroad Co.*, 33 F. 81 (C.C.N.D.Ga. 1887); *Huskins v. Cincinnati, New Orleans & Texas Pacific Railway Co.*, 37 F. 504 (C.C.N.D.Tenn. 1889); *Cooper v. Richmond & Danville Railroad Co.*, 42 F. 697 (C.C.N.D.Ga. 1890). Opposing: *Southworth v. Reid*, 36 F. 451 (C.C.D.Wisc. 1888); *Goldworthy v. Chicago, Milwaukee & St. Paul Railway Co.*, 38 F. 769 (C.C.N.D.Iowa 1889); *Amy v. Manning*, 38 F. 868 (C.C.S.D.N.Y. 1889); *Dennison v. Brown*, 38 F. 535 (C.C.N.D.N.Y. 1889); *Minnick v. Union Insurance Co.*, 40 F. 369 (C.C.W.D.Mich. 1889); *Rike v. Floyd*, 42 F. 247 (C.C.S.D.Ohio 1890); *Niblock v. Alexander*, 44 F. 306 (C.C.D.Ind. 1890); *Paul v. Baltimore & Ohio & Chicago Railroad Co.*, 44 F. 513 (C.C.D.Ind. 1890); *Herndon v. Southern Railroad Co.*, 73 F. 307 (C.C.E.D.N.C. 1896).

21. 38 F. 673 (C.C.E.D.Tenn. 1889).

22. *Huskins v. Cincinnati, New Orleans & Texas Pacific Railway Co.*, 37 F. 504 (C.C.N.D.Tenn. 1889); *Rike v. Floyd*, 42 F. 247 (C.C.S.D.Ohio 1890).

23. 137 U.S. 451 (1890).

24. *Malone v. Richmond & Danville Railroad Co.*, 35 F. 625 (C.C.E.D.N.C. 1888).

25. *In re Pennsylvania Co.*, 137 U.S. 454–55.

26. Ibid., p. 456.

27. Ibid., p. 457.

28. Ibid.

29. Ibid.

30. Ibid.

31. 142 U.S. 459 (1892).

32. Ibid., p. 467.

33. Ibid.

34. Two Justices, Harlan and Field, dissented. 142 U.S. 469.

35. Removal prevented by jurisdictional amount requirement: *Tod v. Cleveland & Mahoning Valley Railway Co.*, 65 F. 145 (C.C.A. 6 1894); *Tucker v. Interstate Life Association*, 17 S.E. 532 (Sup. Ct. N.C. 1893). Removal prevented by tighter timing requirement: *Davis v. Chicago & Northwestern Railway Co.*, 46 F.307 (C.C.N.D.Iowa 1891); *Hobart v. Illinois Central Railroad Co.*, 81 F. 5 (C.C.N.D.Iowa 1897); *Mason v. Interstate Consolidated Street Railway Co.*, 49 N.E. 645 (Sup. Jud. Ct. Mass. 1898).

36. *Wilder v. Virginia, Tennessee & Carolina Steel & Iron Co.*, 46 F. 676, 682–83 (C.C.W.D.Va. 1891) (Fuller, C.J.); *Gann v. Northeastern Railroad Co.*, 57 F. 417, 420 (C.C.N.D.Ga. 1891) (Lamar, J.).

37. *Fisk v. Henarie*, 142 U.S. 459 (1892). Compare the decision below, *Fisk v. Henarie*, 32 F. 417, 421–24 (C.C.D.Oreg. 1887), where plaintiff moved for remand on four separate grounds, including both the lateness of the petition and the lack of complete diversity.

38. 153 U.S. 192, 197 (1894).

39. The successor treatise to Dillon on removal put forward the *Whalen–Thouron* rule as the correct federal rule. Henry Campbell Black, *A Treatise on the Laws and Practice Governing the Removal of Causes from State Courts to Federal Courts* (St. Paul, 1898), pp. 217–20. The major rival treatise, written from a states' rights perspective and critical of expanded federal jurisdiction, conceded that the *Whelan–Thouron* rule was "possibly" the law but maintained that it was, in any event, incorrect. See Moon, *Removal of Causes*, pp. 576–87. Moon's views opposing the minimum diversity rule were considered and rejected in *Seaboard Air Line Railway v. North Carolina Railroad Co.*, 123 F. 629, 631 (C.C.E.D.N.C. 1903), where the court declared that the minimum diversity rule was followed "in nearly all the other circuits." A minority of decisions rejected the *Whelan–Thouron* rule. See, for example, *Anderson v. Bowers*, 43 F. 321 (C.C.N.D.Iowa 1890); *In re Cilley*, 58 F. 977 (C.C.N.H. 1893); *City of Terre Haute v. Evansville & Terre Haute Railroad Co.*, 106 F. 545 (C.C.D.Ind. 1901); *Campbell v. Milliken*, 119 F. 982 (C.C.D.Colo. 1902).

40. *Haire v. Rome Railroad Co.*, 57 F. 321 (C.C.N.D.Ga. 1891); *Hall v. Chattanooga Agricultural Works*, 48 F. 599 (C.C.E.D.Tenn. 1891); *Jackson & Sharp v. Pearson*, 60 F. 113 (C.C.D.Ky. 1892); *City of Detroit v. Detroit City Railway Co.*, 54 F. 1 (C.C.E.D.Mich. 1893) (Taft, J.); *Cassidy v. Atlanta & Charlotte Air Line Railway Co.*, 109 F. 673 (C.C.W.D.N.C. 1901); *Holmes v. Southern Railway Co.*, 125 F. 301 (C.C.W.D.N.C. 1903); *Baird v. Richmond & Danville Railroad Co.*, 18 S.E. 698 (Sup. Ct. N.C. 1893). The minimum diversity rule was accepted, though not applied, in *Boatmen's Bank of St. Louis, Mo. v. Fritzlen*, 135 F. 650 (C.C.A. 8 1905); *Adelbert College of Western Reserve University v. Toledo, Wabash & Western Railway Co.*, 47 F. 836 (C.C.N.D.Ohio 1891); *Bane v. Keefer*, 66 F. 610 (C.C.D.Ind. 1895); *Bonner v. Meikle*, 77 F. 485 (C.C.D.Nev. 1896); *Seaboard Air Line Railway v. North Carolina Railroad Co.*, 123 F. 629 (C.C.E.D.N.C. 1903).

41. *Pollock v. Farmers' Loan & Trust Co.*, 157 U.S. 429, 518, 516 (1895).

42. Ibid., pp. 533–34, 553.

43. *Pollock v. Farmers' Loan & Trust Co.*, 157 U.S. 429, 586, 607 (1895) (Field, J., concurring).

44. 158 U.S. 601, 686, 695 (Brown, J., dissenting). See Arnold M. Paul, *Conservative Crisis and the Rule of Law: Attitudes of Bar and Bench, 1887–1895* (New York, 1969), pp. 159–220; William Lasser, "The Supreme Court in Periods of Critical Realignment," *Journal of Politics* 47 (1985): 1174; Wayne K. Hobson, *The American Legal Profession and the Organizational Society, 1890–1930* (New York, 1986), pp. 255–59.

45. Quoted in Editorial notes, *American Law Review* 30 (1896): 266. On the federal courts in the election of 1896 generally, see Alan F. Westin, "The Supreme Court, The Populist Movement and the Campaign of 1896," *Journal of Politics* 15 (1953): 3.

46. Altgeld's speech was reported in "Current Topics," *Albany Law Journal* 54 (1896): 257, 259.

47. Irving Browne, "The Lawyer's Easy Chair," *Green Bag* 8 (1896): 303.

48. Keller, *Affairs of State,* p. 583; Samuel Eliot Morrison and Henry Steele Commager, *The Growth of the American Republic,* vol. 2 (New York, 1962), pp. 358–61; Stanley L. Jones, *The Presidential Election of 1896* (Madison, WI, 1964), chap. 21.

49. See, for example, *Ober v. Gallagher,* 2 Otto (93 U.S.) 99 (1876); *Blake v. McKim,* 13 Otto (103 U.S.) 336 (1880). The Court refused to decide whether complete diversity was a constitutional requirement in the *Case of the Sewing Machine Companies,* 18 Wall. (85 U.S.) 553, 586–87 (1873). See Moon, *Removal of Causes,* pp. 339–44, esp. n. 5.

50. For example, *Smith v. Lyon,* 133 U.S. 315 (1890); *Fisk v. Henarie,* 142 U.S. 459 (1894); *Shaw v. Quincy Mining Co.,* 145 U.S. 444 (1892); *Martin's Administrator v. Baltimore & Ohio Railroad Co.,* 151 U.S. 673 (1894): "The recent acts of Congress have tended more and more to contract the jurisdiction of the courts of the United States" (p. 687). See Dillon, *Removal of Causes,* 5th ed. (1889), p. 3; Black, *Treatise,* pp. 11–12., 40–45; Moon, *Removal of Causes,* p. 46 and cases cited in n. 4.

Similarly, in the area of review over state court decisions involving federal law issues, the Court narrowed its scope of review between 1888 and 1894 in an apparent effort to cut its docket. Herman Trautman, "Federal Right Jurisdiction and the Declaratory Remedy," *Vanderbilt Law Review* 7 (1954): 445. The Justices also supported the Evarts Act which became law in 1891 and made the decisions of the new courts of appeals final in diversity actions (though allowing the Supreme Court to hear appeals in such cases as a matter of its discretion). The Justices strongly favored a drastic cut in the number of diversity cases the Court would hear. See King, *Melville Weston Fuller,* pp. 148–51.

51. 25 Stat. 433, 434, sec. 2; *Tennessee v. Union & Planters' Bank,* 152 U.S. 454 (1894); *Mexican National Railroad Co. v. Davidson,* 157 U.S. 201 (1895); *Texas & Pacific Railroad Co. v. Cody,* 166 U.S. 606 (1897). Moon, *Removal of Causes,* pp. 104–6; Black, *Treatise,* pp. 31–32 (stating rule less comprehensively). In *Madisonville Traction Co. v. Saint Bernard Mining Co.,* 196 U.S. 239, 245–46 (1905), the Court stated that four decisions between 1888 and 1895 "settled" the rule that "a suit cannot be removed from a state court, unless it could have been brought originally in the Circuit Court of the United States."

52. See n. 51.

53. 137 U.S. 456.

54. 199 U.S. 260 (1905).

55. Ibid., pp. 270–73.

56. *City of Cleveland v. Cleveland, Columbus, Cincinnati & St. Louis Railway Co.,* 147 F. 171 (C.C.A. 6 1906); *Southern Railway Co. v. Thomason,* 146 F. 972 (C.C.A. 4 1906); *Armstrong v. Kansas City Southern Railway Co.,* 192 F. 608 (C.C.W.D.Ark. 1911).

57. Dobie, *Handbook,* p. 388.

58. See, for example, the testimony of various representatives of business interests who testified before Congress in 1932. "Limiting Jurisdiction of Federal Courts," Hearing before the Committee on the Judiciary of the United States House of Representatives, 72 Cong., 1 Sess. (1932). In defending diversity jurisdiction the representatives frequently misstated the law, relied on sweeping but vague and inflated factual allegations, and often placed essentially contradictory assertions on the record.

59. As the subsequent text makes clear, the discussion of local prejudice here refers only to cases within the system of corporate diversity jurisdiction and, in particular, does not include any case where race or ethnicity was a factor.

60. The attorney was appearing before the House Judiciary Committee as part of a major effort by corporate interests to oppose restrictions on diversity jurisdiction. The hearings, in fact, were regarded as unusually important because, shortly before they began, the Senate Judiciary Committee had approved a bill that would abolish diversity jurisdiction. The bank's attorney was attempting to bolster the case for preserving diversity by highlighting the dangers of local prejudice in the state courts. In this critical context and presumably after ample time for consultation and preparation, it seems particularly revealing that he could come up with only one weak example of prejudicial conduct and none that had actually occurred in a state court. "Limiting Jurisdiction of Federal Courts," Hearings before the Committee on the Judiciary of the United States House of Representatives, 72 Cong., 1 Sess. (1932), p. 63 (statement of Washington Bowie, representing the Fidelity & Deposit Co. of Baltimore) (emphasis added).

61. Sen. Doc. No. 338, 62 Cong., 2 Sess. (1912), vol. 2, p. 977 (statement of Gardiner Lathrop, general counsel, Atchison, Topeka & Santa Fe Railroad Co.); Sen. Doc. No. 90, 62 Cong., 1 Sess. (1911), p. 98 (statement of Theodore W. Reath, general solicitor, Norfolk & Western Railway Co.).

62. "Limiting Jurisdiction of Federal Courts," Hearings before the Committee on the Judiciary of the United States House of Representatives, 72 Cong., 1 Sess. (1932), pp. 29, 31 (statement of J. H. Doyle); and p. 11 (statement of Paul Howland).

63. See, for example, Harry N. Scheiber, "Federalism and the American Economic Order, 1789–1910," *Law and Society Review* 10 (1975): 84; Charles W. McCurdy, "American Law and the Marketing Structure of the Large Corporation, 1875–1890," *Journal of Economic History* 38 (1978): 631.

64. 1 Wall. (68 U.S.) 175 (1864).

65. See, for example, "Limiting Jurisdiction of Federal Courts," Hearing before the Committee on the Judiciary of the United States House of Representatives, 72 Cong., 1 Sess. (1932), pp. 35–37 (statement of James A. Emery, general counsel, National Association of Manufacturers), and pp. 53–55 (statement of Paul V. Keyser, counsel of the Investment Bankers Association of America).

66. This, of course, assumes that it was "local prejudice," rather than reasonable interpretations of the law and facts of a case, that was actuating the state courts. In at least some cases that would appear to be a false assumption. See, for example, Charles Fairman, "Justice Samuel F. Miller," *Political Science Quarterly* 50 (1935): 32; Fairman, *Reconstruction and Reunion 1864–1888* (New York, 1971), pp. 910–1116.

67. "Limitation of Venue in Certain Actions Brought Under the Employers' Liability Act," Hearings before Subcommittee No. 4 of the Committee on the Judiciary of the House of Representatives, 80 Cong., 1 Sess. (1947), p. 167 (letter from Louis E. Miller to Hon. Earl Michener, April 1, 1947); see also p. 158 (letter from J. P. Marshall, state legislative representative, Brotherhood of Railroad Trainmen to Hon. John E. Jennings, Jr., February 20, 1947), and p. 152 (letter from F. G. Pellett, state representative, Brotherhood of Railroad Trainmen to Hon. Earl C. Michener, March 20, 1947).

68. Office of the Attorney General of the United States, *Annual Report, 1892,* p. xvii.

69. In his study of state and federal trial courts in Alameda County, California, Lawrence Friedman uncovered some cases that suggest that corporate employees may have used improper or unethical tactics in attempting to influence trials. See Lawrence M. Friedman, "Civil Wrongs: Personal Injury Law in the Late 19th Century," *American Bar Foundation Research Journal* (1987): 351, 371.

70. 137 U.S. 457. The Court subsequently reaffirmed its statements in *Pennsylvania,* but it did nothing to elaborate them. *Fisk v. Henarie,* 142 U.S. 459, 468 (1892); *Bellaire v. Baltimore and Ohio Railroad Co.,* 146 U.S. 117, 118 (1892). See Black, *Treatise,* pp. 228–33; Moon, *Removal of Causes,* pp. 587–91.

71. *Ellison v. Louisville & Nashville Railroad Co.,* 112 F. 805, 810 (C.C.A. 6 1902).

72. Black, *Treatise,* pp. 228–33; Moon, *Removal of Causes,* pp. 587–91; James Hamilton Lewis, *Removal of Causes from State to Federal Courts* (New York, 1923), pp. 362–65. For example, *Herndon v. Southern Railway Co.,* 73 F. 307 (C.C.E.D.N.C. 1896); *Bonner v. Meikle,* 77 F. 485 (C.C.D.Nev. 1896).

73. *P. Schwenk & Co. v. Strang,* 59 F. 209, 211 (C.C.A. 8 1893).

74. *Ellison v. Louisville & Nashville Railroad Co.,* 112 F. 805, 807 (C.C.A. 6 1902).

75. See, for example, the court's awkward and unsatisfactory struggle with the problems of applying the fraudulent joinder doctrine in *Shane v. Butte Electric Railway Co.,* 150 F. 801, 808–11 (C.C.D. Mont. 1906).

76. *City of Detroit v. Detroit City Railway Co.,* 54 F. 1, 19 (C.C.E.D.Mich. 1893) (Taft, J.). In a personal letter in 1922, Taft wrote that "the whole federal system is based on the fear of local prejudice, and therefore the very existence of the federal courts is an intimation not wholly complimentary to state courts, and not wholly satisfactory to the local litigants if they lose" (William Howard Taft to Sir William R. Meredith, August 19, 1922, William Howard Taft Papers, Reel 224). I wish to express my thanks to Professor Robert C. Post for calling this letter to my attention.

77. For example, *Ellison v. Louisville & Nashville Railroad Co.*, 112 F. 805 (C.C.A. 6 1902); *Walcott v. Watson*, 46 F. 529 (C.C.D.Nev. 1891); *Bradley v. Ohio River and Charleston Railway Co.*, 78 F. 387 (C.C.W.D.N.C. 1896) (finding local prejudice but remanding for lack of diversity).

78. *Haire v. Rome Railroad Co.*, 57 F. 321 (C.C.N.D.Ga. 1891); *Carpenter v. Chicago, Milwaukee & St. Paul Railway Co.*, 47 F. 535 (C.C.N.D.Iowa 1891).

79. *Minnick v. Union Insurance Co.*, 40 F. 369 (C.C.W.D.Mich. 1889); *Durkee v. Illinois Central Railroad Co.*, 81 F. 1 (C.C.N.D.Iowa 1897); *Crotts v. Southern Railway Co.*, 90 F. 1 (C.C.W.D.N.C. 1898); *Parks v. Southern Railway Co.*, 90 F. 3 (C.C.W.D.N.C. 1898). Compare *Parker v. Vanderbilt*, 136 F. 246 (C.C.W.D.N.C. 1905).

80. Among the small number of reported cases in which defendants produced evidence of local prejudice, many arose from disputes that had become significant public issues. See, for example, *City of Detroit v. Detroit City Railway Co.*, 54 F. 1 (C.C.E.D.Mich. 1893) (Taft, J.); *County Court of Taylor County v. Baltimore & Ohio Railroad Co.*, 35 F. 161 (C.C.D.W.Va. 1888); *City of Tacoma v. Wright*, 84 F. 836 (C.C.D.Wash. 1898); *Montgomery County v. Cochran*, 116 F. 985 (C.C.M.D.Ala. 1902), rev'd, 199 U.S. 260 (1905).

A special situation apparently arose in North Carolina in suits involving the Southern Railway Company. See *Herndon v. Southern Railroad Co.*, 73 F. 307 (C.C.E.D.N.C. 1896); *Herndon v. Southern Railroad Co.*, 76 F. 398 (C.C.E.D.N.C. 1896); *City of Durham v. Southern Railway Co.*, 121 F. 894 (C.C. E.D..N.C. 1903); *Seaboard Air Line Railway v. North Carolina Railroad Co.*, 123 F. 629 (C.C.E.D.N.C. 1903). See *Crotts v. Southern Railway Co.*, 90 F. 1 (C.C.W.D.N.C. 1898); *Parks v. Southern Railway Co.*, 90 F. 3 (C.C.W.D.N.C. 1898); *Holmes v. Southern Railway Co.*, 125 F. 301 (C.C.W.D.N.C. 1903).

81. *Carson & Rand Lumber Co. v. Holtzclaw*, 39 F. 885, 887 (C.C.E.D.Mo. 1889). Agreeing: *Minnick v. Union Insurance Co.*, 40 F. 369 (C.C.W.D.Mich. 1889).

82. *P. Schwenck & Co. v. Strang*, 59 F. 209, 210 (C.C.A. 8 1893).

83. In 1945, twenty-four federal district and circuit judges in the Ninth Circuit agreed that an actual prejudice standard was workable. They urged Congress to abolish general diversity jurisdiction and maintain only a special diversity jurisdiction based on proof of actual prejudice. See Hearing before the Committee on the Judiciary of the United States Senate on S. 466, 79 Cong., 1 Sess. (1945) (statement of William Denman, judge of the United States Circuit Court for the Ninth Circuit, on behalf of twenty-four circuit and district court judges in the Ninth Circuit). In his private correspondence, Justice Louis D. Brandeis proposed the same idea. See *"Half Brother, Half Son": The Letters of Louis D. Brandeis to Felix Frankfurter*, ed. Melvin I. Urofsky and David W. Levy (Norman, OK, 1991), p. 576.

84. 14 Stat. 27 (1866).

85. Congress modified the original act in 1874. See Rev. Stat. (1874) sec. 641. See also Herman Belz, *Reconstructing the Union: Theory and Practice During the Civil War Era* (Ithaca, NY, 1969); Fairman, *Reconstruction and Reunions;* Harold M. Hyman, *A More Perfect Union: The Impact of the Civil War and Reconstruction* (New York, 1973); Harold M. Hyman and William M. Wiecek, *Equal Justice Under Law: Constitutional Development 1835–1875* (New York, 1982).

86. 23 Fed. Cas. 869 (C.C.W.D.Tx. 1874).

87. Ibid., p. 870.

88. Ibid., p. 871.

89. *Blyew v. United States*, 11 Wall. (80 U.S.) 581, 599 (1871) (Bradley, J., dissenting).

90. 100 U.S. 457, 479, 480, 482 (1879) (Bradley, J., dissenting).

91. Morton Keller, *Affairs of State: Public Life in Late Nineteenth Century America* (Cambridge, MA, 1977), p. 223.

92. Howard N. Rabinowitz, *Race Relations in the Urban South, 1865–1890* (New York, 1978); Leon F. Litwack, *Been in the Storm So Long: The Aftermath of Slavery* (New York, 1981); C. Vann Woodward, *The Strange Career of Jim Crow* (New York, 1974).

93. For example, *Blyew v. United States*, 13 Wall. (80 U.S.) 581 (1871); *United States v. Cruikshank*, 92 U.S. 542 (1875); *United States v. Reese*, 92 U.S. 214 (1876); *Hall v. DeCuir*, 95 U.S. 485 (1878). See William E. Wiecek, *Liberty Under Law: The Supreme Court in American Life* (Baltimore, 1988), pp. 82–109.

94. *Tennessee v. Davis,* 100 U.S. 257 (1879); *Strauder v. West Virginia,* 100 U.S. 303 (1879); *Virginia v. Rives,* 100 U.S. 313 (1879); *Ex parte Virginia,* 100 U.S. 339 (1879).

95. 100 U.S. 318.

96. Ibid., p. 319.

97. Ibid.

98. Ibid., p. 321. In one of the companion cases, *Ex parte Virginia,* 100 U.S. 339 (1880), the Court refused to block a federal prosecution against a state judge who purposely excluded blacks from his juries.

99. Ibid., pp. 321–22.

100. See Anthony G. Amsterdam, "Criminal Prosecutions Affecting Federally Guaranteed Civil Rights: Federal Removal and Habeas Corpus Jurisdiction to Abort State Court Trial," *University of Pennsylvania Law Review* 113 (1965): 793, 814–28, 851–63; Note, "Federal Jurisdiction: The Civil Rights Removal Statute Revisited," *Duke Law Journal* 136 (1967); *Georgia v. Rachel,* 384 U.S. 780 (1966); *City of Greenwood v. Peacock,* 384 U.S. 808 (1966).

101. Wiecek, *Liberty Under Law,* argues bluntly that the Court's decisions construing the rights of the freedmen in the late nineteenth century stemmed from a "results-oriented pro-segregation bias" (p. 103).

102. Sen. Rep. No. 693, 46 Cong., 2 Sess. (1880), p. xxiii.

103. Ibid., p. x, and also see Majority Report, pp. iii–viii; Minority Report, pp. ix–xxv.

104. Ibid., p. iv.

105. Ibid., p. v.

106. Ibid., p. xvii.

107. For an interesting discussion of the Court's views on protecting blacks and other groups, see Aviam Soifer, "The Paradox of Paternalism and Laissez-Faire Constitutionalism: United States Supreme Court, 1888–1921," *Law and History Review* 5 (1987): 249.

108. *Neal v. Delaware,* 103 U.S. 370, 392–93 (1880); *In re Wood,* 140 U.S. 278, 284–86 (1891); *Gibson v. Mississippi,* 162 U.S. 565, 584–85 (1896); *Murray v. Louisiana,* 163 U.S. 101, 105–7 (1896). See Dillon, *Removal of Causes,* 5th ed. (1889), pp. 73–76.

109. 103 U.S. 370 (1880).

110. Ibid., pp. 393–95.

111. Ibid., p. 395.

112. Ibid., pp. 393–94.

113. The Supreme Court was quite aware of the severe limits that circumscribed the effectiveness of an appeal under Section 25 as a general remedy for abuses in the state courts. Indeed, the Court had previously recognized that in practice the difference between the two types of procedural "remedies"—immediate removal to a federal trial court or delayed appeal to the United States Supreme Court after trial and appeal in a state court system—could be of great importance.

Less than a decade before *Rives* and *Neal,* for example, the Court had recognized and dealt forcefully—and quite differently—with a similar type of enforcement and remedy problem. In *Tarble's Case,* 80 U.S. (13 Wall.) 397 (1871), the Justices addressed the question of whether a state judicial officer could issue a writ of habeas corpus for an underage boy held as an enlisted soldier by the United States Army. If state courts were allowed to issue such writs, the Court reasoned, the possibilities of delay, public prejudice, and misuse of state judicial authority could easily render ineffective the federal government's remedy of an appeal to the United States Supreme Court. Because a Section 25 remedy would therefore be inadequate, the Court held that issuance of the writ was beyond the state's authority:

> The experience of the late rebellion has shown us that, in times of great popular excitement, there may be found in every State large numbers ready and anxious to embarrass the operations of the government, and easily persuaded to believe every step taken for the enforcement of its authority illegal and void. Power to issue writs of *habeas corpus* for the discharge of soldiers in the military service, in the hands of parties thus disposed, might be used, and often would be used, to the great detriment of the public service. In many exigencies the measures of the National government might in this way be entirely bereft of

their efficacy and value. An appeal in such cases to this court, to correct the erroneous action of these officers, would afford no adequate remedy. [Ibid., pp. 408–9]

Similarly, Chief Justice John Marshall had made the same point in his classic opinion in *Osborn v. Bank of the United States,* 9 Wheat. (22 U.S.) 738, 822–23 (1824). Marshall stressed the danger that appellate review of state court decisions could, in some kinds of cases, be insufficient to protect federal rights. A formal review of an "insulated point" of law might be inadequate to correct a judgment "after it has received that shape which may be given to it by another tribunal." The court below, in other words, could frame the issues and establish the factual record in ways that would essentially preempt the significance of the legal point on which the appellate court could properly reverse the decision. As a result, Marshall stated, appellate review of state decisions by the United States Supreme Court—as compared with access to a federal forum in the first instance—could be an "insecure remedy."

114. *United States v. Reynolds,* 235 U.S. 133 (1914); William Cohen, "Negro Involuntary Servitude in the South, 1865–1940: A Preliminary Analysis," *Journal of Southern History* 42 (1976): 31, 53–54.

115. Joe Williamson, *The Crucible of Race: Black–White Relations in the American South Since Emancipation* (New York, 1984); Rabinowitz, *Race Relations in the Urban South;* John Cell, *The Highest Stage of White Supremacy: The Origins of Segregation in South Africa and the American South* (New York, 1982); Woodward, *The Strange Career of Jim Crow;* Howard N. Rabinowitz, "More Than the Woodward Thesis: Assessing the *Strange Career of Jim Crow,*" *Journal of American History* 75 (1988): 842; C. Vann Woodward, "*Strange Career* Critics: Long May They Persevere," *Journal of American History* 75 (1988): 857.

116. 163 U.S. 537 (1896).

117. Removal was discussed and denied in *Gibson v. Mississippi,* 162 U.S. 565 (1896); *Charley Smith v. Mississippi,* 162 U.S. 592 (1896); *Murray v. Louisiana,* 163 U.S. 101 (1896); *Williams v. Mississippi,* 170 U.S. 213 (1898). Motions to quash criminal indictments were considered and granted in *Carter v. Texas,* 177 U.S. (1900) and *Rogers v. Alabama,* 192 U.S. 226 (1904) and denied in *Brownfield v. South Carolina,* 189 U.S. 426 (1903) and *Thomas v. Texas,* 212 U.S. 278 (1909). On occasion, the Court seemed apologetic: *Gibson v. Mississippi,* 162 U.S. 591–92. The jury abuses were not confined exclusively to blacks; see *Kentucky v. Powers,* 201 U.S. 1 (1906).

118. Black, *Treatise,* p. 50 (emphasis added).

Chapter 7

1. For example, *Brady v. Indemnity Insurance Co. of North America,* 68 F. 2d 302 (C.C.A. 6 1933); *El Paso & Southwestern Co. v. Riddle,* 287 F. 173 (W.D.Tx. 1923), aff'd 294 F. 892 (C.C.A. 5 1923); *Genuine Panama Hat Works, Inc. v. Webb,* 36 F. 2d 265 (S.D.N.Y. 1929); *National Union Fire Insurance Co. v. Chesapeake & Ohio Railway Co.,* 4 F. Supp. 25 (E.D.Ky. 1933); *Beddings v. Great Eastern Stages,* 6 F. Supp. 529 (E.D.Ill. 1934); *St. Louis-San Francisco Railway Co. v. Oxford,* 298 S.W. 207 (Sup.Ct.Ark. 1927); *St. Louis-San Francisco Railway Co. v. Oxford,* 298 S.W. 207 (Sup.Ct.Ark. 1927); *Culp v. Lincoln National Life Insurance Co.,* 161 S.E. 717 (Sup.Ct.N.C. 1932).

2. For insurance plaintiffs joinder was available only when they could rely on special statutory or contractual provisions. The courts generally held that claims arising under different contracts were separable and that only the parties to an agreement could be joined in an action on a contract. *Des Moines Elevator & Grain Co. v. Underwriters' Grain Association,* 63 F.2d 103 (C.C.A. 8 1933); *Lynch v. Springfield Fire & Marine Insurance Co.,* 15 F.2d 725 (E.D.N.Y. 1926); *Automobile Insurance Co. of Hartford, Conn. v. Harrison,* 7 F. Supp. 846 (S.D.N.Y. 1934); *McVay v. Mutual Benefit Health & Accident Association of Omaha,* 23 F. Supp. 642 (N.D.Okla. 1938). When there were special facts or a statute made insurance companies directly liable to third parties, the tactic could defeat removal. For example, *Morrell v. Lalonde,* 271 F. 19 (D.R.I. 1921); *Hellenthan v. John Hancock Mutual Life Insurance Co.,* 31 F.2d 997 (W.D.Wash. 1929); *Lake v. Texas News Co.,* 51 F.2d 862 (S.D.Tx. 1931).

3. *McAllister v. Chesapeake & Ohio Railway Co.,* 243 U.S. 302 (1917); *Chicago & Alton*

Railroad Co., 243 U.S. 422 (1917); *Lee v. Central of Georgia Railway Co.*, 252 U.S. 109 (1920). But see *Hay v. May Department Stores Co.*, 271 U.S. 318 (1926).

4. *Wilson v. Republic Iron & Steel Co.*, 257 U.S. 92 (1921).

5. Note, "Separation of Causes in Removal Proceedings," *Harvard Law Review* 41 (1928): 1048.

6. Compare, for example, *Forrest v. Southern Railway Co.*, 20 F. Supp. 753 (W.D.S.C. 1937) with *Forest v. Southern Railway Co.*, 20 F. Supp. 851 (W.D.S.C. 1937); and *Hancock v. Missouri–Kansas–Texas Railroad Co.*, 28 F.2d 45 (W.D.Okla. 1928) with *Watson v. Chevrolet Motor Co. of St. Louis*, 68 F.2d 686 (C.C.A. 8 1934).

7. For example, *Leonard v. St. Joseph Lead Co.*, 75 F.2d 390 (C.C.A. 8 1935); *Martin v. Matson Navigation Co.*, 239 F. 188 (W.D.Wash. 1917); *Plunkett v. Gulf Refining Co.*, 259 F. 968 (N.D.Ga. 1919); *Zigich v. Tuolumne Copper Mining Co.*, 260 F. 1014 (D.Mont. 1919); *Scherrer v. Foster*, 5 F.2d 236 (E.D.Ill. 1925); *Henderlong v. Standard Oil Co. of California*, 17 F.2d 184 (N.D.Cal. 1926); *Stokes v. Great Southern Lumber Co.*, 21 F.2d 185 (S.D.Miss. 1927); *Morefield v. Ozark Pipe Line Corporation*, 27 F.2d 890 (N.D.Okla. 1928); *Johnson v. Coast Manufacturing & Supply Co.*, 53 F.2d 271 (S.D.Cal. 1931); *Davis v. St. Louis & San Francisco Railway Co.*, 8 F. Supp. 519 (N.D.Okla. 1934); *Toadvine v. Cincinnati, New Orleans & Texas Pacific Railway Co.*, 20 F. Supp. 226 (E.D.Ky. 1937).

8. For example, *Kraus v. Chicago, Burlington & Quincy Railroad Co.*, 16 F.2d 79 (C.C.A. 8 1926); *Breymann v. Pennsylvania, Ohio & Detroit Railroad Co.*, 38 F.2d 209 (C.C.A. 6 1930); *Martin v. Norfolk & Western Railway Co.*, 43 F.2d 293 (C.C.A. 4 1930); *Johnson v. Noble*, 64 F.2d 396 (C.C.A. 10 1933); *Morris v. E.I. Du Pont de Nemours & Co.*, 68 F.2d 788 (C.C.A. 8 1934); *Beal v. Chicago, Burlington & Quincy Railroad Co.*, 298 F. 180 (E.D.Mo. undated [circa 1924]); *La Flower v. Merrill*, 28 F.2d 784 (N.D.Cal. 1928); *Nelson v. Arcade Investment Co.*, 30 F.2d 695 (D.Minn. 1929); *Donaldson v. Tucson Gas, Electric Light & Power Co.*, 14 F. Supp. 246 (D.Ariz. 1935); *Newton v. Southern Grocery Stores, Inc.*, 16 F. Supp. 164 (E.D.S.C. 1936); Note, "The Content of 'Separable Controversy' for Purposes of Removal to the Federal Courts," *Columbia Law Review* 36 (1936): 794, 800–2.

On occasion the circuit courts of appeals criticized the lower courts for too readily denying remands. The Eighth Circuit, for example, instructed that "doubtful issues of law and fact in the cases are to be tried in the court which has jurisdiction, and are not to be determined in the removal proceedings." Reversing with express direction that the case be remanded, it allowed its displeasure to show. "[I]t is difficult to understand why the appellees should have removed the case or why the lower court should have retained it." *Huffman v. Baldwin*, 82 F.2d 5, 7, 8, (C.C.A. 8 1936). Agreeing: *Norwalk v. Air-Way Electric Appliance Corp.*, 87 F.2d 317 (C.C.A. 2 1937).

9. *Tolbert v. Jackson*, 99 F.2d 513 (C.C.A. 5 1938); *Lake v. Texas News Co.*, 51 F.2d 862 (S.D.Tx. 1931); *Newton v. Southern Grocery Stores, Inc.*, 16 F. Supp. 164 (E.D.S.C. 1936); *Dwinelle v. Union Pacific Railroad Co.*, 16 F. Supp. 891 (D.Colo. 1936).

10. See, for example, William L. Prosser, "Joint Torts and Several Liability," *California Law Review* 25 (1937): 413, 414–18, 430–31, and note the qualification on p. 442; Edson R. Sutherland, "Joinder of Actions," *Michigan Law Review* 18 (1920): 571; Note, "Recent Trends in Joinder of Parties, Causes, and Counterclaims," *Columbia Law Review* 37 (1937): 462; Leon R. Yankwich, "Joinder of Parties in the Light of Recent Statutory Changes," *Southern California Law Review* 2 (1929): 315.

11. Annotation, 98 A.L.R. 1057, 1059–62 (1935).

12. United States Bureau of the Census, *The Statistical History of the United States* (Stamford, CT, 1965), p. 437; Robert A. Kagan, Bliss Cartwright, Lawrence M. Friedman, and Stanton Wheeler, "The Business of State Supreme Courts, 1870–1970," *Stanford Law Review* 30 (1977): 121, 134, 142–45.

13. Kagan et al., "The Business of State Supreme Courts," pp. 134, 142–45; Charles E. Clark and Harry Shulman, *A Study of Law Administration in Connecticut* (New Haven, CT, 1937), chart between pp. 14 and 15, 16, 166–76; Lawrence M. Friedman and Robert V. Percival, "A Tale of Two Courts: Litigation in Alameda and San Benito Counties," *Law & Society* 10 (1976): 281–83, 288; Director of the Administrative Office of the United States Courts, *Annual Report, 1948*, p. 133, Chart C2.

Although automobile tort suits created major problems for the courts, they were often outside the system of corporate diversity litigation. In well over half of the cases individuals sued other individuals, not corporations. The parties were often relatively equal, and they acted without benefit of prior litigation planning. They were citizens of the states where they happened to live, and the site of the accident that brought them together was fortuitous for both. In most cases the parties had no prior relationship that contributed to the ability of either to use informal pressures. They were literally related only by accident.

Insurance companies, of course, were often the real parties in interest, but the litigations were too diverse and conflicting to allow the companies to develop any consistent strategy to exploit the system in such cases. If insurance companies were involved, their interests could be on the plaintiff's side as well as the defendant's and on an individual's side as well as a corporation's. Often insurance companies were on both sides. See Clark and Shulman, *Study of Law Administration in Connecticut,* pp. 174–76. Also see Lawrence Blum, Sheldon Goldman, and Austin Sarat, "The Evolution of Litigation in the Federal Courts of Appeals, 1895–1975," *Law & Society Review* 16 (1981–82): 291, 305–6. By the early 1940s, slightly more than half of the automobile tort cases heard in the federal courts involved foreign corporations. That was, of course, a tiny sample of the total number of suits involving automobiles. Herbert Wechsler, "Federal Jurisdiction and the Revision of the Judicial Code," *Law & Contemporary Problems* 13 (1948): 216, 243.

When individuals brought tort suits involving automobiles against manufacturers or other foreign corporations, joinder continued to be a useful tool for defeating removal. See, for example, *Watson v. Chevrolet Motor Co. of St. Louis,* 68 F.2d 686 (C.C.A. 8 1934); *Haenni v. Craven,* 56 F.2d 261 (S.D.Tx. 1932); *Dwinelle v. Union Pacific Railroad Co.,* 16 F.Supp. 891 (D.Colo. 1936); *Siler v. Morgan Motor Co.,* 15 F.Supp. 468 (E.D.Ky. 1936). For a general summary of the substantive law applicable, see Charles J. Babbitt, *The Law Applied to Motor Vehicles,* 3rd ed. by Arthur W. Blakemore (Washington, DC, 1923) and 4th ed. (Rochester, NY, 1933).

14. Morton Keller, *The Life Insurance Enterprise, 1885–1910: A Study in the Limits of Corporate Power* (Cambridge, MA, 1963), pp. 187–88; Kagan et al., "The Business of the State Supreme Courts," pp. 134, 140 and n. 43. Also see Chapter 9.

15. Kermit L. Hall, *The Magic Mirror: Law in American History* (New York, 1989), pp. 212–14, 216–18, 257–60; Jerold S. Auerbach, *Unequal Justice: Lawyers and Social Change in Modern America* (New York, 1976), pp. 95–101, 102–29; Robert A. Silverman, *Law and Urban Growth: Civil Litigation in the Boston Trial Courts, 1880–1900* (Princeton, NJ, 1981), pp. 115–19, 137, 191 and n. 47; Clark and Shulman, *Law Administration in Connecticut,* pp. 171–73; Frank W. Munger, Jr., "Social Change and Tort Litigation: Industrialization, Accidents, and Trial Courts in Southern West Virginia, 1872–1940," *Buffalo Law Review* 36 (1987): 75, 108–9; Munger, "Miners and Lawyers: Law Practice and Class Conflict in Appalachia, 1872–1920," (unpublished manuscript). Compare H. Laurence Ross, *Settled Out of Court: The Social Process of Insurance Claims Adjustments* (Chicago, 1970), pp. 74–80; John P. Heinz and Edward O. Lauman, *Chicago Lawyers: The Social Structure of the Bar* (New York, 1982), esp. pp. 55–56, 79–83, 90–93, 112, 379–85; Maurice Rosenberg and Michael I. Sovern, "Delay and the Dynamics of Personal Injury Litigation," *Columbia Law Review* 59 (1959): 1115, 1166–68 and works cited on p. 1166, n. 1. For the growth of the night and part-time law school movement in the eighteen-nineties, see Robert Stevens, *Law School: Legal Education in America from the 1850's to the 1980's* (Chapel Hill, NC, 1983), esp. chap. 5.

16. Henry Wade Rogers, "The Ideals of the American Advocate—A Symposium," *Central Law Journal* 58 (1904): 423, 424. In 1905 Henry St. George Tucker, a prominent Virginia attorney, also stressed the close relationship between Christian ethics and the integrity of the bar as well as the need to "fearlessly and ruthlessly" root out "the unworthy member who brings dishonor upon the whole profession." See Henry St. George Tucker, "Review of Legislation of Year 1904–05," *American Law Review* 39 (1905): 801, 809–10, 812.

17. Quoted in William H. Harbaugh, *Lawyer's Lawyer: The Life of John W. Davis* (New York, 1973), p. 118.

Henry W. Taft, the brother of William Howard Taft and a senior partner in a prominent New York law firm, revealed the power and persistence of the elite bar's social attitudes. Looking back over his long career in 1941, Taft attempted what he regarded as a fair-minded commentary on the rapid increase in the number of Jewish lawyers in the city since the 1880s. Although he acknowledged that some social discrimination continued to exist, he attempted to minimize it by claiming that there was little hostility toward those Jews who were willing "to find some reasonable basis for removing from the minds of non-Jewish lawyers the racial prejudice which sometimes appears." He also praised Jewish lawyers for "their characteristic mental acquisitiveness." Henry W. Taft, *Legal Miscellanies: Six Decades of Changes and Progress* (New York, 1941), pp. 77–78.

For the role of ethnic hostility in the bar after the turn of the century, see Auerbach, *Unequal Justice,* chaps. 4, 5; Hall, *The Magic Mirror,* pp. 257–59.

18. Quoted in N.E.H. Hull, "Restatement and Reform: A New Perspective on the Origins of the American Law Institute," *Law and History Review* 8 (1990): 55, 63. See Robert Stevens, *Law School: Legal Education in America from the 1850's to the 1980's* (Chapel Hill, NC, 1983), pp. 98–102 and 125–26, n. 18.

19. David J. Brewer, "A Better Education the Great Need of the Profession," *Yale Law Journal,* 5 (1895): 1, 10.

20. Comment, *Virginia Law Register* 4 (1899): 768, 769.

21. Quoted in Hull, "Restatement and Reform," p. 63.

22. Orla B. Taylor, "The Abuse of Personal Injury Litigation," *Green Bag* 18 (1906): 193, 205.

23. Robert Monaghan, "The Liability Claim Racket," *Law and Contemporary Problems* 3 (1936): 491; *Chunes v. Duluth, Winnipeg & Pacific Railway Co.,* 298 F. 964 (D.Minn. 1924); J. Willard Hurst, *The Growth of American Law: The Lawmakers* (Boston, 1950), pp. 313–15, 320–25; William M. Wherry, "A Study of the Organization of Litigation and of the Jury Trial in the Supreme Court of New York County," *New York University Law Quarterly Review* 8 (1931): 396, 423.

24. J. L. Quackenbush, "The Abuse of Personal Injury Litigation," *Green Bag* 18 (1906): 193, 212.

25. Andrew J. Hirschl, "Personal Injury Actions: The Plaintiff's Standpoint," *Illinois Law Review* 1 (1906): 16, 17, 19.

26. Roger S. Warner, "Employers' Liability as an Industrial Problem," *Green Bag* 18 (1906): 185, 189.

27. Comment, *Yale Law Journal* 16 (1907): 427.

28. Warner, "Employers' Liability as an Industrial Problem," p. 189.

29. Clarence A. Lightner, "The Abuse of Personal Injury Litigation," *Green Bag* 18 (1906): 94.

30. Comment, *Virginia Law Register* 4 (1899): 768.

31. J. W. Donovan, "The Ideals of the American Advocate—A Symposium," *Central Law Journal* 58 (1904): 423, 427.

32. "The Law's Delays," *Green Bag* 17 (1905): 261; "The Abuse of Personal Injury Litigation," *Green Bag* 18 (1906): 193.

33. *Green Bag* 18 (1906): 185.

34. Ibid., p. 189.

35. R. B. Newcomb, "The Abuse of Personal Injury Litigation," *Green Bag* 18 (1906): 196, 197; Percy Werner, "The Abuse of Personal Injury Litigation," *Green Bag* 18 (1906): 201, 202.

36. Quackenbush, "The Abuse of Personal Injury Litigation," pp. 212, 213.

37. Everett P. Wheeler, "The American Judiciary," *Green Bag* 18 (1906): 14, 15. For other early examples of the new mood, see Samuel Maxwell, "To Assimilate the Pleadings, Practice and Procedure in the Federal Courts in Actions at Law and Suits in Equity to the Pleadings, Practice and Procedure of the Courts of Record of the State Where the Action Is Brought," *American Law Review* 35 (1901): 264; Editorial note, *American Law Review* 39 (1905): 598; "How Shall the Increased Business of the Courts of Many of the States Be Provided For?" *Central Law Journal* 63 (1906): 65.

38. Simeon E. Baldwin, "The Ideals of the American Advocate—A Symposium," *Central Law Journal* 58 (1904): 423.

39. Auerbach, *Unequal Justice,* pp. 40–53; Hurst, *Growth of American Law,* pp. 329–33, 361.

For a more general treatment discussing the internal tensions within the bar in the decades around the turn of the century, see Richard Hofstadter, *The Age of Reform: From Bryan to F.D.R.* (New York, 1955), pp. 156–64.

40. In 1917 the ABA passed a resolution urging local bar groups to foster such legal aid societies. By the early 1930s, bar groups were providing some sort of assistance to dozens of such societies. See Hurst, *Growth of American Law,* pp. 153, 365.

41. Sen. Doc. No. 338, 62 Cong., 2 Sess. (1912), vol. 2, p. 653.

42. Ibid., vol. 2, p. 648. Workers seemed often to express their dislike or distrust of personal injury attorneys, even while retaining or defending them when necessary. See Sen. Doc. No. 479, 62 Cong., 2 Sess. (1912), pp. 3, 4, 10, 13, 14. Sen. Rep. No. 553, Part 2, 62 Cong., 2 Sess. (1912), pp. 17, 18.

43. Felix Frankfurter and James M. Landis, *The Business of the Supreme Court: A Study in the Federal Judicial System* (New York, 1928), p. 131, n. 121; Office of the Attorney General of the United States, *Annual Report, 1937,* p. 2. See, for example, H.R. Rep. No. 1721, 70 Cong., 1 Sess. (1928) (Texas; new division sought).

44. Sen. Rep. No. 1843, 70 Cong., 2 Sess. (1929), p. 1; H.R. Rep. No. 2464, 70 Cong., 2 Sess. (1929), p. 1. See Edwin C. Surrency, *History of the Federal Courts* (New York, 1987), pp. 39–40; H.R. Rep. No. 825, 64 Cong., 1 Sess. (1916); "To Change the Judicial Circuits of the United States and to Create a Tenth Judicial Circuit," Hearing before the Committee on the Judiciary of the United States House of Representatives on H.R. 5690, 70 Cong., 1 Sess. (1928), *passim.*

45. U.S. Bureau of the Census, *Statistical History of the United States,* p. 14.

46. The percentages in this and the next two paragraphs are estimates based on the reasonable but artificial assumptions that the locations in which the federal courts sat were the largest cities and counties in the country and that the increase in court locations was relatively steady from year to year over the period. U.S. Bureau of the Census, *Statistical History of the United States,* p. 14; R. D. McKenzie, "The Rise of Metropolitan Communities," in *Recent Social Trends in the United States: Report of the President's Research Committee on Social Trends* (New York, 1933), pp. 445–46.

47. "Judicial Code and Judiciary," Hearings before a Subcommittee of the Committee on the Judiciary of the United States Senate on H.R. 3214, 80 Cong., 2 Sess. (1948), pp. 1–5 (statement of Sen. Spessard L. Holland of Florida); pp. 335–39 (statement of Sen. Claude Pepper of Florida).

48. There is a vast literature on the impact of the automobile on American culture. See, for example, Blaine A. Brownell, "A Symbol of Modernity: Attitudes Toward the Automobile in Southern Cities in the 1920s," *American Quarterly* 24 (1972): 20; James J. Flink, "Three Stages of American Automobile Consciousness," *American Quarterly* 24 (1972): 451; Eli Chinoy, *Automobile Workers and the American Dream* (New York, 1955). Two classic documents are by Robert S. Lynd and Helen M. Lynd, *Middletown: A Study in Modern American Culture* (New York, 1929), and *Middletown in Transition: A Study in Cultural Conflicts* (New York, 1937).

49. Alfred D. Chandler, Jr., ed., *Giant Enterprise: Ford, General Motors, and the Automobile Industry* (New York, 1964), pp. 10–11.

50. U.S. Bureau of the Census, *Statistical History of the United States,* p. 462; John B. Rae, *The Road and the Car in American Life* (Cambridge, MA, 1971), p. 56. See generally John B. Rae, *The American Automobile: A Brief History* (Chicago, 1965); Ralph C. Epstein, *The Automobile Industry: Its Economic and Commercial Development* (New York, 1972).

51. Daniel J. Boorstin, *The Americans: The Democratic Experience* (New York, 1973), pp. 548–55; U.S. Bureau of the Census, *Statistical History of the United States,* p. 462; Rae, *Road and Car in American Life,* p. 50. By the 1920s, too, regional differences in the ratio of automobiles to population were evening out: "The automobile culture became truly national in the 1920's as significant early regional differences in automobility lessened." See James J. Flink, *The Car Culture* (Cambridge, MA, 1975), pp. 141–42.

52. For those without a car, bus service began to offer an alternative that was considerably less expensive and often more convenient than the railroads. Specially designed passenger buses appeared in the mid-1920s, and intercity and interstate bus service became widely available. The production of passenger buses rose from 17,000 in 1925 to almost 59,000 ten years later and then

topped 100,000 in 1940. During the same years, passenger miles grew from 4.3 million in 1926 to 13.6 million in 1941. Intercity bus transportation grew most rapidly in the South and West where rail transportation remained less widely available than in other sections. See U.S. Bureau of the Census, *Statistical History of the United States,* p. 462; Rae, *Road and Car in American Life,* pp. 96–99; Malcolm M. Willey, "The Agencies of Communication," in *Recent Social Trends,* pp. 174–75.

53. The material in this and the following paragraph is from Albert C. Rose, "The Highway from the Railroad to the Automobile," in Jean Labatut and Wheaton J. Lane, eds., *Highways in Our National Life* (Princeton, N.J., 1950), pp. 78, 103, 107; U.S. Bureau of the Census, *Statistical History of the United States,* p. 459; Bruce E. Seeley, *Building the American Highway System: Engineers as Policy Makers* (Philadelphia, 1987), pp. 11–18, 35–46, 59–62, 88–93.

54. "Delay" is, of course, an extremely difficult factor to measure. To a large extent it is subjective, and to a large extent it may be caused by either or both of the parties and for any number of tactical reasons. See, for example, David S. Clark, "Adjudication to Administration: A Statistical Analysis of Federal District Courts in the Twentieth Century," *Southern California Law Review* 55 (1981): 65, 74 and n. 48; Hans Zeisel, Harry Kalven, Jr., and Bernard Buchholz, *Delay in the Court* (Boston, 1959), pp. 3–57; Hans Zeisel, "Delay by the Parties and Delay by the Courts," *Journal of Legal Education* 15 (1962): 27.

55. Clark, "Adjudication to Administration," pp. 108, 114, 120, 126.

56. Ibid., pp. 108, 114.

57. Ibid., pp. 114, 120.

58. Ibid., pp. 108, 114, 120, 126. For numbers based on a different and probably more exact measure developed later, see Will Shafroth, "Federal Judicial Statistics," *Law & Contemporary Problems* 13 (1948): 200, 201. Director of the Administrative Office of the United States Courts, *Annual Report, 1948,* pp. 16–17, 95.

59. See, for example, Henry Wade Rogers, "Legal Ethics," *Yale Law Journal* 16 (1907): 225, 244–45; Editorial, "Overcrowding of the Legal Profession," *Green Bag* 23 (1911): 324.

60. The commission's findings and recommendations are summarized in J. Noble Hayes, "New York," in "The Law's Delays," *Green Bag* 17 (1905): 299.

61. Frederick N. Judson, "The Quarter Century in American Jurisprudence," *American Law Review* 37 (1903): 481, 483–84.

62. Salter [*sic*] Storrs Clark, "Individualism and Legal Procedure," *Yale Law Journal* 14 (1905): 262, 263.

63. Quoted in Alpheus T. Mason, *William Howard Taft: Chief Justice* (New York, 1964), p. 56 (without emphasis added). See, for example, "Chief Justice Taft's Address," *American Bar Association Journal* 8 (1922): 333. The rise of the scientific, or at least scientistic, professional expert in the early twentieth century has been widely studied. Some of the more important works include Robert H. Wiebe, *The Search for Order, 1877–1920* (New York, 1967); Mary O. Furner, *Advocacy and Objectivity: A Crisis in the Professionalization of American Social Science, 1896–1905* (Lexington, KY, 1975); Thomas L. Haskell, *The Emergence of Professional Social Science: The American Social Science Association and the Nineteenth-Century Crisis of Authority* (Urbana, IL, 1977); Robert C. Bannister, *Sociology and Scientism: The American Quest for Objectivity, 1880–1940* (Chapel Hill, NC, 1987); Dorothy Ross, *The Origins of American Social Science* Cambridge, MA, 1991); David A. Hollinger, *Morris R. Cohen and the Scientific Ideal* (Cambridge, MA, 1975); Jerry Israel, ed., *Building the Organizational Society: Essays on Associational Activities in Modern America* (New York, 1972). For the professional manager-administrator, see Alfred D. Chandler, Jr., *The Visible Hand: The Managerial Revolution in American Business* (Cambridge, MA, 1977); Thomas K. McCraw, *Prophets of Regulation: Charles Francis Adams, Louis D. Brandeis, James M. Landis, Alfred E. Kahn* (Cambridge, MA, 1984). For the impact of scientism in the law, see Wayne K. Hobson, *The American Legal Profession and the Organizational Society, 1890–1930* (New York, 1986).

64. Clark, "Adjudication to Administration," pp. 105–6; Frankfurter and Landis, *Business of the Supreme Court,* pp. 144–45.

65. Henry P. Chandler, *Some Major Advances in the Federal Judicial System, 1922–1947* (St. Paul, 1963), p. 317.

66. Clark, "Adjudication to Administration," p. 86.

67. 42 Stat. 837 (1922). See H.R. Rep. No. 482, 67 Cong., 1 Sess. (1921); Mason, *William Howard Taft,* pp. 97–107. Much of the discussion in this and the next paragraphs is based on Frankfurter and Landis, *Business of the Supreme Court,* pp. 217–54; Chandler, *Some Major Advances,* pp. 313–66; Mason, *William Howard Taft, passim;* Peter Graham Fish, *The Politics of Federal Judicial Administration* (Princeton, NJ, 1973), pp. 3–90.

68. 53 Stat. 1223 (1939). See Henry P. Chandler, "The Administration of the Federal Courts," *Law & Contemporary Problems* 13 (1948): 182.

69. Clark, "Adjudication to Administration," p. 70.

70. Fish, *Politics of Federal Judicial Administration,* p. 182.

71. Clark, "Adjudication to Administration," pp. 86–87.

72. Office of the Attorney General of the United States, *Annual Report, 1930,* p. 5, *Annual Report, 1931,* pp. 6–7, *Annual Report, 1934,* pp. 5–6. *Annual Report,* 1937, p. 13.

73. Office of the Attorney General of the United States, *Annual Report,* 1936, p. 5, and see, *Annual Report, 1935,* p. 4.

74. Office of the Attorney General of the United States, *Annual Report, 1938,* pp. 5–6. The Attorney General's interest and research were related to President Franklin D. Roosevelt's plan to "pack" the Supreme Court. The President and his Attorney General based their court reform package largely on the need to overcome delay in the courts, and from 1935 or 1936 until 1938, the problem of delay took on special political resonance. See *Annual Report, 1937,* pp. 1–3 and the responses of the Judicial Conference on pp. 12–17, and *Annual Report, 1938,* pp. 17–22.

75. Clark, "Adjudication to Administration," pp. 114, 120, 126.

76. Emphasizing the "importance of accurate information as a basis for legislation," for example, the *Final Report* of the United States Industrial Commission in 1902 pointed to the growing body of statistical evidence that demonstrated the extreme dangers of industrial labor and highlighted the compelling finding that "in the United States more than twice as many employees are killed in proportion to the number employed as in any European country." H.R. Doc. No. 380, 57 Cong., 1 Sess. (1902), pp. 939, 912.

77. Beginning in 1892, for example, a movement for the enactment of uniform state laws threatened, at least in theory, to wipe out large areas of the federal common law. The National Conference of Commissioners on Uniform State Laws, a group established with the aid of the American Bar Association and supported by much of the legal elite, began the arduous task of trying to unify American law by convincing the states to adopt specially drafted uniform statutes. Composed of unpaid legal specialists appointed by the governors of the states and inspired in good part by the desire to forestall the possibility of national legislation, the commissioners drafted a series of model statutes that covered a range of common law areas. They promulgated their first uniform code, a negotiable instruments statute, in 1896 and introduced several more in the years before World War I. Their success was slow in coming and almost wholly limited to such commercial law areas as sales, negotiable instruments, and warehouse receipts—the core area over which *Swift* gave the federal courts their independent judgment of state common law. See William Twining, *Karl Llewellyn and the Realist Movement* (London, 1973), pp. 272–73; Hobson, *American Legal Profession,* pp. 240–48.

78. See Chapter 9; Keller, *Life Insurance Enterprise,* pp. 194–226, esp. p. 199. For the parol evidence rule, see *Northern Assurance Co. v. Grand View Building Association,* 183 U.S. 308 (1902). *Bank Savings Life Insurance Co. v. Baker,* 244 P. 862 (Sup.Ct.Kan. 1926), illustrates one of the kinds of laws many states passed to protect policyholders.

79. Lubove, "Workmen's Compensation," p. 261; Lester P. Schoene and Frank Watson, "Workmen's Compensation on Interstate Railways," *Harvard Law Review* 47 (1934): 389, 391–92; Edward D. Berkowitz, *Disabled Policy: America's Programs for the Handicapped* (New York, 1987), pp. 16–17; H.R. Doc. No. 380, 57 Cong., 1 Sess. (1902), pp. 912–13; 933–35, 938–39. State laws relating to employers' liabilities are collected in H.R. Rep. No. 1386, 60 Cong., 1 Sess. (1908), pp. 30–75. As late as 1902 only five states had passed employers' liability laws. See Conrad Reno, *A Treatise on the Law of the Employers' Liability Acts,* 2nd ed. (Indianapolis, 1903), p. v.

80. *Tullis v. Lake Erie and Western Railroad Co.,* 175 U.S. 348 (1899); *St. Louis Merchants' Bridge Terminal Railway Co. v. Callahan,* 194 U.S. 628 (1904); *Pittsburgh, Cincinnati, Chicago &*

St. Louis Railway Co. v. Lightheiser, 212 U.S. 560 (1908). See Robert Asher, "Failure and Fulfillment: Agitation for Employers' Liability Legislation and the Origins of Workmen's Compensation in New York State, 1876–1910," *Labor History* 24 (1983): 198, 215–16.

81. *Holden v. Hardy,* 169 U.S. 598 (1898).

82. *Atchison, Topeka & Santa Fe Railroad Co. v. Matthews,* 174 U.S. 96 (1899); *Minnesota Iron Co. v. Kline,* 199 U.S. 593 (1905); *Louisville & Nashville Railroad Co. v. Melton,* 218 U.S. 36 (1910).

83. *Mobile, Jackson & Kansas City Railroad Co. v. Turnipseed,* 219 U.S. 35 (1910). See *Easterling Lumber Co. v. Pierce,* 235 U.S. 380 (1914).

84. *Chicago, Burlington & Quincy Railroad Co. v. McGuire,* 219 U.S. 549 (1911).

85. *Bowersock v. Smith,* 243 U.S. 29, 34 (1917). Agreeing: *The Missouri Pacific Railway Co. v. Castle,* 224 U.S. 541, 544 (1912).

86. Frank W. Munger, Jr., has discussed many of the problems involved in determining why the workmen's compensation movement seemed to triumph so quickly and completely in a relatively short period of time. He points to problems with various theories that have been advanced and emphasizes the difficulty of identifying the "causes" for the success of workmen's compensation. I intend here simply to suggest that the rise of the personal injury bar and the changing social nature of the process of dealing with formal and particularly informal tort claims was a significant factor that has often been overlooked. See Munger, "Social Change and Tort Litigation: Industrialization, Accidents, and Trial Courts in Southern West Virginia, 1872–1940," *Buffalo Law Review* 36 (1987): 75, 109–16, 117–18.

87. For early discussions of the law of workmen's compensation, see James Harrington Boyd, *A Treatise on the Law of Compensation for Injuries to Workmen Under Modern Industrial Conditions* (Indianapolis, 1913); Jeremiah Smith, "Sequel to Workmen's Compensation Acts," *Harvard Law Review* 27 (1914): 235; J. E. Rhodes, II, *Workmen's Compensation* (New York, 1917); L. V. Hill and Ralph H. Wilkin, *Workmen's Compensation Statute Law* (St. Louis, 1923).

88. Lawrence M. Friedman and Jack Ladinsky, "Social Change and the Law of Industrial Accidents," *Columbia Law Review* 67 (1967): 50; James Weinstein, *The Corporate Ideal in the Liberal State: 1900–1918* (Boston, 1968), chap. 2; Robert F. Wesser, "Conflict and Compromise: The Workmen's Compensation Movement in New York, 1890's–1913," *Labor History* 12 (1971): 345; Barbara C. Steidle, " 'Reasonable' Reform: The Attitude of Bar and Bench Toward Liability Law and Workmen's Compensation," in Jerry Israel, ed., *Building the Organizational Society: Essays on Associational Activities in Modern America* (New York, 1972), pp. 31–41; Ernest Angell, "Recovery Under Workmen's Compensation Acts for Injury Abroad," *Harvard Law Review* 31 (1918): 619; Lubove, "Workmen's Compensation"; Roy Lubove, *The Struggle for Social Security, 1900–1935* (Cambridge, MA, 1968), chap. 3; Munger, "Social Change and Tort Litigation," p. 75; Joseph F. Tripp, "An Instance of Labor and Business Cooperation: Workmen's Compensation in Washington State (1911)," *Labor History* 17 (1976): 530; Robert Asher, "Radicalism and Reform: State Insurance of Workmen's Compensation in Minnesota, 1910–1933," *Labor History* 14 (1973): 19; J. E. Rhodes, II, "The Inception of Workmen's Compensation in the United States," *Maine Law Review* 11 (1917): 35; Asher, "Failure and Fulfillment," p. 198.

89. *New York Central Railroad Co. v. White,* 243 U.S. 188, 196 (1917). See *Jeffrey Manufacturing Co. v. Blagg,* 235 U.S. 571 (1915); *Hawkins v. Bleakly,* 243 U.S. 210 (1917); *Mountain Timber Co. v. State of Washington,* 243 U.S. 219 (1917).

90. *Arizona Employers' Liability Cases,* 250 U.S. 400 (1919); Alexander M. Bickel and Benno C. Schmidt, Jr., *The Judiciary and Responsible Government, 1910–1921* (New York, 1984), pp. 581–92; Alexander M. Bickel, *The Unpublished Opinions of Mr. Justice Brandeis: The Supreme Court at Work* (Chicago, 1957), pp. 61–76.

91. Schoene and Watson, "Workmen's Compensation," p. 412; Berkowitz, *Disabled Policy,* p. 15; Hill and Wilkin, *Workmen's Compensation Statute Law,* "Preface," first unpaginated page.

92. Berkowitz, *Disabled Policy,* pp. 20–24. On workmen's compensation generally, see Walter Dodd, *Administration of Workmen's Compensation* (New York, 1936); Herman M. Somers and Anne Somers, *Workmen's Compensation: Prevention, Insurance, and Rehabilitation of Occupational Disability* (New York, 1954). A study of state supreme courts shows that disputes over

workmen's compensation became a major source of litigation. Between 1911 and 1935 they may have accounted for 20 percent of the state tort dockets and from 1940 to 1970, for almost 30 percent. Kagan et al., "Business of the State Supreme Courts," p. 134. Compare Lois R. Sincere, "Processing Workers' Compensation Claims in Illinois," *American Bar Foundation Research Journal* (1982): 1073; Stefan A. Riesenfeld, "Forty Years of American Workmen's Compensation," *Minnesota Law Review* 35 (1951): 525.

93. 27 Stat. 531 (1893), amended 29 Stat. 85 (1896).

94. Kurt Wetzel, "Railroad Management's Response to Operating Employees Accidents, 1890–1913," *Labor History* 21 (1980): 351, 353–54.

95. 32 Stat. 943 (1903).

96. *Johnson v. Southern Pacific Co.,* 196 U.S. 1, 14, 17 (1904). For the opinion below, see *Johnson v. Southern Pacific Co.,* 117 F. 462 (C.C.A. 8 1902).

97. Office of the Attorney General of the United States, *Annual Report, 1905,* pp. 20–21. See *Chicago, Burlington & Quincy Railway Co. v. United States,* 220 U.S. 559 (1911).

98. 36 Stat. 298 (1910).

99. 34 Stat. 1415 (1907).

100. 36 Stat. 913 (1911), amended 38 Stat. 1192 (1915).

101. *St. Louis, Iron Mountain and Southern Railway Co. v. Taylor,* 210 U.S. 281, 295 (1908).

102. *Delk v. St. Louis and San Francisco Railroad Co.,* 220 U.S. 580 (1911); *Chicago Junction Railway Co. v. King,* 222 U.S. 222 (1911); *Chicago, Rock Island and Pacific Railway Co. v. Brown,* 229 U.S. 317 (1913); *Southern Railway Co. v. Crockett,* 234 U.S. 725 (1914); *Texas & Pacific Railway Co. v. Rigsby,* 241 U.S. 33 (1916); *San Antonio & Arkansas Pass Railway Co. v. Wagner,* 241 U.S. 476 (1916); *Spokane & Inland Empire Railroad Co. v. Campbell,* 241 U.S. 497 (1916); *St. Joseph & Grand Island Railway Co. v. Moore,* 243 U.S. 311 (1917). On occasion the Court held that the act did not reach an injury and denied recovery. *Schlemmer v. Buffalo, Rochester and Pittsburgh Railway Co.,* 220 U.S. 590 (1911); *Pennell v. Philadelphia & Reading Railway Co.,* 231 U.S. 675 (1914). The Safety Appliance Act, by itself, did not affect contributory negligence. *Minneapolis, St. Paul & Sault Ste. Marie Railway Co. v. Popplar,* 237 U.S. 369 (1915). See Daunis McBride, *Richey's Federal Employers' Liability, Safety Appliance, and Hours of Service Acts* (Charlottesville, VA, 1916), pp. 526–50.

103. 36 Stat. 1087, 1091 (1911).

104. 38 Stat. 803, 804 (1915).

105. 40 Stat. 451, 456 (1918).

106. 43 Stat. 936, 941 (1925). The statute excepted corporations in which the federal government owned half or more of the stock.

107. 34 Stat. 232 (1906).

108. *Employers' Liability Cases,* 207 U.S. 463 (1908).

109. 35 Stat. 65 (1908). See Sen. Rep. No. 460, 60 Cong., 1 Sess. (1908).

110. *Second Employers' Liability Cases,* 223 U.S. 1 (1912).

111. 36 Stat. 291 (1910).

112. 223 U.S. 50.

113. *Missouri, Kansas and Texas Railway Co. v. Wulf,* 226 U.S. 570 (1913); *Missouri, Kansas & Texas Railway Co. v. West,* 232 U.S. 682 (1914); *Oliver v. Northern Pacific Railway Co.,* 196 F. 432 (E.D. Wash. 1912).

114. See, for example, *Seaboard Air Line Railway v. Horton,* 233 U.S. 492 (1914); *Chesapeake and Ohio Railway Co. v. De Atley,* 241 U.S. 310 (1916); *Chesapeake and Ohio Railway Co. v. Nixon,* 271 U.S. 218 (1926); *Delaware, Lackawanna and Western Railroad Co. v. Koske,* 279 U.S. 7 (1929).

115. For example, *Seaboard Air Line Railway v. Horton,* 233 U.S. 492 (1914); *Atlantic Coast Line Railroad Co. v. Driggers,* 279 U.S. 787 (1929); *McCalmont v. Pennsylvania Railroad Co.,* 283 F. 736 (C.C.A. 6 1922); *Douglas v. Washington Terminal Co.,* 298 F. 199 (C.C.A.D.C. 1924).

116. *Seaboard Air Line Railway v. Horton,* 233 U.S. 492 (1914).

117. 36 Stat. 291 (1910).

118. See Sen. Rep. No. 432, 61 Cong., 2 Sess. (1910); H.R. Rep. No. 513, 61 Cong., 2 Sess. (1910); and see Chapter 8.

119. 36 Stat. 291 (1910). Prior to the 1910 amendments FELA actions were removable. For example, *Clark v. Southern Pacific Co.*, 175 F. 122 (C.C.W.D.Tx. 1909).

120. *Lombardo v. Boston & Maine Railroad Co.*, 223 F. 427, 433 (N.D.N.Y. 1915). For the widespread application of the amendment to deny removal, see, for example, *Teel v. Chesapeake & Ohio Railway Co. of Virginia*, 204 F. 918 (C.C.A. 6 1913); *Symonds v. St. Louis & Southeastern Railway Co.*, 192 F. 853 (C.C.W.D.Ark. 1911); *Saiek v. Pennsylvania Railroad Co.*, 193 F. 303 (C.C.E.D.N.Y. 1911); *Strauser v. Chicago, Burlington & Quincy Railroad Co.*, 193 F. 293 (D.Neb. 1912); *Ullrich v. New York, New Haven & Hartford Railroad Co.*, 193 F. 768 (S.D.N.Y. 1912); *McChesney v. Illinois Central Railroad Co.*, 197 F. 85 (W.D.Ky. 1912); *Kelly's Administratrix v. Chesapeake & Ohio Railway Co.*, 201 F. 602 (E.D.Ky. 1912); *Patton v. Cincinnati, New Orleans & Texas Pacific Railway*, 208 F. 29 (E.D.Tenn. 1913); *Mitchell v. Southern Railway Co.*, 247 F. 819 (N.D.Ga. 1917); McBride, *Richey's Federal Employers' Liability*, 246–51. The state courts applied the amendment similarly: *Missouri, Kansas & Texas Railway Co. of Texas v. Bunkley*, 153 S.W. 937 (Ct.Civ.App.Tx. 1913); *Lloyd v. North Carolina Railroad Co.*, 78 So. 489 (Sup.Ct.N.C. 1913); *Southern Railway Co. v. Puckett*, 85 S.E. 809 (Ct.App.Ga. 1915). The principal exception was *Van Brimmer v. Texas & Pacific Railway Co.*, 190 F. 394 (C.C.E.D.Tx. 1911).

121. *Kansas City Southern Railway Co. v. Leslie*, 238 U.S. 599 (1915); *Southern Railway Co. v. Lloyd*, 239 U.S. 496 (1916); *St. Joseph & Grand Island Railway Co. v. Moore*, 243 U.S. 311 (1917).

122. Sen. Doc. No. 338, 62 Cong., 2 Sess. (1912).

123. H.R. Rep. No. 1441, 62 Cong., 3 Sess. (1913), p. 218.

124. Sen. Rep. No. 553, 62 Cong., 2 Sess. (1912), Part 1; H.R. Rep. No. 1441, 62 Cong., 3 Sess. (1913). The dissenters' views appear in pt. 2 of the Senate report and in "The Views of the Minority" in the House report, p. 215. See Weinstein, *Corporate Ideal in the Liberal State*, p. 59. For general views and particularly for the division among labor groups, see "Employers' Liability and Workmen's Compensation," Hearings before the Committee on the Judiciary of the United States House of Representatives on H.R. 20487 (S. 5382), 62 Cong., 2 Sess. (1913); for example, pp. 467–68 (statement of Samuel Gompers, president of the American Federation of Labor).

125. 38 Stat. 1164 (1915).

126. 41 Stat. 988, 1007 (1920).

127. *Engel v. Davenport*, 271 U.S. 33 (1926); *International Stevedoring Co. v. Haverty*, 272 U.S. 50 (1926). See *Buffalo & Grand Island Ferry Co. v. Williams*, 25 F.2d 612 (C.C.A. 2 1928); *Petterson v. Standard Oil of New Jersey*, 41 F.2d 219 (S.D.N.Y. 1924). On the Seamens' Act, see Bickel and Schmidt, *Judiciary and Responsible Government*, pp. 483–89.

128. Sen. Rep. No. 775, 64 Cong., 1 Sess. (1916), pp. 2, 3. When Congress responded the next year by relieving the Supreme Court of the duty to hear appeals under the FELA and the Safety Appliance Act, it provided plaintiffs with further incremental relief. The act made it much less likely that they would have to bear the burden of a second appeal to the Supreme Court. Congress removed FELA and Safety Appliance Act cases from the category of cases that could be appealed to the Court by writ of error, an appeal as of right, and made them appealable only by the discretionary route of certiorari. 39 Stat. 726 (1916).

129. For example, *Fort Smith & Western Railroad Co. v. Blevins*, 130 P. 525 (Sup.Ct.Okla. 1913).

130. Lawrence Baum, Sheldon Goldman, and Austin Sarat, "The Evolution of Litigation in the Federal Courts of Appeals, 1895–1975," *Law & Society Review* 16 (1981–82): 291, 305. The study does not specifically refer to the 1910 amendment to the FELA or to the Jones Act.

131. The American Law Institute, *A Study of the Business of the Federal Courts: Part II, Civil Cases* (Philadelphia, 1934), Detailed Table 6. The seven districts referred to—which terminated a combined total of 3,325 civil cases during the year—are the District of Colorado, the District of Connecticut, the Northern District of Illinois, the District of Kansas, the Eastern District of Louisiana, the Western District of North Carolina, and the Southern District of West Virginia. The three districts whose FELA terminations are itemized in the text are, respectively, the District of Massachusetts, the Southern District of Ohio, and the Northern District of California. They terminated, respectively, 372, 428, and 1,007 civil cases during 1929–30.

The three other districts in the study—the Eastern District of Michigan, the Southern District of New York, and the Northern District of Ohio—terminated 10, 34, and 122 FELA cases, respectively, in 1929–30. The numbers for the first two districts also are relatively small, as both included heavily populated areas with large dockets. The Michigan district terminated 1,521 civil cases during the year, and the New York district 2,075. The Northern District of Ohio was the exception. It not only terminated an extraordinarily large number of FELA actions, but those actions accounted for more than 10 percent of its 1,124 civil terminations. The numbers in the Ohio district were probably the result of special local factors, most likely the presence in the district of one or more federal judges identified as strongly proplaintiff, a local court system that in critical ways seemed particularly unfavorable to negligence plaintiffs, and quite possibly a local bar that worked aggressively to bring cases into the district for filing in the federal court.

The heavy FELA caseload in the Northern District of Ohio was obviously not the result of a heavier general caseload and was almost certainly not the result of the presence in the district of more potential FELA claims. Consider, in comparison, the Northern District of Illinois, which included Chicago, then the nation's second largest city and a national rail center. It terminated 1,542 civil cases, almost 40 percent more cases than the Northern District of Ohio did, but it did not terminate a single FELA case during 1929–30. Similarly, the Northern District of California, which includes Oakland—another major rail center—and San Francisco, terminated just over a thousand civil cases in 1929–30, yet its civil terminations included only 4 FELA actions. It seems certain that there were many FELA actions brought in both Chicago and Oakland and that those actions must have been brought overwhelmingly in the state courts. See Chapter 8.

132. There are no satisfactory statistics available on forum choice. The estimate in the text is based largely on the material discussed in the preceding note together with the following: Office of the Attorney General of the United States, *Annual Report, 1936,* p. 179, *Annual Report, 1937,* p. 189, *Annual Report, 1938,* p. 233, *Annual Report, 1939,* p. 215; Sen. Doc. No. 68, 74 Cong., 1 Sess. (1935), pp. 10, 25–26; United States Railroad Retirement Board, *Work Injuries in the Railroad Industry, 1938–40* (1947), vol. 1, pp. 43–45; U.S. Bureau of the Census, *Statistical History of the United States,* p. 437; "Workmen's Compensation," Hearings before the Committee on the Judiciary of the United States House of Representatives on H.R. 1, 61 Cong., 1 Sess. (1910), p. 80 (statement of Robert J. Cary, Esq., counsel of the New York Central Lines); "Limitation of Venue in Certain Actions Brought Under the Employers' Liability Act," Hearings before a Subcommittee of the Committee on the Judiciary of the United States Senate on S. 1567 and H.R. 1639, 80 Cong., 2 Sess. (1948), p. 20 (statement of John W. Freels, attorney for the Illinois Central Railroad Co.).

133. Note, "Review by the Supreme Court of Cases Arising Under the Federal Employers' Liability Act," *Yale Law Journal* 42 (1933): 226. See, for example, *Atchison, Topeka & Santa Fe Railway Co. v. Saxon,* 284 U.S. 458, 459 (1932). For state cases purposely construing the act "humanely," see, for example, *Baltimore & Ohio Railroad Co. v. Branson,* 98 A. 225 (Ct.App.Md. 1916); *Schuppenies v. Oregon Short Line Railroad Co.,* 225 P. 501 (Sup.Ct.Idaho 1924).

134. *Pederson v. Delaware, Lackawanna & Western Railroad Co.,* 229 U.S. 146, 152 (1913). See *Illinois Central Railroad Co. v. Behrens,* 233 U.S. 473, 478 (1914).

135. *New York Central and Hudson River Railroad Co. v. Carr,* 238 U.S. 260, 262 (1915).

136. *Pedersen v. Delaware, Lackawanna & Western Railroad Co.,* 229 U.S. 146 (1913); *St. Louis, San Francisco & Texas Railway Co. v. Seale,* 229 U.S. 156 (1913); *North Carolina Railroad Co. v. Zachary,* 232 U.S. 248 (1914).

137. See *Delaware, Lackawanna & Western Railroad Co. v. Yurkonis,* 238 U.S. 439 (1915); *Shanks v. Delaware, Lackawanna and Western Railroad Co.,* 239 U.S. 556 (1916); *Chicago, Burlington & Quincy Railroad Co. v. Harrington,* 241 U.S. 177 (1916); *McCluskey v. Marysville & Northern Railway Co.,* 243 U.S. 36 (1917). Compare *Pedersen v. Delaware, Lackawanna & Western Railroad Co.,* 229 U.S. 146 (1913) with *Raymond v. Chicago, Milwaukee & St. Paul Railway Co.,* 243 U.S. 43 (1917). The question of whether an employee was injured in interstate or intrastate commerce was a jury question. *Pennsylvania Co. v. Donat,* 239 U.S. 50 (1915).

138. *Beutler v. Grand Trunk Junction Railway Co.,* 224 U.S. 85 (1912); *Tweeten v. Tacoma Railway & Power Co.,* 210 F. 828 (C.C.A. 9 1914); *Union Pacific Railroad Co. v. Marone,* 246 F. 916 (C.C.A. 8 1917).

139. 244 U.S. 147 (1917). See *Erie Railroad Co. v. Winfield,* 244 U.S. 170 (1917); *New York Central & Hudson River Railroad Co. v. Tonsellito,* 244 U.S. 360 (1917).

140. *Great Northern Railway Co. v. Alexander,* 246 U.S. 276 (1918).

141. For example, *Moore v. Chesapeake & Ohio Railway Co.,* 291 U.S. 205 (1934).

142. *New York Central and Hudson River Railroad Co. v. Carr,* 238 U.S. 262, 263.

143. *Great Northern Railway Co. v. Alexander,* 246 U.S. 282; *Aldredge v. Baltimore & Ohio Railroad Co.,* 20 F.2d 655 (C.C.A. 8 1927), cert. denied, 275 U.S. 550 (1927).

144. Interstate commerce allegations under the FELA were upheld in *Farmers' Bank & Trust Co. of Hardinsburg, Ky. v. Atchison, Topeka & Santa Fe Railway Co.,* 25 F.2d 23 (C.C.A. 8 1928); *Wabash Railway Co. v. Lindley,* 29 F.2d 829 (C.C.A. 8 1928); *Stafford v. Norfolk & Western Railway Co.,* 202 F. 605 (E.D.Ky. 1913); *Rice v. Boston and Maine Railroad Co.,* 203 F. 580 (N.D.N.Y. 1913); *Smith v. Camas Prairie Railway Co.,* 216 F. 799 (D.Idaho 1914); *Reese v. Southern Railway Co.,* 26 F.2d 367 (N.D.Ga. 1928).

An allegation that plaintiff was injured in interstate commerce prevented removal but was ultimately found unsupported on the merits in *Wabash Railroad Co. v. Hayes,* 234 U.S. 86 (1914); *Great Northern Railway Co. v. Alexander,* 246 U.S. 276 (1918): *Polluck v. Minneapolis & St. Louis Railroad Co.,* 183 N.W. 859 (Sup.Ct.S.D. 1921); *Bailey v. Davis,* 193 N.W. 658 (Sup.Ct.N.D. 1923).

145. Schoene and Watson, "Workmen's Compensation," pp. 408–9; Jerome Pollack, "Workmen's Compensation for Railroad Work Injuries and Diseases," *Cornell Law Quarterly* 36 (1951): 236, 249–50.

146. "Amendments to Federal Employers' Liability Act," Hearings before the Committee on the Judiciary of the United States House of Representatives, 64 Cong., 1 Sess. (1916), p. 5 (statement of W. M. Clark, vice-president and national legislative representative of the Order of Railway Conductors), and see p. 12 (statement of Val Fitzpatrick, vice-president of the Brotherhood of Railroad Trainmen).

147. Sen. Doc. No. 68, 74 Cong., 1 Sess. (1935), pp. 11, 13.

148. Ibid., pp. 8, 14.

149. Ibid., p. 11. The interstate commerce requirement was not the only factor that helped explain the difference. It was also significant that those working on trains tended to be paid more. The study also suggested another possible factor to explain the discrepancy, that train injuries tended to be more serious. Because the differences in settlement and judgment amounts between train and nontrain accidents existed for comparable injuries, including death (pp. 12–13), however, a difference in the seriousness of injuries does not seem to be a plausible explanation. Because the Supreme Court held that only economic loss could be recovered under the FELA, *Chesapeake & Ohio Railway Co. v. Kelly,* 241 U.S. 485 (1916), the difference could not be explained as the result of more liberal federal damages rules.

150. 35 Stat. 66 (1908). The Erdman Act, 30 Stat. 424 (1898), banned programs involving compulsory membership, but it seemed to have only a limited impact on the companies' use of relief departments.

151. 224 U.S. 603 (1912). See *Baltimore & Ohio Railroad Co. v. Gawinske,* 197 F. 31 (C.C.A. 3 1912).

152. Three years later the Court applied the section more broadly, holding that a plaintiff could raise it in a non-FELA action against a nonemployer defendant to defeat a defense based on the joint tortfeasor release rule. *Chicago & Alton Railway Co. v. Wagner,* 239 U.S. 452 (1915). See McBride, *Richey's Federal Employers' Liability,* pp. 56–59. Section 5 did not void otherwise proper releases obtained after an accident as part of an independent settlement of the claim. See, for example, *Patton v. Atchison, Topeka & Santa Fe Railway Co.,* 158 P. 576 (Sup.Ct.Okla. 1916).

153. 237 U.S. 84 (1915).

154. *Baltimore & Ohio Southwestern Railway v. Voigt,* 176 U.S. 498, 511, 513; *Robinson v. Baltimore and Ohio Railroad Co.,* 237 U.S. 85–87.

155. 102 U.S. 451 (1880).

156. *Voigt,* 176 U.S. 512; *Robinson,* 237 U.S. 88.

157. *Robinson,* 237 U.S. 91.

158. Ibid., pp. 92–93.

159. Ibid., p. 94.

160. For example, *Pennsylvania Co. v. Roy,* 102 U.S. 451 (1880).

161. *Taylor v. Wells Fargo & Co.,* 249 F. 110 (C.C.A. 5 1918).

162. Ibid., pp. 113–14.

163. Ibid., p. 114.

164. 254 U.S. 175 (1920).

165. Ibid., p. 187.

166. *Lindsay v. Chicago, Burlington & Quincy Railroad Co.,* 226 F. 23 (C.C.A. 7 1915); *Fowler v. Pennsylvania Railroad Co.,* 229 F. 373 (C.C.A. 2 1916); *Martin v. New York, New Haven & Hartford Railroad Co.,* 241 F. 696 (S.D.N.Y. 1917); *Eubanks v. Southern Railway Co.,* 244 F. 891 (S.D.Fla. 1917).

167. *Hull v. Philadelphia & Reading Railway Co.,* 252 U.S. 475 (1920); *Stevenson v. Lake Terminal Railroad Co.,* 42 F.2d 357 (C.C.A. 6 1930). The approach did not always work: *Linstead v. Chesapeake & Ohio Railway Co.,* 276 U.S. 28 (1928); *Erie Railroad Co. v. Margue,* 23 F.2d 664 (C.C.A. 6 1928).

168. *Chicago, Rock Island & Pacific Railway Co. v. Bond,* 240 U.S. 449 (1916).

169. Wetzel, "Railroad Management's Response," pp. 365–68.

170. Sen. Doc. No. 338, 62 Cong., 2 Sess. (1912), vol. 1, pp. 131, 135.

171. Compare ibid., vol. 1, pp. 131, 135, 139, 143 with Railroad Retirement Board, *Work Injuries,* vol. 1, pp. 43–45.

172. Sen. Doc. No. 338, 62 Cong., 2 Sess. (1912), vol. 1, pp. 131, 135, 139, 143; Sen. Doc. No. 68, 74 Cong., 1 Sess. (1935), pp. 10–14, 19–22. Comparison is necessarily inexact and in some areas impossible because the studies used somewhat different categories and definitions.

173. *Adair v. United States,* 208 U.S. 161 (1908); *Coppage v. Kansas,* 236 U.S. 1 (1915).

174. 245 U.S. 229 (1917).

175. 197 U.S. 544, 570 (1905).

176. 206 U.S. 46 (1907).

177. 213 U.S. 175 (1909).

178. Ibid., p. 191.

179. 215 U.S. 372 (1910).

180. *Southern Railway v. United States,* 222 U.S. 20 (1911); *Texas & Pacific Railway Co. v. Rigsby,* 241 U.S. 33 (1916); *Adams Express Co. v. Croninger,* 226 U.S. 491 (1913); *Charleston & Western Carolina Railway v. Thompson,* 234 U.S. 576 (1914); *Southern Railway Co. v. Railroad Commission of Indiana,* 236 U.S. 439 (1915); *Kansas City Southern Railway v. Van Zant,* 260 U.S. 459 (1923). See Bickel and Schmidt, *Judiciary and Responsible Government,* pp. 202–4, 415–16, 553, and cases cited; Jonathan D. Caspar, "The Supreme Court and National Policy Making," *American Political Science Review* 70 (1976): 50, 56. For a general discussion of the Court's use of the commerce clause to protect the national market see James Willard Hurst, *Law and the Conditions of Freedom in the Nineteenth-Century United States* (Madison, WI, 1967), pp. 44–51.

181. *New York Central Railroad Co. v. Winfield,* 244 U.S. 149, citing *Baltimore & Ohio Railroad Co. v. Baugh,* 149 U.S. 368, 378–79 (1893).

182. 244 U.S. 205 (1917).

183. The following year the Court ruled that state courts were obliged to follow the decisions of the federal courts in construing the maritime law. *Chelentis v. Luckenbach Steamship Co.,* 247 U.S.372 (1918) (denying recovery under a state workmen's compensation act in a removed diversity suit brought under the "savings clause" of Section 9 of the Judiciary Act of 1789). See Bickel and Schmidt, *Judiciary and Responsible Government,* pp. 558–66.

184. 40 Stat. 395 (1917), invalidated in *Knickerbocker Ice Co. v. Stewart,* 253 U.S. 149 (1920); 42 Stat. 634 (1922), invalidated in *Washington v. Dawson & Co.,* 264 U.S. 219 (1924).

185. 44 Stat. 1424 (1927).

186. *Crowell v. Benson,* 285 U.S. 22 (1932). The constant need to determine which claims fell within federal statutes and which without repeatedly forced injured workers to litigate jurisdictional issues. See, for example, *Northern Coal & Dock Co. v. Strand,* 278 U.S. 142 (1928).

187. *Gilvary v. Cugahoga Valley Railway Co.,* 292 U.S. 57 (1934).

188. The Court developed its assumption of risk analysis in *Seaboard Air Line Railway Co. v.*

Horton, 233 U.S. 492 (1914). For later applications, see *Boldt v. Pennsylvania Railroad Co.,* 245 U.S. 440 (1917); *Chesapeake & Ohio Railway Co. v. Nixon,* 271 U.S. 218 (1926); *Toledo, St. Louis & Western Railroad Co. v. Allen,* 276 U.S. 165 (1928); Edward P. Buford, "Assumption of Risk Under the Federal Employers' Liability Act," *Harvard Law Review* 28 (1914): 163; Note, "Assumption of Risk Under the Federal Employers' Liability Act," *Columbia Law Review* 32 (1932): 1384. Political liberals and the railroad brotherhoods argued that the federal courts expanded the employers' defenses under the FELA. For example, "To Amend the Employers' Liability Act," Hearing before Subcommittee No. 4 of the Committee on the Judiciary of the United States House of Representatives, 75 Cong., 1 Sess. (1937), p. 59 (statement of James R. Claiborn, attorney), pp. 65–66 (statement of E. L. Harrigan, deputy president, Brotherhood of Railroad Trainmen).

189. *Chicago, Milwaukee & St. Paul Railway Co. v. Coogan,* 271 U.S. 472, 474 (1926). Agreeing: *Michigan Central Railroad Co. v. Vreeland,* 227 U.S. 59 (1913); *Missouri Pacific Railroad Co. v. Aeby,* 275 U.S. 426 (1927); *Toledo, St. Louis & Western Railroad Co. v. Allen,* 276 U.S. 165 (1928).

190. See, for example, *Chicago, Milwaukee & St. Paul Railway Co. v. Coogan,* 271 U.S. 472 (1926); *Atlantic Coast Line Railroad v. Temple,* 285 U.S. 143 (1932); Maurice G. Roberts, *Injuries to Interstate Employees on Railroads* (Chicago, 1915), pp. 239–41; Felix Frankfurter and James M. Landis, "The Business of the Supreme Court at October Term, 1931," *Harvard Law Review* 46 (1932): 226, 239–49.

191. 47 Stat. 70 (1932).

192. 53 Stat. 1404 (1939). See H.R. Rep. No. 2153, 75 Cong., 3 Sess. (1938); H.R. Rep. No. 1222, 76 Cong., 1 Sess. (1939).

193. *Byers v. Carnegie Steel Co.,* 159 F. 347 (C.C.A. 6 1908).

194. *Southern Railway-Carolina Division v. Bennett,* 233 U.S. 80 (1914); *Minneapolis & St. Louis Railroad Co. v. Gotschall,* 244 U.S. 66 (1917); *Lucid v. E.I. Du Pont de Nemours Powder Co.,* 199 F. 377 (C.C.A. 9 1912); *Philadelphia & Reading Railway Co. v. McKibben,* 259 F. 476 (C.C.A. 3 1919). By 1916 one treatise stated that *res ipsa loquitur* was available in an action under the FELA. See McBride, *Richey's Federal Employers' Liability,* pp. 330–34.

195. *Central Railroad Co. of New Jersey v. Peluso,* 286 F. 661, 666–67 (C.C.A. 2 1923). Agreeing: *Baltimore & Ohio Railroad Co. v. Kast,* 299 F. 419 (C.C.A. 6 1924); *Kaemmerling v. Athletic Mining & Smelting Co.,* 2 F.2d 574 (C.C.A. 8 1924); *Erie Railroad Co. v. Murphy,* 9 F.2d 525 (C.C.A. 2 1925); *Lowery v. Hocking Valley Railway Co.,* 60 F.2d 78 (C.C.A. 6 1932); *Leathem Smith–Putnam Navigation Co. v. Osby,* 79 F.2d 280 (C.C.A. 7 1935).

Chapter 8

1. Harry N. Scheiber, "Federalism and the American Economic Order, 1789–1910," *Law & Society Review* 10 (1975): 57.

2. For the developing relations between the settlement movement and workers, see Allen F. Davis, *Spearheads for Reform: The Social Settlements and the Progressive Movement, 1890–1914* (New York, 1967).

3. "Employers' Liability and Workmen's Compensation," Hearings before the Committee on the Judiciary of the United States House of Representatives on H.R. 20487, 62 Cong., 2 Sess. (1913), pp. 197–98 (statement of T. J. Hoskins, member of the Brotherhood of Locomotive Engineers).

4. "Limitation of Venue in Certain Actions Brought Under the Employers' Liability Act," Hearings before Subcommittee No. 4 of the Committee on the Judiciary of the United States House of Representatives on H.R. 1639, 80 Cong., 1 Sess. (1947), p. 91 (statement of A. E. Lyon, executive secretary, Railway Labor Executives Association).

5. "Limitation of Venue in Certain Actions Brought Under the Employers' Liability Act," Hearings before a Subcommittee of the Committee on the Judiciary of the United States Senate on S. 1567 and H.R. 1639, 80 Cong., 2 Sess. (1948), p. 231 (statement of Warren H. Atherton, Esq., attorney for the Brotherhood of Railroad Trainmen).

The jurisdiction of the Brotherhood of Railroad Trainmen reached half or more of all railroad employees, including both roadmen and yardmen. Members included switchmen, brakemen, baggagemen, yard helpers, and conductors. See Joel Seidman, *The Brotherhood of Railroad Trainmen: The Internal Political Life of a National Union* (New York, 1962), pp. 6–11.

6. "Limitation of Venue in Certain Actions Brought Under the Employers' Liability Act," Hearings before Subcommittee No. 4 of the Committee on the Judiciary of the United States House of Representatives on H.R. 1639, 80 Cong., 1 Sess. (1947), p. 148 (statement of Warren H. Atherton, member of the Brotherhood of Railroad Trainmen); "Limitation of Venue in Certain Actions Brought Under the Employers' Liability Act," Hearings before a Subcommittee on the Judiciary of the United States Senate on S. 1567 and H.R. 1639, 80 Cong., 2 Sess. (1948), pp. 154–55 (statement of A. E. Lyon, executive secretary-treasurer, Railway Labor Executives Association).

7. "Limitation of Venue in Certain Actions Brought Under the Employers' Liability Act," Hearings before a Subcommittee of the Committee on the Judiciary of the United States Senate on S. 1567 and H.R. 1639, 80 Cong., 2 Sess. (1948), pp. 231–32 (statement of Warren H. Atherton, Esq., attorney for the Brotherhood of Railroad Trainmen). The initial contract between the brotherhood and its regional counsel required the counsel to remit 4 percent of their fee to the brotherhood to support the legal aid department. Critics charged that the provision constituted unlawful and unethical fee splitting, and in 1946—after judicial censure of the arrangement—the brotherhood discontinued the practice of accepting the 4 percent (pp. 232–34). See also "Limitation of Venue in Certain Actions Brought Under the Employers' Liability Act," Hearings before Subcommittee No. 4 of the Committee on the Judiciary of the United States House of Representatives on H.R. 1639, 80 Cong., 1 Sess. (1947), pp. 46, 50, 55 (statement of Harry See, national legislative representative, Brotherhood of Railroad Trainmen), pp. 66–67, 71–72 (statement of Warren H. Atherton, Esq., member of the Brotherhood of Railroad Trainmen).

8. "Limitation of Venue in Certain Actions Brought Under the Employers' Liability Act," Hearings before a Subcommittee of the Judiciary of the United States Senate on S. 1567 and H.R. 1639, 80 Cong., 2 Sess. (1948), p. 162 (statement of Harry See, national legislative representative, Brotherhood of Railroad Trainmen); "Limitation of Venue in Certain Actions Brought Under the Employers' Liability Act," Hearings before Subcommittee No. 4 of the Committee on the Judiciary of the United States House of Representatives on H.R. 1639, 80 Cong., 1 Sess. (1947), p. 145 (statement of Warren H. Atherton, member of the Brotherhood of Railroad Trainmen), pp. 156–58 (letter from Jno. F. Scott, Virginia State Legislative Board of the Brotherhood of Railroad Trainmen, to Hon. John J. Jennings, Jr.).

9. Seidman, *Brotherhood of Railroad Trainmen,* p. 157.

10. See, among others, the interesting and sometimes elusive testimony of Burk Finnerty, a New Jersey attorney, who acknowledged representing clients from a number of states, and the critical portrayal of interstate solicitation by D. Lindley Sloan, a Maryland attorney, in "Limitation of Venue in Certain Actions Brought Under the Employers' Liability Act," Hearings before Subcommittee No. 4 of the Committee on the Judiciary of the House of Representatives, 80 Cong., 1 Sess. (1947), p. 97; also see n. 17.

11. *Dennick v. Railroad Co.,* 13 Otto (103 U.S.) 11, 18 (1880). Agreeing: *Stewart v. Baltimore and Ohio Railroad Co.,* 168 U.S. 445, 448 (1897); *St. Louis, Iron Mountain and Southern Railway Co. v. Taylor,* 210 U.S. 281, 285 (1908).

12. *Corfield v. Coryell,* 4 Wash. C.C. 371, 380 (1823); *Ward v. Maryland,* 12 Wall. (79 U.S.) 418, 430 (1870); *Blake v. McClung,* 172 U.S. 239, 252 (1898); *Chambers v. Baltimore and Ohio Railroad Co.,* 207 U.S. 142, 148 (1907). For general discussions, see Note, "The Equal Privileges and Immunities of the Federal Constitution," *Columbia Law Review* 28 (1928): 347; Note, "Discretionary Exercise of Jurisdiction of Suits Between Non-Resident Parties in New York," *Yale Law Journal* 37 (1928): 983; Note, "Constitutional Right of Non-Residents to Sue," *Harvard Law Review* 41 (1928): 387.

13. For torts, see, for example, *Slater v. Mexican National Railroad Co.,* 194 U.S. 120 (1904); *Spokane and Inland Empire Railroad Co.,* 237 U.S. 487 (1915). For contracts, see, for example, *Selover, Bates and Co. v. Walsh,* 226 U.S. 112 (1912); *Manhattan Life Insurance Co. of New York v. Cohen,* 234 U.S. 123 (1914). For statements of the general rule, see *American Banana Co. v.*

United Fruit Co., 213 U.S. 347, 355–56 (1909); *Cuba Railroad Co. v. Crosby,* 222 U.S. 473, 478 (1912). See Harold L. Korn, "The Choice-of-Law Revolution: A Critique," *Columbia Law Review* 83 (1983): 722.

14. See, for example, *Northern Pacific Railroad Co. v. Babcock,* 154 U.S. 190 (1894); Conrad Reno, *A Treatise on the Law of the Employers' Liability Acts* (Indianapolis, 1903), pp. 498–501.

15. *Petersen v. Ogden Union Railway & Depot Co.*, 175 P.2d 744, 746 (Sup.Ct.Utah 1946).

16. "Employers' Liability and Workmen's Compensation," Hearings before the Committee on the Judiciary of the United States House of Representatives on H.R. 20487, 62 Cong., 2 Sess. (1913), p. 198 (statement of T. J. Hoskins, member of the Brotherhood of Locomotive Engineers).

17. "Limitation of Venue in Certain Actions Brought Under the Employers' Liability Act," Hearings before Subcommittee No. 4 of the Committee on the Judiciary of the House of Representatives, 80 Cong., 1 Sess. (1947), p. 102 (statement of Burk Finnerty).

18. For example, Austin W. Scott, "Jurisdiction over Nonresidents Doing Business Within a State," *Harvard Law Review* 32 (1919): 871; Gerard C. Henderson, *The Position of Foreign Corporations in American Constitutional Law: A Contribution to the History and Theory of Juristic Persons in Anglo-American Law* (Cambridge, MA, 1918), pp. 77–100.

19. Compare, for example, *Stewart v. Baltimore and Ohio Railroad Co.*, 168 U.S. 445 (1897) with *Chambers v. Baltimore and Ohio Railroad Co.*, 207 U.S. 142 (1907). See *Atchison, Topeka & Santa Fe Railway Co. v. Sowers*, 213 U.S. 55 (1909); *Galveston Houston & San Antonio Railway Co. v. Wallace*, 223 U.S. 481 (1912); *Tennessee Coal, Iron & Railroad Co. v. George*, 233 U.S. 354 (1914); *Loucks v. Standard Oil Co. of New York*, 120 N.E. 198 (Ct.App.N.Y. 1918) (Cardozo, J.); *Walton v. Pryor*, 115 N.E. 2 (Sup.Ct.Ill. 1917). For a contemporary review of the law, see Archibald H. Davis, "Where May the Injured Sue?" *Virginia Law Review* 2 (1914): 33.

20. The New Jersey Court of Chancery, one of the most influential state courts of equity, reviewed the authorities in *Bigelow v. Old Dominion Copper Mining & Smelting Co.*, 71 A. 153 (Ct.Chan.N.J. 1908). See Ernest J. Messner, "The Jurisdiction of a Court of Equity over Persons to Compel the Doing of Acts Outside the Territorial Limits of the State," *Minnesota Law Review* 14 (1930): 494.

21. It seems likely that wrongful death actions, themselves a product of the late nineteenth century, were among the first types of actions to raise issues concerning interstate forum shopping, at least among the kinds of cases that were involved in the system of corporate diversity litigation. Relatively little note was taken of the phenomenon, however, until after 1910. See, for example, Simeon E. Baldwin, *American Railroad Law* (New York, 1904), pp. 534–39; Joseph A. Joyce and Howard C. Joyce, *A Treatise on Damages* (New York, 1903), vol. 1, pp. 591–604. For an early discussion of the legal issues involved, see editorial note, *Central Law Journal* 60 (1905): 209; "Correspondence," *Central Law Journal* 62 (1906): 13.

22. For example, *New England Mutual Life Insurance Co. v. Woodworth*, 111 U.S. 138 (1884); *Barrow Steamship Co. v. Kane*, 170 U.S. 100 (1898); Note, "Progress in Interstate Adjustment of the Place of Trial of Civil Actions," *Yale Law Journal* 45 (1936): 1100, 1111 and works cited in n. 58; Joseph J. Kalo, "Jurisdiction as an Evolutionary Process: The Development of Quasi In Rem and In Personam Principles," *Duke Law Journal* (1978): 1147.

23. William Laurens Walker, "Foreign Corporation Laws: The Loss of Reason," *North Carolina Law Review* 47 (1968): 1, 13.

24. 145 U.S. 444 (1892).

25. 152 U.S. 454 (1894).

26. 203 U.S. 449 (1906).

27. Henry Campbell Black, *A Treatise on the Laws and Practice Governing the Removal of Causes from State Courts to Federal Courts* (St. Paul, 1898), pp. 154–57, 304–5; B. C. Moon, *The Removal of Causes from the Courts of the Several States to the Circuit Courts of the United States* (New York, 1901), pp. 108–9, 377–78. See, for example, *Virginia-Carolina Chemical Co. v. Sundry Insurance Cos.*, 108 F. 451 (C.C.S.C. 1901); *Rome Petroleum & Iron Co. v. Hughes Specialty Well Drilling Co.*, 130 F. 585 (C.C.N.D.Ga. 1904). But see *Foulk v. Gray*, 120 F. 156 (C.C.S.D.W.Va. 1902).

28. 157 U.S. 201, 208 (1895).

29. 203 U.S. 460. The Attorney General criticized federal venue rules for giving advantage

to corporations. Office of the Attorney General of the United States, *Annual Report, 1892,* pp. xvii–xviii.

30. 36 Stat. 291 (1910).

31. For example, *Garrett v. Louisville & Nashville Railroad Co.,* 197 F. 715 (C.C.A. 6 1912), aff'd 235 U.S. 308 (1914); *Newell v. Baltimore & Ohio Railroad Co.,* 181 F. 698 (C.C.W.D.Pa. 1910); *Cound v. Atchison, Topeka & Santa Fe Railroad Co.,* 173 F. 527 (C.C.W.D.Tx. 1909).

Both the Senate and House reports stated that the general federal venue statute might require a plaintiff to sue hundreds or thousands of miles from his home. "The extreme difficulty, if not impossibility," they explained, "of a poor man who is injured while in railroad employ securing the attendance of the necessary witnesses at such a distant point makes the remedy given by the law of little avail under such circumstances." Sen. Rep. No. 432, 61 Cong., 2 Sess. (1910), p. 4; H.R. Rep. No. 513, 61 Cong., 2 Sess. (1910), p. 6. Hearings on the proposed amendment made it clear that if the spokesmen for the railroads and the unions did not anticipate the kind of forum shopping that subsequently developed, they were nevertheless keenly aware of the practical advantages favorable venue rules provided. See generally "Liability of Common Carriers to Employees," Hearing before the Subcommittee of the Committee on the Judiciary of the United States Senate on H.R. 17263, 61 Cong., 2 Sess. (1910).

32. The concurrent jurisdiction provision should not have been necessary, but it was added to counteract the argument advanced and accepted in at least one state that local courts of general jurisdiction were not required to hear FELA cases. See *Second Employers' Liability Cases,* 223 U.S. 1, 59 (1912). The language in the Court's decision provided some basis to argue that Congress had given such a right to plaintiffs under the FELA and that state courts could not refuse to hear claims brought under the statute (p. 56).

33. 241 U.S. 211 (1916). Agreeing: *Louisville and Nashville Railroad Co. v. Stewart,* 241 U.S. 261 (1916).

34. "Limitation of Venue in Certain Actions Brought Under the Employers' Liability Act," Hearings before Subcommittee No. 4 of the Committee on the Judiciary of the United States House of Representatives on H.R. 1639, 80 Cong., 1 Sess. (1947), p. 149 (statement of Warren H. Atherton, Esq., member of the Brotherhood of Railroad Trainmen).

35. Ernest Angell, "Recovery Under Workmen's Compensation Acts for Injury Abroad," *Harvard Law Review* 31 (1918): 619.

36. Order quoted in *Alabama & Vicksburg Railway Co. v. Journey,* 257 U.S. 111, 112, n. 1. The FELA itself may not have been widely used until after 1910 or 1912. See "Workmen's Compensation," Hearings before the Committee on the Judiciary of the United States House of Representatives on H.R. 1, 61 Cong., 1 Sess. (1910), p. 80 (statement of Robert J. Cary, counsel of the New York Central Lines); Sen. Doc. No. 338, 62 Cong., 2 Sess. (1912), vol. 2, p. 1192 (statement of Benjamin D. Warfield, attorney for the Louisville & Nashville Railroad Co.).

37. *Alabama & Vicksburg Railway Co. v. Journey,* 257 U.S. 112, n. 1.

38. For New York, see, for example, *Hoes v. New York, New Haven & Hartford Railroad Co.,* 66 N.E. 119 (Ct.App.N.Y. 1903); *Pietraroia v. New Jersey & Hudson River Railway & Ferry Co.,* 91 N.E. 120 (Ct.App.N.Y. 1910); *Zeikus v. Florida East Coast Railway Co.,* 128 N.Y.S. 931, aff'd, 128 N.Y.S. 933 (App.Div.1st Dep't N.Y. 1911); *Connelly v. Central Railroad Co. of New Jersey,* 238 F. 932 (S.D.N.Y. 1916); *Philadelphia & Reading Railway Co. v. McKibben,* 243 U.S. 264 (1917); *Wood v. Delaware & Hudson Railroad Corp.,* 63 F.2d 235 (C.C.A. 2 1933). It was generally accepted that New York was a desirable plaintiff's forum because its juries tended to award larger verdicts. For example, Note, "Discretionary Exercise of Jurisdiction of Suits Between Non-Resident Parties in New York," *Yale Law Journal* 37 (1928): 983, 985–86. For Texas, see, for example, *Southern Pacific Co. v. Allen,* 106 S.W. 441 (Ct.Civ.App.Tx. 1907); *St. Louis & San Francisco Railroad Co. v. Kiser,* 136 S.W. 852 (Ct.Civ.App.Tx. 1911); *St. Louis & San Francisco Railroad Co. v. Matlock,* 141 S.W. 1067 (Ct.Civ.App.Tx. 1911); *Lancaster v. Dunn,* 95 So. 385 (Sup.Ct.La. 1922); *Southern Pacific Co. v. Baum,* 38 P.2d 1106 (Sup.Ct.N.M. 1934).

39. *Minneapolis & St. Louis Railroad Co. v. Bombolis,* 241 U.S. 211 (1916).

40. For examples of nonresidents selecting the Missouri forum, see *Illinois Life Insurance Co. v. Prentiss,* 115 N.E. 554 (Sup.Ct.Ill. 1917); *Wabash Railway Co. v. Peterson,* 175 N.W. 523 (Sup.Ct.Iowa 1919); *Bank Savings Life Insurance Co. v. Wood,* 253 P. 431 (Sup.Ct.Kansas 1927);

Cleveland, Cincinnati, Chicago & St. Louis Railway Co. v. Shelly, 170 N.E. 328 (App.Ct.Ind. 1930). For the nonunanimous jury provision, see Missouri Rev. Stat. (1909), Sec. 7280 and *Prentiss,* 115 N.E. 554, above. For Missouri law supporting the right of out-of-state plaintiffs to sue in state, see *State ex rel. Pacific Mutual Life Insurance Co. v. Grimm,* 143 S.W. 483 (Sup.Ct.Mo. 1911); *Gold Issue Mining & Milling Co. v. Pennsylvania Fire Insurance Co.,* 184 S.W. 999 (Sup.Ct.Mo. 1916), aff'd 243 U.S. 93 (1917); *Wells v. Davis,* 261 S.W. 58 (Sup.Ct.Mo. 1924); *State ex rel. Foraker v. Hoffman,* 274 S.W. 362 (Sup.Ct.Mo. 1925), aff'd 274 U.S. 21 (1927); *Shaw v. Chicago & Alton Railroad Co.,* 282 S.W. 416 (Sup.Ct. Mo. 1926); *Kepner v. Cleveland, Cincinnati, Chicago & St. Louis Railway Co.,* 15 S.W. 2d 825 (Sup.Ct.Mo. 1929). Insurance companies seemed to do relatively poorly in Missouri. See Morton Keller, "The Judicial System and the Law of Life Insurance, 1888–1910," *Business History Review* 35 (1961): 317, 323.

41. Georgia, for example, used juries in equity proceedings to reform insurance contracts and seemed particularly willing to impose penalties and attorneys' fees on companies. See Granger Hansell, "The Proper Forum for Suits Against Foreign Corporations," *Columbia Law Review* 27 (1927): 12, 13.

42. *Davis v. Farmers Co-Operative Equity Co.,* 262 U.S. 312, 314, n. 1 (1923).

43. Office of the Attorney General of the United States, *Annual Report, 1929,* p. 5. The report does not refer to the forum shopping problem or to removals.

44. Note, "Action Against Foreign Carrier for Cause Arising Outside of State as Burden upon Interstate Commerce," *Minnesota Law Review* 13 (1929): 485.

45. Ibid., pp. 485, 487–88 (personal jurisdiction); Note, *Michigan Law Review* 31 (1933): 903, n. 1. For joinder, *Mayberry v. Northern Pacific Railroad Co.,* 110 N.W. 356 (Sup.Ct.Minn. 1907); *Doyle v. St. Paul Union Depot Co.,* 159 N.W. 1081 (Sup.Ct.Minn. 1916).

46. *Frye v. Chicago, Rock Island & Pacific Railway Co.,* 195 N.W. 629, cert. denied 263 U.S. 723 (1924).

47. Nonunanimous verdict: *Minneapolis & St. Louis Railroad Co. v. Bombolis,* 241 U.S. 211 (1916). Damages: *Frye v. Chicago, Rock Island & Pacific Railway Co.,* 195 N.W. 629 (Sup.Ct.Minn. 1923), cert denied 263 U.S. 723 (1924).

48. Note, "Progress in Interstate Adjustment of the Place of Trial of Civil Actions," *Yale Law Journal* 45 (1936): 1100, 1114–15. Attorneys representing out-of-state personal injury plaintiffs frequently filed their actions in two or more counties. "The object and purpose of the practice seems to be to ascertain the counties in which juries are most liberal in fixing damages." *Savarin v. Union Pacific Railroad Co.,* 292 F. 157, 162 (D.Minn. 1923).

49. *Njus v. Chicago, Milwaukee & St. Paul Railway Co.,* 49 N.W. 527 (Sup.Ct.Minn. 1891); *Little v. Chicago, St. Paul, Minneapolis & Omaha Railway Co.,* 67 N.W. 846 (Sup.Ct.Minn. 1896); *State ex rel. Prall v. District Court of Waseca County,* 148 N.W. 463 (Sup.Ct.Minn. 1914); *Davis v. Minneapolis, St. Paul & Sault Ste. Marie Railway Co.,* 159 N.W. 1084 (Sup.Ct.Minn. 1916); *State ex rel. Schendel v. District Court of Lyon County,* 194 N.W. 780 (Sup.Ct.Minn. 1923).

50. *Rishmiller v. Denver & Rio Grande Railroad Co.,* 159 N.W. 272 (Sup.Ct.Minn. 1916).

51. *Davis v. Minneapolis, St. Paul & Sault Ste. Marie Railway Co.,* 159 N.W. 1084 (Sup.Ct.Minn. 1916); *State ex rel. Bossung v. District Court, Hennepin County,* 168 N.W. 589 (Sup.Ct.Minn. 1918); *Union Pacific Railroad Co. v. Rule,* 193 N.W. 161 (Sup.Ct.Minn. 1923). Similarly, in 1926 the Supreme Court of Minnesota held that a violation by a Minnesota attorney of an Iowa statute that made it unlawful to solicit tort suits in Iowa for out-of-state prosecution did not require the Minnesota courts to dismiss the solicited suit. *Hovel v. Minneapolis & St. Louis Railway Co.,* 206 N.W. 710 (Sup.Ct.Minn. 1926).

52. See *Savarin v. Union Pacific Railroad Co.,* 292 F. 157 (D.Minn. 1923); *Reed's Administratrix v. Illinois Central Railroad Co.,* 206 S.W. 794 (Ct.App.Ken. 1918); *In re Spoo's Estate,* 183 N.W. 580 (Sup.Ct.Iowa 1921); *Chicago, Milwaukee & St. Paul Railway Co. v. McGinley,* 185 N.W. 218 (Sup.Ct.Wisc. 1921); *Winders v. Illinois Central Railroad Co.,* 223 N.W. 291 (Sup.Ct.Minn. 1929).

53. 298 F. 977 (D.Minn. 1924).

54. Ibid., p. 986.

55. Ibid., p. 983.

56. Ibid., p. 982. A sample of 133 cases brought against another railroad in Minnesota during

1927 and 1928 on out-of-state causes of action sought an average of almost $31,000 each. Note, *Minnesota Law Review* 15 (1930): 83, 94, n. 44.

57. *Chicago, Milwaukee, St. Paul & Pacific Railway Co. v. Wolf*, 226 N.W. 297, 298 (Sup.Ct.Wisc. 1929).

58. Ibid., p. 298.

59. Ibid., p. 299.

60. "Limitation of Venue in Certain Actions Brought Under the Employers' Liability Act," Hearings before a Subcommittee on the Judiciary of the United States Senate on S. 1567 and H.R. 1639, 80 Cong., 2 Sess. (1948), p. 20 (statement of John W. Freels, attorney for the Illinois Central Railroad Co.).

61. "Limitation of Venue in Certain Actions Brought Under the Employers' Liability Act," Hearings before Subcommittee No. 4 of the Committee on the Judiciary of the United States House of Representatives on H.R. 1639, 80 Cong., 1 Sess. (1947), p. 31 (statement of John W. Freels, attorney for the Illinois Central Railroad).

62. Ibid., p. 29. The supporters and defenders of interstate forum shopping traded numerous charges and allegations. The former offered a number of reasons for the emergence of the five major cities as importing centers (the plaintiffs' attorneys were experts; the cities were headquarters for many railroads; the railroads brought large numbers of their seriously injured workers to the hospitals in those cities; medical experts were more readily available; it was necessary to avoid many localities where the railroads were a dominant force). The latter denied those claims and explained the development on the basis of the unlawful and unethical practices that they alleged were common (organized solicitation; champerty and maintenance; misleading and deceiving clients; and unethical cooperation with the brotherhoods' legal aid departments). See hearings cited in n. 60 and 61; and H.R. Rep. No. 613, 80 Cong., 1 Sess. (1947) (pt 1, Majority Report; pt. 2 Minority Report; pt. 3, Minority Views of Mr. Feighan).

63. "Limitation of Venue in Certain Actions Brought Under the Employers' Liability Act," Hearings before Subcommittee No. 4 of the Committee on the Judiciary of the United States House of Representatives on H.R. 1639, 80 Cong., 1 Sess. (1947), p. 7 (statement of Hon. John Jennings, Jr., U.S. Congressman from Tennessee), pp. 101–2 (statement of E. Burke Finnerty, Esq.), p. 109 (statement of Jonas A. McBride, vice-president and national legislative representative, Brotherhood of Locomotive Firemen and Enginemen); "Limitation of Venue in Certain Actions Brought Under the Employers' Liability Act," Hearings before a Subcommittee of the Committee on the Judiciary of the United States Senate on S. 1567 and H.R. 1639, 80 Cong., 2 Sess. (1948), p. 37 (statement of John W. Freels, Illinois Central Railroad Co.), p. 85 (statement of Floyd E. Thompson, Esq.), pp. 169–70 (statement of Samuel D. Jackson, representing the Indiana State Bar Association).

64. "Limitation of Venue in Certain Actions Brought Under the Employers' Liability Act," Hearings before a Subcommittee of the Committee on the Judiciary of the United States Senate on S. 1567 and H.R. 1639, 80 Cong., 2 Sess. (1948), p. 232 (statement of Warren H. Atherton, attorney for the Brotherhood of Railroad Trainmen). The railroads agreed with the assessment. See Chapter 10.

65. Auerbach, *Unequal Justice,* chap. 4; Monaghan, "Liability Claim Racket"; *State ex. rel. Reynolds v. Circuit Court of Milwaukee County, Branch No. 1,* 214 N.W. 396 (Sup.Ct.Wisc. 1927); *Rubin v. State,* 216 N.W. 513 (Sup.Ct.Wisc. 1927); *Matter of Brooklyn Bar Association,* 223 App. Div. 149 (App.Div.2d Dep't N.Y. 1928); *Matter of Bar Association of City of New York,* 222 App. Div. 580 (App.Div.1st Dep't N.Y. 1928); *People v. Culkin,* 162 N.E. 487 (Ct.App.N.Y. 1928); *In re Rowe,* 4 F. Supp. 35 (E.D.N.Y.); *In re O'Neill,* 5 F. Supp. 465 (E.D.N.Y.); *In re McCallum,* 391 Ill. 400 (Sup.Ct.Ill. 1945). For general discussions of the rise of nativism and anti-Semitism in the years after World War I, see John Higham, *Strangers in the Land: Patterns of American Nativism, 1860–1925* (New York, 1963); John Higham, *Send These to Me: Immigrants in Urban America* (Baltimore, 1975); Henry L. Feingold, "Investing in Themselves: The Harvard Case and the Origins of the Third American-Jewish Commercial Elite," *American Jewish History* 77 (1987): 530–53; and the collection of essays published under the title "A Reexamination of a Classic Work in American Jewish History: John Higham's *Strangers in the Land,*" *American Jewish History* 76 (1986): 106–226.

66. Note, *California Law Review* 18 (1930): 159, n. 1; *Murnan v. Wabash Railway Co.*, 158 N.E. 508 (N.Y. 1927).

67. *New York, Chicago & St. Louis Railroad Co. v. Matzinger*, 25 N.E. 2d 349 (Sup.Ct.Ohio 1940); *Pere Marquette Railway Co. v. Slutz*, 256 N.W. 458 (Sup. Ct.Mich. 1934). See Note, *California Law Review* 18 (1930): 159.

68. Ibid., n. 1; *Chambers v. Baltimore & Ohio Railroad Co.*, 207 U.S. 142 (1907); *Loftus v. Pennsylvania Railroad Co.*, 140 N.E. 94 (Sup.Ct.Ohio 1923); *New York, Chicago & St. Louis Railroad Co. v. Matzinger*, 25 N.E. 2d 349, 351 (Sup.Ct.Ohio 1940).

69. Chapter 293 of the Acts of the Thirty Seventh General Assembly, Iowa Code (1927) Sec. 13172; Comp. Stat. Neb. (1929), sec. 28–739. See *Wabash Railway Co. v. Peterson*, 175 N.W. 523 (Sup.Ct.Iowa 1919); *Payne v. Knapp*, 198 N.W. 62 (Sup.Ct.Iowa 1924); Note, *Michigan Law Review* 31 (1933): 902, 905, n. 11.

70. American Bar Association, *Reports* 52 (1927): 292.

71. American Bar Association, *Annual Report* (1937): 1105 and n., 1118.

72. For example, "Limitation of Venue in Certain Actions Brought Under the Employers' Liability Act," Hearings before Subcommittee No. 4 of the Committee on the Judiciary of the United States House of Representatives on H.R. 1639, 80 Cong., 1 Sess. (1947), pp. 127, 136–37 (statement of Thomas B. Gay, president the Virginia State Bar Association and chairman of the Committee on Jurisprudence and Law Reform of the American Bar Association); "Limitation of Venue in Certain Actions Brought Under the Employers' Liability Act," Hearings before a Subcommittee of the Committee on the Judiciary of the United States Senate on S. 1567 and H.R. 1639, 80 Cong., 2 Sess. (1948), pp. 97–98 (statement of Jonathan C. Gibson, vice-president and general counsel, Santa Fe Railway).

73. Monaghan, "Liability Claim Racket." See Letter from John J. Cornwell to Newton D. Baker, April 12, 1932, Newton D. Baker Papers, Box 39, File: "B & O RR 1932," Library of Congress.

74. For example, *Chicago, Rock Island & Pacific Railway Co. v. Schendel*, 270 U.S. 611 (1926); *Chicago, Rock Island & Pacific Railway Co. v. Lundquist*, 221 N.W. 228 (Sup.Ct.Iowa 1928).

75. "Limitation of Venue in Certain Actions Brought Under the Employers' Liability Act," Hearings before Subcommittee No. 4 of the Committee on the Judiciary of the United States House of Representatives on H.R. 1639, 80 Cong., 1 Sess. (1947), p. 68 (statement of Warren H. Atherton, Esq., member of the Brotherhood of Railroad Trainmen).

76. Agreements upheld: *Detwiler v. Chicago, Rock Island & Pacific Railway Co.*, 15 F. Supp. 541 (D.Minn. 1936); *Detwiler v. Lowden*, 269 N.W. 367 (Sup.Ct.Minn. 1936); *Clark v. Lowden*, 48 F. Supp. 261 (D.Minn. 1942); *Herrington v. Thompson*, 61 F. Supp. 903 (W.D.Mo. 1945); *Roland v. Atchison, Topeka & Santa Fe Railway Co.*, 65 F. Supp. 630 (N.D.Ill. 1946). Agreements voided: *Sherman v. Pere Marquette Railway Co.*, 62 F. Supp. 590 (N.D.Ill. 1945); *Petersen v. Ogden Union Railway & Depot Co.*, 175 P.2d 744 (Sup.Ct.Utah 1946); *Krenger v. Pennsylvania Railroad Co.*, 174 F.2d 556 (2d Cir. 1949). In *Boyd v. Grand Trunk Western Railroad Co.*, 338 U.S. 263 (1949), the Supreme Court held such agreements to be invalid under Section 5 of the FELA.

77. "Limitation of Venue in Certain Actions Brought Under the Employers' Liability Act," Hearings before Subcommittee No. 4 of the Committee on the Judiciary of the United States House of Representatives, 80 Cong., 1 Sess. (1947), p. 68 (statement of Warren H. Atherton, Esq., member of the Brotherhood of Railroad Trainmen).

78. Hansell, "The Proper Forum for Suits Against Foreign Corporations," p. 12; Paxton Blair, "The Doctrine of Forum Non Conveniens in Anglo-American Law," *Columbia Law Review* 29 (1929); 1; Roger S. Foster, "Place of Trial in Civil Actions," *Harvard Law Review* 43 (1930): 1217; Roger S. Foster, "Place of Trial—Interstate Application of Intrastate Methods of Adjustment," *Harvard Law Review* 44 (1930): 41; Note, "Progress in Interstate Adjustment of the Place of Trial of Civil Actions," *Yale Law Journal* 45 (1936): 1100, 1235.

79. *Schendel v. McGee*, 300 F. 273 (C.C.A. 8 1924); *Southern Railway Co. v. Cochran*, 56 F.2d 1019 (C.C.A. 6 1932); *Norris v. Illinois Central Railroad Co.*, 18 F.2d 584 (D.Minn. 1925); *Beem v. Illinois Central Railroad Co.*, 55 F.2d 708 (D.Minn. 1930); *Doyle v. Northern Pacific*

Railway Co., 55 F.2d 708 (D.Minn. 1932); *Sacco v. Baltimore & Ohio Railroad Co.*, 56 F.Supp. 959 (E.D.N.Y. 1944). See Note, "The Exercise of Jurisdiction over Foreign Causes of Action Based on the Federal Employers' Liability Acts," *Yale Law Journal* 39 (1930): 388.

80. Messner, "The Jurisdiction of a Court of Equity," p. 494; Note, "Exterritorial [*sic*] Recognition of Injunctions Against Suit," *Yale Law Journal* 39 (1930): 719; Note, "Pendency of Foreign Suit in Personam on Same Cause of Action as Ground for Abatement or Stay," *Yale Law Journal* 39 (1930): 1196; Note, "When Courts of Equity Will Enjoin Foreign Suits," *Iowa Law Review* 27 (1941): 76.

81. Injunction granted: *Weaver v. Alabama Great Southern Railroad Co.*, 76 So. 364 (Sup.Ct.Ala. 1917); *Wabash Railway Co. v. Peterson*, 175 N.W. 523 (Sup.Ct.Iowa 1919); *Northern Pacific Railway Co. v. Richey & Gilbert Co.*, 232 P. 355 (Sup.Ct.Wash. 1925); *Cleveland, Cincinnati, Chicago & St. Louis Railway Co. v. Shelly*, 170 N.E. 328 (App.Ct.Ind. 1930); *Pere Marquette Railway Co. v. Slutz*, 256 N.W. 458 (Sup.Ct.Mich. 1934); *New York, Chicago & St. Louis Railroad Co. v. Matzinger*, 25 N.E.2d 349 (Sup.Ct.Ohio 1940). Injunction denied: *Missouri Pacific Railway Co. v. Harden*, 105 So. 2 (Sup.Ct.La. 1925). On foreign injunctions, for Minnesota, see cases cited in n. 51; *Peterson v. Chicago, Burlington & Quincy Railway Co.*, 244 N.W. 823 (Sup.Ct.Minn. 1932). For Missouri, see *Kepner v. Cleveland, Cincinnati, Chicago & St. Louis Railway Co.*, 15 S.W.2d 825 (Sup.Ct.Mo. 1929); *Lindsey v. Wabash Railway Co.*, 61 S.W.2d 369 (Sup.Ct. Mo. 1933); but compare *State ex. rel. New York, Chicago & St. Louis Railroad Co. v. Nortoni*, 55 S.W.2d 272 (Sup.Ct.Mo. 1932) (the Missouri state court has no jurisdiction to enjoin a railroad company from prosecuting a contempt proceeding in an out-of-state court that had enjoined one of its own citizens from prosecuting an action in Missouri).

82. State courts allowed injunctions against out-of-state FELA plaintiffs in *Reed's Administratrix v. Illinois Central Railroad Co.*, 206 S.W. 794 (Ct.App.Ky. 1918); *Chicago, Milwaukee & St. Paul Railway Co. v. McGinley*, 185 N.W. 218 (Sup.Ct.Wisc. 1921); *New York, Chicago & St. Louis Railroad Co. v. Perdiue*, 187 N.E. 349 (App.Ct.Ind. 1933); *Kern v. Cleveland Cincinnati, Chicago & St. Louis Railway Co.*, 185 N.E. 446 (Sup.Ct.Ind. 1933); *Alspaugh v. New York Chicago & St. Louis Railroad Co.*, 188 N.E. 869 (App.Ct.Ind. 1934); *Louisville & Nashville Railroad Co. v. Ragan*, 113 S.W.2d 743 (Sup.Ct.Tenn. 1938); *New York, Chicago & St. Louis Railroad Co. v. Matzinger*, 25 N.E.2d 349 (Sup.Ct.Ohio 1940). State courts denied injunctions in *Lancaster v. Dunn*, 95 So. 385 (Sup.Ct.La. 1922); *Payne v. Knapp*, 198 N.W. 62 (Sup.Ct.Iowa 1924); *Missouri-Kansas-Texas Railroad Co. v. Ball*, 271 P. 313 (Sup.Ct.Kan. 1928); *Southern Pacific Co. v. Baum*, 38 P.2d 1106 (Sup.Ct.N.M. 1934); *McConnell v. Thomson*, 8 N.E.2d 986 (Sup.Ct.Ind. 1937); *Baltimore & Ohio Railroad Co. v. Inlow*, 28 N.E. 373 (Ct.App.Ohio 1940).

The leading federal case holding that FELA plaintiffs had a statutory right to sue out of state and that state courts could not enjoin their suits was *Chicago, Milwaukee & St. Paul Railway Co. v. Schendel*, 292 F. 326 (C.C.A. 8 1923). See *Southern Railway Co. v. Cochran*, 56 F.2d 1019 (C.C.A. 6 1932); *Chesapeake & Ohio Railway Co. v. Vigor*, 17 F. Supp. 602 (S.D.Ohio 1936), aff'd 90 F.2d 7 (C.C.A. 6 1937), cert. denied 302 U.S. 705 (1937); *Rader v. Baltimore & Ohio Railroad Co.*, 108 F.2d 980 (C.C.A. 7 1940); *Baltimore & Ohio Railroad Co. v. Clem*, 36 F.Supp. 703 (N.D.W.Va. 1941). A leading federal case upholding a state court's right to enjoin an FELA suit pending in another state court was *Ex parte Crandall*, 52 F.2d 650 (S.D.Ind. 1931), aff'd 53 F.2d 969 (C.C.A. 7 1931). Occasionally, federal courts would themselves enjoin out-of-state suits. For example, *Baltimore & Ohio Railroad Co. v. Bole*, 31 F. Supp. 221 (N.D.W.Va. 1940). But more often they would not. For example, *Baltimore & Ohio Railroad Co. v. Clem*, 36 F. Supp. 703 (N.D.W.Va. 1941); *Baltimore & Ohio Railroad Co. v. Halchak*, 71 F.Supp. 224 (W.D.Pa. 1947).

The federal courts seemed to split on whether, in a federal FELA action, they could enjoin the defendant from seeking from a state court in plaintiff's home state an injunction prohibiting the plaintiff from continuing his federal action. Compare *Chicago, Milwaukee & St. Paul Railway Co. v. Schendel*, 292 F. 326 (C.C.A. 1923) with *Bryant v. Atlantic Coast Line Railroad Co.*, 92 F.2d 569 (C.C.A. 2 1937). The Supreme Court did not rule on the injunction issues until the early 1940s. Then, it held that state courts could not enjoin FELA suits in either state or federal courts and that federal courts could not enjoin federal FELA defendants from seeking injunctions against plaintiffs in the state courts of plaintiffs' home states. See Chapter 10.

83. Most notably, more than 20 percent of the cases the railroads identified as "imported" in the years from 1941 to 1946 arose from injuries that occurred within the same state where the action was filed. The roads classified them as imported because they were filed in a judicial district in the state other than the one in which the injury occurred. See "Limitation of Venue in Certain Actions Brought Under the Employers' Liability Act," Hearings before a Subcommittee of the Committee on the Judiciary of the United States Senate, 80 Cong., 2 Sess. (1948), pp. 25–26 (statement of John W. Freels, Illinois Central Railroad Co.). See also *Missouri-Kansas-Texas Railroad Co. v. Ball*, 271 P. 313 (Sup.Ct.Kan. 1928) (80 miles).

84. *Power Manufacturing Co. v. Saunders*, 274 U.S. 490, 492 (1927).

85. See *Missouri Pacific Railway Co. v. Harden*, 105 So. 2, 5 (Sup.Ct.La. 1925); *Miles v. Illinois Central Railroad Co.*, 315 U.S. 698, 705, 706 (Jackson, J., concurring) (in an action involving a railroad's petititon for an injunction to block an out-of-state suit under the FELA, referring to the "rather fantastic fiction that a widow is harassing the Illinois Central Railroad").

86. *Douglas v. New York, New Haven & Hartford Railroad Co.*, 279 U.S. 377 (1929).

87. 230 N.W. 457 (1931).

88. Foster, "Place of Trial," p. 59.

89. Blair, "Doctrine of Forum Non Conveniens," p. 34.

90. For example, ibid.; Foster, "Place of Trial"; Hansell, "Proper Forum for Suits"; Joseph Dainow, "The Inappropriate Forum," *Illinois Law Review* 29 (1935): 867. All four, particularly the first two, were valuable pieces of scholarship. They revealed, however, a strong dislike of interstate forum shopping without considering extenuating social factors, and they seemed to advance arguments that rather consistently favored corporate defendants. The author of the first major law review essay, Paxton Blair, was an associate at the large New York law firm of Cadwalader, Wickersham & Taft at the time he wrote his article. See Allan R. Stein, "Forum Non Conveniens and the Redundancy of Court-Access Doctrine," *University of Pennsylvania Law Review* 133 (1985): 781, 811, n. 127. The articles also stretched to pull together a coherent "doctrine" of *forum non conveniens* from disparate and thin sources. For criticism of their doctrinal efforts, see Stein, "Forum Non Conveniens," pp. 796–800; Alexander M. Bickel, "The Doctrine of Forum Non Conveniens as Applied in the Federal Courts in Matters of Admirality," *Cornell Law Quarterly* 35 (1949): 12; Robert Braucher, "The Inconvenient Federal Forum," *Harvard Law Review* 60 (1947): 908, 911–14. For contemporary analyses of interstate forum shopping with a somewhat different political tone, see Note, "Exercise of Jurisdiction over Foreign Causes"; Note, "Progress in Interstate Adjustment."

91. In such early cases where venue was improper and *Wisner* would have defeated removal (many of which involved commercial disputes between business groups), plaintiffs repeatedly failed to raise the venue objection promptly. This failure strongly suggests that plaintiffs' motive for bringing suit in their chosen forums was something other than the desire to prevent removal. The federal courts held that failure to raise promptly an objection to venue constituted a waiver and upheld the removals. See, for example, *Louisville & Nashville Railroad Co. v. Fisher*, 155 F. 68 (C.C.A. 6 1907); *Hill v. Woodland Amusement Co.*, 158 F. 530 (C.C.D.Dela. 1908) (court nevertheless holds improper venue to be jurisdictional and remands on that ground); *Corwin Manufacturing Co. v. Henrici Washer Co.*, 151 F. 938 (C.C.D.Mass. 1907); *Proctor Coal Co. v. United States Fidelity & Guaranty Co.*, 158 F. 211 (C.C.N.D.Ga. 1907); *Gillespie v. Pocahontas Coal & Coke Co.*, 162 F. 742 (C.C.S.D.W.Va. 1907).

92. Commercial uses: *Kansas Gas & Electric Co. v. Wichita Natural Gas Co.*, 266 F. 614 (C.C.A. 8 1920); *Louisville & Nashville Railroad Co. v. Western Union Telegraph Co.*, 218 F. 91 (E.D.Ky. 1914); *Western Union Telegraph Co. v. Louisville & Nashville Railroad Co.*, 229 F. 234 (N.D.Ga. 1915); *Ostrom v. Edison*, 244 F. 228 (D.N.J. 1917); *Lockport Glass Co. v. H.L. Dixon Co.*, 262 F. 976 (W.D.Pa. 1919); *Gist v. Johnson Carey Co.*, 151 N.W. 382 (Sup.Ct.Wisc. 1915); *Stewart v. Cybur Lumber Co.*, 72 So. 276 (Sup.Ct.Miss. 1916).

93. Plaintiffs defeated removal in *Hubbard v. Chicago, Milwaukee & St. Paul Railway Co.*, 176 F. 994 (C.C.D.Minn. 1910) (FELA suit prior to 1910 amendments); *Bottoms v. St. Louis & San Francisco Railroad Co.*, 179 F. 318 (C.C.N.D.Ga. 1910) (FELA suit prior to 1910 amendments); *Perrette v. Illinois Commercial Men's Association*, 267 F. 583 (W.D.Ky. 1920); *St. Louis & San Francisco Railroad Co. v. Kiser*, 136 S.W. 852 (Ct.Civ.App.Tx. 1911); *St. Louis & San*

Francisco Railroad Co. v. Matlock, 141 S.W. 1067 (Ct.Civ.App.Tx. 1911); *Hershiser v. Chicago, Burlington & Quincy Railroad Co.,* 170 N.W. 178 (Sup.Ct.Neb. 1918); *Southwestern Gas & Electric Co. v. Raines,* 218 S.W. 545 (Ct.Civ.App.Tx. 1920); *Pullman Co. v. Sutherlin,* 104 S.E. 782 (Sup.Ct.Ga. 1920). Plaintiffs failed to defeat removal in *Bagenas v. Southern Pacific Co.,* 180 F. 887 (C.C.N.D.Cal. 1910); *James v. Amarillo City Light & Water Co.,* 251 F. 337 (N.D.Tx. 1918); *Sanders v. Western Union Telegraph Co.,* 261 F. 697 (N.D.Ga. 1919); *Earles v. Germain Co.,* 265 F. 715 (S.D.Ala. 1920). It was also possible to use *Wisner* in connection with assigned claims: for example, *Waterman v. Chesapeake & Ohio Railway Co.,* 199 F. 667 (D.N.J. 1912).

94. Armistead M. Dobie, *Handbook of Federal Jurisdiction and Procedure* (St. Paul, 1928), p. 504.

95. *Webb v. Southern Railway Co.,* 248 F. 618 (C.C.A. 5 1918); *Gopcevic v. California Packing Corp.,* 272 F. 994 (N.D.Cal. 1921); *St. Louis & San Francisco Railroad Co. v. Kitchen,* 136 S.W. 970 (Sup.Ct.Ark. 1911); *St. Louis & San Francisco Railroad Co. v. Hodge,* 157 P. 63 (Sup.Ct.Okla. 1916); *Central Coal & Coke Co. v. Graham,* 196 S.W. 940 (Sup.Ct.Ark. 1917).

96. *St. John v. United States Fidelity & Guaranty Co.,* 213 F. 685 (D.Md. 1914); *Lockport Glass Co. v. H.L. Dixon Co.,* 262 F. 976 (W.D.Pa. 1919); *Southwestern Gas & Electric Co. v. Raines,* 218 S.W. 545 (Ct.Civ.App.Tx. 1920). See Dobie, *Handbook,* p. 505 and n. 17.

97. *Bagenas v. Southern Pacific Co.,* 180 F. 887 (C.C.N.D.Cal. 1910); *Louisville & Nashville Railroad Co. v. Western Union Telegraph Co.,* 218 F. 91 (E.D.Ky. 1914); *Western Union Telegraph Co. v. Louisville & Nashville Railroad Co.,* 229 F. 234 (N.D.Ga. 1915); *Keating v. Pennsylvania Co.,* 245 F. 155 (N.D.Ohio 1917); *James v. Amarillo City Light & Water Co.,* 251 F. 337 (N.D.Tx. 1918); *Sanders v. Western Union Telegraph Co.,* 261 F. 697 (N.D.Ga. 1919); *Earles v. Germain Co.,* 265 F. 715 (S.D.Ala. 1920).

98. In *In re Moore,* 209 U.S. 490, 507 (1908), the Court admitted that *Wisner* contained "unnecessary" language that could give rise to a "future misconception" about venue. It emphasized that *Wisner* did not change the established rule that parties could not confer subject matter jurisdiction on a federal court and that they could allow an action to proceed—assuming that subject matter jurisdiction existed—only by waiving an otherwise valid objection to venue. The general rule was that parties could waive otherwise valid objections to venue. See, for example, *Central Trust Co. v. McGeorge,* 151 U.S. 129 (1894). Two months later, to underscore the point, the Court declared the unnecessary language in *Wisner* to be "overruled." *Western Loan and Savings Co. v. Butte and Boston Consolidated Mining Co.,* 210 U.S. 368, 369 (1908). If that was not bad enough, in another series of decisions between 1909 and 1911, the Court undermined *Wisner* on a second procedural point in the case concerning the use of mandamus as a tool for securing appellate review. *Matter of Tobin,* 214 U.S. 506 (1909); *Ex parte Nicola,* 218 U.S. 506 (1910); *Ex parte Harding,* 219 U.S. 363 (1911).

Within a few years of its appearance, then, *Wisner* seemed a somewhat shaky authority. For a contemporary view of federal venue issues, see Armistead M. Dobie, "Venue in the United States District Court," *Virginia Law Review* 2 (1914): 1.

99. *Bagenas v. Southern Pacific Co.,* 180 F. 887 (C.C.N.D.Cal. 1910).

100. *Jackson v. William Kenefick Co.,* 233 F. 130 (S.D.N.Y. 1913).

101. *Sanders v. Western Union Telegraph Co.,* 261 F. 697 (N.D.Ga. 1919).

102. *Louisville & Nashville Railroad Co. v. Western Union Telegraph Co.,* 218 F. 91, 111 (E.D.Ky. 1914).

103. *Guaranty Trust Co. of New York v. McCabe,* 250 F. 699, 706 (C.C.A. 2 1916) (L. Hand, J., dissenting). See *Jackson v. William Kenefick Co.,* 233 F. 130 (S.D.N.Y. 1913); *Ivanoff v. Mechanical Rubber Co.,* 232 F. 173 (N.D.Ohio 1916); *Keating v. Pennsylvania Co.,* 245 F. 155 (N.D.Ohio 1917); *Earles v. Germain Co.,* 265 F. 715 (S.D.Ala. 1920).

104. *General Investment Co. v. Lake Shore & Michigan Southern Railway Co.,* 260 U.S. 261, 270–79 (1922).

105. 260 U.S. 653 (1923).

106. Ibid., p. 660.

107. Ibid., p. 660. For a contemporary review of federal venue law after *Lee,* see Armistead M. Dobie, "Venue in Civil Cases in the United States District Court," *Yale Law Journal* 35 (1925): 129.

108. For example, *Terral v. Burke Construction Co.,* 257 U.S. 529 (1922). See Chapter 9. *Lee* quickly put an end to the *Wisner* tactic. Compare, for example, *Louisville & Nashville Railroad Co. v. Garnett,* 93 So. 241 (Sup.Ct.Miss. 1922) with *Louisville & Nashville Railroad Co. v. Garnett,* 96 So. 519 (Sup.Ct.Miss. 1923).

109. For example, *Burnrite Coal Briquette Co. v. Riggs,* 274 U.S. 208 (1927). Law, practicalities, and social conditions made the right to remove more valuable to corporations than the venue restrictions that protected them against original federal suits. Compared with the number of plaintiffs who sought to bring actions against foreign corporations in their home state courts, relatively few tried to bring them in out-of-state federal courts.

The practical advantage that *Lee* restored to corporations was based in part on what seemed an inconsistent treatment of the concept of waiver. If it was reasonable to hold that a plaintiff who initiated suit in a foreign state court thereby waived his right to object to federal venue in that same location, it seemed equally reasonable to assume that a defendant who consented to submit to personal jurisdiction in a state thereby waived its right to object to venue in an original federal suit in the same state. The Supreme Court so held in 1939 in *Neirbo Co. v. Bethlehem Shipbuilding Corp., Ltd.,* 308 U.S. 165 (1939). See Chapter 10.

110. Not only was the decision in *Lee* unanimous, but a letter from Justice John H. Clarke, who had retired from the Court less than a year before, to Justice Willis Van Devanter, who wrote the *Lee* opinion, suggests that the decision's practical litigation significance caused little or no conflict among the Justices. Clarke, appointed by Woodrow Wilson in 1916, was a staunch progressive who had repeatedly shown his sympathy for injured workers during his tenure on the Court. Yet, writing to the conservative Van Devanter, Clarke commented that *Lee*

> is in your best vein and does what should have been done years ago. It was one of those unfortunate straddles which some men persuade themselves are very astute & which others let pass rather than oppose. You clear it up finally & make me more confident even than your letter did that all is well. [John H. Clarke to Willis Van Devanter, March 2, 1923, Willis Van Devanter Papers, Library of Congress]

I wish to thank Professor Robert C. Post for calling this letter to my attention.

111. In spite of the consensus that marked the Court's decision in *Lee,* Justice Louis D. Brandeis, at least, had reservations about the decision. Three years after it came down he advised privately that, as part of a general effort to limit diversity jurisdiction, Congress should "take away the jurisdiction established in Lee v. C & O Ry Co." Brandeis to Felix Frankfurter, Feb. 1, 1926, *"Half Brother, Half Son": The Letters of Louis D. Brandeis to Felix Frankfurter,* ed. Melvin I. Urofsky and David W. Levy (Norman, OK, 1991), p. 229. By eliminating the *Lee* rule, Brandeis hoped to find one more way to limit diversity jurisdiction. Although he favored restricting diversity jurisdiction for a variety of reasons, his dislike of the jurisdiction was also fueled by his belief that it unfairly disadvantaged individual plaintiffs who sued corporate defendants.

112. 262 U.S. 312 (1923).

113. Ibid., p. 318.

114. Ibid., pp. 315–16 and n. 2.

115. Ibid., p. 316.

116. Ibid., p. 317.

117. The following year the Court seemed to expand *Davis's* doctrine of commerce clause venue when it reviewed an action brought to enjoin enforcement of a default judgment obtained in an earlier tort action. In *Atchison, Topeka & Santa Fe Railway Co. v. Wells,* 265 U.S. 101 (1924), the Court voided both a Texas garnishment statute as applied and the judgment obtained through its use. The decision suggested that the commerce clause venue doctrine might have jurisdictional significance, as the Court used it not merely to reverse a judgment on appeal but to void a default judgment obtained in a separate action that had ostensibly become final.

118. For general discussions of Brandeis's life and career on the bench, see Alpheus Thomas Mason, *Brandeis: A Free Man's Life* (New York, 1946); Anton Gal, *Brandeis of Boston* (Cambridge, MA, 1980); Nelson L. Dawson, *Louis D. Brandeis, Felix Frankfurter, and the New Deal* (Hamden, CT, 1980); Bruce Allen Murphy, *The Brandeis/Frankfurter Connection: The Secret Political Activities of Two Supreme Court Justices* (New York, 1982); Lewis J. Paper, *Brandeis*

(Englewood Cliffs, NJ, 1983); Philippa Strum, *Louis D. Brandeis: Justice for the People* (Cambridge, MA, 1984); and Leonard Baker, *Brandeis and Frankfurter: A Dual Biography* (New York, 1984). Particularly valuable in understanding Brandeis's evolving views are two collections of letters, both superbly edited by Melvin I. Urofsky and David W. Levy: *Letters of Louis D. Brandeis,* 5 vols. (Albany, NY, 1971–78) and *"Half Brother, Half Son."*

119. Blair, "Doctrine of Forum Non Conveniens," p. 24, n. 110.

120. *Schendel v. McGee,* 300 F. 273 (C.C.A. 8 1924); *Norris v. Illinois Central Railroad Co.,* 18 F.2d 584 (D.Minn. 1925); *Trapp v. Baltimore & Ohio Railroad Co.,* 283 F.655 (E.D.Ohio 1922).

121. *Maverick Mills v. Davis,* 294 F. 404 (D.Mass. 1923); *Griffin v. Seaboard Air Line Railway Co.,* 28 F. 2d 998 (W.D.Mo. 1928).

122. *Hoffman v. Foraker,* 274 U.S. 21 (1927).

123. Ibid., p. 23.

124. 278 U.S. 492 (1929).

125. Ibid., p. 495.

126. 284 U.S. 284 (1932).

127. Ibid., p. 286.

128. Ibid., pp. 286–87.

129. Ibid.

130. The court so held in *Bohn v. Norfolk & Western Railway Co.,* 22 F.Supp. 481 (S.D.N.Y. 1937). For general discussions of the commerce clause venue doctrine, see Note, *California Law Review* 17 (1929): 396; Note, "Due Process, Jurisdiction over Corporations, and the Commerce Clause," *Harvard Law Review* 42 (1929): 1062; Paul E. Farrier, "Suits Against Foreign Corporations as a Burden on Interstate Commerce," *Minnesota Law Review* 17 (1933): 381; Note, *Columbia Law Review* 34 (1934): 1135; Note, *Michigan Law Review* 34 (1936): 979.

131. 262 U.S. 316–17. In its earliest commerce clause venue decisions, the Court gave somewhat conflicting signals regarding the importance of plaintiff's residence. In *Atchison, Topeka & Santa Fe Railway Co. v. Wells,* 265 U.S. 101 (1924), it seemed to enlarge the reach of the *Davis* doctrine by suggesting that the residence of the plaintiff was irrelevant. There, the plaintiff had become a resident of the forum state, and the Court did not trouble to specify when he had done so in vacating his judgment below. The same year, however, in *St. Louis, Brownsville & Mexico Railway Co. v. Taylor,* 266 U.S. 200 (1924), the Court expressly gave weight to plaintiff's residence in refusing to apply the *Davis* doctrine. Its decision refused to prevent a Missouri court from hearing an action against a foreign corporation based on *quasi in rem* jurisdiction over the company's instate property.

132. For example, *Williamson v. Osenton,* 232 U.S. 619 (1914).

133. 279 U.S. 377 (1929).

134. The Court rested its finding of reasonableness on two of the practical reasons that those who opposed interstate forum shopping usually advanced. "There are manifest reasons for preferring residents in access to often overcrowded Courts," it declared, "both in convenience and in the fact that broadly speaking it is they who pay for maintaining the Courts concerned" (ibid., p. 387). See also *Canadian Northern Railway Co. v. Eggen,* 252 U.S. 553, 562 (1920).

135. 279 U.S. 388.

136. *Converse v. Hamilton,* 224 U.S. 243 (1912); *Supreme Council of the Royal Arcanum v. Green,* 237 U.S. 531 (1915); *Modern Woodmen of America v. Mixer,* 267 U.S. 544 (1925); E. Merrick Dodd, Jr., "The Power of the Supreme Court to Review State Decisions in the Field of Conflict of Laws," *Harvard Law Review* 39 (1926): 533; Stephen I. Langmaid, "The Full Faith and Credit Required for Public Acts," *Illinois Law Review* 24 (1929): 383; Edward A. Corwin, "The 'Full Faith and Credit' Clause," *University of Pennsylvania Law Review* 81 (1933): 371.

137. 286 U.S. 145 (1932).

138. See *John Hancock Mutual Life Insurance Co. v. Yates,* 299 U.S. 156 (1936). For general developments, see G. W. C. Ross, "Has the Conflict of Laws Become a Branch of Constitutional Law?" *Minnesota Law Review* 15 (1931): 161; G. W. C. Ross, " 'Full Faith and Credit' in a Federal System," *Minnesota Law Review* 20 (1936): 140.

139. The equal protection clause was much less important than the due process clause. See,

for example, *Kentucky Finance Corp. v. Paramount Auto Exchange Corp.*, 262 U.S. 544 (1923); *Power Manufacturing Co. v. Saunders*, 274 U.S. 490 (1927).

140. For example, *Riverside and Dan River Cotton Mills v. Menafee*, 237 U.S. 189 (1915); *Rosenberg Bros. & Co., Inc. v. Curtis Brown Co.*, 260 U.S. 516 (1923); *James-Dickinson Farm Mortgage Co. v. Harry*, 273 U.S. 119 (1927); *Consolidated Textile Corp. v. Gregory*, 289 U.S. 85 (1933).

141. *Old Wayne Mutual Life Association of Indianapolis v. McDonough*, 204 U.S. 8 (1907); *Simon v. Southern Railway Co.*, 236 U.S. 115 (1915); *Robert Mitchell Furniture Co. v. Selden Breck Construction Co.*, 257 U.S. 213 (1921). In 1922 the Court announced that in dealing with such statutes it would adopt "a construction, where possible, that would exclude from their operation causes of action not arising in the business done by them in the State." See *Missouri Pacific Railroad Co. v. Clarendon Boat Oar Co., Inc.*, 257 U.S. 533, 535 (1922).

142. For example, *New York Life Insurance Co. v. Head*, 234 U.S. 149 (1914); *New York Life Insurance Co. v. Dodge*, 246 U.S. 357 (1918); *Aetna Life Insurance Co. v. Dunken*, 266 U.S. 389 (1924); *Home Insurance Co. v. Dick*, 281 U.S. 397 (1930); *Hartford Accident & Indemnity Co. v. Delta & Pine Land Co.*, 292 U.S. 143 (1934). See also *Mutual Life Insurance Co. of New York v. Liebing*, 259 U.S. 209 (1922).

143. See, for example, for Minnesota: *Gamble-Robinson Co. v. Pennsylvania Railroad Co.*, 196 N.W. 266 (Sup.Ct.Minn. 1923); *Erving v. Chicago & Northwestern Railway Co.*, 214 N.W. 12 (Sup.Ct.Minn. 1927); *Kebbe v. Chicago & Northwestern Railway Co.*, 216 N.W. 513 (Sup. Ct. Minn. 1927); *Gagere v. Chicago & Northwestern Railway Co.*, 220 N.W. 429 (Sup.Ct.Minn. 1928); *Witort v. Chicago & Northwestern Railway Co.*, 226 N.W. 934 (Sup.Ct.Minn. 1929). For Missouri, see, for example, *Wells v. Davis*, 261 S.W. 58 (Sup.Ct.Mo. 1924); *State ex rel. Foraker v. Hoffman*, 274 S.W. 362 (Sup.Ct.Mo. 1925), aff'd 274 U.S. 21 (1927); *Shaw v. Chicago & Alton Railroad Co.*, 282 S.W. 416 (Sup.Ct.Mo. 1926).

144. *Winders v. Illinois Central Railroad Co.*, 226 N.W. 213 (Sup.Ct.Minn. 1929). Agreeing: *Boright v. Chicago, Rock Island & Pacific Railroad Co.*, 230 N.W. 457, 460 (Sup.Ct.Minn. 1930). The Missouri Supreme Court acted similarly in *Bright v. Wheelock*, 20 S.W. 2d 684 (Sup. Ct. Mo. 1929).

145. *Denver & Rio Grande Western Railroad Co. v. Terte*, 284 U.S. 284, 287 (1932); *International Milling Co. v. Columbia Transportation Co.*, 292 U.S. 511, 521 (1934).

146. 284 U.S. 183 (1931).

147. For prior doctrine, see Dobie, *Handbook*, pp. 193–95. For example, *Mexican Central Railway Co. v. Eckman*, 187 U.S. 429 (1903); *Continental Insurance Co. v. Rhoads*, 119 U.S. 237 (1886); *Dodge v. Perkins*, 7 Fed. Cas. 798 (C.C.D.Mass. 1827). The tactic was used in *Prince v. New York Life Insurance Co.*, 24 F. Supp. 41 (D.Mass. 1938).

To defeat interstate forum shopping tactics, the Court was unwilling to twist the venue statutes as far as some lower court judges attempted. In *Chesapeake & Ohio Railway Co. v. Moore*, 64 F. 2d 472 (C.C.A. 7 1933), for example, the Seventh Circuit adopted what seemed an obviously distorted construction of the federal venue laws in an apparent attempt to frustrate—and, it almost seemed, to punish—a railroad worker who had been seriously injured at his job site in Kentucky but who brought his suit in Indiana. James B. Moore alleged that he had fallen under the wheel of a car because of a faulty coupler and pleaded two causes of action in the alternative, one under the FELA and another under a Kentucky employers' liability law similar to the FELA. On both claims he pleaded that the defective coupler violated the federal Safety Appliance Act and thereby established the company's negligence. Although the district court upheld Moore's claims and the jury awarded him a verdict for $30,000, the Seventh Circuit reversed.

Two federal appellate judges and a district judge sitting by designation reasoned that the two claims were brought not under the FELA and state law, respectively, but under the Safety Appliance Act. On that basis they concluded that venue was proper in each of the two claims only under the general federal venue statute, which required suit to be brought in the district of the defendant's residence. Not content with that, the judges also declared that the Safety Appliance Act applied "only to interstate commerce" (ibid., p. 476) and therefore could not apply, in any event, to Moore's state law claim. The appellate court reversed the judgment below with instructions to allow Moore, if he chose, to replead his first claim based solely on the FELA and to replead his second claim solely on Kentucky law. It decided, in other words, to force Moore either to abandon his attempt to rely on the federal Safety Appliance Act or to bring his suit several hundred miles away at the railroad's residence in the Eastern District of Virginia.

The following year, in an opinion by Chief Justice Charles E. Hughes, the Supreme Court curtly reversed. The Seventh Circuit's ruling, it announced on the basis of well-established authority, "cannot be sustained." *Moore v. Chesapeake & Ohio Railway Co.,* 291 U.S. 205, 210 (1934). Regarding the plaintiff's first claim, the Court noted that the FELA was "in *pari materia*" with the Safety Appliance Act and that it made the standards of the latter relevant to claims under the former. The first claim was properly brought under the FELA, then, and the FELA's broad venue provision controlled and allowed suit in Indiana where the company did business. Regarding the second claim, the Court held that state law could incorporate the federal standards mandated in the Safety Appliance Act without transforming the claim into a federal law claim. The plaintiff's second claim therefore was not based on the presence of a federal question but only on diversity of citizenship, and in actions based solely on diversity jurisdiction, venue was proper in the district of residence of either defendant or plaintiff. Because Moore lived in Indiana, venue was proper there. Based on the Seventh Circuit's dictum about the scope of the Safety Appliance Act, the Court easily labeled it "erroneous" (ibid., p. 213). Citing its earlier decisions and quoting the language of the statute, the Court declared that "the scope of the statute was enlarged so as to include all cars 'used on any railroad engaged in interstate commerce' " (ibid., pp. 213–14).

Moore was noteworthy for two reasons. First, the Seventh Circuit's decision strained beyond plausibility to defeat plaintiff and seemed flatly inconsistent with established law. At a minimum it exemplified the extremes to which some lower federal court judges were willing to go to restrict interestate forum shopping. It suggested, too, that the three judges who sat on the case were particularly sympathetic to corporate defendants. Second, the Supreme Court's decision illustrated the relatively narrow limits within which the Court was willing to shape the law to confine interstate forum shopping and the extent to which the Justices were often less favorably disposed toward corporate defendants than were many lower court judges. Whereas three lower court judges had joined the Seventh Circuit's opinion, all nine Justices of the Supreme Court supported the reversal.

The case is also revealing in another way. *Moore* represents a relatively narrow view of the scope of general "federal question" jurisdiction. It held that a federal law issue incorporated into a state law claim was not sufficiently substantial to make the claim "arise under" federal law for purposes of original jurisdiction in the district court. It arguably contrasts with decisions that seem to give a broader scope to federal question jurisdiction. For example, *Smith v. Kansas City Title & Trust Co.,* 255 U.S. 180 (1921). As such, *Moore* has taken on a continued vitality: for example, *Merrill Dow Pharmaceuticals, Inc. v. Thompson,* 478 U.S. 804 (1986). Both the nature of the Seventh Circuit's opinion and the historical context of the Supreme Court's decision, however, suggest that *Moore's* authority as precedent may properly be somewhat less than might at first seem appropriate. In *Moore,* the Court was not attempting to state a general rule or develop a general approach to the question of the proper scope of federal question jurisdiction. Rather, it was forced to reverse an unsupportable and obviously strained decision, and it was attempting to ensure the practical effectiveness of the federal Safety Appliance Act and to clarify in the process important legal issues other than the nature of a "federal question."

148. 292 U.S. 511, 520 (1934).

149. Ibid., p. 517. After *International Milling,* the commerce clause venue doctrine was seldom applied. See Stein, "Forum Non Conveniens," pp. 781, 810 and n. 120.

150. *McKnett v. St. Louis & San Francisco Railway Co.,* 292 U.S. 230 (1934).

151. *Louisville & Nashville Railroad Co. v. Chatters,* 279 U.S. 320 (1929).

152. *Alaska Packers Association v. Industrial Accident Commission of California,* 294 U.S. 532, 547, 548 (1935). See *Ohio v. Chattanooga Boiler & Tank Co.,* 289 U.S. 439 (1933); *Pacific Employers Insurance Co. v. Industrial Accident Commission,* 306 U.S. 493 (1939); Paul A. Freund, *On Law and Justice* (Cambridge, MA, 1968), pp. 183–213.

153. *Broderick v. Rosner,* 294 U.S. 629, 643 (1935).

Chapter 9

1. "Limiting Jurisdiction of Federal Courts," Hearings before the Committee on the Judiciary of the United States House of Representatives, 72 Cong., 1 Sess. (1932), p. 77 (statement of F. G. Dunham, representing the Association of Life Insurance Counsel).

2. Letter from Raymond N. Klass to George W. Norris, October 26, 1933, George W. Norris Papers, Library of Congress, Box 198, File: "Limiting Jurisdiction of Federal Courts (71st & 72nd) Congress."

3. "Limiting Jurisdiction of Federal Courts," Hearings before the Committee on the Judiciary of the United States House of Representatives, 72 Cong., 1 Sess. (1932), pp. 20, 24 (statement of Hobart S. Weaver, attorney for the Association of Life Insurance Presidents).

4. Probably more than 90 percent of all insurance litigation occurred in state courts. See ibid., p. 25 (statement of Hobart S. Weaver, attorney for the Association of Life Insurance Presidents); Morton Keller, "The Judicial System and the Law of Life Insurance, 1888–1910," *Business History Review* 35 (1961): 317, 321.

5. 8 Wall. (75 U.S.) 168 (1868).

6. The Court stated in *Paul:*

It is not too much to say that the wealth and business of the country are to a great extent controlled by [corporations]. And if, when composed of citizens of one State, their corporate powers and franchises could be exercised in other States without restriction, it is easy to see that, with the advantages thus possessed, the most important business of those States would soon pass into their hands. The principal business of every State would, in fact, be controlled by corporations created by other States. [75 U.S. 181–82]

7. 20 Wall. (87 U.S.) 445 (1874).

8. 3 Otto (94 U.S.) 535 (1876).

9. For example, *Chicago & Northwestern Railroad Co. v. Whitton,* 13 Wall. (80 U.S.) 270 (1871); *Hess v. Reynolds,* 113 U.S. 73 (1885); *Goldley v. Morning News,* 156 U.S. 518 (1895).

10. 121 U.S. 186 (1887).

11. 146 U.S. 202 (1892).

12. 202 U.S. 246 (1906).

13. Ibid., p. 257.

14. For example, *Hooper v. California,* 155 U.S. 648 (1895); *New York Life Insurance Co. v. Deer Lodge County,* 231 U.S. 495 (1913).

15. After 1910 the Supreme Court began to develop the doctrine of "unconstitutional conditions," barring states from imposing restrictions that caused the violation of constitutional rights. Although it voided a number of state statutes that attempted to restrict removal, it relied implicitly or explicitly on a constitutional right to conduct interstate business. See, for example, *Western Union Telegraph Co. v. Kansas,* 216 U.S. 1 (1910); *Donald v. Philadelphia & Reading Coal & Iron Co.,* 241 U.S. 329 (1916). The Court explained that the "extremely narrow" rule of *Doyle* and *Prewitt* was limited to cases that "involved state legislation as to a subject over which there was complete state authority." *Harrison v. St. Louis & San Francisco Railroad Co.,* 232 U.S. 318, 332–33 (1914).

16. "Limiting Jurisdiction of Federal Courts," Hearings before the Committee on the Judiciary of the United States House of Representatives, 72 Cong., 1 Sess. (1932), p. 27 (statement of J. H. Doyle, general counsel, National Board of Fire Underwriters); George Richards, *A Treatise on the Law of Insurance,* 3rd ed. (New York, 1910), pp. 162–169. Included among the states that had antiremoval statutes on their books were Georgia, Kansas, Michigan, Nebraska, New Hampshire, Ohio, Illinois, North Carolina, Kentucky, and Wisconsin. See Richards, *Treatise on the Law of Insurance,* 2nd ed. (New York, 1893), App. 24, pp. 582–83; William R. Vance, *Handbook of the Law of Insurance* (St. Paul, 1930), p. 33, n. 81; *Cable v. United States Life Insurance Co.,* 191 U.S. 288 (1903); *Doyle v. Continental Insurance Co.,* 94 U.S. 535 (1876); *Security Mutual Life Insurance Co. v. Prewitt,* 202 U.S. 246 (1906). There were particularly strong motives to regulate insurance companies in the states of the South and the Mississippi Valley. See B. Michael Pritchett, "Northern Institutions in Southern Financial History: A Note on Insurance Investments,"

Journal of Southern History 41 (1975): 391. For a summary of the legal status of corporations in the states after *Prewitt,* see William L. Clark, Jr., *Handbook of the Law of Private Corporations,* 3rd ed. (St. Paul, 1916), pp. 758–70.

17. Generally, legal fraud required proof of an intent to deceive, and equitable fraud required proof only of a material misrepresentation of fact. See, for example, *New York Life Insurance Co. v. Marotta,* 57 F.2d 1038 (C.C.A. 3 1932); George L. Clark, *Equity: An Analysis and Discussion of Modern Equity Problems* (Cincinnati, 1923) pp. 506–28; William F. Walsh, *A Treatise on Equity* (Chicago, 1930), pp. 490–513; George Tucker Bispham, *The Principles of Equity: A Treatise on the System of Justice Administered in Courts of Chancery,* 11th ed., rev. by Joseph D. McCoy (New York, 1931), pp. 176–93.

18. The statutory provision was based on Section 16 of the original Judiciary Act of 1789 and has remained in force continously since that time. See John Norton Pomeroy, *A Treatise on Equity Jurisprudence,* 4th ed. (San Francisco, 1918), vol. 1, pp. 576–78.

19. *Home Insurance Co. v. Stanchfield,* 12 Fed. Cas. 449, 453 (C.C.D.Minn. 1870).

20. Ibid., p. 452.

21. Ibid.

22. Ibid., pp. 451, 452.

23. Ibid., p. 452.

24. 13 Wall. (80 U.S.) 616 (1871).

25. Ibid., p. 620.

26. Ibid., pp. 622–23.

27. 191 U.S. 288 (1903).

28. Ibid., p. 309.

29. Ibid.

30. Ibid., p. 308.

31. Ibid., p. 297.

32. For example, *Riggs v. Union Life Insurance Co. of Indiana,* 129 F. 207 (C.C.A. 8 1904); *Griesa v. Mutual Life Insurance Co. of New York,* 169 F. 509 (C.C.A. 8 1909); *Mechanics' Insurance Co. of Philadelphia v. C.A. Hoover Distilling Co.,* 173 F. 888 (C.C.A. 8 1909); *Niagara Fire Insurance Co. of New York v. Adams,* 198 F. 822 (C.C.A. 1 1912); *Nellis v. Pennock Manufacturing Co.,* 38 F. 379 (C.C.E.D.Pa. 1889). See Pomeroy, *Treatise on Equity Jurisprudence,* 4th ed., vol. 1, pp. 577–78 and notes; John Norton Pomeroy, *Equity Jurisprudence* (San Francisco, 1905), vol. 2, pp. 1151–57; Joseph A. Joyce, *A Treatise on Marine, Fire, Life, Accident and All Other Insurances* (San Francisco, 1897), vol. 2, pp. 1685–91. Sometimes, of course, the courts did find "special circumstances." See *Mutual Life Insurance Co. of New York v. Pearson,* 114 F. 395 (C.C.D.Mass. 1902); *Mutual Life Insurance Co. of New York v. Blair,* 130 F. 971 (C.C.E.D.Mo. 1904).

33. See, for example, the complaints and proposals in Remington Rogers, "Bogus Claimants and Malingerers," American Bar Association, *Address Delivered at the Milwaukee Meeting, Section of Insurance Law* (1934): 15.

34. 257 U.S. 529 (1922).

35. Ibid., pp. 532, 533.

36. Letter from Matthew A. McCullough to George W. Norris, February 21, 1933, George W. Norris Papers, Library of Congress, Box 198, File: "Limiting Jurisdiction of Federal Courts (71st & 72nd) Congress."

37. Letter from J. B. Lewright to George W. Norris, December 12, 1932, George W. Norris Papers, Library of Congress, Box 198, File: "Limiting Jurisdiction of Federal Courts (71st & 72nd) Congress."

38. Letter from Donald Gallagher to George W. Norris, April 16, 1932, George W. Norris Papers, Library of Congress, Box 198, File: "Limiting Jurisdiction of Federal Courts (71st & 72nd) Congress."

39. Letter from A. J. O'Melia to George W. Norris, March 25, 1932, George W. Norris Papers, Library of Congress, Box 198, File: "Limiting Jurisdiction of Federal Courts (71st & 72nd) Congress."

40. The numbers are estimates. See, for example, Office of the Attorney General of the

United States, *Annual Report, 1937,* pp. 188–89; American Law Institute, *A Study of the Business of the Federal Courts: Part II, Civil Cases* (Philadelphia, 1934), p. 56; *Report of the Judicial Conference of Senior Circuit Judges and Annual Report of the Director of the Administrative Office of the United States Courts, 1940* (Washington, DC, 1940), p. 71, and ibid. (1941), p. 96; "Limiting Jurisdiction of Federal Courts," Hearings before the Committee on the Judiciary of the United States House of Representatives, 72 Cong., 1 Sess. (1932), pp. 24–25 (statement of Hobart S. Weaver, attorney for the Association of Life Insurance Presidents). See also Vance, *Handbook on the Law of Insurance,* pp. 454–55; Warren Freedman, *Richards on the Law of Insurance* (New York, 1952), p. 168.

41. Compare George Richards, *A Treatise on the Law of Insurance,* 2nd ed. (New York, 1893), p. 212 (incontestability clauses discussed in three lines) with 3rd ed. (New York, 1910), pp. 531–36 and 4th ed. (New York, 1932), pp. 667–75. The clause began to come into widespread use in the 1890s. William A. Fricke, *Insurance: "A Text Book"* (Milwaukee [?], 1898), pp. 49–50. See, for example, *Great Western Life Insurance Co. v. Snavely,* 206 F. 20 (C.C.A. 9 1913).

42. Vance, *Handbook on the Law of Insurance,* pp. 819–23.

43. *Jefferson Standard Life Insurance Co. v. McIntyre,* 294 F. 886 (C.C.A. 5 1923); *Northwestern Mutual Life Insurance Co. v. Pickering,* 293 F. 496 (C.C.A. 5 1923); *Scharlach v. Pacific Mutual Life Insurance Co.,* 9 F.2d 317 (C.C.A. 5 1925); *Chun Ngit Ngan v. Prudential Insurance Co. of America,* 9 F.2d 340 (C.C.A. 9 1925); *Rose v. Mutual Life Insurance Co. of New York,* 19 F. 2d 280 (C.C.A. 6 1927); *Densby v. Acacia Mutual Life Association,* 78 F.2d 203 (C.C.A.D.C. 1935).

44. 263 U.S. 167 (1923).

45. Ibid., p. 170.

46. Ibid.

47. Ibid., p. 178.

48. For example, *Jefferson Standard Life Insurance Co. v. McIntyre,* 294 F. 886 (C.C.A. 5 1923). *Hurni* lacked broader impact because it was limited to the specific language of the policy and because the terms of incontestability clauses varied considerably. See, for example, *Aetna Life Insurance Co. v. Kentucky,* 31 F.2d 971 (C.C.A. 8 1929).

49. For example, *Mutual Life Insurance Co. of New York v. Conley,* 55 F.2d 421 (D.Minn. 1932).

50. The other new Justices were George Sutherland and Pierce Butler. Classic early cases of the Taft Court include *Traux v. Corrigan,* 257 U.S. 312 (1921); *Bailey v. Drexel Furniture Co.,* 259 U.S. 20 (1922); and *Adkins v. Children's Hospital,* 261 U.S. 525 (1923).

51. 257 U.S. 532–33.

52. *Kline v. Burke Construction Co.,* 260 U.S. 226 (1922). The established law was that removal was solely a statutory right and that it was within the power of Congress to limit or terminate it. Even Justice David J. Brewer, who believed fervently in the central role of the federal courts in American government, acknowledged without pause that the "inferior courts, in number, name, and powers, are creatures of congressional action." Brewer, "The Supreme Court of the United States," *Scribner's Magazine* 33 (1903): 273. Some of the most extreme defenders of removal, however, continued to maintain that it was a constitutional right.

53. Vance, *Handbook on the Law of Insurance,* pp. 25–26 and n. 55.

54. For the industry's desire to curb the power of the jury see, for example, American Bar Association, *Program and Committee Reports, Section of Insurance Law* (1933), p. 36.

55. 38 Stat. 956 (1915), codified as Section 274 of the Judicial Code. The equitable defenses provision appeared in Subsection B.

56. Thomas B. Adams, "Federal Practice as to Equitable Defenses in Actions at Law," *American Bar Association Journal* 10 (1924): 467.

57. Ibid. Taft had attempted to bring about a similar type of reform in dealing with challenges to releases made by tort plaintiffs. The Law and Equity Act probably did not harm such tort plaintiffs who would otherwise have had to start separate equity suits in order to have the releases canceled (see Chapter 2). For federal practice in tort actions under the partially merged procedure that the act brought about, see *Union Pacific Railroad Co. v. Syas,* 246 F. 561 (C.C.A. 8 1917); *Pennsylvania Railroad Co. v. Hammond,* 7 F.2d 1010 (C.C.A. 2 1925) (dictum); *Pringle v.*

Storrow, 9 F.2d 464 (D.Mass. 1925); *Hoad v. New York Central Railroad Co.*, 6 F.Supp. 565 (W.D.N.Y. 1934); *Detwiler v. Chicago, Rock Island & Pacific Railway Co.*, 15 F.Supp. 541 (D. Minn. 1936). The court refused to transfer an action for damages to its equity docket in *Skinkle v. Lehigh Valley Railroad Co.*, 3 F.Supp. 326 (E.D.N.Y. 1933).

58. 260 U.S. 235 (1922).

59. Ibid., p. 245.

60. Ibid., p. 242; and also see pp. 243–44.

61. The Court dealt with related issues in *American Mills Co. v. American Surety Co. of New York*, 260 U.S.360 (1922).

62. 292 F. 53 (C.C.A. 4 1923).

63. *Jones v. Reliance Life Insurance Co. of Pittsburgh, Pa.*, 11 F.2d 69 (C.C.A. 4 1926); *Brown v. Pacific Mutual Life Insurance Co.*, 62 F.2d 711 (C.C.A. 4 1933); *Provident Mutual Life Insurance Co. of Philadelphia v. Parsons*, 70 F.2d 863 (C.C.A. 4 1934); *New York Life Insurance Co. v. Truesdale*, 79 F.2d 481 (C.C.A. 4 1935).

64. *Lincoln National Life Insurance Co. of Fort Wayne, Ind., v. Hammer*, 41 F.2d 12 (C.C.A. 8 1930); *Jamerson v. Alliance Insurance Co. of Philadelphia*, 87 F.2d 253 (C.C.A. 7 1937); *Ruhlin v. New York Life Insurance Co.*, 93 F.2d 416 (C.C.A. 3 1937). Immediately after its decision in *Erie Railroad Co. v. Tompkins*, 304 U.S. 64 (1938), overturning the federal common law (see Chapter 10), the Supreme Court reversed the Third Circuit's decision in *Ruhlin v. New York Life Insurance Co.*, 304 U.S. 202 (1938).

65. *New York Life Insurance Co. v. Seymour*, 45 F.2d 47 (C.C.A. 6 1930); *Harnischfeger Sales Corp. v. National Life Insurance Co.*, 72 F.2d 921 (C.C.A. 7 1934) (accepting the principle stated but reversing an order enjoining plaintiff's state court action on the policy and rejecting *Keeton* on the issue of the availability of injunction relief); *Jensen v. New York Life Insurance Co.*, 59 F.2d 927 (C.C.A. 8 1932), affirming 38 F.2d 524 (D.Neb. 1929) (intermediate appellate opinion, 50 F.2d 512).

66. *Adler v. New York Life Insurance Co.*, 33 F.2d 827 (C.C.A. 8 1929); *Franco v. New York Life Insurance Co.*, 53 F.2d 562 (C.C.A. 5 1931); *Hesselberg v. Aetna Life Insurance Co.*, 75 F.2d 490 (C.C.A. 8 1935); *New York Life Insurance Co. v. Renault*, 11 F.2d 281 (D.N.J. 1926); *New York Life Insurance Co. v. Sisson*, 19 F.2d 410 (W.D.Pa. 1926); *Philadelphia Life Insurance Co. v. Burgess*, 18 F.2d 599 (E.D.S.C. 1927); *Abraham Lincoln Life Insurance Co. v. Kleven*, 33 F.2d 638 (D.Mass. 1928); *Pacific Mutual Life Insurance Co. of California v. Hartman*, 10 F.Supp. 425 (N.D.Okla. 1935); *Equitable Life Insurance Co. of Iowa v. Carver*, 17 F.Supp. 23 (W.D.Wash. 1936).

67. *Perkins v. Prudential Insurance Co. of America*, 69 F.2d 218, 219 (C.C.A. 7 1934).

68. *Peake v. Lincoln National Life Insurance Co.*, 15 F.2d 303 (C.C.A. 8 1926); *New York Life Insurance Co. v. Halpern*, 47 F.2d 935 (W.D.Pa. 1931).

69. *Royal Union Mutual Life Insurance Co. v. Lloyd*, 254 F. 407 (C.C.A. 8 1918); *New York Life Insurance Co. v. Hurt*, 35 F.2d 92 (C.C.A. 8 1929); *New York Life Insurance Co. v. Marotta*, 57 F.2d 1038 (C.C.A. 3 1932); *Phillips-Morefield v. Southern States Life Insurance Co. of Alabama*, 66 F.2d 29 (C.C.A. 5 1933); *State Life Insurance Co. v. Spencer*, 62 F.2d 640 (C.C.A. 5 1933). The courts had considerable scholarly support for using the merger of law and equity to narrow the role of the jury. See Walter Wheeler Cook, "Equitable Defenses," *Yale Law Journal* 32 (1923): 645; Note, *Harvard Law Review* 36 (1923): 474; J. P. McBaine, "Equitable Defenses to Actions at Law in the Federal Court," *California Law Review* 17 (1929): 591. See also *Dunn v. Prudential Insurance Co. of America*, 8 F.Supp. 799 (D.Minn. 1934); *Smith v. St. Paul Fire & Marine Insurance Co.*, 23 F.Supp. 420 (E.D.N.Y. 1938).

70. *Jones v. Reliance Life Insurance Co. of Pittsburgh, Pa.*, 11 F.2d 69 (C.C.A. 4 1926); *Adler v. New York Life Insurance Co.*, 33 F.2d 827 (C.C.A. 8 1929); *Brown v. Pacific Mutual Life Insurance Co.*, 62 F.2d 711 (C.C.A. 4 1933); *Provident Mutual Life Insurance Co. of Philadelphia v. Parsons*, 70 F.2d 863 (C.C.A. 4 1934); *Jamerson v. Alliance Insurance Co. of Philadelphia*, 87 F.2d 253 (C.C.A. 7 1937); *Ruhlin v. New York Life Insurance Co.*, 93 F.2d 416 (C.C.A. 3 1937), rev'd 304 U.S. 202 (1938); *Philadelphia Life Insurance Co. v. Burgess*, 18 F.2d 599 (E.D.S.C. 1927); *Abraham Lincoln Life Insurance Co. v. Kleven*, 33 F.2d 638 (D.Mass. 1928); *Pacific Mutual Life Insurance Co. of California v. Hartman*, 10 F.Supp. 425 (N.D.Okla. 1935).

The injunction cases seemed in at least some instances to be inconsistent with the Supreme Court's decision in *Kline v. Burke Construction Co.*, 260 U.S. 226 (1922), where the Court held that a federal court could not protect its jurisdiction over a contract action based on diversity of citizenship by enjoining a state court action subsequently brought on the same contract. See, for example, Telford Taylor and Everett I. Willis, "The Power of Federal Courts to Enjoin Proceedings in State Courts," *Yale Law Journal* 42 (1933): 1169, 1174.

71. Numerous cases probably fall into this category, but it is usually impossible to determine in any particular case why the policyholder did not bring a separate action at law.

72. *New York Life Insurance Co. v. McCarthy*, 22 F.2d 241 (C.C.A. 5 1927); *Lumbermen's Mutual Casualty Co. v. Bagley*, 62 F.2d 617 (C.C.A. 10 1933); *New York Life Insurance Co. v. Miller*, 73 F.2d 350 (C.C.A. 8 1934); *Continental Casualty Co. v. Yerxa*, 16 F.2d 473 (D.Mass. 1926); *New York Life Insurance Co. v. Feicht*, 29 F.2d 318 (N.D.Ill. 1928).

73. "Limiting Jurisdiction of Federal Courts," Hearings before the Committee on the Judiciary of the United States House of Representatives, 72 Cong., 1 Sess. (1932), p. 28 (statement of J. H. Doyle, general counsel, National Board of Fire Underwriters). See, for example, *Fisher v. Pacific Mutual Life Insurance Co.*, 72 So. 846 (Sup. Ct. Miss. 1916); *Illinois Life Insurance Co. v. Prentiss*, 115 N.E. 554 (Sup. Ct. Ill. 1917); *Bank Savings Life Insurance Co. v. Wood*, 253 P. 431 (Sup. Ct. Kansas 1927).

74. *Pennsylvania Fire Insurance Co. v. Gold Issue Mining Co.*, 243 U.S. 93 (1917).

75. Letters from C. W. Crossan to George W. Norris, April 14, 1933, and November 4, 1933, George W. Norris Papers, Tray 42, Box 8, File: "Limiting Jurisdiction of Federal Courts," Library of Congress.

76. Letters from Raymond N. Klass to George W. Norris, October 26, 1933, and to John P. Robertson, April 13, 1933, George W. Norris Papers, Library of Congress, Box 198, File: "Limiting Jurisdiction of Federal Courts (71st & 72nd) Congress."

77. Compare, for example, *Bernblum v. Travelers Insurance Co.*, 9 F.Supp. 34 (W.D.Mo. 1934) with *Phoenix Mutual Life Insurance Co. of Harford, Conn. v. England*, 22 F.Supp. 284 (W.D.Mo. 1938). A federal statute (28 U.S.C. Sec. 41, Sec. 24 (1) of the Judicial Code) restricted the use of assignments to create diverse citizenship for jurisdictional purposes. It did not, according to its terms, affect the issue of assignments to destroy diverse citizenship. See, Armistead M. Dobie, *Handbook of Federal Jurisdiction and Procedure* (St. Paul, 1928), pp. 224–39, 409–10.

78. *Robbins v. Western Automobile Insurance Co.*, 4 F.2d 249 (C.C.A. 7 1925); *New York Life Insurance Co. v. Marshall*, 23 F.2d 225 (C.C.A. 5 1928); *Application of Hardware Mutual Fire Insurance Co. of Minnesota*, 91 F.2d 13 (C.C.A. 9 1937); *Waltman v. Union Central Life Insurance Co.*, 25 F.2d 320 (N.D.Tx. 1928); *Patrick v. Equitable Life Insurance Society of the United States*, 2 F.Supp. 762 (E.D.Ky. 1933); *Fried v. State Life Insurance Co. of Indianapolis, Ind.*, 10 F.Supp. 369 (W.D.La. 1938).

79. *Henderson v. Maryland Casualty Co.*, 62 F.2d 107 (C.C.A. 5 1932); *Brady v. Indemnity Insurance Co. of North America*, 68 F.2d 302 (C.C.A. 6 1933); *Travelers Protective Association of America v. Smith*, 71 F.2d 511 (C.C.A. 4 1934); *Woods v. Massachusetts Protective Association*, 34 F.2d 501 (E.D.Ky. 1929). Claimants were apparently preparing to refile with discounted claims in *Prudential Insurance Co. of America v. Stack*, 60 F.2d 830 (C.C.A. 4 1932) and *New York Life Insurance Co. v. Driggs*, 72 F.2d 833 (C.C.A. 4 1934). See Note, *Cornell Law Quarterly* 15 (1930): 307.

80. *Johnson v. Home Life Insurance Co. of New York, N.Y.*, 252 N.W. 641 (Sup.Ct.S.D. 1934).

81. For example, *Lynch v. Springfield Fire & Marine Insurance Co.*, 15 F.2d 725 (E.D.N.Y. 1926); *Ivy River Land & Timber Co. v. American Insurance Co. of Newark*, 130 S.E. 864 (Sup.Ct.N.C. 1925) and cases cited.

82. "Limiting Jurisdiction of Federal Courts," Hearings before the Committee on the Judiciary of the United States House of Representatives, 72 Cong., 1 Sess. (1932), p. 57 (statement of J. H. Drake, representing the Association of Casualty and Surety Executives). Note, "The Content of 'Separable Controversy' for Purposes of Removal to the Federal Courts," *Columbia Law Review* 36 (1936): 794, 803. Of course, if the insurance contract allowed a direct action

against the insurer, a plaintiff could jointly sue the alleged tortfeasor and her insurer. For example, *Haenni v. Craven,* 56 F.2d 261 (S.D.Tx. 1932).

83. See Charles E. Clark, "Joinder and Splitting of Causes of Action," *Michigan Law Review* 25 (1927): 393, 398–400.

84. *Daniel v. Burdette,* 24 F.Supp. 218, 221 (W.D.S.C. 1938).

85. For example, *Charlton v. Van Etten,* 55 F.2d 418 (D.Minn. 1932); *Jones v. United States Fidelity & Guaranty Co.,* 19 F.Supp. 799 (N.D.Fla. 1937).

86. There were, of course, a variety of *ad hoc* tactics that claimants attempted. When they seemed to overreach, the federal courts showed little sympathy. See *Evetts v. People's Life Insurance Co.,* 36 F.2d 832 (N.D.Tx. 1929); *Morrow v. Mutual Casualty Co. of Chicago,* 20 F.Supp. 193 (E.D.Ky. 1937).

87. *Aetna Life Insurance Co. of Hartford, Conn. v. Wilson,* 84 F.2d 330 (C.C.A. 4 1936); *La Vecchia v. Connecticut Mutual Life Insurance Co. of Hartford, Conn.,* 1 F.Supp. 588 (S.D.N.Y. 1932); *Small v. New York Life Insurance Co.,* 18 F.Supp. 820 (N.D.Ala. 1937); *Rau v. American National Insurance Co.,* 154 S.W. 645 (Ct.Civ.App.Tx. 1913). See Note, "Federal Jurisdiction: Amount in Controversy in Installment Payment Situations," *California Law Review* 36 (1948): 124.

88. *New England Mortgage Security Co. v. Gay,* 145 U.S. 123, 130 (1892).

89. *Mutual Life Insurance Co. v. Wright,* 276 U.S. 602 (1928), affirming *Wright v. Mutual Life Insurance Co. of New York,* 19 F.2d 117 (C.C.A. 5 1927).

90. Letter from Raymond N. Klass to George W. Norris, October 10, 1933, George W. Norris Papers, Tray 42, Box 8, File: "Limiting Jurisdiction of Federal Courts," Library of Congress.

91. Equity had frequently been invoked in controversies in which the monetary value of disputed practices or rights could not be precisely stated, and in such suits the federal courts applied more flexible rules to determine the true amount in controversy. For example, *Hunt v. New York Cotton Exchange,* 205 U.S. 322 (1907); *Bitterman v. Louisville & Nashville Railroad,* 207 U.S. 205 (1907).

92. *Massachusetts Protective Association, Inc. v. Kittles,* 2 F.2d 211 (C.A.A. 5 1924) (disability); *New York Life Insurance Co. v. Swift,* 38 F.2d 175 (C.C.A. 5 1930); *Jensen v. New York Life Insurance Co.,* 50 F.2d 512 (C.C.A. 8 1931) (disability); *Pacific Mutual Life Insurance Co. of California v. Parker,* 71 F.2d 872 (C.C.A. 4 1934) (disability; equity jurisdiction denied because no incontestability clause); *Shaner v. West Coast Life Insurance Co.,* 73 F.2d 681 (C.C.A. 10 1934) (disability); *New York Life Insurance Co. v. Kaufman,* 78 F.2d 398 (C.C.A. 9 1935) (disability), cert. denied, 296 U.S. 626 (1936); *Jeffress v. New York Life Insurance Co.,* 74 F.2d 874 (C.C.A. 4 1935) (disability); *Bell v. Philadelphia Life Insurance Co.,* 78 F.2d 322 (C.C.A. 4 1935) (insured also sued for declaration that policy was in full force); *Mutual Life Insurance Co. of New York v. Rose,* 294 F. 122 (E.D.Ky. 1923) (aggregate two policies whose individual face values were each less than the jurisdictional minimum), rev'd on other grounds, 19 F.2d 280 (C.C.A. 6 1927); *Mutual Life Insurance Co. v. Thompson,* 27 F.2d 753 (W.D.Va. 1928); *Massachusetts Protective Association Inc. v. Stephenson,* 5 F.Supp. 586 (E.D.Ky. 1933) (disability); *Penn Mutual Life Insurance Co. of Philadelphia,* 5 F.Supp. 1003 (D.Minn. 1934) (disability); *Commercial Casualty Insurance Co. v. Humphrey,* 13 F.Supp. 174 (S.D.Tx. 1935).

93. *Brown v. Pacific Mutual Life Insurance Co.,* 62 F. 2d 711 (C.C.A. 4 1933). The decision appeared so extreme that two commentators in the *Yale Law Journal* termed its reasoning "wholly unsatisfactory." Taylor and Willis, "Power of Federal Courts to Enjoin Proceedings," p. 1181. On the authority of federal courts to enjoin actions in state courts, see Edgar Noble Durfee and Robert L. Sloss, "Federal Injunctions Against Proceedings in State Courts: The Life History of a Statute," *Michigan Law Review* 30 (1932): 1145.

94. *Federal Life Insurance Co. v. Rascoe,* 12 F.2d 693 (C.C.A. 6 1926).

95. *Kimel v. Missouri State Life Insurance Co.,* 71 F.2d 921 (C.C.A. 10 1934); *Kithcart v. Metropolitan Life Insurance Co.,* 1 F.Supp. 719 (W.D.Mo. 1932); *Parks v. Maryland Casualty Co.,* 59 F.2d 736 (W.D.Mo. 1932); *Ginsburg v. Pacific Mutual Life Insurance Co. of California,* 5 F.Supp. 296 (S.D.N.Y. 1933); *Menssen v. Travelers Insurance Co.,* 5 F.Supp. 114 (E.D.N.Y. 1933); *Wyll v. Pacific Mutual Life Insurance Co. of California,* 3 F.Supp. 483 (N.D.Tx. 1933); *Hines v. Fidelity Mutual Life Insurance Co.,* 6 F.Supp. 692 (E.D.N.Y. 1934). See Lawrence J.

Ackerman, "Anticipatory Repudication and Disability Insurance," *University of Newark Law Review* 1 (1936): 47.

96. *Thorkelson v. Aetna Life Insurance Co.*, 9 F.Supp. 570 (D.Minn. 1934); *Ross v. Travelers Insurance Co.*, 18 F.Supp. 819 (E.D.S.C. 1936); *Enzor v. Jefferson Standard Life Insurance Co.*, 14 F.Supp. 677 (E.D.S.C. 1936); *Struble v. Connecticut Mutual Life Insurance Co. of Hartford*, 20 F.Supp. 779 (S.D.Fla. 1937). See the cases reviewed in *Button v. Mutual Life Insurance Co. of New York*, 48 F.Supp. 168 (W.D.Ky. 1943); Note, *Harvard Law Review* 51 (1938): 1109; Note, *Minnesota Law Review* 25 (1941): 356.

97. Letter from William H. Westover to Sen. Norris, April 20, 1933, George W. Norris Papers, Library of Congress, Box 198, File: "Limiting Jurisdiction of Federal Courts (71st & 72nd) Congress."

98. Ackerman, "Anticipatory Repudiation and Disability Insurance," p. 48, n. 14.

99. 39 Stat. 929 (1917); 43 Stat. 976 (1925); 44 Stat. 416 (1926).

100. See Zechariah Chafee, Jr., "Modernizing Interpleader," *Yale Law Journal* 30 (1921): 814; Zechariah Chafee, Jr., "Interpleader in the United States Courts," *Yale Law Journal* 41 (1932): 1134, and *Yale Law Journal* 41 (1932): 42; Zechariah Chafee, Jr., "The Federal Interpleader Act of 1936," *Yale Law Journal* 45 (1936): 963; Ralph V. Rogers, "Historical Origins of Interpleader," *Yale Law Journal* 51 (1942): 924; Geoffrey C. Hazard, Jr., and Myron Moskovitz, "An Historical and Critical Analysis of Interpleader," *California Law Review* 52 (1964): 706.

101. Edwin Borchard, *Declaratory Judgments* (Cleveland, 1934), pp. 244–45.

102. 48 Stat. 955 (1934).

103. Borchard, *Declaratory Judgments*, p. 490.

104. Insurance companies used the device in a range of situations, though they did not always do so successfully. See, for example, *Aetna Casualty & Surety Co. v. Yeatts*, 122 F.2d 350 (C.C.A. 4 1938); *Columbian National Life Insurance Co. v. Foulke*, 13 F. Supp. 350 (W.D.Mo. 1936); *Travelers Insurance Co. v. Helmer*, 15 F. Supp. 355 (N.D.Ga. 1936); *Aetna Life Insurance Co. v. Richmond*, 139 A. 702 (Sup.Ct. of Err. Conn. 1927); *American Motorists' Insurance Co. v. Central Garage*, 169 A. 121 (Sup.Ct.N.H. 1933); *Merchants Mutual Casualty Co. v. Pinard*, 183 A. 36 (Sup.Ct.N.H. 36); *Utica Mutual Insurance Co. v. Glennie*, 230 N.Y.S. 673 (Sup.Ct.N.Y. 1928).

105. Borchard, *Declaratory Judgments*, pp. 119–21; Edwin Borchard, "Recent Developments in Declaratory Relief," *Temple Law Quarterly* 10 (1936): 235, 245.

106. For example, *Davis v. American Foundry Equipment Co.*, 94 F.2d 441 (1938).

107. *Trainor Co. v. Aetna Casualty & Surety Co.*, 290 U.S. 47 (1933); *Mutual Life Insurance Co. of New York v. Johnson*, 293 U.S. 335 (1934). The Court may have been influenced by its review of cases presenting run-of-the-mill issues of contract construction that did not seem particularly appropriate to its docket. For example, *Williams v. Union Central Life Insurance Co.*, 291 U.S. 170 (1934); *Stroehmann v. Mutual Life Insurance Co. of New York*, 300 U.S. 435 (1937).

108. *White v. Sparkill Realty Corp.*, 280 U.S. 500 (1930); *Radio Corporation of America v. Raytheon Manufacturing Co.*, 296 U.S. 459 (1935).

109. 293 U.S. 379 (1935).

110. *Adamos v. New York Life Insurance Co.*, 293 U.S. 386 (1935).

111. *Enelow v. New York Life Insurance Co.*, 293 U.S. 383 (1935).

112. Ibid., p. 385.

113. 296 U.S. 64 (1935).

114. Ibid., p. 67.

115. Ibid., p. 68.

116. Ibid., p. 73. *Di Giovanni* also addressed the question of whether the adequate remedy at law necessary to supplant federal equity had to be available in the federal courts. After *Cable*, the Court had seemed to settle the issue, ruling that the adequate remedy had to be available in a federal court. See *Risty v. Chicago, Rock Island & Pacific Railway Co.*, 270 U.S. 378 (1926), and *Henrietta Mills v. Rutherford County*, 281 U.S. 121 (1930). See also *Smyth v. Ames*, 169 U.S. 466 (1898). *Di Giovanni* pointed out, first, that the rule assumed that a basis for federal jurisdiction otherwise existed and, second, that the lack of an adequate remedy at law in a federal court would not justify the intervention of federal equity if the federal legal remedy were lacking simply because the jurisdictional amount was not satisfied (296 U.S. 69–70).

117. *Mobley v. New York Life Insurance Co.*, 295 U.S. 632 (1935).

118. 297 U.S. 672 (1936).

119. For example, *Brotherhood of Locomotive Firemen & Enginemen v. Pinkston*, 293 U.S. 96 (1934); *KVOS, Inc. v. Associated Press*, 299 U.S. 269 (1936). In 1936 the Court denied certiorari in a case in which the Ninth Circuit decided the issue. *New York Life Insurance Co. v. Kaufman*, 78 F.2d 398 (C.C.A. 9th 1935), cert. denied, 296 U.S. 626 (1936).

The Court did not address the companies' "reserve fund" theory in actions at law brought by policyholders. Although the theory seemed inconsistent with established doctrine, for example, *Berlin v. Travelers Insurance Co. of Hartford, Conn.*, 18 F.Supp. 126 (D.Md. 1937), the Court's decisions in equity in the mid-1930s lent it some plausibility. For example, *Brotherhood of Locomotive Firemen & Enginemen v. Pinkston*, 293 U.S. 96 (1934); *Healy v. Ratta*, 292 U.S. 263 (1934).

The Court also construed the federal interpleader statute broadly and sympathetically. *Dugas v. American Surety Co.*, 300 U.S. 414 (1937).

120. 300 U.S. 203 (1937).

121. *Stewart v. American Life Insurance Co.*, 80 F.2d 600, 85 F.2d 791 (C.C.A. 10 1936).

122. 85 F.2d 792.

123. *Pacific Mutual Life Insurance Co. of California v. Andrews*, 77 F.2d 692 (C.C.A. 8 1935); *New York Life Insurance Co. v. Thompson*, 78 F.2d 946 (C.C.A. 10 1935); *Rohrback v. Mutual Life Insurance Co. of New York*, 82 F.2d 291 (C.C.A. 8 1936); *Nichols v. Pacific Mutual Life Insurance Co. of California*, 84 F.2d 896 (C.C.A. 8 1936); *Metropolitan Life Insurance Co. v. Banion*, 86 F.2d 886 (C.C.A. 10 1936).

124. *New York Life Insurance Co. v. Panagiotopoulos*, 80 F.2d 136, 140 (C.C.A. 1 1935).

125. For example, *Dawson v. Kentucky Distilleries Co.*, 255 U.S. 288 (1921).

126. *American Life Insurance Co. v. Stewart*, 300 U.S. 212.

127. Ibid., p. 214.

128. 85 F.2d 796–98 (Phillips, C. J., dissenting).

129. 300 U.S. 215.

130. Ibid.

131. Ibid., p., 216.

132. *Aetna Life Insurance Co. v. Haworth*, 300 U.S. 227 (1937).

133. The federal courts worked out their answers to these questions over the next quarter-century. See Chapter 10.

134. Compare, for example, *Carpenter v. Edmonson*, 92 F.2d 895 (C.C.A. 5 1937) with *Home Indemnity Co. of New York v. Peters*, 86 F.2d 916 (C.C.A. 5 1936). See Edwin Borchard, "Declaratory Judgments and Insurance Litigation," *Journal of American Insurance* 15 (1938): 18; Note, "The Declaratory Judgment and the Insurance Contract," *Yale Law Journal* 46 (1936): 286. In 1937 there were eighty-four declaratory judgment actions filed in the federal courts. Office of the Attorney General of the United States, *Annual Report, 1937*, p. 189.

Chapter 10

1. 304 U.S. 64 (1938).

2. *Hammer v. Dagenhart*, 247 U.S.251 (1918); *Bailey v. Drexel Furniture Co.*, 259 U.S. 20 (1922).

3. For example, *Duplex Printing Press Co. v. Deering*, 254 U.S. 443 (1921); *Bedford Cut Stone Co. v. Journeyman Stone Cutters' Association*, 274 U.S. 37 (1927).

4. Peter H. Irons, *The New Deal Lawyers* (Princeton, NJ, 1982), pp. 3, 13, 46; Letter from Homer Cummings to The President, November 8, 1933, Franklin D. Roosevelt Papers, OF 41, Box 114, Franklin D. Roosevelt Library, Hyde Park, NY.

5. For example, *Schechter Poultry Co. v. United States*, 295 U.S. 495 (1935) (invalidating the National Industrial Recovery Act); *United States v. Butler*, 297 U.S. 1 (1936) (invalidating the Agricultural Adjustment Act).

6. Letter from Homer Cummings to The President, June 2, 1936, Franklin D. Roosevelt Papers, OF 10, Box 5, Franklin D. Roosevelt Library. The statute was 28 U.S.C. Sec. 3224. See

letter from Homer Cummings to The President, July 19, 1935, Franklin D. Roosevelt Papers, OF 10, Box 4, Franklin D. Roosevelt Library; James McGregor Burns, *Roosevelt: The Lion and the Fox* (New York: 1956), p. 229.

7. The plan called for the addition of a new Justice, up to a total of six, for each Justice on the Court who was over the age of seventy. Although the plan was initially packaged as a remedy for congestion in the courts, Roosevelt's real purpose was transparent. When opposition immediately broke out, Roosevelt quickly confessed the purpose of the plan and stressed the need for a Court that would allow the government to meet the crisis of the depression. His adversaries attacked his proposal as an attempt to destroy the Constitution, subvert the independent judiciary, and establish a presidential dictatorship.

The proposal appears as H. R. Doc. 142, 75 Cong., 1 Sess. (1937). For general discussions, see Joseph Alsop and Turner Catledge, *The 168 Days* (Garden City, NY, 1938); Leonard Baker, *Back to Back: The Duel Between FDR and the Supreme Court* (New York, 1967); Burns, *Roosevelt;* William E. Leuchtenberg, "Franklin D. Roosevelt's Supreme Court 'Packing' Plan," in Harold M. Hollingsworth and William F. Holmes, eds., *Essays on the Deal Deal* (Austin, TX, 1969); Leuchtenberg, "The Origins of Franklin D. Roosevelt's 'Court Packing' Plan," *Supreme Court Review* (1966): 347; Leuchtenberg, "The Constitutional Revolution of 1937," in Victor Hoar, ed., *The Great Depression: Essays and Memoirs from Canada and the United States* (Toronto, 1969); Gregory A. Caldeira, "Public Opinion and the U.S. Supreme Court: FDR's Court-packing Plan," *American Political Science Review* 81 (1987): 1139 and works cited.

8. The Court-packing episode was the greatest political defeat of Roosevelt's presidency. A variety of factors proved too strong for his overtly political and transparently duplicitous scheme. Defections from the Democratic ranks, an intense and powerful lobbying effort, and a series of labor strikes that frightened much of the nation with the specter of lawlessness combined to stall the bill. The longer it stayed in committee, the stronger the opposition seemed to grow. In the heat of the summer, Roosevelt's loyal majority leader in the Senate, who had personally been able to keep a number of southern Democrats out of the opposition, died of a heart attack, and three Justices of the Supreme Court—including Justice Louis D. Brandeis, the leading progressive on the Court—made an extraordinary appearance before Congress to oppose the plan.

9. *West Coast Hotel v. Parrish,* 300 U.S. 379 (1937); *National Labor Relations Board v. Jones & Laughlin Steel Corp.,* 301 U.S. 1 (1937); *Steward Machine Co. v. Davis,* 301 U.S. 548 (1937); *Helvering v. Davis,* 301 U.S. 619 (1937).

10. C. Herman Pritchett, *The Roosevelt Court: A Study in Judicial Politics and Values, 1937–1937* (Chicago, 1969), pp. 300–1.

11. See generally ibid., *passim;* Paul L. Murphy, *The Constitution in Crisis Times, 1918–1969* (New York, 1972), chaps. 4–6.

12. See, for example, Robert Harrison, "The Breakup of The Roosevelt Supreme Court: The Contribution of History and Biography," *Law and History Review* 2 (1984): 165.

13. Rayman L. Solomon, "The Politics of Appointment and the Federal Courts' Role in Regulating America: U.S. Courts of Appeals Judgeships from T.R. to F.D.R.," *American Bar Foundation Research Journal* (1984): 285; Harrison, "Breakup of the Roosevelt Supreme Court," pp. 170–73. For the administration's early interest in the political balance in the federal courts, see letter from Homer Cummings to The President, November 8, 1933, Franklin D. Roosevelt Papers, OF 41, Box 114, Franklin D. Roosevelt Library.

14. Director of the Administrative Office of the United States Courts, *Annual Report, 1940,* Table 4, p. 71, *Annual Report, 1942,* Table 7 (unpaginated), *Annual Report, 1944,* Table 6 (unpaginated), *Annual Report, 1945,* Table C2, p. 82, *Annual Report, 1946,* Table C2, p. 88, *Annual Report, 1947,* Table C2, p. 108, *Annual Report, 1948,* Table C2, p. 132.

The *Annual Report* of the Attorney General reports terminations of FELA cases by the federal courts for half of 1935 and for the years from 1936 to 1939. By "termination" it means the disposition of a case in any way whatever, from voluntary pretrial discontinuance to verdict after trial. Thus, in the absence of data dealing with filings, the figures for "terminations" represent a reasonable proxy for the number of new FELA cases initiated each year. Because civil terminations exceeded civil filings in every year but one between 1930 and 1942, it does not seem likely that figures for terminations would understate the number of new filings each year.

The *Annual Report* states that in half of 1935 the federal courts disposed of 48 FELA actions, and in 1936 through 1939 they disposed of 326, 108, 100, and 102, respectively. The number for 1936 appears to be an aberration. Except for 1936, the federal courts averaged just over 100 FELA terminations per year for four and a half years. Including 1936, they averaged about 146 per year. Office of the Attorney General of the United States, *Annual Report, 1935,* Table 2H, p. 200, *Annual Report, 1936,* Table 2H, p. 179, *Annual Report, 1937,* Table 2H, p. 189, *Annual Report, 1938,* Table 2H, p. 233, *Annual Report, 1939,* Table 2H, p. 215. After the Administrative Office of the United States Courts was established in 1939, the attorney general no longer published FELA statistics.

15. Director of the Administrative Office of the United States Courts, *Annual Report, 1949,* Table C2, p. 130 (944 FELA cases filed), *Annual Report, 1950,* Table C2, p. 142 (1,084 FELA cases filed), *Annual Report, 1951,* Table C2, p. 130 (1,132 FELA cases filed).

16. American Law Institute, *A Study of the Business of the Federal Courts: Part II, Civil Cases* (Philadelphia, 1934), pp. 56, 102; Sen. Rep. No. 1830, 85, Cong., 2 Sess. (1958), p. 26; Administrative Office of the United States Courts, *Annual Report,* for the years 1945 through 1951, Tables C2 and C4; Herbert Wechsler, "Federal Jurisdiction and the Revision of the Judicial Code," *Law & Contemporary Problems* 13 (1948): 216, 243; "Jurisdiction of Federal Courts Concerning Diversity of Citizenship," Hearing before Subcommittee No. 3 of the Committee on the Judiciary of the United States House of Representatives, 85 Cong., 1 Sess. (1957), p. 20.

17. 314 U.S. 118 (1941). See *Oklahoma Packing Co. v. Oklahoma Gas & Electric Co.,* 309 U.S. 4 (1939).

18. *Seas Shipping Co., Inc. v. Sieracki,* 328 U.S. 85, 95 (1946).

19. 326 U.S. 310 (1945).

20. The Court expanded the reach of state jurisdiction again in *Travelers Health Association v. Virginia,* 339 U.S. 643 (1950).

21. 308 U.S. 165 (1939).

22. Ibid., p. 172. See *Freeman v. Bee Machine Co.,* 319 U.S. 448, 455, 461 (1943) (Frankfurter, J., dissenting); Note, "Federal Venue Requirements for Foreign Corporations," *Yale Law Journal* 49 (1940): 724; Note, "Venue of Actions Against Foreign Corporations in the Federal Courts," *Harvard Law Review* 53 (1940): 660.

23. Raymond J. Moore, "Recent Trends in Judicial Interpretation in Railroad Cases Under the Federal Employers' Liability Act," *Marquette Law Review* 29 (1946): 73, 76.

24. *Tiller v. Atlantic Coast Line Railroad Co.,* 318 U.S. 54, 58, 67 (1943). See also *Lilly v. Grand Trunk Western Railroad Co.,* 317 U.S. 481 (1943).

25. For example, *Bailey v. Central Vermont Railway, Inc.,* 319 U.S. 350 (1943); *Tennant v. Peoria & P.U. Railroad Co.,* 321 U.S. 29 (1944); *Lavender v. Kurn,* 327 U.S. 645 (1946).

Bailey is a particularly interesting example of judicial legerdemain by the Roosevelt Court. It upheld a jury verdict even though plaintiff presented no direct evidence to support the claim that the deceased worker had been killed as a result of the railroad's negligence. There were no eyewitnesses, and plaintiff's evidence was slight and required several favorable inferences. Moreover, the defendant railroad presented strong evidence to support its theory that the deceased employee had actually been murdered by someone, probably a hobo, unconnected with the railroad. In this situation the Court not only upheld the verdict for plaintiff but also cited and quoted from *Patton* concerning the employer's duty of care (319 U.S. 353). *Bailey* and *Patton* were from different worlds, and under the evidentiary doctrine the latter decision had established forty-five years earlier the plaintiff could not possibly have prevailed.

26. *Brown v. Western Railway of Alabama,* 338 U.S. 294 (1949); *Dice v. Akron, Canton & Youngstown Railroad Co.,* 342 U.S. 359 (1952).

27. 315 U.S. 1 (1942).

28. Ibid., p. 3.

29. Ibid., p. 7.

30. *Boyd v. Grand Trunk Western Railroad Co.,* 338 U.S. 263, 265 (1949).

31. 314 U.S. 44 (1941).

32. 315 U.S. 698 (1942).

33. 314 U.S. 54.

34. 315 U.S. 704.

35. Ibid., p. 705.

36. Ibid., p. 708 (Frankfurter, J., dissenting).

37. Edward L. Barrett, Jr., "The Doctrines of *Forum Non Conveniens*," *California Law Review* 35 (1947): 380, 388–89.

38. 315 U.S. 705, 706, 707–8 (Jackson, J., concurring).

39. *Southern Railway Co. v. Painter,* 314 U.S. 155 (1941). See *Herb v. Pitcairn,* 324 U.S. 117 (1945).

40. *Magnolia Petroleum Co. v. Hunt,* 320 U.S. 430 (1943).

41. See Elliott E. Cheatham, "Res Judicata and the Full Faith and Credit Clause: Magnolia Petroleum Co. v. Hunt," *Columbia Law Review* 44 (1944): 330; Paul A. Freund, *On Law and Justice* (Cambridge, MA, 1968), pp. 203–6. The Court had problems with the scope of the full faith and credit clause in the 1930s and 1940s (see Chapter 8); *Pacific Employers Insurance Co. v. Industrial Accident Commission,* 306 U.S. 493 (1939); *Pink v. A.A.A. Highway Express, Inc.,* 314 U.S. 201 (1941); *Williams v. North Carolina,* 317 U.S. 287 (1942); Freund, *On Law and Justice,* pp. 183–213; Thomas Reed Powell, "And Repent at Leisure," *Harvard Law Review* 58 (1945): 930; Robert H. Jackson, "Full Faith and Credit—The Lawyer's Clause of the Constitution," *Columbia Law Review* 45 (1945): 1.

The New Deal Court may also have weakened slightly plaintiffs' ability to avoid removal. In *Pullman Co. v. Jenkins,* 305 U.S. 534 (1939), the Court ordered an action remanded to state court but suggested in its discussion a somewhat narrowed scope for the employee joinder tactic. Justice Hugo Black, concurring (p. 542), criticized the majority and maintained that *Thompson* was the controlling authority in the area. The majority's discussion was apparently marked by a concern that state law might exert an undue amount of control over a federal jurisdictional issue. The timing of the case suggests that it may have been an effort to begin sorting out the implications of *Erie Railroad Co. v. Tompkins,* 304 U.S. 64 (1938) and the new Federal Rules of Civil Procedure that went into effect in 1938. Compare *Neirbo,* 308 U.S. 175 (denying that the construction of the venue statute that the Court applied would allow state law to control the federal issue of joinder).

42. *Francis v. Southern Pacific Co.,* 333 U.S. 445, 450 (1948).

43. Although all of the Roosevelt Justices sympathized with the FELA, by the mid-1940s they had split sharply over the extent to which the Court should spend time reviewing appeals under the act. Justices Hugo Black, William O. Douglas, Frank Murphy, and Wiley B. Rutledge often sought to review FELA decisions, especially those that had gone against injured plaintiffs, but the other Justices, of whom Felix Frankfurter was the most outspoken, usually opposed Court review of "mere" negligence issues that presented questions that were essentially factual. As a law professor in the 1920s, Frankfurter had criticized what he regarded as the Supreme Court's waste of time hearing such cases that turned solely on an evaluation of the factual record below. See Felix Frankfurter and James M. Landis, *The Business of the Supreme Court: A Study in the Federal Judicial System* (New York, 1928), pp. 206–10; Sidney Fine, *Frank Murphy: The Washington Years* (Ann Arbor, MI 1984), pp. 311–12, 541–42; Joseph Lash, ed., *From the Diaries of Felix Frankfurter* (New York, 1975) pp. 229–30, 329–33.

For more general discussion of the Roosevelt Court and its breakup, see Alpheus T. Mason, *Harlan Fiske Stone: Pillar of the Law* (New York, 1956), esp. chaps. 34–37; Gerald T. Dunne, *Hugo Black and the Judicial Revolution* (New York, 1977), esp. chaps. 9–12; Harry N. Hirsch, *The Enigma of Felix Frankfurter* (New York, 1981), esp. chap. 5; James F. Simon, *The Antagonists: Hugo Black, Felix Frankfurter and Civil Liberties in Modern America* (New York, 1989), esp. chaps. 3–4.

44. 304 U.S. 64 (1938).

45. Ibid., pp. 74–75.

46. Ibid., p. 75.

47. 276 U.S. 518 (1928).

48. 276 U.S. 533 (Holmes, J., dissenting).

49. Ibid., p. 80.

50. This is not meant to suggest that the litigation tactics of the 1920s and 1930s caused the Court to reverse *Swift*. Here, the point is simply that the litigation context was one factor influencing the Court and that the significance of that context has sometimes been overlooked.

51. "Limitation of Venue in Certain Actions Brought Under the Employers' Liability Act," Hearings before a Subcommittee of the Committee on the Judiciary of the United States Senate on S. 1567 and H.R. 1639, 80 Cong., 2 Sess. (1948), p. 239 (statement of Warren H. Atherton, attorney for the Brotherhood of Railroad Trainmen).

52. 48 Stat. 1064 (1934).

53. For general discussions of the background of the Rules Enabling Act, see Stephen B. Burbank, "The Rules Enabling Act of 1934," *University of Pennsylvania Law Review* 130 (1982): 1015; Stephen N. Subrin, "How Equity Conquered Common Law: The Federal Rules of Civil Procedure in Historical Perspective," *University of Pennsylvania Law Review* 135 (1987): 909.

54. Murphy, *Constitution in Crisis Times,* p. 141; Burns, *Roosevelt,* p. 229; Sen. Docs. Nos. 25–33, 37–44, 75 Cong., 1 Sess. (1937); William H. Harbaugh, *Lawyer's Lawyer: The Life of John W. Davis* (New York, 1973), pp. 365–72.

55. Robert H. Jackson, *The Struggle for Judicial Supremacy: A Study of a Crisis in American Power Politics* (New York, 1941), pp. 118–19.

56. *Miles v. Illinois Central Railroad Co.,* 315 U.S. 707 (1942) (Jackson, J., concurring). While still in private practice in 1930, Jackson was unusual in the bluntness with which he acknowledged the desire of the litigator and trial lawyer for victory on the basis of skill and tactics rather than the merits:

> It is in the field of uncertainty that the lawyer wins fame as a cross-examiner, a persuasive reasoner, a skillful tactician, an artist at enlarging verdicts in doubtful cases. Hence while laymen crave certainty we abhor a proceeding where two and two must always make four—we want a chance by forensic skill to build two and two up to six or hold them down to three, and now and then to get two and two returned by a jury as a cipher. [Robert H. Jackson, "Trial Practice in Accident Litigations," *Cornell Law Quarterly* 15 (1930): 194, 197].

57. *Trainor Co. v. Aetna Casualty & Surety Co.,* 290 U.S. 47 (1933); *Mutual Life Insurance Co. of New York v. Johnson,* 293 U.S. 335 (1934). Also see Chapter 8.

58. *Willing v. Binenstock,* 302 U.S. 272 (1937).

59. *Great Northern Railway Co. v. Sunburst Oil & Refining Co.,* 287 U.S. 358 (1932); *Hawks v. Hamill,* 288 U.S. 52 (1933); *Clark v. Williard,* 292 U.S. 112 (1934).

60. *Boseman v. Connecticut General Life Insurance Co.,* 301 U.S. 196 (1937).

61. *Burns Mortgage Co., v. Fried,* 67 F. 2d 352 (C.C.A. 3 1933).

62. *Burns Mortgage Co., v. Fried,* 292 U.S. 487 (1934). The Court quickly followed its decision in *Fried* in *Marine National Exchange Bank of Milwaukee v. Kalt-Zimmers Manufacturing Co.,* 293 U.S. 357 (1934).

63. *Healy v. Ratta,* 292 U.S. 263, 270 (1934).

64. 292 U.S. 25 (1934).

65. Ibid., p. 35.

66. *Canada Malting Co. v. Paterson Co.,* 285 U.S. 413 (1932).

67. *Rogers v. Guaranty Trust Co. of New York,* 288 U.S. 123 (1933).

68. Note, *"Forum Non Conveniens* and the 'Internal Affairs' of a Foreign Corporation," *Columbia Law Review* 33 (1933): 492; Note, "Extortionate Corporate Litigation: The Strike Suit," *Columbia Law Review* 34 (1908): 1308; Mortimer Hays, "A Study in Trial Tactics: Derivative Shareholders' Suits," *Columbia Law Review* 43 (1943): 275; Note, "The Development of the 'Internal Affairs' Rule in the Federal Courts and Its Future Under *Erie v. Tompkins," Columbia Law Review* 46 (1946): 413.

69. The dissenters were Justices Pierce Butler and James C. McReynolds. Justice Stanley F. Reed wrote a separate concurrence, placing the decision on statutory grounds and avoiding the majority's constitutional language. Justice Benjamin N. Cardozo was ill and did not participate.

70. In general the New Deal Court showed a particular sensitivity to state law and often stressed the need for the federal courts to defer to state policies: *Beal v. Missouri Pacific Railroad Corp.,* 312 U.S. 45 (1941); *American Federation of Labor v. Watson,* 327 U.S. 582 (1946)); to state courts: *Thompson v. Magnolia Petroleum Co.,* 309 U.S. 478 (1940); *Railroad Commission of Texas v. Pullman Co.,* 312 U.S. 496 (1941); *Chicago v. Fieldcrest Dairies, Inc.,* 316 U.S. 168

(1942); *Spector Motor Service, Inc. v. McLaughlin,* 323 U.S. 101 (1944); *Alabama State Federation of Labor v. McAdory,* 325 U.S. 450 (1945); and to state administrative agencies: *Railroad Commission of Texas v. Rowan & Nichols Oil Co.,* 310 U.S. 573 (1940) and 311 U.S. 570 (1941); *Burford v. Sun Oil Co.,* 319 U.S. 315 (1943).

71. For the view of the Roosevelt Court regarding the Tenth Amendment, see, for example, *United States v. Darby,* 312 U.S. 100, 123 (1941); Mason, *Harlan Fiske Stone,* pp. 406–11, 550–56; *Erie v. Tompkins,* 304 U.S. 90–91 (Reed, J., concurring).

72. *Six Companies of California v. Joint Highway District No. 13 of California,* 311 U.S. 180 (1940); *Stoner v. New York Life Insurance Co.,* 311 U.S. 464 (1940); *West v. American Telephone and Telegraph Co.,* 311 U.S. 223 (1940); *Fidelity Union Trust Co. v. Field,* 311 U.S. 169 (1940).

73. 313 U.S. 487 (1941).

74. Ibid., p. 496.

75. 326 U.S. 99 (1945).

76. Ibid., p. 109.

77. *York* unequivocally identified the elimination of forum shopping between state and federal courts in the same state as the dominant purpose of *Erie,* and it created a broadly encompassing pragmatic test that reached not only rules of "substantive" law but also large areas of "procedural" law—whatever rules were likely to affect the outcome of an action. See, for example, *Angel v. Bullington,* 330 U.S. 183, 191 (1947); *Ragan v. Merchants Transfer & Warehouse Co.,* 337 U.S. 530 (1949); *Woods v. Interstate Realty Co.,* 337 U.S. 535 (1949); *Cohen v. Beneficial Industrial Loan Co.,* 337 U.S. 541 (1949).

78. Even the fee schedules in the federal courts, a minor consideration, were altered in the mid-1940s to bring them into closer alignment with the court costs in at least most of the states. See "Jurisdiction of Federal Courts Concerning Diversity of Citizenship," Hearing before Subcommittee No. 3 of the Committee on the Judiciary of the United States House of Representatives, 85 Cong., 1 Sess. (1957), p. 12 and n. 5 ("Report of Committee on Jurisdiction and Venue" of the Judicial Conference of the United States).

79. Distance and geography continue to be factors in some litigations even in the late twentieth century. See Kristin Bumiller, "Choice of Forum in Diversity Cases: Analysis of a Survey and Implications for Reform," *Law & Society Review* 15 (1980–81): 749.

80. United States Railroad Retirement Board, *Work Injuries in the Railroad Industry, 1938–40* (Chicago, 1947), pp. 24–29.

81. 311 U.S. 464 (1940).

Similarly, in *Aetna Casualty & Surety Co. v. Flowers,* 330 U.S. 464 (1947), the Court held that under a state workmen's compensation act that "contemplates a single action for the determination of claimant's rights to benefits and a single judgment for the award granted" (pp. 467–68), an action brought to collect payments due involved the claimant's total potential claim. Both decisions probably reflected the Court's desire to promote judicial economy. Because the system of corporate diversity litigation was disintegrating, neither imposed significant burdens on plaintiffs.

82. See "Developments in the Law: Declaratory Judgments—1941–1949," *Harvard Law Review* 62 (1949): 787, 801–2.

83. In the era of the federal common law, the declaratory judgment would have been particularly useful to insurers, for example, in cases where the claimant might have been able to prevent the company from removing an action on the policy. Two types of cases come to mind: those in which a claimant could have brought an action on a policy for less than the jurisdictional amount (as in disability claims) or those in which she could have arranged the party structure to defeat complete diversity (as when the policyholder and the beneficiary were different individuals, or when a third-party claimant was involved). See "Developments in the Law," pp. 801–2, 852–53.

84. See, for example, *Altvater v. Freeman,* 319 U.S. 359 (1943); *Eccles v. People's Bank of Lakewood Village,* 33 U.S. 426 (1948).

85. *Great Lakes Dredge & Dock Co. v. Huffman,* 319 U.S.293 (1943). The *Great Lakes Dredge* case addressed the particularly touchy issue of federal injunctions against state tax collections, a context that the Court recognized as calling for particular restraint by federal courts.

86. *Maryland Casualty Co. v. Pacific Coal & Oil Co.,* 312 U.S. 270 (1941).

87. 16 U.S. 491 (1942).

88. "Developments in the Law," pp. 852–53.

89. The Court was particularly sensitive to the problem created in federal question cases where parties might be able to circumvent the plaintiff's pleading rule established in *Union & Planters' Bank*. See *Skelly Oil Co. v. Phillips Petroleum Co.*, 339 U.S. 667 (1950).

90. The Court seemed to remain sympathetic to claimants' efforts to maintain their right to trial by jury. See *Ettelson v. Metropolitan Life Insurance Co.*, 317 U.S. 188 (1942). For the opinion below, see *Ettelson v. Metropolitan Life Insurance Co.*, 42 F. Supp. 488 (D.N.J. 1941). In the 1940s, however, the Court was not prepared to rule on the basic constitutional question. For example, *City of Morgantown v. Royal Insurance Co., Ltd.*, 337 U.S. 254 (1949).

91. For example, *Aetna Casualty & Surety Co. v. Quarles*, 92 F. 2d 321 (C.C.A. 4 1937); *Pacific Indemnity Co. v. McDonald*, 107 F. 2d 446 (C.C.A. 9 1939); *(American) Lumbermen's Mutual Casualty Co. of Illinois v. Timms & Howard, Inc.*, 108 F. 2d 497 (C.C.A. 2 1939); *Hargrove v. American Century Insurance Co.*, 125 F. 2d 225 (C.C.A. 10 1942); *Dickinson v. General Accident, Fire & Life Assurance Corp.*, 147 F. 2d 396 (C.C.A. 9 1945). See Fleming James, Jr., "Right to a Jury Trial in Civil Actions," *Yale Law Journal* 72 (1963): 655, 685–86; Jack H. Friedenthal, Mary Kay Kane, and Arthur R. Miller, *Civil Procedure* (St. Paul, 1985), pp. 486, 490; Note, "The Right to Jury Trial Under Merged Procedures," *Harvard Law Review* 65 (1952): 453.

92. "Developments in the Law," pp. 835–36.

93. The principal cases were *Beacon Theatres, Inc., v. Westover*, 359 U.S. 500 (1959) and *Dairy Queen v. Wood*, 369 U.S. 469 (1962). See *Simler v. Connor*, 372 U.S. 221 (1963); John C. McCoid, II, "Procedural Reform and the Right to Jury Trial: A Study of *Beacon Theatres, Inc. v. Westover*," *University of Pennsylvania Law Review* 116 (1967): 1; Charles W. Wolfram, "The Constitutional History of the Seventh Amendment," *Minnesota Law Review* 57 (1973): 639; Martin H. Redish, "Seventh Amendment Right to Jury Trial: A Study in the Irrationality of Rational Decision Making," *Northwestern University Law Review* 70 (1975): 486.

94. 53 Stat. 1404 (1939). The Court upheld the act's broadened coverage in *Reed v Pennsylvania Railroad Co.*, 351 U.S. 502 (1956).

95. United States Bureau of the Census, *The Statistical History of the United States from Colonial Times to the Present* (Stamford, CT, 1965), p. 437.

96. For example, *Union Pacific Railroad Co. v. Utterback*, 146 P. 76 (Sup.Ct.Oreg. 1944). *Kepner* and *Miles* were widely regarded as major factors in guaranteeing the role of interstate forum shopping under the FELA. See "Limitation of Venue in Certain Actions Brought Under the Employers' Liability Act," Hearings before a Subcommittee of the Committee on the Judiciary of the United States Senate on S. 1567 and H.R. 1639, 80 Cong., 2 Sess. (1948), p. 39 (statement of Floyd E. Thompson, Esq.), p. 179 (statement of Hon. John Jennings, Jr., congressman from Tennessee), p. 259 (statement of Edward Dumbauld, special assistant to the Attorney General, Department of Justice); "Limitation of Venue in Certain Actions Brought Under the Employers' Liability Act," Hearings before Subcommittee No. 4 of the Committee on the Judiciary of the United States House of Representatives on H.R. 1639, 80 Cong., 1 Sess. (1947), p. 136 (statement of Thomas B. Gay, president of the Virginia State Bar Association and chairman of the Committee on Jurisprudence and Law Reform of the American Bar Association).

97. *Leet v. Union Pacific Railroad Co.*, 155 P. 2d 42, 46, 48 (Sup.Ct.Cal. 1945). See *In re Waits' Estate*, 146 P. 2d 5 (Sup.Ct.Cal. 1944).

98. The Court denied certiorari in the California case (*Leet*), 325 U.S. 866 (1945), and seemed to approve its statement about the inapplicability of *forum non conveniens* to FELA actions. *Gulf Oil Corp. v. Gilbert*, 330 U.S. 501, 505 (1947) (approving use of *forum non conveniens* in federal actions at law).

99. For example, Glenn R. Winters, "Interstate Commerce in Damage Suits," *Journal of the American Judicature Society* 29 (1946): 135; Forbes B. Henderson, "The 'Exportation' of Personal Injury and Death Claims," *Detroit Bar Quarterly* 13 (1946): 11; Note, "*Forum Non Conveniens*, A New Federal Doctrine," *Yale Law Journal* 56 (1947): 1234; Robert Braucher, "The Inconvenient Federal Forum," *Harvard Law Review* 60 (1947): 908; Note, "New Limitations on Choice of Federal Forum," *University of Chicago Law Review* 15 (1948): 332.

100. H.R. Rep. No. 613, 80 Cong., 1 Sess. (1947). The bill also provided that in the event that a plaintiff could not serve a railroad in either of the two proper districts, he could then bring suit in any district where the company was doing business.

101. H.R. Rep. No. 613, 80 Cong., 1 Sess. (1947), p. 3. By the next year they put the count over 3,100. "Limitation of Venue in Certain Actions Brought Under the Employers' Liability Act," Hearings before a Subcommittee of the Judiciary of the United States Senate, 80 Cong., 2 Sess. (1948), pp. 25–26 (statement of John W. Freels, Illinois Central Railroad Co.).

102. "Limitations of Venue in Certain Actions Brought Under the Employers' Liability Act," Hearings before a Subcommittee of the Committee on the Judiciary of the United States Senate on S. 1567 and H.R. 1639, 80 Cong., 2 Sess. (1948), pp. 98–99 (statement of Jonathan C. Gibson, vice-president and general counsel, Santa Fe Railway Co.).

103. Ibid., pp. 278–79 (supplemental statement of Jonathan C. Gibson, vice-president and general counsel, Santa Fe Railway).

104. Ibid., pp. 173, 260.

105. Ibid., p. 216 (statement of Warren H. Atherton, attorney for the Brotherhood of Railroad Trainmen).

106. Ibid., p. 37 (statement of John W. Freels, attorney for the Illinois Central Railroad Co.). Agreeing: ibid., p. 201 (statement of Frederick W. Brune, chairman of the Committee on Jurisprudence and Law Reform, American Bar Association).

107. 93 *Cong. Rec.* 9193–94 (1947).

108. 93 *Cong. Rec.* 9187 (1947).

109. *Gulf Oil Corp. v. Gilbert,* 330 U.S. 501 (1947); *Koster v. (American) Lumbermen's Mutual Casualty Co.,* 330 U.S. 518 (1947).

The Court seemed to exclude FELA suits from application of the doctrine on the ground that the courts could not, on the basis of *forum non conveniens,* override a statute that offered special venue provisions for actions brought under it. See *Gulf Oil,* 330 U.S. 506.

110. For example, H.R. Rep. No. 2646, 79 Cong., 2 Sess. (1946), pp. A127–28; H.R. Rep. No. 308, 80 Cong., 1 Sess (1947), p. A132.

Drafts of the Revised Code adopted the new transfer provision incorporated in Section 1404 before the Supreme Court adopted *forum non conveniens* in 1947. See, for example, H.R. Rep. No. 2646, 79 Cong., 2 Sess. (1946), "Appendix," p. A127.

111. Ibid., pp. 1–2. The code was enacted on June 25, 1948. See 62 Stat. 869.

112. 8 F.R.D. 439, 441 (1948).

113. Ibid., p. A132.

114. For example, "Limitation of Venue in Certain Actions Brought Under the Employers' Liability Act," Hearings before a Subcommittee of the Committee on the Judiciary of the United States Senate on S. 1567 and H.R. 1639, 80 Cong., 2 Sess. (1948), pp. 257–58 (statement of Hon. Edward J. Devitt, congressman from Minnesota). The arguments and counterarguments of both sides in the House and Senate hearings strongly supported the proposition that no single general rule determining venue would prove just in all or even most cases.

115. For example, H.R. Rep. No. 2626, 79 Cong., 2 Sess. (1946), pp. 2–5.

116. Section 1391.

117. *Hayes v. Chicago, Rock Island & Pacific Railroad Co.,* 79 F. Supp. 821 (D.C. Minn. 1948) (eight actions heard together on motion to transfer).

118. 337 U.S. 55 (1949). A companion case applied the holding of *Collett.* See *Kilpatrick v. Texas & Pacific Railway Co.,* 337 U.S. 75 (1949). A similar question arose under the special venue provision of the Clayton Act. See *United States v. National City Lines, Inc.,* 337 U.S. 78 (1949).

119. *Pope v. Atlantic Coast Line Railroad Co.,* 345 U.S. 379 (1953).

120. Barrett, "Doctrine of *Forum Non Conveniens,*" pp. 388–93; D. H. B., "*Erie,* Forum non Conveniens and Choice of Law in Diversity Cases," *Virginia Law Review* 53 (1967): 381–82.

121. *Missouri ex rel. Southern Railroad Co. v. Mayfield,* 340 U.S. 1 (1950).

122. Parties may and do still use interstate forum shopping for any number of procedural or practical advantages. In some instances, too, where state law provides the rule of decision, parties can try to shop for the most favorable substantive law. Choice-of-law rules limit that possibility,

but they do not preclude it. Insofar as substantive state law is controlling, the Supreme Court has tried to eliminate removal and transfers under Section 1404 as devices for securing a change in the state law to be applied. See, for example, *Van Dusen v. Barrack,* 376 U.S. 612 (1964).

123. Section 1441.

124. Section 1446 (b); H.R. Rep. No. 352, 81 Cong., 1 Sess. (1949), p. 14.

125. H.R. Rep. No. 308, 80 Cong., 1 Sess. (1947), p. A182. See Section 2283.

126. Section 1391.

127. Section 1441(c). Although the difference between the language in the old and new sections was arguably somewhat metaphysical, the official Reviser's notes made clear the intended result of the change: "[I]t will somewhat decrease the volume of Federal litigation." H.R. Rep. No. 308, 80 Cong., 1 Sess. (1947), p. A134. The Supreme Court relied on the statement of intent in eventually construing the new separable controversy section more narrowly than it had the previous version. *American Fire & Casualty Co. v. Finn,* 341 U.S. 6, 9–10 (1951).

128. Section 1446.

129. H.R. Rep. No. 308, 80 Cong., 1 Sess. (1947), p. A133.

130. Ibid., p. A133.

131. Sen. Rep. No. 1830, 85 Cong., 2 Sess. (1958), pp. 7–9; 104 *Cong. Rec.* 12683 (1958).

132. 72 Stat. 415 (1958). Although Congress seemed moved primarily by the desire to cut the federal caseload, the Senate report also stressed the fairness reason for the amendment:

> Very often cases removed to the Federal courts require the workman to travel long distances and to bring his witnesses at great expense. This places an undue burden upon the workman and very often the workman settles his claim because he cannot afford the luxury of a trial in Federal court. [Senate Report No. 1830, 85 Cong., 2 Sess. (1958), p. 9]

The amendment also raised the jurisdictional amount to $10,000.

133. Sen. Rep. No. 1830, 85 Cong., 2 Sess. (1958), p. 4; H.R.Rep. 1706, 85 Cong., 2 Sess. (1958), p. 4. See 104 *Cong. Rec.,* Part 10, 85 Cong., 2 Sess. (1958), p. 12685 (statement of Congressman Emmanuel Celler of New York, chairman, Committee on the Judiciary of the House of Representatives); John J. Parker, "Dual Sovereignty and the Federal Courts," *Northwestern University Law Review* 51 (1956): 407, 411; "Jurisdiction of Federal Courts Concerning Diversity of Citizenship," Hearing before Subcommittee No. 3 of the Committee on the Judiciary of the House of Representatives, 85 Cong., 1 Sess. (1957), p. 14 ("Report of Committee on Jurisdiction and Venue" of the Judicial Conference of the United States).

134. See Walter F. Murphy, *Congress and the Court: A Case Study in the American Political Process* (Chicago, 1962); J. W. Paltason, *Fifty-Eight Lonely Men: Southern Federal Judges and School Desegregation* (Urbana, IL, 1961); C. Herman Pritchett, *Congress Versus the Supreme Court* (New York, 1973); Donald J. Kemper, *Decade of Fear: Senator Hennings and Civil Liberties* (Columbia, MO, 1965); John P. Frank, *Marble Palace: The Supreme Court in American Life* (New York, 1958).

135. 347 U.S. 483 (1954).

136. 101 *Cong. Rec.* "Appendix," p. A1815 (1955) ("Extension of Remarks of Hon. William M. Tuck of Virginia"). See "Jurisdiction of Federal Courts Concerning Diversity of Citizenship," Hearing before Subcommittee No. 3 of the Committee on the Judiciary of the House of Representatives, 85 Cong., 1 Sess. (1957), pp. 5–6 (testimony of William M. Tuck).

137. Sen. Rep. No. 1830, 85 Cong., 2 Sess. (1958), p. 13 (statement of Joseph F. Spaniol, Jr., attorney, Division of Procedural Studies and Statistics, Administrative Office of the United States Courts).

138. The figures, which Congress did not highlight, are calculated from statistics given in Sen. Rep. No. 1830, 85 Cong., 2 Sess. (1958), p. 13, and in "Jurisdiction of Federal Courts Concerning Diversity of Citizenship," Hearing before Subcommittee No. 3 of the Committee on the Judiciary of the House of Representatives, 85 Cong., 1 Sess. (1957), pp. 42–43.

139. "Jurisdiction of Federal Courts Concerning Diversity of Citizenship," Hearing before Subcommittee No. 3 of the Committee on the Judiciary of the House of Representatives, 85 Cong., 1 Sess. (1957), p. 34.

140. Sen. Rep. 530, 72 Cong., 1 Sess. (1932), pp. 4, 3.

141. Sen. Rep. 530, 72 Cong., 1 Sess. (1932), p. 16.

142. In addition to the corporate opposition at the hearings, many companies and trade groups protested any change in diversity jurisdiction. See, for example, George W. Norris Papers, Library of Congress, Washington, DC, Tray 79, Box 8.

143. "Limiting Jurisdiction of Federal Courts," Hearings before the Committee on the Judiciary of the House of Representatives, 72 Cong., 1 Sess. (1932), p. 65 (statement of Washington Bowie, representing the Fidelity & Deposit Co. of Baltimore), p. 45 (statement of James A. Emery, general counsel of the National Association of Manufacturers); also see pp. 5–9 (statement of Paul Howland, chairman of the Committee on Jurisprudence and Law Reform of the American Bar Association).

144. Ibid., p. 87 (statement of Henry M. Ward, Esq.).

145. Letter from William Howard Taft to Willis Van Devanter, April 19, 1928, Willis Van Devanter Papers, Box 33, Library of Congress, Washington, DC.

146. "Jurisdiction of Federal Courts Concerning Diversity of Citizenship," Hearing before Subcommittee No. 3 of the Committee on the Judiciary of the House of Representatives, 85 Cong., 1 Sess. (1957). When asked, the representative of the Judicial Conference volunteered his "impression" that "counsel for large corporate interests that operate through the country would be strongly opposed" to limitations on diversity (p. 35).

147. Note, "Federal Jurisdiction Amount: Determination of the Matter in Controversy," *Harvard Law Review* 73 (1960): 1369, 1370, n. 10.

Chapter 11

1. *Paul v. Virginia,* 8 Wall (75 U.S.) 168 (1869) (denying that corporations were "persons" within the meaning of the privileges and immunities clause and holding that "insurance" did not qualify as "commerce" within the meaning of the commerce clause); *Slaughter-House Cases,* 16 Wall. (83 U.S.) 36 (1873) (holding that the Fourteenth Amendment did not invalidate a state scheme to regulate the business of operating slaughterhouses); *Munn v. Illinois,* 94 U.S. 113 (1877) (upholding the power of the states to regulate warehouse rates).

In upholding the power of the states to restrict foreign corporations in *Paul v. Virginia,* the Court gave voice to the same concerns about corporate size and power that marked its opinion in *Wilkinson, Lockwood, Fort,* and *McCue:*

At the present day corporations are multiplied to an almost indefinite extent. There is scarcely a business pursued requiring the expenditure of large capital, or the union of large numbers, that is not carried on by corporations. It is not too much to say that the wealth and business of the country are to a great extent controlled by them. And if, when composed of citizens of one State, their corporate powers and franchises could be exercised in other States without restrictions, it is easy to see that, with the advantages thus possessed, the most important business of those States would soon pass into their hands. The principal business of every State would, in fact, be controlled by corporations created by other States. [8 Wall. (75 U.S.) 181–82]

2. Much of the statistical overview of the system presented in Chapter 1 was based on the statistics in American Law Institute, *A Study of the Business of the Federal Courts: Part II, Civil Cases* (Philadelphia, 1934).

3. Herbert Wechsler, "Federal Jurisdiction and the Revision of the Judicial Code," *Law & Contemporary Problems* 13 (1948): 216, 243; Administrative Office of the United States Courts, *Annual Report,* 1945–47 (Washington, DC, 1946–48), Tables C2 and C4; Sen. Rep. No. 1830, 85 Cong., 2 Sess. (1958), p. 26.

4. The quarter-century before World War II was also the period that witnessed the emergence of legal realism, an approach to the study of law that stressed the indeterminacy of doctrine and the impact of social and economic factors on the legal process. As interstate forum shopping and similar tactics came into common use, they increasingly highlighted the fact that substantive rules of law conflicted, that forum choice was a factor of major significance, that procedure could be as determinative as was substantive law, and that more sophisticated parties could take special advantage of all of those facts. As early as 1913, Wesley N. Hohfeld, one of the forerunners of

legal realism, addressed the accepted professional view that law and equity were complementary parts of the same overarching and unified system of Anglo-American law.

> [T]he thesis of the present writer is this, while a large part of the rules of equity harmonize with the various rules of law, another large part of the rules of equity—more especially those relating to the so-called exclusive and auxiliary jurisdictions of equity—conflict with legal rules and, as a matter of substance, annul or negative the latter *pro tanto*. [Wesley N. Hohfeld, "The Relations Between Equity and Law," *Michigan Law Review* 11 (1913): 537, 543–44]

Startling to most and heresy to many, Hohfeld's thesis adumbrated a critical approach that would become common by the 1920s and 1930s, reflecting recognition of the kinds of facts that escalating litigation tactics were in the process of making increasingly obvious.

5. See, for example, Judith Resnick, "Managerial Judges," *Harvard Law Review* 96 (1982): 376; Peter Graham Fish, *The Politics of Federal Judicial Administration* (Princeton, NJ, 1973).

6. *Gulf Oil Corp. v. Gilbert,* 330 U.S. 501, 508 (1947).

7. For recent discussions of the problems of attempting to relate law and society by two distinguished legal historians, see Robert W. Gordon, "Critical Legal Histories," *Stanford Law Review* 36 (1984): 57; Lawrence M. Friedman, "The Law and Society Movement," *Law & Society Review* 38 (1986): 763.

8. A clarification may be in order. Although this book's approach may be described metaphorically as ecological, it does not purport to be "scientific" in any strict or meaningful sense, nor does it attempt to apply any particular theory or method used in the biological or other sciences. It certainly does not mean to imply that the idea of an objective and pure "legal science" may be brought to fruition. Compare, for example, Donald Black, *Sociological Justice* (New York, 1989).

9. This book, for example, finds a number of differences between the insurance and tort litigations that national corporations conducted. A more refined analysis would undoubtedly uncover a range of additional significant differences, including differences among various specific companies and individual litigants. Different parties, after all, may have quite different attitudes, resources, goals, or problems that lead them to adopt quite different formal or informal litigation tactics. For example, Frank W. Munger, Jr., "Social Change and Tort Litigation: Industrialization, Accidents, and Trial Courts in Southern West Virginia, 1872–1940," *Buffalo Law Review* 36 (1987): 75, 96–105 (comparing differences between tort litigations involving railroads and coal companies).

10. For example, Paul M. Kurtz, "Nineteenth Century Anti-Entrepreneurial Nuisance Injunctions—Avoiding the Chancellor," *William and Mary Law Review* 17 (1976): 621; Robert G. Bone, "Mapping the Boundaries of a Dispute: Conceptions of Ideal Lawsuit Structure from the Field Code to the Federal Rules," *Columbia Law Review* 89 (1989): 1.

11. Compare, for example, Gary Schwartz, "The Character of Early American Tort Law," *U.C.L.A. Law Review* 36 (1989): 641, with Lawrence M. Friedman and Thomas D. Russell, "More Civil Wrongs: Personal Injury Litigation, 1901–1910," *American Journal of Legal History* 34 (1990): 295.

12. Recent research has begun to emphasize that the relationship between industrialization and legal change in the nineteenth century is much less direct and far more complicated than scholars had previously assumed. See, for example, Lawrence M. Friedman, Robert W. Gordon, Sophie Pirie, and Edwin Whatley, "Law, Lawyers, and Legal Practice in Silicon Valley: A Preliminary Report," *Indiana Law Journal* 64 (1989): 555; Munger, "Social Change and Tort Litigations"; Gordon, "Critical Legal Histories." Compare Lawrence M. Friedman and Jack Ladinsky, "Social Change and the Law of Industrial Accidents," *Columbia Law Review* 67 (1967): 50, with Robert L. Rabin, "The Historical Development of the Fault Principle: A Reinterpretation," *Georgia Law Review* 15 (1981): 925.

13. The discussion in the text is intended only to note points where the book touches on a major and complex historiographical debate. Inevitably, different scholars have described "formalism" and "classical" legal thought with different emphases, and no generally accepted definition of formalism exists. The classic early study is Morton White, *Social Thought in America: The*

Revolt Against Formalism (New York, 1949). Since the text argues that formalism in American legal thought has probably been overemphasized, I should acknowledge my own complicity. See Edward A. Purcell, Jr., *The Crisis of Democratic Theory: Scientific Naturalism and the Problem of Value* (Lexington, KY, 1973), chap. 5. Harry N. Scheiber was one of the first scholars to question the extent to which formalism existed and exerted influence in judicial decisions. He found instrumentalist reasoning common throughout the late nineteenth century, especially in the state courts. See Scheiber, "Instrumentalism and Property Rights: A Reconsideration of American 'Styles of Judicial Reasoning' in the Nineteenth Century," *Wisconsin Law Review* (1975): 1.

For general discussions of "formalism" and "classical" legal thought see Karl N. Llewellyn, *The Common Law Tradition: Deciding Appeals* (Boston, 1960); Morton J. Horwitz, *The Transformation of American Law, 1780–1860* (Cambridge, MA, 1977), chap. 8; Grant Gilmore, *The Ages of American Law* (New Haven, CT, 1977), esp. chap. 3; G. Edward White, *Tort Law in America: An Intellectual History* (New York, 1980), esp. chap. 2; Duncan Kennedy, "Toward an Historical Understanding of Legal Consciousness: The Case of Classical Legal Thought in America, 1850–1940," *Research in Law and Society* 3 (1980): 3; William E. Nelson, *The Roots of American Bureaucracy, 1830–1900* (Cambridge, MA, 1982), pp. 133–48; Thomas C. Grey, "Langdell's Orthodoxy," *University of Pittsburgh Law Review* 45 (1983): 1; Robert W. Gordon, "Legal Thought and Legal Practice in the Age of American Enterprise," in Gerald L. Geison, ed., *Professions and Professional Ideologies in America* (Chapel Hill, NC, 1983), 70–110.

On the question of the social significance of formalism, many scholars, such as Gilmore (p. 66) and White (pp. 61–62), have seen a connection between formalist jurisprudence and the interests of expanding capitalist enterprise in the late nineteenth century. Generally, they argue that formalism was particularly compatible with doctrines of narrow tort liability and that it strengthened and encouraged the judiciary in invalidating government regulatory legislation. Horwitz goes beyond most in insisting (p. 266) on a direct and purposeful connection: "For the paramount social condition that is necessary for legal formalism to flourish in a society is for the powerful groups in that society to have a great interest in disguising and suppressing the inevitably political and redistributive functions of law."

Some scholars have focused more closely on the structure of ideas that constituted formalist legal thought. Kennedy, although not denying the likelihood that connections existed between legal thought and the rise of nineteenth–century capitalism, sees "classical legal thought" as a form of "legal consciousness" that channeled judicial thinking and molded doctrine with "relative autonomy" from social interests (p. 4). Gordon, extending Kennedy's emphasis on the autonomy of legal consciousness, suggests that formalism is best understood as an integrated political ideology produced by lawyers and centered around the "conception of freedom as a set of barriers against coercive intrusion into zones of autonomous conduct" (p. 90).

Other scholars have minimized or even denied a significant relationship between formalism and corporate enterprise. Stressing the generally benevolent and fair intentions of the late nineteenth-century judiciary, Nelson (pp. 150–5) concludes that formalist legal writers did not share "any single well-developed style or method, but an aversion to explicit analysis of policy" (p. 144). Grey emphasizes the importance of a new and politically moderate legal professoriate in fostering "classical" legal thought. He denies that such scholars were "enthusiastic supporters of late nineteenth century big business" (35) and questions whether classical legal thought "actually influenced the course of judicial decision in a pro-business direction" (p. 33).

The comments in the text concern only the extent to which formalism characterized the legal thought of federal judges in the late nineteenth and early twentieth centuries. Later sections of this chapter discuss the related question of the general political role and orientation of the federal courts.

14. It is important to recall that in some cases the Court, by its own admission, structured the law to achieve openly-acknowledged policy goals. In *Tuttle,* for example, it announced the importance of protecting employers from the negligence of their workers, and in *Northern Assurance* it proclaimed the need to protect investors from both policyholders and company agents.

It is also important to note that an emphasis on instrumentalism in judicial decisions does not deny the importance either of legal rules and precedents or of ideology and legal consciousness. Accepted professional canons of practice impose meaningful and often predictable restraints on the ways that lawyers and judges deal with legal materials, and powerful and largely buried preconceptions (paradigms, ideologies, etc.) are inherent aspects of human thought. Instrumentalism does not and cannot exist in a cultural vacuum.

15. Formalism may well have been less an actual method of legal reasoning that judges employed than a distinctive historical phenomenon that resulted from a conflict between divergent versions of reality (world views, paradigms, ideologies) in a time of rapid, massive, and structural social change and relatively acute political-cultural conflict. Those who lived within one world view (which tended to be regarded as normative within established institutions, accepted by socially dominant ethnic groups, and rooted in pervasive elements of middle-class Protestantism, common law tradition, nineteenth–century economic theory, and American national culture) failed to perceive, understand, value, and take account of "facts" and "social consequences" in ways that were consistent with another, newly coalescing world view. Those who shared the emerging world view (which tended to be regarded as normative within the new professional classes, accepted by a range of social outsiders, and rooted in attitudes associated with naturalistic science, Enlightenment rationalism, political egalitarianism, and other elements of Protestantism and American national culture) translated that failure as "formalism." Judges who shared the older world view helped inspire and confirm that translation by increasingly avoiding overt or detailed policy-based analysis as a method of obviating or minimizing clashes (whether theoretical, political, economic, cultural, or moral) with the newer world view. Those who shared the newer world view increasingly saw the term "formalism" as a rhetorically effective label to discredit those who accepted the older world view. As the newer world view came to dominance in the twentieth century, its later adherents came to think of "formalism" as a "real" method of legal reasoning and a "real" jurisprudence that had characterized legal thought during an earlier period.

What those judges who shared the older world view almost certainly did not do, however, was reach their decisions (as opposed to writing their opinions or stating their theories of jurisprudence) by some truly "abstract" method of deduction that ignored social context, conseqences, and values. In one of its allegedly most formalist opinions, for example, the Supreme Court—although failing to engage in detailed policy analysis and relying on reasoning that seemed abstract and deductive—revealed the extent to which its decision reflected both the majority's awareness of the existence of bitterly disputed "social facts" and a commitment to its own substantive social theory.

No doubt, wherever the right of private property exists, there must and will be inequalities of fortune; and thus it naturally happens that parties negotiating about a contract are not equally unhampered by circumstances. This applies to all contracts, and not merely to that between employer and employe [*sic*]. Indeed a little reflection will show that wherever the right of private property and the right of free contract co-exist, each party when contracting is inevitably more or less influenced by the question whether he has much property, or little, or none; for the contract is made to the very end that each may gain something that he needs or desires more urgently than that which he proposes to give in exchange. And, since it is self-evident that, unless all things are held in common, some persons must have more property than others, it is from the nature of things impossible to uphold freedom of contract and the right of private property without at the same time recognizing as legitimate those inequalities of fortune that are the necessary result of the exercise of those rights. [*Coppage v. Kansas,* 236 U.S. 1, 17 (1915)]

16. Robert W. Gordon has begun a promising effort to integrate both substantive and procedural law with broader ideological and social factors. See "Legal Thought and Legal Practice in the Age of American Enterprise, 1870–1920," in Geison, ed., *Professions and Professional Ideologies in America,* esp. pp. 101–7.

17. "Whether or not there is actual local prejudice in the local court is not the question. It is a question of whether an investor has confidence in the local court being entirely free of local prejudice." See "Limiting Jurisdiction of Federal Courts," Hearing before the Committee on the Judiciary of the United States House of Representatives, 72 Cong., 1 Sess. (1932), p. 53 (statement of Paul V. Keyser, counsel of the Investment Bankers Association of America).

18. The situation may well have been similar to the use of delaying tactics in late twentieth-century litigation. No attorney today would publicly admit adopting a tactic simply to delay a lawsuit. To do so would be to admit violating an explicit rule of professional ethics that forbids an attorney to take any action for the sole purpose of delay. Yet, alternative and "acceptable" reasons for using a tactic that happens to delay a suit as a "side effect" are almost always available. The reference in the ethical rule to a "sole" purpose provides a loophole sufficiently wide to allow even the dullest attorney to come up with some other reason for using a tactic and thus to avoid the compulsion of the rule.

19. For example, Wechsler, "Federal Jurisdiction and the Revision of the Judicial Code," pp. 216, 234–37; Henry J. Friendly, "The Historic Basis of Diversity Jurisdiction," *Harvard Law Review* 41 (1928): 483; Henry J. Friendly, *Federal Jurisdiction: A General View* (New York, 1973), pp. 146–52.

Again, this is not to suggest that some local prejudice did not exist or that guaranteeing an unbiased judicial forum is not a proper and desirable federal goal. It is merely to say that federal diversity jurisdiction in the late nineteenth and early twentieth centuries was only partially related to protection against whatever dangers nonresident litigants faced from local bias or prejudice.

On the disputed issue of diversity jurisdiction and the existence of local bias in the mid-twentieth century, see Marvin R. Summers, "Analysis of Factors That Influence Choice of Forum in Diversity Cases," *Iowa Law Review* 47 (1962): 933; Note, "The Choice Between State and Federal Court in Diversity Cases in Virginia," *Virginia Law Review* 51 (1965): 178; Jerry Goldman and Kenneth S. Marks, "Diversity Jurisdiction and Local Bias: A Preliminary Empirical Inquiry," *Journal of Legal Studies* 9 (1980): 93; Kristin Bumiller, "Choice of Forum in Diversity Cases: Analysis of a Survey and Implications for Reform," *Law & Society Review* 15 (1880–81): 749.

20. 196 U.S. 579 (1905).

21. Ibid., p. 586. The Court's statement probably represented a generally shared view. As one federal judge also noted in 1905 while addressing his state's bar association: The Supreme Court adopted the "fiction" of corporate citizenship for diversity purposes "[i]n order to enable the Federal courts to obtain jurisdiction in actions by or against corporations." See Jacob Trieber, "The Jurisdiction of Federal Courts in Actions in Which Corporations Are Parties," *American Law Review* 39 (1905): 564, 567–68.

22. Similarly, the Court's treatment of the jurisdictional amount in equity suits over the years suggests the same conclusion. If cases were socially and economically important, the Court usually found the jurisdictional amount requirement satisfied, even when the specific claims at issue were for small amounts. For example, *Hunt v. New York Cotton Exchange*, 205 U.S. 322 (1907); *Bitterman v. Louisville and Nashville Railroad Co.*, 207 U.S. 205 (1907); *Packard v. Banton*, 264 U.S. 140 (1924)

23. Charles O. Gregory, "Trespass to Negligence to Absolute Liability," *Virginia Law Review* 37 (1951): 259, 382; Leonard W. Levy, *The Law of the Commonwealth and Chief Justice Shaw* (Cambridge, MA, 1957), p. 166; Lawrence M. Friedman, *A History of American Law* (New York, 1973), pp. 407–27; Morton J. Horwitz, *The Transformation of American Law, 1780–1860* (Cambridge, MA, 1977), esp. chap. 3. For critiques of the subsidy thesis, see Rabin, "Historical Development of the Fault Principle"; Gary Schwartz, "Tort Law and the Economy in Nineteenth Century America: A Reinterpretation," *Yale Law Journal* 90 (1981): 1717; Schwartz, "Character of Early American Tort Law."

More recent work is important because it is beginning to change the focus from the formal to the informal legal process in evaluating the subsidy thesis. See, for example, Lawrence M. Friedman, "Civil Wrongs: Personal Injury Law in the Late 19th Century," *American Bar Foundation Research Journal* (1987): 351; Friedman and Russell, "More Civil Wrongs."

24. One law review comment concluded from a study of the fellow servant rule that "litigation on the subject was enormous and the economic benefit of the rule to any class in society, except possibly the lawyers, was doubtful." See Comment, "The Creation of a Common Law Rule: The Fellow Servant Rule, 1837–1860," *University of Pennsylvania Law Review* 132 (1984): 579, 583, n. 21 on p. 584. The view overlooks the critical role of the informal legal process. Even if corporate litigation costs equalled or exceeded the amounts for which companies could have been liable in litigated cases, those litigation costs and their social results—often favorable

substantive law and always the show of financial power and the willingness to use it—helped dissuade approximately 95 percent of injured workers from prosecuting suits to judgment. It was from those instances that national corporations derived the primary economic benefit of the fellow servant rule and similar doctrines of law.

25. See, for example, Werner Z. Hirsch, *Law and Economics: An Introductory Analysis,* 2nd ed. (Boston, 1988). Much of the inspiration for the movement came from the work of Ronald H. Coase, "The Problem of Social Cost," *Journal of Law & Economics* 3 (1960): 1, and Guido Calabresi, *The Costs of Accidents: A Legal and Economic Analysis* (New Haven, CT, 1970). For analyses of the so-called Coase theorem, see, for example, Robert C. Ellickson, "Of Coase and Cattle: Dispute Resolution Among Neighbors in Shasta County," *Stanford Law Review* 38 (1986): 623; Stewart Schwab, "Coase Defends Coase: Why Lawyers Listen and Economists Do Not," *Michigan Law Review* 87 (1989): 1171. Richard A. Posner has perhaps been the most important and indefatigable figure in the law and economics movement. See, for example, Richard A. Posner, *Economic Analysis of Law,* 2nd ed (Boston, 1977); "Some Uses and Abuses of Economics in Law," *University of Chicago Law Review* 46 (1979): 281, and *The Economics of Justice* (Cambridge, MA, 1983). Major contributors have included John Prather Brown, "Toward an Economic Theory of Liability," *Journal of Legal Studies* 2 (1973): 323; Paul H. Rubin, "Why Is the Common Law Efficient?" *Journal of Legal Studies* 6 (1977): 51; George L. Priest, "The Common Law Process and the Selection of Efficient Rules," *Journal of Legal Studies* 6 (1977): 65; Robert Cooter and Lewis Kornhauser, "Can Litigation Improve the Law Without the Help of Judges?" *Journal of Legal Studies* 9 (1980): 139; Mark F. Grady, "A New Positive Economic Theory of Negligence," *Yale Law Journal* 92 (1983): 799; George L. Priest and Benjamin Klein, "The Selection of Disputes for Litigation," *Journal of Legal Studies* 13 (1984): 13.

26. Richard A. Posner, "A Theory of Negligence," *Journal of Legal Studies* 1 (1972): 29.

27. See n. 25. Critics of the law and economics movement have also been numerous. See, for example, A. Mitchell Polinsky, "Economic Analysis as a Potentially Defective Product: A Buyer's Guide to Posner's *Economic Analysis of Law,*" *Harvard Law Review* 87 (1974): 1655; Arthur Allen Leff, "Law And," *Yale Law Journal* 87 (1978): 989; Izhak England, "The System Builders: A Critical Appraisal of Modern American Tort Theory," *Journal of Legal Studies* 9 (1980): 27; Mario J. Rizzo, "The Mirage of Efficiency," *Hofstra Law Review* 8 (1980): 641; Jules L. Coleman, "Efficiency, Exchange, and Auction: Philosophical Aspects of the Economic Approach to Law," *California Law Review* 68 (1980): 221; George L. Priest, "The New Scientism in Legal Scholarship: A Comment on Clark and Posner," *Yale Law Journal* 90 (1981): 1284; Rabin, "Historical Development of the Fault Principle"; Note, "The Inefficient Common Law," *Yale Law Jounral* 92 (1983): 862; Ronald Dworkin, *A Matter of Principle* (Cambridge, MA, 1985), chaps. 12–13; Ronald Dworkin, *Law's Empire* (Cambridge, MA, 1986), chap. 8; Mark Kelman, *A Guide to Critical Legal Studies* (Cambridge, MA, 1987), chaps. 4–5; Herbert Hovenkamp, "Positivism in Law & Economics," *California Law Review* 78 (1990): 815. For a discussion of Posner's work after his appointment to the bench, see George M. Choen, "Posnerian Jurisprudence and Economic Analysis of Law: The View from the Bench," *University of Pennsylvania Law Review* 133 (1985): 1117.

28. Posner, "Theory of Negligence," pp. 29–31.

29. Ibid., p. 32.

30. Ibid., p. 33.

31. Ibid.

32. Ibid., p. 73. Although Judge Posner continues to adhere to the general arguments and analyses in "A Theory of Negligence," he seems to have qualified his views to some extent. For his continued adherence, see William M. Landes and Richard A. Posner, *The Economic Structure of Tort Law* (Cambridge, MA, 1987), pp. 22, 71, 308–9. There, for example, he states that the "doctrinal structure [of late nineteenth-century industrial tort law] seems broadly consistent with efficiency" (p. 309). As a general matter, however, Judge Posner's recent statements seem more tentative than those in his earlier writings. See, for example, p. 24. More important, he would now apparently limit his general conclusions to "the *formal* adequacy of industrial-accident law" as a "model of efficient rules of tort law" (p. 310, emphasis added). He repeats the same qualification on the next page, stating that the rules were efficient "at least formally" (p. 311). The comments seem to moderate or perhaps even withdraw the claim that the rules of late

nineteenth–century tort law brought economically efficient results in practice. In addition, he notes in the same book a problem with one element of the logic of the fellow servant rule. The rule made sense, he suggests, only insofar as it applied to those fellow servants who worked "in some proximity" to the injured employee. If the fellow servant worked closely with the injured person, it would be reasonable to expect that the latter could and should have known of the negligent behavior of the former and taken appropriate steps to protect against it. But, he notes, "most courts rejected the proximity limitation." That rejection, he declares, "is a puzzle" (pp. 309–10). For a discussion of the proximity rule and its rejection by the United States Supreme Court, see Chapter 3.

33. Ibid., p. 92.

34. Posner is, of course, aware of the existence of practical problems and tries to draw evidence from the appellate cases to suggest their nature. Judicial opinions, however, especially appellate opinions, do not generally include significant evidence regarding practical and extra-legal pressures that deflect the ideal working of the legal process. His conclusions, accordingly, minimize their significance. Posner offers several tentative conclusions, however, including his view that the cost of prosecuting claims was generally low, that plaintiffs seemed to have counsel that were as able or more able than defendants' counsel, that the doctrine of *res ipsa loquitur* was commonly used, and that juries seemed to favor plaintiffs. He also acknowledges evidence that small claims may have been uneconomical to pursue. Perhaps of greatest interest, even from appellate cases Posner is able to show that employees were relatively reluctant to sue their employers, that they tended to do so only in the case of particularly serious injuries, and that employers often used relief association funds and releases to prevent their employees from bringing suit (ibid., pp. 74–92).

35. Ibid., pp. 36–73. Posner seems to acknowledge this relatively narrow focus and to accept that it imposes restrictions on the scope of his conclusions. See Landes and Posner, *Economic Structure of Tort Law*, p. 20.

36. Posner, "Theory of Negligence," p. 94.

37. Ibid., p. 93.

38. Ibid., p. 36.

39. Friedman and Russell, "More Civil Wrongs," pp. 307–8; American Law Institute, *Study of the Business of the Federal Courts*, p. 93.

40. The other categories that Posner and the commission use are not comparable. The commission found average awards of $3,515 in permanent partial disability cases (which included single amputations), $11,272 in total permanent disability cases, and $932 in temporary disability cases. Posner found averages of $4,640 in nondeath "bodily injury" cases, and $10,138 in cases involving "amputation or equivalent" (ibid., p. 79). The numbers suggest, though they are by no means clear, that recoveries in appealed cases may have been considerably higher than recoveries in nonappealed cases for most or all types of injuries. See Sen. Doc. No. 338, 62 Cong., 2 Sess. (1912), pp. 131, 135, 139, 143. Posner also mentions two studies of trial courts that found that average damages were only about 80 percent of the amounts awarded in the appellate cases he reviewed. See Posner, "Theory of Negligence," p. 94.

41. Ibid., 93.

42. See, for example, United States Railroad Retirement Board, *Work Injuries in the Railroad Industry, 1938–40* (Chicago, 1947), pp. 39–43; Janusz A. Ordover, "Costly Litigation in the Model of Single Activity Accidents," *Journal of Legal Studies* 7 (1978): 243; George L. Priest, "Selective Characteristics of Litigation," *Journal of Legal Studies* 9 (1980): 399; Keith N. Hylton, "Costly Litigation and Legal Error Under Negligence," *Journal of Law, Economics, and Organization* 6 (1990): 433.

There are, of course, times when Posner appears to draw conclusions about matters beyond the formal law. Those comments, however, generally are confined to instances in which he allows the formal assumptions of his economic theory to take on the appearance of historical description. For example:

Any marked inefficiencies in the common law approach would have been self-correcting. Were there little taste for working in hazardous conditions, we would expect to find

employers voluntarily upgrading the safety of employment conditions in order to econo-
mize on wages. Similarly, if the fellow-servant rule did not accomplish an efficient division
of safety policing functions between employer and employee, we would expect to find the
parties abrogating the rule by contract. Yet the sample contains only one case in which the
basis of a suit for injuries sustained by an employee was an agreement by the employer to
indemnify him for accidental injury regardless of fault. [Posner, "Theory of Negligence,"
p. 71]

Although Posner seems to be discussing actual relations between employers and employees, he is
instead merely recasting the form of his assumptions: that employees were free and able to seek
the kind of employment contract they desired; that employers and employees bargained rationally over the terms of employment; and that some workers preferred hazardous work for higher
wages and in fact received higher commensurate wages. Studies of workers and of labor–
management relations in the late nineteenth and early twentieth centuries do not support a claim
that those assumptions accurately describe actual behavior. See, for example, Daniel J.
Walkowitz, *Worker City, Company Town: Iron and Cotton-Worker Protest in Troy and Cohoes,
New York, 1855–84* (Urbana, IL, 1978); David Montgomery, *Workers' Control in America:
Studies in the History of Work, Technology, and Labor Struggles* (New York, 1979); David Alan
Corbin, *Life, Work, and Rebellion in the Coal Fields: The Southern West Virginia Miners, 1880–
1922* (Urbana, IL, 1981); John Gaventa, *Power and Powerlessness: Quiescence and Rebellion in
an Appalachian Valley* (Urbana, IL, 1980); David L. Carlton, *Mill and Town in South Carolina,
1880–1920* (Baton Rouge, 1982); James C. Cobb, *Industrialization and Southern Society, 1877–
1984* (Lexington, KY, 1984); Jacquelyn Dowd Hall, Robert Korstad, and James Leloudis, "Cotton Mill People: Work, Community and Protest in the Textile South, 1880–1940," *American
Historical Review* 91 (1986): 245; David Emmons, "An Aristocracy of Labor: The Irish Miners of
Butte, 1880–1914," *Labor History* 28 (1987): 275; Shelton Stromquist, *A Generation of Boomers:
The Pattern of Railroad Labor Conflict in Nineteenth-Century America* (Urbana, IL, 1987); Anthony F. C. Wallace, *St. Clair: A Nineteenth-Century Coal Town's Experience with a Disaster-
prone Industry* (New York, 1987). Compare Richard A. Epstein, "The Historical Origins and
Economic Structure of Workers' Compensation Law," *Georgia Law Review* 16 (1982): 775.

    43. As Posner wrote in another context: "Anything that reduces the plaintiff's minimum offer
[to settle] or increases the defendant's maximum offer, such as an increase in the parties' litigation
expenditures relative to their settlement costs, will reduce the likelihood of litigation." See
Richard A. Posner, "An Economic Approach to Legal Procedure and Judicial Administration,"
Journal of Legal Studies 2 (1973): 399, 418. The system of corporate diversity litigation created
strong pressures on plaintiffs to lower their settlement expectations and thereby assisted defendants and reduced the likelihood of litigation.

    44. Posner seems to make that assumption: See "Theory of Negligence," p. 94.

    One might attempt to defend Posner's conclusions that the system reached efficient results by
relying on another assumption: that corporations' total costs equalled the true economic costs of
all injuries over the universe of all claims because the underpayment made to injured persons who
settled their claims on an unfairly discounted basis was made up by the overpayment made to
those who asserted fraudulent claims, used dishonest testimony, or employed other similar types
of abusive tactics against corporate defendants. Such an assumption, however, would not seem to
support Posner's position. First, such a defense would be irrelevant. To the extent that abusive
claims imposed costs on companies, the abuses would have given corporations relatively little
incentive to invest in safety measures as opposed to investing in measures designed to curb the
abuses themselves. Thus, even if companies paid out large amounts as a result of fraudulent
claims, those payments would not have induced them to increase safety precautions to the level of
economic efficiency. Second, even assuming the relevance of the assumption, it seems implausible
as a matter of historical fact. Given the extensive and reliable evidence as to the number of
industrial injuries that occurred, it seems highly unlikely that abusive claims could have constituted more than a tiny percentage of the total claims assertable. That would seem to be especially
true for the injuries that occurred in the years before the turn of the century and in locations other
than a handful of major cities.

45. See, for example, Richard A. Posner, *Economic Analysis of Law,* 2nd ed. (Boston, 1977), pp. 399–417.

46. Posner seems to recognize the dynamic in another context:

The Cournot approach implies, quite reasonably, that an increase either in the plaintiff's stakes or in the effectiveness of his litigation expenditures, or a decrease either in defendant's stakes or in the effectiveness of *his* litigation expenditures, will induce the plaintiff to spend at a higher rate than the defendant, and vice versa.

It is the "vice versa," of course, that is relevant here (Posner, "Economic Approach to Legal Procedure," p. 431).

47. Schwartz, "Tort Law and the Economy." Schwartz qualifies and expands his earlier views concerning the rules of industrial tort law in his "Character of Early American Tort Law."

48. Robert McCloskey, *The American Supreme Court* (Chicago, 1960), p. 195. See also McCloskey, *American Conservatism in the Age of Enterprise, 1865–1910: A Study of William Graham Sumner, Stephen J. Field and Andrew Carnegie* (New York, 1951), pp. 122–26; Sidney Fine, *Laissez Faire and the General Welfare State: A Study of Conflict in American Thought, 1865–1901* (Ann Arbor, MI, 1964), pp. 126–64.

49. Alfred H. Kelly and Winfred A. Harbison, *The American Constitution: Its Origins and Development,* 5th ed. (New York, 1976), p. 485.

50. During the last quarter-century, scholarship dealing with the late nineteenth century has clearly rejected the populist–progressive–New Deal charge that the Court was a "tool" of business interests. Most scholars have concluded that the Justices were generally fair and well intentioned, though certain economic biases may have occasionally influenced them. They agree that the Court was often and usually willing to uphold the regulation of business, and some argue that the Justices were sometimes quite suspicious of corporate claims and activities. For a recent general synthesis reflecting these views, see Kermit Hall, *The Magic Mirror: Law in American History* (New York, 1989), pp. 230–38.

Much recent work has argued that the Court was anxious to restrict corporations whenever they threatened traditional American values of liberty and individual freedom. For example, Charles W. McCurdy, "The *Knight* Decision of 1895 and the Modernization of American Corporation Law, 1869–1903," *Business History Review* 53 (1979): 304; William E. Nelson, *The Roots of American Bureaucracy, 1830–1900* (Cambridge, MA, 1982), pp. 148–55; Michael Les Benedict, "Laissez-Faire and Liberty: A Re-Evaluation of the Meaning and Origins of Laissez-Faire Constitutionalism," *Law & History Review* 3 (1985): 293.

Some have pointed to the origins of the liberal individualism of the judiciary in a Jacksonian opposition to special charters and special interests. For example, Alan Jones, "Thomas M. Cooley and 'Laissez-Faire Constitutionalism': A Reconsideration," *Journal of American History* 53 (1967): 751; Charles W. McCurdy, "Justice Field and the Jurisprudence of Government–Business Relations: Some Parameters of Laissez-Faire Constitutionalism, 1863–1897," *Journal of American History* 61 (1975): 970; David M. Gold, "Redfield, Railroads, and the Roots of 'Laissez-Faire Constitutionalism,'" *American Journal of Legal History* 27 (1983): 255; David M. Gold, "John Appleton of Maine and Commercial Law: Freedom, Responsibility, and Law in the Nineteenth Century Marketplace," *Law and History Review* 4 (1986): 55.

Some have emphasized the roots of the Court's social views in nineteenth-century economic doctrine. For example, Herbert Hovenkamp, "The Political Economy of Substantive Due Process," *Stanford Law Review* 40 (1988): 379; James May, "Antitrust Practice and Procedure in the Formative Era: The Constitutional and Conceptual Reach of State Antitrust Law, 1880–1918," *University of Pennsylvania Law Review* 135 (1987): 495. Others deny that the Court followed any consistent economic theory, including laissez-faire. For example, Lawrence M. Friedman, "Freedom of Contract and Occupational Licensing 1890–1910: A Legal and Social Study," *California Law Review* 53 (1965): 487; Loren P. Beth, *The Development of the American Constitution, 1877–1917* (New York, 1971), pp. 138–41; Robert L. Rabin, "Federal Regulation in Historical Perspective," *Stanford Law Review* 38 (1986): 1189.

Though the different writers cited would surely disagree on numerous points, all seem to agree generally that the Court did not specifically try to help business, that its rulings for the most part were not particularly favorable to corporate interests, and that it was supportive of most legislative and regulatory efforts to control corporate enterprise. For example, John E. Semonche, *Charting the Future: The Supreme Court Responds to a Changing Society, 1890–1920* (Westport, CT, 1978); James May, "Antitrust in the Formative Era: Political and Economic Theory in Constitutional and Antitrust Analysis, 1880–1918," *Ohio State Law Journal* 50 (1989): 257; Morton J. Horwitz, "Progressive Legal Historiography," *Oregon Law Review* 63 (1984): 679.

Perhaps most would also agree that the Court showed some bias in labor cases, particularly those involving injunctions. For example, Semonche, *Charting the Future*, pp. 430–31; David P. Currie, "The Constitution in the Supreme Court: The Protection of Economic Interests, 1889–1910," *University of Chicago Law Review* 52 (1985): 324.

These studies of the Supreme Court seem basically consistent with more recent studies focusing on the development of the common law of torts that stress the extent to which judges sought to restrict corporate actions and expand their liability for wrongs. See, for example, Rabin, "Historical Introduction of the Fault Principle"; Schwartz, "Tort Law and the Economy"; Schwartz, "Character of Early American Tort Law."

51. For example, Rabin, "Federal Regulation in Historical Perspective"; Nelson, *Roots of American Bureaucracy*, pp. 148–55.

52. For example, Aviam Soifer, "The Paradox of Paternalism and Laissez-Faire Constitutionalism: United States Supreme Court, 1888–1921," *Law & History Review* 5 (1987): 249, 251–53, 278–79; Cass R. Sunstein, "Lochner's Legacy," *Columbia Law Review* 87 (1987): 873, 874, 882–83; Stephen A. Siegel, "Understanding the *Lochner* Era: Lessons from the Controversy over Railroad and Utility Rate Regulation," *Virginia Law Review* 70 (1984): 187, 261. Some scholars would probably also argue that many judges—perhaps especially federal appellate judges— tended to reach decisions favorable to business interests as a result of the largely unrecognized and unarticulated promptings of culturally induced and class-biased ideologies. For example, Kennedy, "Toward an Historical Understanding of Legal Consciousness"; Gordon, "Legal Thought and Legal Practice."

53. See, for example, Morton Horwitz, "History and Theory," *Yale Law Journal* 96 (1987): 1825; Martin J. Sklar, *The Corporate Reconstruction of American Capitalism, 1890–1916* (New York, 1988); May, "Antitrust in the Formative Era"; "An Exchange on Critical Legal Studies Between Robert W. Gordon and William E. Nelson," *Law & History Review* 6 (1988): 139.

54. Aside from some extreme political rhetoric, the serious claim is not that federal judges favored corporations out of either direct self-interest or specific intent to assist corporations. Rather, the claim is that federal judges generally shared with businessmen—and with many and perhaps most Americans—certain powerful underlying values and assumptions that disposed them to foster the activities and interests of corporations. Those basic shared values included commitments to the rights of property, the virtues of enterprise, the desirabililty of progress and wealth creation, the rewards of an expanding interstate market, and the triumph of nationalism and American economic power. A letter that Justice Holmes wrote to his friend Sir Frederick Pollock in 1910 suggests the powerful influence that those attitudes most likely had on federal judges as well as on other Americans in the decades around the turn of the century. Holmes commented that he regarded the railroad magnate James J. Hill "as representing one of the greatest forms of human power, an immense mastery of economic details, an equal grasp of general principles, and ability and courage to put his conclusions into practice with brilliant success when all the knowing ones said he would fail." Hill commanded his admiration, Holmes explained, even though "the intense external activity that calls for such powers does not especially delight me." See Mark DeWolfe Howe, ed., *Holmes–Pollock Letters: The Correspondence of Mr. Justice Holmes and Sir Frederick Pollock, 1874–1932* (Cambridge, MA, 1961), vol. 1, p. 167. Even if many Americans, including federal judges, shared Holmes's intellectual misgivings, most probably shared on some level his admiration for the "power," "mastery," "ability," and "courage" that entrepreneurs and their corporate enterprises represented.

55. Compare Charles W. McCurdy, "The Roots of 'Liberty of Contract' Reconsidered: Major Premises in the Law of Employment, 1867–1937," *Yearbook of the Supreme Court Historical Society* (1984): 20.

56. See, for example, Paul Kens, "The Source of a Myth: Police Powers of the States and Laissez Faire Constitutionalism, 1900–1937," *American Journal of Legal History* 35 (1991): 70.

57. Sklar, *The Corporate Reconstruction of American Capitalism;* Rabin, "Federal Regulation in Historical Perspective"; Morton J. Horwitz, "*Santa Clara* Revisited: The Development of Corporate Theory," *West Virginia Law Review* 88 (1985): 173; McCurdy, "*Knight* Decision of 1895."

58. The concern of the Justices, especially of Chief Justice Melville W. Fuller, to restrict the jurisdiction of the Supreme Court itself, was apparent in the support they gave to what became the Evarts Act in 1891. See Willard L. King, *Melville Weston Fuller: Chief Justice of the United States, 1888–1910* (Chicago, 1967), pp. 148–51.

59. *Powers v. Chesapeake and Ohio Railway Co.,* 169 U.S. 92, 100 (1898). Also see Chapters 4 and 5.

60. The Court's treatment of removal under the venue statutes raised such an obvious problem that in 1898 the successor to Judge Dillon's treatise, which consistently supported broad removal jurisdiction, was led to point out the "anomaly" that resulted. The federal court, the treatise explained, "would acquire jurisdiction, by removal from a state court, of a cause of which it is forbidden to take cognizance by the issuance of its own process." Even more interesting, the treatise did not even attempt to offer a rationale for the "anomaly." Henry Campbell Black, *A Treatise on the Laws and Practice Governing the Removal of Causes from State Courts to Federal Court* (St. Paul, 1898), p. 164.

61. For example, *Gold-Washing and Water Co. v. Keyes,* 96 U.S. 199 (1877); *Railroad Co. v. Mississippi,* 102 U.S. 135 (1880); *Tennessee v. Davis,* 100 U.S. 264 (1879); *Feibleman v. Packard,* 109 U.S. 421 (1883). See Herman L. Trautman, "Federal Right Jurisdiction and the Declaratory Remedy," *Vanderbilt Law Review* 7 (1954): 445, 451–54.
Plaintiffs could also remove, of course, under the express language of the statute.

62. Michael G. Collins, "The Unhappy History of Federal Question Removal," *Iowa Law Review* 71 (1986): 717.

63. *Metcalf v. Watertown,* 128 U.S. 586, 588–89 (1888).

64. *Bock v. Perkins,* 139 U.S. 628 (1891). See *Cooke v. Avery,* 147 U.S. 375 (1893). For lower court applications of the rule, see *Lowry v. Chicago, Burlington & Quincy Railroad Co.,* 46 F. 83 (C.C.D.Neb. 1891); *State of South Carolina v. Port Royal & Augusta Railway Co.,* 56 F. 333 (C.C.D.S.C. 1893); *Hurst v. Cobb,* 61 F. 1 (C.C.N.D.Tx. 1894); *Southern Pacific Railroad Co. v. Townsend,* 62 F. 161 (C.C.S.D.Cal. 1894). See also John F. Dillon, *Removal of Causes from State Courts to Federal Courts,* 5th ed. (St. Louis, 1889), pp. 91–95.

65. Collins, "Unhappy History of Federal Question Removal," pp. 755–756.

66. 152 U.S. 454 (1894).

67. Harlan wrote for the two and argued that the Court's construction was "erroneous" and "too narrow." He saw no difficulty with construing the statute more broadly to allow removal when defendants raised a federal right or defense (ibid., p. 464). See Collins, "Unhappy History of Federal Question Removal."

68. Black, *Treatise,* p. 186.

69. 152 U.S. 462.

70. For example, *Chappell v. Waterworth,* 155 U.S. 102 (1894); *Postal Telegraph Cable Co. v. Alabama* 155 U.S. 482 (1894); *East Lake Land Co. v. Brown,* 155 U.S. 488 (1894); *Oregon Short Line & Utah Northern Railroad Co. v. Skottowe,* 162 U.S. 490 (1896); *Texas & Pacific Railroad Co. v. Cody,* 166 U.S. 606 (1897); *Walker v. Collins,* 167 U.S.57 (1897); *Galveston, Houston & San Antonio Railroad Co. v. Texas,* 170 U.S. 226 (1898).

71. 152 U.S. 469.

72. Section 3, 24 Stat. 552 (1887), as corrected by 25 Stat. 433 (1888). See Note, "Power of a Federal Court Receiver to Remove Under Section 33 of the Judicial Code," *Yale Law Journal* 43 (1934): 1325.

73. Albro Martin, "Railroads and the Equity Receivership: An Essay on Institutional Change," *Journal of Economic History* 34 (1974): 685, 705.

74. Dillon, *Removal of Causes,* 5th ed., p. 114.

75. 145 U.S. 593 (1892). See n. 72 re quotation from *Union and Planters' Bank* about *Cox.*

76. *White v. Ewing,* 159 U.S. 36 (1895); *Rouse v. Hornsby,* 161 U.S. 588 (1896); *Oregon Short Line & Utah Northern Railway Co. v. Skottowe,* 162 U.S. 490 (1896); *Bausman v. Dixon,* 173 U.S.

113 (1899); *Pope v. Louisville, New Albany & Chicago Railway Co.*, 173 U.S. 573 (1899); *Chicago, Rock Island & Pacific Railway Co. v. Martin*, 178 U.S. 245 (1900).

77. 152 U.S. 463.

78. The classic case, though generally regarded as construing only the constitutional limit on federal question jurisdiction, not the statutory limit, was *Osborn v. Bank of the United States*, 9 Wheat. (22 U.S.) 738 (1824). There the Court held that a suit involving a bank incorporated by the United States, which was authorized by its charter to sue and be sued, presented a case that arose under federal law. Similarly, in the *Pacific Railroad Removal Cases*, 115 U.S. 1 (1885), the Court held that suits against railroad companies incorporated by the federal government raised federal questions sufficient to support removal. The existence of the federal charter, giving the corporation the right to sue and be sued, meant that suits against the companies involved a federal question. In regard to both decisions, federal jurisdiction existed whether or not the parties disputed the terms of the charters themselves. The federal question that allowed jurisdiction, in other words, did not have to be an issue that was directly involved in the dispute itself.

79. *Gold-Washing and Water Co. v. Keyes*, 96 U.S. 199, 203 (1877).

In the 1889 edition of his treatise Dillon discussed the cases that held that federal incorporation was sufficient to create a federal question. See Dillon, *Removal of Causes*, 5th ed., pp. 92–94. He stated the general rule concerning federal question jurisdiction, however, as follows:

> There must be some question actually involved in the case *depending for its determination upon the correct construction of the Constitution, or some law of Congress, or some treaty of the United States,* in order to sustain the Federal jurisdiction under the clause under consideration, namely, "suits arising under the Constitution, or laws or treaties of the United States." Accordingly, a case relating to the title to land is not one of Federal jurisdiction, although the title may be originally derived under an Act of Congress, if no question arises, or is raised, as to the validity or operative effect of the Act of Congress, and the rights of the parties depend upon State statutes or the general principles of law. [Ibid., p. 94 (italics in original)]

80. *St. Joseph and Grand Island Railroad Co. v. Steele*, 167 U.S. 659 (1897). *See Western Union Telegraph Co. v. Ann Arbor Railroad Co.*, 178 U.S. 239 (1900).

81. The test for a "federal question" sufficient to support jurisdiction was unsettled and changing in the late nineteenth century. See, for example, James H. Chadbourn and A. Leo Levin, "Original Jurisdiction of Federal Questions," *University of Pennsylvania Law Review* 90 (1942): 639; Collins, "Unhappy History of Federal Question Removal." In part, the confusion was due to the fact that federal question jurisdiction in the lower courts was still relatively new and the courts needed time to refine their thinking. It was also due to doctrinal confusion between, first, the limits of federal question jurisdiction allowed in the Constitution and the limits authorized in the Judiciary Act of 1875 and, second, the appropriate constitutional role of the Supreme Court's jurisdiction in reviewing final judgments from state courts and the appropriate role of the lower courts in deciding matters of federal law in the first instance.

In addition to doctrinal and institutional considerations, however, the difficulties also can be traced to the fact that the Court was uncertain as to just what types of cases it wanted the lower courts to hear and what kind it did not. The problems of defining a true "federal question," in other words, were as much social and pragmatic as they were technical or "legal." On the same day in 1885, for example, the Court first denied that a suit brought to enforce a federal judgment presented a federal question sufficient to support jurisdiction in the lower courts, *Provident Savings Life Assurance Association v. Ford*, 114 U.S. 635 (1885), but, second, upheld federal question jurisdiction over railroad corporations chartered by the United States government on the ground that the existence of the federal charters necessarily presented a federal question, *Pacific Railroad Removal Cases*, 115 U.S. 1 (1885). The latter decision seemed to conflate the constitutional and statutory questions. In the context of the Court's decisions of the 1890s, it was not surprising that the Court reaffirmed the ruling of the *Pacific Railroad Removal Cases* in *Texas & Pacific Railway v. Cody*, 166 U.S. 606 (1897).

82. The federal docket increased fairly steadily from 1875 until about 1895. It did not turn down until the full effect of the depression of the 1890s finally reduced the number of new filings.

Thus, in 1894 when it decided *Union and Planters' Bank,* the Court still faced a continuously growing caseload. See American Law Institute, *Study of the Business of the Federal Courts,* p. 33.

Collins, "Unhappy History of Federal Question Removal," provides an illuminating discussion of the doctrinal and legislative background of the Judiciary Act of 1887–88 and of the Court's decision in *Union and Planters' Bank.* The article explains *Union and Planters' Bank* in considerable part, however, by arguing that the Court "had determined, even before 1891, to fashion a general rule of restrictive construction of the 1887 Act" (pp. 764–65). The article does not note the significance of the Court's change in direction in diversity actions after 1892–3 and the likelihood that one of the motives moving the Court in *Union and Planters' Bank* was the desire to cut federal question removal precisely because it was expanding diversity removal.

83. For example, *Jewett v. Whitcomb,* 69 F. 417 (C.C.E.D.Wisc. 1895); *Lund v. Chicago, Rock Island & Pacific Railway Co.,* 78 F. 385 (C.C.D.Neb. 1897); *Tompkins v. MacLeod,* 96 F. 927 (C.C.D.Ky. 1899); *Gilmore v. Herrick,* 93 F. 525 (C.C.N.D.Ohio 1899) (dictum) (Taft, J.); *Winters v. Drake,* 102 F. 545 (C.C.N.D.Ohio 1900); *Hardwick v. Kean,* 26 S.W. 589 (Ct.App.Ky. 1894); *St. Louis, Arkansas & Texas Railway Co. v. Trigg,* 40 S.W. 579 (Sup.Ct. Ark. 1897) (dictum); Black, *Treatise,* pp. 209–11; B. C. Moon, *The Removal of Causes from the Courts of the Several States to the Circuit Courts of the United States* (New York, 1901), pp. 272–77 and cases cited.

84. *Landers v. Felton,* 73 F. 311 (C.C.D.Ky. 1896) (Taft, J.); *Lund v. Chicago, Rock Island & Pacific Railway Co.,* 78 F. 385 (C.C.D.Neb. 1897); *Gableman v. Peoria, Decatur & Evansville Railway Co.,* 82 F. 790 (C.C.D.Ind. 1897), rev'd, 179 U.S. 335, 340 (1900). *But see Shearing v. Trumbull,* 75 F. 33 (C.C.D.Colo. 1895) (receiver may not remove when joined with resident defendant).

85. *Carpenter v. Northern Pacific Railroad Co.,* 75 F. 850 (C.C.D.Wash. 1896); *Sullivan v. Barnard,* 81 F. 886 (C.C.W.D.Mo. 1897); *Shinney v. North American Savings, Loan & Building Co.,* 97 F. 9 (C.C.D.Utah 1899). But see *Gilmore v. Herrick,* 93 F. 525 (C.C.N.D.Ohio 1899); *Ray v. Peirce,* 81 F. 881 (C.C.D.Ind. 1897).

86. The pattern appeared in other areas as well. In the extremely tangled doctrinal area concerning the citizenship for jurisdictional purposes of corporations that were chartered, "adopted," or consolidated by the laws of two or more states, the Court had struggled for decades to distinguish among the types of relationships that foreign corporations could have with states that had not originally chartered them and to work out the results for purposes of determining the citizenship of corporations for diversity purposes. See, for example, *Nashua and Lowell Railroad Corp. v. Boston and Lowell Railroad Corp.,* 136 U.S. 356 (1890). In its decisions before the early 1890s there was some tendency, in addition to much inconsistency and confusion, to find that corporations chartered in one state could, in various ways, be made corporations of other states. For example, *Memphis & C.Railroad Co. v. Alabama,* 107 U.S. 581 (1883); *Martin's Administrator v. Baltimore & Ohio Railroad Co.,* 151 U.S. 673 (1894). By acquiring multiple citizenships, of course, the corporations were deprived of their removal rights in the additional "adopting" states.

In *St. Louis & San Francisco Railroad Co. v. James,* 161 U.S. 565 (1896), discussed in Chapter 1, the Court severely limited the ability of states to "recharter" foreign corporations and thereby make them into domestic corporations for federal jurisdictional purposes. In 1899 in *Louisville, N. A. & C. Railroad Co. v. Louisville Trust Co.,* 174 U.S. 552 (1899), the Court restricted that state power even further, making it clear that the issue of citizenship for federal jurisdiction purposes, absent agreement of the corporation, was largely beyond the control of the states. As one treatise explained in 1901:

> The chief effect, if not the main purpose, of this new doctrine, is to authorize the removal of suits against it, by every re-incorporated railroad company, when sued in the courts of the State of its re-incorporation, if the original company was organized in another state. Such a corporation has heretofore been denied the right to remove such suits, because it was a domestic corporation. [Moon, *Removal of Causes,* p. 337, n. 9 on p. 338]

Also see generally ibid., pp. 332–39, and compare Black, *Treatise,* pp. 165–72; Armistead M. Dobie, *Handbook of Federal Jurisdiction and Procedure* (St. Paul, 1928), pp. 199–204.

87. The number of railroading injuries declined somewhat during the depression, but the number of industrial tort suits apparently rose. Compare United States Bureau of the Census, *A Statis-*

tical History of the United States from Colonial Times to the Present (Westport, CT, 1965), p. 437; Richard A. Posner, "A Theory of Negligence," *Journal of Legal Studies* 1 (1972): 29, 51, 85–91.

88. The question arises, of course, whether the Court acted specifically to protect corporations or more generally to provide neutral federal forums to nonresidents in a time when rising social tensions meant that the dangers of local prejudice would likely be greater. Although such a question cannot be answered precisely, the historical record suggests that both factors were probably involved. It surely seems reasonable to assume that the Justices believed that anticorporate feelings were unusually strong, just as it is obvious from the Court's decisions that the defendants it was protecting were almost exclusively corporations. Whatever the personal motives of the Justices, the fact remains that the Court responded favorably to the pleas of corporations. There was, in contrast, no alteration whatever in the almost nonexistent scope that the Court gave to removal under the Civil Rights Act, even though abuses against blacks in the 1890s were far more extreme and vicious—and were escalating far more quickly—than anything visited on corporate defendants in tort suits.

One might contend that the Court acted in the 1890s in order to preserve the principle of an expansive federal removal jurisdiction. That explanation seems implausible given the Court's decisions in the half-dozen years after 1887, its decisions limiting federal question removal in the 1890s, and its decisions limiting diversity removal jurisdiction after the turn of the century.

89. The same pattern of first expanding corporate removal rights in the 1890s and then restricting them after 1900 appeared in yet another related doctrinal area. In the 1890s the Court expanded diversity removal by restricting the power of the states to "adopt" foreign corporations. Following in the immediate wake of its major decisions restricting diversity removal in 1905–6, the Court—in one of the system's classic types, a wrongful death action against a railroad—broadened somewhat the leeway that the states enjoyed to "adopt" foreign corporations and thereby prevent them from removing. See *Patch v. Wabash Railroad Co.,* 207 U.S. 277 (1907). The Court's changes in attitude from the late 1880s through *Patch* and beyond compounded an already difficult doctrinal problem. See Dobie, *Handbook,* pp. 199–204.

90. 179 U.S. 335, 340 (1900).

91. For the decision below, see *Gableman v. Peoria, Decatur and Evansville Railway Co.,* 82 F. 790 (C.C.D.Ind. 1897).

92. The Court's statement that it was merely "modifying" some of the language in *Cox* was at best highly midleading. Commentators had agreed that *Cox* held that a federally appointed receiver should remove on the ground that any action against him raised a federal question. See, for example, Black, *Treatise,* pp. 209–11; Moon, *Removal of Causes,* pp. 272–77. Many lower courts agreed: for example, *White v. Ewing,* 66 F. 2, 6 (C.C.A. 6 1895). Most revealing, however, in the 1890s the Supreme Court itself agreed. In *Tennessee v. Union and Planters' Bank,* 152 U.S. 454, 463 (1894), the Court clearly identified the significance it saw in its earlier decision. *Cox,* the Court stated,

> maintained the jurisdiction of the Circuit Court of the United States of the action against the receivers, under the act of 1887, upon the ground that the right to sue, without the leave of the court which appointed them, receivers appointed by a court of the United States, was conferred by section 6 of that act, and therefore the suit was one arising under the Constitution and laws of the United States.

In their dissent in *Union and Planters' Bank,* Justices Harlan and Field construed *Cox* similarly (ibid., p. 472).

93. 196 U.S. 239, 245–46 (1905).

94. David S. Clark, "Adjudication to Administration: A Statistical Analysis of Federal District Courts in the Twentieth Century," *Southern California Law Review* 55 (1981): 65, 103. Compare the similar but somewhat different numbers given in American Law Institute, *Study of the Business of the Federal Courts,* Detailed Table 1. Beginning in the 1902 Term, one scholar has noted, the Court showed a new willingness to save itself time by disposing of cases on technicalities without full review (Semonche, *Charting the Future,* p. 152).

95. *Great Southern Fireproof Hotel Co. v. Jones,* 177 U.S. 450 (1900); *Raphael v. Trask,* 194 U.S. 272 (1904).

96. *Patch v. Wabash Railroad Co.*, 207 U.S. 277 (1907).

97. *Macon Grocery Co. v. Atlantic Coast Line Railroad Co.*, 215 U.S. 501 (1910).

98. "Notes," *American Law Review* 35 (1901): 883.

99. For example, *Blake v. McKim*, 103 U.S. 336 (1880); *Hawes v. Oakland*, 104 U.S. 450 (1881).

100. American Law Institute, *Study of the Business of the Federal Courts*, Detailed Table 1.

101. Compare, for example, the Court's discussion in *Hawes* with its opinion in *Doctor v. Harrington*, 196 U.S. 579 (1905).

102. Clark, "Adjudication to Administration," p. 103; American Law Institute, *Study of the Business of the Federal Courts*, p. 33 and Detailed Table 1.

103. In 1905 the Court seemed to expand diversity removal jurisdiction in situations where state actions affecting private property were being reviewed in the state court system. *Madison-ville Traction Co. v. Saint Bernard Mining Co.*, 196 U.S. 239 (1905) (allowing removal in a condemnation proceeding). Compare *Upshur County v. Rich*, 135 U.S. 467 (1890) (denying removal where defendant sought diversity removal of a tax assessment proceeding).

In 1908, three years after *Doctor*, the Court again demonstrated its apparently strong concern to maintain federal jurisdiction over shareholder derivative suits. See *Venner v. Great Northern Railway Co.*, 209 U.S. 24 (1908).

104. In the early 1920s, for example, when docket problems were growing rapidly and the Taft Court was seeking methods of controlling the problem, it handed down its decisions in *Terral* and *Lee*, both of which opened the national courts to new classes of cases. At the same time it also seemed to broaden the reach of federal question jurisdiction. Compare *Smith v. Kansas City Title & Trust Co.*, 255 U.S. 180 (1921) with *Shoshone Mining Co. v. Rutter*, 177 U.S. 505 (1900) and *American Well Works Co. v. Layne & Bowler Co.*, 241 U.S. 257 (1916).

Similarly, in the 1880s, although the Court felt the pressures of a rapidly growing caseload, it nevertheless expanded federal jurisdiction by ensuring that cases involving federally chartered railroads would be cognizable in the national courts. Its decision, in fact, seemed to stretch considerably in finding that the existence of a federal charter conferred jurisdiction on the federal courts. See *Pacific Railroad Removal Cases*, 115 U.S. 1 (1885).

105. See Chapter 5. Among the Justices who sometimes opposed the fellow servant rule, there was noticeable if irregular opposition to the Court's other principal common law decisions. Similarly, with the exception of Justice Rufus W. Peckham (who generally supported the majority's common law decisions) in *Northern Assurance*, the only Justices who dissented in those other common law decisions were those who had also dissented in at least one case that applied the federal fellow servant rule. Although there were no dissents in either *Lewis* or *Patton*, all of the other cases drew at least one dissent as follows:

Voigt: Harlan
Adams: Harlan and (Joseph) McKenna
Dixon: Harlan, McKenna, White, and Fuller
Northern Assurance: Harlan and Fuller (and Peckham)

The only exception was Justice William R. Day who dissented, joined by Harlan (the Court's strongest opponent of the fellow servant rule), in *Prewitt*. Brewer concurred alone and without opinion in *Wisner*.

107. Albro Martin, *Enterprise Denied: Origins of the Decline of American Railroads, 1897–1917* (New York, 1971), pp. 17–21, 22–38.

108. See, for example, Naomi R. Lamoreaux, *The Great Merger Movement in American Business, 1895–1904* (New York, 1985), p. 2.

109. Morton J. Horwitz argued that the Court at the turn of the century was dominated by what he calls "old conservatives" who were hostile to corporate consolidation. See Horwitz, "*Santa Clara* Revisited," pp. 198–203. Martin J. Sklar also emphasized the extent to which the Court between 1897 and 1911 was willing to impose an exceedingly strict construction on the Sherman Antitrust Act in order to minimize corporate opportunities to restrict competition. See Sklar, *Corporate Reconstruction of American Capitalism*. Given those attitudes, it seems reasonable that the merger movement may have helped persuade some of the Justices either that most of

the new consolidated national corporations no longer needed any special protection from the federal courts or, perhaps, that they no longer deserved it.

    . 110. The literature on progressivism is immense. Among the more recent additions that incorporate and cite most of the earlier works are the following: David Sarasohn, *The Party of Reform: Democrats in the Progressive Era* (Jackson, MS, 1989); John F. Reynolds, *Testing Democracy: Electoral Behavior and Progressive Reform in New Jersey, 1880–1920* (Chapel Hill, NC, 1988); Judith Sealander, *Grand Plans: Business Progressivism and Social Change in Ohio's Miami Valley, 1890–1929* (Lexington, KY, 1988); Niels Aage Thorsen, *The Political Thought of Woodrow Wilson, 1875–1910* (Princeton, NJ, 1988); Paul M. Minus, *Walter Rauschenbusch: American Reformer* (New York, 1988); Donald K. Gorrell, *The Age of Social Responsibility: The Social Gospel in the Progressive Era, 1900–1920* (Macon, GA, 1988); Michael E. Teller, *The Tuberculosis Movement: A Public Health Campaign in the Progressive Era* (Westport, CT, 1988); Susan Lehrer, *Origins of Protective Labor Legislation for Women, 1905–1925* (Albany, NY, 1987); James T. Kloppenberg, *Uncertain Victory: Social Democracy and Progressivism in European and American Thought, 1870–1920* (New York, 1986).

    111. Roscoe Pound, "The Causes of Popular Dissatisfaction with the Administration of Justice," *American Bar Association Reports* (1906): 395.

    112. Ibid., p. 411.

    113. Ibid., p. 412.

    114. For example, *American Bar Association Reports* (1907): 505–12; (1908): 27–49, 542–64, (1909): 61–85, 578–609.

    115. William Howard Taft, "The Delays of the Law," *Yale Law Journal* 18 (1908): 28, 30.

    116. Ibid., pp. 30–31.

    117. Ibid., p. 33.

    118. Ibid., p. 37.

    119. Ibid.

    120. Ibid., p. 31.

    121. *Shoshone Mining Co. v. Rutter,* 177 U.S. 505, 513 (1900).

    122. After 1900 a number of courts and judges seemed to grow more sympathetic to tort plaintiffs. Without changing black letter law, for example, the West Virginia Supreme Court of Appeals ruled against railroads and coal companies in a significantly higher percentage of tort suits in the decade after 1900 than it had in the previous decade. See Munger, "Social Changes and Tort Litigation," pp. 97–99.

    It seems reasonable to speculate that some of the Justices may also have been nudged toward restricting diversity jurisdiction by the desire to reduce the presence in the federal courts of the kinds of personal injury cases that so many members of the elite bar found sordid or distasteful. They may have regarded them for social reasons as more "appropriate" to state courts. For a discussion of the essentially moderate and professional roots of legal progressivism, see Richard Hofstadter, *The Age of Reform: From Bryan to F.D.R.* (New York, 1955), pp. 156–64.

    123. Michael Kammen, *A Machine That Would Go of Itself: The Constitution in American Culture* (New York, 1986), pp. 191–92.

    124. 198 U.S. 45 (1905).

    125. Semonche, *Charting the Future,* p. 184.

    126. Woodrow Wilson, *Constitutional Government in the United States* (New York, 1910), p. 153. Concerning the federal common law, Wilson stated:

> The courts of the United States have not the right to impose upon litigants their own interpretations of the fundamental law of a state when that law in no way involves the jurisdiction or the authority of the federal government, and in the trial of ordinary cases between citizens of different states they must hold themselves to the administration of state laws as they are interpreted by the courts of the states in which they originated. [Ibid., pp. 155–56]

    127. *Lochner v. New York,* 198 U.S. 76 (Holmes, J., dissenting). "I like to multiply my skepticisms," he wrote privately the following year, "as against the judicial tendency to read into a Constitution class prejudices naively imagined to be eternal laws." See James Bishop Peabody,

ed., *The Holmes–Einstein Letters: Correspondence of Mr. Justice Holmes and Lewis Einstein, 1903–1935* (New York, 1964), p. 23. For Holmes's attitude toward the political and economic controversies that swirled around the Court at the time see, for example, ibid., pp. 14, 16; Howe, ed., *Holmes–Pollock Letters*, pp. 123–24.

128. *Northern Pacific Railway Co. v. Dixon*, 194 U.S. 338, 352 (1904) (White, J., dissenting).

129. Robert W. Gordon, " 'The Ideal and the Actual in the Law': Fantasies and Practices of New York City Lawyers, 1870–1910," in Gerard W. Gawalt, ed., *The New High Priests: Lawyers in Post–Civil War America* (Westport, CT, 1984), pp. 51–74; Gordon, "Legal Thought and Legal Practice"; Morton J. Horwitz, "Progressive Legal Historiography," *Oregon Law Review* 63 (1984): 679; Horwitz, "History and Theory"; Sklar, *Corporate Reconstruction of American Capitalism*.

130. Black, *Treatise*, pp. 22–26; Moon, *Removal of Causes*, pp. 36–37.

131. A constitutional scholar in 1910 captured the essence of the formalistic approach that the Court used in *Prewitt* to avoid the doctrinal bind it faced:

> There is, to be sure, a causal *nexus* between the exercise of the federal right of removal and of the State's right to withdraw its permission to the foreign corporation to do business within the State's limits. But, legally speaking, there is no connection. Each is an exercise of an independent right. [W. W. Willoughby, *The Constitutional Law of the United States* (New York, 1910), vol. 1, p. 148]

132. For the most part only members of the middle class could have afforded to carry insurance in amounts that would have made them vulnerable to removal. As late as 1932, a quarter-century after *Prewitt,* when insurance coverage had increased severalfold, the average life insurance policy in force in the United States was in an amount of less than $2,400. See "Limiting Jurisdiction of Federal Courts," Hearings before the Committee on the Judiciary of the United States House of Representatives, 72 Cong., 1 Sess. (1932), p. 77 (statement of F. G. Dunham, representing the Association of Life Insurance Counsel).

Given the generally more favorable attitude of the Court, and of most American courts in general, toward insurance claimants as compared to tort plaintiffs, it is not unreasonable to speculate that in the wake of *Cochran* and *Thomson*—both providing major assistance to tort plaintiffs—the Court may have felt the appropriateness of providing similar assistance to insurance claimants. To the exent that those who carried insurance represented in theory at least the thrifty, hardworking, and economically rational classes that deserved consideration if anyone did, the Justices may well have thought that it would be unfair to assist tort plaintiffs without doing the same for insurance plaintiffs. Compare, for example, Gold, "John Appleton of Maine," p. 69:

> Appleton desired a society of independent moral beings, which meant that while individuals had to be allowed to manage their own affairs, they had as well to bear the good or bad consequences of their actions. They had to be self-reliant, but also sober, rational, and prudent because others must not be made to suffer for their misconduct. In sum, they had to be both free and responsible.

Also Robert E. Gamer, "Justice Brewer and Substantive Due Process: A Conservative Court Revisited," *Vanderbilt Law Review* 18 (1965): 615, 635: "But Brewer assumed that when no privileges granted by the government or monopoly backed by law were involved, men should be able to take care of themselves and need not be coddled by protection in matters their own initiative can handle."

133. In the same years the Court was also in effect reconsidering and developing its role vis-à-vis Congress and especially the new federal administrative agencies. See, for example, Rabin, "Federal Regulation in Historical Perspective." In his study of the reconstitution of American national government in the late nineteenth and early twentieth centuries, Stephen Skowronek identifies the years from 1904 to 1906 as the time when national administrative reformers mounted their most sustained and, to that point, most successful challenge to the government's nineteenth-century institutional *status quo*. "The strategic environment for state building," he writes, "was more favorable during the [Theodore] Roosevelt administration than at any other time in the entire scope of this study [from 1877 to 1920]." He continues:

The institutional initiatives that secure Roosevelt's reputation as the premier state builder of his age were concentrated in the period between his landslide election of 1904 and the congressional elections of 1906. From a position of electoral strength and political security, the executive-professional reform coalition pursued a course of redistributing institutional powers and prerogatives away from Congress and the courts toward the President and the bureaucracy. [Skowronek, *Building a New American State: The Expansion of National Administrative Capacities, 1877–1920* Cambridge, MA, 1982), pp. 171–72]

Because diversity jurisdiction pertains more directly to matters of federalism, the discussion focuses on the way the Court altered the role of the national courts vis-à-vis the states and their courts.

134. 198 U.S. 45 (1905). From the time of its announcement to the present, *Lochner* has been regarded as a landmark decision. It was bitterly attacked by progressives and later by New Dealers as the classic example of both the Court's probusiness orientation and its illicit judicial activism on behalf of the social values of the majority Justices. In part, at least, the decision's fame rested on the dissent by Justice Holmes which, in memorably elegant language, seemed to make that same point. More recently, in a political and social world distant from progressivism and the New Deal, the image of *Lochner* has changed somewhat. See, for example, John Hart Ely, *Democracy and Distrust: A Theory of Judicial Review* (Cambridge, MA, 1980), pp. 14–21; Horwitz, "History and Theory," p. 1825; Cass R. Sunstein, "Lochner's Legacy," *Columbia Law Review* 87 (1987): 873. Compare Paul Kens, *Judicial Power and Reform Politics: The Anatomy of Lochner v. New York* (Lawrence, KS, 1990). For an interesting view of *Lochner* from the perspective of nineteenth-century constitutional law, see James L. Kainen, "Nineteenth Century Interpretations of the Federal Contract Clause: The Transformation from Vested to Substantive Rights Against the State," *Buffalo Law Review* 31 (1982): 381.

135. For example, *Santa Clara County v. Southern Pacific Railroad Co.*, 118 U.S. 394 (1886); *Mugler v. Kansas*, 123 U.S. 623 (1887).

136. *Chicago, Milwaukee & St. Paul Railroad Co. v. Minnesota*, 134 U.S. 418 (1890); *Smyth v. Ames*, 169 U.S. 466 (1898).

137. *Allgeyer v. Louisiana*, 165 U.S. 578 (1897).

138. 209 U.S. 123 (1908).

139. The amendment provided: "The Judicial power of the United States shall not be construed to extend to any suit in law or equity, commenced or prosecuted against one of the United States by Citizens of another State, or by Citizens or Subjects of any Foreign State." Although prior to Reconstruction the Court had construed the Eleventh Amendment relatively narrowly, in the 1870s and 1880s it generally enforced it rigorously. In a series of cases brought by bondholders against southern states that had repudiated their public debts, it repeatedly held that the federal courts lacked jurisdiction to hear such suits. To a large extent the results of the cases seemed to reflect another aspect of the end of Reconstruction. See John Orth, "The Interpretation of the 11th Amendment, 1798–1908: A Case Study of Judicial Power," *University of Illinois Law Review* (1983): 423. By 1890 the Court was willing to give the amendment such breadth that it held that it also precluded suits against states brought by a state's own citizens who were raising a federal constitutional claim. See *Hans v. Louisiana*, 134 U.S. 1 (1890). And see generally John V. Orth, *The Judicial Power of the United States: The Eleventh Amendment in American History* (New York, 1987), esp. chap. 8; William F. Duker, "Mr. Justice Rufus W. Peckham and the Case of *Ex parte Young*: Lochnerizing *Munn v. Illinois*," *Brigham Young University Law Review* (1980): 539.

140. *Tindal v. Wesley*, 167 U.S. 204 (1897).

141. *Pennoyer v. McConnaughy*, 140 U.S. 1 (1891); *Fitts v. McGhee*, 172 U.S. 516 (1899).

142. Orth, *Judicial Power of the United States*, pp. 122, 126. Unquestionably, Lawrence Friedman has written, "statutes were challenged in 1900 that would not have been challenged in an earlier generation." See Lawrence M. Friedman, "Freedom of Contract and Occupational Licensing 1890–1910: A Legal and Social Study," *California Law Review* 53 (1965): 487, 532, n. 140.

143. 188 U.S. 537 (1903).

144. The Eleventh Amendment, *Prout* stated, could not "be successfully pleaded as an invincible barrier to judicial inquiry whether the salutary provisions of the Fourteenth Amendment have been disregarded by state enactments" (ibid., p. 543).

145. *Gunter v. Atlantic Coast Line Railroad Co.*, 200 U.S. 273, 283–84 (1906).

146. *Young,* stood, in a sense, as a kind of inverted image of *Virginia v. Rives,* 100 U.S. 313 (1879), which had destroyed civil rights removal. The former opened the doors of the federal courts to those who sought offensively to protect their alleged constitutional rights, whereas the latter closed the doors of the same courts to blacks seeking defensively to protect theirs.

147. In *Willcox v. Consolidated Gas Co.*, 212 U.S. 19 (1909), the Court heard an appeal from a lower court decision invalidating a state rate-making order on constitutional grounds. In its argument before the Court the state agency criticized the lower court for taking jurisdiction, and at the start of their opinion the Justices rebuked the agency for making such an argument and, presumably, strengthened the resolve of the lower courts to hear such cases:

> At the outset it seems to us proper to notice the views regarding the action of the court below, which have been stated by counsel for appellants, the Public Service Commission, in their brief in this court. They assume to criticize that court for taking jurisdiction of this case, as precipitate, as if it were a question of discretion or comity, whether or not that court should have heard the case. On the contrary, there was no discretion or comity about it. When a Federal court is properly appealed to in a case over which it has by law jurisdiction, it is its duty to take such jurisdiction [citation omitted], and in taking it that court cannot be truthfully spoken of as precipitate in its conduct. That the case may be one of local interest only is entirely immaterial, so long as the parties are citizens of different States or a question is involved which by law brings the case within the jurisdiction of a Federal court. The right of a party plaintiff to choose a Federal court where there is a choice cannot be properly denied. . . .
>
> The case before us . . . involves the constitutionality, with reference to the Federal Constitution, of two acts of the legislature of New York, and it is one over which the Circuit Court undoubtedly had jurisdiction under the act of Congress, and its action in taking and hearing the case cannot be the subject of proper criticism. [Ibid, pp. 39–40]

148. For example, Semonche, *Charting the Future,* pp. 184, 223–24.

149. *Barney v. City of New York,* 193 U.S. 430 (1904).

150. *Raymond v. Chicago Union Traction Co.*, 207 U.S. 20, 37 (1907).

151. *Siler v. Louisville & Nashville Railroad Co.*, 213 U.S. 175, 192 (1909).

152. *Home Telephone and Telegraph Co. v. City of Los Angeles,* 227 U.S. 278 (1913). Although it effectively terminated the *Barney* rule, the Court did not expressly overrule the earlier decision. It took half a century before it was prepared to declare formally that *Barney* had been "worn away by the erosion of time" and "contrary authority." *United States v. Raines,* 362 U.S. 17, 26 (1960).

153. Ibid., pp. 284, 285.

154. Ibid., p. 288.

155. *Prentis v. Atlantic Coast Line Co.*, 211 U.S. 210, 228–30 (1908). See *Bacon v. Rutland Railroad Co.*, 232 U.S. 134 (1914).

156. *Siler v. Louisville and Nashville Railroad Co.*, 213 U.S. 174 (1909).

157. *General Oil Co. v. Crain,* 209 U.S. 211 (1908).

158. Ibid., pp. 226–27. The case is somewhat puzzling. It presented a rather eccentric procedural context, and the Court's decision on the same day in *Young* seemed to obviate any pressing need for the decision and to undercut its apparent reasoning. At a minimum, the case reflects both the Court's concern that states might try to prevent judicial review of their actions as well as a commitment to ensure that some form of judicial review would be available to aggrieved parties seeking to challenge state actions.

159. *Johnson v. Southern Pacific Co.*, 196 U.S. 1 (1904).

160. *Northern Securities Co. v. United States,* 193 U.S. 197 (1904).

161. The Roosevelt administration announced the Northern Securities prosecution as a centerpiece of its antitrust enforcement efforts. See, for example, George E. Mowry, *The Era of Theodore Roosevelt and the Birth of Modern America, 1900–1912* (New York, 1958), pp. 131–32.

162. McCurdy, "*Knight* Sugar Decision of 1895." In spite of its new focus on federal law issues, the Court was determined to maintain a rather strict test for the presence of a "federal

question." See *Shoshone Mining Co. v. Rutter,* 177 U.S. 505 (1900). As part of this effort, too, the Court continued to apply rigorously the well-pleaded complaint rule announced in *Union & Planters' Bank.* See, for example, *Louisville & Nashville Railroad v. Mottley,* 211 U.S. 149 (1908). It applied the *Union & Planters' Bank* rule even in potentially significant antitrust cases. See *Minnesota v. Northern Securities Co.,* 194 U.S. 48 (1904). When major social issues arose, however, the Court was willing to apply a looser standard for finding a "federal question." Perhaps the two most striking examples are *In re Debs,* 158 U.S. 564 (1895) (upholding a federal injunction against labor groups on the basis of the national government's obligation to protect interstate commerce and the transportation of mail) and *Ex parte Young,* 209 U.S. 809 (1908) (in which the Court apparently created an implied cause of action under federal law).

163. See Chapter 7. Although there was a significant change in the Court's membership between 1905–6 and the middle of the next decade when many of these decisions came down, the lineup of Justices appeared generally to hold. Those voting for the Court's common law and substantive due process decisions (the "conservative" wing) tended to vote in favor of the other expansions in the Court's lawmaking powers, whereas those who opposed the Court's federal common law and substantive due process decisions (the "progressive" wing) tended—with the significant qualification noted next—to oppose the expansions. Specifically, the dissenters in the cases discussed in the text were as follows:

> *Muhlker:* Fuller, White, Holmes (and Peckham)
> *Kansas v. Colorado:* none (White and McKenna, however, concurred without opinion in the result only)
> *Kuhn:* Holmes, White, and McKenna
> *Hitchman:* Holmes, Brandeis, and Clarke
> *Jensen:* Holmes, Brandeis, Clarke (and Pitney)
> *Winfield:* Brandeis and Clarke (without opinion)

It is noteworthy that, with the exception of *Winfield,* the statutory preemption decisions discussed in Chapter 7 were generally unanimous. Thus, when a congressional statute was at issue, the progressive wing seemed willing to use preemption to broaden its reach. In the absence of congressional action, however, the progressive wing preferred to leave the lawmaking to the states.

164. The Supreme Court's decisions in the 1890s authorized the federal courts to review "state regulatory legislation to ascertain its probable effect on the distribution of corporate assets and liabilities," Charles W. McCurdy noted. "Judicial review of fact in so complex an area as corporate finance added burdensome judicial duties to an already crowded docket" (McCurdy, "Justice Field and the Jurisprudence of Government–Business Relations," p. 1004).

165. The process of change has not been total; its pace has not been steady; and its direction has not been linear. Indeed, jurisdiction remains an area of intensely practical political and social conflict that is subject to repeated backing and filling as the nature of the conflicts, the legal focus of the disputes, and the attitudes of Congress and the membership of the United States Supreme Court change.

The shift from the eighteenth- and nineteenth-century view to the twentieth-century view was, of course, to some extent subtle and largely a matter of emphasis. It also required several decades to work its way into the basic assumptions of the legal profession and, of course, never commanded complete agreement in its implications for most of the specific rules of federal jurisdiction. Indeed, as I suggest throughout the book, jurisdictional issues include social issues, and that fact by itself inevitably leads to disagreements over matters of technical doctrine. In fact, what I have referred to as the twentieth-century view probably was not fully developed until the years of the Warren Court, and then its social implications prompted opposition from those who opposed its major and controversial decisions.

One of the characteristic assumptions of the twentieth-century view is that federal courts are more "suitable" forums for hearing federal law issues than are state courts. Yet, however much most twentieth-century lawyers and judges would agree with that assertion as a general matter, in specific cases many would adamantly dispute its applicability. Under the umbrella of the twentieth-century view, adversaries continue to disagree over jurisdictional issues for a variety of reasons, including, of course, the social results they would likely bring. And even the Warren Court, which emphasized the importance of having federal claims heard in federal courts, continued on occasion to stress the essential role of the state courts in protecting federal rights. See, for example, Martha A. Field, "The Uncertain Nature of Federal Jurisdiction," *William and Mary Law Review* 22 (1981): 683.

Two quotations will suffice to suggest the nature of the assumptions that marked the earlier view as well as their persistence in the first decade of the twentieth century. In 1902 Horace H. Lurton, still on the Sixth Circuit, discussed the relation between the federal and state courts in an address dedicating a new courthouse in Wayne County, Michigan:

> I have referred briefly to the great constitutional functions discharged by both [state and federal] judicial systems, and to the semi-governmental questions involved in the exercise of the jurisdiction of both federal and state tribunals as defenders and upholders of constitutional limitations. There is a wider jurisdiction exercised by both state and federal courts, which concerns only the administration of justice in the innumerable controversies which arise continually between man and man. In the discharge of this high and sacred duty, the judges of the federal and state courts are alike set apart for the exercise of the most exalted functions which man may assume over his fellow-men.

The basic assumptions, of course, are the parallel and equal nature of the state and federal courts, the equal role envisioned for the state courts in enforcing federal rights, and the importance to the federal courts of private law, primarily diversity, cases (the controversies "between man and man"). See Horace H. Lurton, "The Relation of the Federal and the State Judiciary to Each Other," *Michigan Law Review* 1 (1902): 169, 177–78.

Second, in 1910 the *Central Law Journal* discussed and criticized a recent lower federal court case involving the removal of a diversity action. It then commented:

> The more, therefore, the reasons of removal statutes are considered, the more they seem nothing more than whip handles subserving no purpose but to give non-residents special privileges, and incidentally to minister to the importance of lower federal courts, which in administering merely federal law would be not much more than negligible factors.

The assumption was that federal question cases constituted no special or particularly important part of the federal caseload and that diversity cases were the staple business of the national courts. See Comment, *Central Law Journal* 71 (1910): 294.

In the 1920s the work of Felix Frankfurter, then a professor at the Harvard Law School, became one of the most significant academic efforts to push along the process of reconceiving and reorienting federal jurisdictional law. Generally, Frankfurter argued that state courts should hear state law claims, including at least most diversity actions, and that the federal courts should specialize, though not have exclusive jurisdiction, in actions based on federal law questions. See Felix Frankfurter and James M. Landis, *The Business of the Supreme Court: A Study in the Federal Judicial System* (New York, 1928); Felix Frankfurter, "Distribution of Judicial Power Between United States and State Courts," *Cornell Law Quarterly* 13 (1928): 499.

By the 1940s the idea that federal question cases generally belonged in the federal courts had become widely accepted. "The most important function of the federal court system undoubtedly," announced one law review article in its lead sentence, "is the determination of those cases which lawyers commonly refer to as 'federal question' cases." See Ray Forrester, "The Nature of a 'Federal Question'," *Tulane Law Review* 16 (1942): 362. Ten years later another law review article announced:

> Whatever have been the circumstances and needs during the first century of our country's history, there seems to be little doubt that today, with the expanding scope of federal legislation, the exercise of power over [federal question cases] constitutes one of the major purposes of a full independent system of national trial courts.

The lower federal courts were essential to "furthering the rapid, widespread, yet uniform and accurate, interpretation of federal law," and they were the frontline and critical "vindicators of federal law." See Paul J. Mishkin, "The Federal 'Question' in the District Courts," *Columbia Law Review* 53 (1953): 157, 171, 170.

To the extent that the twentieth-century view became associated with the Warren Court and the lower courts came to be seen in particular as the "vindicators" of the expanded constitutional rights that it enforced, the reaction to the Supreme Court's "liberal" and "activist" decisions tended to challenge some parts of that view. We, of course, may be in the middle of a period that will succeed again in redefining our conceptions of the national legal system and of the role of the federal courts in that system. See, for example, Aviam Soifer and H. C. Macgill, "The *Younger* Doctrine: Reconstructing Reconstruction," *Texas Law Review* 55 (1977): 1141; George D. Brown, "Has the Supreme Court Confessed Error on the Eleventh Amendment? Revisionist Scholarship and State Immunity," *North Carolina Law Review* 68 (1990): 867.

Regardless of the reaction, however, it seems extremely unlikely at this point that diversity jurisdiction will recover the importance that it enjoyed in the federal dockets in the eighteenth and nineteenth centuries.

In the late twentieth century Congress has repeatedly amended the judicial code to restrict diversity jurisdiction and expand federal question jurisdiction. In 1980 it abolished the jurisdictional amount in cases brought under general federal question jurisdiction and then eight years later raised the jurisdictional amount in diversity actions to $50,000. In 1988 it also restricted the *Powers* rule by imposing an absolute one-year limit on the time within which defendants can remove diversity suits. In 1990 it abolished removal on the basis of diversity of citizenship under the amended version of the "separable controversy" provision, limiting such removals to actions based on federal question jurisdiction. Similarly, in the same year it also abolished "pendent" and "ancillary" jurisdiction and replaced them with a statutorily defined "supplemental jurisdiction" which extends the jurisdiction of the national courts broadly in cases that present a federal question but restricts such supplemental jurisdiction severely where cases are based only on diversity of citizenship. See John B. Oakley, "Recent Statutory Changes in the Law of Federal Jurisdiction and Venue: The Judicial Improvement Acts of 1988 and 1990," *U.C. Davis Law Review* 24 (1991): 735; Ellen S. Mouchawar, "The Congressional Resurrection of Supplemental Jurisdiction in the Post-*Finley* Era," 42 *Hastings Law Journal* (1991): 1611.

In 1990 a special congressionally-sponsored study committee recommended further severe restrictions on general diversity jurisdiction that would leave it standing only in special cases involving complex multistate elements, interpleader, and aliens. See *Report of the Federal Courts Study Committee* (1990), 38–42.

Indeed, the critical area of disagreement in the latter half of the twentieth century is not between diversity jurisdiction and federal question jurisdiction but between the different kinds of cases that fall within federal question jurisdiction: which of those categories are to be treated favorably and which unfavorably; which shall be accorded a federal forum and a potential federal remedy and which shall be denied those options. For any number of reasons, many of which are "social" and not "legal," the decision to allow or deny a federal forum may be critical and perhaps dispositive to an action's outcome.

166. Throughout the progressive period, and indeed through the rest of the century, the Court continued to enforce the plaintiffs' pleading rule to restrict removals on the basis of a federal question. See, for example, *Louisville & Nashville Railroad v. Mottley,* 211 U.S. 149 (1908).

167. The rule barring defendants with federal rights or defenses from removing on that ground has remained in force since *Union and Planters' Bank.* Lawyers have come to refer to it as the "well-pleaded complaint" rule.

As what I have termed the twentieth-century view of the federal courts became dominant, it made the well-pleaded complaint rule originated in *Union and Planters' Bank* seem a puzzling or inappropriate "anomaly" in federal jurisdictional law. In reaffirming the rule in 1983, for example, the Supreme Court described it as based on "reasons involving perhaps more history than logic." *Franchise Tax Board of California v. Construction Laborers Vacation Trust for Southern California,* 463 U.S. 1, 4 (1983). The Court's description speaks volumes. Although it is surely right that "history" explains the existence of the well-pleaded complaint rule, it is wrong in its implied assumption that history and logic are independent and inconsistent. To the contrary, history creates and shapes the premises and propositions on which logical reasoning operates. When the well-pleaded complaint rule developed, it seemed "logical" to the Justices; it flowed, in other words, with sufficient consistency from the accepted premises that defined their conceptions of the law and the federal judicial system. The rule seems to conflict with "logic" in the late twentieth century, not because history and logic are independent or unrelated—or because contemporary Justices have somehow become more "logical" than their predecessors—but because historical developments have changed the social and institutional premises on which the Justices and other legal writers operate.

One of the most broad-based and thoroughly considered proposals to abandon the well-pleaded complaint rule and allow defendants to remove on the basis of the federal rights that they assert resulted from an elaborate study of federal jurisdiction undertaken in the 1960s by the American Law Institute. See American Law Institute, *Study of the Division of Jurisdiction Between State and Federal Courts* (Washington, DC, 1969), pp. 4, 162–68, 187–94. The ALI stated in part:

> If, as has been suggested above, the justification for original federal question jurisdiction is to protect litigants relying on federal law from the danger that the state courts will not properly apply that law, either through misunderstanding or lack of sympathy, then that jurisdiction should extend to all cases in which the meaning or application of the Constitution, laws, or treaties of the United States, is a principal element in the position of either party—unless there are compelling reasons to the contrary, as there may be in some special types of litigation. This is not now the law. It is the rationale on which the present proposals are based. [p. 168]

For influential mid-century criticisms of *Union and Planters' Bank,* see, for example, James H. Chadbourn and A. Leo Levin, "Original Jurisdiction of Federal Questions," *University of Pennsylvania Law Review* 90 (1942): 639, 671–74; Paul J. Mishkin, "The Federal 'Question' in the District Courts," *Columbia Law Review* 53 (1953): 157, 176–84. Arguably reflecting a growing and long-established consensus at least among law professors, Donald L. Doernberg titled a recent broadside attack on the rule rather more bluntly: "There's No Reason for It; Its Just Our Policy: Why the Well-pleaded Complaint Rule Sabotages the Purposes of Federal Question Jurisdiction," *Hastings Law Journal* 38 (1987): 597. After reviewing the basic issues that the rule raises, one treatise concludes that "the critics of the well-pleaded complaint rule seem to have the better of the argument." Erwin Chemerinsky, *Federal Jurisdiction* (Boston, 1989), p. 236. Even some who see some benefit in the rule nevertheless come down on the side of the critics:

> The well-pleaded complaint rule fulfills a useful and necessary function. Given the limited nature of federal subject matter jurisdiction, it is essential that the existence of jurisdiction be determined at the outset, rather than being contingent upon what *may* occur at later stages in the litigation. By demanding that a federal issue be raised in the complaint, the rule accomplishes this goal. But this achievement may be overshadowed by the fact that because general federal question jurisdiction exists only if a federal issue appears on the face of a well-pleaded complaint, in many cases federal courts are precluded from passing upon important issues of federal law. Therefore, not surprisingly, the rule has been subjected to some rather trenchant criticism. [Jack H. Friedenthal, Mary Kay Kane, and Arthur R. Miller, *Civil Procedure* (St. Paul, 1985), pp. 23–24]

168. See, for example, David J. Brewer, "Protection to Private Property from Public Attack," *New Englander and Yale Review* 55 (1891): 97; "Growth of the Judicial Function," *Report of the Organization and First Annual Meeting of the Colorado Bar Association* (Denver, 1898), pp. 82–93; Address to the Colorado Bar Association, July 2, 1903, *Report of the Sixth Annual Meeting of the Colorado Bar Association* (no publication site, 1903), pp. 46–50; and, "The Right of Appeal," *The Independent* 55 (1903): 2547. The second item may be found in volume 3 of the papers of David J. Brewer, Library of Congress, Washington, DC. The third and fourth items appear in volume 4 of those papers. See generally Arnold M. Paul, "David J. Brewer," in Leon Friedman and Fred L. Israel, eds., *The Justices of the United States Supreme Court, 1789–1969, Their Lives and Major Opinions,* 4 vols. (New York, 1969), p. 1515.

169. David J. Brewer, "A Better Education the Great Need of the Profession," *Yale Law Journal* 5 (1895): 1, 12.

It is necessary to note that Brewer's statement begins with the following introduction: "When in youth I studied the structure of our government, I looked with awe and reverence upon the Supreme Court of the United States." The section quoted in the text immediately follows as part of the sentence.

It was revealing that Brewer placed the origins of his vision in the distant past where it was, of course, quite inaccurate. He probably did so for essentially the same reason that Frankfurter in his *Kepner* dissent repeatedly referred to the doctrine of *forum non conveniens* as "familiar" (see Chapter 10). In truth, both were sponsoring new ideas and hoped to confer on them the authority of some kind of antiquity.

In his speech, Brewer was clearly imagining the historical roots of his version. He was born in 1837, graduated from Yale College in 1856, began reading law with his uncle David Dudley Field the same year, and completed his legal studies in 1858. Thus, if we take his statement literally, his "awe and reverence" for the Supreme Court would have developed at the same time the Court decided the *Dred Scott* case, called down on itself a storm of criticism and even contempt, helped precipitate the Civil War, and then endured for two decades what is generally regarded as the nadir of its prestige and influence. It was probably not until the 1880s that the Court regained the prestige it had lost and not until the 1890s that it began playing a powerful and independent role in American politics and society. Moreover, Brewer's description of the Court's workload in the nineteenth century was obviously and substantially inaccurate. Throughout the century—indeed, in the 1890s when he gave his speech—the Supreme Court continued to hear numerous diversity cases and disputes between individuals. Until 1891, in fact, when Congress established the Circuit Courts of Appeal in the Evarts Act, the Supreme Court regularly heard appeals from the lower courts in diversity actions and was, indeed, the only court that could hear appeals from the circuit courts in removed diversity actions.

For contrasting views of Brewer, see Gamer, "Justice Brewer"; Paul, "David J. Brewer," p. 1515.

170. Brewer supported the Court's decision in the income tax case in 1895, for example, whereas Harlan dissented.

Fearing the "coercion" of the majority and believing that politicians were trimmers, Brewer saw the judiciary as the only bulwark against national disaster, and he repeatedly stressed the need for judicial review of legislative actions. The "urgent need" of the day, Brewer insisted in 1893, was to give "to the judiciary the utmost vigor and efficiency." David J. Brewer, "The Nation's Safeguard," *Proceedings of the New York State Bar Association, Sixteenth Annual Meeting* (New York, 1893), p. 44. Five years later he boasted that the United States Army had not defeated the Pullman strikers but that "it was simply the United States courts that ended the strike." The experience, Brewer maintained, demonstrated "the wisdom of judicial interference." David J. Brewer, "The Nation's Anchor," reprinted in *Albany Law Journal* 57 (1898): 166, 168.

Harlan, though himself deeply committed to the protection of private property, nevertheless showed greater sympathy for the use of the police power, especially by the federal government, and less sympathy for the idea of an activist judiciary that was central to Brewer's thinking. "[T]here is a tendency in some quarters," Harlan warned in 1896, "to look to the Supreme Court of the United States for relief against legislation which is admittedly free from constitutional objection, and which therefore is not liable to criticism except upon grounds of public policy." Although the duty to enforce the Constitution was central, he insisted, "equally imperative and equally sacred is its duty to respect legislative enactments." If courts began to act "simply upon their own view as to the wisdom of legislation," the result would be "the downfall of our government." John M. Harlan, "The Supreme Court of the United States and Its Work," *American Law Review* 30 (1896): 900, 901.

To the extent that the two disagreed, it was Brewer who was generally with the majority in the Court's controversial rulings in the decades around the turn of the century. In the context of the 1890s, however, in diversity actions neither wanted to restrict the access of national corporations to the federal courts.

171. David J. Brewer, "The Supreme Court of the United States," *Scribner's Magazine* 33 (1903): 273, 277.

172. John M. Harlan, "The Position of the Supreme Court of the United States in Our Governmental System," *American Law Review* 37 (1903): 95.

173. Though Brewer and Harlan remained far apart, in light of the newly emerged consensus their actions in two major decisions in 1908 seemed somewhat less surprising than they otherwise might appear. Brewer wrote for a majority that included Harlan in *Muller v. Oregon,* 208 U.S. 412 (1908), distinguishing *Lochner* and upholding a state statute that limited the hours that women could work in factories. Harlan wrote for the majority that included Brewer in *Adair v. United States,* 208 U.S. 161 (1908), invalidating a federal statute that made yellow-dog contracts unenforceable.

174. William T. Lord, "The Ideals of the American Advocate—A Symposium," *Century Law Journal* 58 (1904): 423, 429.

175. Henry St. George Tucker, "Review of Legislation of Year 1904–5," *American Law Review* 39 (1905): 801, 809.

176. John F. Dillon, "Remarks of John F. Dillon at Banquet, at the Hotel Astor, New York, on the Twenty-Fifth Anniversary of the Graduating Class of Columbia Law School, June 12, 1905," *American Law Journal* 39 (1905): 707, 708.

177. Elihu Root, "Some Duties of American Lawyers to American Law," in Root, *Addresses on Government and Citizenship,* ed. Robert Bacon and James Brown Scott (Cambridge, MA, 1916), p. 419.

178. Ibid., p. 421.

179. Ibid., p. 419

180. Ibid., pp. 422–23.

181. Ibid., pp. 423–24.

182. Ibid., p. 424.

183. Ibid., p. 423.

184. Ibid., p. 424.

185. Ibid., p. 425.

186. Ibid., p. 426. Root repeatedly hammered his point:

There is a constant tendency to ignore such limitations [on government] and condone the transgression of them by public officers, provided the thing done is done with good motives from a desire to serve the public. Such a process if general is most injurious. If continued long enough, it results in an attitude of personal superiority on the part of great officers which is inconsistent with our institutions, a destruction of responsibility and independent judgment on the part of lower officers, and a neglect of the habit of asserting legal rights on the part of the people. The more frequently men who hold great power in office are permitted to override the limitations imposed by law upon their powers, the more difficult it becomes to question anything they do; and the people, each one weak in himself and unable to cope with powerful officers who regard any questioning of their acts as an affront, gradually lose the habit of holding such officers accountable, and ultimately practically surrender the right to hold them accountable. [Ibid., p. 426]

187. Tucker, "Review of Legislation," pp. 803–4.

188. Ibid., p. 806.

189. An editorial in one law magazine summarized attitudes as follows:

A somewhat vague opinion pervades the public mind, that the Federal courts, and, in particular, the Supreme Court, form a firm bulwark of important political and civil rights, and a guarantee against aggressions from the executive and the legislative branches of government. It is the object of this article to call attention to some of the considerations which tend to qualify the value of this guarantee.

The editorial then discussed various limitations on federal judicial power, and, in particular, it criticized judicial doctrines of self-limitation. "It is to be regretted that it [the Supreme Court] should have adopted principles for its guidance in administering this imposing power [to declare acts of Congress unconstitutional], which render it of far less utility to the people than it might be." The editorial concluded with a criticism of the Court and an implied exhortation:

> Without injustice to the court, it can, we think, be affirmed, that by its unwillingness to take the risks attendant on a prohibition of unconstitutional legislative action, or on an early prevention of executive steps looking to the enforcement of unconstitutional laws, the court has very much curtailed its utility as a guardian of fundamental rights. And it has also been illogical. The most inferior executive officer, a sheriff or constable, or marshall, a tax-assessor or collector, in performing what he thinks his duty is acting out his own judgment, or the judgment of some superior officer. It ought to matter not, how high or low in the official hierarchy such officer may be. If his only authority is an unconstitutional law, he is altogether without authority, and the court should be ready to forbid the highest as the lowest executive officer, from doing acts for which only an unconstitutional statute can be vouched. [Editorial, "The Federal Courts as Guardians of Constitutional Rights," *The Forum,* 9 (1905): pp. 185, 206, 207]

Index

Abb, Frank, 37
Abb v. Northern Pacific Railway Co., 37
Adams. See Northern Pacific Railway Co. v. Adams (1904)
Addams, Jane, quoted, 109
Administrative law, 265
Administrative Office of the United States Courts, founded in 1939, 159
Aetna Casualty & Surety Co. v. Flowers (1947), 389n81
Aetna Life Insurance Co., 35
Aetna Life Insurance Co. v. Haworth (1937)
  expands opportunities for insurance companies to use declaratory judgment as tactical device, 216
  holds federal Declaratory Judgment Act constitutional, 215
Aetna Life Insurance Co. v. Moore (1913), 72
Alabama
  in Fifth Circuit, 56
  Supreme Court of, 146–47
Alabama Great Southern Railway Co. v. Thompson (1906). *See also* Joinder; Tort Joinder tactic
  allows particularly broad use of tort joinder tactic, 274, 275
  and *Cable v. United States Life Insurance Co.*, 204
  and *Cochran v. Montgomery County*, 136
  designed to settle issue of tort joinder tactic, 273
  and *Ex parte Wisner*, 182
  impact of, 119–21
  limited by lower federal courts, 120, 122–24, 148–49
  mentioned, 252, 275, 277
  protects workers from federal fellow servant rule, 250
  and *Security Mutual Life Insurance Co. v. Prewitt*, 201
  supported by "conservative" Justices on Supreme Court, 124–25
  typical of Supreme Court's jurisdictional rulings after turn of century, 126, 245, 267, 272
  upholds tort joinder tactic, 117
Alaska Packers Association v. Industrial Acci-

dent Commission of California (1935), 198, 246
Alliance Against Accident Fraud, 152
Altgeld, John Peter, 135
Ambulance chasing, 151, 153, 154, 178
American Association of Railroads, 234
American Bar Association
  adopts code of ethics, 153
  defends diversity jurisdiction in 1932, 242
  helps draft Law and Equity Act of 1915, 207
  joins fight against interstate forum shopping, 188
  mentioned, 277, 290
American Express Co., 38
American Federation of Labor, 234
American Law Institute (ALI), 21, 88–89, 167, 220, 246–47, 414n167
American Law Review, 26, 62
American Life Insurance Co. v. Stewart (1937), 214
American Railroad Law (Baldwin), 30, 40
American Railway Union, 109
Amidon, Charles F., 123–24, 341n135
Amount in controversy. *See* Jurisdictional amount
Anticipatory breach of contract
  adopted by Sixth Circuit, 211
  becomes plaintiffs' tactic, 211
  rejected by Supreme Court, 214
Antiremoval statutes (state)
  enacted in approximately twenty states, 201–2
  invalidated by Supreme Court, 201, 205
  upheld by Supreme Court, 201–2
Antiremoval tactics, 209, 210. *See also* Claim discounting; Joinder; Tort joinder tactic
Anti-Semitism, 150–51
Antitrust law, 265
Appellate courts, federal. *See* Circuit Courts of Appeals
Arizona, in Ninth Circuit, 56
Arkansas, in Eighth Circuit, 56
Arrowsmith v. Nashville & Ducatur Railroad Co. (1893), 110
Association of American Law Schools, 151
Association of Life Insurance Presidents, 200

419